Handbook of Research on Diagnosing, Treating, and Managing Intellectual Disabilities

Rejani Thudalikunnil Gopalan
Gujarat Forensic Sciences University, India

A volume in the Advances in Psychology, Mental Health, and Behavioral Studies (APMHBS) Book Series

Information Science REFERENCE
An Imprint of IGI Global

Published in the United States of America by
Information Science Reference (an imprint of IGI Global)
701 E. Chocolate Avenue
Hershey PA, USA 17033
Tel: 717-533-8845
Fax: 717-533-8661
E-mail: cust@igi-global.com
Web site: http://www.igi-global.com

Library of Congress Cataloging-in-Publication Data

Library of Congress Cataloging-in-Publication Data

Names: Gopalan, Rejani Thudalikunnil, 1974- editor.
Title: Handbook of research on diagnosing, treating, and managing intellectual disabilities / Rejani Thudalikunnil Gopalan, editor.
Description: Hershey : Information Science Reference, 2016. | Includes bibliographical references and index.
Identifiers: LCCN 2016002937| ISBN 9781522500896 (hardcover) | ISBN 9781522500902 (ebook)
Subjects: LCSH: Intellectual disabilities | Mental retardation--Diagnosis. | Mental retardation--Treatment. | Disability evaluation.
Classification: LCC RC570 .H347 2016 | DDC 362.2--dc23 LC record available at http://lccn.loc.gov/2016002937

This book is published in the IGI Global book series Advances in Psychology, Mental Health, and Behavioral Studies (APMHBS) (ISSN: pending; eISSN: pending)

British Cataloguing in Publication Data
A Cataloguing in Publication record for this book is available from the British Library.

All work contributed to this book is new, previously-unpublished material. The views expressed in this book are those of the authors, but not necessarily of the publisher.

For electronic access to this publication, please contact: eresources@igi-global.com.

Advances in Psychology, Mental Health, and Behavioral Studies (APMHBS) Book Series

Bryan Christiansen
PryMarke, LLC, USA

ISSN: pending
EISSN: pending

Mission

The complexity of the human mind has puzzled researchers and physicians for centuries. While widely studied, the brain still remains largely misunderstood.

The **Advances in Psychology, Mental Health, and Behavioral Studies (APMHBS)** book series presents comprehensive research publications focusing on topics relating to the human psyche, cognition, psychiatric care, mental and developmental disorders, as well as human behavior and interaction. Featuring diverse and innovative research, publications within APMHBS are ideally designed for use by mental health professionals, academicians, researchers, and upper-level students.

Coverage

- Treatment & Care
- Developmental Disorders
- Psychiatry
- Human Behavior
- Socialization
- Personality Disorders
- Mental Health & Disorders
- Emotional Health
- Neurological Disorders
- Cognition

IGI Global is currently accepting manuscripts for publication within this series. To submit a proposal for a volume in this series, please contact our Acquisition Editors at Acquisitions@igi-global.com or visit: http://www.igi-global.com/publish/.

The Advances in Psychology, Mental Health, and Behavioral Studies (APMHBS) Book Series (ISSN pending) is published by IGI Global, 701 E. Chocolate Avenue, Hershey, PA 17033-1240, USA, www.igi-global.com. This series is composed of titles available for purchase individually; each title is edited to be contextually exclusive from any other title within the series. For pricing and ordering information please visit http://www.igi-global.com/book-series/advances-psychology-mental-health-behavioral/110200. Postmaster: Send all address changes to above address.

Titles in this Series

For a list of additional titles in this series, please visit: www.igi-global.com

Neuroeconomics and the Decision-Making Process
Bryan Christiansen (PryMarke LLC, USA) and Ewa Lechman (Gdansk University of Technology, Poland)
Business Science Reference • copyright 2016 • 354pp • H/C (ISBN: 9781466699892) • US $195.00 (our price)

Integrating Technology in Positive Psychology Practice
Daniela Villani (Università Cattolica del Sacro Cuore, Italy) Pietro Cipresso (Università Cattolica del Sacro Cuore, Italy & I.R.C.C.S. Istituto Auxologico Italiano, Italy) Andrea Gaggioli (Università Cattolica del Sacro Cuore, Italy & I.R.C.C.S. Istituto Auxologico Italiano, Italy) and Giuseppe Riva (Università Cattolica del Sacro Cuore, Italy & I.R.C.C.S. Istituto Auxologico Italiano, Italy)
Information Science Reference • copyright 2016 • 447pp • H/C (ISBN: 9781466699861) • US $185.00 (our price)

Global Perspectives on Youth Gang Behavior, Violence, and Weapons Use
Simon Harding (Middlesex University, UK) and Marek Palasinski (Liverpool John Moores University, UK)
Information Science Reference • copyright 2016 • 425pp • H/C (ISBN: 9781466699380) • US $185.00 (our price)

Exploring the Collective Unconscious in the Age of Digital Media
Stephen Brock Schafer (Digipen Institute of Technology, USA)
Information Science Reference • copyright 2016 • 316pp • H/C (ISBN: 9781466698918) • US $175.00 (our price)

Psychosocial Studies of the Individual's Changing Perspectives in Alzheimer's Disease
Cordula Dick-Muehlke (University of California, Irvine, USA) Ruobing Li (University of California, Irvine, USA) and Myron Orleans (California State University, Fullerton, USA)
Medical Information Science Reference • copyright 2015 • 434pp • H/C (ISBN: 9781466684782) • US $225.00 (our price)

Psychological and Social Implications Surrounding Internet and Gaming Addiction
Jonathan Bishop (Centre for Research into Online Communities and E-Learning Systems, Swansea, UK)
Information Science Reference • copyright 2015 • 335pp • H/C (ISBN: 9781466685956) • US $195.00 (our price)

Handbook of Research on Innovations in the Diagnosis and Treatment of Dementia
Panagiotis D. Bamidis (Aristotle University of Thessaloniki, Greece) Ioannis Tarnanas (Aristotle University of Thessaloniki, Greece) Leontios Hadjileontiadis (Aristotle University of Thessaloniki, Greece) and Magda Tsolaki (Aristotle University of Thessaloniki, Greece)
Medical Information Science Reference • copyright 2015 • 511pp • H/C (ISBN: 9781466682344) • US $245.00 (our price)

IGI GLOBAL
DISSEMINATOR OF KNOWLEDGE
www.igi-global.com

701 E. Chocolate Ave., Hershey, PA 17033
Order online at www.igi-global.com or call 717-533-8845 x100
To place a standing order for titles released in this series, contact: cust@igi-global.com
Mon-Fri 8:00 am - 5:00 pm (est) or fax 24 hours a day 717-533-8661

Editorial Advisory Board

List of Reviewers

List of Contributors

Table of Contents

Detailed Table of Contents

The relationship between communication and cognition which has been explored since mid-1900s is a highly contentious topic. Hypotheses from various researchers have experienced a gradual shift from cognitive/innate bases to social perspective of acquisition and development of speech and language skills in individuals with intellectual disability. This acquisition tends to be delayed or deviant (qualitative and /or quantitative). In the recent years, research in this area is experiencing a paradigm shift evolving from 'incapacity' to 'functioning' which is obvious in the clinical practice of assessment and intervention of speech and language skills in these individuals. Further, the rehabilitation process is experiencing a transition from clinician directed to child-oriented or hybrid approaches of intervention. This chapter will be a comprehensive document of recent trends in research and practice related to acquisition of language, assessment and intervention of communication difficulties for professionals working with intellectual disability.

The Chapter begins with an attempt to understand disability aspect in general and assessment aspect extensively. This chapter would attempt to observe both classic and latest trends of assessment techniques. Since it was observed that the recent trends concentrate extensively on global concept, the present chapter would include assessment categories on different dimensions of ability, emotions and behaviors such as intelligence, achievement, adaptive, social behavior and emotional adjustment, communication/ language, sensory status, motor skills, and health status. The adaptivity skills will be emphasized more since it was observed adaptive skills plays a crucial role in the children with intellectual disability. in this current chapter a number of critical issues concerning the assessment of children with intellectual disabilities, including definitional problems, psychometric factors, and practical difficulties would be proposed to help students, counselors, teachers and psychologists.

Intellectual disability (intellectual developmental disorder) is characterized by deficits in general mental abilities, such as reasoning, problem solving, planning, abstract thinking judgment, academic learning, and learning from experience (DSM V). This neuro developmental disorder is one of the conditions with onset in the developmental period. This condition has been classified into four categories on the basis of the individual's IQ (Intelligence quotient). The objective of the present paper is to highlight some of the areas that are related to the concerns for the people with intellectual disability. The paper focuses on the following topics: 1) Legal services, 2) Challenges faced by parents, 3) Health issues, 4) Sexual knowledge, 5) Marriage, 6) Quality of life, 7) Old age, 8) Attitude of society towards the individual with intellectual disability, 9) Implications, management and prevention for future improvement for individuals with intellectual disability.

Intellectual Disability is sub-average intellectual ability with impaired adaptive functioning, which starts before the age of 18. They have IQ below. There are many issues which require attention while dealing with ID like human resources, quality training of clinical psychologists in India, the conflicts among the team approach, acceptance in the family and society and many more. There are 1.5 million people with intellectual disability in India. However, experts working in the field of developmental disabilities feel that prevalence is much higher. The population with ID is increasing but the resources to deal with these issues are few. The mental health profession is a multidisciplinary one. The psychiatrist, the clinical psychologist and the psychiatric social worker all have their significant role in the management of ID. There is a long way to go. There are many things that can be offered but what we need is acceptance in our society of such people and Awareness towards Intervention.

History on PWID indicates influence of various psycho-social, biological, religious and educational factors for the existence of stereotypical attitudes towards PWID. Across the world until the mid-80's they were a marginalized group of people who were discriminated from others' who considered themselves as "normal". But since the early part of the 21st century significant efforts have been reported across countries in integrating and mainstreaming the PWID in the community at large. To attain this challenging milestone attitude plays a very significant role. Families of PWID undergo high levels of stress and emotional reactions resulting from daily care demands, emotional distress, interpersonal difficulties (family discord), financial hardships as well as social isolation which call for intervention not just for the intellectually disabled but also with the family members. Positive attitude among the health and all professionals with humane qualities such as empathy, genuineness, unconditional positive regard towards the PWID leads to positive expectation and better outcome. Interestingly in developing countries stereotypes are based on ignorance and families find it extremely difficult to disclose the presence of Intellectual Disability (ID) as it is considered to be a 'loss of face'' and is believed to tarnish the family reputation. Hence, families often adopt strategies to hide the existence of a disability, which in turn delays the treatment, and rehabilitation of PWID. Along with parents and family members other stakeholders like siblings and relatives, teachers, educationists, health professionals and general public's attitudes towards

The chapter summarizes key issues in vocational rehabilitation for individuals with intellectual disability, nature of vocational rehabilitation in in mild, moderate and severe intellectual disability, principles of rehabilitation for individuals with intellectual disability, assessment of intellectual disability and it's limitations. Then the chapter reviews the need for vocational rehabilitation, assessment required for rehabilitation and barriers of vocational rehabilitation for individuals with intellectual disability. the chapter then covers vocational rehabilitation process and preparation of the individual for rehabilitation. The chapter ends with social skills training and newer trends in rehabilitation like use of virtual reality and sensory integration.

This chapter focuses on the use of assistive technology in persons with Intellectual Disabilities (IDs). Persons with IDs have significant limitations, both in intellectual functioning and in adaptive behaviors. The use of assistive technology is essential to help persons with IDs and make them independent in all spheres of life. Assistive technology devices and services can be used to teach, train, rehabilitate, and empower persons in a variety of daily activities viz. new learning, home living, employment, health and safety, communication, social activities, protection and leisure. Empirical studies suggest that assistive technology is effective in improving the quality of life of persons with IDs and make them less dependent on others. This chapter investigates the available research evidence on the use of assistive technology in IDs, discusses utilizations, impediments/barriers, implications and suggests recommendations for future research.

Intellectual Disability (ID) can be caused by a variety of factors, which may lead to a variety of signs and symptoms. Individuals with ID are living in societies where during the past decade there is a steady increase in the amount of research focused on civil law, criminal law and mental health. In this chapter, there will be a theoretical presentation of the research on ID regarding criminal law and the different forms of aggressive behavior such as sexual violence, homicide, theft, arson and alcohol-drug abuse. There will be information on research regarding civil law and the most common problems for individuals with ID, such as financial capacity and capacity for medical consent. Finally, there will be a section for the most important issues regarding the trial and conviction for individuals with ID and a presentation of a recent research on attitudes toward ID and legal issues. The above will be examined through the prism of current neuropsychological data, while cross-cultural restrictions will be discussed.

Preface

Intellectual Disability (ID, previously known as mental retardation) is a condition of arrested or incomplete development of the mind. ID is especially characterized by impairment of skills manifested during the developmental period, which contribute to the overall level of intelligence, i.e. cognitive, language, motor, and social abilities.

In the past decades, research in the area of intellectual disability has helped in a phenomenal way to change the attitude toward the condition as well delivery in various multidisciplinary services to affected individuals. New ways for assisting these individuals with focus in understanding and managing significant issues and thereby integrating them into the mainstream society has been the aim every research being conducted.

Keeping it in mind this book is designed with the objective of providing students and professionals who work with individuals with intellectual disability a literature which focus on historical development of intellectual disability as a debilitating condition, awareness and attitudes toward intellectual disability, issues pertaining to mental health, schooling, sexuality, parenthood, crime and law, and quality of life of individuals with intellectual disability, issues faced by family members, assessment and management, psychosocial treatment, use of assistive technology and vocational rehabilitation.

To be more specific, Chapter 1 gives an overall view about the history, changes in terminology, classification, epidemiology, etiology, comorbidities and management of intellectual disability. Also, current understanding and latest trends and issues are highlighted.

Chapter 2 deals with developmental vulnerability and mental health. It gives an account of the prevalence of psychiatric disorders and its nature in individuals with intellectual disability. It looks into the consequences of this comorbid condition on individuals, families and the wider community, and also the various challenges in identifying and managing these concerns. Issues such as applicability of standardised psychiatric classification systems, gaps in service delivery models and access to such services, as well as unmet training need are also focussed in this chapter.

Chapter 3 concentrates on the topic school bullying and students with intellectual disabilities. The history of research in school bullying which has looked into the nature, extent, causes, and consequences of school bullying and recent research on cyber bullying, bullying using information and communication technologies, research on school bullying involvement among students with disabilities, particularly those with intellectual disabilities is provided in this chapter. Along with multidisciplinary research details the chapter also has recommendations for public policy and prevention programs as well as future research.

Chapter 4 discusses the mental health issues among family members of children with mental disability. It looks into the types of problems faced by the children with mental disability, their parents and siblings, including the possible impact on mental health of the family. The chapter as well discusses the impact of mental health difficulties in parents and its impact on parenting. It intends to highlight the need to recognise parents who are struggling, what professionals should look for in their assessment of families with children with intellectual disabilities.

Chapter 5 deals with stress and adjustment issues in the family of children intellectual disability. It looks into wellbeing, coping and overall adjustment of parents, siblings and other family members of children with intellectual disability and also research carried out in this area. Intervention techniques for helping families cope with issues associated with having a member with intellectual disability is also discussed.

Chapter 6 deals with stress and resilience in parents of intellectually disabled children. It presents a study which attempted to find out the factors of stress that could act against the resilience in the parents of intellectually disabled children. The sample consisted of 50 parents of intellectually disabled children from different panchayats in the Calicut, Kannur, Wayanad districts in the state of Kerala, India. Results of the study indicate that extra-familial stress was a negative predictor of resilience in the parents of the intellectually disabled children. Further, the parents who were in a late part of the young adulthood period and old were relatively more resilient than the parents who were in the earlier part of the young adulthood period.

Chapter 7 focuses on the role of family members as caregivers of individuals with intellectual disabilities. It looks into the experience of caregivers of persons with intellectual disabilities, factors that exacerbate caregiver stress and facilitate caregiver gain while reviewing the research in this field, and research about parents, siblings and grandparents as caregivers in different cultural settings. Factors with regard to parents such as age, severity, birth order, problem solving and coping mechanism, experiences of both mothers and fathers, their marital relationship, bereavement experiences are also focussed. Experience of siblings is explored in depth with regards to their feelings towards a sibling with Intellectual Disability, expectations about responsibly etc. Finally, the role of stigma, families in context, poverty, support staff and guidelines for caregivers and support system are also explored

Chapter 8 explores the quality of life of people with intellectual disability. The need to understand the quality of life of people with intellectual disability is crucial as this mental disability is considered to be a major setback for any individual and his/her family. It needs to be highlighted here, that the families of people with intellectual disability also play a crucial role. New research reviews are required to bring policy changes and better tools.

Chapter 9 outlines 21st century perspective of assessment and management of communication skills in individuals with intellectual disability. The development of communication skills according to different perspectives, communication skills in individuals with intellectual disability and associated issues, their assessment and intervention is covered comprehensively in this chapter.

Chapter 10 covers issues and recent trends in the assessment and management of intellectual disability in childhood. It is an attempt to understand disability aspect in general and assessment aspect extensively. Both the classic and latest trends of assessment techniques have been looked into. It include assessment categories on different dimensions of ability, emotions and behaviours such as intelligence, achievement, adaptive, social behaviour and emotional adjustment, communication/language, sensory status, motor skills, and health status. The issues concerning the assessment of children with intellectual disabilities, including definitional problems, psychometric factors, and practical difficulties is emphasized and measures would be proposed to help students, counsellors, teachers, and psychologists.

Chapter 11 explores the concerns for individuals with intellectual disability in India. It focuses on topics like legal services available for persons with intellectual disability, challenges faced by parents, health issues, sexual knowledge, marriage, quality of life, and old age, attitude of society towards the individual with intellectual disability, implications, management and prevention for future improvement for individuals with intellectual disability.

Chapter 12 provides awareness towards intervention for intellectual disability. There are many issues which require attention while dealing with ID like human resources, quality training of clinical psychologists in India, the conflicts among the team approach, acceptance in the family and society and many more. There are 1.5 million people with intellectual disability in India. However, experts working in the field of developmental disabilities feel that prevalence is much higher. The population with ID is increasing but the resources to deal with these issues are few. The mental health profession is a multidisciplinary one. The psychiatrist, the clinical psychologist and the psychiatric social worker all have their significant role in the management of ID. There is a long way to go. There are many things that can be offered but what we need is acceptance in our society of such people and Awareness towards Intervention.

Chapter 13 discusses about attitude towards People With Intellectual Disabilities (PWID). It delves into the history on PWID to understand the existence of stereotypical attitudes towards PWID. This chapter also presents with the stress, stress related issues faced by families of PWID. It discusses how families often cope with these issues and its effect on providing timely assistance and rehabilitation of PWID. Also, attitude of stakeholders like siblings and relatives, teachers, educationists, health professionals, general public and future recommendations for service and research are also discussed.

Chapter 14 deals with psycho-social treatment of intellectual disability and current trends in it. Applied Behaviour Analysis has the most research evidence base for treatment of challenging behaviours and improving the quality of life of these individuals. Applied Behaviour Analysis adopts a systematic approach in assessment and treatment of challenging behaviours. In recent years, 'parenting' has also emerged as a dominant theme among researchers and practitioners. Emerging research evidences are also favouring 'parenting skill based programmes' grounded in behavioural research as intervention strategies to obtain better developmental outcomes for individuals with intellectual disability.

Chapter 15 covers recent trends and issues in vocational rehabilitation of people with intellectual disability. The rights of people with disabilities have been given new attention with the entry into force of the United Nations Convention on the Rights of Persons with Disabilities (CRPD) in May 2008. The various policies, issues and trends in vocational rehabilitation of people with intellectual disabilities in existence in different countries need to be examined along with different models in existence to develop appropriate executable models whereby such rehabilitation services could be made available early in life to such individuals and after training they could be provided with supported employment or integrated employment as the case may be.

In chapter 16 the vocational rehabilitation of persons with intellectual disability, recent trends and associated issues is discussed. A summary of key issues in vocational rehabilitation for individuals with intellectual disability, nature of vocational rehabilitation in in mild, moderate and severe intellectual disability, principles of rehabilitation for individuals with intellectual disability, assessment of intellectual disability and it's limitations. It reviews the need for vocational rehabilitation, assessment required for rehabilitation and barriers of vocational rehabilitation for individuals with intellectual disability. The vocational rehabilitation process and preparation of the individual for rehabilitation is covered subsequently. Finally, it presents social skills training and newer trends in rehabilitation like use of virtual reality and sensory integration.

Chapter 17 focuses on the use of assistive technology to empower persons with intellectual disabilities. It highlights the importance of using assistive technology is to help persons with intellectual disabilities and make them independent in all spheres of life. Empirical studies suggest that assistive technology is effective in improving the quality of life of persons with intellectual disability and ensures independence for them. This chapter is an investigation of available research evidence on the use of assistive technology in intellectual disability, discusses utilizations, impediments/barriers, implications and suggests recommendations for future research.

Chapter 18 concentrates on crime and legal issues among intellectually disabled individuals. It presents with research on criminal law and the different forms of aggressive behaviour such as sexual violence, homicide, theft, and arson and alcohol-drug abuse associated with intellectual deficiency. This chapter also provides information on research regarding civil law and the most common problems for individuals with intellectual deficiency, such as financial capacity and capacity for medical consent, issues regarding the trial and conviction for individuals with intellectual deficiency and also recent research on attitudes toward intellectual deficiency and legal issues. Neuropsychological and cross-cultural perspectives of the issues are also presented.

Chapter 19 reviews literature with regard to parents with intellectual disability. It also attempts to review literature on the data available about parents and issue of parenting with intellectual disability in the Indian context while concentrating on directions for future research. Research studies' focussing on parents with intellectual disability is scarce. Available research primarily addresses the question of whether or not individuals with intellectual disability can be adequate parents or reports on methods for improving their parenting skills. There has been relatively negligible work in the Indian context with regard to parents with intellectual disability.

Finally, Chapter 20 deals with sexuality, parenting skills, and associated issues in persons with Intellectual Disability. Sexuality has an active role in the development, evolution, emotional balance and affective stability of the individual. It has a significant role in interpersonal and couple's relationships. As intellectually disabled person approach puberty their control of behaviour and expression of sexuality may manifest in unacceptable ways. Persons with intellectual disabilities are at increased risk for physical, sexual and emotional abuse. This chapter focuses on the issues related to sexual feelings and its expression among intellectually disabled people and the risk for sexual abuse. The necessity of sex education and components of sex education for different group is also explained in detail. The chapter also addresses the parenting skills and problems related with parenthood among individuals with intellectual disability.

This handbook was aimed to provide the latest empirical research findings in the area of Intellectual disability focusing on epidemiology, assessment, causes, and comorbidities, intellectual disabilities at various stages (childhood, adolescence, and adulthood), educational and vocational issues, sexuality, marriage and parenting issues, forensic issues, stigma, and mental health problems among family members. It would also provide a fresh approach and comprehensive knowledge on ID and its various aspects and I think the chapters have done justice to the objective of the handbook.

I am hopeful that the target audience of this Handbook (composed of professionals and researchers working in the mental health area such as clinicians ([especially Psychiatrists, Clinical Psychologists, Pediatricians], academicians, special educators, social workers, Psychiatric nurses, rehabilitation centres, and students in the area of mental health) would be benefited from this handbook. This handbook is useful for Universities, hospitals, and the public. Moreover, it would provide a deep knowledge on ID and its various issues from a developmental approach and it is valuable as it deals with their sexual issues, marriage, parenting skills and issues faced by the family members. It will further enrich our current knowledge of intellectual disabilities. I hope this handbook will be another stepping stone to understand intellectual disabilities in a more comprehensive way.

The research works cited in this book is referenced according to APA guidelines.

I express my gratitude towards all who have contributed and joined with me in the process of writing this book. I would like to thank my son Harikrishnan for his patience, husband and family members for their encouragements and support. Special thanks to all authors, reviewers and editorial members for their constant support and enthusiasm. My heartfelt thanks to the publisher for their continuous support and suggestions.

Rejani Thudalikunnil Gopalan
Gujarat Forensic Sciences University, India

Chapter 1
Intellectual Disability: From History to Recent Trends

Rejani Thudalikunnil Gopalan
Gujarat Forensic Sciences University, India

ABSTRACT

Intellectual Disability (ID, also known as mental retardation) is a condition of arrested or incomplete development of the mind. ID is especially characterized by impairment of skills manifested during the developmental period, which contribute to the overall level of intelligence, i.e. cognitive, language, motor, and social abilities. This chapter focused to give an overall view about its history, changes in terminology, classification, epidemiology, etiology, comorbidities and management. Current understanding and latest trends and issues were highlighted.

HISTORY OF INTELLECTUAL DISABILITY

Intellectual Disability (ID, also known as mental retardation) is a condition of arrested or incomplete development of the mind. ID is especially characterized by impairment of skills manifested during the developmental period, which contribute to the overall level of intelligence, i.e. cognitive, language, motor, and social abilities (WHO, 1992). It occurs in 2-3% of the general population. Prevalence of mild level of intellectual disability is seven to ten times more than severe level of intellectual disability.

The understanding about intellectual disability, mainly its features, causes and intervention has a long history. Both modern and ancient cultures presumed that demon possession caused ID. Similarly, some cultures thought ID was a punishment by God. There were some exceptions. As early as 1500 B.C. some physicians understood IDs as a medical problem. Although translation is imprecise, the therapeutic papyri of Thebes (Luxor), Egypt, 1500 B.C. reference disabilities of the mind due to brain damage. Ancient Greeks and Romans looked upon the condition as a burden on society. Accordingly, persons with ID were treated atrociously. The ancient Greeks and Romans commonly killed infants believed to be defective. Others were sold for entertainment. Since demonic possession or God's wrath was believed the cause, they were treated as less than human. (Reynolds, Zupanick, & Dombeck, 2013).

DOI: 10.4018/978-1-5225-0089-6.ch001

Not much literature is available on mentioning intellectual disability in the past, especially prior to 1700. Jean-Marc Itard (1774-1838) is considered as the pioneer of systematic instruction for intellectually disabled as he tried to educate the boy named Victor with cognitive impairment. The special education for less abled children slowly gained popularity and Edouard Seguin (1812-1880) established an educational program in Paris which emphasized physiological and moral education.One of the major changes occurred in the history of Intellectual disability is the Eugenics movement in the late 19th century. "Eugenics" comes from the Greek words for "good" and "origin," or "good birth" and it is a social philosophy advocating the improvement of human genetic traits through the promotion of higher rates of sexual reproduction for people with desired traits (positive eugenics), or reduced rates of sexual reproduction and sterilization of people with less-desired or undesired traits (negative eugenics), or both (Osborn & Frederick, 1937).The term eugenics was first coined by Francis Galton in the late 1800's and he believed that desirable traits could pass through generations based on his studies on intelligence among upper class of Britain. He found that their desired traits such as superior intelligence are hereditary and passes through generations and favored the idea of selective breeding or humanity could be improved by encouraging the fittest members of society to have more children (Norrgard, 2008). The movement became popular in America in the early part of 20th century and it resulted in a negative attitude towards disabled people including mentally ill and intellectually disabled or feeble-minded individuals as they were considered to polluting the gene pool of the country. Such individuals were seen as a threat to society and the probable cause of most of the criminal activity and social problems of the country. In many states, support for the Eugenics movement resulted in legislation requiring mandatory sterilization, incarceration, and in many cases, the castration of persons with disabilities. In each state, hundreds of thousands of people with mental illness or intellectual disabilities were placed in institutions, the largest of which housed as many as 20,000 people (Felty, 2007).

In addition to this, the development of intelligence tests also made remarkable contribution in the history of Intellectual disability. During the early 1900s, Alfred Binet and Theodore Simon developed the first intelligence test as result of the request by the French government to find students with academic difficulties in the school. Terman standardized this test with sample from America and published in 1916, was called the Stanford-Binet Intelligence Scale. Psychological testing, especially intelligence tests used to identify intellectual deficiency and institutionalization was considered as the major remedy for the problem of intellectual disability.On his study on Kallikak family, Goddard (1912) found that feeblemindedness" was inherited which also encouraged institutionalization and sterilization of intellectually disabled people.

Researches on causes of intellectual disability lead to finding of multiple etiological factors which reflected well on its improved management techniques. The changes in terminology used describe intellectual disability also reflected our understanding about it different dimensions including social stigma. The ideas of normalization evolved in the Scandinavian countries during 1950s-1960s, originated by Niels Eric Bank Mikkelsen. Bank Mikkelsen, who is known as father of Normalization Principle, was the pioneer of the deinstitutionalization movement in the Scandinavian countries. He firstly implemented his ideas of normalization in Denmark, during the 1950s to 1960s. This movement emphasized for providing all the opportunities to all persons with disabilities which are available to a non-disabled person in society, which had a profound positive effect on the lives of the people with disabilities including Intellectually disabled individuals (Kumar, 2013).

The deinstitutionalization movement of the 1970s reflected a concern for the civil rights of mentally retarded.Although deinstitutionalization has been positive for the majority of patients, it also has severe shortcomings. Expectations that community care would lead to fuller social integration have not been achieved; many remain without work, have limited social contacts, and often live in sheltered environments (Fuller, 1997).

Efforts of community integration of disabled individual including intellectually disabled are continuing in different dimensions in terms of education, vocational rehabilitation, social welfare and legal safety. All over the world efforts are taken place in these dimensions and governments, parents organizations, community service centers are working towards this goal though variation can be noticed in developed and developing /under developed countries.

Terminology

Earlier the term simpleton was used to describe people with intellectual disability and it was introduced by S. G. Howe (1846), which was replaced by the term moroninvented by Henry Goddard. Changes reflected in the classification of intellectually disabled individuals in to moron (IQ of 51–70), imbecile (26–50), and idiot (0–25) based on IQ tests. For over 50 years, the most frequently used term to refer to individuals with intellectual disabilities was mental retardation. This term reflected widespread and long-term use in the wake of the elimination of the labels of feeblemindedness, moron, imbecile, and idiot (Polloway & Lubin, 2009). Retarded comes from the Latin retardare,which means "to make slow, delay, keep back, or hinder." Mental retardation replaced older terms such as feeblemindedness, idiocy, and mental subnormality that had become pejorative. Now, over 5 decades later, the term 'mental retardation' is being eliminated for similar reasons (Harris, 2013).

The ICD-10 conceptualization of Mental Retardation is replaced with the concept of intellectual developmental disorders (IDD) in ICD-11. The diagnostic term of mental retardation is replaced by Intellectual Disability In DSM 5. The term "intellectual disability" (ID) has widely replaced MR for policy, administrative and legislative purposes in many countries (Carulla, 2011). A federal statute in the United States (Public Law 111-256, Rosa's Law) replaces the term mental retardation with intellectual disability in law and public policy.

Classification

In ICD-10 criteria, Intellectual disability/mental retardation comes under Mental and Behavioural disorders (F70-F99), specifically from F70 to F79. According to ICD-10 criteria, the coding for degree of mental retardation are: F70 Mild Mental Retardation, F71 Moderate Mental Retardation, F72 Severe Mental Retardation, F73 Profound Mental Retardation, F78 Other Mental Retardation and F79 Unspecified Mental Retardation. In mild mental retardation or intellectual disability, the approximate IQ range from 50 to 69 (in adults, mental age from 9 to under 12 years). This group may have somelearning difficulties in school and many adults will be able to work and maintain good social relationships and contribute to society. In moderate level of intellectual disability or Moderate Mental Retardation, the approximate IQ range from 35 to 49 (in adults, mental age from 6 to under 9 years). This category shows marked developmental delays in childhood but most can learn to develop some degree of independence in self-care and acquire adequate communication and academic skills. Adults will need varying degrees of support to live and work in the community. Under severe Mental Retardation or severe level of Intellectual disability, the approximate IQ range from 20 to 34 (in adults, mental age from 3 to under 6 years).This group needs continuous need of support. In Profound Mental Retardation or profound (IQ under 20 (in adults, mental age below 3 years) which results in severe limitation in self-care, continence, communication and mobility (ICD-10, WHO).

In ICD-11 criteria, the term is used asIntellectual Developmental Disorders and the term defines as 'a group of developmental conditions characterized by significant impairment of cognitive functions, which are associated with limitations of learning, adaptive behavior and skills. The levels of severity (mild, moderate, severe, or profound) are proposed to remain unchanged in ICD-11 (Salvador-Carulla, Reed, Vaez-Azizi et al., 2011).

In DSM 5, the diagnostic term of mental retardation is replaced by Intellectual Disability (Intellectual Developmental Disorder) whichis the equivalent term for the ICD-11 diagnosis of Intellectual Developmental Disorders (DSM-5, p. 33). According to DSM 5, Intellectual Disability (Intellectual Developmental Disorder) is a disorder with onset during the developmental period that includes both intellectual and adaptive functioning deficits in conceptual, social, and practical domains.There are three criteria to be considered for making a diagnosis such as deficits in intellectual functions, deficits in adaptive functioning and the onset of intellectual and adaptive deficits during the developmental period. The severity levels for intellectual disability are mild, moderate severe and profound.

There are lot of changes can be noticed in terms of diagnostic criteria in DSM –IV and DSM 5 on Intellectual disability. Apart from change in terms of terminology, reduced importance placed on the intelligence tests or score. According to DSM-IV significantly sub average intellectual functioning; an IQ of approximately 70 or below, is required but DSM 5 emphasis more on adaptive functions. In DSM –IV, onset is considered to be before the age of 18 which is changed as onset of intellectual and adaptive deficits during the developmental period.

Critical components of intelligence proposed in both DSM-5 and the ICD-11 are verbal comprehension, working memory, perceptual reasoning, and cognitive efficacy. The diagnosis in DSM-5 will emphasize both clinical judgment and standardized intelligence testing; however, less emphasis is expected to be placed on the IQ score, but greater emphasis will be placed on the adaptive reasoning in academic, social, and practical settings. The requirement for both intellectual deficits and adaptive deficits that fail to meet the standards for personal independence are proposed to remain in DSM-5, with greater emphasis on linking intellectual deficits to adaptive deficits through adaptive reasoning in the three domains listed (Harris, 2013).

Epidemiology

Epidemiology is essentially the study of a disorder in a given population. Epidemiological research may investigate the causes of a disease, the natural history of a disease, the characteristics of a disease, influenced by such factors as age, sex, social class and ethnic background.Research may be used to test the efficacy and efficiency of healthcare intervention to prevent or treat the disorder. It may also assist in healthcare planning (Prasher & Routhu, 2003, 2011). Estimation of intellectual disability is important to understand its causes and management.

Prevalence of ID has been reported around 1-3% population in the world (Schalock, Borthwick-Duffy, Bradley, Buntinx, Coulter, Craig, *et al.*, 2010).Studies have noticed that highest prevalence is in low income countries (16.41/1000 population), whereas for middle- and high-income countries is around 15.94 and 9.21/1000 population, and the prevalence of ID is more among child/adolescent population (18.30/1000) in comparison with an adult population (4.94/1000) (Harris and Maulik *et al.,* 2013).

The prevalence of intellectual disability across Asia appears to be consistent with western estimates at 0.06-1.3% (Jeevanandam, 2009). Prevalence of intellectual disability in India is around 2% for mild level of intellectual disability and 0.5% for severe level of intellectual disability (defined as IQ less than 50) (Srinath & Girimaji, 1999). The causes of severe level of intellectual disability can be determined in 60-70% of cases, as compared to mild level of intellectual disability where 35-55% remain idiopathic (Kabra & Gulati, 2003).A recent study noticed that overall, India has a prevalence of 10.5/1000 in ID. Urban population has slightly higher rate (11/1000) than rural (10.08/1000; $P = 0.044$). Age was found to be highly correlated with prevalence of ID in rural children as well as in children and adults in urban population. The possibility of confounding or the existence of covariates for children in urban settings was noted. Results of this study match findings in other epidemiological studies (Lakhan, Ekúndayò, & Shahbazi, 2015).

Variations in estimation of ID are noticed in many countries.For example, according to census results in 2011, the prevalence of ID is around 13/1000 population in Iran. The prevalence of ID is showed according to age and gender. In general, the prevalence of ID among men (5.3/1000) is more than women (3.5/1000), and it has the highest rate for adolescents and young people. The results in comparison to other studies showed that the prevalence of ID in Iran is lower than global estimates significantly. Because of the different definitions of ID and data collection methods, rates are different in Iran as compared with other countries (Soltani, Khosravi & Salehiniya, 2015).

From an epidemiologic perspective, ID prevalence rates vary according to the definitions and classification system being used. Using IQ<70 as the only criteria, researchers estimated that in the United States the prevalence of ID was around 3%. However, by including other criteria such as deficits in adaptive behavior, or defining less severe ID as learning disabilities, or accounting for variable rates of case identification and mortality across different age-groups, the estimates were reduced to 1% (King et al. 2009). Increasing the IQ cut-off score from 70 to 75 almost doubles the number of PWID because of the general population distribution of intelligence. Even across different states within the U.S., prevalence rates among school children vary, from 3.2/1000 in New Jersey to 25.4/1000 in Kentucky, due to varying case definitions, level of completed education, and income level of the family (Massey and McDermott 1995). Intellectual disability is also conceptualized differently across cultures and countries and this is reflected in the many definitions used across countries (WHO 2007).

Over the past 50 years the prevalence and incidence of mental retardation have been affected by changes in the definition of mental retardation, improvements in medical care and technology, societal attitudes regarding the acceptance and treatment of an individual with mental retardation, and the expansion of educational services to children with disabilities from birth through age 21. The theoretical approach to determining the prevalence of mental retardation uses the normal bell curve to estimate the number of individuals whose IQ falls below the established criterion score. For example, 2.3% of the population of the United States has an IQ score below 70, and 5.5% has an IQ score below 75. However, this estimate does not account for adaptive behaviour skills. Assuming a normal distribution for intelligence with a mean of 100, 2.3% of children would be expected to have an IQ score greater than 2 standard deviations below the mean on an intelligence test, for an estimated prevalence of 23 per 1000. However, prevalence as ascertained from community samples has been shown to be closer to 10 per 1000 (Armatas, 2009 ;Yeargin-Alsoppet al 2008).

Etiology

Though hereditary was considered as the single most reason for ID in earlier days, studies in over many decades found multiple causes and risk factors. These include genetic conditions, metabolic disorders, birth related complications, exposure to toxins, Iodine deficiency (cretinism), and malnutrition.

A recent study reported that genetic factors are responsible for up to 40% developmental disability cases, such as global developmental delay/intellectual disability (GDD/DI). Chromosomal abnormalities and fragile X syndrome are the most frequent causes of developmental disabilities and the techniques employed to detect such genetic disorders should be used as first line investigations of GDD/DI (Miclea, Peca, Cuzmici, Pop, 2015). Previous studies noted that single-gene disorders which are associated with atypical or dysmorphic physical characteristics which include fragile X syndrome, neurofibromatosis, tuberous sclerosis, Noonan's syndrome and Cornelia de Lange's syndromecould lead to intellectual disabilities (Sultana et al., 1995; Jones & Smith, 1997). Because of the high prevalence of developmental disabilities, the high genetic contribution to this type of pathology and insufficient referral for genetic consultation, the American and more recently the European guidelines on this group of diseases state that genetic testing is essential and should become a standardized diagnostic practice (Miclea, Peca, Cuzmici, Pop, 2015).

Pre- and post-natal exposure to toxins can cause intellectual disabilities, especially lead, mercury or radiations. Diseases like whooping cough, measles, or meningitis can cause mental disability if medical care is delayed or inadequate (Ardinger & Holmes, 2000; Aicardi, 1998).

Birth related complications can cause intellectual disabilities.Several complications and diseases of pregnancy,delivery, and infancy have been found to be more prevalent among the intellectually disabled-than among normal children (Costeff, Cohen, Weller, & Kleckner, 1981). A recent study reported high rate of (74%) pre-natal, peri-natal and post-natal complications among intellectually disabled children (Gopalan, Sharma & Unnikrishnan, 2014).Pregnant mothers who use alcohol or drugs during pregnancy or exposure to anticonvulsants,diseases in mother such us heart and kidney disease and diabetes and placental dysfunction, congenital infections such as cytomegalovirus, toxoplasmosis, herpes, syphilis, rubella and human immunodeficiency virus; prolonged maternal fever in the first trimester; untreated maternal phenylketonuria (PKU), low-birth-weight, complications of pregnancy or during deliverycan leads to intellectual deficits (Strømme & Hagberg, 2007; Piecuch et al., 1997; Kolevzon, Gross & Reichenberg, 2007).

Studies also shown that intellectual disability is related with Iodine deficiency, malnutrition, male gender, rural back ground, socioeconomic disadvantage,family history of intellectual disability and mental illness, and increased maternal age (Gopalan, Sharma & Unnikrishnan, 2014; Wines, 2006; Emerson & Hatton, 2007; Heikura, Taanila, Hartikainen, Olsen, Linna, Von Wendt, & Järvelin, 2008).

Comorbidities

Intellectual disability is often seen as a predisposing factor for psychiatric disorders and high rates of comorbidity with psychiatric disorders with emotional and behavioural disorders.The risk of psychopathology was found to be significantly increased by moderate intellectual disability, limitations in adaptive behavior, impaired language development, poor socialization, living with one biological parent, and low socio-economic status of the family, child's physical symptoms, family dysfunction, andprevious parental mental health (Gopalan, Sharma & Unnikrishnan, 2014; Kolaitis, 2008; Koskentausta, Iivanainen & Almqvist, 2007; Wallander, Dekker, & Koot, 2006).

Management

Management of ID requires a detailed case history and assessments. The clinical history must put an emphasis on healthcare during the prenatal, perinatal and postnatal period, genealogical tree for at least three generations and an intentional search for family antecedents of mental delay and psychiatric illnesses and congenital abnormalities. Physical exam should focus on secondary abnormalities and congenital malformations, somatometric measurements and neurological and behavioral phenotype evaluations. The clinical exam should include: head circumference evaluation (microcephaly or macrocephaly may provide useful clues to etiology) and height measurement (short stature could indicate fetal alcohol syndrome or tall stature may suggest fragile X syndrome or Sotos syndrome), neurological consultation (evaluation of muscle tone, coordination, tendon reflexes, abnormal movements, or other modifications), ophthalmologic and otolaryngology evaluation, skin changes (pigmentation abnormalities), facial and extremity dysmorphology or internal malformations assessment (Katz, Lazcano-Ponce, 2008; Moeschler & Shevell, 2006).

Intellectual disability is not curable but early identification and managing children with developmental delays may improve the outcomes. The mainstay of ID treatment is the development of a comprehensive management plan for the condition. By considering the comorbidities and multiple disabilities, special inputs would be required from multiple sources such as special educators, language therapists, behavioral therapists, occupational therapists, and community services that provide social support and respite care for families affected by ID. Though no scientifically approved medicines were found to improve the cognitive function of people with ID, they would be benefited from pharmacological treatment for comorbidities such as ADHD, epilepsy, and/or aggressive behaviours.

REFERENCES

Aicardi, J. (1998). The etiology of developmental delay. *Seminars in Pediatric Neurology*, *5*(1), 15–20. doi:10.1016/S1071-9091(98)80013-2 PMID:9548636

Armatas, V. (2009). Mental retardation: Definitions, etiology, epidemiology and diagnosis. *Journal of Sport and Health Research.*, *1*(2), 112–122.

Carulla, L. S., Reed, G. M., Vaezazizi, L. M., Cooper, S. N., Leal, R. M., Bertelli, M., & Saxena, S. et al. (2011). Intellectual developmental disorders: Towards a new name, definition and framework for "mental retardation/intellectual disability" in ICD-11. *World Psychiatry; Official Journal of the World Psychiatric Association (WPA)*, *10*(3), 175–180. doi:10.1002/j.2051-5545.2011.tb00045.x PMID:21991267

Costeff, H., Cohen, B. E., Weller, L., & Kleckner, H. (1981). Pathogenic factors in idiopathic mental retardation. *Developmental Medicine and Child Neurology*, *23*(5), 484–493. doi:10.1111/j.1469-8749.1981.tb02022.x PMID:7196853

Einfeld, S. L., & Tonge, B. J. (1996). Population prevalence of psychopathology in children and adolescents with intellectual disability: II epidemiological findings. *Journal of Intellectual Disability Research*, *40*(2), 99–109. doi:10.1111/j.1365-2788.1996.tb00611.x PMID:8731467

Emerson, E. (2003). Prevalence of psychiatric disorders in children and adolescents with and without intellectual disability. *Journal of Intellectual Disability Research*, *47*(1), 51–58. doi:10.1046/j.1365-2788.2003.00464.x PMID:12558695

Emerson, E., & Hatton, C. (2008). Poverty, socio-economic position, social capital and the health children with intellectual disability. *Journal of Intellectual Disability Research*.

Fuller, T.E. (1997). Deinstitutionalization: A Psychiatric "Titanic". In *Out of the Shadows: Confronting America's Mental Illness Crisis*. John Wiley & Sons.

Goddard, H. H. (1912). *The Kallikak family: A study in the heredity of feeble-mindedness*. New York: Macmillan. doi:10.1037/10949-000

Gopalan, R. T., Sharma, R., & Unnikrishnan, M. P. (2014). Socio-Demographic and Clinical Features of Children with Intellectual Disability and Their Parents-an Indian Study. *International Neuropsychiatric Disease Journal*, *2*(6), 289–302. doi:10.9734/INDJ/2014/10610

Harris, J. C. (2006). *Intellectual Disability: Understanding Its Development, Causes, Classification, Evaluation, and Treatment*. New York: Oxford University Press.

Harris, J. C. (2013). New Terminology for Mental Retardation in DSM-5 and ICD-11. *Current Opinion in Psychiatry*, *26*(3), 260–262. doi:10.1097/YCO.0b013e32835fd6fb PMID:23507999

Heikura, U., Taanila, A., Hartikainen, A. L., Olsen, P., Linna, S. L., Von, W. L., & Järvelin, M. R. (2006). Intellectual disability: A prospective longitudinal population-based study. *Intellectual Disability Research*, *50*(4), 259–268. doi:10.1111/j.1365-2788.2005.00792.x PMID:16507030

Jeevanandam, L. (2009). Perspectives of intellectual disability in Asia: Epidemiology, policy, and services for children and adults. *Current Opinion in Psychiatry*, *22*(5), 462–468. doi:10.1097/YCO.0b013e32832ec056 PMID:19625968

Jones, K. L., & Smith, D. W. (1997). *Smith's recognizable patterns of human malformation* (5th ed.). Philadelphia: Saunders.

Kabra, M., & Gulati, S. (2003). Mental retardation. *Indian Journal of Pediatrics*, *70*(2), 153–158. doi:10.1007/BF02723745 PMID:12661811

Katz, G., & Lazcano-Ponce, E. (2008). Intellectual disability: Definition, etiological factors, classification, diagnosis, treatment and prognosis. *Salud Pública de México*, *50*(2), 132–141. PMID:18470340

Kolevzon, A., Gross, R., & Reichenberg, A. (2007). Prenatal and Perinatal Risk Factors for Autism: A Review and Integration of Findings. *Archives of Pediatrics & Adolescent Medicine*, *161*(4), 326–333. doi:10.1001/archpedi.161.4.326 PMID:17404128

Kumar, A. (2013). Normalization: Guiding Principle of Equal Opportunities in Education for Children with Disabilities in India. *American Journal of Epidemiology*, *167*, 169–177.

Maulik, P. K., Mascarenhas, M. N., Mathers, C. D., Dua, T., & Saxena, S. (2011). Prevalence of intellectual disability: A meta-analysis of population-based studies. *Research in Developmental Disabilities*, *32*(2), 419–436. doi:10.1016/j.ridd.2010.12.018 PMID:21236634

Miclea, D. L., Cuzmici, Z., & Pop, I. V. (2015). Genetic testing in patients with global developmental delay / intellectual disabilities. *A review Med.*, *88*(3), 288–292. PMID:26609258

Moeschler, J. B., & Shevell, M. (2006). Clinical genetic evaluation of the child with mental retardation or developmental delays. *Pediatrics*, *117*(6), 2304–2316. doi:10.1542/peds.2006-1006 PMID:16740881

Norrgard, K. (2008). Human testing, the eugenics movement, and IRBs. *Nature Education*, *1*(1), 170.

Osborn, F. (1937). Development of a Eugenic Philosophy. *American Sociological Review*, *2*(3), 389–397. doi:10.2307/2084871

Piecuch, R. E., Leonard, C. H., Cooper, B. A., & Sehring, S. A. (1997). Outcome of extremely low birth weight infants (500 to 999 grams) over a 12-year period. *Pediatrics*, *100*(4), 633–639. doi:10.1542/peds.100.4.633 PMID:9310517

Polloway, E. A., & Lubin, J. (2009). Feeblemindedness. Encyclopedia of American Disability History of children and adolescents with intellectual disabilities in Britain: A replication. *Journal of Intellectual Disability Research*, *51*, 866–874.

Prasher, V. P., & Routhu, S. K. (2003). Epidemiology of learning(intellectual) disability and comorbid conditions. *Psychiatry*, *2*, 8.

Reynolds, T., Zupanick, C. E., & Dombeck, M. (2013). *Historical and Contemporary Perspectives on Intellectual Disabilities*. Intellectual Disabilities.

Salvador-Carulla, L., Reed, G. M., & Vaez-Azizi, L. M. (2011). Intellectual developmental disorders: Towards a new name, definition and framework for 'mental retardation/intellectual disability' in ICD-11. *World Psychiatry; Official Journal of the World Psychiatric Association (WPA)*, *10*(3), 175–180. doi:10.1002/j.2051-5545.2011.tb00045.x PMID:21991267

Sandberg, N. M., & Ahlström, G. (2015). Prevalence of older people with intellectual disability in Sweden: A spatial epidemiological analysis. *Journal of Intellectual Disability Research*, *59*(12), 1155–1167. doi:10.1111/jir.12219 PMID:26306552

Schalock, R. L., Borthwick-Duffy, S. A., Bradley, V. J., Buntinx, W. H., Coulter, D. L., & Craig, E. M. (2010). *Intellectual Disability: Definition, Classification, and Systems of Supports*. Washington, DC: ERIC.

Schalock, R. L., & Ruth, A. (2007). The Renaming of Mental Retardation: Understanding the Change to the Term Intellectual Disability. *Intellectual and Developmental Disabilities*, *45*(2), 116–124. doi:10.1352/1934-9556(2007)45[116:TROMRU]2.0.CO;2 PMID:17428134

Soltani, S., Khosravi, B., & Salehiniya, H. (2015). Prevalence of intellectual disability in Iran: Toward a new conceptual framework in data collection. *Journal of Research in Medical Sciences*, *20*(7), 714–715. doi:10.4103/1735-1995.166234 PMID:26622264

Srinath, S., & Girimaji, S. C. (1999). Epidemiology of child and adolescent mental health problems and mental retardation. *Nimhans Journal*, *17*, 355–366.

Strømme, P., & Hagberg, G. (2007). Aetiology in severe and mild mental retardation: A population-based study of Norwegian children. *Developmental Medicine and Child Neurology*, *42*(2), 76–86. doi:10.1111/j.1469-8749.2000.tb00050.x PMID:10698323

Sultana, S. A. G., Lam-Po-Tang, T. R. L., Wright, F., Linderman, R., & Purvis-Smith, S. (1995). Fragile X mental retardation in an Indonesian family. *Medical Journal of Indonesia*, *4*, 17–17. doi:10.13181/mji.v4i1.885

Wallander,J.L., Dekker, M.C., Koot, H.M.,(1992) *Variations in prenatal sociodemographic factors associated with intellectual disability*. Academic Press.

World Health Organization. (1992). International statistical classification of diseases and related health problems (10th ed.). Geneva: WHO.

Chapter 2
Mind the Gap:
Developmental Vulnerability and Mental Health

Valsamma Eapen
University of New South Wales, Australia & South West Sydney Local Health District, Australia

Amelia Walter
University of New South Wales, Australia & South West Sydney Local Health District, Australia

ABSTRACT

Individuals with Intellectual Disability (ID) experience higher rates of psychiatric disorders than the general population, although findings are mixed with regard to the determinants of this increased prevalence. Despite growing recognition of the prevalence of mental health problems among individuals with ID, and the consequences this comorbidity carries for individuals, families and the wider community, there are multiple challenges in identifying and managing these concerns. Accurate diagnosis and effective intervention is currently hindered by factors including the applicability of standardised psychiatric classification systems, gaps in service delivery models and access to such services, as well as unmet training needs.

INTRODUCTION

Despite increased recognition of the prevalence and impact of psychiatric disorders among individuals with Intellectual Disability (ID), the early assessment and treatment of these remains a challenge. This is particularly caused by limitations in current assessment and diagnostic systems, and further development and refinement of standardised diagnostic systems is critical. Furthermore, in order for intervention to be effective, it must address the multiple risk and resilience factors underlying ID and comorbid mental health problems. Therefore, from a public health perspective, rates of comorbid psychiatric disorders should be taken into account when planning for provision of services. Similarly, intervention research should consider the role of comorbidity in predicting outcomes, while basic science research would benefit from increasing understanding of these comorbidities by delineating possible heterogeneous

DOI: 10.4018/978-1-5225-0089-6.ch002

aetiological and neurobiological determinants. This chapter will review and synthesise the literature on the prevalence, impact and determinants of the comorbidity of ID and psychiatric disorders, and discuss important considerations to improve accurate identification and effective management of these concerns.

BACKGROUND

Intellectual Disability (ID) is characterised by deficits in both intellectual and adaptive functioning beginning during childhood or adolescence (APA, 2013). Adaptive behaviour includes conceptual skills (e.g., language, money and time concepts), social skills (e.g., interpersonal skills and social problem solving), and practical skills (e.g., activities of daily living and occupation) (Maulik, Mascarenhas, Mathers, Dua, & Saxena, 2011).

A recent meta-analysis found that the overall global prevalence of ID was approximately 1%, with higher prevalence rates found in low- and middle-income countries, and among child and adolescent populations (Maulik et al., 2011). Social gradients and ethnic disparities have been reported in previous research on the prevalence of ID. For example, lower socio-economic status (SES) has been found to be associated with a marked increase in the prevalence of ID, particularly mild ID (Emerson, 2012; Leonard et al., 2005; Leonard & Wen, 2002; Roeleveld & Zielhuis, 1997; Stromme & Magnus, 2000), and higher rates of ID have been found among African-American and Indigenous Australian children (Croen, Grether, & Selvin, 2001; Leonard, Petterson, Bower, & Sanders, 2003; Leonard et al., 2005; Yeargin-Allsopp, Drews, Decouflé, & Murphy, 1995). In a recent epidemiological study to estimate the burden of disease caused by ID in Australia, the authors estimated that ID was responsible for 1.7% of the total disease burden in all Australians, and 5.5% of the total disease burden in Indigenous Australians (Begg et al., 2007; Vos, Barker, Stanley, & Lopez, 2007). Of particular concern is the evidence that an "inverse care law" applies, in that the greater number of risk factors a child may have for ID, the less access they have to preventative and comprehensive health care (Woolfenden et al., 2013). This creates a vicious cycle whereby the risk factors that may predispose a child to ID are also the same risk factors that may mean they are likely to miss out on timely and effective identification and intervention.

CHALLENGES IN THE ASSESSMENT AND MANAGEMENT OF PSYCHIATRIC DISORDERS AMONG INDIVIDUALS WITH INTELLECTUAL DISABILITY

Prevalence of Psychiatric Disorders among Individuals with Intellectual Disability

In a recent systematic review, Einfeld, Ellis, and Emerson (2011) found that between 30 and 50% of children and adolescents with ID had a comorbid mental disorder, and that the relative risk of mental disorder associated with ID, when compared to children and adolescents without ID, ranged from 2.8 to 4.5. Consistent with these findings, a secondary analysis of the 1999 and 2004 Office for National Statistics surveys of the mental health of British children and adolescents estimated that the 3% of British children with ID accounted for 14% of total child and adolescent psychiatric morbidity (Emerson &

Hatton, 2007b). Comparing 641 children with ID and 17 774 children without ID, this research found that the prevalence of psychiatric disorders was observed to be 36% among children with ID and 8% among children without (Odds Ratio/OR=6.5). Increased prevalence among children with ID was particularly marked for autism spectrum disorder (OR=33.4), hyperkinesis (OR=8.4) and conduct disorders (OR=5.7). Furthermore, a cumulative effect was observed, with research suggesting that the greater the number of social or environmental risk factors a child with ID is exposed to (e.g., low SES, stressful life events, poor parental mental health), the higher their risk of having mental health problems such as emotional or conduct disorders (Emerson & Hatton, 2007b).

Other studies have also noted an increased relative risk for psychiatric disorders among children and adolescents with ID, and this has been found across a range of diagnoses including anxiety and mood disorders, behaviour disorders and attention deficit hyperactivity disorder (Dekker & Koot, 2003a; Emerson, 2003; Emerson & Hatton, 2007b). A secondary analysis of the 1999 Office for National Statistics survey of the mental health of children and adolescents in Great Britain found that the prevalence of any diagnosed ICD-10 disorder, as well as specific disorders such as conduct disorder, anxiety disorder, hyperkinesis and pervasive developmental disorders, was significantly greater among children with ID than among their non-ID peers (Emerson, 2003). This study noted that there were no statistically significant differences between children with and without ID with regard to rates of depressive disorders, eating disorders or psychosis.

Longitudinal studies suggest that comorbid psychiatric disorders among children with ID persist through to adolescence and adulthood (Chadwick, Kusel, Cuddy, & Taylor, 2005; Einfeld et al., 2006; Richardson & Koller, 1996; Tonge & Einfeld, 2000). For example, in a 14-year longitudinal study of children with ID in Australia, high initial levels of behavioural and emotional disturbance decreased only slowly over time, with 31% of participants continuing to meet criteria for a psychiatric disorder in young adulthood (Einfeld et al., 2006). Greater decreases in psychopathology were found among males rather than females, and in participants with mild ID compared to those with severe or profound ID.

Overall findings with regard to rates of mental disorder among adults with ID have been somewhat inconsistent, partially due to differing methods for assessing psychiatric comorbidity. In their meta-analysis, Maulik et al. (2011) found that studies based on diagnosing psychiatric comorbidity using psychological assessments or scales showed higher prevalence compared to those using standard diagnostic systems and disability instruments. When ICD-10 or DSM-IV-TR criteria have been applied, reported rates of psychiatric disorder among adults with ID have been comparable to those found in the general population (Cooper, Smiley, Morrison, Williamson, & Allan, 2007; Deb, Thomas, & Bright, 2001); however, the utility of these criteria among individuals with ID has been questioned (Einfeld & Tonge, 1999; Sturmey, 1995). When psychiatric diagnoses were made by consultant psychiatrists on the basis of clinical interviews, Cooper et al. (2007) found that 41% of adults with ID met diagnostic criteria for at least one mental disorder. This is a significantly higher point prevalence rate than that observed in the general population, where rates have been estimated to be approximately 13.2% (Andrews, Henderson, & Hall, 2001). Indeed, reviews generally indicate a three to four-fold increased prevalence of psychiatric problems among individuals with ID compared to the general population (Harris, 2006). As for children and adolescents, a number of psychiatric disorders have been found to be more common among adults with ID than among the general population, including anxiety and affective disorders, psychotic disorders, and behavioural problems (Maulik & Harbour, 2010).

Impact of Psychiatric Disorders among Individuals with Intellectual Disability

Psychopathology associated with ID carries significant consequences for individuals with ID, their families and the wider community. For individuals themselves, for example, the dual disability of ID and psychiatric disorder is a major cause of failure of transition to school programs and community residential placements (Bruininks, Hill, & Morreau, 1988; Einfeld et al., 2006), leads to restricted participation in recreational and educational programs (Parmenter, Einfeld, Tonge, & Dempster, 1998), and is associated with reduced workplace opportunities following school (Anderson, Lakin, Hill, & Chen, 1992). Robust evidence indicates that a lack of early detection and intervention has significant implications for the future academic, behavioural and social functioning of children with ID (Bouras, 2011).

Interactions between social environment, family, ID and mental health problems are complex and not unidirectional. It is known that families experiencing additional life stress prior to having children are more likely to have children with ID (Eapen, Al-Gazali, Bin-Othman, & Pramathan, 1998). This is particularly the case with respect to Indigenous families, those from culturally and linguistically diverse backgrounds, and those with a parent who has ID or a mental illness (Leonard et al., 2011; Leonard et al., 2005; To et al., 2004). Hence, a vicious cycle of the development of ID and mental health problems can be seen at an individual level or in population groups experiencing adversity (Whitehouse, Durkin, Jaquet, & Ziatas, 2009; Whitehouse, Watt, Line, & Bishop, 2009). This confluence of factors generates a significant health burden for individuals, families, and communities, as well as inequity in child health resulting in significant health and economic impacts.

The long-term support of individuals with ID places a considerable burden on families and carers (Bourke et al., 2008; Miodrag & Hodapp, 2010), and mothers in particular are at increased risk of mental health problems (Abbeduto et al., 2004). Several studies have found that parents of children and adolescents with ID have higher levels of child-related stress and depression than parents of typically developing children (Browne & Bramston, 1998; Dyson, 1997; Olsson & Hwang, 2001; White & Hastings, 2004), and key short- and long-term outcomes for families of individuals with ID may be mediated, at least in part, by mental health (Eapen, 2014). For example, the mental wellbeing of parents of children and young adults with ID has been shown to be more strongly influenced by the severity of their child's comorbid mental health disorders including emotional and behavioural problems than by the severity of their ID (McIntyre, Blacher, & Baker, 2002; Tonge & Einfeld, 2003). Mental health problems among children and young adults with ID have also been shown to significantly predict parents' feelings of dissatisfaction with the family situation (Maes, Broekman, Došen, & Nauts, 2003), mothers' perceived negative impact of their child on the family, and the family's decision to seek out-of-home placement (Maes et al., 2003; McIntyre et al., 2002). It is interesting to note that stress did not account for significant additional variance in this decision-making (McIntyre et al., 2002), suggesting that mental health problems can significantly impact on the family's ability to care for a young person with ID without requiring out-of-home care arrangements. This adds to the social and financial burden of ID on families and societies, and has significant implications for service provision and policy development.

ID is also associated with reduced life expectancy and poorer quality of life (Begg et al., 2007), and high economic costs for governments and families (Doran et al., 2012). It ranks within the top 20 sources of burden of disease (Begg et al., 2007) and is among the 20 most costly disorders (Polder, Meerding, Bonneux, & Van Der Maas, 2002). This burden is compounded when ID is associated with a comorbid mental health disorder, leading to greater economic burden for provision of health care and education, in addition to further reductions in capacity for employment and earning.

Determinants of Mental Health Problems in Intellectual Disability

Given the high prevalence of mental health disorders among individuals with ID, and the impact of this dual diagnosis on individuals, families and the community, there has also been interest in examining specific variables that may influence this comorbidity.

Available evidence from the literature suggests that most variance in developmental vulnerability is associated with the social determinants of health and their interaction with an individual's innate biological susceptibility to adversity (Guralnick, 1997; Zeanah, Boris, & Larrieu, 1997). Cumulative exposure to risk factors over time in the absence of protective factors can result in changes in neuronal circuitry with long-term consequences (Eapen, 2014). For example, there is evidence of altered brain architecture found in children exposed to abusive environments or who have a history of sensory deprivation, as well as an association between the impact of less extreme adverse environments on brain architecture linked with language and reading skills (Hackman, Farah, & Meaney, 2010; Marmot et al., 2010). Such risk and protective factors have their maximum effect during *critical* or *sensitive* periods, especially in the first five years of life (Maggi, Irwin, Siddiqi, & Hertzman, 2010; Siddiqi, Irwin, & Hertzman, 2007). While brain plasticity offers an opportunity for maximum gains with appropriate intervention during the early years, this becomes increasingly difficult the further we move away from childhood.

There is also emerging evidence of a transactional relationship between genes and the environment (A. E. Sameroff, 2009), suggesting that individuals with certain genetic profiles may be more sensitive to favourable and unfavourable environmental influences than those without such genetic makeups (Mitchell et al., 2013). In other instances the behavioural or mental health problem may be part of the behavioural phenotype of the underlying genetic condition as is the case with Lesch-Nyhan syndrome and self-injurious behaviours, Fragile X syndrome and disruptive behaviours, Williams syndrome and exceptional conversational verbal abilities and excessive empathy, Prader-Willi syndrome and temper tantrums and obsessive-compulsive features, and Angelman syndrome and happy affect and hyperactivity (Cassidy & Morris, 2001). Further, when the condition is associated with dysmorphic features or changes in physical appearance, such as short stature or excessive growth, or delayed sexual development or functioning, affected individuals can suffer from low self-esteem and this can, in turn, lead to secondary emotional or behavioural difficulties.

Due to the transactional and inter-dependent relationship between these factors, developmental vulnerability should be understood, assessed and treated with consideration given to the cumulative impact of multiple factors, both risk and protective, including those related to the individual child, family, psychosocial status, neighbourhood, and service systems and policy (Eapen, 2014). The occurrence and nature of mental health comorbidity in children with ID is therefore influenced by the interaction between biological and environmental risk and protective factors, with the overall risk increasing as the number of risk factors increases (Eapen, 2014).

Exposure to a range of social and environmental risk factors such as poverty, living in a single-parent household, exposure to negative life events, low parental education, and poor maternal mental and physical health, has been found to be associated with increased prevalence of emotional and conduct disorders among children both with and without ID (Emerson & Hatton, 2007b). Importantly, however, exposure to these risk factors was found to be significantly higher among children with ID, with 46% of them having been exposed to three or more potential risk factors compared to 24% of children without ID. While there is limited evidence regarding the specific factors predicting the presence of mental health problems in individuals with ID (Costello & Bouras, 2006), these findings are consistent with the prevailing view that individuals with ID are more vulnerable to psychosocial stress than people without ID, and are therefore more likely to develop psychiatric symptomatology (Deb et al., 2001).

Similar findings were reported by Emerson (2003), who conducted a secondary analysis of data from 10 438 children aged between five and 15 years from the 1999 ONS survey of the Mental Health of Children and Adolescents in Great Britain (Meltzer, Gatward, Goodman, & Ford, 2000). Specific family characteristics were found to be associated with increased rates of particular psychiatric diagnoses, and children living in families belonging to lower social classes, and those from single-parent and lower-income households, were found to be at increased risk for a range of psychiatric disorders, including emotional disorders, anxiety disorders, depression and conduct disorders. A further study specifically examining the contribution of socioeconomic position to the health and mental health status of children and adolescents with ID, using the same sample, found that between-group differences in socioeconomic position and household composition accounted for 24% of the increased risk for poor health, 23% of the increased risk for conduct disorder and 37% of the increased risk for emotional disorder among children and adolescents with ID (Emerson & Hatton, 2007a). The authors concluded that socioeconomic disadvantage may account for a significant proportion of the increased risk for poorer physical and mental health among children and adolescents with ID. Another study, however, failed to find significant differences in the prevalence of psychiatric disorders between children classified as low SES and those classified as medium to high SES (Dekker & Koot, 2003b).

Factors related to parents, including parental mental health and parenting practices, have also been found to be an important determinant of mental health problems in children and adolescents with ID (Dekker & Koot, 2003b; Emerson, 2003). Children whose primary carers reported more frequent use of punitive strategies and who had higher scores on the General Health Questionnaire (a measure assessing risk of developing psychiatric disorders) were more likely to have a range of psychiatric disorders, including an emotional disorder, an anxiety disorder, a conduct disorder and hyperkinesis (Emerson, 2003).

In a systematic review, Einfeld et al. (2011) discuss individual factors that have been associated with mental disorder in children and adolescents with ID. Factors that have been most commonly examined include age, gender and severity of ID, but findings have been largely inconsistent. With regard to age, some studies have found higher rates of psychiatric disorder in younger children when compared to teenagers (Molteno, Molteno, Finchilescu, & Dawes, 2001), but others studies have shown no significant relationships between age and overall rates of mental disorder (Einfeld & Tonge, 1996a, 1996b). Other studies have examined age effects for particular psychiatric disorders. Older children with ID (aged 11 – 16 years) have been found to be more likely to have an emotional disorder, including a depressive disorder, while younger children (aged 5 – 10 years) were more likely to have hyperactivity or a pervasive developmental disorder (Emerson, 2003; Emerson & Hatton, 2007b). Among adults with ID, increasing age has been found to be associated with a higher likelihood of psychiatric illness (Cooper, 1997; Deb et al., 2001).

Mixed findings have also been noted with regard to the association between gender and risk of mental disorders among children and adolescents with ID. Some studies have found no effect of gender on overall rates of mental disorder (Einfeld & Tonge, 1996a, 1996b; Molteno et al., 2001), but other studies have reported significantly higher overall rates of mental health problems among male children and adolescents with ID (Emerson, 2003; Stromme & Diseth, 2000). Further, some studies of children and adolescents with ID have found that males are significantly more likely to have conduct disorder and hyperactivity than females with ID (Emerson, 2003; Emerson & Hatton, 2007b), while others have shown no gender effects for anxiety, mood or disruptive disorders (Dekker & Koot, 2003a). In a study of adults with ID, female gender was associated with increased prevalence of psychiatric disorder (Cooper et al., 2007).

The literature is also unclear about how the severity of ID affects an individual's vulnerability to developing different psychiatric disorders (Costello & Bouras, 2006). Among children and adolescents, several studies have reported no statistically significant association between severity of ID and risk of psychiatric disorder (Einfeld & Tonge, 1996a, 1996b; Stromme & Diseth, 2000), but one study found higher rates of mental disorder in participants with more severe ID (Molteno et al., 2001). Findings are also mixed in adults. Some studies have shown higher rates of psychiatric illness among people with severe ID (Cooper et al., 2007; Gostason, 1985; Lund, 1985), others among individuals with mild ID (Borthwick-Duffy & Eyman, 1990; Iverson & Fox, 1989), and others have found no evidence either way (Corbett, 1979). Intellectual functioning has also been examined, with findings suggesting that depressive feelings, anxiety and antisocial behaviours are more common among those with higher IQs, while psychotic, self-absorbed and autistic behaviours are more likely to be found in children with lower IQs (Dekker & Koot, 2003b). The impact of physical disability on psychiatric illness is also unclear. Some studies have found that physical disability is associated with an increased prevalence of mental disorder (Deb et al., 2001), while others report that the absence of severe physical disability and immobility is associated with greater prevalence of psychiatric illness (Cooper et al., 2007).

Challenges in Identification of Psychiatric Disorders among Individuals with Intellectual Disability

There are a number of obstacles to the valid and reliable identification of mental health problems in people with ID (Hatton, 2002). Firstly, standardised psychiatric classification systems are often adopted in studies of mental health problems in people with ID (Costello & Bouras, 2006); however, the applicability of these to this population is questionable. Two factors have been posited to influence the applicability of standardised psychiatric assessment criteria to individuals with ID: linguistic abilities and the presentation of mental health problems (Costello & Bouras, 2006).

Current diagnostic systems such as ICD-10 and DSM-5 rely upon verbal accounts of an individual's symptoms. The utility of these systems is therefore limited by the linguistic skills of the individual being assessed. As Costello and Bouras (2006) note, some features of psychiatric illness are complex, requiring a high level of verbal fluency to describe and differentiate between symptoms. Therefore, the use of these existing diagnostic symptoms may not be appropriate among people with ID, particularly those with severe ID who frequently have limited or no language skills. When examining mental health among individuals with ID, it is therefore necessary to assess the individual's non-verbal behaviour, in addition to gathering historical information and observations from other people such as family members or carers. Importantly, the validity of this information is also dependent on the particular psychiatric condition in question, with informants likely to be more aware of disorders with clear behavioural manifestations rather than subjectively experienced phenomena such as thought disorder or anxiety (Costello & Bouras, 2006).

In addition to concerns with regard to linguistic abilities, the use of standardised classification systems among individuals with ID assumes that mental health problems present in the same way in this population as they do in the general population; however, this may not be the case and may also depend on the severity of ID. For example, in a review of mood disorders among patients with ID, Hurley (2006) reported that individuals with mild ID had a fairly typical presentation and could be assessed using standard practices with minor accommodations. An atypical presentation of mood disorders, however, including increased behavioural problems such as aggression, was more frequent in individuals with moderate to profound ID. Due to limitations in the use of standardised diagnostic symptoms, various instruments (including both self- and informant-report measures) have been either designed specifically or adapted for use with individuals with ID (for a review, see Hatton, 2002).

Differential diagnosis between symptoms that may be an expression of underlying brain damage and those that are related to a psychiatric disorder may also be particularly important when working with individuals with ID (Costello & Bouras, 2006). Disturbances of emotion, attention, activity and thought, and associated behavioural problems, may occur as part of the ID and it is often difficult to ascertain whether these additional difficulties are due to a comorbid psychiatric disorder. For example, it is important to distinguish between ID and the negative symptoms of schizophrenia such as slowness of thought and poverty of speech (Clarke, Littlejohns, Corbett, & Joseph, 1989).

It is likely that many individuals with ID have mental health problems that remain undetected and therefore untreated (Taylor, Hatton, Dixon, & Douglas, 2004). Einfeld et al. (2006), for example, found that only 10% of young adults with ID and definite psychiatric disorder had received specialist mental health intervention. Insufficient numbers of professionals with appropriate training and necessary expertise may impede accurate diagnosis and the adequate provision of mental health services to people with ID (Maulik & Harbour, 2010; McCarthy & Boyd, 2002). Diagnostic overshadowing, where a clinician regards the ID as a sufficient explanation for an individual's presenting symptoms rather than attributing them to a psychiatric disorder and making a dual diagnosis, may be partly responsible for the under-recognition of dual disability in clinical settings (Tonge & Einfeld, 2000). Recognition of comorbid psychopathology requires detailed interviews using sensitive assessment techniques by specialist staff (Maulik & Harbour, 2010).

Furthermore, in the general population, identification of a mental health problem is often prompted by the failure of an individual to maintain social roles such as employment and parenting. In contrast, individuals with ID generally have fewer societal role expectations and the severity of their symptoms therefore does not necessarily relate to the degree of impairment in daily life (Costello & Bouras, 2006). This reduces the chances that mental health problems will be recognised by carers, and means that conditions such as anxiety and depression may cause significant distress to an individual yet remain undiagnosed.

The prevalence, persistence and consequences of comorbid mental health problems in individuals with ID necessitate improvements in the availability of early assessment and diagnostic services for these individuals and their families, for whom there are currently significant gaps in service provision (McCarthy & Boyd, 2002).

Challenges in Management of Psychiatric Disorders among Individuals with Intellectual Disability

The significant comorbidity between ID and mental health disorders poses considerable challenges to individuals with ID and their families, and for service providers (Eapen & Jairam, 2009), including not only significant barriers in the detection of mental health problems among individuals with ID but also the unique challenges in the management of these concerns. Some of the specific challenges in this regard include the lack of an interdisciplinary service model; lack of dedicated 'space' within mainstream mental health services for individuals with ID; lack of a clear transition model from childhood to adult services; and lack of staff training and expertise. Such deficiencies in service provision, and the associated cognitive, emotional and behavioral problems, combine to increase rates of unemployment, social isolation and depression in individuals with ID and their families, and the consequent healthcare burden for communities and governments.

There is an acute need to be aware of the impact of ID and associated mental health difficulties not only on the individual, but also on the wellbeing of his or her family. Several studies have found that parents of children with ID report higher levels of child-related stress than parents of typically developing children (Browne & Bramston, 1998; Dyson, 1997). Parental stress may result from life events that may impact on any family such as marital breakdown, but also from family life-cycle transitions that may be especially relevant to families of children with disabilities, such as the diagnosis of the child's disability, starting school, transition from child to adult services, and increasing age and infirmity of parents (Hastings & Beck, 2004). It has been assumed that the extra stress of caring for a child with disabilities places parents at an increased risk for depression. Indeed, mothers of children with ID have been found to have higher depression scores than mothers of typically developing children, although no significant differences were found in reported depressive symptoms among fathers (Olsson & Hwang, 2001).

Thus, one of the primary targets of intervention when working with children with ID and their families should be to reduce stress and increase wellbeing among parents. This is also important because it is likely that parents of children with ID who report high levels of stress may engage in parenting behaviour that may negatively affect outcomes both in the child with ID and his or her siblings (Hastings & Beck, 2004), thus maintaining a vicious cycle. Indeed, it is likely that complex and multidirectional relationships exist between parents' wellbeing, psychological coping styles, parenting practices, and their child's behavioural problems, and comprehensive and effective intervention should aim to target these various factors.

Several factors have been found to explain stress among parents of children with ID. For example, research has suggested that child characteristics, such as the frequency or severity of behaviour problems, may lead to parental stress (Hassall, Rose, & McDonald, 2005; Hastings, 2002). For example, in a study of Australian children with a disability, the severity of children's behaviour was associated with parents' experience of greater stress in relation to their child, and their own personal wellbeing (Gavidia-Payne, Richdale, Francis, & Cotton, 1997). Thus, interventions that are successful at improving skills or reducing problem behaviours in children with ID also seem to benefit parental wellbeing (Gavidia-Payne & Hudson, 2002; Hastings & Beck, 2004). Other studies, however, have found that different factors are more important in predicting parental stress than child characteristics. For example, the way in which parents define their situation, and the resources available to them, have been found to predict significantly more variance in stress levels in mothers (29% and 42% respectively) and fathers (37% and 33% respectively) than any characteristics of the child, which accounted for only 2% of variance in maternal stress and 8% of variance in paternal stress (Saloviita, Itälinna, & Leinonen, 2003). Similarly, significant variance in mothers' parenting stress has been found to be explained by parental locus of control and parenting satisfaction (Hassall et al., 2005). These findings are encouraging, as changing parents' attitudes and perceptions may be an easier intervention target than ameliorating the child's disability and associated difficulties (Saloviita et al., 2003).

Recent reviews suggest that behavioural family interventions that train parents to respond contingently to child behaviour indicate positive results among both children with ID and their parents (Gavidia-Payne & Hudson, 2002; Hastings & Beck, 2004). For example, Stepping Stones Triple P (Sanders, Mazzecchelli, & Studman, 2003), an adaptation of the Triple P Positive Parenting Program for families of children with developmental disabilities, has been found to lead to fewer maternal-reported child behaviour problems, improved maternal and paternal parenting style, and decreased maternal stress, with gains maintained at the six-month follow-up (Roberts, Mazzucchelli, Studman, & Sanders, 2006). Similarly, parents of children with ID who have been trained in behavioural principles, such as limit setting and use of consequences and rewards, have been found to report increases in their self-efficacy in managing their child's behaviour, as well as lower levels of stress (Feldman & Werner, 2002). While parent training programs have been found to be beneficial, some research has suggested that families with additional psychosocial stressors such as lack of employment and poor marital adjustment may make the least gains (Baker, Landen, & Kashima, 1991).

Hastings and Beck (2004) have also reviewed other interventions for stress reduction in parents of children with ID, including parent-to-parent interventions, and group interventions with parents. Although descriptions of various models have been published, strong evaluation data has rarely been reported for parent-to-parent interventions. One exception is a controlled trial of the Parent-to-Parent model (Singer et al., 1999), in which a parent who has experience caring for a child with a disability is paired with and provides emotional support and information to another parent of a child with ID. Although no measure of parental stress was used, the study found that parents' positive perceptions of their child and his or her impact on the family improved significantly in the treatment group, and parents' ratings of progress towards the resolution of their main need showed a clear improvement (Singer et al., 1999). Aside from the value of formal or informal networks of parents, research has also investigated the efficacy of group interventions for decreasing stress among parents of children with ID. Most group interventions have involved elements of cognitive-behavioural therapy (CBT), and suggest a reasonable evidence base for the use of CBT techniques in improving the wellbeing of parents of children with ID (for a review, see Hastings & Beck, 2004). For example, mothers assigned to a Life Skills Training group where sessions focused on CBT techniques including coping and communication skills, problem solving and decision making, and skills to manage and control social networks, had reduced depression and stress and improved social support compared to mothers who were assigned to a non-directive parent support group (Kirkham & Schilling, 1990). Further, mothers in the Life Skills Training group maintained lower depression scores and higher levels of social support at a two-year follow-up (Kirkham, 1993). Furthermore, there is increasing evidence of the buffering role of informal support in the management of young people with ID and mental health problems and their families. For example, parents of adolescents with ID who perceived greater helpfulness from informal supports (e.g., spouse, extended family, friends) reported lower stress, anxiety and depression, even after controlling for child characteristics (White & Hastings, 2004). Typical appropriate supports provided by services for children with ID and their families such as respite services, case management and provision of key workers are also likely to contribute to reductions in parental stress (Hastings & Beck, 2004). Further, the establishment of early family-school partnerships is important in promoting positive outcomes among children with developmental delays and should not be overlooked as children transition to school (McIntyre, Blacher, & Baker, 2006). The importance of school-based intervention programs for mental health difficulties, including among children and adolescents with ID, has been recognised (Christensen et al., 2011). School-based interventions, such as the NSW School-Link initiative in NSW, Australia (NSW Ministry of Health, 2015), and targeted policies, such as the No Child Left Behind Act ("No Child Left Behind Act of 2001," 2002) are vital in ensuring effective intervention is provided to children and adolescents with comorbid mental disorders and ID.

Having a brother or sister with ID is a risk factor for sibling adjustment problems (Rossiter & Sharpe, 2001). Within their families, siblings may experience extra caregiver burden, differential treatment, and an imbalance of family resources (Lobato & Kao, 2002). Outside their families, siblings may experience limited access to information about the child's condition, negative peer reactions, and disruptions in age-appropriate peer and family activities (Lobato & Kao, 2002). Thus, siblings of children with ID may also require formal support. Studies have investigated the efficacy of combined group interventions for siblings and parents of children with ID that are designed to increase the siblings' understanding of and adjustment to ID. These studies have found significant improvements in siblings' knowledge of the child's disorder, siblings' self-competence, and sibling connectedness, and decreases in parent-reported behavioural problems among siblings (Lobato & Kao, 2002, 2005). Several of these improvements have been shown to be maintained at three-month follow-up (Lobato & Kao, 2002, 2005). Open communication and sharing age-appropriate information with siblings appears to be the best approach, as this reduces uncertainty and confusion, helps the development of family-centred problem solving skills, and allows siblings to support parents in the best way they can. If there are issues of risk to the sibling in terms of violent or aggressive behaviours, appropriate safety steps should also be taken.

Despite this range of interventions, there are significant challenges in providing a comprehensive and integrated service for those with ID and mental health problems. For example, studies from the UK have shown that young people with severe ID and mental health problems fall between a number of healthcare providers, including child and adolescent mental health services, specialist ID services and paediatricians (McCarthy & Boyd, 2002). Working with children with ID and their families likely necessitates a multidisciplinary approach, potentially involving physiotherapy for motor development and coordination, occupational therapy for proprioception and sensory integration, speech therapy for receptive, expressive and pragmatic communication, psychology for assistance with thoughts, feelings and behaviour including social interaction, and medical specialists for assistance with physical health difficulties, just to name a few. In this regard, it is worth noting that severity of ID is associated with an increase in associated medical conditions and complications, with the relationship being complex as they interact with one another and can result in secondary medical and behavioural complications (O'Brien, Barnard, Pearson, & Rippon, 2002). Collaboration and clear communication is also needed between families, health providers, and the various other agencies involved in the patient's care including education, housing and financial support services. Due to the multidisciplinary nature of services required for children with ID and their families, a model where one person works closely with the family and can mediate between the family and various services or professionals may lead to the most positive outcomes for parents (Hastings & Beck, 2004). However, there is often no collaboration or communication to enable a continuum of care. This is further compounded by the fact that different disciplines and agencies use different models of care ranging from patient-centred to those involving the family. Often there is no continuity between various services such as acute inpatient units, emergency departments, outpatient and community services, education services, vocational centres, the juvenile justice system and disability services. Families may be expected to go from one specialist to another, and navigating the complex health system is a significant challenge for both patients and their carers.

Hatton (2002) reviewed the literature on psychosocial interventions for adults with ID and comorbid mental health problems. Individual and group intervention studies using modified CBT, including one small waiting list controlled trial (Rose, West, & Clifford, 2000), have found reductions in anger and aggressive behaviour among adults with ID. Adaptations of CBT have also shown reasonable outcomes in reducing depression and anxiety among adults with ID, but the reviewed research is limited to case studies and case series (Hatton, 2002). When implementing CBT with adults with ID, Hatton (2002) discusses the importance of assessing the individual's capacity to give informed consent. Wong, Clare, Holland, Watson, and Gunn (2000) found that people with ID and people with dementia were less able to make an informed consent decision than people with a chronic mental health problem or a comparison group. All participants benefited when the informed consent decision-making task was simplified by presenting information as separate elements and reducing the level of expressive verbal ability required to respond (Wong et al., 2000). These considerations may be particularly important when working with adults with comorbid ID and mental health problems. Further, consideration must be given to the person's suitability to engage in CBT, including assessment of communication skills, cognitive aptitude, ability to identify emotions, and capacity to understand the CBT model (Hatton, 2002). Enhancing skills including communication, emotion recognition, problem solving and social skills can lead to increased independence and self-determination, which in turn can improve overall quality of life among individuals with ID (Nota, Ferrari, Soresi, & Wehmeyer, 2007). Assistance with housing, employment, social networks and independent living skills also deserve attention.

Risk management is also important when working with individuals with comorbid ID and mental health problems. One particular area that warrants attention is the issue of behavioural change associated with sexual development, which can lead to sexualised behaviours and offending. Social stories appropriate to the mental age of the person with ID and sexual health education are critical in these situations. CBT has also been found to be successful in changing attitudes in sex offenders with ID (Hatton, 2002). Planning for emergencies and crisis situations is an important consideration of treatment, and having a safety plan with contact numbers of case workers or members of the treating team in case a crisis happens can put the mind at ease for both the patient and the family.

While randomised controlled trials concerning the effectiveness of psychotropic medications for people with ID and comorbid mental health problems are virtually absent (Hatton, 2002), psychopharmacology is a treatment option although this is also associated with challenges. It is to be noted that individuals with ID are often more at risk of developing side effects. One example of the potential complexities when treating people with ID who also have mental health problems is evident when these individuals are treated with second generation antipsychotics (SGAs) which considerably decrease the lifespan due to increased risk of weight gain, cardiometabolic changes, metabolic syndrome and related side effects of SGAs. In either case, attention should also be given to an integrated and comprehensive physical health care plan for people with ID and mental health problems. While such a plan would be a policy direction to aspire to, research is needed in order to understand gaps in attitudes, awareness, training of staff, resources, and service delivery options.

While various interventions have been found to show efficacy, Dosen (2007) argues that a monodisciplinary treatment approach to behavioural and psychiatric problems in persons with ID, such as psychotropic medication or behaviour modification alone, has yielded limited success. He argues for an integrative diagnostic and treatment approach consisting of four dimensions – biological, psychological, social and developmental – for people with ID and mental health problems, where the focus should not be primarily directed towards the symptoms of the disorder but towards restoring a person's mental wellbeing. For individuals with an established dual diagnosis of both ID and a psychiatric disorder, treatment goals should include preventing further disability, restoring premorbid functioning, and improving quality of life through restoration of functionality, independent living and rehabilitation.

SOLUTIONS, RECOMMENDATIONS, AND FUTURE RESEARCH DIRECTIONS

A developmental-bio-psycho-social-cultural model of service delivery and training and education of professionals involved in the care of people with ID is critical for early identification and appropriate management of comorbid mental health problems. People with ID and mental health problems are some of the most vulnerable people in society and they are often let down by the health care system, funding and service delivery models. Efforts to intervene in a more coordinated and integrated way can significantly improve their outcomes. Further, both the patient and the family or caregiver would need support, advocacy and case management. This would require coordination rather than separate services across types of difficulty, age groups, treatment modalities and disciplines. This should include a focus on the individual in a family context and using skill building models for developmental gains and appropriate management of maladaptive behaviours through an integrated multidisciplinary and multiagency collaborative service.

In order to plan effective and comprehensive prevention and intervention strategies for young people with ID and mental health disorders, it is important that there is a better understanding of the complex interplay of both risk and protective factors at different levels, including individual child factors, family, neighbourhood and society, as well as services, systems and policies. Given that no factor acts in isolation, and that there is an interaction of these factors at multiple bio-ecological levels, and at multiple time points along the life course, it is essential to have rigorous and relevant epidemiological and statistical techniques that can apply a bio-ecological model using a life course approach (Woolfenden et al., 2014). A cumulative risk index, being the sum of individual risk factors, is one way of conceptualising how risk factors interact over a life course (A. J. Sameroff & Seifer, 1983), but in this model all risk factors are given an equal weight which is a significant disadvantage when compared to a regression model. Structural Equation Modelling and Multilevel Modelling techniques, on the other hand, are based on a proposed hypothesis and, using regression techniques, variables including time are grouped into hierarchical levels (Diez Roux, 2004), and measured to see which model fits best. Future research exploring risk factors should where possible use composite theoretical models, longitudinal study designs and multilevel modelling in order to tease apart risk factors at different levels including individual, family and neighbourhood as well as society, services, systems and policy factors, which might increase vulnerability of people with ID to develop mental health problems. In this context, it is noteworthy that the occurrence of mental health comorbidity in children with ID, and the nature and type of such comorbidity, is shaped by the interplay of biological and environmental risk and resilience factors, mediated by the life course issues as to when these factors are in operation in the child's life. Eapen (2014) has described such a model of a Developmental Risk Index where appropriate weighted scoring is given to different microsystem (child's most immediate or proximal environment), mesosystem (reciprocal relationships and interconnections), exosystem (distal factors that indirectly impact on the child and their family) and macrosystem (societal, cultural and service or policy) factors. Future studies should also explore biological risk factors including genetic factors, perinatal events, trauma, toxins, infections and immunological factors. Research should also focus on early identification processes that accurately assess the nature and reasons behind behavioural and emotional problems encountered in the context of ID; for example challenging behaviours may be due to the underlying brain pathology, or due to speech and language difficulties resulting in communication problems, or due to lack of stimulation and opportunities resulting in poor quality of life. Such a comprehensive assessment would no doubt facilitate the development of an individualised multidisciplinary treatment model and better outcomes.

CONCLUSION

There are significant challenges in the detection and characterisation of comorbid mental health problems in the context of ID. For example, for those with limited language and cognitive abilities, can the same diagnostic criteria and measures be used? Identifying the nature and extent of mental health problems is further compounded by the lack of measures specific for ID. There are also difficulties in identifying the nature and extent of ID and the consequent impact on function (measurement of adaptive behavior), as there is considerable variability in the terms and definitions as well as the diagnostic criteria and assessments across settings and across the different parts of the globe. While some of these issues could be addressed through better training of professionals, there are also significant barriers in service delivery models and access to services. In this regard, there are significant gaps in the availability of evidence based intervention programs in general for children with ID and mental health problems. In particular, the needs of those with behavioural or mental health problems and chronic and complex health care problems are not met by mainstream services. There is an urgent need to have a consensus on a statement of minimum standards of care, with clear policy objectives, program outlines and comprehensive training of staff, followed by evaluation of its implementation. Improved longitudinal outcomes will only be possible for people with ID and psychiatric disorders if there are opportunities for access to integrated services including better identification and treatment models, and improved knowledge and awareness of health-related conditions for people with ID, enhanced parent or carer support, as well as changes within health and disability service systems to ensure universal coverage of quality services.

REFERENCES

Abbeduto, L., Seltzer, M. M., Shattuck, P., Krauss, M. W., Orsmond, G., & Murphy, M. M. (2004). Psychological well-being and coping in mothers of youths with Autism, Down Syndrome, or Fragile X Syndrome. *Journal Information*, *109*(3). PMID:15072518

Anderson, D. J., Lakin, K. C., Hill, B. K., & Chen, T. (1992). Social integration of older persons with mental retardation in residential facilities. *American Journal of Mental Retardation*. PMID:1562307

Andrews, G., Henderson, S., & Hall, W. (2001). *Prevalence, comorbidity, disability and service utilisation* (Vol. 178). Academic Press.

APA. (2013). Diagnostic and Statistical Manual of Mental Disorders - Fifth Edition (DSM-5). Washington, DC: American Psychiatric Publishing.

Baker, B. L., Landen, S. J., & Kashima, K. J. (1991). Effects of parent training on families of children with mental retardation: Increased burden or generalized benefit? *American Journal of Mental Retardation*. PMID:1930946

Begg, S., Vos, T., Barker, B., Stevenson, C., Stanley, L., & Lopez, A. (2007). *Burden of disease and injury in Australia, 2003*. Australian Institute of Health and Welfare AIHW.

Borthwick-Duffy, S. A., & Eyman, R. K. (1990). Who are the dually diagnosed? *American Journal of Mental Retardation*. PMID:2340136

Bouras, N. (2011). Mental health problems and related issues for people with developmental and intellectual disability. *Current Opinion in Psychiatry*, *24*(5), 365–366. doi:10.1097/YCO.0b013e328349d249 PMID:21778881

Bourke, J., Ricciardo, B., Bebbington, A., Aiberti, K., Jacoby, P., Dyke, P., . . . Leonard, H. (2008). Physical and mental health in mothers of children with Down syndrome. *The Journal of Pediatrics, 153*(3), 320-326.

Browne, G., & Bramston, P. (1998). Stress and the quality of life in the parents of young people with intellectual disabilities. *Journal of Psychiatric and Mental Health Nursing*, *5*(5), 415–421. PMID:10067490

Bruininks, R. H., Hill, B. K., & Morreau, L. E. (1988). *Prevalence and implications of maladaptive behaviors and dual diagnosis in residential and other service programs. In Mental retardation and mental health* (pp. 3–29). Springer.

Cassidy, S. B., & Morris, C. A. (2001). Behavioral phenotypes in genetic syndromes: Genetic clues to human behavior. *Advances in Pediatrics*, *49*, 59–86. PMID:12214780

Chadwick, O., Kusel, Y., Cuddy, M., & Taylor, E. (2005). Psychiatric diagnoses and behaviour problems from childhood to early adolescence in young people with severe intellectual disabilities. *Psychological Medicine*, *35*(05), 751–760. doi:10.1017/S0033291704003733 PMID:15918352

Christensen, H., Calear, A., Tait, R., Gosling, J., Griffiths, K., & Murray, K. (2011). *School based intervention programs and shared care collaborative models targeting the prevention of or early intervention in child and adolescent mental health problems: An Evidence Check rapid review*. NSW Ministry of Health.

Clarke, D. J., Littlejohns, C. S., Corbett, J. A., & Joseph, S. (1989). Pervasive developmental disorders and psychoses in adult life. *The British Journal of Psychiatry*, *155*(5), 692–699. PMID:2611600

Cooper, S. A. (1997). Psychiatry of elderly compared to younger adults with intellectual disabilities. *Journal of Applied Research in Intellectual Disabilities*, *10*(4), 303–311. doi:10.1111/j.1468-3148.1997.tb00025.x

Cooper, S. A., Smiley, E., Morrison, J., Williamson, A., & Allan, L. (2007). Mental ill-health in adults with intellectual disabilities: Prevalence and associated factors. *The British Journal of Psychiatry*, *190*(1), 27–35. doi:10.1192/bjp.bp.106.022483 PMID:17197653

Corbett, J. A. (1979). Psychiatric morbidity and mental retardation. In F. E. James & R. P. Snaith (Eds.), *Psychiatric illness and mental handicap* (pp. 11–25). London: Royal College of Psychiatry, Gaskell.

Costello, H., & Bouras, N. (2006). Assessment of mental health problems in people with intellectual disabilities. *The Israel Journal of Psychiatry and Related Sciences*, *43*(4), 241. PMID:17338443

Croen, L. A., Grether, J. K., & Selvin, S. (2001). The epidemiology of mental retardation of unknown cause. *Pediatrics*, *107*(6), e86–e86. doi:10.1542/peds.107.6.e86 PMID:11389284

Deb, S., Thomas, M., & Bright, C. (2001). Mental disorder in adults with intellectual disability. 1: Prevalence of functional psychiatric illness among a community-based population aged between 16 and 64 years. *Journal of Intellectual Disability Research*, *45*(6), 495–505. doi:10.1046/j.1365-2788.2001.00374.x PMID:11737536

Dekker, M. C., & Koot, H. M. (2003a). DSM-IV disorders in children with borderline to moderate intellectual disability. I: Prevalence and impact. *Journal of the American Academy of Child and Adolescent Psychiatry*, *42*(8), 915–922. doi:10.1097/01.CHI.0000046892.27264.1A PMID:12874493

Dekker, M. C., & Koot, H. M. (2003b). DSM-IV Disorders in Children With Borderline to Moderate Intellectual Disability. II: Child and Family Predictors. *Journal of the American Academy of Child and Adolescent Psychiatry*, *42*(8), 923–931. doi:10.1097/01.CHI.0000046891.27264.C1 PMID:12874494

Diez Roux, A. V. (2004). The Study of Group-Level Factors in Epidemiology: Rethinking Variables, Study Designs, and Analytical Approaches. *Epidemiologic Reviews*, *26*(1), 104–111. doi:10.1093/epirev/mxh006 PMID:15234951

Doran, C. M., Einfeld, S. L., Madden, R. H., Otim, M., Horstead, S. K., Ellis, L. A., & Emerson, E. (2012). How much does intellectual disability really cost? First estimates for Australia. *Journal of Intellectual & Developmental Disability*, *37*(1), 42–49. doi:10.3109/13668250.2011.648609 PMID:22339044

Dosen, A. (2007). Integrative treatment in persons with intellectual disability and mental health problems. *Journal of Intellectual Disability Research*, *51*(1), 66–74. doi:10.1111/j.1365-2788.2006.00868.x PMID:17181604

Dyson, L. L. (1997). Fathers and mothers of school-age children with developmental disabilities: Parental stress, family functioning, and social support. *American Journal of Mental Retardation*, *102*(3), 267–279. doi:10.1352/0895-8017(1997)102<0267:FAMOSC>2.0.CO;2 PMID:9394135

Eapen, V. (2014). Developmental and mental health disorders: Two sides of the same coin. *Asian Journal of Psychiatry*, *8*, 7–11. doi:10.1016/j.ajp.2013.10.007 PMID:24655619

Eapen, V., Al-Gazali, L. I., Bin-Othman, S., & Pramathan, T. (1998). Learning disorders in school-going children–detection and diagnosis. *Journal of Tropical Pediatrics*, *44*(4), 192–193. doi:10.1093/tropej/44.4.192 PMID:9718902

Eapen, V., & Jairam, R. (2009). Integration of child mental health services to primary care: challenges and opportunities. *Mental Health in Family Medicine, 6*(1), 43.

Einfeld, S. L., Ellis, L. A., & Emerson, E. (2011). Comorbidity of intellectual disability and mental disorder in children and adolescents: A systematic review. *Journal of Intellectual & Developmental Disability*, *36*(2), 137–143. doi:10.1080/13668250.2011.572548 PMID:21609299

Einfeld, S. L., Piccinin, A., Mackinnon, A., Hofer, S., Taffe, J., Gray, K., & Tonge, B. et al. (2006). Psychopathology in young people with intellectual disability. *Journal of the American Medical Association*, *296*(16), 1981–1989. doi:10.1001/jama.296.16.1981 PMID:17062861

Einfeld, S. L., & Tonge, B. (1999). Observations on the use of the ICD-10 Guide for Mental Retardation. *Journal of Intellectual Disability Research*, *43*(5), 408–412. doi:10.1046/j.1365-2788.1999.043005408.x PMID:10546965

Einfeld, S. L., & Tonge, B. J. (1996a). Population prevalence of psychopathology in children and adolescents with intellectual disability: I rationale and methods. *Journal of Intellectual Disability Research*, *40*(2), 91–98. doi:10.1111/j.1365-2788.1996.tb00610.x PMID:8731466

Einfeld, S. L., & Tonge, B. J. (1996b). Population prevalence of psychopathology in children and adolescents with intellectual disability: II epidemiological findings. *Journal of Intellectual Disability Research*, *40*(2), 99–109. doi:10.1111/j.1365-2788.1996.tb00611.x PMID:8731467

Emerson, E. (2003). Prevalence of psychiatric disorders in children and adolescents with and without intellectual disability. *Journal of Intellectual Disability Research*, *47*(1), 51–58. doi:10.1046/j.1365-2788.2003.00464.x PMID:12558695

Emerson, E. (2012). Deprivation, ethnicity and the prevalence of intellectual and developmental disabilities. *Journal of Epidemiology and Community Health*, *66*(3), 218–224. doi:10.1136/jech.2010.111773 PMID:20889590

Emerson, E., & Hatton, C. (2007a). Contribution of socioeconomic position to health inequalities of British children and adolescents with intellectual disabilities. *Journal Information*, *112*(2). PMID:17295554

Emerson, E., & Hatton, C. (2007b). Mental health of children and adolescents with intellectual disabilities in Britain. *The British Journal of Psychiatry*, *191*(6), 493–499. doi:10.1192/bjp.bp.107.038729 PMID:18055952

Feldman, M. A., & Werner, S. E. (2002). Collateral effects of behavioral parent training on families of children with developmental disabilities and behavior disorders. *Behavioral Interventions*, *17*(2), 75–83. doi:10.1002/bin.111

Gavidia-Payne, S., & Hudson, A. (2002). Behavioural supports for parents of children with an intellectual disability and problem behaviours: An overview of the literature. *Journal of Intellectual & Developmental Disability*, *27*(1), 31–55. doi:10.1080/13668250120119626

Gavidia-Payne, S., Richdale, A., Francis, A., & Cotton, S. (1997). *The Parenting Hassles Scale: Measuring stress in parents of children with disabilities.* Paper presented at the 121st Annual Meeting of the American Association on Mental Retardation, New York.

Gostason, R. (1985). Psychiatric illness among the mentally retarded. *Acta Psychiatrica Scandinavica*, *318*(suppl 71), 1–117. doi:10.1111/j.1600-0447.1985.tb10511.x PMID:3893045

Guralnick, M. J. (1997). Effectiveness of early intervention for vulnerable children: A developmental perspective. *American Journal of Mental Retardation*, *102*(4), 319–345. doi:10.1352/0895-8017(1998)102<0319:EOEIFV>2.0.CO;2 PMID:9475942

Hackman, D. A., Farah, M. J., & Meaney, M. J. (2010). Socioeconomic status and the brain: Mechanistic insights from human and animal research. *Nature Reviews. Neuroscience*, *11*(9), 651–659. doi:10.1038/nrn2897 PMID:20725096

Harris, J. C. (2006). *Intellectual disability: Understanding its development, causes, classification, evaluation, and treatment.* Oxford University Press New York.

Hassall, R., Rose, J., & McDonald, J. (2005). Parenting stress in mothers of children with an intellectual disability: The effects of parental cognitions in relation to child characteristics and family support. *Journal of Intellectual Disability Research*, *49*(6), 405–418. doi:10.1111/j.1365-2788.2005.00673.x PMID:15882391

Hastings, R. P. (2002). Parental stress and behaviour problems of children with developmental disability. *Journal of Intellectual & Developmental Disability*, *27*(3), 149–160. doi:10.1080/1366825021000008657

Hastings, R. P., & Beck, A. (2004). Practitioner review: Stress intervention for parents of children with intellectual disabilities. *Journal of Child Psychology and Psychiatry, and Allied Disciplines*, *45*(8), 1338–1349. doi:10.1111/j.1469-7610.2004.00357.x PMID:15482495

Hatton, C. (2002). Psychosocial interventions for adults with intellectual disabilities and mental health problems: A review. *Journal of Mental Health (Abingdon, England)*, *11*(4), 357–374. doi:10.1080/09638230020023732

Hurley, A. D. (2006). Mood disorders in intellectual disability. *Current Opinion in Psychiatry*, *19*(5), 465–469. doi:10.1097/01.yco.0000238471.84206.0a PMID:16874117

Iverson, J. C., & Fox, R. A. (1989). Prevalence of psychopathology among mentally retarded adults. *Research in Developmental Disabilities*, *10*(1), 77–83. doi:10.1016/0891-4222(89)90030-9 PMID:2928581

Kirkham, M. A. (1993). Two-year follow-up of skills training with mothers of children with disabilities. *American Journal of Mental Retardation*. PMID:7681675

Kirkham, M. A., & Schilling, R. F. II. (1990). Life skills training with mothers of handicapped children. *Journal of Social Service Research*, *13*(2), 67–87. doi:10.1300/J079v13n02_05

Leonard, H., Glasson, E., Nassar, N., Whitehouse, A., Bebbington, A., Bourke, J., & Bower, C. et al. (2011). Autism and intellectual disability are differentially related to sociodemographic background at birth. *PLoS ONE*, *6*(3), e17875. doi:10.1371/journal.pone.0017875 PMID:21479223

Leonard, H., Petterson, B., Bower, C., & Sanders, R. (2003). Prevalence of intellectual disability in Western Australia. *Paediatric and Perinatal Epidemiology*, *17*(1), 58–67. doi:10.1046/j.1365-3016.2003.00469.x PMID:12562473

Leonard, H., Petterson, B., De Klerk, N., Zubrick, S. R., Glasson, E., Sanders, R., & Bower, C. (2005). Association of sociodemographic characteristics of children with intellectual disability in Western Australia. *Social Science & Medicine*, *60*(7), 1499–1513. doi:10.1016/j.socscimed.2004.08.014 PMID:15652683

Leonard, H., & Wen, X. (2002). The epidemiology of mental retardation: Challenges and opportunities in the new millennium. *Mental Retardation and Developmental Disabilities Research Reviews*, *8*(3), 117–134. doi:10.1002/mrdd.10031 PMID:12216056

Lobato, D. J., & Kao, B. T. (2002). Integrated sibling-parent group intervention to improve sibling knowledge and adjustment to chronic illness and disability. *Journal of Pediatric Psychology*, *27*(8), 711–716. doi:10.1093/jpepsy/27.8.711 PMID:12403861

Lobato, D. J., & Kao, B. T. (2005). Brief report: Family-based group intervention for young siblings of children with chronic illness and developmental disability. *Journal of Pediatric Psychology*, *30*(8), 678–682. doi:10.1093/jpepsy/jsi054 PMID:16260437

Lund, J. (1985). The prevalence of psychiatric morbidity in mentally retarded adults. *Acta Psychiatrica Scandinavica*, *72*(6), 563–570. doi:10.1111/j.1600-0447.1985.tb02655.x PMID:4083061

Maes, B., Broekman, T. G., Došen, A., & Nauts, J. (2003). Caregiving burden of families looking after persons with intellectual disability and behavioural or psychiatric problems. *Journal of Intellectual Disability Research*, *47*(6), 447–455. doi:10.1046/j.1365-2788.2003.00513.x PMID:12919195

Maggi, S., Irwin, L. J., Siddiqi, A., & Hertzman, C. (2010). The social determinants of early child development: An overview. *Journal of Paediatrics and Child Health*, *46*(11), 627–635. doi:10.1111/j.1440-1754.2010.01817.x PMID:20796183

Marmot, M. G., Allen, J., Goldblatt, P., Boyce, T., McNeish, D., Grady, M., & Geddes, I. (2010). *Fair society, healthy lives: Strategic review of health inequalities in England post-2010*. Academic Press.

Maulik, P. K., & Harbour, C. K. (2010). Epidemiology of intellectual disability. *International Encyclopaedia of Rehabilitation.*

Maulik, P. K., Mascarenhas, M. N., Mathers, C. D., Dua, T., & Saxena, S. (2011). Prevalence of intellectual disability: A meta-analysis of population-based studies. *Research in Developmental Disabilities*, *32*(2), 419–436. doi:10.1016/j.ridd.2010.12.018 PMID:21236634

McCarthy, J., & Boyd, J. (2002). Mental health services and young people with intellectual disability: Is it time to do better? *Journal of Intellectual Disability Research*, *46*(3), 250–256. doi:10.1046/j.1365-2788.2002.00401.x PMID:11896810

McIntyre, L. L., Blacher, J., & Baker, B. L. (2002). Behaviour/mental health problems in young adults with intellectual disability: The impact on families. *Journal of Intellectual Disability Research*, *46*(3), 239–249. doi:10.1046/j.1365-2788.2002.00371.x PMID:11896809

McIntyre, L. L., Blacher, J., & Baker, B. L. (2006). The transition to school: Adaptation in young children with and without developmental delays. *Journal of Intellectual Disability Research*, *50*(5), 349–361. doi:10.1111/j.1365-2788.2006.00783.x PMID:16629928

Meltzer, H., Gatward, R., Goodman, R., & Ford, T. (2000). *Mental health of children and adolescents in Great Britain*. London: The Stationery Office. doi:10.1037/e622732007-001

Miodrag, N., & Hodapp, R. M. (2010). Chronic stress and health among parents of children with intellectual and developmental disabilities. *Current Opinion in Psychiatry*, *23*(5), 407–411. doi:10.1097/YCO.0b013e32833a8796 PMID:20592593

Mitchell, C., McLanahan, S., Brooks-Gunn, J., Garfinkel, I., Hobcraft, J., & Notterman, D. (2013). Genetic differential sensitivity to social environments: Implications for research. *American Journal of Public Health*, *103*(S1), S102–S110. doi:10.2105/AJPH.2013.301382 PMID:23927507

Molteno, G., Molteno, C. D., Finchilescu, G., & Dawes, A. R. L. (2001). Behavioural and emotional problems in children with intellectual disability attending special schools in Cape Town, South Africa. *Journal of Intellectual Disability Research*, *45*(6), 515–520. doi:10.1046/j.1365-2788.2001.00368.x PMID:11737538

No Child Left Behind Act of 2001, 20 U.S.C., Pub. L. No. 107-110 (2002).

Nota, L., Ferrari, L., Soresi, S., & Wehmeyer, M. (2007). Self-determination, social abilities and the quality of life of people with intellectual disability. *Journal of Intellectual Disability Research*, *51*(11), 850–865. doi:10.1111/j.1365-2788.2006.00939.x PMID:17910537

NSW Ministry of Health. (2015). *NSW School-Link Strategy and Action Plan 2014-2017*. Sydney, Australia: NSW Ministry of Health.

O'Brien, G., Barnard, L., Pearson, J., & Rippon, L. (2002). Physical health and clinical phenotypes. *Physical Health of Adults with Intellectual Disabilities*, 35-62.

Olsson, M. B., & Hwang, C. P. (2001). Depression in mothers and fathers of children with intellectual disability. *Journal of Intellectual Disability Research*, *45*(6), 535–543. doi:10.1046/j.1365-2788.2001.00372.x PMID:11737541

Parmenter, T. R., Einfeld, S. L., Tonge, B. J., & Dempster, J. A. (1998). Behavioural and emotional problems in the classroom of children and adolescents with intellectual disability. *Journal of Intellectual & Developmental Disability*, *23*(1), 71–77. doi:10.1080/13668259800033591

Polder, J. J., Meerding, W. J., Bonneux, L., & Van Der Maas, P. J. (2002). Healthcare costs of intellectual disability in the Netherlands: A cost-of-illness perspective. *Journal of Intellectual Disability Research*, *46*(2), 168–178. doi:10.1046/j.1365-2788.2002.00384.x PMID:11869388

Richardson, S. A., & Koller, H. (1996). *Twenty-two years: Causes and consequences of mental retardation*. Harvard University Press.

Roberts, C., Mazzucchelli, T., Studman, L. J., & Sanders, M. R. (2006). Behavioral family intervention for children with developmental disabilities and behavioral problems. *Journal of Clinical Child and Adolescent Psychology*, *35*(2), 180–193. doi:10.1207/s15374424jccp3502_2 PMID:16597214

Roeleveld, N., & Zielhuis, G. A. (1997). The prevalence of mental retardation: A critical review of recent literature. *Developmental Medicine and Child Neurology*, *39*(2), 125–132. doi:10.1111/j.1469-8749.1997.tb07395.x PMID:9062428

Rose, J., West, C., & Clifford, D. (2000). Group interventions for anger in people with intellectual disabilities. *Research in Developmental Disabilities*, *21*(3), 171–181. doi:10.1016/S0891-4222(00)00032-9 PMID:10939316

Rossiter, L., & Sharpe, D. (2001). The siblings of individuals with mental retardation: A quantitative integration of the literature. *Journal of Child and Family Studies*, *10*(1), 65–84. doi:10.1023/A:1016629500708

Saloviita, T., Itälinna, M., & Leinonen, E. (2003). Explaining the parental stress of fathers and mothers caring for a child with intellectual disability: A double ABCX model. *Journal of Intellectual Disability Research*, *47*(4-5), 300–312. doi:10.1046/j.1365-2788.2003.00492.x PMID:12787162

Sameroff, A. E. (2009). *The transactional model of development: How children and contexts shape each other*. American Psychological Association. doi:10.1037/11877-000

Sameroff, A. J., & Seifer, R. (1983). Familial risk and child competence. *Child Development*, *54*(5), 1254–1268. doi:10.2307/1129680 PMID:6354632

Sanders, M. R., Mazzecchelli, T. G., & Studman, L. J. (2003). *Practitioner's Manual for Standard Stepping Stones Triple P: For Families with a Child who has a Disability*. Brisbane, Australia: Triple P International.

Siddiqi, A., Irwin, L. G., & Hertzman, C. (2007). *The total environment assessment model of early child development. Evidence Report for the World Health Organization's Commission on the Social Determinants of Health*. OMS.

Singer, G. H. S., Marquis, J., Powers, L. K., Blanchard, L., DiVenere, N., Santelli, B., & Sharp, M. et al. (1999). A multi-site evaluation of parent to parent programs for parents of children with disabilities. *Journal of Early Intervention*, *22*(3), 217–229. doi:10.1177/105381519902200305

Stromme, P., & Diseth, T. H. (2000). Prevalence of psychiatric diagnoses in children with mental retardation: Data from a population-based study. *Developmental Medicine and Child Neurology*, *42*(04), 266–270. doi:10.1017/S0012162200000451 PMID:10795566

Stromme, P., & Magnus, P. (2000). Correlations between socioeconomic status, IQ and aetiology in mental retardation: A population-based study of Norwegian children. *Social Psychiatry and Psychiatric Epidemiology*, *1*(35). PMID:10741531

Sturmey, P. (1995). DSM-III-R and persons with dual diagnoses: Conceptual issues and strategies for future research. *Journal of Intellectual Disability Research*, *39*(5), 357–364. doi:10.1111/j.1365-2788.1995.tb00539.x PMID:8555711

Taylor, J. L., Hatton, C., Dixon, L., & Douglas, C. (2004). Screening for psychiatric symptoms: PAS-ADD Checklist norms for adults with intellectual disabilities. *Journal of Intellectual Disability Research*, *48*(1), 37–41. doi:10.1111/j.1365-2788.2004.00585.x PMID:14675229

To, T., Guttmann, A., Dick, P. T., Rosenfield, J. D., Parkin, P. C., Tassoudji, M., & Harris, J. K. et al. (2004). Risk markers for poor developmental attainment in young children: Results from a longitudinal national survey. *Archives of Pediatrics & Adolescent Medicine*, *158*(7), 643–649. doi:10.1001/archpedi.158.7.643 PMID:15237063

Tonge, B., & Einfeld, S. (2000). The trajectory of psychiatric disorders in young people with intellectual disabilities. *The Australian and New Zealand Journal of Psychiatry*, *34*(1), 80–84. doi:10.1046/j.1440-1614.2000.00695.x PMID:11185949

Tonge, B., & Einfeld, S. L. (2003). Psychopathology and intellectual disability: The Australian child to adult longitudinal study. *International Review of Research in Mental Retardation*, *26*, 61–91. doi:10.1016/S0074-7750(03)01002-4

Vos, T., Barker, B., Stanley, L., & Lopez, A. (2007). *The burden of disease and injury in Aboriginal and Torres Strait Islander peoples 2003: Centre for Burden of Disease and Cost-Effectiveness*. School of Population Health, University of Queensland.

White, N., & Hastings, R. P. (2004). Social and professional support for parents of adolescents with severe intellectual disabilities. *Journal of Applied Research in Intellectual Disabilities*, *17*(3), 181–190. doi:10.1111/j.1468-3148.2004.00197.x

Whitehouse, A. J. O., Durkin, K., Jaquet, E., & Ziatas, K. (2009). Friendship, loneliness and depression in adolescents with Asperger's Syndrome. *Journal of Adolescence*, *32*(2), 309–322. doi:10.1016/j.adolescence.2008.03.004 PMID:18692233

Whitehouse, A. J. O., Watt, H. J., Line, E. A., & Bishop, D. V. M. (2009). Adult psychosocial outcomes of children with specific language impairment, pragmatic language impairment and autism. *International Journal of Language & Communication Disorders*, *44*(4), 511–528. doi:10.1080/13682820802708098 PMID:19340628

Wong, J. G., Clare, I. C. H., Holland, A. J., Watson, P. C., & Gunn, M. (2000). The capacity of people with a 'mental disability'to make a health care decision. *Psychological Medicine*, *30*(02), 295–306. doi:10.1017/S0033291700001768 PMID:10824650

Woolfenden, S., Goldfeld, S., Raman, S., Eapen, V., Kemp, L., & Williams, K. (2013). Inequity in child health: The importance of early childhood development. *Journal of Paediatrics and Child Health*, *49*(9), E365–E369. PMID:23551940

Woolfenden, S., Williams, K., Eapen, V., Mensah, F., Hayen, A., Siddiqi, A., & Kemp, L. (2014). Developmental vulnerability–don't investigate without a model in mind. *Child: Care, Health and Development*. PMID:25088700

Yeargin-Allsopp, M., Drews, C. D., Decouflé, P., & Murphy, C. C. (1995). Mild mental retardation in black and white children in metropolitan Atlanta: A case-control study. *American Journal of Public Health*, *85*(3), 324–328. doi:10.2105/AJPH.85.3.324 PMID:7892913

Zeanah, C. H., Boris, N. W., & Larrieu, J. A. (1997). Infant development and developmental risk: A review of the past 10 years. *Journal of the American Academy of Child and Adolescent Psychiatry*, *36*(2), 165–178. doi:10.1097/00004583-199702000-00007 PMID:9031569

KEY TERMS AND DEFINITIONS

Cognitive-Behavioural Therapy: A type of psychotherapy that helps individuals to identify and teaches skills to modify unhelpful thinking patterns, feelings and behaviours.

Indigenous Australians: The original inhabitants of the Australian continent and nearby islands, including Aboriginal people and Torres Strait Islanders.

Intellectual Disability: A disability characterised by significantly impaired intellectual and adaptive functioning, formerly known as Mental Retardation.

Multidisciplinary: Drawing on expertise from multiple disciplines to accurately define and manage complex situations including health concerns.

Chapter 3
School Bullying and Students with Intellectual Disabilities

Michelle F. Wright
Masaryk University, Czech Republic

ABSTRACT

School bullying research began in the 1970s through seminal research conducted on these experiences among Norwegian boys. From this initial research, multiple studies have been conducted over the past forty years, revealing the nature, extent, causes, and consequences of school bullying. More recent investigations have also focused on cyberbullying, bullying using information and communication technologies (e.g., cell phones). Little attention has been given to school bullying involvement among students with disabilities, particularly those with intellectual disabilities. These studies suggest that these students experience internalizing (e.g., depression, anxiety, loneliness) and externalizing (e.g., aggression, antisocial behaviors) difficulties associated with their involvement in school bullying. The aim of this chapter is to review multidisciplinary research concerning school bullying among students with intellectual disabilities and to make recommendations for public policy and prevention programs as well as future research.

INTRODUCTION

Students with disabilities benefit from inclusion in the same schools as their nondisabled peers. Research findings also suggest that nondisabled peers benefit from this inclusion as well (Buckley, Bird, Sacks, & Archer, 2002; Lindsay & McPherson, 2012; Richardson, 1996; Sailor, Wolf, Choi, & Roger, 2009; Tomasik, 2007). Therefore, disabled and nondisabled students benefit from having an inclusive school environment where there is potential for social interactions among a variety of students with different backgrounds. There is also evidence that such inclusion does not reduce test scores, grades, or instructional time, further suggesting the necessity of inclusion for students with disabilities (Sirlopu et al., 2008; Stahmer, Carter, Baker, & Miwa, 2003; Salend & Duhaney, 1999; York, Vandercook, MacDonald, Heise-Neff, & Caughey, 1992).

DOI: 10.4018/978-1-5225-0089-6.ch003

The total number of students with disabilities in inclusion education varies based on students' location within the United States. In particular, students from the Eastern United States are more frequently assigned to segregated classrooms (Kurth, 2014). In addition, some states (e.g., Iowa, Minnesota, West Virginia) favor inclusion, while other states (e.g., Florida, New Jersey, South Carolina) prefer the restrictive setting for students with disabilities. Overall, 50% of disabled students from the ages of 6 to 11 are in regular classrooms around 80% of the day, while 30% of disabled students from the ages of 12 and higher are in such classrooms (Maryland Coalition for Inclusive Education, 2011). Regardless of the differences in these rates, it is clear that a variety of students with disabilities spend some time learning in the regular classroom.

Although there are benefits to the inclusion of students with disabilities in the school environment, additional attention is needed to promote a more welcoming environment as these students are often victims of school bullying (Mishna, 2003). Welcoming school environments are not always something students with disabilities experience as bullying is frequently a direct result of their disability, especially if the students' disability is more visible in inclusion environments (Verdugo, Bernejo, & Fuertes, 1995; Waldman, Swerdloff, & Perlman, 1999; Whitney, Smith & Thompson, 1994). In addition, students with disabilities are also rejected by their peers, a risk factor associated with victimization and bullying perpetration (Fox, 1989; Kistner & Gatlin, 1989; Martlew & Hodson, 1991; Morrison, Furlong, & Smith, 1994). Being rejected by one peers can lead to isolation and other consequences, such as depression, loneliness, and anxiety. Furthermore, peer rejection can affect academic engagement and achievement, which are vital to the long-term functioning of these students.

Some students with disabilities are also vulnerable to school bullying involvement because they have inadequate protection in the inclusion environment and due to their tendency to react aggressively (Lagerheim, 1986; Nabuzoka & Smith, 1993; Sprafkin & Gadow, 1987). Many times this inadequate protection stems from these students being socially rejected by their peers, which diminishes their odds of having good quality friendships, a protective factor associated with reduced bullying incidences. Reacting aggressively to benign situations or in situations when it is not warranted increases children's and adolescents' risk of being rejected by their peers. This increased risk also makes them vulnerable to victimization and aggression. Students with intellectual disabilities are also at risk for victimization because they have fewer resources to cope with this experience (Cunningham, Clark, Heaven, Durrant, & Cunningham, 1989; Lagerheim, 1986; Nabuzoka & Smith, 1993; Zeitlin & Williamson, 1990).

The purpose of this chapter is to examine school bullying perpetration and victimization among students with intellectual disabilities in elementary, middle, and high schools. The chapter utilizes multidisciplinary qualitative, quantitative, and mixed-design research methodologies drawn from psychology, special education, sociology, social work, and criminology to review research on students with intellectual disabilities' involvement in school bullying, incorporating both cross-sectional and longitudinal research designs. This chapter has six main purposes, including describing:

1. **The Nature of School Bullying:** Discussion of the definition, forms and types, prevalence rates, and associated psychosocial adjustment difficulties;
2. The prevalence and consequences of school bullying among students with disabilities;
3. The predictors of school bullying among students with intellectual disabilities;
4. **Solutions and Recommendations:** Description of public policy and school bullying prevention programs concerning students with intellectual disabilities;

5. **Future Research Directions:** The focus is on longitudinal research designs as well as recommending more research dedicated to understanding risk factors and protective factors associated with school bullying involvement among students with intellectual disabilities;
6. **Conclusion:** Final remarks concerning the state of the literature on school bullying among students with intellectual disabilities.

THE NATURE OF SCHOOL BULLYING

School bullying is a common experience for many students in the United States and throughout the world. It is defined as the intentional use of physical force or power against another person or group (Espelage & Swearer, 2003; Hemphill, Tollit, Kotevski, & Florent, 2015; Hong et al., 2014). It includes behaviors which cause physical and/or psychological harm and that are perceived as unwanted by the target of these behaviors. Over the last forty years, research on school bullying has been evolving, providing an important foundation for understanding the nature, extent, causes, consequences, intervention strategies, and the prevention of these behaviors (Hymel & Swearer, 2015). The recent attention given to school bullying by the public is the result of many high profile cases and news reports regarding school shootings and victims committing suicide. Although some of the research awareness and concern over school bullying is the result of the 1999 Columbine school shooting, the study of school bullying began in Norway during the 1970s. This systematic study of school bullying began with Olweus's 1973 book, *Aggression in the Schools: Bullies and Whipping Boys*. In his book, Olweus described boys' experiences with school bullying in Scandinavian countries. Most of the earliest research spurred by Olweus's book occurred across Europe as a result of the 1978 translation of his book into English. The book generated further interest and 10 years later the first European conference was held on school bullying. At this time, Olweus developed an intervention campaign designed to prevent school bullying among Norwegian students. Other European countries, like England, Wales, and Scotland, launched similarly designed intervention programs. A couple of years later, research and awareness began in Canada, the United States, Australia, and New Zealand. Most current research has focused attention on school bullying in Asia, Africa, and South America.

The typically used definition of school bullying comes from Olweus's work (1993). Like the definition provided in the previous paragraph, Olweus's definition emphasizes three essential elements of school bullying, including:

1. The behavior is aggressive and negative (i.e., it is unwanted and causes emotional distress to the victim),
2. The behavior is carried out repeatedly (i.e., it occurs often and over time), and
3. The behavior occurs in a relationship where there is an imbalance of power between the individuals involved.

School bullying behaviors are further delineated into two modes, direct and indirect. Direct forms of school bullying include physical aggression in which the victim is openly attacked, while indirect forms include social exclusion or social rejection. Indirect forms of bullying are often employed by girls while direct forms are more often used by boys (Banks, 1997; Brighi, Guarini, Melotti, Galli, & Genta, 2012; Carbone-Lopez, Esbensen, & Brick, 2010; Carney & Merrell, 2001; Crick & Grotpeter, 1995; Ericson,

2001). Socialization processes throughout childhood and adolescence are thought to account for gender differences in the usage of direct and indirect forms of bullying. As a result of these gender differences in bullying involvement, researchers argue that it is important to distinguish between indirect and direct forms of school bullying.

Other researchers, like Underwood and colleagues (2001), suggest that referring to some school bullying behaviors as indirect implies that the behavior does not involve direct or overt interaction with the victim, which might diminish beliefs about the severity of this type of bullying. By diminishing the belief that indirect forms of bullying are severe, schools, parents, and students might not take these behaviors seriously and consider them harmful to victims' well-being. Instead of using the terminology of indirect bullying, some researchers utilize social aggression to categorize the indirect forms of school bullying that Olweus described. As a result of the different forms of school bullying, researchers have categorized these behaviors into four types, including physical (e.g., pushing, hitting), verbal (e.g., name-calling), relational (e.g., exclusion, spreading rumors), and damage to property (Olthof & Goossens, 2008; Wang, Iannotti, Luk, & Nansel, 2010). Bullying can also include bullying in other contexts, such as those behaviors which occur electronically. Electronic forms of bullying are referred to as cyberbullying, and typically these behaviors are perpetrated or experienced through social networking websites, email, chatrooms, or chat programs (Lapidot & Dolev-Cohen, 2015; Waasdorp & Bradshaw, 2015). Sexual bullying is another type of bullying which can occur in the school setting. It occurs when a person is bullied based on his or her sex or sexual activity, and it can include physical, verbal, or emotional forms (Duncan, 1999).

Another important element of the school bullying definition is that the behaviors occur among school-aged students, 5 to 18 years of age, and it doesn't include aggression or bullying perpetrated by siblings. The definition also does not include bullying that might occur within romantic relationships. Furthermore, the definition excludes any bullying and abuse which might be perpetrated by adults or behaviors directed to adults. Children and adolescents can hold a variety of different roles in the bullying situation. They can be victims, bullies, bully-victims (both victim and perpetrator), bystanders (i.e., witnesses to the bullying situation), and uninvolved (Noorden, Haselager, Cillessen, & Bukowski, 2015; Psalti, 2012). Students experience a variety of academic and psychosocial adjustment consequences associated with the specific role they have in school bullying. In particular, bully-victims usually have the worst psychological, social, behavioral, and academic outcomes when compared to victims, bullies, bystanders, and uninvolved children and adolescents, with victims having worse outcomes than the other roles.

Prevalence rates of school bullying vary, depending on the definitions employed, samples used, the measurement of school bullying, and the age of the participants. Variations found in the general population range from 13% to 75% based on a variety of factors that impact students' reporting of school bullying, such as the definitions used, the measurement of school bullying, and their reluctance to admit to perpetrating and/or experiencing school bullying (Swearer, Siebecker, Johnsen-Frerichs, & Wang, 2010). Usually, researchers report prevalence rates between 30% and 32%, with 10.6% of students categorized as victims, 13.0% as bullies, and 6.3% as bully-victims (Dinkes, Kemp, Baum, & Snyder, 2009; Nansel et al., 2001). Research has also revealed that boys were more likely to report victimizing others when compared to girls while girls were more likely to report being victimized (Charach, Pepler, & Ziegler, 1995; Craig & Pepler, 1995). However, when researchers specified different forms of bullying, girls were more often involved in relational forms, while boys were more often engaged in physical forms (Banks, 1997; Brighi et al., 2012; Carbone-Lopez et al., 2010; Carney & Merrell, 2001; Crick & Grotpeter, 1995; Ericson, 2001). Furthermore, relational forms of school bullying increase in adolescence, while physical forms tend to decrease from childhood into adolescence (Boyes, Bowes, Cluver, Ward, & Badcock, 2014; Bradshaw, Waasdrop, & Johnson, 2015; Ryoo, Wang, & Swearer, 2015). Findings from these studies underscore the importance of consideration both gender and age when examining school bullying involvement.

Researchers, parents, and educators are particularly concerned with school bullying because of its linkages to academic (e.g., poor academic achievement, lower academic engagement), behavioral (e.g., delinquency), and psychosocial (e.g., depression, anxiety, loneliness) adjustment difficulties. School bullying victimization is a strong predictor of interpersonal problems and internationalizing emotional problems, such as anxiety, depression, and loneliness (Graham, Bellmore, & Mize, 2006; Hawker & Boulton, 2000; Kelly et al., 2015; Nishina, Juvonen, & Witkow, 2005; Perren, Dooley, Shaw, & Cross, 2010; Thomas et al., 2015). Such psychosocial problems contribute to victimized students' poor academic performance, often as a result of frequent absences from school and impaired concentration (Card & Hodges, 2008; Espelage, Low, & Jimerson, 2014; Hong et al., 2014; Nishina et al., 2005). Victims might not attend school because they fear further victimization. In addition, their concentration is impaired because they might repeatedly ruminate over their experience and be concerned about the chances of experiencing other attacks. Victimized students are also at risk for psychiatric problems and suicidal ideation (Dickerson Mayesa et al., 2014; Kumpulainen, Rasanen, & Puura, 2001; Rigby & Slee, 1991; Skapinakis et al., 2011). It is unclear whether victimization is a cause of psychiatric problems and suicidal ideation or whether psychiatric problems and suicidal ideation reduce children's and adolescents' coping abilities, leading them to be vulnerable to victimization. Many victimized children believe that they deserve to be bullied, which further contributes to the helplessness they feel, creating a vicious cycle of peer victimization. This cycle might make it difficult for them to believe that they can ever escape victimization.

Students who bully others also experience depression and suicidal ideation, and they are also at risk for antisocial behavioral tendencies, such as abusing drugs, drinking alcohol, and property theft (Hertz, Donato, & Wright, 2013; Kaltiala-Heino, Rimpela, Marttunen, Rimpela, & Rantanen, 1999; Cummings, Pepler, Mishna, & Craig, 2006). They also engage in academic misconduct, such as cheating and skipping school, and have lower academic achievement (Atik & Guneri, 2013; Berthold & Hoover, 2000; Carlson & Cornell, 2008; Rigby & Cox, 1996). Later in life, bullies are likely to be diagnosed with a psychiatric problem and to engage in substance abuse and criminal misconduct (Baldry & Farrington, 2000; Kumpulainen et al., 2001; Luukkonen, Riala, Hakko, & Rasanen, 2010; Nansel et al., 2001; Radliff, Wheaton, Robinson, & Morris, 2012; Rigby & Cox, 1996). Although there are overlaps in negative adjustment consequences between bullies and victims, there are differences in the type of consequences experienced. For instance, bullies typically experience more externalizing problems, while victims usually experience more internalizing problems.

Bully-victims experience the highest levels of these externalizing (e.g., antisocial behavior, rage, anger) and internalizing (e.g., depression, anxiety, loneliness) behaviors when compared to students who are either bullies or victims only (Kelly et al., 2015; Marini et al., 2009; Ozdemir & Stattin, 2011; Sansone & Sansone, 2008). Given that bully-victims experience elevated levels of internalizing and externalizing problems when compared to bullies and victims, it is imperative that researchers consider the multiple roles that students can have in school bullying. Nowadays, the education of students with disabilities occurs in schools with their peers without disabilities. Because peer victimization is a concern in the school environment, researchers began to focus their attention on investigating the school bullying experiences of disabled students.

PREVALENCE AND CONSQUENCES OF SCHOOL BULLYING AMONG STUDENTS WITH INTELLECTUAL DISABILITIES

Although many studies have been conducted on school bullying involvement among the general population of students, less attention has been given to examining students with disabilities' involvement in these behaviors, especially those with intellectual disabilities. The lack of attention to these students might be the result of the mistaken belief that such students cannot adequately express their opinions about their experiences with peers. As a result, some researchers might not include students with disabilities in their samples. Furthermore, ethical considerations might require special provisions for including students with disabilities in research, and many researchers might not have the resources necessary to ensure that they have the tools to aid in data collection that would allow these students' participation.

Most of the research on school bullying among students with disabilities utilizes school-aged samples of children and adolescents with disabilities between the ages of 5 and 18. Such research is important as there are consistent findings concerning students with disabilities being at an increased risk for school bullying when compared to their peers without disabilities (Rose, Espelage, & Monda-Amaya, 2009; Rose, Monda-Amaya, & Espelage, 2011; Sheard, Clegg, Standen, & Cromby, 2001). In particular, some research indicates that these students are more vulnerable to school bullying in comparison to nondisabled peers, while other research suggests that there are no differences in their risk for experiencing school bullying. The researchers that conclude that students with disabilities are more prone to school bullying propose that these students are at an increased risk for peer victimization because they have fewer resources to cope with this experience. Having better coping strategies makes it easier for students with disabilities to handle the challenges that they encounter and to "bounce back" from such challenges.

When compared to the general population of students, students with disabilities are 5 times more likely to report victimization by school bullying (Rose et al., 2009; Rose et al., 2011). In addition, research indicates that students with disabilities were more likely to experience peer victimization when placed in remedial classes and regular education classes when compared to students without disabilities. To explain these results, Rose and colleagues (2009; 2011) proposed that these students' physical or mental disability makes them particularly salient in the classroom, increasing the likelihood that they will be noticed and that others will be aware that they are different in some way. Being different from the average, might heightened the chance that students with disabilities will be victimized.

In one of the few longitudinal studies to examine school bullying among students with disabilities, students between the ages of 3 and 6 were followed for three years (Son, Parish, & Peterson, 2012). Employing parent reports, Son and colleagues found that 19% of 3 and 4 year olds experienced one or more types of peer victimization, and that 25% of 5 year olds experienced one or more types of peer victimization. The experience of peer victimization increased to 30% at the age of 6. The developmental trajectory of peer victimization reveals increases in these experiences from elementary to middle school, with declines beginning in early high school. Similar to their peers without disabilities' experiences with school bullying, peer victimization peaks in middle school. The patterns concerning the increase in peer victimization experiences from ages 3 to 6 is not unique among students with disabilities, but the odds of exposure are a bit higher than among students without disabilities. In particular, 34.1% of students with disabilities in one sample reported peer victimization compared with 24.5% in elementary school and 26.6% in high school (Blake et al., 2012). Other research revealed that rates of victimization among children with disabilities peaked in 3rd grade and declined afterward, somewhat in contrast to findings from the previous research (Bear, Mantz, Glutting,Yang, & Boyer, 2015). So far, only one study has examined the prevalence rates of cyberbullying involvement among students with intellectual disabilities. In their study, Didden et al. (2009) found that between 4% and 9% of students with intellectual disabilities were involved in cyberbullying as either the perpetrator or the victim.

Students with disabilities are also at an elevated risk of school bullying perpetration (Carter & Spencer, 2006; Doren, Bullis, & Benz, 1996; Estell et al., 2009; Rose et al., 2009; Whitney et al., 1994). Students with disabilities also report more incidences of physical bullying, sexual abuse, and emotional abuse (Cappadocia, Weiss, & Pepler, 2012; Mishna, 2003; Reiter, Bryen, & Shachar, 2007). For example, Whitney and colleagues (1994) found that one-third of students with disabilities in their sample engaged in school bullying perpetration when compared to one-sixth of students without disabilities. In another study comparing prevalence rates between students with disabilities and students without, Dickson and colleagues (2005) found that 28% of students with disabilities in their sample reported being victims of school bullying when compared to 9.8% of students without. Given that students with disabilities are more likely to be exposed to school bullying, they might experience extreme distress from such exposure. This distress might reduce their ability to deal with peer victimization, making them utilize ineffective coping strategies. One such way they might cope with peer victimization is by aggressing against others, maybe even those responsible for their victimization.

Thus far, much of the research reviewed on school bullying perpetration among students with disabilities did not specify whether school bullying was a function of revenge, meaning that the bully was retaliating against someone who had previously bullied him or her first. This provoked type of school bullying is more common among students with disabilities, and they are more often classified as bully-victims (Carter & Spencer, 2006; Reiter & Lapidot-Lefler, 2007; Roberts & Smith, 1999; Whitney et al., 1994; Van Cleave & Davis, 2006). Considering that students with disabilities are at risk for being bully-victims, it is important for research to focus more attention on these students' experiences with school bullying as bully-victims experience the worse psychological, social, behavior, and academic consequences. Thus, students with disabilities who are bully-victims might be at an elevated risk for these consequences.

The statistics discussed in the previous paragraphs involve studies in which researchers combined samples of students with physical disabilities as well as intellectual and social disabilities without delineating different types of disability (Dawkins, 1996; Llewellyn, 2000). Such a consideration is important as risk factors associated with disability, like aggressiveness, anger, hostility, low impulsive control, hyperactivity, poor social information processing, poor social skills, low self-esteem, and social rejection, are what contribute to school bullying involvement, and these factors vary depending on the specific type of disability (Kavale & Forness, 1995; Kavale & Forness, 1996; Lewandowski & Barlow, 2000; McNamara, Willoughby, Chalmers, & YLC-CURA, 2005; Nabuzoka, 2003; Rose & Espelage, 2012). Therefore, it is important to take into consideration the type of disability that students might have when examining their experience of school bullying.

Students with intellectual disabilities typically have more problems with anger, aggression, information processing, and self-control than students with other types of disabilities (Jahoda, Pert, & Trower, 2006a; Jahoda, Pert, & Trower, 2006b; Novaco & Taylor, 2004). Among students with mild developmental and intellectual disabilities, Reiter and Lapidot-Lefler (2007) found that half of the 12 through 18 year old students in their sample were involved in school bullying as perpetrators. About 83% of students in their sample were victims of physical, social, and verbal forms of school bullying. Similar patterns were found in later studies, citing prevalence rates between 50% and 80% among students with mild developmental and intellectual disabilities (Emerson, 2010; Glumbic & Zunic-Pavlovic, 2010).

Variations in prevalence rates might be the result of measurement and definitional differences among the studies. Despite such variations, it is clear that researchers need to delineate the type of disability when examining school bullying. Such a consideration is also important for research comparing students with disabilities to students without disabilities.

The research is mixed as to whether students with intellectual disabilities are more at risk for peer victimization in special education placement settings or inclusive placement settings. In particular, research indicates that rates of peer victimization are much higher in more restrictive special education placements (Norwich & Kelly, 2004; Rose et al., 2009), while other studies reveal that inclusive placements relate to greater school bullying involvement (Sterzing, Shattuck, Narendorf, Wagner, & Cooper, 2012; Whitney, Nabuzoka, & Smith, 1992; Zablotsky, Bradshaw, Anderson, & Law, 2013). Furthermore, research on cyberbullying suggested that placement in special education settings increased the risk of cyberbullying involvement among students with intellectual disabilities (Didden et al., 2009). Additional research attention should be given to understanding their experience of cyberbullying as children and adolescents, even students with intellectual disabilities, are spending more time utilizing information and communication technologies, a known risk factor associated with cyberbullying involvement (Flander, Stimac, Bagaric, & Vinscak, 2014; Kopecky, 2014; Lindfors, Kaltiala-Heino, & Rimpela, 2012; Mishna, Khoury-Kassabri, Gadalla, & Daciuk, 2012; Sourander et al., 2010).

Students with disabilities are at risk for a variety of adjustment difficulties resulting from their involvement in school bullying. In this literature, students with disabilities experience depression, anger, hostility, and lower self-esteem as a result of their bullying involvement, no matter their role as victims or perpetrators (Bauminger, Solomon, & Rogers, 2010; Larkin, Jahoda, MacMahon, & Pert, 2012; Rose, Forber-Pratt, Espelage, & Aragon, 2013). Similar patterns were found for victims and perpetrators of cyberbullying (Didden et al., 2009). They also experience increased levels of loneliness, delinquency, greater difficulties in their social interactions with their peers, and higher levels of social exclusion and peer rejection (Andreou, Didaskalou, & Vlachou, 2013; Jahoda et al., 2012; Nadeau & Tessier, 2006; Pearl & Bay, 1999). In addition, Davis and Nixon (2010) found that students with disabilities were more likely to experience severe trauma as a result of peer victimization when compared to students without disabilities. The associations between adjustment difficulties and school bullying are much stronger when students with disabilities are identified as bully-victims. In particular, Farmer and colleagues (2012) found that students with disabilities who were classified as bully-victims were at an increased risk for experiencing emotional (e.g., depression) and behavioral (e.g., antisocial behavior) problems when compared to students who were identified as either victims or bullies. Taken together, this research indicates that more consideration should be given to predictors of students with disabilities' involvement in school bullying as understanding such predictors can help to identify students who are at an increased risk for experiencing these behaviors. Identification of these students is important as specific intervention strategies can be implemented to mitigate their involvement in school bullying. In addition, identifying such students could help with including them in school bullying prevention programs.

PREDICTORS OF SCHOOL BULLYING AMONG STUDENTS WITH INTELLECTUAL DISABILITIES

Little attention has been given to the risk factors related to students with intellectual disabilities' involvement in school bullying. In the literature, behavioral problems (e.g., uncontrolled anger) are risk factors associated with school bullying perpetration among students with disabilities (Reiter & Lapidot-Lefler, 2007). In particular, temper tantrums, unruly and quarrelsome behavior, and a tendency to lie and steal increase these students' school bullying involvement as bullies and as bully-victims. Other findings revealed that emotional and interpersonal problems (e.g., poor social skills) increase these students' vulnerability to peer victimization. Their higher levels of depression, anxiety, and loneliness, and frequent conflicts within their friendships are significant predictors of peer victimization as well (Matheson, Olsen, & Weisner, 2007; Zeedyk, Rodriguez, Tipton, Baker, & Blacher, 2014). Students with intellectual disabilities also have lower adaptive behaviors and poorer social skills (i.e., social problems, social withdrawal), which increase their risk for peer victimization (Neece & Baker, 2008). Because they have lower adaptive behavioral skills, they might not be able to effectively deal with changes in their routine, which could reduce their ability to cope with changes. Their reduced capacity to cope might increase their susceptibility to peer victimization. Furthermore, having poorer social skills might also make students with intellectual disabilities particularly salient to the peer group as well. Some members of this group might notice the lack of social skills among students with intellectual disabilities, making them perceive these students as targets, especially easy targets, for school bullying. Another study found that poor social skills increased students with intellectual disabilities' susceptibility to peer victimization from middle childhood through early adolescence (Christensen, Fraynt, Neece, & Baker, 2012). Given that bullying increases in early adolescence, it might be likely that having poor social skills makes these students particularly vulnerable to peer victimization. Findings from Christensen et al. (2012) demonstrate the need for social skills training programs for these students as a lack of such skills perpetuates the cycle of peer victimization. Therefore, it is important for schools, parents, researchers, and the government to join together to help mitigate students with disabilities' involvement in school bullying.

SOLUTIONS AND RECOMMENDATIONS

To better understand and prevent school bullying among students with intellectual disabilities, federal programs should be developed to help fund research and bullying prevention incentives (Flynt & Morton, 2007). Access to funding can make conducting research on bullying among students with intellectual disabilities more feasible for researchers who might not have the funds necessary to revise data collection tools to fit this population. Furthermore, increased funding can also help researchers design more large-scale projects devoted to understanding more about school bullying among students with intellectual disabilities.

Research plays a major role in the development of bullying prevention programs and additional funds should be allocated to better serve students with intellectual disabilities in anti-bullying efforts. Individualized Education Programs could also be a source of bullying prevention. Expanding technical assistance within these programs can help to protect students with intellectual disabilities from school bullying involvement as well as provide effective ways for addressing specific bullying behaviors related to students' disabilities. Furthermore, school-wide bullying prevention programs should be modified to accommodate students with intellectual disabilities in an effort to guarantee that these students benefit from such programs. Most bullying prevention and intervention strategies have not be empirically evaluated for application to students with intellectual disabilities. However, the available programs do have some evidence that they decrease anger as well as school bullying victimization and perpetration among students with intellectual disabilities (Rose, West, & Clifford, 2000; Whitney et al., 1994).

Many programs are designed and implemented for use with students without disabilities. Therefore, the application and effectiveness of such programs for students with intellectual disabilities is untestable, making the implementation of these programs particularly problematic, especially if the cost of implementation is high.

Social policy should also mandate the development of a system used to notify parents of incidences involving school bullying. The aims of such a system would be to notify parents of their children's involvement in bullying, as either victims or perpetrators, as well as when other children are involved in these incidences. This notification system might be especially important for students with intellectual disabilities who might have communication issues which could prevent their reporting of school bullying incidences to their parents. For instance, an incident might have occurred at school, but parents could only have an awareness of the event, not really knowing what happened. It might be difficult for a student with intellectual disabilities to explain the event to their parents, which might make parents panic. Receiving information from the notification system might reduce parents' worries and their complaints to schools.

FUTURE RESEARCH DIRECTIONS

Based on the literature reviewed in this chapter, there are some clear gaps concerning students with intellectual disabilities' involvement in school bullying that should be addressed in future research. First, much of the literature involves cross-sectional designs, making it difficult to draw conclusions concerning the long-term extent, causes, and consequences of school bullying among students with intellectual disabilities. Such research can help to determine the risk factors associated with school bullying involvement and the long-term outcomes of students with intellectual disabilities' involvement as bullies and victims. Furthermore, this longitudinal research will shed light on whether students with intellectual disabilities experience more severe consequences associated with their involvement in school bullying when compared to their peers without intellectual disabilities. Longitudinal designs will also be helpful for testing prevention and intervention programs that are specifically designed to be sensitive to students with intellectual disabilities.

Second, much of the research does not compare school bullying involvement among students with different intellectual disabilities, which is important as some individuals might be more susceptible to these behaviors when compared to other individuals with intellectual disabilities. That is, students with physical disabilities might experience school bullying at different rates when compared to students with intellectual disabilities. This knowledge might also be important for the development of more sensitive prevention and intervention programs. In addition, some disabilities might differentially relate to different risks for school bullying involvement from childhood to adolescence. For example, students with physical disabilities might experience different levels of psychological, social, behavioral, and academic difficulties after experiencing school bullying in comparison to students with intellectual disabilities.

Another topic worth investigating is the role of protective factors. It is currently unknown whether there are protective factors associated with school bullying among students with intellectual disabilities. Understanding these protective factors might benefit the development of prevention programs and intervention strategies as they can be promoted to reduce these students' involvement in school bullying.

CONCLUSION

In summary, the literature reveals that students with intellectual disabilities are involved in school bullying as victims, perpetrators, and bully-victims. Furthermore, the research also suggests that they experience victimization by school bullying more often than their peers without intellectual disabilities. They also have similar risk factors and adjustment difficulties related to their experience of school bullying as their nondisabled peers. More research needs to be conducted to provide a better understanding of students with disabilities' involvement in school bullying and the associated risk factors and psychosocial adjustment difficulties. Such research is important as it serves as a foundation for the much needed policies and prevention and intervention programs aimed at reducing school bullying involvement among students with intellectual disabilities.

ACKNOWLEDGMENT

This work was supported by the project "Employment of Best Young Scientists for International Cooperation Empowerment" (CZ.1.07/2.3.00/30.0037), co-financed from European Social Fund and the state budget of the Czech Republic.

REFERENCES

Andreou, E., Didaskalou, E., & Vlachou, A. (2013). Bully/victim problems among Greek pupils with special educational needs: Associations with loneliness and self-efficacy for peer interactions. *Journal of Research in Special Educational Needs.*

Atik, G., & Guneri, O. Y. (2013). Bullying and victimization: Predictive role of individual, parental, and academic factors. *School Psychology International*, *34*(6), 658–673. doi:10.1177/0143034313479699

Baldry, A. C., & Farrington, D. (2000). Bullies and delinquents: Personal characteristics and parental styles. *Journal of Community & Applied Social Psychology*, *10*(1), 17–31. doi:10.1002/(SICI)1099-1298(200001/02)10:1<17::AID-CASP526>3.0.CO;2-M

Banks, R. (1997). *Bullying in Schools*. Washington, DC: U.S. Government Printing Office.

Bauminger, N., Solomon, M., & Rogers, S. J. (2010). Externalizing and internalizing behaviors in ASD. *Autism Research*, *3*(3), 101–112. doi:10.1002/aur.131 PMID:20575109

Bear, G. G., Mantz, L. S., Glutting, J. J., Yang, C., & Boyer, D. E. (2015). Differences in bullying victimization between students with and without disabilities. *School Psychology Review*, *44*(1), 98–116. doi:10.17105/SPR44-1.98-116

Berthold, K., & Hoover, J. (2000). Correlates of bullying and victimization among intermediate students in Midwestern USA. *School Psychology International*, *21*(1), 65–79. doi:10.1177/0143034300211005

Blake, J. J., Lund, E. M., Zhou, Q., Kwok, O., & Benz, M. (2012). National prevalence rates of bully victimization among students with disabilities in the United States. *School Psychology Quarterly*, *27*(4), 2100–2222. doi:10.1037/spq0000008 PMID:23294235

Boyes, M. E., Bowes, L., Cluver, L. C., Ward, C. L., & Badcock, N. A. (2014). Bullying victimization, internalizing symptoms, and conduct problems in South African children and adolescents: A longitudinal investigation. *Journal of Abnormal Child Psychology*, *42*(8), 1313–1324. doi:10.1007/s10802-014-9888-3 PMID:24882504

Bradshaw, C. P., Waasdorp, T. E., & Johnson, S. L. (2015). Overlapping verbal, relational, physical, and electronic forms of bullying in adolescence: Influence of school context. *Journal of Clinical Child and Adolescent Psychology*, *44*(3), 494–508. doi:10.1080/15374416.2014.893516 PMID:24738548

Brighi, A., Guarini, A., Melotti, G., Galli, S., & Genta, M. L. (2012). Predictors of victimization across direct bullying, indirect bullying and cyberbullying. *Emotional & Behavioural Difficulties*, *17*(3-4), 375–388. doi:10.1080/13632752.2012.704684

Buckley, S., Bird, G., Sacks, B., & Archer, T. (2002). A comparison of mainstream and special school education for teenagers with Down syndrome: Effects of social and academic development. *Down's Syndrome: Research and Practice*, *2*(2), 46–54.

Cappadocia, M. C., Weiss, J. A., & Pepler, D. (2012). Bullying experiences among children and youth with autism spectrum disorders. *Journal of Autism and Developmental Disorders*, *42*(2), 266–277. doi:10.1007/s10803-011-1241-x PMID:21499672

Carbone-Lopez, K., Esbensen, F. A., & Brick, B. T. (2010). Correlates and consequences of peer victimization: Gender differences in direct and indirect forms of bullying. *Youth Violence and Juvenile Justice*, *8*(4), 332–350. doi:10.1177/1541204010362954

Card, N. A., & Hodges, E. V. E. (2008). Peer victimization among schoolchildren: Correlations, causes, consequences, and considerations in assessment and intervention. *School Psychology Quarterly*, *23*(4), 451–461. doi:10.1037/a0012769

Carlson, I. W., & Cornell, D. W. (2008). Differences between persistent and desistent middle school bullies. *School Psychology International*, *29*(4), 442–451. doi:10.1177/0143034308096433

Carney, A., & Merrell, K. (2001). Bullying in schools: Perspectives on understanding and preventing an international problem. *School Psychology International*, *21*(3), 364–382. doi:10.1177/0143034301223011

Carter, B. B., & Spencer, V. G. (2006). The Fear Factor: Bullying and Students with Disabilities. George Mason University. *International Journal of Special Education*, *21*(1). Retrieved from http://www.forockids.org/PDF Docs/Bullying.pdf

Charach, A., Pepler, D., & Ziegler, S. (1995). Bullying at school. *Education Canada*, *37*, 12–18.

Christensen, L., Fraynt, B., Neece, C. L., & Baker, B. L. (2012). Bullying adolescents with intellectual disability. *Journal of Mental Health Research in Intellectual Disability*, *5*(1), 49–65. doi:10.1080/19315864.2011.637660

Craig, W. M., & Pepler, D. J. (1995). Peer processes in bullying and victimization: An observational study. *Exceptionality Education Canada*, *5*, 81–95.

Crick, N. R., & Grotpeter, J. K. (1995). Relational aggression, gender, and social-psychological adjustment. *Child Development*, *66*(3), 710–722. doi:10.2307/1131945 PMID:7789197

Cummings, J., Pepler, D. J., Mishna, F., & Craig, W. M. (2006). Bullying and victimization among children with exceptionalities. *Exceptionality Education Canada*, *16*, 193–222.

Cunningham, C. E., Clark, M. L., Heaven, R. K., Durrant, J., & Cunningham, L. H. (1989). The effects of coping-modelling problem solving and contingency management procedures on the positive and negative interactions of learning disabled and attention deficit disordered children with an autistic peer. *Child & Family Behavior Therapy*, *11*(3-4), 89–106. doi:10.1300/J019v11n03_06

Davis, S., & Nixon, C. (2010). *The youth voice research project: Victimization and strategies*. Retrieved from: http://njbullying.org/documents/YVPMarch2010.pdf

Dawkins, J. L. (1996). Bullying, physical disability and the pediatric patient. *Developmental Medicine and Child Neurology*, *38*(7), 603–612. doi:10.1111/j.1469-8749.1996.tb12125.x PMID:8674911

Dickerson Mayes, S., Baweja, R., Calhoun, S. L., Syed, E., Mahr, F., & Siddiqui, F. (2014). Suicide ideation and attempts and bullying in children and adolescents: Psychiatric and general population samples. *Crisis*, *35*(5), 301–309. doi:10.1027/0227-5910/a000264 PMID:25115491

Dickson, K., Emerson, E., & Hatton, C. (2005). Self-reported anti-social behaviour: Prevalence and risk factors amongst adolescents with and without intellectual disability. *Journal of Intellectual Disability Research*, *49*(11), 820–826. doi:10.1111/j.1365-2788.2005.00727.x PMID:16207279

Didden, R., Scholte, R. H. J., Korzilius, H., De Moor, J. M. H., Vermeulen, A., O'Reilly, M., & Lancioni, G. E. et al. (2009). Cyberbullying among students with intellectual and developmental disability in special education settings. *Developmental Neurorehabilitation*, *12*(3), 146–151. doi:10.1080/17518420902971356 PMID:19466622

Dinkes, R., Kemp, J., Baum, K., & Snyder, T. (2009). *Indicators of school crime and safety: 2009 (NCES 2010–012/NCJ 228478)*. Washington, DC: National Center for Education Statistics, Institute of Education Sciences, U.S. Department of Education, and Bureau of Justice Statistics, Office of Justice Programs, U.S. Department of Justice.

Doren, B., Bullis, M., & Benz, M. R. (1996). Predictors of victimization: Experiences of adolescents with disabilities in transition. *Exceptional Children*, *63*, 7–18.

Duncan, N. (1999). *Sexual bullying: Gender conflict and pupil culture in secondary schools*. New York, NY: Routledge.

Emerson, E. (2010). Self-reported exposure to disablism is associated with poorer self-reported health and well-being among adults with intellectual disabilities in England: A cross-sectional survey. *Public Health*, *124*(12), 682–689. doi:10.1016/j.puhe.2010.08.020 PMID:21035153

Ericson, N. (2001). *Addressing the problem of juvenile bullying*. Washington, DC: U.S. Government Printing Office. doi:10.1037/e317892004-001

Espelage, D. L., Low, S. K., & Jimerson, S. R. (2014). Understanding school climate, aggression, peer victimization, and bully perpetration: Contemporary science, practice, and policy. *School Psychology Quarterly*, *29*(3), 233–237. doi:10.1037/spq0000090 PMID:25198615

Espelage, D. L., & Swearer, S. M. (2003). Research on school bullying and victimization: What have we learned and where do we go from here? *School Psychology Review*, *32*, 365–383.

Estell, D. B., Farmer, T. W., Irvin, M. J., Crowther, A., Akos, P., & Boudah, D. J. (2009). Students with exceptionalities and the peer group context of bullying and victimization in late elementary school. *Journal of Child and Family Studies*, *18*(2), 136–150. doi:10.1007/s10826-008-9214-1

Farmer, T. W., Irvin, M. J., Motoca, L. M., Leung, M., Hutchins, B. C., Brooks, D. S., & Hall, C. M. (2015). Externalizing and internalizing behavior problems, peer affiliations, and bullying involvement across the transition to middle school. *Journal of Emotional and Behavioral Disorders*, *23*(1), 3–16. doi:10.1177/1063426613491286

Farmer, T. W., Petrin, R., Brooks, D. S., Hamm, J. V., Lambert, K., & Gravelle, M. (2012). Bullying involvement and the school adjustment of rural students with and without disabilities. *Journal of Emotional and Behavioral Disorders*, *20*(1), 19–37. doi:10.1177/1063426610392039

Flander, G. B., Stimac, D., Bagaric, E. S., & Vinscak, M. (2014). Patterns of and copying with cyberbullying in Croatia. *The International Journal of Person Centered Medicine.*

Flynt, S. W., & Morton, R. C. (2007). Bullying prevention and students with disabilities. *National Forum of Special Education Journal, 19*(1), 1-6.

Fox, C. L. (1989). Peer acceptance of learning disabled children in the regular classroom. *Exceptional Children*, *56*(1), 50–59.

Glumbic, N., & Zunic-Pavlovic, V. (2010). Bullying behavior in children with intellectual disability. *Procedia: Social and Behavioral Sciences*, *2*(2), 2784–2788. doi:10.1016/j.sbspro.2010.03.415

Graham, S., Bellmore, A. D., & Mize, J. (2006). Peer victimization, aggression, and their co-occurrence in middle school: Pathways to adjustment problems. *Journal of Abnormal Child Psychology*, *34*(3), 363–378. doi:10.1007/s10802-006-9030-2 PMID:16648999

Hawker, D. S., & Boulton, M. J. (2000). Twenty years' research on peer victimization and psychosocial maladjustment: A meta-analytic review of crosssectional studies. *Journal of Child Psychology and Psychiatry, and Allied Disciplines*, *41*(4), 441–455. doi:10.1111/1469-7610.00629 PMID:10836674

Hemphill, S. A., Tollit, M., Kotevski, A., & Florent, A. (2015). Bullying in schools: Rates, correlates and impact on mental health. In J. Lindert & I. Itzhak (Eds.), *Violence and mental health: Its manifold faces* (pp. 185–205). Springer. doi:10.1007/978-94-017-8999-8_9

Hertz, M. F., Donato, I., & Wright, J. (2013). Bullying and suicide: A public health approach. *The Journal of Adolescent Health*, *53*(1), S1–S3. doi:10.1016/j.jadohealth.2013.05.002 PMID:23790194

Hong, J. S., Davis, J. P., Sterzing, P. R., Yoon, J., Choi, S., & Smith, D. C. (2014). A conceptual framework for understanding the association between school bullying victimization and substance misuse. *The American Journal of Orthopsychiatry*, *84*(6), 696–710. doi:10.1037/ort0000036 PMID:25545436

Hong, J. S., Peguero, A. A., Choi, S., Lanesskog, D., Espelage, D. L., & Lee, N. Y. (2014). Social ecology of bullying and peer victimization of Latino and Asian youth in the United States: A review of the literature. *Journal of School Violence*, *13*(3), 315–338. doi:10.1080/15388220.2013.856013

Hymel, S., & Swearer, S. M. (2015). Four decades of research on school bullying. *The American Psychologist*, *70*(4), 293–299. doi:10.1037/a0038928 PMID:25961310

Jahoda, A., Pert, C., & Trower, P. (2006a). Socioemotional understanding and frequent aggression in people with mild to moderate intellectual disabilities: Recognition of facial affect and role-taking abilities. *American Journal of Mental Retardation*, *111*(2), 77–89. doi:10.1352/0895-8017(2006)111[77:SUAFAI]2.0.CO;2 PMID:16466287

Jahoda, A., Pert, C., & Trower, P. (2006b). Frequent aggression and attribution of hostile intent in people with mild to moderate intellectual disabilities: An empirical investigation. *American Journal of Mental Retardation*, *111*(2), 90–99. doi:10.1352/0895-8017(2006)111[90:FAAAOH]2.0.CO;2 PMID:16466288

Kaltiala-Heino, R., Rimpela, M., Marttunen, M., Rimpela, A., & Rantanen, P. (1999). Bullying, depression, and suicidal ideation in Finnish adolescents: School survey. *British Medical Journal*, *319*(7206), 438–451. doi:10.1136/bmj.319.7206.348 PMID:10435954

Kavale, K. A., & Forness, S. R. (1995). Social skill deficits and training: A meta-analysis of the research in learning disabilities. *Advances in Learning and Behavioral Disabilities*, *9*, 119–160.

Kavale, K. A., & Forness, S. R. (1996). Social skill deficits and learning disabilities: A meta-analysis. *Journal of Learning Disabilities*, *29*(3), 226–237. doi:10.1177/002221949602900301 PMID:8732884

Kelly, E. V., Newton, N. C., Stapinski, L. A., Slade, T., Barrett, E. L., Conrod, P. J., & Teesson, M. (2015). Suicidality, internalizing problems and externalizing problems among adolescent bullies, victims and bully-victims. *Preventive Medicine: An International Journal Devoted to Practice and Theory*, *73*, 100–105. doi:10.1016/j.ypmed.2015.01.020 PMID:25657168

Kistner, J. A., & Gatlin, D. F. (1989). Sociometric differences between learning-disabled and nonhandicapped students: Effects of sex and race. *Journal of Educational Psychology*, *81*(1), 118–120. doi:10.1037/0022-0663.81.1.118

Kopecky, K. (2014). Cyberbullying and other risks of internet communication focused on university students. *Procedia: Social and Behavioral Sciences*, *112*, 260–269. doi:10.1016/j.sbspro.2014.01.1163

Kumpulainen, K., Rasanen, E., & Puura, K. (2001). Psychiatric disorders and the use of mental health services among children involved in bullying. *Aggressive Behavior*, *27*(2), 102–110. doi:10.1002/ab.3

Kurth, J. A. (2014). Educational placement of students with autism: The impact of state of residence. *Focus on Autism and Other Developmental Disabilities*.

Lagerheim, B. (1986). Preparing disabled children for coping with adolescent stress. *International Journal of Adolescent Medicine and Health*, *2*(4), 309–316.

Lapidot-Lefler, N., & Dolev-Cohen, M. (2015). Comparing cyberbullying and school bullying among school students: Prevalence, gender, and grade level differences. *Social Psychology of Education*, *18*(1), 1–16. doi:10.1007/s11218-014-9280-8

Larkin, P., Jahoda, A., MacMahon, K., & Pert, C. (2012). Interpersonal sources of conflict in young people with and without mild to moderate intellectual disabilities at transition from adolescent to adulthood. *Journal of Applied Research in Intellectual Disabilities*, *25*(1), 29–38. doi:10.1111/j.1468-3148.2011.00652.x PMID:22473946

Lewandowski, L. J., & Barlow, J. R. (2000). Social cognition and verbal learning disabilities. *Journal of Psychotherapy in Independent Practice*, *4*(4), 35–47. doi:10.1300/J288v01n04_04

Lindfors, P. J., Kaltiala-Heino, R., & Rimpela, A. H. (2012). Cyberbullying among Finnish adolescents – a population-based study. *BMC Public Health*, 1. PMID:23176715

Lindsay, S., & McPherson, A. C. (2012). Strategies for improving disability awareness and social inclusion of children and young people with cerebral palsy. *Child: Care, Health and Development*, *38*(6), 809–816. doi:10.1111/j.1365-2214.2011.01308.x PMID:21880056

Llewellyn, A. (2000). Perceptions of mainstreaming: A systems approach. *Developmental Medicine and Child Neurology*, *42*(2), 106–115. doi:10.1017/S0012162200000219 PMID:10698328

Luukkonen, A. H., Riala, K., Hakko, H., & Rasanen, P. (2010). Bullying behavior and substance abuse among underage psychiatric inpatient adolescents. *European Psychiatry*, *25*(7), 382–389. doi:10.1016/j.eurpsy.2009.12.002 PMID:20435448

Marini, Z. A., Dane, A. V., Bosacki, S. L., & Cura, Y.-. (2006). Direct and indirect bully-victims: Differential psychosocial risk factors associated with adolescents involvement in bullying and victimization. *Aggressive Behavior*, *32*(6), 551–569. doi:10.1002/ab.20155

Martlew, M., & Hodson, J. (1991). Children with mild learning difficulties in an integrated and in a special school: Comparisons of behavior, teasing and teachers' attitudes. *The British Journal of Educational Psychology*, *61*(3), 355–372. doi:10.1111/j.2044-8279.1991.tb00992.x PMID:1786214

Maryland Coalition for Inclusive Education. (2011). *Quality indicators for inclusive building based practices.* Retrieved from: http://www.mcie.org/usermedia/application/8/quality-indicators---building-based-practices-(2011).pdf

Matheson, C., Olsen, R. J., & Weisner, T. (2007). A good friend is hard to find: Friendship among adolescents with disabilities. *American Journal of Mental Retardation*, *112*(5), 319–329. doi:10.1352/0895-8017(2007)112[0319:AGFIHT]2.0.CO;2 PMID:17676957

McNamara, J. K., Willoughby, T., & Chalmers, H. (2005). Psychosocial status of adolescents with learning disabilities with and without comorbid attention deficit hyperactivity disorder. *Learning Disabilities Research & Practice*, *20*(4), 234–244. doi:10.1111/j.1540-5826.2005.00139.x

Mishna, F. (2003). Learning disabilities and bullying: Double jeopardy. *Journal of Learning Disabilities*, *36*(4), 336–347. doi:10.1177/00222194030360040501 PMID:15490906

Mishna, F., Khoury-Kassabri, M., Gadalla, T., & Daciuk, J. (2012). Risk factors for involvement in cyber bullying: Victims, bullies, and bully-victims. *Children and Youth Services Review*, *32*(1), 63–70. doi:10.1016/j.childyouth.2011.08.032

Morrison, G. M., Furlong, M. J., & Smith, G. (1994). Factors associated with the experience of school violence among general education, leadership class, opportunity class, and special day class pupils. *Journal of Education and Treatment of Children*, *17*, 356–369.

Nabuzoka, D. (2003). Teacher ratings and peer nominations of bullying and other behavior of children with and without learning difficulties. *Educational Psychology*, *23*(3), 307–321. doi:10.1080/0144341032000060147

Nabuzoka, D., & Smith, P. K. (1993). Sociometric status and social behaviour of children with and without learning difficulties. *Journal of Child Psychology and Psychiatry, and Allied Disciplines*, *34*(8), 1435–1448. doi:10.1111/j.1469-7610.1993.tb02101.x PMID:8294529

Nadeau, L., & Tessier, R. (2006). Social adjustment of children with cerebral palsy in mainstream classes: Peer perception. *Developmental Medicine and Child Neurology*, *48*(05), 331–336. doi:10.1017/S0012162206000739 PMID:16608539

Nansel, T. R., Overpeck, M., Pilla, R. S., Ruan, W. J., Simons-Morton, B., & Scheidt, P. (2001). Bullying behaviors among US youth: Prevalence and association with psychosocial adjustment. *Journal of the American Medical Association*, *285*(16), 2094–2100. doi:10.1001/jama.285.16.2094 PMID:11311098

Neece, C., & Baker, B. L. (2008). Predicting maternal parenting stress in middle childhood: The roles of child intellectual status, behavior problems and social skills. *Journal of Intellectual Disability Research*, *52*(12), 1114–1128. doi:10.1111/j.1365-2788.2008.01071.x PMID:18513339

Nishina, A., Juvonen, J., & Witkow, M. (2005). Sticks and stones may break my bones, but names will make me sick: The consequences of peer harassment. *Journal of Clinical Child and Adolescent Psychology*, *34*, 37–48. doi:10.1207/s15374424jccp3401_4 PMID:15677279

Noorden, T. H. J., Haselager, G. J. T., Cillessen, A. H. N., & Bukowski, W. M. (2015). Empathy and involvement in bullying in children and adolescents: A systematic review. *Journal of Youth and Adolescence*, *44*(3), 637–657. doi:10.1007/s10964-014-0135-6 PMID:24894581

Norwich, B., & Kelly, N. (2004). Pupils' views on inclusion: Moderate learning difficulties and bullying in mainstream and special schools. *British Educational Research Journal*, *30*(1), 43–65. doi:10.1080/01411920310001629965

Novaco, R. W., & Taylor, J. L. (2004). Assessment of anger and aggression among male offenders with developmental disabilities. *Psychological Assessment*, *16*(1), 42–50. doi:10.1037/1040-3590.16.1.42 PMID:15023091

O'Brennan, L. M., Bradshaw, C. P., & Sawyer, A. L. (2009). Examining development differences in the social-emotional problems among frequent bullies, victims, and bully/victims. *Psychology in the Schools*, *46*(2), 100–115. doi:10.1002/pits.20357

Olthof, T., & Goossens, F. A. (2008). Bullying and the need to belong: Early adolescents' bullying-related behavior and the acceptance they desire and receive from particular classmates. *Social Development*, *17*(1), 24–46.

Olweus, D. (1978). *Aggression in the schools: Bullies and whipping boys*. Washington, DC: Hemisphere Press.

Olweus, D. (1993). *Bullying at school: What we know and what we can do*. Blackwell Publshing.

Ozdemir, M., & Stattin, H. (2011). Bullies, victims, and bully-victims: A longitudinal examination of the effects of bullying-victimization experiences on youth well-being. *Journal of Aggression, Conflict and Peace Research*, *3*(2), 97–102. doi:10.1108/17596591111132918

Pearl, R., & Bay, M. (1999). Psychosocial correlates of learning disabilities. In V. L. Schwean & D. H. Saklofske (Eds.), *Handbook of psychosocial characteristics of exceptional children* (pp. 443–470). New York, NY: Kluwer Academic / Plenum Publishers. doi:10.1007/978-1-4757-5375-2_17

Perren, S., Dooley, J., Shaw, T., & Cross, T. (2010). Bullying in school and cyberspace: Associations with depressive symptoms in Swiss and Australian adolescents. *Child and Adolescent Psychiatry and Mental Health*, *23*(4), 28. doi:10.1186/1753-2000-4-28 PMID:21092266

Psalti, A. (2012). Bullies, victims, and bully-victims in Greek schools: Research data and implications of practice. *Hellenic Journal of Psychology*, *9*(2), 132–157.

Radliff, K. M., Wheaton, J. E., Robinson, K., & Morris, J. (2012). Illuminating the relationship between bullying and substance use among middle and high school youths. *Addictive Behaviors*, *37*(4), 569–572. doi:10.1016/j.addbeh.2012.01.001 PMID:22277772

Reiter, S., Bryen, D., & Shachar, I. (2007). Adolescents with intellectual disabilities as victims of abuse. *Journal of Intellectual Disabilities*, *11*(4), 371–387. doi:10.1177/1744629507084602 PMID:18029413

Reiter, S., & Lapidot-Leflet, N. (2007). Bullying among special education students with intellectual disabilities: Differences in social adjustment and social skills. *Journal of Intellectual & Developmental Disability*, *45*(3), 174–181. doi:10.1352/1934-9556(2007)45[174:BASESW]2.0.CO;2 PMID:17472426

Richardson, S. O. (1996). Coping with dyslexia in the regular classroom: Inclusion or exclusion. *Annals of Dyslexia*, *46*(1), 37–48. doi:10.1007/BF02648170 PMID:24234266

Rigby, K., & Cox, I. K. (1996). The contributions of bullying and low self-esteem to acts of delinquency among Australian teenagers. *Personality and Individual Differences*, *21*(4), 609–612. doi:10.1016/0191-8869(96)00105-5

Rigby, K., & Slee, P. T. (1991). Bullying among Australian school children: Reported behaviour and attitudes to victims. *The Journal of Social Psychology*, *131*(5), 615–622. doi:10.1080/00224545.1991.9924646 PMID:1798296

Roberts, C. M., & Smith, P. R. (1999). Attitudes and behavior of children towards peers with disabilities. *International Journal of Disability Development and Education*, *46*(1), 35–50. doi:10.1080/103491299100713

Rose, C. A., & Espelage, D. L. (2012). Risk and protective factors associated with the bullying involvement of students with emotional and behavioral disorders. *Behavioral Disorders*, *37*(3), 133–148.

Rose, C. A., Espelage, D. L., & Monda-Amaya, L. E. (2009). Bullying and victimization rates among students in general and special education: A comparative analysis. *Educational Psychology*, *29*(7), 761–776. doi:10.1080/01443410903254864

Rose, C. A., Forber-Pratt, A. J., Espelage, D. L., & Aragon, S. R. (2013). The influence of psychosocial factors on bullying involvement of students with disabilities. *Theory into Practice*, *52*(4), 272–279. doi:10.1080/00405841.2013.829730

Rose, C. A., Monda-Amaya, L. E., & Espelage, D. L. (2011). Bullying perpetration and victimization in special education: A review of the literature. *Remedial and Special Education*, *32*(2), 114–130. doi:10.1177/0741932510361247

Rose, J., West, C., & Clifford, D. (2000). Group intervention for anger in people with intellectual disabilities. *Research in Developmental Disabilities*, *21*(3), 171–181. doi:10.1016/S0891-4222(00)00032-9 PMID:10939316

Ryoo, J. H., Wang, C., & Swearer, S. M. (2015). Examination of the change in latent statuses in bullying behaviors across time. *School Psychology Quarterly*, *30*(1), 105–122. doi:10.1037/spq0000082 PMID:25111466

Sailor, W., Wolf, N., Choi, H., & Roger, B. (2009). Sustaining positive behavior support in a context of comprehensive school reform. In W. Sailor, G. Dunlop, G. Sugai, & R. Horner (Eds.), *Handbook of positive behavior support* (pp. 633–669). New York: Springer Publishing. doi:10.1007/978-0-387-09632-2_26

Salend, S. J., & Duhaney, L. M. G. (1999). The impact of inclusion on students with and without disabilities and their educators. *Remedial and Special Education*, *20*(2), 114–126. doi:10.1177/074193259902000209

Sansone, R. A., & Sansone, L. A. (2008). Bully victims: Psychological and somatic aftermaths. *Psychiatry*, *5*(6), 62–64. PMID:19727287

Sheard, C., Clegg, J., Standen, P., & Cromby, J. (2001). Bullying and people with severe intellectual disability. *Journal of Intellectual Disability Research*, *45*(5), 407–415. doi:10.1046/j.1365-2788.2001.00349.x PMID:11679046

Sirlopu, D., Gonzalez, R., Bohner, G., Siebler, F., Ordonnez, G., Millar, A., & De Tezanos-Pinto, P. et al. (2008). Promoting positive attitudes toward people with Down syndrome: The benefit of school inclusion programs. *Journal of Applied Social Psychology*, *38*(11), 2710–2736. doi:10.1111/j.1559-1816.2008.00411.x

Skapinakis, P., Bellos, S., Gkatsa, T., Magklara, K., Lewish, G., Araya, R., & Mavreas, V. et al. (2011). The association between bullying and early stages of suicidal ideation in late adolescents in Greece. *BMC Psychiatry*, *11*(1), 1–9. doi:10.1186/1471-244X-11-22 PMID:21303551

Son, E., Parish, S. L., & Peterson, N. A. (2012). National prevalence of peer victimization among young children with disabilities in the United States. *Children and Youth Services Review*, *34*(8), 1540–1545. doi:10.1016/j.childyouth.2012.04.014

Sourander, A., Klomek, A. B., Ikonen, M., Lindroos, J., Luntamo, T., Koskelainen, M., & Helenius, H. et al. (2010). Psychosocial risk factors associated with cyberbullying among adolescents: A population-based study. *Archives of General Psychiatry*, *67*(7), 720–728. doi:10.1001/archgenpsychiatry.2010.79 PMID:20603453

Sprafkin, J., & Gadow, K. (1987). An observational study of emotionally disturbed and learning-disabled children in school settings. *Journal of Abnormal Child Psychology*, *15*(3), 393–408. doi:10.1007/BF00916457 PMID:3668086

Sterzing, P. R., Shattuck, P. T., Narendrof, S. C., Wagner, M., & Cooper, B. P. (2012). Bullying involvement and autism spectrum disorders: Prevalence and correlates of bullying involvement among adolescents with an autism spectrum disorder. *Archives of Pediatrics & Adolescent Medicine*, *166*(11), 1058–1064. doi:10.1001/archpediatrics.2012.790 PMID:22945284

Swearer, S. M., Siebecker, A. B., Johnsen-Frerichs, L., & Wang, C. (2010). Assessment of bullying/victimization: The problem of comparability across studies and across methodologies. In S. R. Jimerson, S. M. Swearer, & D. L. Espelage (Eds.), *Handbook of bullying in schools: An international perspective* (pp. 305–327). New York, NY: Routledge.

Tomasik, M. (2007). Effective inclusion activities for high school students with multiple disabilities. *Journal of Visual Impairment & Blindness*, *101*(10), 657–659.

Underwood, M. K., Galen, B. R., & Paquette, J. A. (2001). Top ten challenges for understanding gender and aggression in children: Why can't we all just get along? *Social Development*, *10*, 248–266.

Van Cleave, J., & Davis, M. M. (2006). Bullying and peer victimization among children with special health care needs. *Pediatrics*, *118*(4), 1212–1219. doi:10.1542/peds.2005-3034 PMID:17015509

Verdugo, M. A., Bermejo, B. G., & Fuertes, J. (1995). The maltreatment of intellectually handicapped children and adolescents. *Child Abuse & Neglect*, *19*(2), 205–215. doi:10.1016/0145-2134(94)00117-D PMID:7780782

Waasdorp, T. E., & Bradshaw, C. P. (2015). The overlap between cyberbullying and traditional bullying. *The Journal of Adolescent Health*, *56*(5), 483–488. doi:10.1016/j.jadohealth.2014.12.002 PMID:25631040

Waldman, H. B., Swerdloff, M., & Perlman, S. P. (1999). A "dirty secret": The abuse of children with disabilities. *ASDC Journal of Dentistry for Children*, *66*(3), 197–202. PMID:10476359

Wang, J., Iannotti, R. J., Luk, J. W., & Nansel, T. R. (2010). Co-occurrence of victimization from five subtypes of bullying: Physical, verbal, social exclusion, spreading rumors, and cyber. *Journal of Pediatric Psychology*, *35*(10), 1103–1112. doi:10.1093/jpepsy/jsq048 PMID:20488883

Whitney, I., Nabuzoka, D., & Smith, P. K. (1992). Bullying in schools: Mainstream and special needs. *Support for Learning*, *7*(1), 3–7. doi:10.1111/j.1467-9604.1992.tb00445.x

Whitney, I., Smith, P. K., & Thompson, D. (1994). Bullying and children with special educational needs. In P. K. Smith & S. Sharp (Eds.), *School bullying: Insights and perspectives* (pp. 213–240). London: Routledge.

York, J., Vandercook, T., MacDonald, C., Heise-Neff, C., & Caughey, E. (1992). Feedback about integrating middle school students with severe disabilities in general education classes. *Exceptional Children*, *58*(3), 244–257. PMID:1839896

Zablotsky, B., Bradshaw, C. P., Anderson, C., & Law, P. A. (2013). The association between bullying and the psychological functioning of children with autism spectrum disorders. *Journal of Developmental and Behavioral Pediatrics*, *34*(1), 1–8. doi:10.1097/DBP.0b013e31827a7c3a PMID:23275052

Zeedyk, S. M., Rodrigeuz, G., Tipton, L. A., Baker, B. L., & Blacher, J. (2014). Bullying of youth with autism spectrum disorder, intellectual disability, or typical development: Victim and parent perspectives. *Research in Autism Spectrum Disorders*, *8*(9), 1173–1183. doi:10.1016/j.rasd.2014.06.001 PMID:25285154

Zeitlin, S., & Williamson, G. (1990). Coping characteristics of disabled and nondisabled young children. *The American Journal of Orthopsychiatry*, *60*(3), 404–411. doi:10.1037/h0079183 PMID:2143354

ADDITIONAL READING

Basquill, M., Nezu, C. M., Nezu, A. M., & Klein, T. L. (2004). Aggression-related hostility bias and social problem-solving deficits in adult males with mental retardation. *American Journal of Mental Retardation*, *109*(3), 255–263. doi:10.1352/0895-8017(2004)109<255:AHBASP>2.0.CO;2 PMID:15072517

Ebeling, H., & Nurkkala, H. (2002). Children and adolescents with developmental disorders and violence. *International Journal of Circumpolar Health*, *61*(0), 51–60. doi:10.3402/ijch.v61i0.17502 PMID:12585820

Fenning, R. M., Baker, J. K., Baker, B. L., & Crnic, K. A. (2007). Parenting children with borderline intellectual functioning: A unique risk population. *American Journal of Mental Retardation*, *112*(2), 107–121. doi:10.1352/0895-8017(2007)112[107:PCWBIF]2.0.CO;2 PMID:17295551

Horner-Johnson, W., & Drum, C. E. (2006). Prevalence of maltreatment of people with intellectual disabilities: A review of recently published research. *Mental Retardation and Developmental Disabilities Research Reviews*, *12*(1), 57–69. doi:10.1002/mrdd.20097 PMID:16435331

Loveland, K. A., & Kelley, M. L. (1988). Development of adaptive behavior in adolescents and young adults with autism and Down syndrome. *American Journal of Mental Retardation*, *93*, 84–92. PMID:2970861

Luckasson, R., Borthwick-Duffy, S., Buntinx, W. H. E., Coulter, D. L., Craig, E. M., Reeve, A., & Tasse, M. J. et al. (2002). *Mental retardation: Definition, classification, and systems of supports*. Washington, DC: American Association on Mental Retardation.

Mitchell, L. M., & Buchele-Ash, A. (2000). Abuse and neglect of individuals with disabilities: Building protective supports through public policy. *Journal of Disability Policy Studies*, *10*(2), 225–243. doi:10.1177/104420730001000206

Murphy, N. (2011). Maltreatment of children with disabilities: The breaking point. *Journal of Child Neurology*, *26*(8), 1054–1056. doi:10.1177/0883073811413278 PMID:21775619

Nettelbeck, T., & Wilson, C. (2002). Personal vulnerability to victimization of people with mental retardation. *Trauma, Violence & Abuse*, *3*(4), 289–306. doi:10.1177/1524838002237331

Olweus, D. (1991). Bully/victim problems among school children: Some basic facts and effects of a school-based intervention program. In D. Pepler & K. Rubin (Eds.), *The development and treatment of childhood aggression* (pp. 411–448). Hillsdale, NJ: Erlbaum.

Chapter 4
Mental Health Issues among Family Members of Children with Mental Disability

Aili Hanim Hashim
University Malaya, Malaysia

Manveen Kaur
University Malaya, Malaysia

Norharlina Bahar
Hospital Selayang, Malaysia

Wan Salwina Wan Ismail
University Kebangsaan Malaysia, Malaysia

ABSTRACT

Parenting children with intellectual disabilities is challenging. Many of these children are misunderstood, while parents are often blamed for the difficulties. The reality is that parents of such children are themselves unable to understand the nature of their child's difficulties, what more to cope with the child. The child's difficulties poses challenge for the parents and siblings, and many parents struggle. The chapter will discuss types of problems faced by the children with mental disability, their parents and siblings, including the possible impact on mental health of the family. The chapter will as well discuss the impact of mental health difficulties in parents and its impact on their parenting. The chapter hopes to highlight the need to recognize parents who are struggling, what should professionals looked for in their assessment of families with children with intellectual disabilities. Identifying families who are struggling is important as the family environment has an impact on functioning and, consequently, service needs of the child.

INTRODUCTION

Looking after children[1] with intellectual disabilities (ID) is challenging. Adults often misunderstand these children. A lot of children with ID look healthy thus it confuses others why they are not behaving or evolving similarly to their peers.

Moreover, parents are often blamed for the difficulties i.e. that they are not doing enough for their child. The reality is many parents of children with ID are themselves unable to understand why their child is struggling or facing continuous difficulties, what more how to manage them. In most instances, the child's difficulties pose many challenges for the parents and siblings, and many parents struggle to cope.

DOI: 10.4018/978-1-5225-0089-6.ch004

The chapter discusses the mental health difficulties faced by the family of children with ID, specifically the impact on parents.

The section hopes to highlight the need to recognize parents with children with ID who are struggling and what medical and mental health professionals should look for in their assessment of these families. This issue is important as the family environment impact on the child's functioning and consequently on the services needed by the children and their family.

UNDERSTANDING CHILDREN WITH INTELLECTUAL DISABILITY

Intelligence or the mental capacity of an individual is important to all humans. We use this ability to acquire and apply knowledge and skills to help us think, learn and deal with things around us effectively. In many cultures, children are particularly judged based on their intellectual abilities especially their academic performance.

Many more children with ID are surviving now than they did a century ago (DeWeaver and Kropf, 1992). Thus, in the recent years, children who are delayed or are slower in their development in their development have received a lot of attention and interest.

Affected children with reduced cognitive development struggle to understand concepts, to remember and utilize things expected of them. They are unable to learn as good or as fast as other children of the same age group. The other chapters of the book discuss these deficits and difficulties.

The presentation of the difficulties varies according to the severity of deficiency present, which corresponds approximately to the level of IQ scores (American Psychiatric Association, 2013; American Association on Intellectual & Developmental Disabilities, 2012). Categorized as mild, moderate, severe and profound difficulties, are discussed elsewhere in the book.

The reduced ability to adapt to the daily demands of the social environment (World Health Organization, 1992) affects all areas of their daily living. The children struggle even with simple things such as their daily routine, with mental abilities e.g. reading, remembering things taught and tasks expected of them. Reasoning, planning and thinking about things or issues does not come quickly. Subsequent impairment is seen across all activities of daily living e.g. in their personal care, keeping their schedules/routines and personal safety. Going about carrying out their day-to-day tasks is a struggle as they are unable to comprehend and remember there is a routine to follow, and how to go about it. The children frequently need assistance from people around them with their daily routines, e.g. handle school and doing their schoolwork. They often need repeatedly to be told what to do, how to behave, how to do things or tasks, etc. Thus, daily life is a struggle for the children and their family. It is hard for them to understand how things work, how to go about things and to decide even on simple issues. Evidently parents worry or become anxious when their child lacks behind their peers.

The deficits in global functioning *impact their quality of life* with a significant number of the children severely impaired in their everyday functioning (American Psychiatric Association, 1994; Einfeld et al., 2006; American Association on Intellectual & Developmental Disabilities, 2012). In many situations and to most people, these children are seen as being "childish" and not of their biological age. It is frustrating for people around them as the child is unable to cope well without help. As they do not live up to the expectations of their parents, teachers, comparisons are often made. Despite the aid given, they continue to be behind their peers. Their differences are often highlighted, with many pushed and punished to do better. Often they are labeled as being defiant, stubborn, lazy, etc.

Consequences of Having Deficits in Intellectual Disability

Children with ID experience more physical, emotional and behavioral problems and manifest more social issues when compared to typically developing children (Dekker et al., 2002; E. and Hatton, 2007; Witwera and Lecavaliera, 2008; Mazzucchelli and Sanders, 2011; Vrijmoeth et al., 2011; Gray et al., 2011).

Parents with children with mental disabilities will have to deal with:

1. **Behavioural and Emotional Problems:** (Parmenter et al., 1998; Crnic et al., 2004; Witwera and Lecavaliera, 2008; Emerson et al., 2014) Parents often report their child's behaviours as being problematic at home and in social settings, describing their children as:
   a. Being uncooperative, not listening to them.
   b. Being stubborn.
   c. Unable to follow through with requests or tasks.
   d. Not being able to verbalise their daily experience and needs adequately.
   e. Constantly relying on others.
   f. Eating difficulties i.e. fussy with food.
   g. Unable to cope well when left on their own.

A central theme of the child's problems emerges as the child struggles to keep up with the many age's appropriate expectations. Their inability to organize their behavior in a coherent and consistent manner and to address the tasks expected of them becomes frustrating for many adults (Fenning et al., 2014; Schuiringa et al., 2015). The problematic behaviors are more visible over time as the child ages. The child is seen becoming more dependent on others and unable to cope when left on their own.

Other challenging behaviours faced by parents are, some of the children are self-absorbed and often prefers to be by themselves while others are more disruptive and aggressive in their interaction (Molteno et al., 2001; Einfeld et al., 2006; Alimovic, 2013; Emerson et al., 2014).

Further common and distressing behaviours are self-injurious behaviors, and extreme or erratic in their mood and intimidating others (Einfeld et al., 2006; Allen, 2008). They often are provoking others, using inappropriate or abusive words, while some display rather inappropriate behaviours in public. The presence of these behaviors causes added distress to their parents who often worry about possible harm to the child and others. The child risk being socially excluded displaying such actions.

2. **Social Difficulties:** (Cermak and Aberson, 1998; Kemp and Carter, 2002; Fenning et al., 2014) Social skills are learned. These skills or socially acceptable behaviours are necessary for humans to have to help them fit into their environment and to be accepted (Elliott and Gresham, 1993; Cermak and Aberson, 1998). These behaviours include being appropriate with others, having good self and emotional control, being cooperative and responsible, etc. (Elliott and Gresham, 1993; Cermak and Aberson, 1998).

In social settings, children with ID have more problems settling in their environment (Howell et al., 2007), they seemed inappropriate or unable to handle themselves in social settings (Guralnick et al., 2006; Howell et al., 2007). The behaviours exhibited make them seen as being a problematic child. Not only does it hinders them making and keeping relationships, these behaviours often feed into the social stigma that the children are already recognized for (Howell et al., 2007; Ali et al., 2012).

3. **Difficulties in Areas of Scholastic Attainment:** (Parmenter et al., 1998; E. and Hatton, 2007; Fenning et al., 2014) The difficulties are evident as the child enters preschool and by the time they reach primary school, many continue to struggle even with basic reading and writing, as well as managing tasks expected of them. While in some children with ID they may eventually learn to read or recognize words, they are not as fluent or as quick as their normally functioning peers. Most importantly the child would not be able to comprehend what they read or write, and they need constant help to organize and complete their tasks.

If the parents were less concerned about their child's performance at pre-school level by the time the child is in primary school and struggling to keep up, many parents start to worry. In children with mild intellectual disability, being in school is stressful. Parents, teachers and even peers see them behaving and performing way below their biological age. Invariably, they are given more classes or opportunities to try to catch up to their peers, and often they fail. Their worries increase over time as many parents begin to recognize despite the time and aid given the child continues to struggle.

Adults may not realize the child is having the disability and what the disability entails. Commonly, the expectation placed on the child is similar to that of a normally functioning child. It does not help the child or their parents with the school putting expectations on the child to perform. Many adults, parents, and teachers included believe all children have the same thinking ability. Adults feel knowledge and success will be gained with child learning and working hard. Parents experience countless negative contacts with the school, and this worsens, as adults are not aware of the actual matter of the disorder. A lot of more are not receptive about the disability dismissing it as the child not putting in enough effort or having no interest.

Likewise, parents become more concerned as they realize their child actually cannot cope with the typical school program. While some parents are more appropriate in dealing with the difficulties, others continue to push their child to deliver. They are made to attend more tuition classes hoping the child to catch eventually up. At some stage, some parents begin to recognize and worry will their child ever be able to cope with high school.

Many parents rightly worry about what employment prospects would be suitable for their child. The reality is that many will be at the risk of being unemployed; they will continue to rely on their families in their adulthood as most do not establish enough finances on their own, or have anyone to help look after them (Wells et al., 2003; Wolfe et al., 2014).

IMPACT OF CO-MORBIDITY

Additionally, children with ID are prone to develop psychiatric disorders (Deb et al., 2001; Einfeld et al., 2006; Witwera and Lecavaliera, 2008; Bakken et al., 2010; Tremblay et al., 2010; Reardon et al., 2015). The presence of a psychiatric diagnosis signifies more challenging behaviours (Moss et al., 2000; Myrbakk and von Tetzchner, 2008; Bakken et al., 2010; Baker et al., 2010; Caplan et al., 2015). In addition to increasing impairment in their functioning (Dekker and Koot, 2003; Einfeld et al., 2011).

In the other chapters of the book the presence of co-morbidity is discussed.

IMPACT OF HAVING A CHILD WITH ID

Most couples are ecstatic with the arrival of a new child in their family. Parents are often bursting with optimistic expectations and plans for the new-born child. Every parent hopes for a healthy child thus when told their child is having difficulties, and the difficulties may be life long, these feelings of joy and hopes inevitably fades (Feniger-Schaal and Oppenheim, 2013; Barak-Levy and Atzaba-Poria, 2013).

It is traumatic for any parent learning that one's child has a disability (Kazak and Marvin, 1984; Pianta and Marvin, 1996; Sheeran et al., 1997; Schuengel et al., 2009). The news of having a child with a disability often place them into a quandary and at times crisis (Sheeran et al., 1997; Nimbalkar et al., 2014). Many are left feeling confused, helpless and at times angry. They go through a mixture of reactions from shock, anger, denial, guilt and even rejection of the possible truth (Kazak and Marvin, 1984; Trute, 1990; Pianta and Marvin, 1996; Schuengel et al., 2009). Blacher (1984) reports parents go through a period of mourning, i.e. grieving and sadness for the loss of a healthy child (Schuengel et al., 2009) while some parents feeling stress and anxious.

They try to comprehend what they are facing i.e. the reality of their child's disability and their wish and desire to have a healthy and manageable child (Trute, 1990; Pianta & Marvin, 1996; Marvin & Pianta, 1996; Sheeran et al., 1997; Jessop et al., 1998). Some may feel they are punished for sins in their past while others blame their spouses or partners and feel despair.

The process of grief continues with differences in parental expectations and the disability of the child (Wikler, 1981; Eakes, 1995). Bruce et al. (1994) describe parents going through a continuing sense of loss with the presence of the disability being an ongoing source of stress, with mothers more affected than fathers. Eakes (1995) and other researchers (Trute, 1990; Bruce et al., 1994; Eakes et al., 1998) speak of parents going through chronic sorrow. They not only have they to come to terms with the loss of a normal functioning child, they invariably have to go through the tedious process of many medical examinations and procedures, and at the same time continuing to look after their child.

The sense of loss continues throughout the child's life and may resurface when other non-disabled peers experience significant life events (Trute, 1990; Bruce et al., 1994) such as delivery of a healthy child, wedding and for some family gatherings.The presence of prolonged and complicated emotional reactions of anxiety and sorrow may interfere with the parents' availability as caregivers for their child (Schuengel et al., 2009).

It is not surprising many parents have difficulties with receiving or accepting their child's diagnosis. Many children with borderline to mild ID look very ordinary. Their developmental delay may be very subtle and not as visible as a child with more severe ID. When told their child is struggling many parents may be dismissive of the news or disagrees with the results of the assessment.

In some families, there are often difficulties in the parents themselves during their childhood days e.g. delay in talking, not interested in academics. They could survive their childhood. These scenarios make it harder for parents to comprehend the difficulties in their child.

The presence of a broad range of difficulties impacts the child and on the lives of their family (Baker et al., 2003; Baker et al., 2005; McConkey et al., 2008; Woodman et al., 2011; Fenning et al., 2014; Reardon et al., 2015). Having a child with ID requires many life adjustments for the parents and family (Gupta and Harpreet, 2010). Various demands persist throughout childhood and possibly into adult years.

These changes and needs will inevitably affect the family. The child may not be the only factor that affects his family's life and dynamics. Researchers have shown the parents' behavior, parenting styles, and mental health positively or negatively affects the child's development.

1. **Parenting, Family Functioning, and Relationship:** It is challenging to deal with a less independent child. Handling the child is time-consuming and requires a lot of patience to handle their daily needs. Added to this, the presence of self-injurious, aggressive and destructive behaviours increases the family distress (MacLean Jr. et al., 2010; Petty et al., 2014).

The unique caretaking demands, limitation on family opportunities, financial constraint, can result in *emotional distress* for all family members.

The parenting quality mutually affects the child maladaptive behaviors. The child's social (e.g. disruptive or aggressive behaviors) and personal maladaptive behaviors (e.g. stereotyped or abusive behaviors) influence and are influenced directly by parenting behaviors (Floyd & Zmich, 1991).

The presence of responsive mother-child behavior certainly helps with more proper performance of the child's social behavior seen (Hauser-Cram et al., 1999). Fenning et al. (2014) found among parents of children with borderline ID they were negative and demanding in dealing with their child's problematic behaviors. Kennedy (1994) and Granic and Patterson (2006) are among researchers who found a significant link between *negative-controlling parenting corresponded with an exacerbation of child behavioral difficulties*. Even though in the short term the use of physical punishment often leads to increase in desirable behavior, in the long-term it has been shown to be associated with increased deviant behavior, aggressiveness, and delinquency (Straus & Stewart, 1999; Straus & Donnelly, 2001).

Even in children with ID, an encouraging environment can provide the children with learning more adaptive and functioning behavior. Ainsworth et al. (1978) and Ainsworth (1985) speaks about how the environment stimulates and encourages certain behaviors with Bandura (1991) hypothesizing children learn behaviors from the environment by watching, observing and imitating actions of others. Research have consistently shown the association between maternal distress and increasing challenging behavior in children (Nihira et al., 1985; Orsmond et al., 2003). This finding is not surprising as maternal distress not associated with a calm state. Distress mothers are often impatient and more punitive methods used to handle the child's daily hassles.

Fittingly Nihira et al. (1985) observed *parenting quality and child maladaptive behaviors* mutually influence each other. Hauser-Cram et al. (1999) strongly showed early-related aspects of the family environment are predictive of the child's communication, social and daily living skills. The presence of family connectedness and being responsive helps with the development of the child's social and communicative skills (Hauser-Cram et al., 1999).

The family and the home environment is essential for the child's development (Bowlby, 1988a; Bowlby, 1988b). Bradley et al. (2001) found learning occurs and is affected by the presence of types of stimulation, maternal responsiveness and perception and the use of harsh punishment.

2. **Interaction with the Child:** (Fenning et al., 2014; Robinson and Neece, 2015) The parent-child relationship plays a crucial role in the mental health development of every child (Bowlby, 1989; Bowlby, 1988a). A critical component of any parent-child relationship is the emotional element of parents' expression (Ainsworth, 1985). The child develops better in their social development with expressions of positive emotions (Ainsworth, 1985).

The magnitude of stress and worries about their child and their future, impact the parents' appraisal and subsequent handling of their child. Adding to the parents concerns is the child's behavior. The high levels of parental stress invariably create an environment associated with more negative emotion expression. It is highly likely appropriately expressed feelings are present. The presence of more negative emotion expression will impact the functioning of the parents' and siblings' relationship with the child.

3. **The Families' Finances:** (Ouyang et al., 2014; Goudie et al., 2014; Ou et al., 2015; Emerson and Hatton, 2007) In many cases, the child with ID requires added costs (Emerson & Hatton, 2007) from daily needs, medical, and educational expenses. The increase in expenses is likely to cause financial stress to the couple/ parents. The family's financial status is often associated with caring for children and the more severe the disability, the greater the likelihood of finance-related problems is (Emerson & Hatton, 2007; Goudie et al., 2014). The financial difficulties are much related to:
    a. Higher expenditure related to the direct cost of handling and raising the child.
    b. Cutting back on work or working hours.
    c. Single parent or as a couple.
    d. Health and insurance coverage.

Emerson and Hatton (2007) states, commonly *the strength of the relationship between families* supporting a child with disability lessens the very high rates of disadvantage faced by lone parents.

Health and insurance coverage helps cover medical costs and alleviates the family's finances. However, not all children with a disability receive health and insurance coverage.

4. **Relationship of the Couple:** (Kersh et al., 2006; Robinson & Neece, 2015) The quality of their marriage and conflicts. The daily handling of the child added with the presence of challenging behaviors not only affect the parents' emotional well-being, but it also affects their marital relationship (Baker et al., 2005; Robinson & Neece, 2015). Having a special need child/ children may result in the couple being distant to each other or it may bring the couple closer and strengthens the marriage (Baker et al., 2005; McCarthy et al., 2006). The latter is not surprising as the presence of both parents working together helps relief the stress of just one parent handling the child. Likewise, better quality of marital relationship undoubtedly helps reduce the stress as parents share the responsibility and supports each other.
5. **The Stress Level of the Family:** Having a child with ID is stressful on the family (Lopez et al., 2008; Al-Krenawi et al., 2011; Ritzema & Sladeczek, 2011; Robinson & Neece, 2015) Parents reported having higher levels of child-related stress than parents of typically developing children (Gallagher et al., 2008; Azar & Badr, 2010; Cramm & Nieboer, 2011; Gray et al., 2011; Lin et al., 2014; Gallagher & Hannigan, 2014). Hence, it is not surprising, parents of children with ID have poorer levels of both mental and physical health (Bourke-Taylor et al., 2012; Bazzano et al., 2015).

The stress is related to a mix of issues i.e. the child's diagnosis, their condition and added with the increase in the care-giving necessity that is often daily. The stress often persists throughout childhood and into the adult years.

Invariably stress occurs with the continuous and significant challenge with looking after the child (Dabrowska & Pisula, 2010; Pisula, 2011). The presence of the behaviors already discussed above frequently tests the parents' capacity to manage the child effectively. Often tasks need to be done repetitively and broken down into simpler steps for the child to be able to follow. Frequently parents have to keep in mind of their child's limitation. Recurrently there will be a crisis to attend to and often this requires instant and quick respond by the parents to manage the crises.

Very often the experience of the child-related stress begins in the preschool period with parents having to face and handle the hassles daily (Azad et al., 2013) e.g. getting the child up, bath and dressed. The child will need help as he/ she has trouble seeing how things or how events are and how they relate to each other. They require more structure and support for basic skills and tasks, such as dressing, getting ready for school, playing or interacting with others and even feeding them.

The stress level remains relatively stable and then increases over time until about middle childhood. This increase in the stress level is mainly related to the emergence of behavior issues (Baker et al., 2002; Azad et al., 2013). It is not surprising as the presence of more challenging behavior, stresses the parents more (Baker et al., 2005). The children required closer supervision with the emergence of their difficult behaviors.

Children with ID have heightened levels of problematic or challenging behaviors (Emerson et al., 2014), with a correlation seen between the child's cognitive ability and severity of behavior problems (Baker et al., 2002; Crnic et al., 2004). Furthermore, the occurrence of high levels of behavior problems with low levels of social skills put mothers of children with ID at the most risk for high-stress levels (Neece & Baker, 2008).

They are more likely to be destructive, over-activity, self-injury, sleeping difficulties, physical aggression, attention-seeking behavior and having temper tantrums (Crnic et al., 2004). Frequently the behavior problems are as a result of the child trying to cope with the demands and expectations placed on them. Many are unable to make sense of what the expectations are, why and how they will cope. They are unable to communicate their stress and distress. Thus, the behavioral problems often emerge as a sign of them communicating their distress. While in others, the emergence of behavioral problems is indicative of the presence of psychiatric disorders (Bakken et al., 2010; Caplan et al., 2015).

Many of these behaviors are exhausting, time-consuming for the family. The child invariably needs constant care to ensure their safety. Studies support parents' psychological health and well-being tends to decrease as children's behavior problems increase (Hastings, 2003; Baker et al., 2005; McCarthy et al., 2006; Robinson & Neece, 2015). Also, research supports many more mothers experience higher levels of stress than fathers (McCarthy et al., 2006; Bourke-Taylor et al., 2010; Lee, 2013; Fairthorne et al., 2015) and they report higher depressive scores (Olsson & Hwang, 2001; Lee, 2013).

Interestingly, studies found as the child settles e.g. in a more structured school environment or receives school-base intervention and the child spends more time in school, parenting stress reduces (Blacher et al., 2009). However if the child is unable to cope with the requirements of school as the school place many new demands on their academic, social, and self-regulatory skills, the parents' stress level increases (Eisenhower et al., 2007; Azad et al., 2013).

Many parents are often left wondering how else to handle the child, as, despite many reminders or teaching, instructions are still poorly understood and forgotten. The prolonged period and energy invested in dealing with the child invariably result in the parents' questioning their parenting ability and self-worth. It is shared many parents report handling one's child is challenging and tiring. It often evokes a mixture of emotions in the individual. Thus, it is not unexpected many parents report feeling they have failed. They see they are not able to change the situation added to them not able to get the help they need.

Additionally, parents often worry as there are many concerns about their child with fears of the child's future being the greatest concerns of many parents (Hallum, 1995). Parents as well as many other fears concerning their child (Hallum, 1995) e.g. sex behavior, menstruation, etc. Doctors are asked again and again by the same parents what will happen to their child? Can they look after themselves? Who will take care of them? The reality of parental concerns and the stress for their child increases as the child grows older (Hallum, 1995). Parents concerns are legitimate. Continuous learning problems and delays in development occur, and the delay limits the child's prospects independence and self-directed functioning.

Similarly, the parents' personal and social satisfactoriness is much reduced as their routines often include being mindful of their child who struggles with day-to-day tasks (Plant & Sanders, 2007; Ritzema & Sladeczek, 2011). Handling the child invariably adds further strain and stress for the parent. The physically demanding and repetitive tasks are time-consuming and often disrupt family routines and activities as well. It takes a longer time to get the child ready and having to wait frequently for others is tiring for a lot of people. Adjustments are required to accommodate the needs of the child and it not only affects the parents but the whole family. Thus, it is not surprising a high portion parents of children with ID are anxious and depressed (Azeem et al., 2013).

Stress and worries are an important determinant of family functioning, interaction and relationship thus consequently their wellbeing (Deater-Deckard, 2005; Gerstein et al., 2009). Any parent feeling overwhelmed by the continuous stress of handling the daily hassles and challenges of their child will invariably have greater problems managing and interacting with their child/children. Stressful parents have negative implications for the family. When stress, their parenting is often characterized by more harsh and critical attitudes when handling their child. Added to this is the presence of inconsistent discipline (Deater-Deckard, 2005). It would be difficult for parents to react more positively and calmly when upset or stressed.

The presence of other vulnerabilities in the family e.g. ongoing conflicts or presence of mental health problems places the family at increased risk of having more difficulties in coping and making the adjustments needed.

Parental stress, ill-health or continuing conflicts within the family even interferes with getting adequate help or intervention programs for the child. When one or both parents disagree about their child's difficulties, along with the stigma of receiving help from mental health facilities and special education, many families do not seek or refuse the help.

However when parents can cope well with the unique childcare demands, they can enhance social and emotional adjustment of the child. When this occurs, it as well avoids distress and disruption for the other family members (Bourke-Taylor et al., 2012).

Among factors, which may affect the stress, level, and functioning of the family are:

1. The more challenging the child's behavior is, the higher is the stress level (Bourke-Taylor et al., 2010). Many of these behavioral problems have been shown to persist into adolescence and adulthood, and this aggravates the stress level (Einfeld et al., 2006; Gray et al., 2011).

The thoughts often wondered by parents are: "What will my child's life be as an adult? Will college or employment be possible?" "Who will look after my child when I am no longer around?"

Longitudinal studies show increasing behavior, and mental health problems in an adult with ID are associated with maternal depression and pessimism (Orsmond et al., 2003; Gray et al., 2011). Parents experience increase stress as their child ages. Gray et al. (2011) found mothers of older children (above 12 years old) report feeling more distress compared to mothers with younger children with mild disability.

Behavior problems are harder to manage in older children. With increasing age, there is the lack of school and post-schooling options, and with the worsening of behavioral problems concerns may arise with regards to living arrangements. In events of much self-injurious behavior and aggression, the capacity of families to continue to provide care is more challenging (Orsmond et al., 2003).

Likewise, the presence of family cohesiveness and harmony helps with more positive social-emotional functioning (Hauser-Cram et al., 1999; Floyd and Zmich, 1991).

Interestingly the onset of psychopathology and its chronicity has been shown in several studies to be predicted by family dysfunction, parental mental health treatment, and the child's physical symptoms (Wallander et al., 2006; Koskentausta et al., 2007).

Other factors, which affect the stress level and functioning of the family, are:

2. The level of disability (Mitchell and Hauser-Cram, 2008; DeLambo et al., 2011; Esbensen, 2011). The child's features and level of disabilities often predict their cognitive, social and daily living difficulties and needs.

While some children may not require much aid or added resources, there are some with chronic physical, developmental, or psychiatric condition who will need health and other related services. This group of children with special needs will require extensive caregiving "burden," namely time, money, and total commitment required from their caregivers due to their increased dependency.

Schuiringa et al. (2015) state the frequency and severity of the child's difficulties are strongly associated with the parent–child relationship. The elevated level and frequency of behavioral problems and severity of disability add considerable challenge to the extent that mothers of an adult with ID report more caregiving burden and were more pessimistic about the future caring for their adult son or daughter (Orsmond et al., 2003). The presence of maternal pessimism invariably affects their quality in the parent–adult child relationship and additionally mothers were found to have greater levels of anxiety and depression.

3. The age of the parents.
4. The mother's appraisal of the difficulties including the mothers' sense of empowerment (Bourke-Taylor et al., 2010; Bourke-Taylor et al., 2012). The mother's perception includes that of her managing the child's disability and needs, along with other family matters.

Mothers are often the primary carers of children in families. Thus, it is not surprising there is a significant link between the functional status of the child and the mental health status of the mother. Mothers of children with ID experience poorer psychological well-being compared to mothers with normal healthy functioning children (Hauser-Cram et al., 2001; Baker et al., 2002; Mitchell and Hauser-Cram, 2008; Eisenhower et al., 2013; Fairthorne et al., 2015). Additional to this, mothers have been shown to experience more restriction in their personal freedom and development (Holroyd, 1974; Holroyd and McArthur, 1976) as often they are the main caregivers. Invariably the child's behavior problems are a chronic stressor for the mother. If the mothers' appraisal of the events is positive and she copes appropriately using positive and supportive parenting, it will help in the child's social-emotional adjustment.

Over the last decade, despite more employment opportunity for women to enter the work force, many mothers leave their job or are unemployed when having a special child (Shearn and Todd, 2000; Gray et al., 2011). Having a special need child greatly affects many mothers' decision to seek employment. Shearn and Todd (2000) found work restrictions were due to the timing and nature of work, lack of adequate and affordable childcare and even finding suitable employment. Unmet maternal expectations in work and minimal to none child-care opportunities are factors of distress for mothers when thinking about working (Gray et al., 2011).

With the change in parenting practices over the years with more fathers taking extra responsibility and interest in child-care matters. It has been helpful for many mothers in such practicing household. The fathers are around to share mothers' stress of handling the child's behaviors (McCarthy et al., 2006) and most importantly provide some respite for the other parent.

5. Single-parent and two-parent families (Olsson and Hwang, 2001). Being in a single-family home, invariably the single parent has many tasks to shoulder, from finances to being solely responsible for their child/ children. Single mothers and having children with ID were more vulnerable to severe depression than in mothers living with partners.
6. Family functioning particularly parenting behaviors and coping styles (Irazábal et al., 2011; Dabrowska and Pisula, 2010; Schuiringa et al., 2015)
7. Participation in health promoting activities (Mitchell and Hauser-Cram, 2008; Bourke-Taylor et al., 2012)
8. Availability of support (Bernard, 2009; Dabrowska and Pisula, 2010; Bourke-Taylor et al., 2012)
9. Social exclusion: research suggests for children with ID, the risk of social exclusion is higher (Emerson, 2015)
10. Being able to work or be financially stable (Brehaut et al., 2004; Bourke-Taylor et al., 2010; Dyson, 2010; Irazábal et al., 2011; Bourke-Taylor et al., 2012)

As the child develops and times moves on, the family must begin coping with long-term uncertainty regarding the child's present and future functioning (Kazak and Marvin, 1984). The level of parents' functioning is much affected by the parents' reaction to the diagnosis and the difficulties and invariably their level of acceptance (Sheeran et al., 1997). Pianta and Marvin (1996) suggest a link between resolutions of receiving the child's diagnosis with the subsequent managing of the difficulties. The presence of difficulties and challenges, impact the interaction of the parents with their child with ID with parents expressing less positive interaction and engagement with the child compared to a child with healthy development (Fenning et al., 2014). Most families attempt to make things as practical and manageable as possible.

The Impact on Siblings

It is not easy having a brother or sister with disability (Scelles, 1997; Dyson, 1999; Meyer et al., 2011; Petalas et al., 2012; De Caroli and Sagone, 2013). Siblings of children ID faced numerous challenges and similar to their parents. They often experience a range of emotions (Dyson, 1999; Hosseinkhanzadeh and Yeganeh, 2013).

The situation of siblings with their brothers or sisters with ID and the function of the type of disability of the child is not a simple relationship (De Caroli and Sagone, 2013). Over time, the siblings become aware something is not right with their sibling. Siblings become subtly aware they have a brother or sister who needs a significant portion of the family time and attention. They become conscious their parents are not physically or mentally available to them even to participate in their daily activities. Many parents speak of certain periods when the children with ID are struggling. They have to make numerous hospital visits and recognize their other off-springs face additional demands due to their unavailability (Dyson, 1999; Hosseinkhanzadeh and Yeganeh, 2013).

Another period when the parents' attention is turned more on their child with the disability and the child experiences significant physical and psychological changes while their non-effected siblings are similarly going through their development from childhood to adolescent (Dyson, 1999). The non-affected siblings may develop behaviour problems as a result of:

1. Role strains (Farber, 1959).
2. High parental expectations (Gath and Gumley, 1987) and pressure to make up for the deficiency of the siblings with disabilities (Farber, 1959; Cleveland and Miller, 1977; Gath and Gumley, 1987).
3. Reduced parental attention and family resources (Sieman, 1984).

Children who have a sibling(s) with disabilities often take on added or unique roles. Taking on this role may restrict their developmental occurring in the transition from childhood to adolescence (Dyson, 1999). Siblings are often involved in the caregiving responsibilities (Longo and Bond, 1984; Sherman and Cocozza, 1984; Dyson, 1999; Wolfe et al., 2014). Many children speak about having to look after their affected siblings while parents have to go out to get things, and even to accompany their parents and affected sibling(s) for hospital visits. While some children may not mind, there are others who report feeling unattended or neglected and others feeling angry or upset at the added responsibility.

Studies show mixed results with regards to impact on non-affected siblings, with studies showing in the unaffected siblings may be at risk of developing:

1. Lesser social competency due to stress related to caring for a brother or sister with disabilities (Cleveland and Miller, 1977; McHale and Gamble, 1989; Wolfe et al., 2014).
2. Lower self-esteem.
3. Greater social withdrawal.

Another issue, which may affect the siblings, is the stigma associated with having a sibling with ID (Hughes et al., 2005; Ali et al., 2012; Jones et al., 2012). People with disabilities are at increased risk of societal stigma, and discrimination just because of the need for personal assistance with daily living. Many siblings find it difficult to manage public perceptions of the sibling and family. The unaffected siblings may themselves be teased or isolated by their peers, neighbors, etc. The teasing and stigma may impact their relationship with their sibling, giving rise to feelings of fear and resentment towards their sibling.

Dyson (2010) showed the unaffected siblings might have an accelerated growth as they take on responsibilities earlier in their childhood. This was significant among female siblings who were noted to be more protective, caring and understanding of others.

Family Outcome

Parents eventually become aware of the impact of their inability to support, be available or to give the attention needed by the non-disabled siblings. These thoughts including pessimism about the future may affect the parent–child relationship including among siblings of children with ID and their psychosocial functioning (Abbott and Meredith, 1986; Scelles, 1997; Orsmond et al., 2003).

The disability and difficulties can severely disrupt family functioning leading to some families breakdown and in some instances, the institutionalization of the child (Blacher and Bromley, 1990; Chan and Sigafoos, 2001). It is never easy thinking of placing any child in an out of the home facility, and it stresses them (Cramm and Nieboer, 2011). However with worsening of their psychological well-being or the child's condition, some parents are unable to meet the long-term needs of their child.

Although many families do not cope well with the challenges of caring for a child with disability, there are families who have made positive adjustments and report positive experiences (Holroyd, 1974; Kazak and Marvin, 1984; Abbott and Meredith, 1986; Kishore, 2011; De Caroli and Sagone, 2013; Mandleco et al., 2003). In these instances, the family is brought together and is closer in their bonds. The presence of more positive environment is linked to parents who are competent and supportive, paving the way for the off-springs to learn and model positive coping skills and express emotions. The positive adaptation is associated with better family functioning, as parent optimism, positive affect, a better internal locus of control, and the use of meaning-focused and problem-focused coping strategies (Bourke-Taylor et al., 2012; McConnell et al., 2014). The positive environment results in the siblings benefiting from the association and dealing with the affected child in a more helping, and caregiving roles.

The collaborative relationship between parents and their children's doctors has been found to be significant in helping parents cope (Galil et al., 2006; Horrell et al., 2006; Mitchell and Hauser-Cram, 2008; Bourke-Taylor et al., 2012; Fairthorne et al., 2015). The majority of these children with ID live at home with their family. In some children, the problem of co-morbid psychopathology is indeed substantial and persistent which suggests the need for intervention (Einfeld et al., 2006; Gray et al., 2011). Mitchell and Hauser-Cram (2008) found a significant association with utilization and satisfaction with children's health services helps parents cope not just with their child's difficulties as well as a reduction in the parents' stress level.

The Role of Professionals

In the recent years, advocates for support for these families have risen. A significant number of children with ID and their families need professional help (Dekker and Koot, 2003; Jansen et al., 2013). Many children with ID eventually age and live with or under the supervision of their family for the majority of their lives (Abbott and Meredith, 1986; Orsmond et al., 2003). Invariably, parents and siblings are their mainstay of their emotional and physical support (Abbott and Meredith, 1986; Orsmond et al., 2003; Dyson, 2010).

As the discussion shows, *support for families having children with ID is crucial.* The developmental course, chronicity, and associated difficulties of the disorder highlight to medical and mental health practitioners the impact of the disability on the child and their family. Numerous reports suggest the need to understand the bio-psychosocial factors that can contribute to improvements and declines in the functioning of families of children with ID. Families are often able to cope better with the presence of child-care needs, including therapeutic and educational opportunities that can assist the children's skills development and inclusion. Even to this time, having a child with ID is a source of shame and guilt. Many still hold the prejudice the parents are to blame, or one or both parents are deficient. This lack of understanding of the child's condition and the probable cause precipitates social ostracism and deprives the family's to obtain the help and support that may be valuable to them.

Reports as well suggest the need to *intervene early* in children and intervene swiftly with the presentation of symptoms suggestive of psychopathology (Floyd and Gallagher, 1997). Improved detection and intervention of any associated difficulties potentially reduce both the human suffering and economic burden to the family. Pianta and Marvin (1996) found in parents with unresolved parental reaction to the crisis, and, in this case, is to the child's diagnosis and condition, they feel more stressful handling their child, compared to parents who were able to resolve the crisis. They also found the link with the resolution of the matter with the quality of attachment to their child. The change is not surprising as in their assessment of and the picture they have of their child and their difficulties they face, affect how they interact with the child.

Additionally despite the advancement in the medical field and improved knowledge dissemination, many parents who turn to professionals for help are frequently met with disappointment, frustration, and further confusion. Many professionals have little or no knowledge of the condition; while some minimize or dismiss the situation, telling parents, "their child will outgrow the difficulties,"

Roos (1977) speaks of unhelpful professional attitudes as:

1. Lack of expertise and ignorant of technology advancement.
2. Sense of hopelessness and "incurable" disease.
3. Lack of acceptance of such a diagnosis/disorder.
4. Reluctance to share proper information with the clients.

The presence of such unhelpful attitudes may result in many parents opting to therapist or doctor shopping in the hope of finding more satisfactory answers. Worst still they will not get any help or intervention.

The assessment of these children should be multidisciplinary in nature, involving a range of experienced professionals. Children with ID require a multidisciplinary team consisting of primary care doctors, speech therapists, physical and occupational therapists, social workers, education staff, neurologists/developmental pediatricians, psychologists, child psychiatrists and others. The ultimate aim of treatment is to enable the child to achieve their full potential regarding the disability and maintaining emotional well-being. Given their complex needs, the treatment has to be multi-modal.

Once the diagnosis is determined, an individualized program is constructed for the child. An integral component of the treatment is to involve the family. Parents need therapeutic and educational opportunities, which hopefully can assist their child's skill development and inclusion into the schools.

Bernard (2009) proposed the assessment should consider:

1. A functional analysis of the behavioral disturbance i.e. what factors could precipitate, aggravate or predispose to the challenging behaviors.
2. The overall cognitive level of the child and specific areas of deficit and needs including academic needs.
3. Psychiatric assessment entails looking at any underlying psychopathology including emotional, behavioral, mood disorders and the presence of psychosis.
4. An organic workout e.g. hematological, biochemical, etc.
5. Family functioning and assessment of risk. A critical evaluation covers factors affecting the family from within and factors outside the environment. The intervention has to be tailored.

Clark and Ladd (2000) and Fenning et al. (2014) are among many researchers who believes in parents and caregivers impact on their children's emotional and social development. The influence of caregivers mainly is linked to the parents' role in their child's developmental deficits, vulnerabilities, and outcomes.

Likewise, there is a strong relationship between the functional status of the child and the mental health status of the mother, particularly in families with a child with chronic illness or difficulties (Jessop et al., 1998).

The central role played by the child within the family unit, the nature of his/her relationships with siblings and other family members, along with the parental perceptions and expectations of their child, has to be explored. In return, the treating team cannot ignore the emotional needs of parents, siblings, and the need to examine the impact of the child on the entire family unit. Supportive psychotherapy, family therapy, parent work and parenting skills to the caregivers/parents, are modalities of treatment that mental health professionals can offer to the families. Often as parents grieve upon the realization of a loss of a healthy child, as discussed above, occurs. Aid can be provided to facilitate the process of working through, acceptance and possibly recovery for parents and families.

Pianta and Marvin (1996) added the resolution of the matter, impacts the parents' mental representation of strategies in managing their difficulties When parents reconcile and able to adjust what they want for their children, themselves and their family with what their circumstances is, they can meet their challenges better.

Interestingly Pianta and Marvin (1996) found a significant link between the presence of a support system including marital and partner relationship with eventual acceptance and working towards resolution of the crisis. This finding makes sense as the existence of other crisis e.g. marital conflict, distracts the family towards finding a possible intervention for their child with difficulties. The presence of a supportive person as well provides the comfort and security needs for the adult in times of their crisis. Consequently, for the adults having a good mental health state helps with the presence of parental optimism and having appropriate coping style (Baker et al., 2005).

Clinicians and mental health professionals working with children and their families need to be aware of the impact of family functioning on the child and their family. Ignoring and not being aware of family dysfunctions and not utilizing family intervention strategies, may lead to the family decompensating (Di Nuovo and Buono, 2007). In the work done by Pianta and Marvin (1996) found the way parents learned the diagnosis of their child's chronic difficulties have significant implication for practitioners and the bearer of news. Parents report feeling angry and resentful when hearing or knowing the news:

1. From Letters between practitioners not intended for parents.
2. Knowing from someone else other than their health care providers.
3. The use of highly technical information and not well understood by them.
4. Secrets or truth kept away from them.
5. Being made to wait months to know the diagnosis.

Health care providers need to aware of factors within the child's environment that could precipitate and perpetuate challenging behaviors. The presence of the child's communication difficulties, sensory difficulties, co-morbid medical disorders, restricted range of coping strategies, and effects of medications, have an astounding impact on the child's behavior. As discussed, these children often have high rates of mental health difficulties, which often lead to them presenting at child psychiatric services (Edelstein and Glenwick, 1977). These conditions are often unrecognized and undiagnosed.

Equally important to keep in mind is that behavioral problems among children, in turn, predict parental stress and exacerbates dysfunction within families. Clinicians need to be on the alert that some behaviors may be more distressing to families than other (Nimbalkar et al., 2014). If parental stress is not recognized and treated, this can, in turn, lead to a worsening of behavioral difficulties in the child (Baker et al., 2003; Eisenhower et al., 2013).

Treatment of children and adolescents with such difficulties needs a diverse approach. Supportive therapy for parents/caregivers and parent work are modalities of treatment that mental health professionals need to offer. Issues that can be tackled and offered help are parenting skills, balancing the needs of siblings, understanding the interplay of relationships within the family, and the patterns of management of the child. Other areas of emphasis are limit setting, the need for consistency of implemented measures, the capability to advocate for services, and the participation in support activities such as parents' organizations. Parents receiving help have favorable developmental and behavioral outcomes (Jansen et al., 2013; McConnell et al., 2014; Cantwell et al., 2014).

Group therapy has been helpful especially in anger management and social skills training. It is essential any information presented to the child have to be in a way comprehensible to the child. Indications of therapy often include conflicts, distress over one's impairments in social skills, and dealing with losses or difficulties in relationships. In addition, parent support groups are beneficial to parents to facilitate understanding and acceptance to enable them to cope better.

Other modalities of treatment are Applied Behavioral Analysis. This technique is a natural science-based approach that aims to change socially significant behavior based on the fundamental principles of learning, i.e. respondent and operant conditioning. This technique is the first-line psychosocial treatment for behavioral and psychiatric disorders in people with ID (Rush and Frances, 2000; Mafifei-Almodovar and Sturmey, 2012). Cognitive Behavior Therapy (CBT) consists of behavioral interventions, including skills training, self-instruction, relaxation training, and cognitive interventions, such as reframing maladaptive patterns of thinking. CBT has become increasingly popular as a treatment for anger and depression.

Clinicians offer pharmacological treatment to treat difficult behaviors. Medications employed range from the use of mood stabilizers, antidepressants and antipsychotic medications that are used to treat self-injurious behaviors, psychotic symptoms, agitation or severe mood disorders. Clinicians are still faced with limited choices, as there is still a dearth of research in this area.

In conclusion, treating young people with ID is indeed complex. The diversity of needs of the child requires a multifaceted treatment, with collaboration with health professionals from various specialties. Healthcare professionals need to tailor their treatment according to the family's values and ensure compatibility with their aims too. The role of mental health professionals is essential, in understanding the needs of the child, understanding his or her role in the family, and playing a role in supporting the family as a whole. The task that clinicians undertake is indeed challenging, and yet rewarding, when young people can resume living enriching and fulfilling lives.

REFERENCES

Abbott, D. A., & Meredith, W. H. (1986). Strengths of parents with retarded children. *Family Relations*, *35*(3), 371–375. doi:10.2307/584363

Ainsworth, M. D. (1985). Attachments across the life span. *Bulletin of the New York Academy of Medicine*, *61*, 792–812. PMID:3864511

Ainsworth, M. S., Blehar, M. C., & Everett Waters, E. et al.. (1978). *Patterns of attachment: A psychological study of the strange situation*. New York: Lawrence Erlbaum.

Al-Krenawi, A., Graham, J. R., & Al Gharaibeh, F. (2011). The impact of intellectual disability, caregiver burden, family functioning, marital quality, and sense of coherence. *Disability & Society*, *26*(2), 139–150. doi:10.1080/09687599.2011.543861

Ali, A., Hassiotis, A., Strydom, A., & King, M. (2012). Self stigma in people with intellectual disabilities and courtesy stigma in family carers: A systematic review. *Research in Developmental Disabilities*, *33*(6), 2122–2140. doi:10.1016/j.ridd.2012.06.013 PMID:22784823

Alimovic, S. (2013). Emotional and behavioural problems in children with visual impairment, intellectual and multiple disabilities. *Journal of Intellectual Disability Research*, *57*(2), 153–160. doi:10.1111/j.1365-2788.2012.01562.x PMID:22563696

Allen, D. (2008). The relationship between challenging behaviour and mental ill-health in people with intellectual disabilities: A review of current theories and evidence. *Journal of Intellectual Disabilities*, *12*(4), 267–294. doi:10.1177/1744629508100494 PMID:19074934

American Association on Intellectual & Developmental Disabilities. (2012). *Definition of Intellectual Disability*. Author.

American Psychiatric Association. (1994). *Diagnostic and Statistical Manual of mental disorders: DSM-IV*. Washington: D.C. American Psychiatric Association.

American Psychiatric Association. (2013). *Diagnostic and Statistical Manual of Mental Disorders: DSM-V*. American Psychiatric Publishing, Incorporated.

Azad, G., Blacher, J., & Marcoulides, G. A. (2013). Mothers of children with developmental disabilities: Stress in early and middle childhood. *Research in Developmental Disabilities*, *34*(10), 3449–3459. doi:10.1016/j.ridd.2013.07.009 PMID:23920028

Azar, M., & Badr, L. K. (2010). Predictors of coping in parents of children with an intellectual disability: Comparison between Lebanese mothers and fathers. *Journal of Pediatric Nursing*, *25*(1), 46–56. doi:10.1016/j.pedn.2008.11.001 PMID:20117676

Azeem MW, Dogar IA, Shah S, et al. (2013) Anxiety and Depression among Parents of Children with Intellectual Disability in Pakistan. *Journal of the Canadian Academy of Child and Adolescent Psychiatry, 22*(4), 290-296.

Baker, B. L., Blacher, J., Crnic, K. A., & Edelbrock, C. (2002). Behavior problems and parenting stress in families of three-year-old children with and without developmental delays. *American Journal of Mental Retardation*, *107*(6), 433–444. doi:10.1352/0895-8017(2002)107<0433:BPAPSI>2.0.CO;2 PMID:12323068

Baker, B. L., Blacher, J., & Olsson, M. B. (2005). Preschool children with and without developmental delay: Behaviour problems, parents' optimism and well-being. *Journal of Intellectual Disability Research*, *49*(8), 575–590. doi:10.1111/j.1365-2788.2005.00691.x PMID:16011551

Baker, B. L., McIntyre, L. L., Blacher, J., Crnic, K., Edelbrock, C., & Low, C. (2003). Pre-school children with and without developmental delay: Behaviour problems and parenting stress over time. *Journal of Intellectual Disability Research*, *47*(4-5), 217–230. doi:10.1046/j.1365-2788.2003.00484.x PMID:12787154

Baker, B. L., Neece, C. L., Fenning, R. M., Crnic, K. A., & Blacher, J. (2010). Mental disorders in five-year-old children with or without developmental delay: Focus on ADHD. *Journal of Clinical Child and Adolescent Psychology*, *39*(4), 492–505. doi:10.1080/15374416.2010.486321 PMID:20589561

Bakken, T. L., Helverschou, S. B., Eilertsen, D. E., Heggelund, T., Myrbakk, E., & Martinsen, H. (2010). Psychiatric disorders in adolescents and adults with autism and intellectual disability: A representative study in one county in Norway. *Research in Developmental Disabilities*, *31*(6), 1669–1677. doi:10.1016/j.ridd.2010.04.009 PMID:20493660

Bandura, A. (1991). Social cognitive theory of self-regulation. *Theories of Cognitive Self-Regulation*, *50*, 248–287.

Barak-Levy, Y., & Atzaba-Poria, N. (2013). Paternal versus maternal coping styles with child diagnosis of developmental delay. *Research in Developmental Disabilities*, *34*(6), 2040–2046. doi:10.1016/j.ridd.2013.02.026 PMID:23584184

Bazzano, A., Wolfe, C., Zylowska, L., Wang, S., Schuster, E., Barrett, C., & Lehrer, D. (2015). Mindfulness Based Stress Reduction (MBSR) for parents and caregivers of individuals with developmental disabilities: A community-based approach. *Journal of Child and Family Studies*, *24*(2), 298–308. doi:10.1007/s10826-013-9836-9

Bernard, S. H. (2009). Mental health and behavioural problems in children and adolescents with learning disabilities. *Psychiatry*, *8*(10), 387–390. doi:10.1016/j.mppsy.2009.06.017

Blacher, J. (1984). Sequential stages of parental adjustment to the birth of a child with handicaps: Fact or artifact? *Mental Retardation*, *22*, 55–68. PMID:6234448

Blacher, J., Baker, B. L., & Eisenhower, A. S. (2009). Student–teacher relationship stability across early school years for children with intellectual disability or typical development. *American Journal on Intellectual and Developmental Disabilities*, *114*(5), 322–339. doi:10.1352/1944-7558-114.5.322 PMID:19928015

Blacher, J., & Bromley, B. E. (1990). Correlates of out-of-home placement of handicapped children: Who places and why? *Journal of Children in Contemporary Society*, *21*, 3–41. doi:10.1300/J274v21n03_02

Bourke-Taylor, H., Law, M., Howie, L., & Pallant, J. F. (2010). Development of the Child's Challenging Behaviour Scale (CCBS) for mothers of school-aged children with disabilities. *Child: Care, Health and Development*, *36*(4), 491–498. doi:10.1111/j.1365-2214.2009.01055.x PMID:20047597

Bourke-Taylor, H., Pallant, J. F., Law, M., & Howie, L. (2012). Predicting mental health among mothers of school-aged children with developmental disabilities: The relative contribution of child, maternal and environmental factors. *Research in Developmental Disabilities*, *32*(6), 1732–1740. doi:10.1016/j.ridd.2012.04.011 PMID:22699247

Bowlby, J. (1988a). *A secure base: clinical applications of attachment theory*. Hove, New York: Brunner-Routledge, Taylor & Francis Group.

Bowlby, J. (1988b). *A secure base: Parent-child attachment and healthy human development*. New York: Basic Books.

Bowlby, J. (1989). *The Making and Breaking of Affectional Bonds*. New York: Routledge, Taylor and Francis Group.

Bradley, R. H., Corwyn, R. F., Burchinal, M., McAdoo, H. P., & Garcia Coll, C. (2001). The home environments of children in the United States Part II: Relations with behavioral development through age thirteen. *Child Development*, *72*(6), 1868–1886. doi:10.1111/1467-8624.t01-1-00383 PMID:11768150

Brehaut, J. C., Kohen, D. E., Raina, P., Walter, S. D., Russell, D. J., Swinton, M., & Rosenbaum, P. et al. (2004). The health of primary caregivers of children with cerebral palsy: How does it compare with that of other Canadian caregivers? *Pediatrics*, *4*(2), e182–e191. doi:10.1542/peds.114.2.e182 PMID:15286255

Bruce, E. J., Schultz, C. L., Smyrnios, K. X., & Schultz, N. C. (1994). Grieving related to development: A preliminary comparison of three age cohorts of parents of children with intellectual disability. *The British Journal of Medical Psychology*, *67*(1), 37–52. doi:10.1111/j.2044-8341.1994.tb01769.x PMID:7515655

Cantwell, J., Muldoon, O. T., & Gallagher, S. (2014). Social support and mastery influence the association between stress and poor physical health in parents caring for children with developmental disabilities. *Research in Developmental Disabilities*, *35*(9), 2215–2223. doi:10.1016/j.ridd.2014.05.012 PMID:24927515

Caplan, B., Neece, C. L., & Baker, B. L. (2015). Developmental level and psychopathology: Comparing children with developmental delays to chronological and mental age matched controls. *Research in Developmental Disabilities*, *37*, 143–151. doi:10.1016/j.ridd.2014.10.045 PMID:25498740

Cermak, S. A., & Aberson, J. R. (1998). Social skills in children with learning disabilities. *Occupational Therapy in Mental Health*, *13*(4), 1–24. doi:10.1300/J004v13n04_01

Chan, J. B., & Sigafoos, J. (2001). Does respite care reduce parental stress in families with developmentally disabled children? *Child and Youth Care Forum*, *30*(5), 253–263. doi:10.1023/A:1014467226528

Clark, K. E., & Ladd, G. W. (2000). Connectedness and autonomy support in parent–child relationships: Links to children's socioemotional orientation and peer relationships. *Developmental Psychology*, *36*(4), 485–498. doi:10.1037/0012-1649.36.4.485 PMID:10902700

Cleveland, D. S., & Miller, N. B. (1977). Attitudes and life commitments of older siblings of mentally retarded adults: An exploratory study. *Mental Retardation*, *15*, 38–41. PMID:875727

Cramm, J. M., & Nieboer, A. P. (2011). Psychological well-being of caregivers of children with intellectual disabilities: Using parental stress as a mediating factor. *Journal of Intellectual Disabilities*, *15*(2), 101–113. doi:10.1177/1744629511410922 PMID:21750213

Crnic, K., Hoffman, C., Gaze, C., & Edelbrock, C. (2004). Understanding the emergence of behavior problems in young children with developmental delays. *Infants and Young Children*, *17*(3), 223–235. doi:10.1097/00001163-200407000-00004

Dabrowska, A., & Pisula, E. (2010). Parenting stress and coping styles in mothers and fathers of preschool children with autism and Down syndrome. *Journal of Intellectual Disability Research*, *54*(3), 266–280. doi:10.1111/j.1365-2788.2010.01258.x PMID:20146741

De Caroli, M. E., & Sagone, E. (2013). Siblings and disability: A study on social attitudes toward disabled brothers and sisters. *Procedia: Social and Behavioral Sciences*, *93*, 1217–1223. doi:10.1016/j.sbspro.2013.10.018

Deater-Deckard, K. (2005). Parenting stress and children's development: Introduction to the special issue. *Infant and Child Development*, *13*(2), 111–115. doi:10.1002/icd.383

Deb, S., Thomas, M., & Bright, C. (2001). Mental disorder in adults with intellectual disability: Prevalence of functional psychiatric illness among a community-based population aged between 16 and 64 years. *Journal of Intellectual Disability Research*, *46*(6), 495–505. doi:10.1046/j.1365-2788.2001.00374.x PMID:11737536

Dekker, M. C., & Koot, H. M. (2003). DSM-IV Disorders in Children With Borderline to Moderate Intellectual Disability. I: Prevalence and Impact. *Journal of the American Academy of Child and Adolescent Psychiatry*, *42*(8), 915–922. doi:10.1097/01.CHI.0000046892.27264.1A PMID:12874493

Dekker, M. C., Koot, H. M., & van der Ende, J. et al.. (2002). Emotional and behavioral problems in children and adolescents with and without intellectual disability. *Journal of Child Psychology and Psychiatry, and Allied Disciplines*, *43*(8), 1087–1098. doi:10.1111/1469-7610.00235 PMID:12455929

DeLambo, D., Chung, W., & Huang, W. (2011). Stress and age: A comparison of Asian American and Non-Asian American parents of children with developmental disabilities. *Journal of Developmental and Physical Disabilities*, *23*(2), 129–141. doi:10.1007/s10882-010-9211-3

DeWeaver, K. L., & Kropf, N. P. (1992). Persons with mental retardation: A forgotten minority in education. *Journal of Social Work Education*, *28*, 36–46.

Di Nuovo, S. F., & Buono, S. (2007). Psychiatric syndromes comorbid with mental retardation: Differences in cognitive and adaptive skills. *Journal of Psychiatric Research*, *41*(9), 795–800. doi:10.1016/j.jpsychires.2006.02.011 PMID:16697412

Dyson, L. (2010). Unanticipated effects of children with learning disabilities on their families. *Learning Disability Quarterly*, *33*(1), 43–55. doi:10.1177/073194871003300104

Dyson, L. L. (1999). The psychosocial functioning of school-age children who have siblings with developmental disabilities: Change and stability over time. *Journal of Applied Developmental Psychology*, *20*(2), 253–271. doi:10.1016/S0193-3973(99)00016-7

Eakes, G. G. (1995). Chronic sorrow: The lived experience of parents of chronically mentally ill individuals. *Archives of Psychiatric Nursing*, *9*(2), 77–84. doi:10.1016/S0883-9417(95)80004-2 PMID:7755411

Eakes, G. G., Burke, M. L., & Hainsworth, M. A. (1998). Middle range theory of chronic sorrow. *Journal of Nursing Scholarship*, *30*(2), 179–184. doi:10.1111/j.1547-5069.1998.tb01276.x PMID:9775562

Edelstein, T. M., & Glenwick, D. S. (1977). Referral reasons for psychological services for adults with mental retardation. *Research in Developmental Disabilities*, *18*(1), 45–59. doi:10.1016/S0891-4222(96)00037-6 PMID:9085429

Einfeld, S. L., Ellis, L. A., & Emerson, E. (2011). Comorbidity of intellectual disability and mental disorder in children and adolescents: A systematic review. *Journal of Intellectual & Developmental Disability*, *36*(2), 137–143. doi:10.1080/13668250.2011.572548 PMID:21609299

Einfeld, S. L., Piccinin, A. M., Mackinnon, A., Hofer, S. M., Taffe, J., Gray, K. M., & Tonge, B. J. et al. (2006). Psychopathology in young people with intellectual disability. *Journal of the American Medical Association*, *296*(16), 1981–1989. doi:10.1001/jama.296.16.1981 PMID:17062861

Eisenhower, A., Blacher, J., & Baker, B. L. (2013). Mothers' perceived physical health during early and middle childhood: Relations with child developmental delay and behavior problems. *Research in Developmental Disabilities*, *34*(3), 1059–1068. doi:10.1016/j.ridd.2012.12.002 PMID:23306002

Eisenhower, A. S., Baker, B. L., & Blacher, J. (2007). Early student–teacher relationships of children with and without intellectual disability: Contributions of behavioral, social, and self-regulatory competence. *Journal of School Psychology*, *45*(4), 363–383. doi:10.1016/j.jsp.2006.10.002 PMID:21490876

Elliott, S. N., & Gresham, F. M. (1993). Social skills interventions for children. *Behavior Modification*, *17*(3), 287–313. doi:10.1177/01454455930173004 PMID:8343100

Emerson, E., Blacher, J., Einfeld, S., Hatton, C., Robertson, J., & Stancliffe, R. J. (2014). Environmental risk factors associated with the persistence of conduct difficulties in children with intellectual disabilities and autistic spectrum disorders. *Research in Developmental Disabilities*, *35*(12), 3508–3517. doi:10.1016/j.ridd.2014.08.039 PMID:25238636

Emerson, E., & Hatton, C. (2007). The socio-economic circumstances of children at risk of disability in Britain. *Disability & Society*, *22*(6), 563–580. doi:10.1080/09687590701560154

Emerson, E., & Hatton, C. (2007). Mental health of children and adolescents with intellectual disabilities in Britain. *The British Journal of Psychiatry*, *191*(6), 493–499. doi:10.1192/bjp.bp.107.038729 PMID:18055952

Esbensen, A. J. (2011). Families of individuals with intellectual disability and comorbid mental health problems. *Journal of Mental Health Research in Intellectual Disabilities*, *4*(3), 140–157. doi:10.1080/19315864.2011.597018

Fairthorne, J., Jacoby, P., Bourke, J., de Klerk, N., & Leonard, H. (2015). Onset of maternal psychiatric disorders after the birth of a child with intellectual disability: A retrospective cohort study. *Journal of Psychiatric Research*, *61*, 223–230. doi:10.1016/j.jpsychires.2014.11.011 PMID:25499469

Farber, B., & Kirk, S. A. (1959). Effects of a severely retarded child on family integration. *Monographs of the Society for Research in Child Development*, *24*(2), 1–112. doi:10.2307/1165597

Feniger-Schaal, R., & Oppenheim, D. (2013). Resolution of the diagnosis and maternal sensitivity among mothers of children with Intellectual Disability. *Research in Developmental Disabilities*, *34*(1), 306–313. doi:10.1016/j.ridd.2012.08.007 PMID:22983017

Fenning, R. M., Baker, J. K., & Bruce, L. et al.. (2014). Parent-child interaction over time in families of young children with borderline intellectual functioning. *Journal of Family Psychology*, *28*(3), 326–335. doi:10.1037/a0036537 PMID:24707801

Floyd, F. J., & Gallagher, E. M. (1997). Parental stress, care demands, and use of support services for school-age children with disabilities and behavior problems. *Family Relations*, *46*(4), 359–371. doi:10.2307/585096

Floyd, F. J., & Zmich, D. E. (1991). Marriage and the parenting partnership: Perceptions and interactions of parents with mentally retarded and typically developing children. *Child Development*, *62*(6), 1434–1448. doi:10.2307/1130817 PMID:1786726

Galil, A., Bachner, Y. G., Merrick, J., Flusser, H., Lubetzky, H., Heiman, N., & Carmel, S. (2006). Physician-parent communication as predictor of parent satisfaction with child development services. *Research in Developmental Disabilities*, *27*(3), 233–242. doi:10.1016/j.ridd.2005.03.004 PMID:15998579

Gallagher, S., & Hannigan, A. (2014). Depression and chronic health conditions in parents of children with and without developmental disabilities: The growing up in Ireland cohort study. *Research in Developmental Disabilities*, *35*(2), 448–454. doi:10.1016/j.ridd.2013.11.029 PMID:24361813

Gallagher, S., Phillips, A. C., Oliver, C., & Carroll, D. (2008). Predictors of psychological morbidity in parents of children with intellectual disabilities. *Journal of Pediatric Psychology*, *33*(10), 1129–1136. doi:10.1093/jpepsy/jsn040 PMID:18430761

Gath, A., & Gumley, D. (1987). Retarded children and their siblings. *Journal of Child Psychology and Psychiatry, and Allied Disciplines*, *28*(5), 715–730. doi:10.1111/j.1469-7610.1987.tb01554.x PMID:2959672

Gerstein, E. D., Crnic, K. A., Blacher, J., & Baker, B. L. (2009). Resilience and the course of daily parenting stress in families of young children with intellectual disabilities. *Journal of Intellectual Disability Research*, *53*(12), 981–997. doi:10.1111/j.1365-2788.2009.01220.x PMID:19874449

Goudie, A., Narcisse, M. R., Hall, D. E., & Kuo, D. Z. (2014). Financial and psychological stressors associated with caring for children with disability. *Families, Systems & Health*, *32*(3), 280–290. doi:10.1037/fsh0000027 PMID:24707826

Granic, I., & Patterson, G. R. (2006). Toward a comprehensive model of antisocial development: A dynamic systems approach. *Psychological Review*, *113*(1), 101–131. doi:10.1037/0033-295X.113.1.101 PMID:16478303

Gray, K. M., Piccinin, A. M., Hofer, S. M., Mackinnon, A., Bontempo, D. E., Einfeld, S. L., & Tonge, B. J. et al. (2011). The longitudinal relationship between behavior and emotional disturbance in young people with intellectual disability and maternal mental health. *Research in Developmental Disabilities*, *32*(3), 1194–1204. doi:10.1016/j.ridd.2010.12.044 PMID:21295442

Gupta, R.K., & Harpreet, K. (2010). Stress among parents of children with intellectual disability. *Asia Pacific Disability Rehabilitation Journal,* 21.

Guralnick, M. J., Hammond, M. A., Connor, R. T., & Neville, B. (2006). Stability, change, and correlates of the peer relationships of young children with mild developmental delays. *Child Development*, *77*(2), 312–324. doi:10.1111/j.1467-8624.2006.00872.x PMID:16611174

Hallum, A. (1995). Disability and the transition to adulthood:Issues for the disabled child, the family, and the pediatrician. *Current Problems in Pediatrics*, *25*(1), 12–50. doi:10.1016/S0045-9380(06)80013-7 PMID:7720408

Hastings, R. P. (2003). Child behaviour problems and partner mental health as correlates of stress in mothers and fathers of children with autism. *Journal of Intellectual Disability Research*, *47*(4-5), 231–237. doi:10.1046/j.1365-2788.2003.00485.x PMID:12787155

Hauser-Cram, P., Warfield, M. E., & Shonkoff, J. P. et al.. (2001). Children with disabilities: A longitudinal study of child development and parent wellbeing. *Monographs of the Society for Research in Child Development*, *66*, 1–131. doi:10.1111/1540-5834.00151 PMID:11677873

Hauser-Cram, P., Warfield, M. E., Shonkoff, J. P., Krauss, M. W., Upshur, C. C., & Sayer, A. (1999). Family influences on adaptive development in young children with Down syndrome. *Child Development*, *70*(4), 979–989. doi:10.1111/1467-8624.00071 PMID:10446730

Holroyd, J. (1974). The Questionnaire on Resources and Stress: An instrument to measure family response to a handicapped family member. *Journal of Community Psychology*, *2*(1), 92–94. doi:10.1002/1520-6629(197401)2:1<92::AID-JCOP2290020133>3.0.CO;2-A

Holroyd, J., & McArthur, D. (1976). Mental retardation and stress on the parents: A contrast between Down's syndrome and childhood autism. *American Journal of Mental Deficiency*, *80*, 431–436. PMID:129006

Horrell, S.C.V., MacLean, W.E., & Conley, V.M. (2006). Patient and parent/guardian perspectives on the health care of adults with mental retardation. *Mental Retardation, 44*(4), 239-248.

Hosseinkhanzadeh, A. A., & Yeganeh, T. (2013). A study of the siblings relationships in families with mentally disable children. *Procedia: Social and Behavioral Sciences*, *84*, 864–868. doi:10.1016/j.sbspro.2013.06.663

Howell, A., Hauser-Cram, P., & Kersh, J. E. (2007). Setting the stage: Early child and family characteristics as predictors of later loneliness in children with developmental disabilities. *American Journal of Mental Retardation*, *112*(1), 18–30. doi:10.1352/0895-8017(2007)112[18:STSECA]2.0.CO;2 PMID:17181387

Hughes, K., Bellis, M. A., Jones, L., Wood, S., Bates, G., Eckley, L., & Officer, A. et al. (2005). Prevalence and risk of violence against adults with disabilities: A systematic review and meta-analysis of observational studies. *Lancet*, *379*(9826), 1621–1629. doi:10.1016/S0140-6736(11)61851-5 PMID:22377290

Irazábal, M., Marsà, F., & García, M. et al.. (2011). Family burden related to clinical and functional variables of people with intellectual disability with and without a mental disorder. *Research in Developmental Disabilities*, *32*, 796–803. PMID:22245729

Jansen, S. L., van der Putten, A. A., & Vlaskamp, C. (2013). What parents find important in the support of a child with profound intellectual and multiple disabilities. *Child: Care, Health and Development*, *39*(3), 432–441. doi:10.1111/j.1365-2214.2012.01381.x PMID:22515566

Jessop, D. J., Riessman, C. K., & Stein, R. E. (1998). Chronic childhood illness and maternal mental health. *Journal of Developmental and Behavioral Pediatrics*, *9*, 147–156. PMID:3403730

Jones, L., Bellis, M. A., Wood, S., Hughes, K., McCoy, E., Eckley, L., & Officer, A. et al. (2012). Prevalence and risk of violence against children with disabilities: A systematic review and meta-analysis of observational studies. *Lancet*, *380*(9845), 899–907. doi:10.1016/S0140-6736(12)60692-8 PMID:22795511

Kazak, A. E., & Marvin, R. S. (1984). Differences, difficulties and adaptation: Stress and social networks in families with a handicapped child. *Family Relations*, *33*(1), 67–77. doi:10.2307/584591

Kemp, C., & Carter, M. (2002). The social skills and social status of mainstreamed students with intellectual disabilities. *Educational Psychology*, *22*(4), 391–411. doi:10.1080/0144341022000003097

Kennedy, C. H. (1994). Manipulating antecedent conditions to alter the stimulus control of problem behavior. *Journal of Applied Behavior Analysis*, *27*(1), 161–170. doi:10.1901/jaba.1994.27-161 PMID:8188556

Kersh, J., Hedvat, T. T., Hauser-Cram, P., & Warfield, M. E. (2006). The contribution of marital quality to the well-being of parents of children with developmental disabilities. *Journal of Intellectual Disability Research*, *50*(12), 883–893. doi:10.1111/j.1365-2788.2006.00906.x PMID:17100949

Kishore, M. T. (2011). Disability impact and coping in mothers of children with intellectual disabilities and multiple disabilities. *Journal of Intellectual Disabilities*, *15*(4), 241–251. doi:10.1177/1744629511431659 PMID:22158461

Koskentausta, T., Iivanainen, M., & Almqvist, F. (2007). Risk factors for psychiatric disturbance in children with intellectual disability. *Journal of Intellectual Disability Research*, *51*(1), 43–53. doi:10.1111/j.1365-2788.2006.00871.x PMID:17181602

Lee, J. (2013). Maternal stress, well-being, and impaired sleep in mothers of children with developmental disabilities: A literature review. *Research in Developmental Disabilities*, *34*(11), 4255–4273. doi:10.1016/j.ridd.2013.09.008 PMID:24080069

Lin, L.-P., Hsu, S.-W., Kuo, M.-T., Wu, J.-L., Chu, C., & Lin, J.-D. (2014). Onset aging conditions of adults with an intellectual disability associated with primary caregiver depression. *Research in Developmental Disabilities*, *35*(3), 632–638. doi:10.1016/j.ridd.2013.12.013 PMID:24467811

Longo, D. C., & Bond, B. (1984). Families of the handicapped child: Research and practice. *Family Relations*, *33*(1), 57–65. doi:10.2307/584590

Lopez, V., Clifford, T., & Minnes, P. et al.. (2008). Parental stress and coping in families of children with and without developmental delays. *Journal on Developmental Disabilities*, *14*, 99–103.

MacLean, W. E. Jr, Tervo, R. C., Hoch, J., Tervo, M., & Symons, F. J. (2010). Self-Injury among a community cohort of young children at risk for intellectual and developmental disabilities. *The Journal of Pediatrics*, *157*(6), 979–983. doi:10.1016/j.jpeds.2010.05.052 PMID:20630541

Mafifei-Almodovar, L., & Sturmey, P. (2012). Evidence-based practice and crisis intervention. In D. D. Reed, R. F. D. DiGennaro, & J. K. Luiselli (Eds.), *Handbook of crisis intervention for individuals with developmental disabilities*. New York: Springer.

Mandleco, B., Olsen, S. F., Dyches, T., & Marshall, E. (2003). The relationship between family and sibling functioning in families raising a child with a disability. *Journal of Family Nursing*, *9*(4), 365–396. doi:10.1177/1074840703258329

Marvin RS and Pianta RC. (1996) Mothers' reactions to their child's diagnosis: Relations with security of attachment. *Journal of Clinical Child Psychology, 25*(4), 436-445.

Mazzucchelli, T. G., & Sanders, M. R. (2011). Preventing behavioural and emotional problems in children who have a developmental disability: A public health approach. *Research in Developmental Disabilities, 32*(6), 2148–2156. doi:10.1016/j.ridd.2011.07.022 PMID:21831592

McCarthy, A., Cuskelly, M., van Kraayenoord, C. E., & Cohen, J. (2006). Predictors of stress in mothers and fathers of children with fragile X syndrome. *Research in Developmental Disabilities, 27*(6), 688–704. doi:10.1016/j.ridd.2005.10.002 PMID:16361079

McConkey, R., Truesdale-Kennedy, M., Chang, M.-Y., Jarrah, S., & Shukri, R. (2008). The impact on mothers of bringing up a child with intellectual disabilities: A cross-cultural study. *International Journal of Nursing Studies, 45*(1), 65–74. doi:10.1016/j.ijnurstu.2006.08.007 PMID:17022985

McConnell, D., Savage, A., & Breitkreuz, R. (2014). Resilience in families raising children with disabilities and behavior problems. *Research in Developmental Disabilities, 35*(4), 833–848. doi:10.1016/j.ridd.2014.01.015 PMID:24491480

McHale, S. M., & Gamble, W. C. (1989). Sibling relationships of children with disabled and nondisabled brothers and sisters. *Developmental Psychology, 25*(3), 421–429. doi:10.1037/0012-1649.25.3.421

Meyer, K. A., Ingersoll, B., & Hambrick, D. Z. (2011). Factors influencing adjustment in siblings of children with autism spectrum disorders. *Research in Autism Spectrum Disorders, 5*(4), 1413–1420. doi:10.1016/j.rasd.2011.01.027

Mitchell, D. B., & Hauser-Cram, P. (2008). The well-being of mothers of adolescents with developmental disabilities in relation to medical care utilization and satisfaction with health care. *Research in Developmental Disabilities, 29*(2), 97–112. doi:10.1016/j.ridd.2006.12.002 PMID:17267176

Molteno, G., Molteno, C. D., Finchilescu, G., & Dawes, A. R. L. (2001). Behavioural and emotional problems in children with intellectual disability attending special schools in Cape Town, South Africa. *Journal of Intellectual Disability Research, 45*(6), 515–520. doi:10.1046/j.1365-2788.2001.00368.x PMID:11737538

Moss, S., Emerson, E., & Kiernan, C. et al.. (2000). Psychiatric symptoms in adults with learning disability and challenging behaviour. *The British Journal of Psychiatry, 177*(5), 452–456. doi:10.1192/bjp.177.5.452 PMID:11060000

Myrbakk, E., & von Tetzchner, S. (2008). Psychiatric disorders and behaviour problems in people with intellectual disability. *Research in Developmental Disabilities, 29*(4), 316–332. doi:10.1016/j.ridd.2007.06.002 PMID:17616450

Neece, C., & Baker, B. (2008). Predicting maternal parenting stress in middle childhood: The roles of child intellectual status, behaviour problems and social skills. *Journal of Intellectual Disability Research, 52*(12), 1114–1128. doi:10.1111/j.1365-2788.2008.01071.x PMID:18513339

Nihira, K., Mink, I. T., & Meyers, C. E. (1985). Home environment and development of slow-learning adolescents: Reciprocal relations. *Developmental Psychology*, *21*(5), 784–794. doi:10.1037/0012-1649.21.5.784

Nimbalkar, S., Raithatha, S., & Shah, R. (2014). *A qualitative study of psychosocial problems among parents of children with cerebral palsy attending two tertiary care hospitals in Western India*. ISRN Family Medicine.

Olsson, M. B., & Hwang, C. P. (2001). Depression in mothers and fathers of children with intellectual disability. *Journal of Intellectual Disability Research*, *45*(6), 535–543. doi:10.1046/j.1365-2788.2001.00372.x PMID:11737541

Orsmond, G. I., Seltzer, M. M., Krauss, M. W., & Hong, J. (2003). Behavior problems in adults with mental retardation and maternal well-being: Examination of the direction of effects. *American Journal of Mental Retardation*, *108*(4), 257–271. doi:10.1352/0895-8017(2003)108<257:BPIAWM>2.0.CO;2 PMID:12780337

Ou, J.-J., Shi, L.-J., & Xun, G.-L. et al.. (2015). Employment and financial burden of families with preschool children diagnosed with autism spectrum disorders in urban China: Results from a descriptive study. *BMC Psychiatry*, *15*, 42–57. PMID:25608486

Ouyang, L., Grosse, S. D., Riley, C., Bolen, J., Bishop, E., Raspa, M., & Bailey, D. B. Jr. (2014). A comparison of family financial and employment impacts of fragile X syndrome, autism spectrum disorders, and intellectual disability. *Research in Developmental Disabilities*, *35*(7), 1518–1527. doi:10.1016/j.ridd.2014.04.009 PMID:24755230

Parmenter, T. R., Einfeld, S. L., Tonge, B. J., & Dempster, J. A. (1998). Behavioural and emotional problems in the classroom of children and adolescents with intellectual disability. *Journal of Intellectual & Developmental Disability*, *23*(1), 71–77. doi:10.1080/13668259800033591

Petalas, M. A., Hastings, R. P., Nash, S., Hall, L. M., Joannidi, H., & Dowey, A. (2012). Psychological adjustment and sibling relationships in siblings of children with Autism Spectrum Disorders: Environmental stressors and the Broad Autism Phenotype. *Research in Autism Spectrum Disorders*, *6*(1), 546–555. doi:10.1016/j.rasd.2011.07.015

Petty, J. L., Bacarese-Hamilton, M., Davies, L. E., & Oliver, C. (2014). Correlates of self-injurious, aggressive and destructive behaviour in children under five who are at risk of developmental delay. *Research in Developmental Disabilities*, *35*(1), 36–45. doi:10.1016/j.ridd.2013.10.019 PMID:24216345

Pianta, R. C., Marvin, R. S., Britner, P. A., & Borowitz, K. C. (1996). Mothers' resolution of their children's diagnosis: Organized patterns of caregiving representations. *Infant Mental Health Journal*, *17*(3), 239–256. doi:10.1002/(SICI)1097-0355(199623)17:3<239::AID-IMHJ4>3.0.CO;2-J

Pisula, E. (2011). Parenting stress in mothers and fathers of children with autism spectrum disorders. In A Comprehensive Book on Autism Spectrum Disorders. InTech. doi:10.5772/18507

Plant, K. M., & Sanders, M. R. (2007). Predictors of care-giver stress in families of preschool-aged children with developmental disabilities. *Journal of Intellectual Disability Research*, *51*(2), 109–124. doi:10.1111/j.1365-2788.2006.00829.x PMID:17217475

Reardon, T. C., Gray, K. M., & Melvin, G. A. (2015). Anxiety disorders in children and adolescents with intellectual disability: Prevalence and assessment. *Research in Developmental Disabilities*, *36*, 175–190. doi:10.1016/j.ridd.2014.10.007 PMID:25462478

Ritzema, A.M., & Sladeczek, I.E. (2011). Stress in parents of children with developmental disabilities over time. *Journal of Developmental Disabilities, 17*, 21-34.

Robinson, M., & Neece, C. L. (2015). Marital satisfaction, parental stress, and child behavior problems among parents of young children with developmental delays. *Journal of Mental Health Research in Intellectual Disabilities*, *8*(1), 23–46. doi:10.1080/19315864.2014.994247

Roos, P. (1977). Parents of mentally retarded people. *International Journal of Mental Health*, *6*(1), 96–119. doi:10.1080/00207411.1977.11448758

Rush, A. J., & Frances, A. T. (2000). The expert consensus guidelines: Treatment of psychiatric and behavioral problems in mental retardation. *American Journal of Mental Retardation, 105*, 159–1228.

Scelles, R. (1997). The impact of a person's disability on his or her sibling. *International Journal of Rehabilitation Research. Internationale Zeitschrift fur Rehabilitationsforschung. Revue Internationale de Recherches de Readaptation*, *20*(2), 129–137. doi:10.1097/00004356-199706000-00002 PMID:9226496

Schuengel, C., Rentinck, I. C. M., Stolk, J., Voorman, J. M., Loots, G. M. P., Ketelaar, M., & Becher, J. G. et al. (2009). Parents' reactions to the diagnosis of cerebral palsy: Associations between resolution, age and severity of disability. *Child: Care, Health and Development*, *35*(5), 673–680. doi:10.1111/j.1365-2214.2009.00951.x PMID:19320906

Schuiringa, H., van Nieuwenhuijzen, M., & de Castro, B. O. et al.. (2015). Parenting and the parent–child relationship in families of children with mild to borderline intellectual disabilities and externalizing behavior. *Research in Developmental Disabilities*, *32*, 1–12. doi:10.1016/j.ridd.2014.08.018 PMID:25262097

Shearn, J., & Todd, S. (2000). Maternal employment and family responsibilities: The perspectives of mothers of children with intellectual disabilities. *Journal of Applied Research in Intellectual Disabilities*, *13*(3), 109–131. doi:10.1046/j.1468-3148.2000.00021.x

Sheeran, T., Marvin, R. S., & Pianta, R. C. (1997). Mothers' resolution of their child's diagnosis and self-reported measures of parenting stress, marital relations, and social support. *Journal of Pediatric Psychology*, *22*(2), 197–212. doi:10.1093/jpepsy/22.2.197 PMID:9114643

Sherman, B. R., & Cocozza, J. J. (1984). Stress in families of the developmentally disabled: A literature review of factors affecting the decision to seek out-of-home placements. *Family Relations*, *33*(1), 95–103. doi:10.2307/584594

Sieman, M. (1984). Siblings of the chronically ill or disabled child. *The Nursing Clinics of North America*, *19*, 295–307. PMID:6233538

Straus, M. A., & Stewart, J. H. (1999). Corporal punishment by American parents: National data on prevalence, chronicity, severity, and duration, in relation to child and family characteristics. *Clinical Child and Family Psychology Review*, *2*(2), 55–70. doi:10.1023/A:1021891529770 PMID:11225932

Straus, M. S., & Donnelly, D. A. (2001). *Beating the devil out of them. Corporal punishment in American families and its effects on children*. New Brunswick, NJ: Transaction Publishers.

Tremblay, K. N., Richer, L., Lachance, L., & Côté, A. (2010). Psychopathological manifestations of children with intellectual disabilities according to their cognitive and adaptive behavior profile. *Research in Developmental Disabilities*, *31*(1), 57–69. doi:10.1016/j.ridd.2009.07.016 PMID:19700260

Trute, B. (1990). Child and parent predictors of family adjustment in households containing young developmentally disabled children. *Family Relations*, *39*(3), 292–297. doi:10.2307/584874

Vrijmoeth, C., Monbaliu, E., & Lagast, E. (2011). Behavioral problems in children with motor and intellectual disabilities: Prevalence and associations with maladaptive personality and marital relationship. *Research in Developmental Disabilities*, *32*, 1027–1038. PMID:22502827

Wallander, J. L., Dekker, M. C., & Koot, H. M. (2006). Risk factors for psychopathology in children with intellectual disability: A prospective longitudinal population-based study. *Journal of Intellectual Disability Research*, *50*(4), 259–268. doi:10.1111/j.1365-2788.2005.00792.x PMID:16507030

Wells, T., Sandefur, D., & Hogan, D. P. (2003). What happens after the high school years among young persons with disabilities? *Social Forces*, *82*(2), 803–832. doi:10.1353/sof.2004.0029

Wikler, L. (1981). Chronic stresses of families of mentally retarded children. *Family Relations*, *30*(2), 281–288. doi:10.2307/584142

Witwera, A. N., & Lecavaliera, L. (2008). Psychopathology in children with intellectual disability: Risk markers and correlates. *Journal of Mental Health Research in Intellectual Disabilities*, *1*(2), 75–96. doi:10.1080/19315860801988327

Wolfe, B., Song, J., Greenberg, J. S., & Mailick, M. R. (2014). Ripple effects of developmental disabilities and mental illness on nondisabled adult siblings. *Social Science & Medicine*, *108*, 1–9. doi:10.1016/j.socscimed.2014.01.021 PMID:24607704

Woodman, A. C., Mawdsley, H. P., & Hauser-Cram, P. (2011). Parenting stress and child behavior problems within families of children with developmental disabilities: Transactional relations across 15 years. *Research in Developmental Disabilities*, *32*, 264–276. PMID:25462487

World Health Organization. (1992). *The ICD-10 classification of mental and behavioral disorders: clinical descriptions and diagnostic guidelines*. Geneva, Switzerland: WHO.

ENDNOTE

1 Children denote anyone below age of 18 years old.

Chapter 5
The Stress and Adjustment in the Family of Intellectually Disabled Children

Babita Prusty
Amity University, India

ABSTRACT

ABSTRACT Intellectual disability is a disorder, in which children exhibit intellectual insufficiency as well as inadequate adaptive skills, in conceptual, social, and practical domains, manifested during developmental period. The wellbeing, coping and overall adjustment of parents, siblings and other family members of children with intellectual disabilities is worth studying not only because of understanding of the children suffering from disability but also because of helping, reducing burden and enhancing a healthy physical and mental life of the family members. Research suggests that parents of children with, typical development, but their mental health in general might be complicated as well. Certain therapeutic techniques like Psychodynamic therapy, family therapy and behavioral therapies could be used for helping such families.

INTRODUCTION: A PERSPECTIVE OF FAMILY

A View about Parents

When a member of a family becomes seriously sick, it is said the whole family becomes sick. It is the pivotal point of this chapter to explore the consequences of intellectual disability in the context of family. The role of parents and the role of siblings are of prime importance in such a family as a primary caregiver. Even though the pediatrician, psychologist, nurse, psychiatrist, special educator, and other necessary community agents have a very essential role in the management of intellectual disability, the role of family is of utmost importance irrespective of the nature of disabilities. Research suggest that parents of children with disability not only experience higher levels of stress compared to families of children with typical development, but their mental health in general might be complicated as well. Parents may

DOI: 10.4018/978-1-5225-0089-6.ch005

experience depression, anxiety (Beckman 1991; Dyson 1991; Emerson 2003; Bristol &Schopher 1984; Hoppes 1990), higher levels of hopelessness, failure, guilt (Jones 1997; Powers 1989; Tommasone & Tommasone 1989), they report less parental skills and less marital satisfaction (Rodrigue et al., 1990).

Parents' psychological well-being is of prime importance. Research emphasized on intervention programs to reduce in parental stress (Davis, 1985; Schilling & Schinke 1984), because high levels of parental stress may have a negative impact on the functioning of the child with disability. Parents may behave ways that have a negative impact on children (Hastings 2002). Studies suggest that parents who experience higher levels of stress interact differently with their children, compared to parents who experience lower levels of stress, and they respond differently to their child's problematic behavior (Conger, R., Patterson, G.R., & Ge, X., 1995). According to Floyd & Phillipe (1993) self-reported depression from parents was a strong predictor for their efforts to manage actively and successfully their child's problematic behaviors. The child with intellectual disabilities is not the only one who affects his family's life and dynamics. The family also affects positively or negatively the child's development. Research suggests that higher levels of parental stress predict less positive outcomes from the early intervention programs for children with disabilities (Brinker, R. P., Seifer, R, & Smeroff, A. J. 1994)., whereas early interventions for children with disabilities are more successful when family problems, parental stress included, are addressed before the intervention program begins. Thus knowing and dealing with parental stress is important for professionals. At last, not only it seems that parental stress interferes with success of intervention programs for children with developmental disabilities. (Robbin et al 1991; Brinker et al 1994), but parents as well, while experiencing high levels of stress, have less positive outcomes from intervention programs designed to improve parental skills (Rhodes 2003; Baker et al 2002).

A View about Siblings

Although there are many positive outcomes of growing up with a sibling having a psychological or behavioral disorder, typical siblings can potentially experience harmful effects of managing and coping with the special demands and stresses of having a sibling with these kinds of difficulties. In order to better understand families, researchers have shown an increasing interest in investigating sibling relationships. Relationships between siblings can be life's most influential and longest lasting relationships.

Understanding Intellectual Disabilities

Intellectual disability involves impairments of general mental abilities that impact adaptive functioning in three domains. These domains determine how well an individual copes with everyday task. These domains are mentioned below. (American Psychiatric Association, 2013).

- **Conceptual Domain:** It includes skills in language, reading, writing, math, reasoning, knowledge, and memory.
- **Social Domain:** It includes empathy, social judgment, interpersonal communication skills, the ability to make and retain friendships, and similar capacities.
- **Practical Domain:** It revolves around self-management in areas such as personal care, job responsibilities, money management, recreation, and organizing school and work tasks.

While intellectual disability does not have a specific age requirement, an individual's symptoms must begin during the developmental period and are diagnosed based on the severity of deficits in adaptive functioning. The disorder is considered chronic and often co-occurs with other mental conditions like depression, attention-deficit/hyperactivity disorder, and autism spectrum disorder (Table 1) (DSM-V, 2013).

Children suffering from intellectual disabilities differ according to their level of disabilities.

Understanding the difficulties the children themselves face along with their family members and attempting for preparing strategies for solving their problem is not an easy task. Moreover it requires an understanding of problem category wise (Levels of retardation) (Table 2).

Table 1. Classification of persons with intellectual disabilities

Medical	Educational
1. Infection and Intoxication 2. Trauma or Physiological agent 3. Metabolism of Nutrition	1. Educable 2. Trainable 3. Custodial
4. Gross brain disease (Post-natal) 5. Unknown Prenatal Influence	**Psychological**
6. Chromosomal Abnormalities 7. Gestational Disorder 8. Psychiatric Disorder 9. Environmental influence 10. Other influences	1. Mild 2. Moderate 3. Severe 4. Profound

(National Institute for the Mentally Handicapped, 1989).

Table 2. Characteristics of persons with various levels of intellectual disabilities

Severity Levels	Mild	Moderate	Severe	Profound
Intelligence Quotient (IQ)	55-69	40-54	25-39	< 25
Mental Age(MA)	8-10yr	5-8yr	3-5yr	3 yr
Educational Category	Educable	Trainable	Custodial (Dependent)	Custodial (Life Support)
Prevalence within the population of Intellectual disabilities	90%	6%	3%	1%
Functional Skills	1. Most of them manage unskilled jobs. 2. Capable of showing social behavior of adolescents. 3.With special training & proper care they can be taught to be independent	1. Their speed of learning is quite slow. 2. With constant support of their family they manage to live safely. 3.They can learn moderately simple skills	1. Most of them are permanently institutionalized & require constant care &support. 2. They are incapable of doing anything independently. 3. They even face problem in learning simple task .	1. Completely incapable of looking after themselves 2. Gross Physical disorder 3. Not able to learn even simplest skill.

(Mohanty, G., 1989).

Associated Problems in Intellectual Disabilities

Apart from Intelligence and adaptive problems, the people suffering from intellectual disabilities have wide ranged medical, psychiatric and psychological complications.

Associated Medical Conditions

- **Infections and Parasitic Diseases:** Diseases coming under this are Tuberculosis of the nervous system, congenital syphilis, Sub acute sclerosingpanencephalitis, Mosquito-borne viral encephalitis, Japanese encephalitis, other viral encephalitis, not elsewhere classified,congenitaltoxoplasm osis, Toxoplasma meningoencephalitis etc. (World Health Organization, 1996).
- **Benign Neoplasm:** Haemangioma and lymphangioma, etc.
- **Disease of the Blood:** Anemia, Vitamin B12 deficiency, Folate deficiency anemia, Thalassemia, Sickle-cell disorders etc. (ICD-10,1996).
- **Endocrine Nutritional and Metabolic Disorders:** Congenital iodine-deficiency syndrome, hypothyroidism, Disorders of aromatic amino-acid metabolism (includes phenylketonuria), Disorders of branched-chain amino-acid metabolism and fatty acid metabolism, Lactose intolerance, disorders of carbohydrate metabolism, Disorders of sphingolipid metabolism and other lipid storage disorders, Disorders of glycosaminoglycan metabolism, Disorders of glycoprotein metabolism, Disorders of lipoprotein metabolism and other lipidaemias, Disorders of purine and pyrimidine metabolism, Disorders of porphyria and bilirubin metabolism, etc.
- **Diseases of the Nervous System:** Encephalitis, myelitis and encephalomyelitis, Epilepsy, Status epilepticus, infantile cerebral palsy. Other degenerative diseases of basal ganglia, Hemiplegia, Paraplegia and tetraplegia, Hydrocephalus Toxic encephalopathy etc. (World Health Organisation, 1996).
- **Disease of the Circulatory System:** Sequelae of subarachnoid hemorrhage, Sequelae of intracerebral hemorrhage, Sequelae of other no traumatic intracranial hemorrhage etc. (World Health Organization, 1996).
- **Diseases of the Musculoskeletal System:** Kyphosis and lordosis & Scoliosis (World Health Organisation, 1996).
- **Congenital Abnormalities, Deformation and Chromosomal Disorders:** Congenital syphilis, Hypothyroidism,Phenylketonuria, Epilepsy, Cerebral Palsy, Congenital cytomegalovirus, Kernicterus, Microcephaly, Spina Bifida, Tuberose Sclerosis, De Lange Syndrome,Cornelia de Lange Syndrome, Brachmann de Lange Syndrome, Prader-Willi Syndrome, Rubenstein-Taybi Syndrome, Down's Syndrome Fragile X syndrome, intracranial injury etc. (World Health Organisation, 1996).

Associated Psychiatric Disorders

In intellectual disabilities there are many comorbid psychiatric conditions (World Health Organisation,1996):

- **Psychotic Disorders:** Schizophrenia, schizotypal and delusional disorders, Acute and transient psychotic disorders Schizoaffective disorders etc.

- **Affective Disorders** Mania, Depressive episode, cyclothimia, dysthymia etc.(World Health Organisation,1996).
- **Neurotic DISORDERS** Neurotic, stress-related and somatoform disorder, Phobic anxiety disorders (Agoraphobia, Socialphobias), other anxiety disorders(Panic disorder, Generalized anxiety disorder, Mixed anxiety and depressive disorder, Obsessive-compulsive disorder, Reaction to severe stress, and adjustment disorder, Post-traumatic stress disorder) etc.
- **Dissociative (Conversion) Disorders:** Dissociative amnesia, fugues, stupor, Trance and possession disorders Dissociative motor disorder, Dissociative convulsions (World Health Organisation, 1996).
- **Somatoform Disorders:** Somatization disorder, Hypochondriacaldisorder, Somatic autonomic dysfunction Persistent somatoform pain disorder, Neurasthenia, Depersonalisation-derealisation syndrome (World Health Organisation, 1996).
- **Other Psychiatric Disorders:** Personality disorders, Kleptomania, Trichotillomania, Gender identity disorder, Disorders of sexual preference, Exhibitionism, Voyeurism, Pedophilia, Childhood autism, Hyperkinetic disorders, Conduct disorders, Separation anxiety disorder of childhood, Social anxiety disorder of childhood, Sibling rivalry disorder, Elective mutism, Tic disorders, Nonorganic enuresis Nonorganic encopresis, Feeding disorder of infancy and childhood, Pica of infancy and childhood, stereotyped movement disorder, stuttering (Stammering) Cluttering etc. (ICD-10; World Health Organisation, 1996).

Family Dealing with Intellectual Disabilities

From the above description about the co morbid medical and psychiatric condition, the magnitude of difficulty in the lives of people suffering from intellectual disability and their primary caregivers, parents & other family members can be very well understood (World Health Organization, 1996).

Families are the primary caregivers of course and long term care giving most often changes care giving to burden. Several studies have highlighted the stress of having an intellectually disabled child in the family. Hewett in 1975 noted that the moment of crisis starts as soon as the parents learn that their child is permanently handicapped. Begab and Richardson (1975) observed that trauma of having a retarded child presents a serious disruptive force to the family life style. Hannam (1975) reported that the presence of intellectual disabled child alters the normal chores of the family. Holroyd and Guthrie (1979) found that mothers generally feel burdened and the family members deprived of normal family life because of the presence of a handicapped.

Disability: A Challenge for Parents

International human rights conventions recognize the right of children to family life in the community (United Nation,1989,2006).In the vast majority of instances children with intellectual disability are cared for by their parents who (along with other family members)serve as their most constant and lifelong caregivers. They play a critical role in shaping the life experiences of their children.

Mothers

Plenty of researches available on mother as a care giver, and the effect of her continuous care on her physical and mental health.Abundant research available in the context of disability.Mother has a major role in the building up of his disabled child, and mother is the person who is worst affected because of the long term, continuous, committed and strenuous pressure of care taking of the disabled child. This pressure of the mother increases along with the increase in severity of disability.

A study by Ryan (2005), evaluated how mothers are impacted and shaped by the reactions of others towards their child with a disability, and the role of appraisal and interpretation of the situation. All mothers within this study reported several occasions where their child with a disability was confronted with stares as well as rude and insensitive comments when they were in public. Some mothers interpreted such reactions as a direct reflection of their incompetence as a parent and their inability to control their child's behavior; whereas others perceived the reactions of others as permissible and understandable given that their child was behaving in a manner that might be considered out of the ordinary.

It is a general notion that mothers of disabled child experience more stress and anxiety as compared to the mothers of a normally developing child.

Fathers

The presence of a disabled child has an impact on physical, psychological, social as well as financial life of the whole family. As generally father is the primary bread earner in any family a financial pressure is also there in fathers of a disabled child.

Although very little research has been conducted with fathers of children with disabilities, existing studies suggest that having a disabled child may have important implications for fathers' well-being and involvement with their children. The researches revealed that fathers though experience psychological distress with a child, withdisabilities; their level of disability is generally less than that of the mothers (Emerson et al., 2010; Gerstein et al., 2009; MacDonald & Hastings, 2010; Olsson & Hwang, 2008; Saloviita et al., 2003). It all depends on how involved a father is with a disabled child. The more the involvement the more will be the stress, both physical and mental. Many studies however have found a long range of effects the presence of a disabled child has.

Several studies have reported that having a child with a disability has adverse effects on fathers' well-being. Fathers often have intense reactions to their child's initial diagnosis and many report experiencing existential conflicts (e.g., reconsidering the purpose of life) as they attempt to adapt to the situation (Blacher,1984, Hornby, G,1992,1992b). Some evidence suggests that fathers of children with disabilities experience poorer psychological functioning (e.g., higher rates of depression, personality difficulties) than do fathers of nondisabled children (Brown&Pacini, 1989; Cummings, 1976; Eisenberg,1957).

It is revealed from past researches that fathers of disabled child has lower self-esteem as compared to a typically developing child.(Cummings,1976;Davis,May,1991;Meyer,Vadasky,Fewell,1982).Fathers of children with disabilities often experience guilt, disappointment, lack of control, inferiority, and isolation, which lower their overall sense of well-being. (Davis & May, 1991, Lamb & Billings,1997).

Factors Associated with Adjustment of Parents of Children with Disabilities

Parental Satisfaction and Self-Efficacy

Studies on parenting efficacy highlights on parent's confidence on their ability to fulfill their parenting role and effectively growing up their children. There are two parameters basically, what the situation is & how one perceives the situation. The stress of parents with a disabled child may be more, but if parents perceive it as possible to deal with the child effectively in the possible manner, then the stress is less. Studies done in this field revealed that parents of a child with intellectual disability who felt satisfied with their parenting role, reported lower level of stress than those who are less satisfied (Nalavany, Glidden & Ryan, 2009).

Self-efficacy in parents is the confidence of parents on their parenting style. Of course to a great extent it depends on the ability of the child itself, but if under a defined circumstance the parents feel satisfied with their approach of handling their children's issue, they experience less stress.

- **Family Functioning:** The parents experience relatively lesser stress in a family, which is supportive and cohesive. Also relationships within families influence their children's social-emotional functioning. (Shonkoff & Phillips, 2000).
- **Marital Functioning:** In a family, the relationship of father with mother is of prime importance. It includes mutual understanding, cooperation and also their physical relationship. When a couple have a child with intellectual disabilities, they are mostly busy with taking care of their child, find lesser time for each other. Even though there are plenty of researches showing the difference to be not very significant between the marital functioning of normal children with that of the intellectually disabled children (Risdal and Singer, 2004).Provided supporting evidence in this context.
- **The Aspects of Siblings:** The relationship between siblings is considered to be one of the most enduring relationships within families. When it comes to sibling of a child with intellectual disabilities, it is again much more important. Researchers suggest that not only normal children, even the disabled children imitate and learn more from their siblings and peer groups than parents. (Smith,2001). Parents experience stress not only because of physical and mental exhaustion due to care taking of their disabled child, also because of the guilt associated with it, that they cannot do justice with their normal child. But parents experience satisfaction if the sibling relationship is good, and no party getting adversely impacted by the critical situation. Luckily recent researchers have found that siblings have favorable self-concepts and they develop additional strength because of their siblings with intellectual disabilities or any other such disabilities. (Van Riper, 2000, Skotko & Levine, 2006).
- **Community Perception:** Disability is typically viewed as a burden, a curse and negative aspect of life in our country. Such kind of notion leads to stigma. Broadly our individual perception, dealing and coping all are result of society reaction or perception to the disability at large. Disability in any member of the family restricts the family to join others in the community outside family in the celebration of kind. Sometimes it becomes a shame or embarrassment for the whole family to invite anybody to the family. Thus not only family life but also social life becomes disrupted.
- **Siblings:** Apart from parents, the next are the siblings who affect and can get affected by their siblings, who have some disabilities. Families having children with disabilities have to face ongoing challenges that can impact various aspects of family life, as well as the adjustment and well-being of family members, including siblings (Dykens, 2005; O'Brien, Duffy, & Nicholl, 2009; Schuntermann, 2007). Research has consistently shown that while most siblings adjust relatively well to having a brother or sister with a disability, other siblings have a limited capacity to mentally, socially and physically adapt to the environment, leaving them vulnerable to adjustment difficulties (Ferraioli & Harris, 2010; Jackson, Richer & Edge, 2008).

Factors Associated with the Adjustment of Siblings of Children with Disabilities

Emotional and Behavioral Problems

Researchers contend that most behavior problems can manifest either internally or externally (Achenbach & Edelbrock, 1983; Mash & Wolfe, 2002; Rossiter & Sharpe, 2001).Emotional distress are internal difficulties (internalized problem) and are characterized by depression, somatic complaints, and anxiety (Achenbach & Edelbrock, 1983; Dishion & Stormshak, 2007) and externalising problems are characterised by distress being directed towards others, and encompasses verbal aggression, non-compliance, oppositional defiance and conduct problems (Achenbach & Edelbrock, 1983; Mash & Wolfe, 2002). Several studies have shown that both internalizing and externalizing problems are common in siblings of children with various disabilities, including autism, Down syndrome, and intellectual disability (Cuskelly & Dadds, 1992; Hasting, 2003; Rossiter & Sharpe, 2001; Verte, Roeyers, & Busse, 2003). A meta-analysis by Williams in 1997 reported an increased risk of adjustment problems for siblings. In addition, siblings were found to be at an increased risk of having internalizing and externalizing behaviors when compared with siblings without a brother or sister with a chronic illness. In a studyby Petalas, Hastings, Nash, Lloyd and Dowey in 2009 found siblings of children with both an intellectual disability and autism have more behavioral and emotional problems when compared to normative data.

These findings are consistent with a recent study conducted by Wood, Sherman, Hamiwka, Blackman and Wirrell (2008). But many studies did not find any difference in stressandadjustment of disability population and normative population. It can be concluded that disability may not be a risk factor in itself for the development of sibling psychopathology. Rather, studies on sibling adjustment may represent typical developmental variability in association with a range of risk and protective factors as they are experienced in the general population. It follows that it may be more informative to utilize concepts and measures that are sensitive to the experiences of siblings of children with disabilities (Stoneman, 2005), and not necessarily bound by categorical conceptualizations of psychopathology.

Self-Esteem

Researchers now contend that sibling psychological adjustment encompasses dimensions beyond externalizing and internalizing behaviors (Moore & Keyes, 2003). One aspect related to adjustment found in the literature on typical development is concerned with the notion of how children perceive themselves (Mash & Wolfe, 2002; Moore & Keyes, 2003). This is referred to as self-concept, and encompasses knowledge and evaluation of one's own values, qualities and strengths. Self-concept is closely related to self-esteem, which has been defined as one's own judgement of self-worth (Berk, 2006; Mash & Wolfe, 2002).In the context of disability, it has been found out that siblings of children with a disability have an increased risk of lowering self-confidence and self-worth when compared to their peers who grow up without a sibling with a disability (Gamble & McHale, 1989). Other studies in this area have revealed that siblings of children with disabilities are indistinguishable from their peers in regards to self-concept and self-esteem (Rodrigue, Geffken, & Morgan, 1993; Singhi, Malhi, & Dwarka, 2002; Verte et al., 2003). Mates in 1990 found that when reported by parents and teachers, siblings (aged between 5 and 17 years) of children with autism had comparable scores to the normative sample on a measure of self-concept. Recent reviews have also suggested that some siblings are not only indistinguishable but find psychological strength from growing up with a brother or sister with a disability (Gallo, Breitmayer, Knafl, & Zoeller, 1993; Stoneman, 2005). Faux (1993) found that when compared with their counterparts, siblings of children with disabilities demonstrated increased empathy for others, were less self-centered, and were protective of their brother or sister with a disability. Research has consistently demonstrated that self-concept and self-esteem are influenced by a range of factors, including the opinions that others make of us, and comparisons and perceptions of the way one is similar to or different to those around them (Berk, 2006; Bos, Muris, Mulkens, & Schaalma, 2006).

Social Competence and Peer Relationships

The development of peer relationships and social competence constitutes another area of investigation in sibling psychological adjustment (Mandleco, Olsen, Dyches, & Marshall,2003). Current findings suggest no apparent differences in social competence between individuals with typically developing siblings and those with a brother or sister with a developmental disability (Grissom & Borkowski, 2002).

Contrary to these findings, other studies have found that when compared to siblings of children without disabilities, those with a brother or sister with a disability are likely to demonstrate greater social competence (Mandleco et al., 2003). Mandleco and colleagues (2003) investigated 78 parent-sibling dyads (half with and the other half without a family member with a disability) aged between 4 and 11 years. When compared to the siblings of children without disabilities, siblings growing up with a brother or sister with a disability demonstrated more cooperation, assertion and self-control in the classroom, as rated by their school teachers. This highlights potential positive consequences of growing up with a brother or sister with a disability, an area that has begun to gain further attention in the literature.

Studies by various dimensions of psychological adjustment highlight that having a brother or sister with a disability is not a risk factor for maladjustment in itself, and that many children can benefit and thrive in a positive way from having a sibling with a disability.(Stawski, Auerbach, Barasch, Lerner, & Zimin, 1997). However, it is possible that when multiple factors are present (e.g., parental conflict, minimal resources, lack of knowledge about disability), it may be more difficult for the typically developing sibling to address environmental and family experiences associated with a sibling with a disability, which in turn may impact adjustment.

Factors Associated with Sibling Adjustment

Sibling Factors

During the last decade in the field of research, factors such as cognitive and behavioral coping responses, and stress have gained significant attention in the development of adaptive and maladaptive adjustment (Harmer Cox, Marshall, Mandleco, & Olsen, 2003; Mash & Wolfe, 2002). Investigators have started to extend these findings and find out the role of these variables in the initiation of psychopathology and adjustment in the siblings of children with disabilities (Harmer Cox et al., 2003). Supportersof this research postulate that it is the constant hassles and frustrations that are encountered on a daily basis that are stressful, and increase the likelihood of adjustment problems more so than major life events. (Caltabiano, Byrne, Martin, &Sarafino, 2002; Giallo & Gavidia-Payne, 2006).This paradigm has been applied to different cohorts across the lifespan, including first-year university students, adolescents and adults, with results consistently finding an association between hassles and uplifts, and health and wellbeing

(Caltabiano et al., 2002). Research dealing with daily hassles and frustrations for siblings has generally been confined to the child with a disability, overlooking experiences and interactions at a family and wider social community level (Giallo & Gavidia-Payne, 2006). Again, little effort has been devoted to relating such experiences to the results (e.g., self-concept, internalizing and externalizing problems), and thus the relationship between daily hassles and uplifts and sibling adjustment remains unclear.

Family Factors

Families of children with disabilities face ongoing challenges and stressful life experience, which adversely affect their family life. (Blacher, Neece, & Paczkowski, 2005; Guralnick, 2004). While some people have good resilience & coping, others are not very efficient in dealing with this and become a prey to stress & anxiety. (Smith, Oliver, &Innocenti, 2001). This can have implications for the health and wellbeing of all family members, including siblings. These assumptions have been generally framed within *family systems theory,* which emphasizes the importance of family interaction and how family members are impacted by one another (Rosenbaum, King, Law, King, & Evans, 1998; Turnbull, Turnbull, Erwin, & Soodak, 2006). According to proponents of this theory, a child with a disability can *directly* impact the psychological development and functioning of their typically developing sibling.

It is also based on the premise that siblings of children with disabilities can be *indirectly* influenced by the family environment, as well as interactions and relationships with other family members such as parents (Turnbull et al., 2006). Consistent with the view regarding indirect influences in the family context, parents of young children with disabilities are often exposed to a range of stressors, which may include coming to terms with their child's diagnosis, the long-term implications of the child's disability, networking the best professional supports, and finding the resources needed to partake in these programs (Guralnick, 2004). Meeting these demands while simultaneously promoting the wellbeing of other family members can be a difficult task for parents and the cumulative effect of these stressors can precipitate episodes of depression, anxiety, and marital problems at a parent level. This in turn is likely to impede on parental confidence and parent-child interactions, resulting in adverse psychological outcomes for siblings (Benson & Karlof, 2009; Ishizaki et al., 2005; Kagan & Lewis, 1996).

Given the extra demands and resources needed to care for a child with a disability, parents are often apprehensive about whether typically developing siblings are receiving adequate attention (Naylor & Prescott, 2004; Parker & Stimpson, 2002; Strohm, 2002). While differential parent treatment is evident in most families, Bischoff and Tingstrom (1991) found that siblings of children with a brother or sister with a disability reported greater inconsistency in parenting than their counterparts with typically developing siblings. That is, children perceived that when compared to themselves, the child with a disability was receiving more parental attention and preferential treatment. Different treatment can have a negative impact on psychological adjustment, as demonstrated by McHale and Gamble (1989). These authors found that typically developing siblings are vulnerable to experiencing anxiety and depression if they perceive that their brother or sister with a disability is being treated more favorably. Wolf and colleagues (1998) reported that greater perceptions of differential treatment were associated with internalizing and externalizing behavior problems across siblings of children with a brother or sister with a disability. This finding has been replicated in families of children without disabilities, with differential treatment being associated with low self-esteem and adjustment problems (McHale, Updegraff, Jackson-Newsom, Tucker, & Crouter, 2000). Rivers and Stoneman (2008), in the study described earlier, also investigated the role of differential treatment, and its interaction with sibling level factors, including temperament.

These authors found that persistence influenced how siblings viewed parenting practices. Siblings who scored lower on persistence (as measured by parents and siblings) reported greater dissatisfaction with differential parenting than their counterparts who were higher on persistence. This in turn had a negative impact on the perceived quality of the sibling relationship, and had the potential to influence adjustment (Brody, 2004). The spillover effect into sibling adjustment has been supported by literature focusing on typical sibling dyads where no sibling has a disability, and as such may be evident in families of children with disabilities (Jenkins & Smith, 1990).

It is noted that siblings who score high on persistence are less likely to be concerned about the amount of time parents are spending with the child with an autism spectrum disorder when they are preoccupied with other activities and not concerned about spending time alone. Conversely, when the child with a disability has elevated scores on persistence and is engaged in other activities, parents may be more able to dedicate additional time to the sibling. This is turn is likely to result in more favorable options of parenting practices, and consequently the sibling relationship and adjustment. While Rivers and Stoneman (2008) obtained a measure of sibling satisfaction with differential parenting, few studieshave elicited information from siblings and identified whether typically developing siblings are able to provide an accurate reflection of what is occurring within the family unit, and further how this influences their psychological adjustment. This is a critical question as it may be siblings' perceptions and the attributions that typically developing siblings attach to parental practices that determine whether such treatment has an adverse effect on their psychological adjustment. In a sample of 21 typicallydeveloping siblings of children with cancer, Havermans and Eiser (1994) found that 12siblings identified that they were receiving differential treatment from their parents, which they attributed to the child's illness. While some of these children reported feeling 'jealous' and believed that they were being 'left out' from activities, others perceived that their sibling with cancer 'needed more attention' and that 'it was fair'. As a result of these positive thoughts (e.g., brother/sister with a disability needed it more) around differential parenting, these siblings were not as distressed about the additional attention that their sibling with cancer was receiving when compared to those siblings with more negative thoughts (e.g., being left out).

Social Support

Research has consistently shown that social supports can *directly* and *indirectly* (e.g., through parent-sibling interactions) influence sibling psychological adjustment (Hastings, Thomas, & Delwiche, 2002). Social support can be defined as an interpersonal exchange between two or more people that is intended to enhance wellbeing (Caltabiano et al., 2002). Both informal and formal support falls under the umbrella of social support. Formal supports encompass professionals, for example the early childhood intervention team (e.g., psychologists, speech therapists, occupational therapists), whereas informal supports include people such as grandparents and friends. Within the general population, social support has been found to serve as a buffer to mental and physical illness and has been associated with decreased feelings of loneliness (Caltabiano et al., 2002). Loneliness is characterized by an upsetting feeling that occurs subsequently to perceiving that one's social needs (e.g., the quantity and even more so the quality) are not being fulfilled by one's social relationships (Hawkley & Cacioppo, 2010). When compared to their counterparts who feel socially connected, lonely individuals perceive their environment as threatening, anticipate that they will encounter negative social interactions, and focus on negative social experiences. In an attempt to protect themselves, lonely individuals avoid social situations and consequently opportunities to engage with other people. This is often referred to as the self-reinforcing loneliness loop, which has been shown to be associated with a range of feelings including anger, anxiety, decreased feelings of self-esteem, and depression. Neurobiological changes as a consequence of loneliness have also started to gain attention (Hawkley & Cacioppo, 2010). The direct association between social support, perceived social connectedness, decreased feelings of loneliness and psychological adjustment in siblings of children with disabilities has been considered, however studies have been scarce (Mascha & Boucher, 2006). In one of the few studies that have been conducted in this area, Kaminsky and Dewey (2002) recruited a sample of 90 siblings aged between eight and 18. A primary aim of this study was to ascertain whether feelings of loneliness and socialsupport were associated with psychological adjustment across three groups, including siblings of children with autism, Down syndrome, and those without a brother or sister with a disability . This study fund that perceptions of social support were consistent across the three groups, and that decreased feelings of loneliness, as measured by the Loneliness and Social Dissatisfaction Questionnaire, were associated with higher levels of social support, as measured by the Social Support Scale for Children. Interestingly this study found that both social support and social connectedness were not associated with psychological adjustment, as measured by the Achenbach Child Behaviour Checklist. Kaminsky and Dewey (2002) provide an explanation for this, hypothesizing that this finding may be the result of a well-adjusted sample. Research has also revealed that siblings exhibit more positive feelings and develop an enhanced tolerance towards their brother or sister with a disability when professionals include typically developing siblings into their programs (Mascha & Boucher, 2006). Mascha and Boucher (2006) indicate that this is associated with siblings having an opportunity to explore and express their emotions about the child with a disability and their impact on the family system. In the absence of feeling connected to a secure social network, siblings may be vulnerable to depressive symptoms which may be further exacerbated if they are subjected to a challenging environment outside the home.

Little research has been conducted on siblings' perceived level of loneliness and its association with psychosocial adjustment. This is of particular concern considering that loneliness in children and adolescents has been associated with adjustment problems, anxiety, depression, and increased rates of suicide and absenteeism from school (Davis, 1990). Given the trajectory of loneliness, research is needed to ascertain if siblings of children with disabilities are at an increased risk of loneliness and further how this relates to their adjustment.

The Wider Social Community

A large body of research has identified risk and protective factors at a family level that have been shown to be associated with sibling adjustment (Giallo & Gavidia-Payne, 2006). Given these family level-findings, and the interactive nature of the multiple systems that children operate within, it is possible that factors outside the family context may contribute to the psychological adjustment of brothers or sisters of children with a disability. Conceptually, this is a context which has the potential to nurture and reinforce positive psychological outcomes in children. Despite the rationale and theoretical argument (e.g., Bronfenbrenner's Ecological Systems Theory) that sibling adjustment is shaped by siblings' experiences and interactions within the wider social system, few studies have focused on community level factors, andsibling adjustment (Barr & McLeod, 2010). Mascha and Boucher (2006) conducted a qualitative study with 14 siblings (10females and four males) of children with either Autism of Asperger's syndrome, with siblingsranging in age from 11 to 18 years (mean = 14.73 years). The primary aim of this study was to elicit information from siblings about those aspects of growing up with a brother or sisters with a disability they find rewarding, and those that they find difficult to deal with. Using asemi-structured interview format, information was obtained about siblings' experience bothwithin and outside the family environment. Results indicated that 72% of individuals with a sibling with a disability were bothered by the attitudes of others, and also embarrassed as a result of their sibling behaving inappropriately in public or in the presence of their friends. In the same vein, other research indicates that siblings are often reluctant to invite friends over to their houses or go out as a family as they are fearful of what may happen whilst they are outside of the home (Seligman, 1983). Opperman and Alant(2003) conducted a qualitative study that focused on the experiences of 19 adolescents (aged between 12 and 15 years) growing up with a brother or sister with a severe disability. These authors found that 89% of participants felt that others did not accept their sibling with a disability without discrimination. A comment that supports this contention includes "...the boy told a lot of other people and they started to tease him...I don't like that" (Opperman & Alant, 2003, p. 447). Consistent with these findings, Pit-ten Cate and Loots (2000) found that the awkward reactions of outsiders were associated with feelings of annoyance and distress in a sample of 10 to 18-year-old individuals who had a sibling with a physical disability (e.g., spina bifida, cerebral plasy). Furthermore, the majority of siblings in Stalker and Connors (2004) study reported adverse reactions to seeing their sibling with a disability being 'abused 'or 'humiliated' by others, and often took steps to protect their sibling or retaliate against the perpetrators. In a recent study, Barr and McLeod (2010) considered siblings' experiences within the wider community, focusing on their interactions with strangers, peers and also the family. Using thematic analysis, the contributions made to a children's internet sibling support site were analysed. Results revealed that siblings were embarrassed when stared at by strangers, and were upset by the negative attitudes strangers have towards people with a disability. At a peer level, siblings felt that their friends had difficulties relating to them, used words that upset them, and described being teased about having a brother or sister with a disability.

Considering that it is often difficult to change societal views and reactions towards individuals with a disability, support provided to family members may need to focus on altering the way in which they interpret the actions of others in order to promote greater psychological adjustment..Further research needs to consider sibling perceptions of outsiders' reactions, and understand sibling experiences, including both hassles and uplifts within a community context. To date and with few exceptions (Barr & McLeod, 2010), siblings have not been interviewed abouttheir own experiences, and have not been encouraged to talk openly about the broad range of hassles and uplifts that they encounter on a daily basis. Further, no study has examined siblings' self-reported experiences outside the family environment and linked these experiences to sibling psychological outcomes. Without this information, it is difficult to obtain a holistic understanding of the broad range of experiences that siblings encounter across the multiple systems that they operate, and subsequently the risk and protective factors associated with adjustment.

Disability Factors

Children with disabilities are unique and have specific characteristics that influence sibling adjustment in diverse ways (Macks & Reeve, 2007). When evaluating sibling adjustment, researchers have typically collapsed a small number of children with different disabilities into one group and have overlooked the individual differences that are associated with different disability types (Fisman, Wolf, Ellison, & Freeman, 2000). This is a shortcoming of the research in this area as specific child characteristics such as the severity of the child's disability, defined as the degree of disruption on daily life due to impairment of child functioning across different developmental domains, may be one of the explanations behind why some children adjust more favourably to having a sibling with a disability than others (Floyd & Gallagher, 1997). For instance, a child with more severe disabilities may require greater support and parental attention, which may result in increased stress, and consequently influence parent-sibling interactions and adjustment. Challenging behaviours, including those exhibited by many children with autism and other disabilities, is a key aspect of severity and is another child characteristic that may be troublesome for siblings and the family system as a whole (Floyd & Gallagher, 1997). For parents, child behavioural difficulties including self-injurious behaviours and aggression towards others have been associated with a variety of negative outcomes including increased feelings of burden, depressive symptoms, and poorer family quality of life (Davis & Gavidia- Payne, 2009). Thepresence of behavioural problems has been associated with greater disruptions in family functioning and few recreational activities as parents and siblings are often worried that the child with a disability may act out in public (Ishizaki et al., 2005; Ross and Cuskelly, 2006) found that aggression is the most common type of stressor that siblings of children with autism have to manage in their interactions with their brother or sister, with 84% reporting that it was a concern. Consequently, it may be more informative to focus on how behavioural problems impact sibling adjustment rather than focusing exclusively on disability group membership (Floyd & Gallagher, 1997).Other unique characteristics of a child's disability may influence the nature of the sibling relationship and provide an explanation for the variability in sibling psychological adjustment (Stoneman, 2005). Kaminsky and Dewey (2001) compared sibling relationships in families of children with autism, Down syndrome, and typically developing children, and found that sibling relationships in families of children with autism were characterised by less intimacy, prosocial behaviour and nurturance. Building on this finding, Hastings (2003) reported that siblings of children with autism had more behavioural problems and displayed less pro-social behaviour when compared to siblings of typically developing children. Further research into the area of specific disability characteristics (e.g., behaviour of the child with a disability, severity, disability type), may provide a greater understanding of the variability across measures of sibling adjustment.

Demographic Factors

Demographic characteristics and their association with sibling adjustment have received considerable attention within the sibling literature (Macks& Reeves, 2007). Several studies have revealed that the psychological adjustment of siblings of children with disabilities is dependent on factors such as gender, birth-order, socioeconomic status (SES) and family size (Macks& Reeves, 2007). However, in a similar fashion to other research studies with siblings, findings have been mixed, with some reporting that there are no associations between demographic variables and sibling adjustment (Gold, 1993). Macks and Reeves (2007) recently compared the psychosocial and emotional development of 51 siblings of children of with autism with 35 siblings of typically developing children. Results revealed that multiple demographic risk factors were predictive of psychosocial and emotional adjustment difficulties for siblings of children with autism.

The demographic characteristics found to have a compounding effect on sibling adjustment included being male from a low SES, being older than the child with autism, and having only one sibling. Researchers have endeavored to find an explanation for this finding, with some advocating that in families where there is more than one sibling, household chores and responsibilities are likely to be shared, and siblings will have others they can relate to and compare themselves against (Randall & Parker, 1999). However, some researchers have found no relationship between family size and sibling adjustment (Mates, 1990), whilst others have found that scores on measures of depression and anxiety in siblings of children with disabilities increase as a function of family size (Thompson, Curtner, & O'Rear, 1994).

Socioeconomic status may need to be taken into consideration when assessing the relationship between family size and sibling adjustment. Socioeconomic status has been consequently families with higher incomes may have more resources available to them to meet the needs of all family members (Turnbull & Turnbull, 1990). Despite these findings, other studies have generated contrasting results. Van Riper (2000) recruited 41 siblings of children with Down syndrome, and found that demographic characteristics such as family income, sibling age, age of the child with Down syndrome, and number of children in thefamily were not associated with sibling adjustment.

The studies by Macks and Reeves (2007) and Van Riper (2000) also investigated sibling age and birth order effects as possible correlates of sibling adjustment. Hamana, Ronen and Feigin (2000) controlled for age, and assessed self-control, anxiety, and loneliness in 62 siblings (aged between nine and 18 years) of children with cancer. The results revealed that younger siblings, aged between nine and 16 years reported greater feelings of loneliness than their older counterparts (aged between 14 and 18). By contrast, Madan-Swain, Sexson, Brown and Ragab (1993) found that older siblings were more withdrawn and perceived themselves to be less involved with the family than their younger counterparts.

In an investigation of sibling birth order, Hastings (2003) recruited 22 families of children with autism, and found that typically developing siblings who were younger than their brother or sister with autism engaged in less pro-social behaviour than their typically developing counterparts who were older than their sibling with a disability. By contrast, Hamana and colleagues (2000) found no association between birth order and scores on sibling adjustment with respect to anxiety. This demonstrates that different factors may be contributing to various sibling outcomes, and as such researchers need to extend beyond measuring sibling adjustment as a single construct.

Training and Management of Parents and Siblings

Singerand others in 2007 did a meta-analysis on different interventions and found that parents respond the best to the treatment system which combines all different treatment approach like, cognitive behavioral, parental psycho-education, individualized programming etc. In common with the general research literature on parents of children with behavior problems, most parenting skills training in the field of intellectual disability and autism uses behavioral methods. The focus is typically on skills for managing difficult behavior as well as skills for building more positive child behaviors

Psychodynamic Approach

- **Training on Healthy Coping:** Coping is a way of life. Coping mechanism is the mechanism to reduce stress or anxiety. Dealing everyday with the people with severe disability will be very much trouble some. . The family members of a child with disability have to develop healthy coping mechanisms not only for dealing with their children effectively but staying stress freely.

In an psychological perspective people mainly understand defense mechanism as a few standardised set of mechanisms as projection, rationalization, reaction formation, sublimation etc. But any mode of action by somebody in order to reduce anxiety or defend oneself from stress can be a proper defense mechanism. We mostly read about these as these are the most common one. Healthy and mature mechanisms like, sublimation, displacement or even humour can be utilized in order to get rid of stress and boost self confidence (Mohanty, 1989).

- **Acceptance:** It is the best way to maintain the normalcy in life. Parents & elder siblings do feel bad, angry at times, guilty at times about their disabled family member. But a critical analysis is imperative in this regard to think and analyze the situation. On many situations we have less control and at times even no control. Parents should not worry on such things as this will not help in any way. Rather quick acceptance will give better results in such situations (Hayes, Strosahl & Wilson,2011).
- **Develop Realistic Expectation:** People should understand the nature of the disability and the working limits of their disabled children thoroughly. When they gather all these information, gradually they will develop realistic expectation. Along with the acquisition of realistic expectation, their anxiety level will lower down. Also they will stop comparing their normally developing child or children with that of the child who has problem (HayesStrosahl& Wilson,2011).
- **Sharing Problems:** Sharing their problems honestly to a group of people on whom the y can confide will be really helpful. Not only this way their problems gradually will be lessened but also they will come to learn new copings and will get a new hopes for living life meaningfully (Singh. A, 2004).
- **Ego Analysis and Ego Strengthening:** The layman understanding of "Ego" is very different from a psychological understanding of "Ego". "Ego" is the most responsible department of human psyche whose function determines the nature of the person. It majorly does three types of actions. These are,
    - Maintaining balance between Id and Super ego.
    - Applying defense mechanisms.
    - Managing all higher Cognitive Processes (thinking, reasoning, planning etc) (Hall & Lindzey, 2004).

In simpler terms when we do Ego analysis we understand our inner self thoroughly.

We understand our needs, our aspirations, our current situations, our problems; we understand each bit of everything that matters to our happiness, our well being.

When we go for an "Ego Analysis", simply by our own understanding, or by the help of any healer (psychological or spiritual) we we what we are doing and what we should do for our betterment. Thus we understand and realize the gap. When we realize the lacune in our thought and action we feel urged to make some concrete action plan in order to eradicate the darkness which has shadowed our life (Wolberg, L.R, 2013).

When at conscious level Ego becomes strong, it gradually starts working even at unconscious level, which is presumed to occupy most levels of human psyche.

Thus with this insight parents with all stress, negative, pessimistic thought and action will gradually feel motivated to do corrective actions for their children, also will try to contribute for themselves and will be able to maintain a peaceful & meaningful life.

Family Systems Approach

- **Family Counselling and Family Therapy:** Both family counselling and family therapy can be therapeutically applied to parents of a disabled child depending upon the situations. Family Therapy is the suitable application of psycho-therapy in a familial situation. It can be Structural, Systemic, Strategic, behavior therapy, Cognitive behavior therapy or psychodynamic therapy to recognized family members who ever require the therapy. Family Therapy is highly indicated for the family members with a disabled child in the family as all the basic family dynamics of a family like, leadership, family structure, roles, responsibility, communication etc gets impaired in such family (Schwartz. R, 2001).

    - **Systemic Family Therapy:** Interest in using Systemic approach in families with intellectual disabilities has grown since 1980s. Higher emotional stress at different life cycle transition, which might get exuberated by the experience of discrimination and blame. These difficulties may more appropriately addressed through family therapy as it considers life cycles and power issues as integral. Secondly there are often concerns about the interaction with the wider care system (Fidell, 2000). Families are often involved with many activities which can impair the boundary between the parental and agency responsibility(Vetere& others 2003). The Systemic approach is very useful here in negotiating the complexity of relationships and communications between different subsystems which can be confusing for family members.(Mitchell & Slopper,2000).Turner & Black 1980),Schulman (1988)., all gave examples where systemic family therapy have been successfully used with children and families.
    - **Behavioural Family Therapy:** Behavioral principles were used in family to reduce stress in parents, siblings, and even the children suffering from intellectual disabilities. The unwanted stress, anxiety, maladaptive coping styles are modified & new adaptive patterns & positive behavioral approach to leave in peace and satisfaction are taught through proper applications of reinforces and punishers. Deep relaxation with relaxing imagery is of great use in this context. Supporting evidences are provided by Keith Marshall, Jan Ferris(2012).
    - **Bownian Family Therapy:** Bownian family therapy is based on several basic assumptions like differentiation of self, nuclear family emotional system, triangles, family Projection Process, multigenerational transmission process, emotional cut-off, sibling position and societal emotional Process etc. All these assumptions are of vital importance in resolving the most frequently occurring problems and difficulties in the families of intellectual disabilities. Parents often feel stressed because of having a intellectually disabled child because of the perception of society, and expectations. Multigenerational transmission and societal emotional process, these two principles are basically orienting the family members of such issues and resolving the same. Family projection processes is a very effective methodology for spreading awareness amongst the parents on their maladaptive style of dealing, also teaches them healthy coping mechanisms for a better life. As a whole Brownian model is extremely effective in dealing with all varieties of problems occurring in a family .(Bowen M, 1978).
    - **Strategic Family Therapy:** In BSFT, whenever possible, preserving the family is desirable. While family preservation is important, two goals must be set: to eliminate or reduce the adolescent's use of drugs and associated problem behaviors, known as "symptom focus," and to change the family interactions that are associated with the adolescent's drug abuse, known as

"system focus." An example of the latter occurs when families direct their negative feelings toward the drug-abusing youth. The parents' negativity toward the adolescent directly affects his or her drug abuse, and the adolescent's drug abuse increases the parents' negativity. At the family systems level, the counselor intervenes to change the way family members act toward each other (i.e., patterns of interaction). This will prompt family members to speak and act in ways that promote more positive family interaction, which, in turn, will make it possible for the adolescent to reduce his or her drug abuse and other problematic behaviors. (Szapocznik,Schwartz, Muir &Brown,, 2012).

CONCLUDING REMARK

Having a child with an intellectual disability can impose financial, social and physical stress on the family (Mak & Ho, 2007). Research has shown that caregivers of children with disabilities experience greater stress than caregivers of children without disabilities (Hassall, Rose, & McDonald, 2005). Similarly, Baker et al. (2003) have shown that parents of young children with developmental delays report experiencing greater stress than parents of children without delays. Although a number of factors can contribute to the increased level of stress experienced by caregivers of children with delays, severity of the child's behavior problems is often the strongest predictor of parental stress (Baker et al., 2003; Floyd & Gallagher, 1997; Hassall, Rose, & McDonald, 2005; Nachshen, Garcin, & Minnes, 2005).

Having a major role in the care and management of their children, it is eminent to identify the stressors in the parents and other involved family member and to take necessary course of action, in terms of parental training and therapies etc. Parental Counselling, Psycho-education, parental training, and various types of psychotherapies starting from Psychoanalytic to positive psychotherapies and family therapies are best suited in this regard.

REFERENCES

Achenbach, T. M., & Edelbrock, C. (1983). *Manual for the child behavior checklist and revised child behaviour profile*. Burlington, VT: Queen City Printers.

Baker, B. L., Blacher, J., Crnic, K., & Edelbrock, C. (2002). Behavior problems and parenting stress in families of three-year-old children with and without developmental delays. *American Journal of Mental Retardation*, *107*(6), 433–444. doi:10.1352/0895-8017(2002)107<0433:BPAPSI>2.0.CO;2 PMID:12323068

Baker, B. L., McIntyre, L. L., Blacher, J., Crnic, K., Edelbrock, C., & Low, C. (2003). Pre-school children with and without developmental delay: Behaviour problems and parenting stress over time. *Journal of Intellectual Disability Research*, *47*(4-5), 217–230. doi:10.1046/j.1365-2788.2003.00484.x PMID:12787154

Barr, J., & McLeod, S. (2010). They never see how hard it is to be me: Siblings' observations of strangers, peers and family. *International Journal of Speech-Language Pathology*, *12*(2), 162–171. doi:10.3109/17549500903434133 PMID:20420357

Beckman, P. J. (1991). Comparison of mothers' and fathers' perceptions of the effect of young children with and without disabilities. *American Journal of Mental Retardation, 95*, 585–595. PMID:2043351

Begab, M. J., & Richardson, S. A. (1975). *The mentally retarded and society: A social Perspective*. London University Press.

Benson, P., & Karlof, K. L. (2009). Anger, stress proliferation, and depressed mood among parents of children with ASD: A longitudinal replication. *Journal of Autism and Developmental Disorders, 39*(2), 350–362. doi:10.1007/s10803-008-0632-0 PMID:18709548

Berk, L. E. (2006). *Child development* (7th ed.). Boston: Allyn & Bacon.

Bischoff, L. B., & Tingstrom, D. H. (1991). Siblings of children with disabilities: Psychological and behavioral characteristics. *Counselling Psychology Quarterly, 4*(4), 311–321. doi:10.1080/09515079108254439

Blacher, J., Neece, C. L., & Paczkowski, E. (2005). Families and intellectual disability. *Current Opinion in Psychiatry, 18*(5), 507–513. doi:10.1097/01.yco.0000179488.92885.e8 PMID:16639109

Bos, A. E. R., Muris, P., Mulkens, S., & Schaalma, H. P. (2006). Changing self-esteem in children and adolescents: A roadmap for future interventions. *Netherlands Journal of Psychology, 62*(1), 26–33. doi:10.1007/BF03061048

Bowen, M. (1978). *Family therapy in clinical practice*. New York: Aronson.

Brinker, R. P., Seifer, R., & Smeroff, A. J. (1994). Relations among maternal stress, cognitive development, and early intervention in middle and low SEC infants with developmental disabilities. (I). *American Journal of Mental Retardation, 98*, 463–480. PMID:8148123

Bristol, M. M., & Schopler, E. (1984). A Developmental Perspective on Stress and Coping in Families of Autistic Children. *Journal of Educational and Social Research.*

Brody, G. (2004). Siblings' direct and indirect contributions to child development. *Current Directions in Psychological Science, 13*(3), 124–126. doi:10.1111/j.0963-7214.2004.00289.x

Brown, R. T., & Pacini, J. N. (1989). Perceived family functioning, marital status, and depression in parents of boys with attention deficit disorder. *Journal of Learning Disabilities, 22*(9), 581–587. doi:10.1177/002221948902200911 PMID:2809411

Caltabiano, M. L., Sarafino, E. P., Byrne, D., & Martin, P. R. (2002). *Health Psychology: Biopsychosocial Interactions*. Milton: John Wiley & Sons.

Conger, R., Patterson, G. R., & Ge, X. (1995). It takes two to replicate: A mediational model for the impact of parents' stress on adolescent adjustment. *Child Development, 66*(1), 80–97. doi:10.2307/1131192 PMID:7497831

Cummings, S. T. (1976). The impact of the child's deficiency on the father: A study of fathers of mentally retarded and chronically ill children. *The American Journal of Orthopsychiatry, 46*(2), 246–255. doi:10.1111/j.1939-0025.1976.tb00925.x PMID:1266948

Cuskelly, M., & Dadds, M. (1992). Behaviour problems in children with Down syndrome and their siblings. *Journal of Child Psychology and Psychiatry, and Allied Disciplines*, *33*(4), 749–761. doi:10.1111/j.1469-7610.1992.tb00910.x PMID:1534811

Davis, B. (1990). Loneliness in children and adolescents. *Issues in Comprehensive Pediatric Nursing*, *13*(1), 59–69. doi:10.3109/01460869009009745 PMID:2391259

Davis, H. (1985). Counselling parents of children who have intellectual disabilities. *Early Child Development and Care*, *22*(1), 19–35. doi:10.1080/0300443850220102

Davis, K., & Gavidia-Payne, S. (2009). The impact of child, family, and professional support characteristics on the quality of life in families of young children with disabilities. *Journal of Intellectual & Developmental Disability*, *34*(2), 153–162. doi:10.1080/13668250902874608 PMID:19404836

Davis, P. B., & May, J. E. (1991). Involving fathers in early intervention and family support programs: *Issues and strategies. Children's Health Care*, *20*(2), 87–92. doi:10.1207/s15326888chc2002_3

Dishion, T. J., & Stormshak, E. (2007). Intervening in children's lives: An ecological, family- centered approach to mental health care. Washington, DC: Academic Press.

Dyken, E. M. (2005). Happiness, well-being, and character strengths: Outcomes for families and siblings of persons with mental retardation. *American Association on Mental Retardation*, *43*, 360–364. PMID:16131234

Dyson, L. L. (1991). Families of young children with handicaps: Parental stress and family functioning. *American Journal of Mental Retardation*, *95*, 623–629. PMID:1829374

Eisenberg, L. (1957). The fathers of autistic children. *The American Journal of Orthopsychiatry*, *27*(4), 715–724. doi:10.1111/j.1939-0025.1957.tb05539.x PMID:13470021

Emerson, E. (2003). Mothers of children and adolescents with intellectual disability: Social and economic situation, mental health status, and the self-assessed social and psychological impact of the child's difficulties. *Journal of Intellectual Disability Research*, *47*(4-5), 385–399. doi:10.1046/j.1365-2788.2003.00498.x PMID:12787168

Emerson, E. (2004). Poverty and children with intellectual disabilities in the world's richer countries. *Journal of Intellectual & Developmental Disability*, *29*(4), 319–337. doi:10.1080/13668250400014491

Faux, S. A. (1993). Siblings of children with chronic physical and cognitive disabilities. *Journal of Pediatric Nursing*, *8*, 305–317. Retrieved from http://www.sciencedirect.com.ezproxy.lib.rmit.edu.au/science/journal/08825963 PMID:8271152

Ferraioli, S. J., & Harris, S. L. (2010). The impact of autism on siblings. *Social Work in Mental Health*, *8*(1), 41–53. doi:10.1080/15332980902932409

Fisman, S., Wolf, L., Ellison, D., & Freeman, T. (2000). A longitudinal study of children with chronic disabilities. *Canadian Journal of Psychiatry*, *45*, 369–375. PMID:10813071

Floyd, F. J., & Gallagher, E. M. (1997). Parental stress, care demands, and use of support services for school-age children with disabilities and behavior problems. *Family Relations*, *46*(4), 359–371. doi:10.2307/585096

Floyd, F. J., & Gallagher, E. M. (1997). Parental stress, care demands, and use of support services for school-age children with disabilities and behavior problems. *Family Relations*, *46*(4), 359–371. doi:10.2307/585096

Floyd, F. J., & Phillippe, K. A. (1993). Parental interactions with children with and without mental retardation: Behavior management, coerciveness, and positive exchange. *American Journal of Mental Retardation*, *97*, 673–684. PMID:7686014

Gallo, A. M., Breitmayer, B. J., Knafl, K. A., & Zoeller, L. H. (1993). Mothers' perceptions of sibling adjustment and family life in childhood chronic illness. *Journal of Pediatric Nursing*, *8*, 318–324. PMID:8271153

Gamble, W. C., & McHale, S. M. (1989). Coping with stress in sibling relationships: A. comparison of children with disabled and nondisabled siblings. *Journal of Applied Developmental Psychology*, *10*(3), 353–373. doi:10.1016/0193-3973(89)90035-X

Gerstein, E. D., Crnic, K. A., Blacher, J., & Baker, B. L. (2009). Resilience and the course of daily parenting stress in families of young children with intellectual disabilities. *Journal of Intellectual Disability Research*, *53*(12), 981–997. doi:10.1111/j.1365-2788.2009.01220.x PMID:19874449

Giallo, R., & Gavidia-Payne, S. (2006). Child, parent and family factors as predictors of adjustment for siblings of children with a disability. *Journal of Intellectual Disability Research*, *50*(12), 937–948. doi:10.1111/j.1365-2788.2006.00928.x PMID:17100954

Gold, N. (1993). Depression and social adjustment in siblings of boys with autism. *Journal of Autism and Developmental Disorders*, *23*(1), 147–163. doi:10.1007/BF01066424 PMID:8463194

Grissom, M. O., & Borkowski, J. G. (2002). Self-efficacy in adolescents who have siblings with or without disabilities. *American Journal of Mental Retardation*, *107*(2), 79–90. doi:10.1352/0895-8017(2002)107<0079:SEIAWH>2.0.CO;2 PMID:11853525

Guralnick, M. J. (2004). Family investments in response to the developmental challenges of young children with disabilities. In A. Kalil & T. Deleire (Eds.), *Family investments in children's potential: Resources and parenting behaviors that promote success* (pp. 119–137). Mahwah, NJ: Lawrence Erlbaum.

Hall, C.S., Lindzey, G., & Campbell, J.B. (2004). Sigmund Freud's Classical Psychoanalytic Theory. In *Theories of Personality*. John Wiley & Sons, Inc.

Hamana, R., Ronen, T., & Feigin, R. (2000). Self-control, anxiety, and loneliness in siblings of children with cancer. *Social Work in Health Care*, *31*(1), 63–83. doi:10.1300/J010v31n01_05 PMID:10989875

Harmer Cox, A., Marshell, E., Mandlesco, B., & Olsen, S. (2003). Coping responses to daily life stressors of children who have a sibling with a disability. *Journal of Family Nursing*, *9*(4), 397–413. doi:10.1177/1074840703258328

Hassall, R., Rose, J., & McDonald, J. (2005). Parenting stress in mothers of children with an intellectual disability: The effects of parental cognitions in relation to child characteristics and family support. *Journal of Intellectual Disability Research*, *49*(6), 405–418. doi:10.1111/j.1365-2788.2005.00673.x PMID:15882391

Hastings, R. P. (2003). Brief report: Behavioral adjustment of siblings of children with autism. *Journal of Autism and Developmental Disorders, 33,* 99-104. doi: 0162- 3257/03/0200-0099/0

Hastings, R. P., Thomas, H., & Delwiche, N. (2002). Grandparent support for families of children with Downs syndrome. *Journal of Applied Research in Intellectual Disabilities*, *15*, 97–104. doi:10.1046/j.1360-2322.2001.00097.x

Havermans, T., & Eiser, C. (1994). Siblings of children with cancer. *Child: Care, Health and Development*, *20*(5), 309–322. doi:10.1111/j.1365-2214.1994.tb00393.x PMID:7988001

Hawkley, L. C., & Cacioppo, J. T. (2010). Loneliness matters: A theoretical and empirical review of consequences and mechanisms. *Annals of Behavioral Medicine*, *40*(2), 218–227. doi:10.1007/s12160-010-9210-8 PMID:20652462

Hayes, S. C., Strosahl, K. D., & Wilson, K. G. (2011). *Acceptance and Commitment Therapy and Mindfulness for Chronic Pain: Model, Process, and Progress*. Retrieved from the Web:https://www.apa.org/pubs/journals/releases/amp-a0035623.pdf

Hewett, S. (1975). Telling the family; A review of some relevant research and opinion. In S. Berie & W. Cuy (Eds.), *Right from the start: A service for families with young handicapped*. London: National Society for Mentally Handicapped Children.

Hoppes, K., & Harris, S. L. (1990). Perceptions of Child Attachment and Maternal Gratification in Mothers of Children with Autism and Down Syndrome. *Journal of Clinical Child Psychology*, *19*(4), 365–370. doi:10.1207/s15374424jccp1904_8

Hornby, G. (1992). A review of fathers' accounts of their experiences of parenting children with disabilities. *Disability, Handicap & Society*, *7*(4), 363–374. doi:10.1080/02674649266780431

Ishizaki, Y., Ishizaki, T., Ozawa, K., Fukai, Y., Hattori, Y., Taniuchi, S., & Kobayashi, Y. (2005). Psychosocial problems among siblings of children with disabilities in Japan: Psychosocial association between mothers and siblings. *Journal of Developmental and Physical Disabilities*, *17*(2), 119–132. doi:10.1007/s10882-005-3684-5

Jackson, C., Richer, J., & Edge, J. A. (2008). Sibling psychological adjustment to type 1 diabetes mellitus. *Pediatric Diabetes*, *9*(4pt1), 308–311. doi:10.1111/j.1399-5448.2008.00385.x PMID:18466212

Jenkins, J., & Smith, M. A. (1990). Factors protecting children living in disharmonious homes: Maternal reports. *Journal of the American Academy of Child and Adolescent Psychiatry*, *29*(1), 60–69. doi:10.1097/00004583-199001000-00011 PMID:2295580

Jones, G. (1997). Disabling Children: Autism, the Effect on Families and Professionals. *Educational and Child Psychology*, *14*(3), 71–76.

Kagan, C., & Lewis, S. (1996). Families with parents who have multiple commitments. In M. Moore, J. Sixsmith, K. Knowles, C. Kagan, S. Lewis, S. Beazley, & U. Rout (Eds.), *Children's reflections of family life* (pp. 29–51). London: The Falmer Press.

Kaminsky, L., & Dewey, D. (2002). Psychosocial adjustment in siblings of children with autism. *Journal of Child Psychology and Psychiatry, and Allied Disciplines*, *43*(2), 225–232. http://onlinelibrary.wiley.com/journal/ doi:10.1111/1469-7610.00015 PMID:11902601

Lamb, M. E., & Billings, L. A. L. (1997). Fathers of children with special needs. In M. E. Lamb (Ed.), *The role of the father in child development* (3rd ed., pp. 179–190). New York: John Wiley & Sons.

MacDonald, E. E., Hastings, R. P., & Fitzsimons, E. (2010). Psychological Acceptance Mediates the Impact of the Behaviour Problems of Children with Intellectual Disability on Fathers' Psychological Adjustment. *Journal of Applied Research in Intellectual Disabilities*, *23*(1), 27–37. doi:10.1111/j.1468-3148.2009.00546.x

Macks, R. J., & Reeve, R. E. (2007). The adjustment of non-disabled siblings of children with autism. *Journal of Autism and Developmental Disorders*, *37*(6), 1060–1067. doi:10.1007/s10803-006-0249-0 PMID:17072750

Madan-Swain, A., Sexson, S. B., Brown, R.T., & Ragab, A. (1993). Family adaptation and coping among siblings of cancer patients, their brothers & sisters and nonclinical controls. *American Journal of Family Therapy*, *21*, 60–70.

Mak, W. S., & Ho, S. M. (2007). Caregiving perceptions of Chinese mothers of children with intellectual disability in Hong Kong. *Journal of Applied Research in Intellectual Disabilities*, *20*(2), 145–156. doi:10.1111/j.1468-3148.2006.00309.x

Mandleco, B., Olsen, S. F., Dyches, T., & Marshall, E. (2003). The relationship between family and sibling functioning in families raising a child with a disability. *Journal of Family Nursing*, *9*(4), 365–396. doi:10.1177/1074840703258329

Marshall, K., & Ferris, J. (2012). Utilizingbehavioral family therapy (BFT) to help support the system around a person with intellectual disability and complex mental health needs: A case study. *Intellect Disabil.*, *16*(2), 109–118. doi:10.1177/1744629512443619 PMID:22496309

Mascha, K., & Boucher, J. (2006). Preliminary investigation of a qualitative method of examining siblings' experiences of living with a child with ASD. *British Journal of Developmental Disabilities*, *52*(102), 19–28. doi:10.1179/096979506799103659

Mash, E. J., & Wolfe, D. A. (2002). *Abnormal Child Psychology* (3rd ed.). Belmont, CA: Wadsworth Group. American Psychiatric Association.

Mates, T. E. (1990). Siblings of autistic children: Their adjustment and performance at home and in school. *Journal of Autism and Developmental Disorders*, *20*(4), 545–553. doi:10.1007/BF02216059 PMID:2279972

McHale, S. M., & Gamble, W. C. (1989). Sibling relationships of children with disabled and non-disabled brothers and sisters. *Developmental Psychology*, *25*(3), 421–429. doi:10.1037/0012-1649.25.3.421

McHale, S. M., Updegraff, K. A., Jackson-Newsom, J., Tucker, C. J., & Crouter, A. C. (2000). When does parents' differential treatment have negative implications for siblings? *Social Development*, *9*(2), 149–172. doi:10.1111/1467-9507.00117

Meyer, D., Vadasky, P., & Fewell, R. (1982). Involving fathers of handicapped infants: Translating research into program goals. *Journal of the Division for Early Childhood, 5.*

Mohanty, G. (1989). Mental Retardation. In *Text Book of Abnormal Psychology*. New Delhi: Kalyani Publishers.

Mohanty, G. (1989). *The Ego and its DefenseMechanism. Text book of Abnormal Psychology*. New Delhi: Kalyani Publishers.

Moore, K. A., & Keyes, C. L. M. (2003). Introduction. In M. H. Bornstein, L. Davidson, C. L. M. Keyes, & K. A. Moore (Eds.), *Wellbeing: Positive development across the life- course* (pp. 1–11). Mahwah, NJ: Lawrence Erlbaum.

Nachshen, J. S., Garcin, N., & Minnes, P. (2005). Problem behaviour in children with intellectual disabilities: Parenting stress, empowerment and school services. *Mental Health Aspects of Developmental Disabilities*, *8*, 105–114.

Nalavany, B. A., Glidden, L. M., & Ryan, S. D. (2009). Parental satisfaction in the adoption of children with learning disorders: The role of behavior problems. *Family Relations*, *58*(5), 621–633. doi:10.1111/j.1741-3729.2009.00579.x

Naylor, A., & Prescott, P. (2004). Invisible children? The need for support groups for siblings of disabled children. *British Journal of Special Education*, *31*(4), 199–206. doi:10.1111/j.0952-3383.2004.00355.x

O'Brien, I., Duffy, A., & Nicholl, H. (2009). Impact of childhood chronic illnesses on siblings: *A literature review. British Journal of Nursing (Mark Allen Publishing)*, *18*, 1360–1365. PMID:20081690

Olsson, M. B., & Hwang, C. P. (2008). Relationships Among Risk, Sense of Coherence, and Well-Being in Parents of Children With and Without Intellectual Disabilities. *Journal of Policy and Practice in Intellectual Disabilities*, *5*(4), 227–236. doi:10.1111/j.1741-1130.2008.00184.x

Opperman, S., & Alant, E. (2003). The coping of the adolescent siblings of children with severe disabilities. *Disability and Rehabilitation*, *25*(9), 441–454. doi:10.1080/0963828031000069735 PMID:12745939

Parker, J., & Stimpson, J. (2002). *Sibling rivalry, sibling love*. London: Hodder & Stoughton.

Petalas, M. A., Hastings, R. P., Nash, S., Lloyd, T., &Dowey, A. (2009). Emotional and behavioural adjustment in siblings of children with intellectual disability with and without autism. *Autism, 13*, 417-483. doi: 10.1177/1362361309335721

Pic-ten Care, L. M., & Loors, G. M. P. (2000). Experiences of siblings of children with physical disabilities: An empirical investigation. *Disability and Rehabilitation*, *22*, 399–408. doi:10.1080/096382800406013 PMID:10894203

Randall, P. E., & Parker, J. (1999). *Supporting the families of children with autism*. Chichester, UK: Wiley & Sons.

Rhodes, P. (2003). Behavioural and family systems interventions in developmental disability: Towards a contemporary and integrative approach. *Journal of Intellectual & Developmental Disability*, *28*(1), 51–64. doi:10.1080/1366825031000086894

Risdal, D., & Singer, G. H. (2004). Marital adjustment in parents of children with disabilities: A historical review and meta-analysis. *Research and Practice for Persons with Severe Disabilities*, *29*(2), 95–103. doi:10.2511/rpsd.29.2.95

Rivers, J., & Stoneman, Z. (2003). Sibling relationships when a child has autism: Marital stress and support coping Disorders. *Journal of Autism and Developmental*, *33*, 383-394. doi: 0162-3257/03/0800-0383/0

Robbins, F. R., Dunlap, G., & Plienis, A. J. (1991). Family Characteristics, FamilyTraining and the Progress of Young Children with Autism. *Journal of Early Intervention*, *15*(2), 173–184. doi:10.1177/105381519101500206

Rodrigue, J. R., Geffken, G. R., & Morgan, S. B. (1993). Perceived competence and behavioural adjustment of siblings of children with autism. *Journal of Autism and Developmental Disorders, 23,* 665–674. doi: 0162-3257/93/0900-0665

Rodrigue, J. R., Morgan, S. B., & Gefken, G. (1990). Families of Autistic Children: Psychological Functioning of Mothers. *Journal of Clinical Psychology*, *19*, 371–379.

Rosenbaum, P. L., King, S., Law, M., King, G., & Evans, J. (1998). Family-centred service: A conceptual framework and research review. *Physical & Occupational Therapy in Pediatrics*, *18*, 1–20. Retrieved from http://informahealthcare.com.ezproxy.lib.rmit.edu.au/loi/pop

Ross, P., & Cuskelly, M. (2006). Adjustment, sibling problems and coping strategies of brothers and sisters of children with autistic spectrum disorder. *Journal of Intellectual & Developmental Disability*, *31*(2), 77–86. doi:10.1080/13668250600710864 PMID:16782592

Rossiter, L., & Sharpe, D. (2001). The siblings of individuals with mental retardation: A quantitative integration of the literature. *Journal of Child and Family Studies*, *10*(1), 65–84. doi:10.1023/A:1016629500708

Ryan, S. (2005). People don't do odd, do they? Mothers making sense of the reactions of others towards their learning disabled children in public places. *Children's Geographies*, *3*(3), 291–305. doi:10.1080/14733280500352920

Saloviita, T., Italinna, M., & Leinonen, E. (2003). Explaining the parental stress of fathers and mothers caring for a child with intellectual disability: A double ABCX model. *Journal of Intellectual Disability Research*, *47*(4-5), 300–312. doi:10.1046/j.1365-2788.2003.00492.x PMID:12787162

Schilling, R. F. II, & Schinke, S. P. (1984). Personal coping and social support for parents of handicapped children. *Children and Youth Services Review*, *6*(3), 195–206. doi:10.1016/0190-7409(84)90060-4

Schulman, B. H., & Mosak, H. H. (1988). *Manual for Life Style Assessment*. Muncie, IN: Accelerated Development.

Schuntermann, P. (2007). The sibling experience: Growing up with a child who has pervasive developmental disorder or mental retardation. *Harvard Review of Psychiatry*, *15*(3), 93–108. doi:10.1080/10673220701432188 PMID:17510829

Schwartz, R. (2001). *Introduction to Internal Family Systems Model.* Trailheads Publications Oak Park.

Seligman, M. (1983). Siblings of handicapped persons. In M. Seligman (Ed.), *The Family with a Handicapped Child: Understanding and Treatment* (pp. 147–174). Orlando, FL: Grune & Stratton, Inc.

Shonkoff, J. P., & Phillips, D. A. (2000). *Committee on Integrating the Science of Early Childhood Development. From Neurons to Neighborhoods: The Science of Early Childhood Development.* Washington, DC: National Academies Press.

Singer, G. H., Ethridge, B. L., & Aldana, S. I. (2007). Primary and secondary effects of parenting and stress management interventions for parents of children with developmental disabilities: A meta-analysis. *Mental Retardation and Developmental Disabilities Research Reviews, 13*(4), 357–369. doi:10.1002/mrdd.20175 PMID:17979202

Singh, A. (2004). *Hand book of Behavioral Sciences.* New Delhi: Galgotia Publishers.

Singhi, P., Malhi, P., & Dwarka, P. (2002). Psychological adjustment of siblings of children with disabilities. *Journal of Personality and Clinical Studies, 18*, 9–18.

Skotko, B. G., & Levine, S. P. (2006). What the other children are thinking: Brothers and sisters of persons with Down syndrome. *American Journal of Medical Genetics, 143*(C), 180–186. doi:10.1002/ajmg.c.30101 PMID:16823778

Smith, T. B., Oliver, M. N. I., & Innocenti, M. S. (2001). Parenting stress in families of children with disabilities. *The American Journal of Orthopsychiatry, 71*(2), 257–261. doi:10.1037/0002-9432.71.2.257 PMID:11347367

Stalker, K., & Connors, C. (2004). Children's perceptions of their disabled siblings: "She's different but it's normal for us. *Children & Society, 18*(3), 218–230. doi:10.1002/chi.794

Stawski, M., Auerbach, J. G., Barasch, M., Lerner, Y., & Zimin, R. (1997). Behavioral problems of children with chronic physical illness and their siblings. *European Child and Adolescent Psychiatry Journal, 6*(1), 20–25. doi:10.1007/BF00573636 PMID:9112043

Stoneman, Z. (2005). Siblings of children with disabilities: Research themes. *Mental Retardation, 43*, 339–350. PMID:16131231

Strohm, K. (2002). *Siblings: Brothers and sisters of children with special needs. Kent Town.* Wakefield Press.

The ICD-10 Classification of Mental and Behavioral Disorders Clinical descriptions and diagnostic guidelines. (2004). World Health Organization.

The UN Convention on the Rights of the Child. (n.d.). *Tenth Report of the session 2002-03.* House of Commons. London: The Stationery Office Limited.

Thompson, A., Curtner, M., & O'Rear, M. (1994). The psychosocial adjustment of well siblings of chronically ill children. *Children's Health Care, 23*(3), 211–226. doi:10.1207/s15326888chc2303_5

Tommasone, L., & Tommasone, J. (1989). *Adjusting to Your Child's Diagnosis.* Bethesda, MD: Woodbine House.

Turnbull, A., Turnbull, R., Erwin, E., & Soodak, L. (2006). *Families, professionals and exceptionality: Positive outcomes through partnerships and trust* (5th ed.). Upper Saddle River, NJ: Pearson/Merrill Prentice Hall.

Van Riper, M. (2000). Family variables associated with wellbeing in siblings of children with Down Syndrome. *Journal of Family Nursing*, *6*(3), 267–286. doi:10.1177/107484070000600305

Verte, S., Roeyers, H., & Busse, A. (2003). Behavioral problems, social competence and Self-concept in siblings of children with autism. *Child: Care, Health and Development*, *29*(3), 193–205. doi:10.1046/j.1365-2214.2003.00331.x PMID:12752610

Vetere, A., & Dallos, R. (2003). *Working Systemically with Families*. London: Karnac.

Walsh, F. (2003). Family resilience: A framework for clinical practice. *Family Process*, *42*(1), 1–18. doi:10.1111/j.1545-5300.2003.00001.x PMID:12698595

Williams, P. D. (1997). Siblings and pediatric chronic illness: A review of the literature. *International Journal of Nursing Studies*, *34*(4), 312–323. doi:10.1016/S0020-7489(97)00019-9 PMID:9306166

Wolberg, L. R. (2013). *The Techniques of Psychotherapy*. Chevy Chase, MD: International Psychotherapy Institute E-Books.

Wolf, L., Fisman, S., Ellison, D., & Freeman, T. (1998). Effect of sibling perception of differential parental treatment in siblings dyads with one disabled child. *Journal of the American Academy of Child and Adolescent Psychiatry*, *37*(12), 1317–1325. doi:10.1097/00004583-199812000-00016 PMID:9847505

Wood, L. W., Sherman, E., Hamiwka, L. D., Blackman, R. N., & Wirrell, E. (2008). Depression, anxiety, and quality of life in siblings of children with intractable epilepsy. *Epilepsy & Behavior*, *13*(1), 144–148. doi:10.1016/j.yebeh.2008.03.012 PMID:18456563

KEY TERMS AND DEFINITIONS

Bowen's Family Therapy: A Psychoanalytic oriented therapy in which the values, thoughts, and experiences of family members are deeply analysed based on certain core principles of this approach.

Ego Analysis: A Psychoanalytic technique in which ego functioning is analysedfor deeper understanding the client.

Family Therapy: Proper application of Psychotherapy in family members involved in a mental health issue in a family.

Intellectual Disability: Refers to a disability, featured by marked deficient intelligence & social adaptability, manifested during developmental period.

Psychiatric Disorders: A mental illness that interferes with personal, occupational, professional and social life of the person significantly.

Strategic Family Therapy: A time limited psychotherapy in which scientific strategies are made for each specific problem in a family.

Systemic Family Therapy: A psychotherapy in which positive changes are brought in terms of the systems of basic family dynamics.

Chapter 6
Stress and Resilience in Parents of Intellectually Disabled Children

K. R. Santhosh
Jain University, India

ABSTRACT

The present study is an attempt to find out the factors of stress that could act against the resilience in the parents of intellectually disabled children. The sample consisted of 50 parents of intellectually disabled children from different panchayats in the Calicut, Kannur, Wayanad districts in the state of Kerala, India. Resilience in the parents was measured using "Bharathiar University Resilience Scale" developed by Annalakshmi (2009). To measure stress among the parents "Stress Scale for Parents of mentally challenged (SPMC)", developed by Rejitha, Biji and Jayan (2005) was used. As per the results, extra-familial stress was a negative predictor of resilience in the parents of the intellectually disabled children. Results further indicated that the parents who were in a late part of the young adulthood period and old were relatively more resilient than the parents who were in the earlier part of the young adulthood period.

INTRODUCTION

Raising a child with an intellectual disability is a stressful experience for parents (Khadi & Hidangmayum, 2012). Numerous psychological and social factors contribute to this distress (Gohel, Mukherjee, & Choudhary, 2011). It starts by the birth of such a child, which is considered as an accident faced by the family. Initially, it will be difficult to accept as a reality. Later, during the commencement of acceptance, parents and close relatives will start formulating different complex speculations regarding the observation of the society on them. Intrapersonal and interpersonal responses to the accepted reality are deeply associated with their identification regarding these speculations as either true or false. These speculations, as well as certain stressors, will together intervene in such a way that it would reduce hope and expectations and ultimately, the self-esteem of the parents. Distress in the parents is thus multidimensional, and the whole of this distress is more than the sum of its parts.

DOI: 10.4018/978-1-5225-0089-6.ch006

Major stressors faced by the parents include problem behaviours of the children, financial difficulties, the dilemma to face the professionals, flaws in one's own parenting style etc. Among these, the most prominent stressor that negatively influences the quality of life of the parents is the problem behaviour of the intellectually disabled children (Mulder, Tudor, & Walsh, 2013). According to Gohel, Mukherjee and Choudhary (2011), one of the commonly held thoughts to avoid this stressor is by separating the child from the family. There are also parents who had reported high suicidal ideation due to this stressor. The problem behavior is a factor that has the capability to moderate pain among the parents and their stress. Significant interaction effects have been identified between these two factors.

Other most important stressor is financial difficulties with regards to the treatment of the child which are typically expensive (Serrata, 2012). In a country like India, therapeutic supports for the intellectually disabled children from psychologist and related professionals are not yet fully recognized. Financial support from the part of the government seems to be more biased to the special education sector, which can only make very little contribution to the cognitive and intellectual advancement in the children. Hence, parents have to depend on their own daily income to provide necessary therapeutic provisions.

For some of the parents, however, managing child care routines and day-to-day household tasks are not as stressful as the interactions they had to make with the school and mental health professionals (Singer and Todis, 1991). Even though inclusive education methods are encouraged, many of the private sector schools hesitate to make it a choice for practice. Reduced academic performance of the children will be considered as a sin in at least some of the institutions. Parents also will be showing reluctance to accept the reality that their children are not pacing up with the peers.

Mulder, Tudor and Walsh (2013) reported that an overprotective parenting style is sometimes a stressor for the parents themselves. Diagnosis of disability in the children will make some parents to act overprotective. This may bring a sense of crisis in each and every behaviour modulations in their children. However, stress and resilience among the parents may differ with respect to the disorder. For instance, according to Abbeduto, Krauss, Murphy, Orsmond, Seltzer and Shattuck (2004) mothers of fragile X syndrome children have reduced levels of well-being when compared to the mothers of down-syndrome children, but increased levels related to the mothers of autistic children. Hence, the disorder itself may be considered as one of the stressors.

Behavioural responses of the parents of intellectually disabled children to their experiences of stress used to vary. In general, they are reported to undergo high levels of frustration and dissatisfaction (Heiman, 2002). Heavier does the daily stressors and hassles, greater will be the tendency among the mothers and fathers to view their marriages negatively. (Gavidia-Payne & Stoneman, 2006). The inverse correlation between stress and marriage quality in the parents with autistic children has been noted by Serrata (2012) also. In the study by Abmedani and Hock (2012) exclusively among the parents of the children with autism spectrum disorder, lower levels of relationship satisfaction were identified. Negative marital interaction and low relationship satisfaction among the parents could result in an unconstructive relationship with the children (Floyd & Zmich, 1991). However, this will not be reflected in their self-reports (Floyd & Zmich, 1991).

Ahmedani and Hock (2012), when compared the social and ecological contexts of the parents, understood that they are poor in maintaining the social capital, especially in their relationship with the neighbors. Their social participation and employment status seemed to be lower when compared to the parents of the normal children, even though they were similar in education, physical health and marital status (Floyd, Greenberg, Hong, Pettee, & Seltzer, 2001). As the protective factors associated with the social support is lacking, they have a high proneness to psychosocial problems (Serrata, 2012), when compared to the parents of normal children. Availability and maintenance of resources for coping are important in order to demonstrate resilience (Bradshaw, Stuart, & Zablotsky, 2013).

Literature provides information regarding the gender differences in the experience of and response to thestress of the parents. The stress in the father was more associated with the temperament of the child and the interpersonal relationship they have with others. Mothers' stress was linked with personal consequences of general parenting (Krauss, 1993). They were identified to be suffering from significantly more daily hassles than did fathers (Gavidia-Payne & Stoneman, 2006). Further, they were more in self-criticism, emotional stress and search for social support. They were subjected to undergo a complex process of adaptation (Rogner & Wessels, 1994).

Considering within gender findings, mothers of children with Autism spectrum disorder were more vulnerable to have high levels of stress and unfortunate mental health compared to mothers of children without the same (Bradshaw, Stuart, & Zablotsky, 2013). Being a mother of a child with disability apart from another child with autism spectrum disorders had severe symptoms of depression and anxiety and lower family adaptability and cohesion compared with mothers who have a single child suffering from autism spectrum disorders (Lin, Orsmond, & Seltzer, 2007).

According to Heiman (2002), all the parents, however, wish to bring positive changes in their social life sticking themselves on to different methods to reach solutions. One such method which generally practiced by the parents is acoercive family process (Blumberg, Horner, Irvin, Laverty, Lucyshyn, & Sprague, 2004). Through coercions, a parent is but reinforcing the problem behaviour of the child. The child, here, in turn, reinforces the ineffective parenting practices. Two types of coercive processes routinely used by the parents are attention driven coercive processes and escape-driven coercive processes. In the former one, parents will be occupied with non-child-centered tasks. In the latter one, parent demands are common (Blumberg, Horner, Irvin, Laverty, Lucyshyn, & Sprague, 2004). Whatever may be the practices, most of the parents like to have a strong belief in the child and in the child's future. They wished to have an optimistic outlook. Many of them were inclined towards a realistic view and showed acceptance of the disability (Heiman, 2002).

Having a higher education does not seem to help in reducing the stress. Floyd, Greenberg, Hong, Pettee and Seltzer (2001) noticed that despite standard educational and occupational attainment and marriage, the parents of the children with intellectual disability, compared to the normal parents, had high proneness to psychosocial problems during the midlife (Floyd, Greenberg, Hong, Pettee, & Seltzer, 2001). However, education seems to be one of the mediating or moderating factors that could influence certain regional or cultural inputs to resilience. For instance, in the study by Upadhyaya and Havalappanavar (2008), conducted in India, extrinsic protective factors of the parents included higher education level, non-agricultural occupation, higher income and urban status of the family. According to McGrail and Rieger (2013), cohesion among the family members and flexibility in them are influenced by the education level and a number of the children in the family. However, much information to have authentic discussions regarding this fact is lacking in the currently available literature.

Most of the parents are trying their level best to maintain the optimal level of resilience (Heiman, 2002). According to Greef and van der Walt (2010), the most significant resilience factors identified among parents include family belief systems, positive outlook of the parents, family hardiness, resourcefulness, flexible and committed family environment, predictable and open communication patterns, social support and higher socio-economic status (Greef & van der Walt, 2010). Bauman (2004) explored the subjective experiences of families (10 parents) of children with intellectual disability and identified that social support and empowerment-oriented practices by professionals having a mediating effect on family stress.

Participation in the programs that could bring certain kind of progress among the children along with the other similar parents and the profession is identified to be helpful in making them feel accepted, respected and resilient (Crowe, Cunningham-Sabo, Helitzer, & Vanleit, 2002). Coping skills were enhanced among the parents who attend activities and programmes to assist them to bring up the children in an improved way. The newly learned coping skills from different programmes increased the capability of the parents to support themselves and their children. It enabled them to be relieved from the over-expectations about their responsibilities. Further, it increased self-care practices (Crowe, Cunningham-Sabo, Helitzer, & Vanleit, 2002).

There is a high probability in using problem-focused coping strategies among them when compared to emotion-focused coping methods (Upadhyaya & Havalappanavar, 2008). However, fathers who reported to be irritated in a daily basis due to the child's disability showed a lesser tendency to adopt problem-focused coping strategies (Gavidia-Payne & Stoneman, 2006). Lesser the hassles, higher is the tendency in fathers to be more positive and to use problem-focused coping strategies (Gavidia-Payne & Stoneman, 2006). As per the study done by Upadhyaya and Havalappanavar (2008), fathers, comparing to mothers of intellectually disabled children, are higher in problem solving, positive distraction, negative distraction, acceptance-redefinition and social support.

In the case of mothers, personal support networks would help a lot (Krauss, 1993). Coping resources of the mothers, in the form of emotional and social supports from the neighborhoods, helped them capable of overcoming high-stress levels and the risk of poor mental health (Bradshaw, Stuart, & Zablotsky, 2013). It is common among the mothers seeking shelter in religion and faith. Such mothers are identified to show more of the habit of denial and blaming (Upadhyaya & Havalappanavar, 2008). Mothers who had the first child intellectually disabled achieved more mastery than the mothers who had a disabled second child (Rogner & Wessels, 1994).

There are resilient parents among whom none of the stressors could hamper their wellness. Study conducted by Geffken, Morgan and Rodrigue (1992), in three groups of 20 fathers, matched on the child's adaptive behaviour, age equivalent, gender, birth order, family size and socioeconomic status, showed that the subjects' level of perceived parenting competence, marital satisfaction and social support were similar to those reported by fathers of normally developing children. As per the findings of Singer and Todis (1991), some of the effective stress management techniques used by parents were household organizational systems and keeping contact with other families in the same situation. Families who had a positive appraisal of life circumstances more successfully adjusted to potentially stressful situations (Singer & Todis, 1991).

Thus, literature is splendid with the reports of the factors that enhance the stress and challenge the resilience of the parents of the intellectually disabled children. At the same time, it lacks information regarding the factors of stress that reduces or bring down the resilience in the parents. The present study attempts to fill this gap. The study further inquires if the age of the parents has a significant influence on their resilience. Hypotheses formulated for the study follows.

Aim of the Present Study

To find out if stress has influences on the resilience of the parents with intellectually disabled children.

Objectives

1. To find out if there is a significant relationship between stress and resilience in the parents of intellectually disabled children.
2. To find out if factors of stress include the factors that could predict resilience in the parents of intellectually disabled children.

HYPOTHESES

1. There is no significant relationship between stress and resilience in the parents of intellectually disabled children.
2. Factors of stress do not include the factors that predict resilience in the parents of intellectually disabled children.
3. Parents who are in early adulthood do not differ from the parents who are in late adulthood and old age in their resilience.

METHOD

Sample

50 parents of the intellectually disabled children were selected purposively from different child mental health clinics at Kozhikode, Kannur and Wayanad district in the state of Kerala, India. Only the parents who have their children living along with them in the same house were considered in the sample. Parents who were diagnosed to have a psychiatric disorder and who had regular usage of substances were excluded from the study.

Measures

1. BU Resilience Scale (Form A), developed by Annalakshmi (2009) consists of 30 Likert-type items. The scale purports to measure resilience with reference to seven domains including duration for getting back to normalcy, reaction to negative events, response to risk factors (specifically, disadvantaged environment) in life, perception of effect of past negative events, defining problems, hope/confidence in coping with future and openness to experience and flexibility. The scale has adequate reliability (reliability coefficient of Spearman-Brown, 0.84; Guttman, 0.84; and Cronbach α, 0.86) as found on a sample of 577 post-graduate students. The scale was validated against Friborg's Resilience Scale for Adults ($r = 0.401$) and Bell's Adjustment Inventory ($r = -0.392$). Higher scores indicate higher resiliency and lower scores indicate lower resiliency.
2. Stress Scale for Parents of mentally challenged (SPMC); developed by Rejitha, Biji & Jayan (2005) consist of 20 items. The scale purports to measure stress with reference to four domains such as financial, intra-familial, extra-familial and emotional factors. The scale is reported to be reliable and valid by the authors. In the present sample, the scale indicated adequate internal reliability (Cronbach $\alpha = .73$).

RESULTS

To find out if there is a significant relationship between stress and resilience in the parents of intellectually disabled children, correlation analysis was administered. Results are given in Table 1.

As per the results of correlation analysis resilience among the parents of intellectually disabled children has a significant moderate negative correlation ($r = -0.47$, $p < 0.01$) with their extra-familial stress. Resilience has a significant moderate negative correlation ($r = 0.4$, $p < 0.01$) with anoverall stress score of the parents of intellectually disabled children.

To find out if extra-familial stress can predict resilience in the parents of intellectually disabled children, one variable regression analysis was done. Table 2 summarizes the results.

Results indicated that extra-familial stress can predict ($\beta = -0.473$, $t = 3.72$, $p < 0.01$) resilience in the parents of intellectually disabled children. Extra-familial stress has a negative relationship with resilience. Hence, when extra-familial stress increases, resilience decreases.

To find out if parents who are in early adulthood differ from the parents who are in late adulthood and old age in their resilience, the t-test is used. Table 3 summarizes the results of the t-test.

Table 1. Correlation analysis: relationship between the resilience and various factors of stress in parents of intellectually disabled children

Variables	Stress				Overall Stress
	Financial	Intra-Familial	Extra-Familial	Emotional	
Intra-familial	0.34*				
Extra-familial	0.21	0.58**			
Emotional	-0.08	0.09	-0.15		
Overall stress	0.48**	0.80**	0.78**	0.34**	
Resilience	0.06	-0.20	-0.47**	-0.163	-0.40**

**P < 0.01, *P < 0.05.

Table 2. Regression model: factors of stress predicting resilience

DV	Predictors	B	T	F	R^2	ΔR^2
Resilience	Extra-familial stress	-0.473	3.724**	13.87**	0.224	0.208

**P < 0.01.

Table 3. Summary of the group statistics which differentiate parents in early adulthood from the parents in late adulthood and old age in their resilience

DV	Age	N	Mean	S.D.	"t"
Resilience	Late adulthood	23	98.69	10.64	3.07**
	Early adulthood	27	89.48	10.35	

**P < 0.01.

As per the findings, parents in the late adulthood differ ($t = 3.07$, $p < 0.01$) from the parents in the early adulthood in their resilience. Parents in the late adulthood ($M = 98.69$, $S.D. = 10.64$) is higher in resilience when compared to the parents in the early adulthood ($M = 89.48$, $S.D. = 10.35$).

DISCUSSION

The present study found that extra-familial stress could reduce resilience. The anxiety of the parents regarding the speculations of the society on them may be contributing to this extra-familial stress. Because of the same extra-familial stress, they may be showing hesitation in interacting with the school authorities and the professionals (Singer and Todis, 1991). These interactions will always make them feel the reality of the disability of their child. During transactions, comparison with other normal children may arrive unintentionally. The comparisons may lead them to the feelings of pessimism, hostility, and shame. Denial, projection of blame, guilt, grief, withdrawal, rejection, and acceptance are the usual parental reactions. Some parents also experience helplessness, feelings of inadequacy, anger, shock and guilt whereas others go through periods of disbelief, depression, and self-blame (Chandramuki, Krishna Shastry, & Vranda, 2012).

However, parents who are older are more capable in accepting the reality. Hence, the results, parents those who are in the later part of the young adulthood and older are better in their resilience. They are capable in maintaining their life in the optimal level of normality. Similar results were found out by Gandotra (1985) when the parents aged less than 35years were compared with parents above 35 years. Results of the study indicated that lower be the age of parents, higher was the stress. Younger parents, as a result, may hesitate to take the child to the professionals. They may be de-motivated to send their children for education too. This would lead to the deprival of on-time psychological intervention and exposure to education, which could help a lot to bring the child to the mainstream.

CONCLUSION AND RECOMMENDATION

The study shows that extra-familial stress is a predictable factor that could reduce the resilience in the parents of the intellectually disabled children. The study also reveals that parents who are in the younger stages of young adulthood are more vulnerable to stress. However, the findings cannot be generalized, as the sample is selected from a limited part of the population. At the same time, the study brings out a specific factor that may be active in most of the similar population. Further inquiries comparing the same factors of stress and resilience have to be done in different cohorts. In the case of repeated results, intervention strategies that could help the parents overcome extra-familial stress shall be designed and tested. More researches to find out the factors which could help enhance the resilience of the parents of intellectually disabled people are recommended.

REFERENCES

Abbeduto, L., Krauss, M. W., Murphy, M. M., Orsmond, G., Seltzer, M. M., & Shattuck, P. (2004). Psychological well-being and coping in mothers of youths with autism, Down syndrome, or fragile X syndrome. *American Journal of Mental Retardation*, *109*(3), 237–254. doi:10.1352/0895-8017(2004)109<237:PWACIM>2.0.CO;2 PMID:15072518

Ahmedani, B. K., & Hock, R. (2012). Parent perceptions of autism severity: Exploring social ecological context. *Disability and Health Journal*, *5*(4), 298–304. doi:10.1016/j.dhjo.2012.06.002 PMID:23021742

Blumberg, E. R., Horner, R. H., Irvin, L. K., Laverty, R., Lucyshyn, J. M., & Sprague, J. R. (2004). Validating the construct of coercion in family routines: Expanding the unit of analysis in behavioral assessment with families of children with developmental disabilities. *Research and Practice for Persons with Severe Disabilities*, *29*(2), 104–121. doi:10.2511/rpsd.29.2.104 PMID:26321883

Bradshaw, C. P., Stuart, E. A., & Zablotsky, B. (2013). The association between mental health, stress and coping supports in mothers of children with autism spectrum disorders. *Journal of Autism and Developmental Disorders*, *43*(6), 1380–1393. doi:10.1007/s10803-012-1693-7 PMID:23100053

Chandramuki, K. S., & Vranda, M. N. (2012). Attitudes of parents towards children with specific learning disabilities. *Disability, CBR and Inclusive Development, 23*(1), 63-69.

Crowe, T. K., Cunningham-Sabo, L. D., Helitzer, D. L., & Vanleit, B. (2002). Perceived changes in self image and coping strategies of mothers of children with disabilities. *The Occupational Therapy Journal of Research*, *22*(1), 25–33. doi:10.1046/j.0045-0766.2001.00276.x

Floyd, F. J., Greenberg, J. S., Hong, J., Pettee, Y., & Seltzer, M. M. (2001). Life course impacts of parenting a child with a disability. *American Journal of Mental Retardation*, *106*(3), 265–286. doi:10.1352/0895-8017(2001)106<0265:LCIOPA>2.0.CO;2 PMID:11389667

Floyd, F. J., & Zmich, D. E. (1991). Marriage and the parenting partnership: Perceptions and interactions of parents with mentally retarded and typically developing children. *Child Development*, *62*(6), 1434–1448. doi:10.2307/1130817 PMID:1786726

Gavidia-Payne, S., & Stoneman, Z. (2006). Marital adjustment in families of young children with disabilities: Associations with daily hassles and problem-focused coping. *American Journal of Mental Retardation*, *111*(1), 1–14. doi:10.1352/0895-8017(2006)111[1:MAIFOY]2.0.CO;2 PMID:16332152

Geffken, G. R., Morgan, S. B., & Rodrigue, J. R. (1992). Psychosocial adaptation of fathers of children with autism, down syndrome and normal development. *Journal of Autism and Developmental Disorders*, *22*(2), 249–263. doi:10.1007/BF01058154 PMID:1385591

Gohel, M., Mukherjee, S., & Choudhary, S. K. (2011). Psychosocial impact on the parents of mentally retarded children in Anand District. *Healthline*, *2*(2), 62–66.

Greef, A. P., & van der Walt, K. J. (2010). Resilience in families with an autistic child. *Education and Training in Autism and Developmental Disabilities*, *45*(3), 347–355.

Heiman, T. (2002). Parents of Children with Disabilities: Resilience, Coping and Future Expectations. *Journal of Developmental and Physical Disabilities*, *14*(2), 159–171. doi:10.1023/A:1015219514621

Khadi, P. B., & Hidangmayum, N. (2012). Parenting stress of normal and mentally challanged children. *Karnataka Journal of Agricultural Sciences*, *25*(2), 256–259.

Krauss, M. W. (1993). Child related and parenting stress: Similarities and differences between mothers and fathers of children with disabilities. *American Journal of Mental Retardation*, *97*(4), 393–404. PMID:8427694

Lin, L. Y., Orsmond, G. I., & Seltzer, M. M. (2007). Mothers of adolescents and adults with autism: Parenting multiple children with disabilities. *Intellectual and Developmental Disabilities*, *45*(4), 257–270. doi:10.1352/1934-9556(2007)45[257:MOAAAW]2.0.CO;2 PMID:17627373

McGrail, J. P., & Rieger, A. (2013). Coping humor and family functioning in parents of children with disabilities. *Rehabilitation Psychology*, *58*(1), 89–97. doi:10.1037/a0031556 PMID:23438005

Mulder, E., Tudor, M. E., & Walsh, C. E. (2013). Predictors of parent stress in a sample of children with ASD: Pain, problem behaviour, and parental coping. *Research in Autism Spectrum Disorders*, *7*(2), 256–264. doi:10.1016/j.rasd.2012.08.010

Rogner, J., & Wessels, E. T. (1994). Coping strategies of mothers and fathers with a first or second born mentally handicapped child. *Praxis der Kinderpsychologie und Kinderpsychiatrie*, *43*(4), 125–129. PMID:8016022

Serrata, C. A. (2012). Psychosocial aspects of parenting a child with autism. *Journal of Applied Rehabilitation Counseling*, *43*(4), 29–35.

Singer, G., & Todis, B. (1991). Stress and stress management in families with adopted children who have severe disabilities. *The Journal of the Association for Persons with Severe Handicaps*, *16*(1), 3–13.

Upadhyaya, G. R., & Havalappanavar, N. B. (2008). Coping in parents of the mentally challanged. *Journal of the Indian Academy of Applied Psychology*, *34*(2), 221–225.

KEY TERMS AND DEFINITIONS

Extra-Familial Stress: Stress, which includes speculations (cognitive responses) following with an alarm reaction and resistance (physiological response), experienced by an individual regarding the feelings of the members outside the family, about something thought to be bad in his or her family.

Intellectual Disability: Deficiency in intelligence that makes an individual disabled to function normally in his or her life.

Parents of Intellectually Disabled Children: Biological mother and thebiological father who live with the children with a psychological or medical diagnosis of intellectual disability.

Resilience: The power within an individual, assisted by the protective factors extrinsic or intrinsic to the individual, which helps him or her to maintain wellness, or to bounce back to normalcy, even after facing tremendous setbacks in life.

Stress: A combination of psychological (cognitive) and psychological responses made by the individual to the potential stressors.

Stressor: Factors, those are extrinsic or intrinsic to the individual, which bring challenges to the expected equilibrium of life.

Chapter 7
Family Members as Caregivers of Individuals with Intellectual Disabilities:
Caregiving for Individuals with Intellectual Disabilities

Krishna Shailesh Vora
Jamnabai Narsee School, India

ABSTRACT

Whenever you have an individual suffering from any disorder, whether emotional, behavioural or intellectual; the prime focus is almost always the individual experiencing it first hand. Often we tend to neglect the sacrifices or adjustments made by the family members. Caregiver stress is one of the phenomena explored here along with experiences of individual family members and the resources available to make it easier for them. Resources could be in terms of finances, emotional support, personality strengths or the society they live in. Another unlikely term explored over here is that of Caregiver Gain which is recently being given attention due to it. This chapter explores the unique experiences of parents, siblings, grandparents as well as support staff as caregivers of individuals with Intellectual Disabilites. We also have a look at traits that help cope with the caregiving process.

INTRODUCTION

This chapter will be focussing on experiences of people who are related to individuals with Intellectual Disabilities and their positive and negative experiences as caregivers.

DOI: 10.4018/978-1-5225-0089-6.ch007

DIFFICULTIES FACED BY INDIVIDUALS WITH INTELLECTUAL DISABILITIES

A child or an adult with intellectual disability is likely to have a relatively lower mental capacity, memory, learning, problem solving, ability to initiate or sustain on a task, reading, math and so on. These would have impact in direct functioning in daily life.

Concepts such as language (reading, writing communication), number sense, time and money, self-care, etc. may not be well developed. Difficulties can also be commonly seen in social life. It is often hard for them to take responsibility for appropriate social behaviour, tend to be gullible, lack interpersonal skills which affect their ability to form and sustain relationships, lack social inhibitors, are unable to follow or obey rules and are also easily victimised. Daily skills are harder for them than most people and issues such as personal care, hygiene, healthcare, travelling independently, following routines, communicating needs, persisting and carrying out tasks, etc. In view of these difficultis let us have a look at Caregivers and their experience (Daily et al, 2000)

CAREGIVERS

A caregiver is any person who takes on the responsibility of assisting someone with a mental, emotional or physical disability. Their services can be paid or unpaid. In case when it's paid, it is usually a nurse or a social worker. Unpaid services are usually given by family members, close relatives' or neighbours if they have grown up together (Feinberg et al, 2001).

Typical duty of a caregiver in this case would be managing medicines, taking over additional household responsibilities, talking to doctors, psychologists and other parties involved to ensure best treatment and adjustment. Depending on the severity of Intellectual Disability a caregiver may even have to help take care of basic necessities such as hygiene, dressing up, presentation, etc. Additional concerns would be getting the person with Intellectual Disability to become as independent as possible along with a means to occupy him/her with any vocational activity. While caregiving can be a humbling and enriching experience, it can often lead to fatigue, exhaustion and burn out. There has been increasing research on the experiences of caregivers and what can be done to ease their burden. It is also difficult to care while simultaneously feeling worry, anxiety about the care, wanting to help but missing out on leisure time, feeling guilty for wishing things to be different, etc.

Though the research is this field is limited, we are going to try and focus here on experiences of caregivers.

Caregiver Stress and Caregiver Gain

For most people caring for their loved ones comes naturally. However, caring for the intellectual, emotional and physical well-being of a child with mental retardation can be overpowering. As the child grows, so does responsibilities and thus there is simultaneous increase in work load, increase in feelings of burden, guilt of not being able to do a perfect job or physical exhaustion, negligence of personal needs or needs of other family members all comes into foray.

Though the term does not enter the Diagnostic and Statistical Manual of Mental Disorders, it is a term used frequently by mental health professionals. *Caregiver stress* may manifest itself in a variety of ways such as feeling overwhelmed, feeling tired all the time, becoming easily angry or upset, depression, frequent headaches, bodily pain or other physical problems etc. In fact, roughly 40-70% of caregivers suffer from depression (Zarit, 2006).

Another effect of having a child with disability is its impact on activities such as recreational activities, shopping, dining out and family vacations (Cherry, 1989; Bauman, 2004), activities that most of us would take for granted.

Contrary to instinct, one cross sectional study involving 900 caregivers found that even after two years older women showed increase in cognitive functions such as memory and processing speeds compared to those who were not caregivers. Though the participants may have been high on these cognitive functions to begin with, the process of caregiving may have helped them develop them further. The same study by Dr. Fredman et al (2012) found that high intensity caregivers maintained stronger physical performance than non-caregivers simply because they performed more physical functions. Caregivers also scored at the level of people who were 10 years younger. Hence the term 'caregiver gain' came into use. Apart from the above mentioned rewards, emotional and spiritual well being, increased sense of purpose, family cohesiveness are other untangible rewards(Stainton & Besser 1992). Various studies by Abbott & Meredith (1986), Trivette, Dunst et al (1990) etc. found that families with children with intellectual disability tend to demonstrate higher resilience and find it easier to mobilize resources to cope with challenges. Many other researchers such as Dunlap & Hollingworth, 1977; Hancock et al. 1990, etc. show how families have been strengthened from the experience of living with a child with difficulty.

A qualitative study by Stainton (1998), shows the positive impact that children with Intellectual Disabilities can have on their families. Their study identified nine core themes such as

1. Source of joy and happiness.
2. Source of increased sense of purpose and priorities.
3. Expanded personal and social networks, and community involvement.
4. Source of increased spirituality.
5. Source of family unity and closeness.
6. Source of increased tolerance and understanding.
7. Source of personal growth and strength.
8. Positive impacts on others/community.
9. Interaction with professionals and the service system.

Parents as Caregivers

Experience of both mothers and fathers as caregivers will be focussed on along with other variables such as age of the caregiver, age of the individual receiving care, marital adjustment among parents etc.

Caregiving in Different Cultures

Depending on the culture one finds themselves in, access to information, support system, living in a different culture, all of this has an impact on the caregiver. In a study of Latino families it was found that young children with disabilities are at increased risk for lack of access to services. Immigration could also reduce the amount of social support available to the family. For Latino mothers of children with mental retardation depression increased as key sources of support were lost, family problems existed, inhabiting in isolated environment and lack of acculturation. When needs of 200 Latino parents of children with intellectual disability was assessed, around 70% of them expressed a need for information regarding services available for their child, both now and in future, psychoeducation about the child's disabilities, how to teach and handle their child, explaining the condition to siblings etc (Bailey et al, 1999)

A study of 100 parents in a district in Gujarat, India, found that unemployed fathers had significantly more negatively affected relationships compared to employed fathers. However, the overall research found that more than 50% of the parents has positive impact in terms of patience, tolerance, empathy and sensitivity. It also showed that 98% of parents received help from family members, relatives and neighbours (Gohel et al, 2011)

Caregiving perceptions of 212 Chinese mothers of children with Intellectual Disabilities residing in Hong Kong was looked into by Ho & Mak (2007). It was found that problem focussed coping was related to positive perceptions while emotion-focussed coping was related to negative perceptions. Meanwhile relationship focussed coping was related to both negative and positive perceptions. They also found that relationship focused coping would be more suitable to understand caregivers in a collectivistic cultures.

Similarly, another research by Kerenhappachu & Godishala (2014), which compared 30 mothers of children with Intellectual Disabilities with a control group found that mothers experienced a significant amount of burden especially in the areas of general strain, emotional involvement and disappointment and there is a significant lag in the amount of support they seeked and actually received.

An Indian study found that burden due to effects of interaction on family was more in the group where children had both Autism and Intellectual Disability than with families who had just children with only Intellectual Disability. On the other hand, burden was more in the group with children with only Intellectual Disability due to finances and effects of physical health of other family members (Suresh et al, 2014).

Another study exploring child related and cultural distress among Latina Caregivers of children with Intellectual Disabilities also found that associations between child behaviour problems and maternal distress was moderated by single parent status, lower English usage and higher familism (Long, Kao et al 2015).

MULTIPLE CHILDREN WITH INTELLECTUAL DISABILITY AND BIRTH ORDER

Kimura & Yamazaki (2013) explored experiences of mothers who had multiple children with Intellectual Disabilities. They used interpretative phenomenological analysis with 10 participants to find three superordinate themes of accumulating mental and physical fatigue, abandoning hope for having a normal family and an attempt to search for positive experiences in parenting more than one child with intellectual disabilities. They often struggled to accept the disability in another child especially when it was diagnosed post several years whether they suspected it or not. Mothers still tried to reframe their negative perceptions.

Rogner & Wessels (1994) looked at birth order of the child with Intellectual Disability and its relationship to the coping strategies of the mother and the father. Among 25 families having two children or one child with intellectual disability they found that if the first child was handicapped, mothers coped more with mastery than mothers of a second born handicapped child. Mothers also showed relatively more emotional stress, criticising of self, experienced frequent ups and downs in the process of adaptation.

- **Age of the Child with Intellectual Disability:** Studies by Bristol and Schopler (1984) & Suelzle & Keenan (1981) found that parents of older children with Intellectual Disabilities went through more stress than those with children of younger age. On the other hand, some researchers such as Townsend, Noelkar, Deimling & Bass put forward an adaptation model of caregiving which hypothesizes better adjustment to caregiving role over time. Indeed one such research by Seltzer and Krauss (1989) found that 462 mothers caring for an offspring with Intellectual Disability were found to be healthier and had better morale.

- **Severity of Intellectual Disability:** a study by Bhargava, Dhiman, & Shetty (2007) confirm that levels of stress and burden increase with the increase in severity of Intellectual Disabilities. The more profound the disability, higher the amount of stress experienced by the mothers. Multiple stressors seemed to exacerbate the amount of stress experienced. While fathers were seen to experience less amount of stress probably owing to lower involvement with the care taking process.

Blacher, Nihira, Meyers (1987), predicted that higher the severity (i.e. lower the IQ score) higher would be the stress levels. Family routine was more severely disrupted for families with children with significant disability along with poorer family adjustment and coping. On the contrary, severity of Intellectual Disability didn't have more adverse impact on marital adjustment.

- **Reciprocity from the Child:** At times, reciprocity from the child with Intellectual Disabilities can also play a role in caregiver stress or the lack of it. A study by Hellen and Factor (1993) found that parents perceived burden was reduced in accordance with support that they received from their offsprings Intellectual Disabilities.

Pain Experienced by Those with Intellectual Disabilities

also leave a negative emotional impact on Caregivers especially when they are dissatisfied with how the health care service managed the pain of individuals with Intellectual Disabilities. Findlay, Williams, Baum & Scior (2014) found exactly that. Using semi-structured interviews information was collected from 11 caregivers caring for adults with Intellectual Disabilities who were suspected to be or were definitely in pain. They found superordinate themes from the caregivers' experiences. It looked at how they tried to reduce pain, their perceptions of pain experience, emotional impact of pain, how they suffered in silence, searched for meaning of this pain, and knowledge and skills required to identify and manage pain. Some of the caregivers also spoke about dissatisfaction with the way pain was managed by health care givers (Findlay et al, 2014)

Fathers as Caregivers

Research on fathers as caregivers has been little but informative. Initial research has found mother as the primary caretaker and fathers have been consistently neglectful. This presumption has been eventually invalidated (Kazak,1986). Various studies by Beckman (1991), Trute (1995), Heller et al (1997) and Krauss (1993) found that compared to mothers, fathers of children with disabilities report fewer depressive symptoms, higher self esteem, lower subjective burden and less of a sense of role restriction. Possible reason for this could be that parents follow traditional gender roles where mother, who is the homemaker, acts as a primary caregiver and the father is the breadwinner and hence can escape much of household responsibilities and other chores related to caregiving.

Study by Brubaker et al (1999) indicated that fathers had more concern than mothers about their physical ability to take care of the child. A longitudinal study by Krauss and Seltzer (1999) on 461 families found fathers shared less burden. Out of 31 possible tasks fathers helped with 4 tasks on an average while mothers did 11 tasks. Fathers were more likely to provide help with tasks that would traditionally fall in the male domain such as home repairs, use of stairs, ambulation difficulties to walk indoors etc. which were done by mothers too. In case the mother dies or becomes incapacitated, the father takes on the role of the primary caregiver including all activities of daily living. Though siblings would also contribute, the role of father in such circumstances was much larger. (Gordon et al,1997).

PROBLEM SOLVING AND COPING MECHANISM

Essex, Seltzer and Krauss (1999) explored differences in coping and well-being among mothers and fathers of children with intellectual disabilities who are aging. This longitudinal study examined 133 mothers and fathers who had children with intellectual disabilities in the age range of 19 to 53. Mothers and fathers were found to be similar in their average levels of subjective burden and depressive symptoms. Fathers were more pessimistic about the future of their son or daughter compared to mothers. This was contradictory to research which expected mothers to show more levels of stress. Mothers were more likely to use problem focussed coping while both were equally likely to use emotion focussed coping. With behavioural issues, mothers using problem focussed coping were much less pessimistic than those who used less of it. With fathers, problem focused and emotion focused solving did not have much impact on depressive symptoms. Their depressive symptoms increased as a function of the age of their son and daughter i.e. it increased with their age and they also experienced functional limitations. Increase in burden for fathers happened when they are more likely to use emotion focused coping along with their son and daughter having severe functional limitations. The type of coping that the father adopted had no direct bearing on their pessimism.

A study by Costigan, Flyod, Harter and McClintok (1997), focused on problem solving abilities of 165 families of children with Intellectual Disabilities and compared it to a group of 52 families with children with typical growth and development. While parents of both groups were equally participative, parents of children with Intellectual Disabilities spent far more time in behaviour management activities. Single parents were unable to allot more time to problem solving probably since they were required to play multiple roles and found them taxing.

- **Literacy of Parents:** A study on 62 parents found that gender and educational level may affect stress and coping. No significant difference in psychological stress and coping levels between mothers and fathers was found. Parents with higher education level had higher levels of coping with less stress. Educated mothers were more likely to seek external support, professional help, give their child timely and appropriate treatment, were aware of workshops and seminars that were available to help enhance coping strategies and deal with problems effectively (Kumar, 2008). A study in Secunderabad, India found that literacy of parents had a positive correlation with duration of follow up (Narayan et al, 1993). A study in Bangalore explored mental health literacy with caregivers and found shocking results where 61.5% believed that people with mental health problems are responsible for their problems and half of them expressed shame over having such a family member. Psychoeducation would be necessary to bust myths and change attitudes (Poreddi et al, 2015). Gatab and Maleki (2013) also found correlationship between parent's literacy level with degree of stress.

- **Aging Parents:** Hayden and Heller (1997) compared how younger and older caregivers fared on service and support utilisation, coping strategies and the amount personal burden experienced. Younger care givers were more likely to seek outside help and hold high expectations of the service system and hence also reported more unmet service needs. They were also more likely to mobilize family to acquire and accept help. While older caregivers sought spiritual support and experienced significantly less burden. Both demonstrated highly developed effective problem solving skills.

Study by Cant, Gething, Kendig, Llewellyn & McConnell (2010) had contradictory findings. They assessed health status and coping of 64 older parent caregivers of children with Intellectual Disabilities in Australia. Health status did not significantly differ from Australian population norms. Though younger parent carers reported relatively poorer mental health. The study identified both stress and satisfaction where satisfaction and good health stemmed from having a partner and large close support system of friends, family and neighbours as well as lower work load.

- **Expressed Emotion:** is hostile, critical and overinvolved emotional attitude of a family member while caring for another family member who has a disorder.(Brown & Rutter, 1966) Hastings and Llyod (2007) reviewed 11 published studies of EE to find that expressed emotion may lead to behavioural problems in both carers as well as individuals with intellectual disabilities. High expressed emotion may be due to the result of interaction between carers and those with Intellectual Disabilities. They also acknowledge that expressed emotion maybe normal for those who experience a huge deal of stress during the caregiving process and mention a lack of research in this area.
- **Perspectives:** Griffith & Hastings (2014) selected 17 studies for meta synthesis which found five primary themes of love, crisis management, low expectations and high hopes for future, altered identity and support. Carers spoke about excessive demands that the process of caregiving placed on them while also experiencing a lot of love for the family member who had Intellectual Disabilities. Though they reported good support practices, it was found that they often caused additional problems and high stress levels for caregivers.
- **Marital Relationships:** usually reports have been found of strained marital relationships. Friedrich & Friedrich (1981) found that families of children with disabilities reported more stress, less religiosity, less psychological well-being, less social support and lower marital satisfaction. Severity of Intellectual Disabilities is another variable that plays a role in stress levels.

Floyd & Zmich (1991) explored the quality of parents marital bond and thereby their ability to work for the children with Intellectual Disability. Their study showed an interesting contrast. During interaction between the parents and the parent and child, significantly more negative functioning was observed on the contrary this was not the case in self reports of marriage and parenting. Indeed marital and parenting expectations may have tonned down the negative sentiments of parents. It was also found that negative marital interaction could predict unpleasant parent child interactions.

Payne & Stoneman (2006) focussed on marital adjustment among families with young children with disabilities. They also looked into its relationship to daily hassles and problem focussed coping. When daily stressors and hassles were higher, marriages were viewed negatively by both husbands and wives. Mothers experienced more daily hassles than did fathers. Both were equally likely to use problem focussed strategies. When fathers reported use of problem focussed strategies along with fewer daily hassles, overall marital adjustment for both mothers and fathers was found to be better.

On contrary, some couples have shown increased marital quality (Kazak & Marvin, 1984). In fact, divorces rates of parents with children with Intellectual difficulties is not significantly different than normal families as noted by Winkler, 1981. Another study showed marital quality in normal range with high cohesion and lower conflict (Trute and Hauch, 1988, pg 188). Also the relationship between parents was one of the key factors for support.

Interviews with 84 Latino and 37 white mothers found that partner emotional support predicted life satisfaction and parenting self-efficacy. Income was not a significant variable. (Cohen et al 2015). These findings can provide guidance in terms of interventions to strength the relationship between the parents to make the whole situation far less stressful.

CONVERSATION ABOUT INTELLECTUAL DISABILITY

Talking to their children about their intellectual disability can also be a stressful experience for parents. Out of 50 parents included in the study (Jones, Oseland, Morris, Larzelere 2014), 66% reported talking to their adolescent children about how they differed from others and/or what their disability meant. Some of these conversations came post or as a response to the child with intellectual disability being bullied. Also parents who had more knowledge about the causes of the disorder were more likely to talk to their children about their disability. Researchers suggest that professionals should consider how to promote more proactive interaction between parents and children so that parents do not have to experience an additional stress or struggle to explain it to their children.

Bereavement Experiences

People with Intellectual Disabilities would be at a higher risk of early death hence parents may often outlive their children with Intellectual Disabilities. In depth interviews with 13 parents who had experienced such as loss (Todd, 2007) found that parents experienced a deep sense of loss after the death of their child with Intellectual Disabilities and lost contact with the world they were too invested in earlier, there was no room for parents to experience their grief and receive emotional support along with the sense that professionals withdrew from the services thereafter. Another study by Hastings et al (2008) explored the experiences of nine mothers whose child with Intellectual Disability had died using semi-structured interviews. Five themes of loss, benefit finding, coping, sources of support, medical relationships emerged. Support from similarly bereaved parents was a preferable source of support but not found easily. Mothers also preferred to continue working within the world of Intellectual Disability even after the death of their child.

Positive Impact of Caregiving

An interesting study by Dunst, Trivette, Hamby and Pollock (1990) studied how variables such as family and personal well being, child behaviour characterisitics, social support interact to lead to adjustment or stress. They spoke about the concept of embeddedness that looks at the child as a part of the family and the family as unit which is a part of a larger social unit. Keeping these variables in mind, they found that social support in the form of information, psycho education, physical material resources seemed to have protective functions for negative stress reactions.

A study on young adults with severe mental retardation found that positive impact had an inverse relationship with behaviour problems i.e. more the behavioural problems with the child, lesser was the positive impact and vice versa. Parent ethnicity also has an impact on positive experiences. Latina mothers reported higher positive impact than Anglo mothers despite discussion happening in context of cultural beliefs. (Blachera, Baker 2007).

One study went a step ahead and looked at whether support provided by adult with Intellectual Disabilities would influence caregiving appraisals. Using surveys and interviews with 80 caregivers, they found that greater support from the adult with Intellectual Disabilities to caregivers led to less burden and greater satisfaction (Heller, Miller, Factor, 1997).

FAMILIES IN A CONTEXT

Bronfenbrenner (1979) examined subsystems such as macrosystem, exosystem and mesosystem and their impact on families with children with disabilities. Based on that Bauman (2004) explored subjective experiences of ten families where themes of empowerment and disempowerment related to four systems i.e. microsystem (family system), mesosystem, exosystem and macrosystem emerged. Among the themes of empowerment, support from family and friends, commitment to children even as they grew older, family unity and comments such as 'we are a blessed family' emerged, use of counselling services, receiving occasional encouragement (e.g. a teacher informing that the child has been the student of the month). Creativity and spirituality were other empowering themes that emerged along with friends, neighbours, co-workers who understood their situation and provided emotional and instrumental support.

Feelings of disempowerment was gauged from behaviour of extended family members who showed low tolerance for the behaviour of the child with difficulty, the child having limited ability to express pain and discomfort, more perceived responsibility by the mother, both parents being at different stages of acceptance or grief. School meetings were often perceived stressful by the parents and experiencing a disrespecting attitude by public school personnels, they did, however, report more satisfaction for an individualized family plan than an individualised educational plan. Social stigma and/or intolerance was also found to be disempowering.

Some other research that tried to look at the experience of the family as a whole. One such study by Mink, Blacher, and Nihira (1988) proposed a taxonomy for families of children with special needs. After examining 97 families with children with Intellectual Disabilities they proposed five types of families such as Cohesive Oriented, Control Oriented, Responsive to Child-Oriented, Moral-Religious Oriented and Achievement Oriented. They argued that interventions be customised according to the criteria that family belongs to. It provides a good starting point for working with families as a whole but hasn't addressed the possibility of a family coming under two or more categories simultaneously.

The family as a whole is also interested that children with Intellectual Disabilities have a successful transition into adulthood. A research by Henninger & Taylor (2014) investigated family perspectives on transition. Using content analysis on the responses of the family to a survey, a variety of themes came up such as being able to live independently, maintaining friendships and employment etc. but besides focussing only on the developmental tasks, the families also wished for a fit between the person with Intellectual Disabilities as well as his or her environment.

Siblings as Caregivers

A sibling of a child with special needs may feel a wide range of emotions such as neglect, hurt, burden of work, possibly embarrassment, wish for a better companion, resentment, confusion, anger, happiness, resilience, lowered or increased self-esteem, development of emotional maturity, positive growth experience, nurturance, etc. Indeed one study showed that mothers and fathers consistently reported that siblings of children with Intellectual Disabilities were more negatively impacted compared to siblings of typically developing children (Neece, Blacher, Baker, 2010).

In case of an adult with mental retardation, the question of who will assume the responsibility of him arises. Most often, after parents, it is assumed that the siblings will take over. Zetlin (1986) found that an adult with Intellectual Disability is emotionally more dependent on a non-disabled sibling. Ongoing studies by Seltzer and Krauss found that 86% of siblings are likely to provide affective support while 25% provide instrumental support. Siblings were also more likely to provide instrumental support to a sibling with less severe mental retardation.

Using a mailed questionnaire expectations about responsibility for future caregiving was drawn from 119 siblings of adults with Intellectual disabilities (along with 61 siblings of adults with serious mental illness). Though 60 percent of siblings expected to take responsibility only 1/3rd of them were able to do so. Involvement in the lives of their siblings was limited by competing family responsibilities while closeness to family of origin led to greater involvement (Greenberg et al, 1999)

Siblings of children with disabilities often experience neglect due to greater parental attention demanded by those with learning difficulties (Corter, Pepler et al, 1992; Lobato, Miller et al 1991). Structured observations show how siblings of children with disabilities express feelings of being deprived of parent's time and attention. Parents tend to provide differential treatment since the child with disability will tend to have more needs. Hence in this scenario it isn't the case of favouritism but as a justified response by the parent in order to take care of children with disabilities.

Poverty

Zigler and Hodapp (1986) proposed subgroups of children classified as having intellectual disabilities due to non-organic causes. The first one being children who have psychosocial Intellectual Disability in traditional sense, may be living in poverty and have at least one sibling and a parent with intellectual disability (Grossman, 1980). Farber (1986) put across a valid question. He wondered how only one or more sibling raised in poverty succumbed to mental retardation while others didn't and they had differing intellectual capacities. In fact, Plomin (1986) found that non shared familial experiences may account for variation among the siblings: birth order, different approaches to caregiving, idiosyncratic behaviour unique to only a specific sibling, sibling influences etc. Children also create their own unique environments by specifically choosing the way they respond and seek specific contexts (Scarr & McCartney, 1983). Owing to the existence of poverty, a new term has been coined- new morbidity which refers to a range of negative outcomes, including intellectual disabilities that are the result of societal ills and colleagues (Haggerty, Roughman, & Pless, 1975). Baumesiter & Kupstas found that New morbidity arises from behavioural, environmental and biological forces which act to produce experiences that collectively affect generations. Indeed, these children live in families which are poverty stricken, have multiple stressors, highly disorganised environments etc. which increased negative outcomes. Yet two siblings may develop different intellectual abilities has been addressed above.

Overall, siblings may experience both positive and negative feelings toward a sibling with Intellectual Disability. At times it would be peer pressure that may act as a threat to their self-esteem and provoke a need to avoid being identified with their sibling (Kaplan, 1969). The degree to which the sibling understands his or her own impairment, the approach to discipline that is adopted by parents, whether normal siblings are allowed to talk freely to their parents about their siblings disability are all the variables that can play a role in creating a positive or negative experience for the children. Some of the other negative experiences may include anger, feeling guilt over feeling anger and fear of being viewed in the same light. Positive experiences include developing greater tolerance, sensitivity to prejudice and compassion towards others (Grossman, 1972)

Moyson and Roeyers (2012) looked into the quality of life of siblings of children with Intellectual Disabilities from the perspective of the siblings themselves. Qualitative research and phenomenology based interviews were used to gauge an understanding of the sibling's frame of reference. Nine domains of sibling quality life that emerged were private time, forbearance, trust in well-being, joint activities, acceptance, mutual understanding, exchanging experiences, dealing with the outside world and social support.

National web based (Hodapp et al, 2010) surveys in US of 1160 adult male and female siblings of individuals with disabilities found that most reported fairly positive relationship with their siblings, close contact, good health and benefits from being a sibling to someone with a disability. Though women reports indicated that they benefitted more from the sibling relationship, they married much later, divorced less and had their first child in a much later age (Hodapp, Urbano, Burke, 2010).

Greenberg, Seltzer, Orsmond, Krauss (1999) found using a mailed questionnaire to collect data from 119 siblings of adults with Intellectual Disabilities. Almost 60 percent of the siblings of adults with Intellectual Disabilities would assume responsibility of primary caregiving. Closeness to the family of origin along with demands and constraints of midlife would determine the extent to which siblings were involved in the present as well as future.

Study by Findler et al (2009) explored psychological growth among siblings focused on the potential of positive growth. They examined 101 siblings of children with Intellectual Disabilities to find higher levels of growth with self-differentiation and perceived paternal acting as important contributors to this growth.

Approach to Stigma

Intellectual Disabilities come with a societal stigma attached to it. Indeed its one the harsh realities which impact caregiving in many ways. Which is why one of the reasons why the term Mental Retardation could have been replaced would be due to use of the words 'mental' and 'retarded' as a derogatory terms. It would be necessary to look at this disability in a larger context and understand how social perception of this disability has an impact on the family's experience of it. The kind culture one resides in will also determine how much stigma one experiences of being related to mentally retarded child. Owing to the large scale impact of stigma, it warranted the need for a different section altogether.

Undesirable mental traits and physical appearance can often arouse fear, derision, repulse, rejection, avoidance etc. though there is a greater degree of acceptance in the society over the past few decades (Rees, Spreen, & Harndek 1991). Another challenge faced by parents is that of social isolation. Peers, family friends and others may fail to comprehend the needs of the child with an intellectual disability (Friedrich, Greenberg, & Crnic, 1983). They would thus miss out on sharing of child care which typical parents would do. E.g. it would be harder for them to find a playdate than it would be for a normal child. Kazak and Wilcox, 1984 found that social outings such as shopping for meals etc. may also be relatively harder.

Initial studies of caregivers of children with Intellectual Disabilities revealed stigma, loss of face and increased anxiety level. A study by Chiu et al (2014), tried to go beyond this study and tested 211 caregivers in two Chinese cities. They found evidence that cultural values do not directly influence someone's mental wellbeing but works through the experience of stigma which brings about anxiety through experience of actual stigma or perceived stigma. Stigma therefore can be seen as an added stress for the caregiver which may have an adverse impact on their caregiving.

A follow up study by Yang X in (2015)China with primary caregivers of people with Intellectual Disabilities explored internalised self-stigma among family caregivers. It was found that stigmatized feelings would hurt caregivers in the Chinese context more than the cognitive thoughts. Caregivers with higher face concern are more likely than others to experience feelings of shame, self-blame and powerlessness and suffered poorer mental health. Those coming from low socio economic groups were especially vulnerable.

There is always a concern that negative societal attitude may be internalised by the family members. According to Ryckman & Handerson (1965), for parents, children may be a psychological extensions of themselves and hence the way their children are perceived is considered personally. The children with Intellectual Difficulties then become an object of shame rather than parental pride. Similarly, siblings also tend to view both their brothers and sisters as their extension but to a lesser degree (Grossman, 1972). Roos (1963) found that if a child or sibling has unwanted traits, it is hard not to view them without feelings of shame, hostility and as poor reflectors of them, at least initially. They would also tend to experience guilt at the same time for feeling so. All of these would have an impact on their self-esteem. In an interesting study of adaption by Mintzer, Als, Tronick and Brazelton, (1985) showed that the parents with children with significant difficulties did not have a positive view till they saw the child as a separate individual. They described their initial experience as a series of assaults to their self-esteem which impaired their parenting. The birth itself was a shock with the following period characterized by disequilibrium. It is also important to note that behaviour of children which are key to their bond with the parents such as responding to parents, smiling, low eye contact etc. may also act as a stressor.

In another study it was found that Taiwanese employees had general positive attitudes and positive affective reactions towards people with Intellectual Disabilities and these positive reactions increased with longer work contact (Hsu, Huang et al, 2015).

Grandparents

Literature review shows that grandparents tend to mirror the reactions of the parents i.e. those of shock, grief and anger when they first find out that their grandchild has a disability. They do eventually become a part of the family system and give instrumental and emotional support. Of course this depends on a lot of factors such as residential proximity, how much they understand about the child's disability and emotional relationship they have with the child and the family. Their support is increased when they gain access to appropriate information regarding the disability, experience good communication as well as the availability of support groups (Lee, Gardner 2010).

From the grandparent's perspective, a lot of studies seem to show positive consequences such as pride in grandchildren's achievement, satisfaction, deep sense of devotion, and change in lifestyle habits such as increased exercise, healthier diet, decline in smoking and alcohol use, gratification, feeling useful, improved relations with family etc. (Burton, 1992; Minkler and Roe, 1993; Pruchno, 1999).

A National Survey in 1992-94 in US found that 25% of grandparent caregivers suffer from depression. Problems are exacerbated when grandparents belonged to an ethnic minority. e.g. 60 % of African American grandparents in Burton's study (1992) found that 61% were smoking more than before, most of them were anxious all the time or depressed and for 36% medical problems had worsened. Minkler & Roe (1993) observed how there is a delay or failure to seek health services for their own health for grandparents who are caregivers.

Caregiving is often an added burden to an already difficult course of life for grandparents (Kaplan, Strawbridge, Wallhagen, Shema; 1996). Janicki, McCallion et al, surveyed 164 grandparents caring for 208 children with developmental delays or disabilities. On an average of 7 years they had cared for at least one grandchild and data for these parents showed that caregiving was a consuming role, they experienced uncertainty, were constantly worried about the future and were unable to access sufficient formal and informal supports. Their ages ranged from 42 to 82 and vast majority of them were female and African Americans.

One study compared 74 urban Latino grandparents as caregivers of children with special needs with grandparents of children without special needs. It was found that grandparents caring for children with special needs had significantly higher number of depressive symptoms despite holding known risk and protective factors constant (Burnette, 2000).

Awareness about services available is crucial especially when child grows out of the school system and grandparents may be unable to keep up with caregiving due to their age and health issues or in case of death. In those cases, where they do know about the services, grandparents of grandchildren with developmental disabilities have faced systems that are unresponsive to their needs. Lack of sufficient transportation to agencies, long waiting periods, and poor access to documentation that is needed may add to their frustration (McCallion et al., 2000).

McCallion et al. (2000) also looked into calls over a nine month period to 800 hotline of New York City Department of Aging Grandparents Resource Centre. They found that grandparents of grandchildren with disabilities typically indicated five major support needs that were hard to meet i.e. financial, guardianship, respite care, emotional support and problems coordinating with a variety of social systems that includes health care, educational supports and housing. The issue of guardianship would create more problems depending upon the policies. Some policies would not allow grandchildren as dependents on insurance policy unless their grandparents have legal custody (Casper & Bryson, 1998).

At times, grandparents playing the role of an additional caregiver seems to alleviate stress levels of mothers that care for children with Intellectual disabilities. Indeed maternal depression was observed where mothers received less emotional support from grandparents, were younger in age and had poorer physical health. Grandparents of younger children were more likely to provide instrumental support rather than grandparents of adult children (Heller, Hsieh, Rowistz, 1999).

A study by Liona Findler (2014) examined the contributions of internal and external resources as being factors that contributed to stress or personal growth. 94 grandparents of those with Intellectual Disabilities along with 105 grandparents of children without intellectual disability completed a variety of scales on the parameters of perceived social support & stress, level of differentiation, multidimensional experience of grandparenthood etc. Surprisingly group differences showed higher negative emotions in grandparents of children without intellectual disability. Growth was often found to be related to gender, symbolic and behavioural aspects of grandparenting. While stress was related to cost of grandparenting, internal resource of self-differentiation, and external resource of social support.

Support Staff as Caregivers

A survey of ninety seven Community based direct support professionals (DSP) found that those who worked with aging adults showed significantly lower empowerment than those who worked with a younger age group. They were also comparatively at higher risk of attrition. This study compared variables of control, job stress & satisfaction, perceived organizational support, organizational commitment turnover etc. (Laws, Kolomer, Gallagher, 2014)

Support staff working with individuals with intellectual disability and challenging behavior tended to experience high levels of work stress. A study explored the potential of using acceptance and mindfulness based stress-management for support staff to see if they showed improvement in their well-being, thought suppression, psychological inflexibility, distress and perceived work stressors. 66 support staff randomly assigned to intervention group were compared to 54 support staff in the control group. Thought suppression was greatly reduced along with reductions in levels of distress which stayed constant after six weeks. There was however, no change in well being or psychological inflexibility (McConachie et al 2014).

One study explored positive perceptions that were held by 101 support staff working with adults with Intellectual Disabilities by a new measure The Staff Positive Contributions Questionnarie (SPCQ) and found that positive perceptions do exist and may need more theoretical explanations (Hastings, Horne, 2004). Another study that expanded on this one, with a staff of 926 found General positive factors and positive work motivations which was associated with high levels of personal accomplishments. Other burnout variables found were emotional exhaustion & depersonalization. (Lunsky, Hastings et al, 2014)

It was found that 43 caregivers who worked for around 3 years, could give very reliable assessment of pain experienced by 187 individuals with intellectual disabilities living in residential facility. (Fogel et al, 2015).

GUIDELINES FOR CAREGIVERS AND SUPPORT SYSTEM

In this section we explore researches that have explored practices, ideas and qualities that caregivers need to develop to make the process of caregiving a decent one.

Blacher et al (1987), parents experience confusion and disorientation regarding what to expect when raising a child with intellectual difficulty. Since every child comes with unique set of challenges, discipline tactics have to be largely customised. Parents need to adjust their expectations regarding following of verbal directions and it would help if involvement with educational institutions system needs to be enhanced.

A couple of researches that investigated coping styles found that 'positive outlook' and 'acceptance' of child aided coping (Meredith, 1986). Other analyses found that realistic appraisal of disability, identifying positive contributions made by children and inner strength also helped in coping (Hancock et al. 1990; Mullins 1987). Keeping these in mind, it would be advisable to use cognitive therapy to help reframe your perspective of the situation and that's exactly what Summers and colleagues (1989) suggest i.e. adapting positive subjective perceptions help in coping during stressful times.

Trivette, Dunst, Hamby and LaPointe (1996) reviewed research regarding empowerment. They interviewed 74 mothers out of which 77% were mothers of those with intellectual disabilities. According to researchers, empowerment would mean the family's belief in the capacity to acquire additional competencies as and when required. They found that parents who were involved in planning and treatment of children felt a sense of satisfaction, competence, efficacy and sense of control. Owing to their findings they suggest that the empowerment philosophy by the provider was related to parent perception which stemmed from family centred practice. Another interesting study by Trivette, Dunst, Deal, Hamer, and Propst (1990) focussed on a strength based approach They advocate the need for the clinician to build on strengths of the family rather than just focussing on things that need to be fixed. After much review of literature regarding it they agreed on the following 12 qualities of strong families.

1. Commitment to the well-being and growth of each family member.
2. Appreciation for the small things that each family member does well.
3. Time commitments made for formal and informal activities together.
4. A sense of purpose for understanding good times and bad times.
5. A sense of congruence regarding goals and needs.
6. The ability to communicate with one another that emphasizes positive interactions.
7. A varied repertoire of coping strategies.
8. Problem solving strategies that result in meeting needs.
9. Clear rules, values and beliefs.
10. Flexible and adaptable roles.
11. To be able to see positive aspects in life.
12. Balance between internal and external family resources.

Active participation in the treatment is seen as more important for parents than traditional treatment skills such as empathy and listening. Trivette, Dunst, and Hamby (1996) showed that feelings of self efficacy and empowerment can be increased with increase decision making, choice and self-determination for parents. Indeed they found that perceived control could help predict people's motivation and performance.

A Focus group research by Freedman, Litchfield, and Warfield (1995), looked into perspectives of mothers with children (in the range of 4 to 32) with Intellectual Disabilities related to their work life. Surprisingly work was viewed as a welcome relief as it provided a distraction from stressors at home and provided a sense of control, predictability or competence which was in contrast to constant unpredictability at home. Many parents pursued education or work in humanities inspired by the needs they encountered at home while those who were particularly influenced by the disability made no changes since the then system worked for them. It is interesting to see how additional work in a different context can seem to have a buffering effect on daily stressors. Part time work would be a solid recommendation to create a space that is different from home environment.

Families with children with Intellectual Disabilities will have multiple needs that need to be addressed simultaneously such as mental health, medical needs, and developmental needs of the child apart from other familial needs. Experiences so frequently taken for granted by normal families such as having a social life, planning an outing, scheduling a wide range of appointments and activities, finances-all of these can act as stressors. Hodap and Zigler (1993) suggested specific macrosystem and exosystem solely on the basis of their field experience to make it easier for these families to function.

1. Encourage insurance companies to look at healthcare more broadly.
2. Promote the family as a unit of service rather than the individual child.
3. Advocate for Medicaid to cover more home-based services for these families.

Though these are simple directives and there is no suggestion for future research, it is a good starting point for policies that address the family as a whole.

Support for family has been very frequently seen as a need for families with children with disabilities especially in the case of infants and toddlers. Social support acts as a buffer to stress that comes along with raising a child with disability. Beckman, Newcomb, Frank, Brown, Flier (1993) propose a system of developing a flexible model that addresses the family as a unit to bridge the gap between the existing practices and idea practices. To move our services from being individual oriented to family oriented. They give an example of Project Assist, a family centered program where parents of children with disabilities receive individual, group and instrumental support. Instrumental support often includes consultation, advocacy for Individualized Educational Planning, medication and health issues and other welfare systems for the child.

Some research which exclusively looked into grandparents as caregivers, even though they weren't the primary caregivers suggested a program that targets the needs of grandparents caring for children with developmental disabilities (McCallion et al., 2000). This intervention was successful in bringing down symptoms of depression and increase their sense of caregiving mastery and sense of empowerment. It included the following components.

1. Grandparent support group.
2. Consumer-developed manual of locally based services.
3. Peer support from other grandparents.
4. Active case management from the participating agencies.

The society of teachers of Family Medicine has recognized that family physicians need to be trained to care for persons with Intellectual Disabilities. Their survey found that 84% of programs provide residents with such trainings and 60% instruct residents in this area. Most directors ranked it as important. (Tyler, Snyder, Zyzanski, 1999). Another research which propagates looking at family as a whole.

Magana, Li, Miranda, Paradiso (2015) developed a culturally sensitive health education intervention for Latina mothers who care for both youth and adults with Intellectual Disabilities. This intervention was introduced because Latina mothers who took care of persons with Intellectual Disabilities over the lifespan struggled to take care of their own health needs. Participants who went through the intervention showed greater increases in self-care, self-efficacy, nutrition and overall health behaviours. This research shows that culturally relevant interventions can help reduce stressors among caregivers.

CONCLUSION

This chapter sheds light into the lives and experiences of caregivers. Though we know a lot of variables that come into play to contribute to caregiver gain and caregiver stress, we are only just beginning to scratch the surface of the possible research in this field. Further research about the experiences of caregivers with regards to cultural context, availability of support, literacy levels, stigma, psychoeducation, age, societal perceptions etc. is recommended to help facilitate the development of better rehabilitative systems for both individuals with Intellectual disabilities and their caregivers.

REFERENCES

Baroff & Olley. (2012). Mental Retardation: Nature, Cause and Management. Routledge.

Bauman, S. (2004). Parents of children with Mental Retardation: Coping Mechanisms and Support needs, Greenberg, Krauss, Osmond, Seltzer; 1999, Siblings of Adults with Mental Illness or Mental Retardation: Current Involvement and Future Caregiving. *Psychiatric Services (Washington, D.C.)*, *50*, 1214–1219.

Besser, S. (1998). The positive impact of children with an intellectual disability on the family. Journal of intellectual & Developmental Disability, 23(1), 57-70.

Blacher, J., Baker, B. L., & MacLean, W. E. Jr. (2007, September). Positive Impact of Intellectual Disability on Families. *American Journal of Mental Retardation*, *112*(5), 330–348. doi:10.1352/0895-8017(2007)112[0330:PIOIDO]2.0.CO;2 PMID:17676958

Bray, N. W. (1997). Article. *International Review of Research in Mental Retardation*, *20*(111), 112.

Burack, Hodapp, & Zigler. (1988). Handbook of Mental Retardation and Development. Cambridge University Press.

Cant, R., Gething, L., Kendig, H., Llewellyn, G., & McConnell, D. (2010). Health status and coping strategies among older parent-carers of adults with intellectual disabilities in an Australian sample. *Research in Developmental Disabilities: A Multidisciplinary Journal, 31*(6), 1176-1186.

Chiu, M. Y., Yang, X., Wong, H. T., & Li, J. H. (2014). The mediating effect of affective stigma between face concern and general mental health - The case of Chinese caregivers of children with intellectual disability. *Research in Developmental Disabilities*, *36C*, 437–446.

Cohen, S. R., Holloway, S. D., Domínguez-Pareto, I., & Kuppermann, M. (2015, January). Support and Self-Efficacy Among Latino and White Parents of Children With ID. *American Journal on Intellectual and Developmental Disabilities*, *120*(1), 16–31. doi:10.1352/1944-7558-120.1.16 PMID:25551264

Daily, D. K., Ardinger, H. H., & Holmes, G. E. (2000, February). Identification and evaluation of mental retardation. *American Family Physician*, *61*(4), 1059–1067, 1070. PMID:10706158

Essex, E., Seltzer, M., & Krauss, M. (1999). Differences in coping effectiveness and well-being among aging Mothers and Fathers of Adults with Mental Retardation. *American Journal of Mental Retardation*, *104*(6), 545–563. doi:10.1352/0895-8017(1999)104<0545:DICEAW>2.0.CO;2 PMID:10587735

Findler, L. (2014, February). The Experience of Stress and Personal Growth Among Grandparents of Children With and Without Intellectual Disability. *Intellectual and Developmental Disabilities*, *52*(1), 32–48. doi:10.1352/1934-9556-52.1.32 PMID:24635690

Findler, L., Vardi, A., & Taylor, S. J. (2009, February). Psychological Growth Among Siblings of Children With and Without Intellectual Disabilities. *Intellectual and Developmental Disabilities*, *47*(1), 1–12. doi:10.1352/2009.47:1-12 PMID:19170414

Floyd, F. J., & Zmich, D. E. (1991). Marriage and the parenting partnership: Perceptions and interactions of parents with mentally retarded and typically developing children. *Child Development*, *62*(6), 1434–1448. doi:10.2307/1130817 PMID:1786726

Gavidia-Payne, S., & Stoneman, Z. (2006). Marital adjustment in families of young children with disabilities: Associations with daily hassles and problem-focused coping. *American Journal of Mental Retardation*, *111*(1), 1–14. doi:10.1352/0895-8017(2006)111[1:MAIFOY]2.0.CO;2 PMID:16332152

Gohel, Mukherjee, & Choudhary. (2011). *Psychosocial impact on the Parents of mentally retarded children in Anand District*. Indian Association of Preventive and Social Medicine.

Griffith, G. M., & Hastings, R. P. (2014, September). Hastings RP. 'He's hard work, but he's worth it'. The experience of caregivers of individuals with intellectual disabilities and challenging behaviour: A meta-synthesis of qualitative research. *Journal of Applied Research in Intellectual Disabilities*, *27*(5), 401–419. doi:10.1111/jar.12073 PMID:24105755

Hastings, R., Horne, S., & Felce, D. (2004, January). Positive Perceptions Held by Support Staff in Community Mental Retardation Services. *American Journal of Mental Retardation*, *109*(1), 53–62. doi:10.1352/0895-8017(2004)109<53:PPHBSS>2.0.CO;2 PMID:14651449

Hastings, R. P., Huws, J. C., Reilly, D. E., & Vaughan, F. L. (2008). "When your child dies you don't belong in that world any more." Experiences of mothers whose child with an intellectual disability has died. *Journal of Applied Research in Intellectual Disabilities*, *21*(6), 546–560. doi:10.1111/j.1468-3148.2008.00427.x

Hayden, M. E., & Heller, T. (1997, October). Support, Problem-Solving/Coping Ability, and Personal Burden of Younger and Older Caregivers of Adults With Mental Retardation. *Mental Retardation*, *35*(5), 364–372. doi:10.1352/0047-6765(1997)035<0364:SPAAPB>2.0.CO;2 PMID:9339065

Heller, T., Hsieh, K., & Rowitz, L. (2000). Grandparents as Supports to Mothers of Persons with Intellectual Disability. *Journal of Gerontological Social Work, 33*(4).

Henninger, N. A., & Taylor, J. L. (2014, April). Family Perspectives on a Successful Transition to Adulthood for Individuals With Disabilities. *Intellectual and Developmental Disabilities*, *52*(2), 98–111. doi:10.1352/1934-9556-52.2.98 PMID:24725109

Ho, G. S. M., & Mak, W. W. S. (2007). Caregiving perceptions of Chinese mothers of children with intellectual disability in Hong Kong. *Journal of Applied Research in Intellectual Disabilities*, *20*(2), 145–156. doi:10.1111/j.1468-3148.2006.00309.x

Hodapp, R. M., Urbano, R. C., & Burke, M. M. (2010, February). Urbano RC, Burke MM, Adult female and male siblings of persons with disabilities: Findings from a national survey. *Intellectual and Developmental Disabilities*, *48*(1), 52–62. doi:10.1352/1934-9556-48.1.52 PMID:20503816

Hodapp, R. M., Urbano, R. C., & Burke, M. M. (2010, February). *Adult female and male siblings of person with disabilities*: Findings from a national survey. *Intellectual and Developmental Disabilities*, *48*(1), 52–62. doi:10.1352/1934-9556-48.1.52 PMID:20503816

Hsu, T.-H., Huang, Y.-T., Liu, Y.-H., Ososkie, J., Fried, J., & Bezyak, J. (2015, March). Taiwanese Attitudes and Affective Reactions Toward Individuals and Coworkers Who Have Intellectual Disabilities. *American Journal on Intellectual and Developmental Disabilities*, *120*(2), 110–124. doi:10.1352/1944-7558-120.2.110 PMID:25715181

Jan, S. (1999, September). Siblings of Adults with Mental Illness or Mental retardation: Current Involvement and Expectation of Future caregiving. *Psychiatric Services (Washington, D.C.)*, *50*(9).

John, K. (2011). *People with disabilities and their siblings: Building Concepts of Support and Transition*. American Association on Intellectual and Development Disabilities Annual Conference.

Jones, J. L., Oseland, L. M., Morris, K. L., & Larzelere, R. E. (2014, November). Parent report of conversations with their adolescents with intellectual disability. *Journal of Applied Research in Intellectual Disabilities*, *27*(6), 521–530. doi:10.1111/jar.12090 PMID:24677601

Kerenhappachu, M.S., & Sridevi. (2014). Caregiver's Burden and Perceived Social Support in Mothers of Children with Mental Retardation. *International Journal of Scientific and Research Publications, 4*(4).

Kimura, M., & Yamazaki, Y. (2013, October). Yamazaki Y., The lived experience of mothers of multiple children with intellectual disabilities. *Qualitative Health Research*, *23*(10), 1307–1319. doi:10.1177/1049732313504828 PMID:24022734

Laws, C. B., Kolomer, S. R., & Gallagher, M. J. (2014, December). Age of Persons Supported and Factors Predicting Intended Staff Turnover: A Comparative Study. *Inclusion*, *2*(4), 316–328. doi:10.1352/2326-6988-2.4.316

Long, K. A., Kao, B., Plante, W., Seifer, R., & Lobato, D. (2015, March). Cultural and Child-Related Predictors of Distress Among Latina Caregivers of Children With Intellectual Disabilities. *American Journal on Intellectual and Developmental Disabilities*, *120*(2), 145–165. doi:10.1352/1944-7558-120.2.145 PMID:25715183

Lukmanuel Hakeem & Subathra. (2013). A Study on the Attitude of Siblings Towards Their Mentally Retarded Brother/Sister. *Indian Journal of Applied Research, 3*(1).

Lunsky, Y., Hastings, R. P., Hensel, J., Arenovich, T., & Dewa, C. S. (2014, August). Perceptions of Positive Contributions and Burnout in Community Developmental Disability Workers. *Intellectual and Developmental Disabilities*, *52*(4), 249–257. doi:10.1352/1934-9556-52.4.249 PMID:25061769

Magaña, S., Li, H., Miranda, E., & Paradiso de Sayu, R. (2014). Improving health behaviours of Latina mothers of youths and adults with intellectual and developmental disabilities. *Journal of Intellectual Disability Research*, *59*(5), 397–410. doi:10.1111/jir.12139 PMID:24761812

Matthew, P. (2000). Characteristics of the Grandparents and the Children with Disabilities for Whom They Care. *Journal of Gerontological Social Work*, *33*(3), 35–55. doi:10.1300/J083v33n03_03

McCallion, P., Janicki, M., Grant-Griffin, L., & Kolomer, S. R. (2000). Grandparent carers II: Service needs and service provision issues. *Journal of Gerontological Social Work*, *33*(3), 57–84. doi:10.1300/J083v33n03_04

McConachie, D. A., McKenzie, K., Morris, P. G., & Walley, R. M. (2014, June). Acceptance and mindfulness-based stress management for support staff caring for individuals with intellectual disabilities. *Research in Developmental Disabilities*, *35*(6), 1216–1227. doi:10.1016/j.ridd.2014.03.005 PMID:24685937

Moyson, T., & Roeyers, H. (2012, January). Roeyers H., 'The overall quality of my life as a sibling is all right, but of course, it could always be better'. Quality of life of siblings of children with intellectual disability: The siblings' perspectives. *Journal of Intellectual Disability Research*, *56*(1), 87–101. doi:10.1111/j.1365-2788.2011.01393.x PMID:21366753

Neece, C. L., Blacher, J., & Baker, B. L. (2010, July). Impact on Siblings of Children With Intellectual Disability: The Role of Child Behavior Problems. *American Journal on Intellectual and Developmental Disabilities*, *115*(4), 291–306. doi:10.1352/1944-7558-115.4.291 PMID:20597724

Poreddi, BIrudu, Thimmaiah, & Math. (2015). Mental health literacy among caregivers of persons with mental illness: A descriptive survey. *Journal of Neurosciences in Rural Practice, 6*(3), 355-360.

Richard, P. (2007). Hastings andTracey Lloyd, Expressed emotion in families of children and adults with intellectual disabilities, Mental Retardation and Developmental Disabilities Research Reviews. *Special Issue: Families of Children with Developmental Disabilities*, *13*(4), 339–345.

Rogner, J., & Wessels, E. T. (1994). Coping strategies of mothers and fathers with a first- or second-born mentally handicapped child. *Praxis der Kinderpsychologie und Kinderpsychiatrie*, *43*(4), 125–129. PMID:8016022

Sethi, S., Bhargava, S. C., & Dhiman, V. (2007). Study of level of stress and burden in the caregivers of children with mental retardation. *Eastern Journal of Medicine*, *12*, 21–24.

Suresh, A. P., Benjamin, T. E., Crasta, J. E., Alwinesh, M. T., Kanniappan, G., Padankatti, S. M., & Russell, P. S. et al. (2014). Comparison of burden among primary care-givers of children with autism and intellectual disability against children with intellectual disability only in a hospital population in India. *Indian Journal of Pediatrics*, *81*(Suppl 2), S179–S182.

Todd, S. (2007). Silenced grief: Living with the death of a child with intellectual disabilities. *Journal of Intellectual Disability Research*, *51*(8), 637–648. doi:10.1111/j.1365-2788.2007.00949.x PMID:17598877

Tyler, C. V. Jr, Snyder, C. W., & Zyzanski, S. J. (1999, October). Caring for Adults With Mental Retardation: Survey of Family Practice Residency Program Directors. *Mental Retardation*, *37*(5), 347–352. doi:10.1352/0047-6765(1999)037<0347:CFAWMR>2.0.CO;2 PMID:10581920

Venkatesh Kumar, G. (2008, July). Psychological Stress and Coping Strategies of the Parents of Mentally Challenged Children. *Journal of the Indian Academy of Applied Psychology*, *34*(2), 227–231.

Weissman-Fogel. (2015, March 31). Pain experience of adults with intellectual disabilities - caregiver reports. *Journal of Intellectual Disability Research*.

Yang, X. (2015, March 23). No matter how I think, it already hurts: Self-stigmatized feelings and face concern of Chinese caregivers of people with intellectual disabilities. *Journal of Intellectual Disabilities*, *19*(4), 367–380. doi:10.1177/1744629515577909 PMID:25801087

KEY TERMS AND DEFINITIONS

Caregiver: A caregiver is any person who takes on the responsibility of assisting someone with a mental, emotional or physical disability.

Caregiver Gain: High tolerance, compassion, sense of fulfilment and satisfaction and other positive experiences as a result of caring for someone with mental, emotional or a physical disability is called caregiver gain.

Caregiver Stress: Stress, fatigues, exhaustion and other negative experiences as a result of caring for someone with mental, emotional or a physical disability is called caregiver stress.

Expressed Emotion: Expressed emotion is hostile, critical and overinvolved emotional attitude of a family member while caring for another family member who has a disorder.

Problem Solving: Problem solving is the ability to be able to deal with problem in an effective manner.

Stigma: Stigma is a negative label attached to a person who is different from others. Negative attitudes may also lead to discrimination and negative behaviour towards the individual who is stigmatised.

Chapter 8
Quality of Life of People with Intellectual Disability

Jamila Firdaus
Navrachana Higher Secondary School, India

Mansi Jadeja
Gujarat Forensic Sciences University, India

ABSTRACT

Intellectual Disability, according to DSM-V is defined as a "disorder with onset during the developmental period that includes both intellectual and adaptive functioning deficits in conceptual, social and practical domains." Clinical judgment and individually administered standardized tests confirm deficits in intellectual functions such as reasoning, problem solving, planning, abstract thinking, judgment, academic learning and learning from experience. Adaptive functioning is also deficit as the individual needs assistance in one or more activities of daily living such as communication, social participation and independent living across multiple environments such as home, school, work and community. The need to understand the quality of life of people with intellectual disability is crucial as this mental disability is considered to be a major setback for any individual and his/her family. It needs to be highlighted here, that the families of people with intellectual disability also play a crucial role. New research reviews are required to bring policy changes and better tools.

INTRODUCTION: INTELLECTUAL DISABILITY

The term Intellectual Disability has its roots in the term 'mental retardation' and 'developmental disability' (Health Commission, 1981; Thompson & O'Quinn, 1979; Wolfe, 1992) and its epidemiology is usually developmental or subsequent to traumatic brain injury. Individuals may have mild, moderate or severe intellectual disabilities depending on the assessments of their cognitive abilities (Arthur, 1998; Hogg & Sebba, 1987).Intellectual disability could be defined as an inability to carry out everyday adaptive functions which make living simple. These deficits could result in difficulties in communication, social participation and independent living across multiple environments such as home, school, workplace

DOI: 10.4018/978-1-5225-0089-6.ch008

and community. On more complex level, intellectual functions of reasoning, problem solving, planning, abstract thinking, judgment, academic learning and learning from experiences could also be hindered.

According to the DSM-V, intellectual disability is defined as a ''disorder with onset during the developmental period that includes both intellectual and adaptive functioning deficits in conceptual, social and practical domains" (DSM-V, 2013).The World Health Organization's definitions of impairment, disability and handicap are generally regarded as authoritative, although multiple interpretations militate against a consensus (Bowe, 1978; Fulcher, 1989; Smyer, McHale, Birkel, & Madle, 1988). A very basic disagreement is whether the disability is a personal tragedy for the individual or is it more of a social problem arising because of disabling barriers within the environment (Abberley, 1987; Bickenbach, 1993; Gleeson, 1995).

Many terms, definitions and various descriptions of people with an intellectual disability see them in a 'deficit perspective'. Such a perspective does not give much importance to the social place, humanity and abilities of people with intellectual disabilities (Bickenbach, 1993; Schalock, 2004). On the other hand, the 'similarity perspective' focuses on capabilities. It supports the argument that all persons can learn, irrespective of the degree or complexity of their disabilities (Oliver, 1996). Various authors have postulated that even very disabled people are capable of making choices that are meaningful and realistic.

General definitions of quality of life prevail in the literature reviews. Schalock (1997) referred to perceived quality of life as satisfaction with the main areas of one's own life. Brown (1994) stated that enhancement of quality of life was related to reduction in the discrepancy between an individual's achieved and unmet needs. Brown (1998) also mentioned that quality of life is the extent to which individuals have increasing control of their environments. Heal (1994) described it in terms of global satisfaction with one's lifestyle and control over resources that produced satisfaction.

A strong literature review supports the idea that conceptualization and assessment of quality of life of people with intellectual disability should be done in a manner similar to those which are done for people without such a disability. Schalock's (1999) core dimensions of quality of life of people with intellectual disability included emotional well-being, personal development, physical well being, self-determination, social inclusion and rights. Emphasis was also put upon individual improvement rather than population improvement (Brown, 1998; Cummins, 1996; Zapf, 1987). It was also argued that people with intellectual disabilities should be more involved in decision-making about policies and programs aimed at improving their quality of life (Brown, 1995; Brown, McLinden, & Porter, 1998,Goode andHogg (1994), Nankervis (1997), Schalock (2002), and Schalock and Verdugo (2002).

Fabian (1991) identified three approaches of quality of life. The first two approaches view quality of life as an objective social indicator for specific groups and viewing it as a broad subjective measure of life satisfaction. The third approach is a measure of adaptive functioning which was identified as an alternative for individuals who were unable to self report or whose life experiences were inequitably limited.

RELATIONSHIP BETWEEN INTELLECTUAL DISABILITY AND QUALITY OF LIFE

People may have difficulty in "knowing" a person with an intellectual disability. It is usually difficult to understand what their feelings, interests, wants, preferences and inner life is like. Several authors have attempted to have a look at these aspects and have described that "knowing" a person with intellectual disability would emerge when a person spends more time with the disabled person. This 'knowing" would become a central part of the quality of relationship and create a better understanding (Gustiatas & Young, 1986; Goode, 1984; Keenan, 1992; & Sacks, 1995).

There is growing concern for a need to ensure that all individuals with an intellectual disability enjoy life as beautifully as others and share equal rights. Such rights cover many aspects of life out of which quality of living or quality of life is a part. The relationship between intellectual disability and quality of life is a deep one. One may wonder as to how a person with an intellectual disability would communicate and express his/her feelings regarding various aspects of quality of life? One would at least require basic level of intelligence in order to carry this out.

Quality of Life

Quality of Life can be considered as a concept that identifies what is important, necessary and satisfying in human existence. The concept dates back many hundreds of years. The earliest known reference to Quality of Life is made by Aristotle who used the term 'eudemonia' or 'the good life'. However, this notion did not enter into social sciences, particularly sociology and psychology, as a defining concept until the beginning of the 20th century and only began being researched in the field of disability in the 1980's and 1990's. Since this time there has been a large growth in the use of the concept and its application within the field of intellectual and allied disabilities (Brown et al. 1989; Schalock 1990; Goode 1994; Felce & Perry 1996; Cummins 1996).

Quality of Life is an integrating concept, which takes into account a number of previous approaches and concepts such as normalization, inclusion, and empowerment, though the development of Quality of Life is resulting in some modification to those practices. For example, the application of personal choice within a developmental framework may set limits for some individuals on the degree to which they wish or feel comfortable with inclusion. Thus it is important to recognize individual and family variability. there are further principles integrated within this holistic concept including, for example, self-image, lifespan, perception, inter and intra personal variability (Schalock & Verdugo 2002; Brown & Brown 2003; Turnbull et al. 2004). Domains cover all areas of individual and family living. Examples are health, finance, community, family, employment, education (see Felce & Perry 1996; Brown et al. 2003, 2006). It is recognized that all of the domains are linked and are activated through such principles as choice. For example, recreation and leisure may for some people the best way to improve physical health and employment. It is this notion of holism that makes Quality of Life an interesting prism through which to examine policies and practices for individuals with disabilities, their families and social network (Brown & Brown 2003).

Although different researchers have categorized Quality of Life of comprising of different domains, each set of Quality of Life domains cover the major areas of life functions. Much used in international public policy are the domains used by the World Health Organization: physical health, psychological well-being, social relations and environment (Murphy et al. 2000). Brown & Brown (2003) consolidated these ideas for practice in disability services into three core domains and nine sub-domains: Being (namely physical, psychological and spiritual well-being), Belonging (namely physical, social and community belonging) and Becoming (namely practical, leisure and growth becoming). Another widely used set of domains is described by Schalock & Verdugo (2002), namely: emotional well-being, interpersonal relations, material well-being, personal development, physical well-being, self-determination, social inclusion, and rights. The various domains discussed by different researchers have a wide degree of commonality though different labels are sometimes employed. All the recent domain structures cover similar ground and reflect the particular context involved.

Many authors have regarded quality of life as a multidimensional concept that covers life satisfaction and other aspects like psychological and subjective well being (Abbey & Andrews, 1986; Headey & Wearing, 1992; Pavot & Diener, 1993). Quality of life seems to be more than the subjective experience of life satisfaction. Schalock (1996) explained three definitions of quality of life which were most representative:

1. Quality of life is experienced when a person's basic needs are met and he has opportunities to pursue and achieve goals.
2. Quality of life is a multidimensional concept involving a number of core dimensions relating to well being.
3. Quality of life reflects a person's desired conditions of living and health and wellness.

The terms subjective well being and subjective quality of life refer to the perceptions of the individual. Life satisfaction means the degree to which the individual's life is perceived to match some implicit or explicit internal standard or referent (Evans, 1994). Subjective quality of life is a personal phenomenon more closely related to the broader concept of quality of life.

Researches in the 1980s focused on individuals with intellectual disability affected by deinstitutionalization (Hughes, 1995; Parmenter, Cummins, Shaddock & Stancliffe, 1994; Richmond, 1983; Schalock, 1994). Clear links between quality of life and normalization, deinstitutionalization, integration, choice and empowerment were established (Brown, 1994; Edgerton, 1996; Goode & Hogg, 1994; Goode, 1992; Parmenter, 1995; Romney, 1994; Schalock, 1994).

The broad emphasis in quality of life research during 1990s was to improve population quality of life. The World Health Organization placed the study and improvement of population quality of life as a primary goal (Evans, 1994). Researchers sought to inform decision-making for public programs and services that purported to improve quality of life (Cheng, 1988; Evans, 1994; Faden & Laplege, 1992; Goodinson & Singleton, 1989; Halpern, 1993; Hatton, 1998; Hughes & Hwang, 1996; Social Policy Directorate, 1994).

Communication

Individuals with intellectual disability are most varied, particularly in terms of their abilities to communicate with others around them (Cirrin & Rowland, 1985).Thus, it becomes important to understand the different communication challenges faced by these people in order to understand them and their quality of life. Communicative competence is crucial (Butterfield, Arthur, & Linfoot, 1992) and so establishing meaningful communication is a major challenge for their families, caregivers and service providers (Feil, 1993).

Researchers have developed specific strategies to minimize these communication deficits. The life sharing approach described by Goode and Hogg (1994) is a method in which adult clients and caregivers share and record life histories and biographies to enhance communication and understanding. Systematic gathering of information from communication partners was utilized by Shaddock, Dowse, Richards and Spinks (1998) to represent the views of adults with intellectual disability at formal tribunal hearings.

Literature demonstrates consensus that communicative behaviors of people with intellectual disability are diverse and frequently difficult to interpret (Arthur, 1998; Goode, 1997). Contemporary research about communication training recognized the potential of communicative intent of subtle, idiosyncratic and non-symbolic behaviors. Some learners communicate effectively without the need for conventional symbols (Carter & Hook, 1998). The most ethical approach seems to be of that in which communication with these individuals is taken seriously and they are considered as an authentic communicator (Tetzchner and Jensen, 1999).

In 1988 the NINDS (NIH) estimated that 90% of children with severe ID manifested some type of language disorder (McLean et al., 1999); likewise adults with mild to moderate ID often exhibit difficulties with speech and language (Cheslock et al., 2008). Research has shown that adults with ID exhibit deficits in multiple aspects of communication, including written, expressive, and receptive modes (Berry, 1972; Merrill & Mar, 1987; Abbeduto, Furman, & Davies, 1989; Abbeduto & Nuccio, 1991; Merrill & Jackson, 1992a; Merrill & Jackson, 1992b; Belva et al., 2012). This may be due to the fact that individuals with ID have reduced cognitive resources compared to typical peers (Kail, 1992; Koul & Clapsaddle, 2006). In areas such as health care, individuals with ID often face cognitive challenges in communicating their needs, understanding and adherence to recommendations or treatments (Ward, Nichols, & Freedman, 2010). Given the communicative challenges faced by individuals with ID, it stands to reason that the most effective ways to communicate with these people may be different from the ways in which information is routinely communicated with persons who do not have ID.

In order to determine the most appropriate interventions and approaches to communication with an individual with ID, it is necessary to understand the degree of communicative impairment that exists for that individual. Recent studies have shown that while a general trend can be observed in which those with more severe ID tend to possess fewer communicative skills (Cascella 2004), there exists significant heterogeneity in the communicative abilities among those with severe ID (Carlesimo, Marotta, & Vicari, 1997; McLean, Brady, & McLean, 1996; McLean et al., 1999; van der Meer et al., 2011). Among those with mild ID, some are relatively unimpaired and effectively fall within what may be considered the normal range of communicative function. These individuals have even been included within normative samples of standardized speech-language tests (Cascella 2006).

An individualized functional approach has been used successfully to devise alternative communication methods to improve information exchange with individuals with locked-in syndrome, another group for whom communication often poses significant challenges (Soderholm, Meinander, & Alaranta, 2001). Functional assessment research has become an important component in treating challenging behaviors in individuals with ID (Matson et al., 2011a), with inherently communicative functions such as attention, and demands being incorporated into the functional assessment (Matson et al., 2011). Functional communication training has also exceeded criteria as a well-established treatment for addressing problem behavior in children with ID and has been characterized as likely, though not proven, to be efficacious with adults (Kurtz et al., 2011).

Subjective Well-Being

Over the past two decades, researchers have drawn attention to the importance of the quality of life of people with intellectual disabilities. Subjective well being and feelings of happiness are considered as key components of quality of life. Subjective well being refers to the global experience of positive reactions to one's life (Diener & Lucas, 2000).

Researchers in the intellectual disability field have focused on improving people's objective and external conditions such as the services they are offered, their physical conditions, their employment or political advocacy and others. Such improvements may not lead to enduring well being in people with intellectual disabilities (Dykens, 2006). The concept of well being has been applied to people with intellectual disabilities. Several studies have found that levels of subjective well being in people with intellectual disability are similar to those in people who do not have intellectual disability (Cummins, 2001; Shephard-Jones, 2005; Emerson & Hatton, 2008).

Functional life skills such as social abilities, communication, affective skills and emotional competence together make up the ability to adapt with everyday life (Gumpel, 1994; O'Reilly, 2004; Smith & Matson, 2010). Deficiencies in these skills can curb people with intellectual disability to live up to their personal and professional potentials. It might cause lower well being and happiness. Intellectually disabled people have more limited social and emotional adaptive skills (Arthur, 2003; La Malfa, 2009).

FAMILIES HAVING A PERSON WITH AN INTELLECTUAL DISABILITY

Literature review focuses on data collected from various countries and consist of perceptions given by primary caregivers, mostly mothers. The overall aim of society, through government policy and community services, is to enable the child with a disability to function as effectively as possible, and also to enable parents and other siblings to function effectively, and wherever possible, live lives of quality (Brown & Brown, 2003).

Family is the environment which enables an individual to develop and grow effectively. The issue is not just the child with an intellectual disability but also the family and the interaction of disability in the family which matters as a whole. Thus, it is important to know as to how disability affects those in the family who are not disabled and how can we develop ways of improving these negative effects in order to make each member function optimally.

Researchers (e.g., Andrews, 1974) have recognized for a long time that perceptions are a major driving force of human behaviour, that is, what is perceived and believed affects how the individual or, in this case family members behave. This includes how a family is affected by its belief and value system, the nature of disability services, whether they are private or public; health and the satisfaction of health in the family, and so on. There are often pressing challenges, for the disability of one member of the family negatively influences the behaviour or resources of the family as a whole, for example, when a mother has to give up her job to look after her child.

It seems plausible that intervention and support in one key area is likely to improve other aspects of family functioning and therefore overall family satisfaction. Key areas differ to some extent from family to family, or over time in the same family, arguing for an individual approach to support. There are families where internal aspects of family life are positive and the challenges largely arise from outside the family, e.g., community reaction, lack of support, and lack of appropriate respite when required. These challenges necessitate careful and considered observation, reflection, and flexibility on the part of policy and service personnel. Additionally, combining intervention and/or support in more than one domain, e.g., Family Health and support for the family in terms of enjoyment of life (Leisure and Recreation or Career Preparation) is likely to have greater and possibly wide-ranging effects on a family's overall satisfaction and quality of life. This would need much close collaboration between different service groups and would require much greater coordination of policy between different departments and agencies. If such arguments are correct such an approach:

1. Requires an accent on service and support across agencies; and
2. Should have long-term economic savings, since such coordinated intervention might be expected to have holistic benefits, such as an increase in family overall health and economic viability.

However, as stressed by Brown and Brown (2009), such intervention and coordination should critically involve the family perception of needs and choices.

Other children in the family also face the impact of a child with an intellectual disability in terms of studying and calling friends at home. Inviting guests or neighbours at home is also difficult because of major behavioural disturbances. This could also lead to decreased support from neighbours and other community members. All this results into the families and the person with intellectual disability being cut-off from the necessary support and community interactions. Such arguments raise important questions regarding why many organizations and individuals go to a great extent to advocate for inclusive policies (Brown & Brown, 2003).

Thus, it is important to being a fundamental change in how we set the policies, administer disability services and then carry out practices at the managerial and frontline levels. It is also means that we need to bring a change in how we educate the personnel. It is essential to understand the lifestyle of families with children having intellectual disability and the major reasons of family disruption.

Elderly Person with Intellectual Disability

Aging is a process which is affected by various biological and social factors and is expressed very uniquely in each individual. Since longevity is increasing, this process of aging includes people with intellectual disability. The context of family is important when we consider the aging process as it plays a fundamental role in the care-giving for the older adults.

Researches conducted on families in the field of intellectual disability have usually focused on stress and burden associated with the care-giving process from a parental (maternal) perspective and the negative impact of disability on the family (Haley &Perkins, 2004; Hatton & Emerson, 2003). Research and literature also focuses on co-resident parents and adults with intellectual disability and need for future planning (Bigby & Balandin, 2004; Bigby, 2004). New policies need to be developed in order to bring a change in the care-givers role considering the changing demands (Hogg, Lucchino, Wang, Janicki, & Group, 2000).

Relations within the family keep changing and these remain an important source of support and provide a sense of belongingness. Family support and positive perceptions are aspects that seem to have a positive influence on the quality of life. Familial support and routine though being an integral part of the family relations, keeps varying from one family to another. Practical, emotional and/or financial aids are provided by and to various members of the family. For e.g. adult siblings provide emotional and practical support to aging parents. Many siblings will also likely carry on with familial support responsibilities for their brother or sister with a disability when parents are no longer able(Bigby, 1997; Dew, Llewellyn, & Balandin, 2004).Reciprocal support between parents and offspring with a disability may also occur regardless of living arrangement, as has been found in research involving co-resident families (Heller,

Miller, &Factor, 1997). Furthermore, some parents anticipate their offspring with a disability may be a source of support, as they themselves age and need help with daily living.

Another important aspect of familial relations is routine. Routine seems to provide predictability and structure to familial contact and support. Depending on the family, routines can occur on a daily, weekly or seasonal basis. For e.g. parent going for grocery shopping while child is in school. Routines are also significant to older aged families of adults with a disability (Knox & Bigby, 2007). Family routines and rituals are, indeed, an important aspect of family life (Fiese et al., 2002) and maintaining some routines may better support families through various transitions (Zisberg, Young, Schepp, & Zysberg, 2007).

MEASURING QUALITY OF LIFE

Direct interviewing approaches could be used for individuals with mild or moderate level of intellectual disability. Contemporary assessment tools include The Lifestyle Satisfaction Scale (Heal & Chadsey-Rusch, 1985), The Quality of Life Questionnaire (Schalock & Keith, 1993) among others. With people who have severe intellectual disability, direct interviewing is inappropriate. The validity and reliability of these assessments could be interrupted if these are used with individuals who have some verbal skills, acquiescence, inconsistency and last-option responding (Baroff, 1986; Felce & Perry, 1996; Heal & Sigelman, 1992; Matikka & Vesala, 1997). Such issues are exacerbated when an individual has atypical expressions, lacks formal communication skills, or tends to acquiesce (Matikka & Vesala, 1997). The validity of interview methods could be enhanced if the data is gathered from multiple interviews with familiar others (Heal & Sigelman, 1992).

To measure one's quality of life, one could be asked generally regarding how satisfied that person is with his/her life. This could be done in person, through the means of a questionnaire or by using a validated instrument or technique. Since quality of life is a concept which is a multidimensional, researchers usually seek to measure and assess it using multiple domains and indicators (Andrews, 1980; Brown, 1994; Cummins, 2000; Erikson & Uusitalo, 1987; Felce & Perry, 1996; Hughes, 1995; Parmenter, 1994, 1995; Sen, 1993; Solomon 1980; Zapf, 1987). Debate continues on whether subjective quality of life can or should be measured across multiple measures or whether a simple global measure is valid and achievable (Felce & Perry, 1996; Romney, 1994; Travers & Richardson, 1993).

Principles on assessment and measurement include the recognition and measurement of individual quality of life, which includes the recognition of valued personal experiences and circumstances, which reflect domains that contribute to a full and interconnected life.

Subjective and objective, both methods have been used to measure and assess quality of life. Objective methods include observable and quantifiable indicators whereas subjective methods use an individual's perceptions and qualitative assessments of happiness or satisfaction (Land, 1983; Lyons, 2000; Schussler & Fisher, 1985).

More instruments that measure QOL need to be developed and rigorously validated. This is especially the case for high-needs disability populations like those individuals that exhibit challenging behavior or have severe to profound ID, as it is questionable whether existing measures can be used with these populations.

Research on quality of life has played a role as a 'change agent' during the past few decades, primarily as a sensitizing notion, broadening to a conceptual framework for assessing quality outcomes and enhancing quality of life through understanding, support and intervention (Lyons, 2010; Schippers &

Tubben, 2008). The very first criteria for research on quality of life is the use of a multidimensional approach which has several domains, with anticipated cross-cultural validity that allows research to be more clearly directed to specific areas.

Out of the various components of research, the first is conceptualization. It describes what quality of life is, namely a multidimensional construct, influenced by personal and environmental factors and their interactions (Schalock& Verdugo, 2002). These components are interrelated although, it is recognized that there is variability from person to person. They result from individual perception and choice, and change over an individual's life span (Brown & Brown, 2003).

The second component of application focuses on the enhancement of well being within the context of those involved, thus implying a wide variety of settings as well as a variety of individual and group purposes. Professional practices should reflect quality of life principles resulting in personally valued quality of life outcomes that are based on sound professional skills and methods such as observation and the measurement of choices that are important to the person (Brown, 2009; Brown & Brown, 2009). All the components need to be interactive. Working in any of the components requires effective assessment and feedback for adjustment to a total research or support program. It requires that the approach must be fully interdisciplinary from a research or a professional perspective. For example, what professionals learn from application often has an impact on measurement strategies and techniques and could result into re-conceptualization.

For effective research on quality of life, a criterion of creating a balance between qualitative and quantitative methods and triangulation of those methods, using assessment of both subjective (perceptual) and objective parameters. A systems perspective is also helpful which integrates the micro-level, meso-level and macro-level in which persons with disabilities live, so that predictors and causal factors in their lives could be identified (Lyons, 2010). Quality of life research requires active involvement of people with disabilities and their social network. Inter and Intra variability is critical in quality of life researches.

EVIDENCE-BASED PRACTICES

Assessing the quality of life of people with intellectual disability is an essential part of managing these individuals. More important is to provide help to them on the basis of research evidence which would make us reach higher probabilities of being sure of treatment. There are two essential ideas in evidence-based practices: first, interventions should have clear empirical support and second, personal outcomes should be used to guide organizational change and quality improvement. The quality of life conceptual and measurement model can serve as a basis for evidence-based practices (Veerman & Van Yperen, 2007).It consists of four levels of evidence: descriptive, theoretical, indicative and causal.

Descriptive

The essential elements of the intervention are made to be explicit and are summarized in program practices and standards as follows-

- A holistic, multi-dimensional approach.
- A focus on the community and organizations being bridges to the community.

- The use of best practices that are empirically based strategies that reduce the discrepancy (i.e., mismatch) between people and the environments through functional skill training, the use of assistive technology devices, accessing natural supports, and environmental modification/accommodation.
- The use of individualized support strategies and their alignment with core quality of life domains.
- The application of quality of life principles.
- The use of quality of life-focused program practices as listed above.
- The measurement of personal outcomes as a key component of evidence-based practices.
- The demonstration of fidelity to the conceptual and measurement model.
- The alignment of assessed support needs to quality of life domains.
- The use of personal outcomes to guide organizational quality improvement.

Theoretical

Here, the intervention has a plausible rationale which explains why it should work. It defines the concept operationally and establishes parameters for program planning and implementation. The theoretical rationale for why an emphasis on quality of life should work is found in the extensive international research (e.g., Brown & Brown, 2005; Cummins, 2005; Schalock et al., 2007) which suggests strongly that one's quality of life is:

1. Multi-dimensional and has the same components for all people;
2. Influenced by personal and environmental factors; and
3. Enhanced by self-determination, inclusion, individualized supports, and purpose in life.

Indicative

The indicative aspect includes intervention strategies which lead to the desired outcome. This level of evidence is reflected in:

1. Studies (e.g., Bonham et al., 2004; Perry & Felce, 2005) which demonstrate that personal outcomes are enhanced when QOL principles and QOL-related program practices are employed; and
2. The publishing of service provider profiles that show longitudinal changes in quality of life outcomes for all service recipients (Keith & Bonham, 2005; State of Nebraska Health and Human Services, 2006).

Causal

This aspect states that either the outcome is caused by or related to the intervention or that there is clear evidence showing which component of the intervention are predictive of the outcomes. There has been considerable work determining the significant predictors of QOL-related outcomes for persons with ID/DD. Across a number of studies (Schalock et al.,2007; Schalock et al., 2008a, b), personal characteristics (such as IQ and adaptive behaviour levels), program practices (e.g., enabling choices, rights, self-determination, availability of transportation, and community inclusion), and setting characteristics (e.g., residential and employment status, setting size, and operational culture) are significant predictors of QOL outcomes.

CONCLUSION

People with Intellectual Disability are the most able individuals when they are brought up in families where they are given "Ownership" to perform their best with support from families and caregivers. Every experience ranging from the most difficult situation to the most achievable milestones in areas of Cognitions, social skills and emotional wellbeing is the essence of defining a Quality Life and Spiritual Wellbeing for each one of them and their families. Learning from others experiences helps families gather strength and reinforces positive living in enabling their Children with Intellectual Disabilities. Parent Support groups and sharing of Case Studies about living dynamic changes of growth and development in areas of wellbeing with limited intellectual potential is the greatest rewarding experience on planet earth in terms of Survival for these Special Ones. It is important to keep engaging the inner soul with the external social environment so that there is no deprivation or depression coming in the way of Quality living in them. Every new experience of pain and resistance when supported with care and love by the family members and caregivers gives a define meaning to the lives of Individuals with Intellectual Disability.

REFERENCES

Abbeduto, L., Furman, L., & Davies, B. (1989). Relation between the receptive language and mental age of persons with mental retardation. *American Journal of Mental Retardation*, *93*, 535–543. PMID:2706121

Abberley, P. (1987). The concept of oppression and the development of a social theory of disability. *Disability, Handicap & Society*, *2*(1), 5–19. doi:10.1080/02674648766780021

Abbey, A., & Andrews, F. M. (1986). Modeling the psychological determinants of life quality. In F. M. Andrews (Ed.), *Research on the quality of life*. Ann Arbor, MI: Institute for Social Research, University of Michigan.

Andrews, F. M. (1974). Social indicators of perceived life quality. *Social Indicators Research*, *1*(3), 279–299. doi:10.1007/BF00303860

Arthur, M. (1998). *Socio-communicative variables and behaviour states in students with the most severe and multiple disabilities: An observational study*. (Unpublished PhD dissertation). Macquarie University, Sydney, Australia.

Belva, B. C., Matson, J. L., Sipes, M., & Bamburg, J. W. (2012). An examination of specific communication deficits in adults with profound intellectual disabilities. *Research in Developmental Disabilities*, *33*(2), 525–529. doi:10.1016/j.ridd.2011.10.019 PMID:22119701

Berry, P. B. (1972). Comprehension of possessive and present continuous sentences by nonretarded, mildly retarded, and severely retarded children. *American Journal of Mental Deficiency*, *76*, 540–544. PMID:5012135

Bickenbach, J. E. (1993). *Physical disability and social policy*. Toronto: University of Toronto Press.

Bigby, C. (1997). Parental substitutes? The role of siblings in the lives of older people with intellectual disability. *Journal of Gerontological Social Work*, *29*(1), 3–21. doi:10.1300/J083v29n01_02

Bigby, C. (2004). *Ageing with a Lifelong Disability: A Guide to Practice, Program and Policy Issues for Human Services Professionals*. London: Jessica Kingsley.

Bigby, C., & Balandin, S. (2004). Issues in researching the ageing of people with intellectual disability. In E. Emerson, C. Hatton, T. Thompson, & T. R. Parmenter (Eds.), *The International Handbook of Applied Research in Intellectual Disabilities* (pp. 221–236). West Sussex, UK: Wiley. doi:10.1002/9780470713198.ch10

Bonham, G. S., Basehart, S., Schalock, R. L., Marchand, C. B., Kirchner, N., & Rumenap, J. M. (2004). Consumer-based quality of life assessment: The Maryland Ask Me! Project. *Mental Retardation*, *42*(5), 338–355. doi:10.1352/0047-6765(2004)42<338:CQOLAT>2.0.CO;2 PMID:15335259

Bowe, F. (1978). *Handicapping America: Barriers to Disabled People*. New York: Harper and Row.

Brown, I. (2006). *Family Quality of Life Survey: Main caregivers of people with intellectual or developmental disabilities*. Toronto: Surrey Place Centre.

Brown, I., & Brown, R. I. (2003). *Quality of Life and Disability: An Approach for Community Practitioners*. London, UK: Jessica Kingsley.

Brown, I., & Brown, R. I. (2009). Choice as an aspect of quality of life for people with intellectual disabilities. *Journal of Policy and Practice in Intellectual Disabilities, 6*, 10-17.

Brown, N., McLinden, M., & Porter, J. (1998). Sensory needs. In P. Lacey & C. Ouvry (Eds.), *People with profound and multiple learning disabilities: A collaborative approach to meeting complex needs* (pp. 29–38). London: David Fulton.

Brown, R. I. (1995). Measuring new dimensions through quality of life: The personal equation. *Evaluation Journal of Australasia*, *7*(1), 14–23.

Brown, R. I. (1998). *Conceptualisation of quality of life: An overview*. Paper presented at the 1998 Australian Society for the Study of Intellectual Disability (ASSID) Conference: Conceptualisation of quality of life workshop, Flinders University of South Australia, Adelaide, Australia.

Brown, R. I., Bayer, M. B., & MacFarlane, C. (1989). *Rehabilitation programs: Performance and Quality of Life of adults with developmental handicaps*. Toronto: Lugus Productions.

Brown, R. I., & Brown, I. (2005). The application of quality of life. *Journal of Intellectual Disability Research*, *49*(10), 718–727. doi:10.1111/j.1365-2788.2005.00740.x PMID:16162116

Butterfield, N., Arthur, M., & Linfoot, K. (1992). Meeting communication needs in communication programming for students with severe intellectual disability: The creating communicative contexts manual. *Special Education Perspectives*, *1*(1), 35–43.

Carlesimo, G. A., Marotta, L., & Vicari, S. (1997). Long-term memory in mental retardation: Evidence for a specific impairment in subjects with Down's syndrome. *Neuropsychologia*, *35*(1), 71–79. doi:10.1016/S0028-3932(96)00055-3 PMID:8981379

Carter, M., & Hook, J. (1998). Communication programming for students with high support needs: A model for deciding what to teach. *Special Education Perspectives*, *7*(1), 42–55.

Cascella, P. W. (2004). *Receptive communication abilities among adults with significant intellectual disability*. Taylor & Francis Ltd.

Cascella, P. W. (2006). Standardised speech-language tests and students with intellectual disability: A review of normative data. *Journal of Intellectual & Developmental Disability*, *31*(2), 120–124. doi:10.1080/13668250600681503 PMID:16782597

Cheslock, M. A., Barton-Hulsey, A., Romski, M., & Sevcik, R. A. (2008). Using a speech-generating device to enhance communicative abilities for an adult with moderate intellectual disability. *Intellectual and Developmental Disabilities*, *46*(5), 376–386. doi:10.1352/2008.46:376-386 PMID:19090639

Cirrin, F. M., & Rowland, C. M. (1985). Communicative assessment of non-verbal youths with severe/profound mental retardation. *Mental Retardation*, *23*(2), 52–62. PMID:3990553

Cummins, R. A. (1996). Assessing quality of life. In R. L. Schalock (Ed.), *Quality of life. Volume Conceptualization and measurement*. Washington, DC: American Association on Mental Retardation.

Cummins, R.A. (1996). The domains of life satisfaction: An attempt to order chaos. *Social Indicators Research, 38*, 303-28.

Cummins, R. A. (2005). Moving from the quality of life concept to a theory. *Journal of Intellectual Disability Research*, *49*(10), 699–706. doi:10.1111/j.1365-2788.2005.00738.x PMID:16162114

Dew, A., Llewellyn, G., & Balandin, S. (2004). Post-parental care: A new generation of siblingcarers. *Journal of Intellectual & Developmental Disability*, *29*(2), 176–179. doi:10.1080/13668250410001709520

Evans, D. R. (1994). Enhancing quality of life in the population at large. *Social Indicators Research*, *33*(1-3), 47–88. doi:10.1007/BF01078958

Fabian, E. S. (1991). Using quality-of-life indicators in rehabilitation program evaluation. *Rehabilitation Counseling Bulletin*, *34*(4), 344–356.

Feil, N. (1993). *The validation breakthrough*. Sydney: McLennan & Petty.

Felce, D., & Perry, J. (1996). Exploring current conceptions of quality of life. In R. Renwick, I. Brown, & M. Nagler (Eds.), *Quality of life in health promotion and rehabilitation: Conceptual approaches, issues, and applications* (pp. 51–62). Thousand Oaks, CA: Sage Publications.

Fiese, B., Tomcho, T., Douglas, M., Josephs, K., Poltrock, S., & Baker, T. (2002). A review of 50 years of research on naturally occurring family routines and rituals: Cause for celebration? *Journal of Family Psychology*, *16*(4), 381–390. doi:10.1037/0893-3200.16.4.381 PMID:12561283

Fulcher, G. (1989). Disability: A social construction. In G. Lupton & J. Najman (Eds.), *Sociology of health and illness: Australian readings*. Melbourne: Macmillan.

Gleeson, B. (1995). Disability: A state of mind? *The Australian Journal of Social Issues*, *30*(1), 10–23.

Goode, D. A. (1994). *A world without words: The social construction of children born deaf and blind*. Philadelphia, PA: Temple University Press.

Goode, D. A., & Hogg, J. (1994). Towards an understanding of holistic quality of life in people with profound intellectual and multiple disabilities. In D. Goode (Ed.), *Quality of life for persons with disabilities: International perspectives and issues* (pp. 197–207). Cambridge, MA: Brookline Books.

Gustiatas, R., & Young, E. W. D. (1986). *A time to be born, a time to die: Conflicts and ethics in an intensive care nursery*. Reading, MA: Addison-Wesley.

Haley, W., & Perkins, E. (2004). Current status and future directions in family caregiving and aging people with intellectual disabilities. *Journal of Policy and Practice in Intellectual Disabilities*, *1*(1), 24–30. doi:10.1111/j.1741-1130.2004.04004.x

Hatton, C., & Emerson, E. (2003). Families with a person with intellectual disabilities: Stress and impact. *Current Opinion in Psychiatry*, *16*(5), 497–501. doi:10.1097/00001504-200309000-00002

Headey, B., & Wearing, A. (1992). *Understanding happiness: A theory of subjective well-being*. Melbourne: Longman Cheshire.

Health Commission of New South Wales. (1981). *Circular 81/8*. Sydney: Health Commission of New South Wales.

Heller, T., Miller, A., & Factor, A. (1997). Adults with mental retardation as supports to their parents: Effects on parental caregiving appraisal. *Mental Retardation*, *35*(5), 338–346. doi:10.1352/0047-6765(1997)035<0338:AWMRAS>2.0.CO;2 PMID:9339062

Hogg, J., Lucchino, R., Wang, K., Janicki, M. P., & Group, W. (2000). *Healthy Ageing: Adults with Intellectual Disabilities: Ageing & Social Policy*. Geneva: World Health Organization.

Hogg, J., & Sebba, J. (1987). Profound retardation and multiple impairment: *Development and learning* (vol. 1). Rockville, MD: Aspen Publishers.

Keenan, B. (1992). *An evil cradling*. London: Vintage Press.

Keith, K. D., & Bonham, G. S. (2005). The use of quality of life data at the organization and systems level. *Journal of Intellectual Disability Research*, *49*(part 10), 799–805. doi:10.1111/j.1365-2788.2005.00755.x PMID:16162131

Knox, M., & Bigby, C. (2007). Moving towards midlife care as negotiated family business: Accounts of people with intellectual disabilities and their families "Just getting along with their lives together". *International Journal of Disability Development and Education*, *54*(3), 287–304. doi:10.1080/10349120701488749

Koul, R., & Clapsaddle, K. C. (2006). Effects of repeated listening experiences on the perception of synthetic speech by individuals with mild-to-moderate intellectual disabilities. *AAC: Augmentative & Alternative Communication*, *22*, 112–122. PMID:17114169

Kurtz, P. F., Boelter, E. W., Jarmolowicz, D. P., Chin, M. D., & Hagopian, L. P. (2011). An analysis of functional communication training as an empirically supported treatment for problem behavior displayed by individuals with intellectual disabilities. *Research in Developmental Disabilities*, *32*(6), 2935–2942. doi:10.1016/j.ridd.2011.05.009 PMID:21696917

Matson, J. L., Horovitz, M., Kozlowski, A. M., Sipes, M., Worley, J. A., & Shoemaker, M. E. (2011). Person characteristics of individuals in functional assessment research. *Research in Developmental Disabilities*, *32*(2), 621–624. doi:10.1016/j.ridd.2010.12.012 PMID:21211941

McLean, L. K., Brady, N. C., & McLean, J. E. (1996). Reported communication abilities of individuals with severe mental retardation. *American Journal of Mental Retardation*, *100*, 580–589. PMID:8735572

McLean, L. K., Brady, N. C., McLean, J. E., & Behrens, G. A. (1999). Communication forms and functions of children and adults with severe mental retardation in community and institutional settings. *Journal of Speech, Language, and Hearing Research: JSLHR*, *42*(1), 231–240. doi:10.1044/jslhr.4201.231 PMID:10025557

Merrill, E. C., & Mar, H. H. (1987). Differences between mentally retarded and nonretarded persons' efficiency of auditory sentence processing. *American Journal of Mental Deficiency*, *91*, 406–414. PMID:3812610

Murphy, B. 2000 Australian WHOQoL instruments: User's manual and interpretation guide. Melbourne, Australia: Australian WHOQoL Field Study Centre.

Nankervis, K. (1997). *Keynote Address*. Paper presented at the Annual Conference, Australian Society for the Study of Intellectual Disability, Hobart, Australia.

Oliver, M. (1996). *Understanding disability: From theory to practice*. London: Macmillan Press. doi:10.1007/978-1-349-24269-6

Perry, J., & Felce, D. (2005). Factors associated with outcomes in community group homes. *American Journal of Mental Retardation*, *110*(2), 121–135. doi:10.1352/0895-8017(2005)110<121:FAWOIC>2.0.CO;2 PMID:15762822

Sacks, O. (1995). *An anthropologist on Mars*. Sydney: Pan Macmillan Australia.

Schalock, R. L. (Ed.). (1990). *Quality of Life: Perspectives and issues*. Washington, DC: American Association on Mental Retardation.

Schalock, R. L. (1997). The concept of quality of life in 21st century disability programmes. In R. I. Brown (Ed.), *Quality of life for people with disabilities: Models, research and practice* (2nd ed.; pp. 327–340). Cheltenham, UK: Stanley Thornes.

Schalock, R. L. (1999, September). *The application of the concept of quality of life: IASSID Quality of Life Consensus Document: Discussion draft.* Paper presented at the 35th National Conference of the Australian Society for the Study of Intellectual Disabilities, Sydney, Australia.

Schalock, R. L. (2002, June). *The concept of quality of life: What we know and do not know.* Paper presented at the Inaugural IASSID [International Association for the Scientific Study of Intellectual Disabilities] Europe Quadrennial Conference, Dublin, Ireland.

Schalock, R. L. (2004). Quality of life: What we know and what we don't know. *Journal of Intellectual Disability Research*, *48*(3), 203–216. doi:10.1111/j.1365-2788.2003.00558.x PMID:15025663

Schalock, R. L., Bonham, G. S., & Verdugo, M. A. (2008). The conceptualization and measurement of quality of life: Implications for program planning and evaluation in the field of intellectual disabilities. *Evaluation and Program Planning*, *31*(2), 181–190. doi:10.1016/j.evalprogplan.2008.02.001 PMID:18394704

Schalock, R. L., Gardner, J. F., & Bradley, V. J. (2007). *Quality of life for persons with intellectual and other developmental disabilities: Applications across individuals, organizations, communities, and systems.* Washington, DC: American Association on Intellectual and Developmental Disabilities.

Schalock, R. L., & Verdugo, M. A. (2002). *Handbook on quality of life for human services practitioners.* Washington, DC: American Association on Mental Retardation.

Schalock, R. L., Verdugo, M. A., Bonham, G. S., Fantova, F., & Van Loon, J. S. (2008). Enhancing personal outcomes: Organizational strategies, guidelines, and examples. *Journal of Policy and Practice in Intellectual Disabilities*, *5*(4), 276–285. doi:10.1111/j.1741-1130.2007.00135.x

Smyer, M. A., McHale, S. M., Birkel, R., & Madle, R. A. (1988). Impairments, handicapping environments, and disability: A life-span perspective. In P. S. Van Hasselt, P. S. Dtrain, & M. Herson (Eds.), *Handbook of developmental and physical disabilities* (pp. 9–20). New York: Permagon.

Söderholm, S., Meinander, M., & Alaranta, H. (2001). Augmentative and alternative communication methods in locked-in syndrome. Journal of Rehabilitation, 33, 235-239.

State of Nebraska Health and Human Services. (2006). *Nebraska developmental disabilities provider profiles.* Lincoln, NE: State of Nebraska Health and Human Services, Division of Developmental Disabilities.

Thompson, R. J., & O'Quinn, A. N. (1979). Developmental disabilities: Etiologies, manifestations, diagnoses, and treatments. New York: Oxford.

Turnbull, A. P., Brown, I., & Turnbull, R. H. (Eds.). (2004). *Families and people with mental retardation and quality of life: International perspectives.* Washington, DC: American Association on Mental Retardation.

Veerman, J. W., & Van Yperen, T. A. (2007). Degrees of freedom and degrees of uncertainty:A developmental model for the establishment of evidence-based youth care. *Evaluation and Program Planning*, *30*(2), 212–221. doi:10.1016/j.evalprogplan.2007.01.011 PMID:17689326

Ward, R. L., Nichols, A. D., & Freedman, R. I. (2010, November). Uncovering Health care Inequalities among adults with intellectual and developmental disabilities. *Health & Social Work*, *35*(4), 280–290. doi:10.1093/hsw/35.4.280 PMID:21171535

Wolfe, P. S. (1992). Challenges for service providers. In P. J. McLaughlin & P. Wejman (Eds.), *Developmental disabilities: A handbook for best practice* (pp. 124–141). Boston: Andover Medical.

Zapf, W., Glatzer, W., Noll, H. H., Habich, R., Berger-Schmitt, R., & Breuer, S. et al.. (1987). German social report: Living conditions and subjective well-being, 1978–1984. *Social Indicators Research*, *19*, 1.

Zisberg, A., Young, H., Schepp, K., & Zysberg, L. (2007). A concept analysis of routine: Relevance to nursing. *Journal of Advanced Nursing*, *57*(4), 442–453. doi:10.1111/j.1365-2648.2007.04103.x PMID:17291208

Chapter 9
Assessment and Management of Communication Skills in Individuals with Intellectual Disability: Perspectives in the 21st Century

Krupa M.
Sri Ramachandra University, India

Prakash Boominathan
Sri Ramachandra University, India

ABSTRACT

The relationship between communication and cognition which has been explored since mid-1900s is a highly contentious topic. Hypotheses from various researchers have experienced a gradual shift from cognitive/innate bases to social perspective of acquisition and development of speech and language skills in individuals with intellectual disability. This acquisition tends to be delayed or deviant (qualitative and /or quantitative). In the recent years, research in this area is experiencing a paradigm shift evolving from 'incapacity' to 'functioning' which is obvious in the clinical practice of assessment and intervention of speech and language skills in these individuals. Further, the rehabilitation process is experiencing a transition from clinician directed to child-oriented or hybrid approaches of intervention. This chapter will be a comprehensive document of recent trends in research and practice related to acquisition of language, assessment and intervention of communication difficulties for professionals working with intellectual disability.

INTRODUCTION, BACKGROUND, AND MOTIVATION

Communication is an indispensable and integral part of daily living for any person. The ability (including the skills and deficits) to communicate is a complicated interactive phenomenon which is an outcome of coordinated actions between several entities such as anatomical, physiological, cognitive, linguistic and

DOI: 10.4018/978-1-5225-0089-6.ch009

psychological components of the individual and the environment. The acquisition is further augmented with appropriate modelling and stimulation from the communication partners. This chapter will focus on the relationship between cognition and language; challenges in communication due to intellectual disability; and contemporary methods of assessment and management of communication difficulties in individuals with intellectual disability. The chapter does not intend to provide the readers with an exhaustive review of literature in this area, however, will to a great extent share the current intellectual climate prevailing in this part of world.

Research in the area of intellectual disability (Abbeduto, 2003) has been taking a three pronged evolution. The first one began with general shift in approach to focus on the subtypes of intellectual disability based on etiology than variation based on severity of intellectual disability. This allowed combining medical etiologies and behavioural description of intellectual disabilities. For instance, better language skills in individuals with William Syndrome against individuals with intellectual disability due to seizural disorders can be explained through this approach. The second focuses on the relationship between language and thought. Chomsky (1959), a nativist hypothesised language development to be driven by learning mechanisms that operate with minimal input from general faculties of mind. The third addressed predominantly on the manipulations of the environmental factors. These may be useful during assessment and intervention of communication skills in individuals with intellectual disability. Current trends in research focus predominantly on longitudinal observations and single case studies.

Language and Cognition: The Relationship

The relationship between the development of cognition and language has been debated in the literature. The cognitive theory of language development hypothesizes that language and cognition are linked developmentally in a 'strong' or in 'weak' form (Klein & Moses, 1999; Bohannon & Bonvillian, 2005). The 'strong' form hypothesis postulates that cognition is the major pre-requisite for language development while the 'weak' form, also known as 'interactionist' model warrants language and cognition as inter-linked and inter-dependent along with other social and linguistic variables (Kamhi & Johnston, 1982; Owens, 2005; Reed, 2005). This provides evidence in considering intellectual disability from a 'delayed' and 'quantitative' perspective in 'strong' form hypothesis, to the need for presence of certain linguistic capacities for language development in the 'weak' form hypothesis. Thus, language development depends not only on cognition, but also on socio-linguistic pre-requisites (Cromer, 1991). This is evident in early stages of sensorimotor development in children with intellectual disability where a delayed and not a deviant pattern of language acquisition is observed, especially in object permanence, first word stage, etc (Greenwald & Leonard, 1979; Kahn, 1984; Mahoney & Snow, 1983; Martin, McConkey, & Martin, 1984). An Indian study (Krupa, Perumal, & Kripa, 2009) conducted on language development (semantic intentions) in children below two years of age indicated a non-linear relationship between language and cognition in children with intellectual disability despite being matched for mental age. On a similar line, Finch-Williams, highlighted earlier in 1984 that language may not develop to the extent predicted by cognitive achievements, especially in individuals with severe and profound retardation. Evidences suggest that some cognitive skills continue to develop till early adulthood (Silverstein et al, 1982) and reaches a plateau at a specific age of an individual. The same is observed with language development as well.

In contrary to the postulates putforth by the proponents of the cognitive theory of language acquisition, Vyogotsky (1962) suggested that language takes the lead role thereby facilitating the development of cognition. In addition to this, Luria (1961,1963) proposed a three-stage theory drawing a relationship between language and motor control. The first stage beginning at birth and continuing till 3 years of age witnesses children use language to communicate but not to control their own behaviour; second being 3-4 ½ years where communication serves to increase desired actions; and third stage runs beyond 4 ½ years, where language is used to direct behaviour of others. Luria's postulates and the study conducted by Milgram and Furth (1968) evidenced stagnated development at second stage in individuals with intellectual disability and only few reaching to third stage with support, due to dissociation of verbal mediation ability from motor system. Cognition-language relationship is an inconsistent one in individuals with intellectual disability. In close to half of these individuals, both receptive and expressive language levels are similar to cognitive levels (Owens, 2004). Among the remaining individuals, 25% of them have comprehensive language skills on par with cognitive levels, while expression lags. In the remaining 25%, the language comprehension and expression may be similar to cognitive levels. This provides evidence for both quantitative and qualitative differences in individuals with intellectual disability when compared to typically developing peers. Thus, cognitive skills play a major role in the development of language and the vice versa. Further, pre-linguistic skills such as attention and concentration are reported to be a major prerequisite for the development of communication.

Role of Attention and Memory in Language Comprehension

Individuals with intellectual disability often do not have difficulty in attending to stimuli, however, the challenge is in choosing the stimuli which requires attention, i.e. the ability to discriminate. As a result, these individuals tend to miss attending to the expected stimuli (Henry & Gudjonsson, 1999; Westling & Fox, 2000). Further, it is known that individuals with intellectual disability have difficulty in both short and long term memory, especially in storing information for retrieval. These individuals find it easier to remember already organised and categorised information than unrelated information. Further, the difficulty in the ability to associate, organise and categorise during learning leads to challenges in retrieval thereby resulting in the need for explicit teaching-learning process (Roseberry-McKibbin, 2007).

Visual information is better learnt and remembered when compared to auditory information. Further, generalisation of learnt information or behaviour is also challenging. The relationship between phonological memory skills and vocabulary acquisition is strong especially till 6 years of age (Gathercole & Baddeley, 1993). This is obvious in individuals with Down syndrome who experience challenges in verbal memory and strengths in visuo-spatial memory (Jarrold, Baddeley, & Phillips, 2002; Wang & Bellugi, 1994) and the vice versa in individuals with William syndrome (Grant et al., 1997; Wang & Bellugi, 1994). Further, Kail (1992) suggests that the speed of processing information is significantly different between typically developing individuals and individuals with intellectual disability. These differences are likely to influence the development of communication in individuals with intellectual disability.

Development of Communication: Delay or Deviant Controversy

Development of communication begins around the 3rd month after birth as pre-speech vocalisations and vocal play called as babbling and lalling. This is further reinforced by the caregiver's acknowledgment and reaction to the same. A classic study on children between 12 and 24 months reported that the change in mean length of utterance is more with respect to form than content (Miller & Yoder, 1974). The competency with respect to precision of communication improves during this phase. Further, social dependency to communicate facilitates expressive language development in young children. Speech is not just considered as a cognitive act, but also as a social act (Vygotstky, 1962). Thus, the development of language is the outcome of interaction between experience and level of cognitive development (Kahn, 1984; Miller, 1981).

Delay in the development of language skills is one of the first signs of intellectual disability (Paul & Norbury, 2012). An observation from Indian population by Subbarao (1992) detailed that no specific or typical pattern of communication is exclusive for individuals with intellectual disability. This is mainly because these individuals tend to exhibit a wide range and variety of challenges in communication. Further, research also indicates that the speech and language profile ranges from minimal comprehension and no expression to fairly good comprehension and expression (with reduced clarity) used for day to day living. Individuals with intellectual disability tend to develop speech and language skills in the same sequence as normal children do, however, at a slower pace.

The available evidence suggests that individuals with intellectual disability are likely to experience and exhibit specific difficulties or delays in the structural aspects of language especially in syntax, sentence length and complexity. These individuals exhibit similar patterns of development for vowels and consonants during first 15 months of age. The emergence of language tend to follow a definite order until 10-15 months of age. Kumin, Councill, and Goodman (1994) observed varied patterns in the emergence of language skills between 10 months and 8 years. This is often due to the challenges faced in phonemic processing and sequencing which influence auditory discrimination and production of sounds (Fowler, 1990; Jarrold & Baddeley, 2002). Further, hypotonia affects the precision of speech sound production, including voice, resonance and fluency (Kumin, 2014; Leddy,1999; Rosenfeld-Johnson,1999). The production also gets influenced by inappropriate planning and sequencing of motor movements (Kumin, 2014; Kumin & Adams, 2000).

MAIN FOCUS OF THE CHAPTER

Language and Communication Skills in Individuals with Intellectual Disability

Language disorders are common in individuals with intellectual disability i. All individuals with an IQ less than 20, 90% individuals with IQ between 21 and 50 and about 45% in 51-70 demonstrate difficulties in various parameters of language (Carrow-Woolfolk & Lynch, 1982). Similar observations were made later by Abbeduto and Boudreau (2004), Owens (2004) and Paul and Norbury (2012). Several researches in the past have hypothesized and provided evidences for qualitative and quantitative differences in language skills of individuals with intellectual disability. Beginning with early developmental milestones, these children tend to attain their speech milestones at a slower pace when compared to their typically developing peers. However, the pattern is often not compromised. This difference is observed to be quantitative till 10 years of age and qualitative beyond that (Owens, 2004). Further, a retrospective analysis of 300 individuals with intellectual disability at the National Institute for the Mentally Handicapped, India by Subbarao and Srinivas (1989) revealed 81.24% individuals having speech and language deficits. Among these individuals 30% of them had no verbal output, while 60.67% were barely verbal. All these individuals expressed delay in the development of speech and language skills. Further, 52% of them had articulation deficits affecting the clarity of speech, 39.33% were observed to have voice problems, while 13% had fluency defects. Bharatraj (1987) reported that the percentage of speech and hearing defects in individuals with intellectual disability were 37% in mild, 21% in moderate, 16% in severe degree. Speech and language defects were observed and reported to be higher in males than females. Despite several deficits in receptive language skills, even adults with profound intellectual disability tend to have stronger abilities in comprehension than expression (Belva et al., 2012). Considering the comprehensive language, literature (Bilsky, 1986; Merrill & Mar, 1987) reports that individuals with intellectual disability take longer duration to process information when compared to typically developing peers. The challenges faced by these individuals are often semantic-analytic in nature than phonological. Further, it is reported that words tend to be heard as separate units of sounds thus affecting the comprehension of the word as a whole. The controversy based on delay and difference in the acquisition of language in individuals with intellectual disability continues to exist till date. Abbeduto, Furman, and Davies (1989) indicated that the receptive language levels of individuals with intellectual disability are often one or more years below the non-verbal mental age which is indicative of cognitive- verbal language relationship. Despite maintaining the sequence of acquisition of syntactic structures similar to typically developing children (Lamberts & Weener, 1976; Dewart, 1979), the comprehension deficits in sentence patterns continue to persist even when matched for language ages (Dewart, 1979). Usually the comprehension deficits around 7 and 9 years of age are restricted to complex syntactic forms such as passives and comparatives (Abbeduto et al., 1989). Research reports evidences for the receptive language skills in individuals with intellectual disability in natural communication environment as being similar to mental age and language aged matched peers. These individuals often understand requests which are indirectly said (Abbeduto et al., 1989). The language characteristic of individuals with intellectual disability can be broadly classified based on the form (phonology as in how sounds combine to form words; morphology as in how suffixes and prefixes are added; syntax as in how words combine to form sentences), content (semantics) and use (pragmatics) of language. Further, a greater frequency of occurrence, but a lesser variety of phonological processes are evident in these children. Literature has also reported difficulties in speech aspect of communication related to clarity of speech; and quality of voice, especially in individuals with syndromic conditions such as Down syndrome. The sections below will detail specific challenges with respect to language in individuals with intellectual disability.

Challenges in Form: Phonology, Morphology, and Syntax

Phonological errors common in individuals with intellectual disability include simplification of productions such as deletion of the last consonant in the word called final consonant deletion, omission of a consonant in a sound cluster termed as cluster reduction (Bernthal & Bankson, 2004; Pena-Brooks & Hegde, 2000). Further, these individuals may not understand or use bound morphemes (suffixes and prefixes) which indicate plural (Eg: -s, -es), possession (Eg: ‘s), past tense (-ed) and other forms (Eg: un-, -ly, etc). The sentence pattern used is usually restricted and simple thereby sounding more telegraphic. These are usually due to delay in development leading to restricted number of vocabulary when compared to typically developing peers. Syntactic patterns used by individuals with intellectual disability depend on the severity of the retardation. Often individuals with mild intellectual disability tend to perform similarly while using bound morphemes, sentence structures and so on. Clausal-syntax development and use of interrogatives (questions) do develop in these individuals, but at a slower pace (Kamhi & Johnston, 1982; McLeavey et al., 1982). These children tend to use shorter, less complex sentences with fewer elaborations and relative clauses (Abbeduto & Boudreau, 2004).

Challenges in Content

Studies on the content (semantic) aspect of language in individuals with intellectual disability indicate a trend of using more nouns than verbs, adjectives and adverbs. Further, usage of prepositions, pronouns, conjunctions and figurative languages are challenging. The vocabulary and thinking of individuals with intellectual disability are often restricted to concrete ones (Karlin, & Strazzula, 1952) which is evident in challenges in tasks pertaining to understanding and using idioms, metaphors and other abstract or indirect use of language. Rosenberg (1982) reports that these individuals tend to acquire the semantic relations and indirect forms of language in the same pattern as typically developing children, but at a slower pace. Further, an Indian study (Bailoor & Subbarao, 2013) on semantic intentions and relations in 4 to 7 year old individuals with intellectual disability did indicate a significant delay in expressing semantic intentions. This concreteness could be associated with the cognitive delay thereby indicating severe impairment in individuals with severe to profound retardation. The development of vocabulary often keeps increasing to a point and plateaus beyond the same indicating reduced vocabulary size in individuals with intellectual disability, compared to typically developing individuals. These challenges are often related to the memory aspect of pre-linguistic skills.

Challenges in Pragmatics

The early development of pragmatics (social use of communication) begins with parent-child interaction during feeding, early vocation and play (Reed, 2005). The speech acts, especially assertive communication acts (such as request for information, directives to perform an action, unsolicited comments or statements, etc) are often not used by individuals with intellectual disability. Evidences from literature (Abbeduto & Rosenberg, 1980; Owings & McManus, 1980) state that despite the initial delay in acquisition, most individuals with mild or moderate retardation tend to acquire all the speech acts by adulthood. These individuals exhibit striking difference between the number of speech acts in the repertoire and the speech acts actually used during any conversation. Mingling in a group of peers with skills such as initiating a conversation, taking turns, waiting for turn, following conversational repair strategies (repairing a communication breakdown) etc are highly challenging for these individuals (Bedrosian & Prutting, 1978; Sinson & Wetherick, 1982). However, individuals with mild retardation do modify their speech while communicating with moderate retarded individuals, similar to what is done by typically developing children matched for mental age (Guralnick & Paul-Brown, 1986). Pragmatic development tends to lag behind cognitive development, however not with a qualitative difference (Abedutto & Boudreau, 2004). Further, an Indian study by Subbarao (1992) postulated that predicting overall language performance based merely on mental age may not be appropriate as communication performances are not uniform across this population. Further, referential communication represent results which indicate individuals with intellectual disability either performing similar to their typically developing counterparts or way inferior than what may be assumed from their intelligence (Abbeduto, Davies, Solesdy, & Furman, 1991). Often these individuals neither request for clarification nor respond appropriately for rectifying a communication breakdown (Abbeduto, Davies, Solesdy, & Furman, 1991). Similar to other language skills, individuals with mild to moderate retardation tend to use this skill when needed, however may miss out subtle cues, especially non-verbal ones (Abbeduto & Rosenberg, 1980; Paul & Cohen, 1984). Vocal clashing which refers to simultaneous verbal outputs is often observed during caregiver-child interaction of children with intellectual disability (Berger & Cunningham, 1983). Taking turns is usually not of great concern in these individuals, despite having no information to be added (Abbeduto, 1991). Challenges in adding information on the topic discussed or on a new topic could be due to a variety of reasons such as lack of or restricted knowledge in the topic discussed or not understanding the social relevance of topic maintenance or inability to link cognition and language. Individuals with intellectual disability do find it difficult to generalise (functional use of new behaviour) a learnt behaviour across contexts and people (Calculator & Dollaghan, 1982). These individuals tend to experience challenges in constructing coherent narratives (Degabriele & Walsh, 2010; Murfett, Powell & Snow, 2008).

Challenges in Speech Parameters

Addressing the controversy on the relationship between speech clarity and language acquisition, Fey (1986) reported reduced frustration thereby leading to improved linguistic output in children, when speech clarity gets better. These children experience difficulty in correct combination of speech sounds and tend to have persistent phonological processes even at adolescent or adult life. Further, the errors in speech production tend to be severe in conversation than isolated productions (Stoel-Gammon, 2000). Adolescent individuals tend to have more difficulty with intelligibility of speech (Rosin et al., 1988) due to anatomical and physiological factors, neurofunctional patterns, and perceptual symptoms (Kumin, 2006). Further, these individuals tend to have inappropriate voice as described by too loud, too soft, inconsistent, and uncontrolled or inappropriate to the occasion due to lack of awareness. Further, breakdown in the flow of speech is common in verbal individuals with Down syndrome due to disrupted neural organisation (Devenny & Silverman, 1990). The dissociation between right hemisphere speech perception and production makes it more difficult (Table 1).

These characteristic features in the communication skills of individuals with intellectual disability may vary based on associated syndromic conditions such as difficulty in syntax and morphology in children with Down Syndrome; difficulty in semantic but better syntax and morphology in children with William Syndrome; difficulty in verbal and non-verbal pragmatics in children with Fragile X Syndrome. Further, several studies have reported that individuals with Down Syndrome tend to exhibit far better receptive languages skills than expressive skills (Abbeduto et al., 2001; Abbeduto & Murphy, 2004; Rice, Warren, & Betz, 2005). In addition to this, several researches have putforth the prevalence of behavioural problems in individuals with intellectual disability due to difficulty in making the communication partner understand their needs and thoughts. This happens vice-versa too, where some individuals tend to lag in their communication skills because of behavioural issues.

ASSESSMENT OF LANGUAGE AND COMMUNICATION

Philosophies

The traditional methods of speech and language assessment was predominantly static one point assessment and considered the inabilities than abilities. Traditional formal assessment used test materials with norm reference, most of which were developed based on the middle class, literate and Western framework. Many of these methods of language assessment do not truly reflect the nature of language behaviour in these individuals (Roseberry-McKibbin, 2007). One point assessments and judgements are often insufficient and less reliable. A preferred alternate that several clinicians began to use was a

Table 1. Summary of speech and language characteristics in individuals with intellectual disability

Parameter	Component	Profile in Individuals with ID
Language		
Form	Phonology	• Phonological processes persists beyond permissible age • Persistence of phonological processes such as consonant deletion, cluster reduction, assimilation, etc. beyond age • Inadequate awareness of rules governing combination of sounds in specific language
	Morphology	• Inadequate understanding and usage of grammatical morphemes (suffixes, prefixes indicating plural, tense, gender, person, etc) • Omission or inapproriate use of morphemes
	Syntax	• Shorter mean length of utterance • Simple and direct sentences • Reduced use of relative clauses
Content	Semantics	• Understanding and usage of more concrete word classes such as nouns, verbs • Difficulty in understanding and using relative and abstract word classes such as prepositions, comparatives, adverbs, adjectives, etc. • Literal meaning are considered
Use	Pragmatics	• Restricted use of variety in speech acts • Limited or no usage of conversational repair • Tend to be less assertive
Speech		
Fluency	Continuity of speech	Fluency difficulties such as sound syllable repetitions, prolongations and blocks especially in individuals with Down syndrome
	Rate of speech	Rate of speech may be very slow and prolonged or very fast and cluttered
Voice	Loudness	• Inadequate or inappropriate loudness • Inappropriate manipulation of loudness
	Pitch	Inconsistent, and uncontrolled or inappropriate manipulation of voice parameters like pitch & quality
	Quality	Hoarse voice leading to lesser clarity of speech
Articulation		• Inappropriate sound combinations • Substitution, omission, distortion of phonemes • More errors and reduced intelligibility in conversation than in isolated sound production
Prosody	Stress, Rhythm & Intonation	• Reduced and inappropriate stress on words • Often monotonous intonation

dynamic approach to assessment. Here, the individual's ability to learn when instructed, following 'test-teach-retest' approach was followed. The transfer from static to dynamic assessment led to the shift from 'What' a child knows to 'How' a child learns (Pena, Iglesias, & Lidz, 2001).

In recent years, research in the area of intellectual disability is experiencing a paradigm shift leading to changes in methods and measures to assess speech and language skills in these individuals. The fifth edition of the widely used Diagnostic and Statistical Manual criteria for individuals with Intellectual Disability 5 (2013) indicates the disorder to be developmental in nature. With the World Health Organisation approved taxonomy of International Classification of Functioning, Disability and Health (WHO, 2001), the evolution is obvious from 'incapacity' to 'functioning'. The sections on 'Body Function' and 'Activity and Participation' in ICF classification covers 'Mental functions'; 'Communication', 'Interpersonal interactions and relationships' related to intellectual disability. The severity qualifiers facilitate in documenting the extent of problem and its impact on the individual's everyday activities. The section on 'Environmental factors' involve eliciting information on the influence of communication, environment, etc. on the language development. This will allow to devise strategies to modify external factors and empower caregivers of individuals with intellectual disability to facilitate communication. ICF conceptualises intellectual disability on an integrative and interactional approach (WHO, 2001; Buntinx & Schalock, 2010; Schalock, 2011; Salvador-Carulla et al., 2011). Further, the ICF-CY (ICF-Children and Youth) developed by WHO (2007) includes development, behaviour and context during the first 20 years of life which is crucial in the assessment and management of individuals with intellectual disability. These warrant the need for a multidisciplinary approach to the assessment and management of individuals with intellectual disability.

Team Members

A comprehensive evaluation by a multidisciplinary team is essential in individuals with intellectual disability. An ideal team would include a clinical psychologist, special educator, speech language pathologist, occupational and physiotherapists; social worker and medical professionals as per need. The clinical and behavioural manifestation of the individual will dictate the range of assessments necessary. Such an evaluation answers several queries related to child's developmental and communicative behaviours in the minds of clinicians, caregivers, parents and family (Plante & Beason, 1999).The role of speech pathologists begins with profiling the child's speech and language skills through intensive assessment, plan appropriate objectives for intervention and execute the same. Adequate guidance and counselling to the family and immediate environment including school is taken care by a speech pathologist (Baroff, 1986), and other relevant professionals.

Types of Assessments

Assessment of language skills can be done either as a screening or diagnostic procedure. Screening procedure is a quick process to obtain brief profile of a child's communication skills. Screening procedures can be formal (standardised with established norms) or informal (non-standardised but tailor-made for clinic or child). By the end of the process, decision on the need for indepth comprehensive analysis or no intervention can be made. Often a brief conversation or reading accompanied with history obtained from the parents facilitate in arriving at a reliable conclusion. Screening procedures carry advantages of being cost-effective and time saving, especially when done for a larger group of population. Often children who fail in screening are referred for a complete evaluation. Most clinicians prefer an initial screening followed by a detailed diagnostic assessment (Kelly & Rice, 1986; Klein, 1984; McCauley & Swisher, 1984b).

Components of Assessment

Case History

Irrespective of following a formal or informal method of testing, case history is an integral part of every language assessment. This is useful in gathering background information starting with identification details to stimulation at home and other environments; birth and medical histories which will facilitate in understanding the individual and the disorder better (Plante & Beason, 1989). In addition, information on the description of the communication disorder, child's language levels, history of regression, prior assessment and rehabilitation, family constellation and communication patterns gets to be accounted through this process. Information on cultural and linguistic background is essential to compare with normative data if available. Further, case history helps in gathering subjective information from the informant (who is usually the parent or caregiver) on the specific characteristic of the disorder which lead to the concern, strengths and weakness of the individual possible cause for the disorder and its manifestation. This information will also facilitate in identifying concerns in daily activities which may require immediate intervention. Case history can be carried out in an interview format or as an open or close ended questionnaire formats. Neverthless, interview method provides scope for gathering specific information, freedom to inquire on insufficient information and discussions wherever needed. The face validity of this method is better than questionnaire method, provided the clinician is sufficiently skilled. Questions pertaining to case history and parental interview should often be straight forward without hesitation inorder to avoid embarrassment and discomfort. A thorough case history reduces the occurrence of cultural-linguistic bias.

Information on the perceived problem of the children by the caregiver is likely to augment the assessment thereby helping in structuring intervention plan accordingly. The expectation caregivers have on their children also indicate their awareness of the challenges and the willingness to work towards changing the same. Further, information on strategies used for facilitating communication in children will help in providing appropriate parental guidance. Information on the languages exposed to at home, school and other frequently exposed environments is important in terms of assessment and management. These information improve the validity of the assessment procedure. On the other hand, incase of very young children who are difficulty to test, information from caregivers or parents are important, for the diagnosis and rehabilitation is based on the same. Research report of greater accuracy in parental information on vocabulary of their children when compared to other measures of vocabulary used by SLPs (Beeghly, Jernberg, & Burrows, 1989; Dale, 1991) and less accurate ones with respect to understandability or intelligibility (Kwiatkowski & Shriberg, 1992). A commonly used parental questionnaire which was standardized on Western population and is being translated to various languages across the world is Children's Communication Checklist -2 (CCC-2, Bishop, 2006). In most clinical practice, such structured method to gather information from parents or caregivers is not mandatorily followed.

Observation

Observation of a child's behaviour provides valuable information during the process of diagnosis. This observation if often done and recommended to be carried out throughout the diagnostic process. The findings of the observation may be ideal when done in a natural environment such as home, school, etc. The communication acts observed during various level and type of play the child gets engaged in, provides information regarding language, cognitive and social functioning of the child. Assessment done by observing a child for a duration of 25-30 minutes in a variety of situations over a period of two to four sessions tend to provide a better insight about the child's communication skills and more reliable findings. In addition, for older individuals, a thorough observation in the classroom will give an understanding into the child's functional usage of communication.

Play-Based Observation

The development of play is reported to have strong correlation with sensorimotor, cognitive and early communication skills (Lifter & Bloom, 1989). Assessment of symbolic play, especially in toddlers has been proved to correlate with language development in children with and without language delays (Snyder & Scherer, 2004). This kind of assessment usually yield better representative sample for analysis as the data collection is recommended to occur in an informal atmosphere using toys which the child is free to explore. Further, the focus is on child's functional communication skills. Observation is an essential part of play based intervention as it is an indicator of the use of language to achieve communication outcomes. Various types of play such as dramatic (taking role in pretend game), fantasy or creative (creating props), exploratory (exploring properties and functions of materials), manipulative (manipulate and explore materials), physical (explore movements and its combinations), games with rules (following instructions to reach shared objective in a game). This play behaviour should ideally be conducted in a familiar environment with a familiar person to give a 'real picture' of everyday communication (Weitzner-Lin, 2004).

Formal Assessment

There are several standardised tests available to assess different components of language. The focus, quality and suitability of these tests are highly variable; and thus requires the clinician to have adequate knowledge and skill to identify the best suitable material, assess and interpret the results. For example, a material apt for assessing syntax in specific may not provide information on overall language status of the child. This would require a decision on choosing norm- or criterion-reference test. Norm-reference tests are used to compare a child's performance with that of a group of typically developing peers; while criterion-reference compares a child's performance against a standard or criterion for behaviour. Further, measures such as sensitivity, specificity, reliability and validity of the test material makes a clinician choose them for assessment.

Peabody Picture Vocabulary Test 4 (Dunn & Dunn, 2006); Pre-school Language Scale 5 (Zimmerman, Steiner, & Pond, 2011), Comprehensive Evaluation of Language Fundamentals (Semel, Wiig & Secord, 2004), Denver Developmental Screening Test (Frankenburg, Dodds & Archer, 1990), Bayley Scales of Infant Development 3 (Bayley, 2005), Bankson Language Screening Test 2 (Bankson, 1990) are a few commonly used standardised tests for Western and few cross cultural population. Language Assessment Tool (Subbarao, 1986); Assessment of Language Development (Lakanna, Venkatesh, & Bhat, 2008); Linguistic Profile Test (Karanth, 1986), Madras Developmental Programming System (Jeyachandran & Vimala, 1983) are some materials standardised on Indian population. The contents and contexts need to be considered while making a choice of a standardised test.

Irrespective of the standardised test used for assessment, certain considerations are to be kept in mind such as providing instructions in a simple and familiar language, repeating, rephrasing and explaining instructions, practice items, omitting biased items, continuing the test even after the ceiling in a particular parameter/measure is arrived as there could be chances of scattered scores in children with intellectual disability. Devoting more than one session for testing, having a familiar person during assessment, getting explanation for wrong answers, multiple scoring system in different languages the child is exposed to are some of other considerations that a clinician should keep in mind while performing a language assessment.

It is important that the sample taken for assessment be representative and spontaneous. Representative in terms of including maximum possible forms of verbal and non-verbal behaviours in the child's repertoire. Obtaining the sample in a natural environment such as home and with a familiar person (Eg: Caregiver) is likely to yield a better spontaneous response for analysis. Collecting the language sample in various environments over a period of time will provide better representative information. It is essential to consider the cultural background (Genesee, Paradis, & Crago, 2004) as in some cultures talking to an elder person with eye contact or calling the individual by name is considered disrespectful, while in others it is considered more as a casual behaviour. Observing the child with different conversation partners will provide information on the competency of the child to modify speech according to the communication partner. In a condition where the speech language pathologist does not speak the child's language, commissioning another SLP to obtain language sample may be required. Usage of age appropriate materials (toys and books) that interests the child during the interaction can motivate better responses. The analysis will include evaluation of the content (semantics), forms (phonology, morphology, syntax) and social use of language (pragmatics). Controlling the factors influencing the representativeness of a language sample will provide an appropriate sample. In summary, a combination of procedures such as observation in natural and structured environment, administering language test, parental questionnaire, caregiver interview will provide reliable and representative information for analysis and diagnosis.

ASSESSMENT OF VARIOUS PARAMETERS OF LANGUAGE

A thorough assessment of all aspects of language is important in individuals with intellectual disability (Owens, 2004). Assessment of form include assessing the range of sounds (phonemes) in the child's verbal repertoire. An in-depth analysis of the child's knowledge in combining these phonemes and usage of language specific rules will give an insight on the phonological profile. Once the language sample is obtained, informal approach to assess morphology and syntax begins with obtaining average number of words used per utterance. The usage of suffixes, prefixes also need to be documented. In addition, understanding and usage of various types of sentences used such as active form, passive form, questioning, statements, requests, etc should be assessed. Assessment of syntax can be complicated considering its diversity and complexity in the specific language. The assessment of syntax includes both comprehension and expression. Comprehension and usage of various types of sentences such as statements (declarative), questions (interrogatives), etc and sentences that convey emotions such as exclamatory are assessed to evaluate the form.

Most formal tests tend to assess the knowledge of words which often provides all or none result (Crais, 1990). In reality the process of acquiring language continues through the life. Factors such as type of task, manner of cueing, ability of the SLP to conduct and interpret the test may influence the results. Thus it is essential to consider these variables while profiling a child's communication. Often a naming or a description is used for assessing the word knowledge. Skills such as categorical understanding (naming lexicals in a category, providing synonym or antonym), word association (naming associated noun or verb), stating similarities and differences, telling all about the word/picture, explaining figurative language, multiple meaning, etc are used for assessing semantics.

The most challenging part of assessment is the use of language (pragmatics) in daily activities. Considering the rules of interaction followed with culturally and linguistically matched peers may provide sufficient information for profiling a child's pragmatics. Skills such as initiation, maintenance and termination of conversation, usage of conversational repair strategy, modifying language appropriate to communication partner and environment have to be included in the complete profile of communication (Roseberry-McKibbin, 2007). Often tasks such as story-telling and topic discussions are used for assessing pragmatics. However, these may not provide information on the ability of the child to answer to questions and ask questions (Owens, 2004). Pragmatic use of language is difficult to assess in a single environment or in a specific time. This has also led to unavailability of norms for the same.

In addition to these, assessment of speech continuity and clarity are essential to profile the speech and language of the individual. Intellectual disability is often associated with Down Syndrome, and cerebral palsy where the palate may be high-arched, tongue could be bulky and muscle tone is inappropriate thereby affecting the clarity of speech. A thorough examination of the oral motor structures such as lips, tongue, palate, mandible, maxilla, teeth for abnormality in structure and function will provide valuable information to the assessment (Table 2).

Communication Intervention in Individuals with Intellectual Disability

The methods of language intervention in individuals with intellectual disability significantly depend on the severity of the disorder. Though the intervention is based on specific language skills and is personalised, the broad objective is to facilitate communication and improve quality of life. Several

Table 2. Summary of formal and informal assessment of speech and language skills

<table>
<tr><th>Parameter</th><th>Formal Assessment</th><th>Informal Assessment</th></tr>
<tr><td colspan="3">Language</td></tr>
<tr><td>Form (Phonology, morphology, syntax)</td><td rowspan="3">Specific parameter:
• Assessment of Phonological Processes – Revised – Preschool phonological Screening (Hodson, 1986)
• Quick Screening of Phonology (Bankson & Bernthal, 1990)
• Semantics, Morphology, Syntax: Test of Language Proficiency (Karanth, 1986)
• Semantics: MacArthur Communication Development Inventory (Fenson et al, 1993)
Overall receptive and expressive language skills:
• Preschool Language Scale-5 (Zimmerman, Steiner, & Pond, 2011)
• Communication and Symbolic Behaviour Scale (Wetherby & Prizant, 1993)
• Clinical Evaluation of Language Fundamentals (Wiig, Secord, & Semel, 1992)
• Language Assessment Tool (Subbarao, 1986)
• Assessment of Language Development (Lakanna, Venkatesh, & Bhat, 2008)</td><td>• Phonological awareness
• Phonological manipulation
• Average number of morphemes/utterance
• Usage of grammatical morphemes (person, number, gender, tense)
• Understanding and use of different types of sentences (statements, questions, exclamatory, etc.)</td></tr>
<tr><td>Content</td><td>• Word meanings
• Word classes: nouns, verbs, prepositions, adjectives, adverbs, pronouns, conjunctions</td></tr>
<tr><td>Use</td><td>• Using known language when required
• Modifying communication based on person, situation and context
• Utterance act, propositional acts; illocutionary and perlocutionary acts</td></tr>
<tr><td colspan="3">Speech</td></tr>
<tr><td>Fluency</td><td rowspan="4">• Stuttering Severity Instrument (Riley, 2009)
• Acoustic analysis of various parameters of voice using software such as PRAAT, Multidimensional Voice Profile, etc.
• Test of articulation in regional languages
• Arizona Articulation Proficiency Scale (Fudala & Reynolds, 2000)
• Photo Articulation Test (Pendergast, Dickey, Selman & Soder, 1997)
• Deep Test of Articulation (McDonald, 2006)</td><td rowspan="4">• Flow of speech, clarity and quality from a general conversation or narration
• Repetition of sentences or words
• Pitch, loudness and quality of voice
• Intelligibility
• Variations of pitch & loudness
• Use of emphasis and tone to convey emotions</td></tr>
<tr><td>Prosody</td></tr>
<tr><td>Voice</td></tr>
<tr><td>Articulation</td></tr>
</table>

studies (Cole, Mills, & Kelley, 2005; Cole, Coggins, & Vanderstoep, 1999) have extensively researched the relationship between communication intervention and child's development in cognitive and social domains. These have determined the need to establish and plan objectives for intervention based on cognition and language levels. Most intervention programmes focus on language levels (Girolametto, Weitzaman, & Clements-Baartman, 1998; Yoder & Warren, 2002). However, the best way to plan intervention is based on child's specific language skills. An ideal intervention plan comprises of receptive and expressive language skills.

Several behavioural problems arise in individuals with intellectual disability due to difficulty in communicating their needs. Thus, it is believed and proven that addressing the communication difficulties will indirectly improve the child's behaviours too. Functional Communication Training (Franzone, 2009), a systematic approach based on the relationship between behaviour and communication is used to reduce the frequency of undesirable behaviour and thereby facilitate communication to a great extent. This technique replaces less clear communication forms such as reaching and leading with more conventional communication forms such as verbalising, pointing, signing and picture exchange. This involves the identification of interfering behaviour through functional behavioural assessment. The challenging part of this training is the appropriate replacement of new set of behaviours which are acceptable by multiple communication partners. Fading the prompts used during the shaping of response is another challenge.

Despite developing adequate vocabulary and sentence structures for basic communication, most individuals with intellectual disability tend to have poor speech clarity/intelligibility. This is often due to structural or functional abnormality such as bulky tongue (especially in individuals with Down Syndrome), hypotonicity of oral structures, etc. Managing the intelligibility part of speech is often done through the earliest form of facilitating communication development including alternative forms (Bondy & Frost, 1994; Kay-Raining Bird, Gaskell, Dallaire, Babineau, & Macdonald, 2000) and gesturing (Yoder & Warren, 1998). Often alternative modes of communication are chosen easier than verbal modes by these individuals. This could possibly be due to ease of imitating gross motor movements than precise articulatory movements.

Language intervention usually focuses on earliest forms of pre-speech communication behaviours expressed through conventional gestures, joint attention and pre-speech vocalisations, which often fade off or shape to meaningful communication in a due course of time. Linking these communication behaviours with speech-like vocalisations, especially canonical vocalisations improve communication to a greater extent. While planning communication intervention for individuals with intellectual disability, it is essential to consider the developmental levels including cognitive, social and emotional domains. For researchers and clinicians working with the 'delay' perspective, setting the ceiling based on cognitive age while working on language skills facilitates better scope for prognosis. When the language age reaches the mental age, the scope for improvement reduces thus leading to change in the approach for intervention. If cognition is considered to be a major pre-requisite for language development, it is essential to stimulate the cognitive skills prior to commencing language therapy. Further, children with less than 2.5 morphemes/utterance tend to respond better with approaches such as milieu teaching (via elicited production prompts) than responsive interaction (Eg: expansions and growth recasts where new semantic, phonological and syntactic information are added to child's utterance) (Yoder et al. 1998).

The earliest forms of therapies for communication were predominantly trainer-oriented where the speech therapist had the complete control on the stimuli, activities and reinforcement. Over the years, several individualised plan based on child-oriented therapies were introduced. Studies on the effectiveness of different methods indicated significant prognosis while using a combination of trainer-oriented and child-oriented methods, known as 'hybrid methods'. Further, recent randomised control trials indicate that various versions of parent mediated milieu teaching have been positive, but with minimal effects and inconsistency across participants (e.g., Warren & Brady, 2007; Yoder & Stone, 2006; Yoder & Warren, 2001). However, the effective reaching and use of technique is debatable (Warren et al., 2008; Warren, Fey, & Yoder, 2007).

Intensity of Intervention

The extent of intensive stimulation may influence the prognosis of communication behaviours in individuals with intellectual disability. However, empirical evidences for supporting the linear relationship between the intensity of intervention and prognosis of communication skills are minimal. This could be influenced by several other factors such as approach used for intervention (child-oriented versus clinician-directed), child's learning history, responsiveness of the caregiver in child's activities of daily living, the objective worked upon, knowledge and skill of the clinician, involvement of the parent in generalising learnt behaviour to other situations (Brady & Warren,, 2003).

The duration need not necessarily relate to the intensive aspect of the intervention, but the quality does. One-on-one intervention proves to be more intensive than group of small or bigger size to improve vocabulary and length of utterance. However, a group intervention may be more intensive for improving social use or pragmatics of language.

Role of Communication Partner

Facilitators of communication in young children are adults such as parents, grandparents or caregivers who spend quality time with the children (Craig, 1983). Communication being an interactive process, the role of communication partner (the caregiver in specific) is highly crucial for facilitating communication in individuals with intellectual disability. They are the first facilitators and models of communication for young children. Several factors including the amount of intervention (Alston & St. James-Roberts, 2005), responsiveness (Warren & Brady, 2007), linguistic input (Weizman & Snow, 2001), and learning strategies used (Smith, Landry, & Swank, 2000) influence the development of communication in these children. Several researches have been conducted on the maternal linguistic input and its impact on children's communication skills. Rondal and Turnure (1976) observed that maternal linguistic input provided by mothers of children with Down Syndrome was similar to the ones provided by typically developing children matched for length of utterance. It is known that caregiver-child interaction plays a vital role in the development of language skills in young children. This interaction is often dominated and compensated by the caregivers due to the significant communication deficits in individuals with intellectual disability. The communicative behaviours of the caregivers, parents and teachers are a reactive response to children's conduct. Among the several modules of parent-training programmes examined by Roberts and Kaiser (2011) the most common approach was putforth by Hanen Program (Manolson, 1992). Earlier studies reported similar results between therapist mediated and parent mediated intervention for communication, while the recent studies report of better generalisation and practice when parents were provided with structured objectives, constant monitoring and appropriate feedback (Kaiser & Roberts, 2013). The variation in service delivery range from one on one to group parent empowerment programmes. Several parent empowerment programmes have compared different methods of intervention which focussed on specific strategies. These reflected changes in both caregivers and children's pragmatic acts and utterances including environmental arrangement and incidental teaching. Yoder and Warren (2001) report caregivers' communicative responsiveness prior to and during intervention determines the progress of therapy. Parent training programme may tend to reduce the directedness and increase responsiveness of mothers of children with developmental delays (Girolametto et al., 1998). Further, this also leads to children being more assertive, use more vocabulary, take turns and exhibit responsive conversational acts.

Researches reveal that intervention programmes which involve the caregivers or parents provide better prognosis than the ones dealing only with children (Searcy, 2012). Working on a parent empowerment or guidance programme along with the SLP ensures there is a continuum and effective transfer and implementation of the target behaviours. It is crucial to remember that the caregivers/parents also require necessary feedback on their interaction with the children. It is evident that the caregiver's communication skills with reference to knowledge, skill and attitude does play a major role in facilitating communication in their children. The role of SLP does not restrict only to modifying child's language skills, but also to make the communication between the caregiver-child dyad an effective one.

Communication intervention begins with facilitating comprehension in children with intellectual disability which depends on the severity of the disorder, associated features if any and its clinical manifestation. For example, an individual with hearing loss associated with intellectual disability, the intervention is often focussed on auditory identification, localisation, discriminations at initial stages. The difficulty in discrimination is often associated with attending to fewer dimensions of stimuli than what is required for distinguishing them (Paul & Norbury, 2012). This can be remediated through direct instruction. Operant conditioning approach to intervention of specific language skills works better in individuals with severe or profound intellectual disability (Reed, 2005). Some researches support script based intervention while the others the vice-versa (Kim & Lombardino, 1991). A conversational observation is likely to yield positive behaviours such as smiling, laughing, engagement in activities with more verbal output than during other tasks such as imitation or stimulus response tasks. Stimulus response approach reinforcement follows the protocol of questions or instructions putforth by the SLP for which the child is expected to response and receive the reinforcement. Thus, most SLPs prefer this structured approach as it increases the probability of occurrence of the target behaviour. However, the child tends to be passive in this model as the SLP manipulates the environment and activities making it unidirectional. These trainer-oriented approaches tend to provide less opportunity for functional use of language (Fey, 1986). Nevertheless research has evidence for improvement in language skills, especially form and content when dealt with structured approaches. However, the challenge arises during generalisation of the learnt behaviour from clinic to a natural environment (Hunt & Goetz, 1988) which doesn't happen on its own. The language assessment and intervention prior to 20th century has focussed more on language content and structure, with minimal emphasis on the use of language. The prognosis gets measured in the child being a successful communicator than on the number of responses. Further, the strategies used by the SLP and the caregiver is closely linked to those used in the natural language-learning environment.

Often child-oriented intervention approaches facilitate comprehension better than clinician-centered methods (Paul et al., 2011). In such situation clinician follows the child's lead in providing adequate stimulation by commenting, repeating or rephrasing child's utterances (Reed, 2005) focussing both on comprehension and expression. Following these by both parents tend to improve both comprehensive and expressive language skills.

Intervention of Meaning

Lexical teaching may be the first aspect of language to be worked on by clinicians. It is also essential to combine the facilitative strategies with syntax inorder to appreciate better prognosis (Miller, 1984). The natural acquisition of language in these children is often restricted to nouns as they are concrete. Thus, it is essential for the intervention to focus on other classes of words such as verbs, adjectives, adverbs and also venture into lexical categories not familiar to the child. One of the common communication characteristic observed in individuals with intellectual disability is echolalia. Echolalia refers to parrot-like speech, i.e. the individual repeats whatever is uttered by the communication partner without understanding the meaning. This could be immediate or delayed based on when the child utters the word. The primitive form of echolalia is observed during 9-10 months where infants begin to imitate sounds produced by adults. These often follow a question or requests with immediate behavioural consequences (Baroff, 1986). Management of echolalia works best with behavioural modification approach which capitalises the echoic response by echoing the expect response. However, generalisation is a debatable aspect in this approach. Thus, a combination of cognitive and behavioural approach have been proved to reduce the occurrence of echolalia.

Intervention of Syntax: Sentence Structure

Among the different approaches to language intervention, the clinician-directed/trainer-oriented and hybrid approaches work best for intervention of syntax. In a hybrid approach, the child is let to choose the activity and the clinician follows it to mediate towards the objective. Some examples of hybrid approaches are mand model and incidental teaching techniques (Paul et al., 2011). In the mand model, the speech pathologist or caregiver asks a question, followed by mand/prompts and models to facilitate verbal output by the child; and finally concludes with verbal acknowledgement and expansion. Similarly, the incidental teaching approach is best dealt by a caregiver as the language expansion happens during any daily activity or routine. Systematic commenting (focussed bombardment of target form but with no expectation of response from the child) is another technique used widely for improving syntax of young children. In contrary, the trainer oriented approach follows operant conditioning principles. Clinician directed or trainer oriented techniques work with prompting, shaping, reinforcing and drilling.

Intervention of Pragmatics: Use of Language

Any learnt behaviour is essential to be used in a functional everyday situation for short or long term. Thus, it is important to empower the child to use the learnt behaviour or word in an appropriate context with appropriate communication partner. This is often difficult in individuals with intellectual disability (Kaiser & Hancock, 2003). Thus, effective intervention for these individuals should focus on learning a wide variety and range of language skills which is simultaneously generalised using multiple therapists, forms and settings. Language facilitation works best in natural communication environment rather than a communication drill (Reed, 2005). However, often these individuals tend to be passive conversationalists which leads the intervention to focus on increasing the range and frequency of assertive behaviours (Fey, 1986). It is crucial for communicative behaviours to be consistent, adequate in frequency and occur in response to natural stimuli thereby expressing its nature than as being learnt. Pragmatics being contextual use of language cannot be adequately facilitated through a single room therapy session, as it involves inter-personal problem solving of judging what a listener needs to know (Abbeduto, 1991). The important consideration here is that the skill being generalised is established prior to its functional usage. The best way to work on pragmatics is group intervention or involve other children or adult during the therapy session such as peer-mediated intervention (Goldstein, & Ferrell, 1987).

Intervention of Speech Aspect of Communication

Depending on the severity of intellectual disability and the extent of verbal communication, intervention of the speech aspect of communication is considered. Due to the significant language difficulties in these individuals, the speech aspect such as understandability and flow are often worked simultaneously. Some researchers (Reed, 2005) report that irrespective of the retardation, the intervention of speech remains the same. However, certain modifications may be incorporated to suit the individual's cognitive difficulty. Due to decreased tone in oral and facial muscles and structures, oral motor stimulation is highly recommended for individuals with Down syndrome to improve vegetative skills, oral awareness and decrease drooling (Swift & Rosin, 1990).

Selection of Materials for Intervention

Selecting materials that will be of interest to children, engage them and motivate for sustained participation that will facilitate communication is challenging. Choosing materials corresponding to the mental age of children with intellectual disability may not be of interest. Thus, arises the discrepancy on choosing materials appropriate to chronological or mental age. A realistic object or drawing is often accepted than others. Very young children with an average utterance length of less than two words would prefer toys including car, utensils, doll, ball etc, while a slightly older child of 2-4 word utterance length might be inclined to use doll house and talk about events or people from immediate space and time. Further, choosing appropriate reinforcement, providing them at adequate intervals, fading gradually plays a major role in intervention of communication (Table 3) (Hegde, 1998).

Table 3. Strategies to facilitate communication in individuals with intellectual disability

Parameters of Language		**Tips to Facilitate Communication**
Form	Phonology Morphology Syntax	• Use simple sentences while communicating • Create opportunities to speak • Respond only if spoken in phrases or sentences
Content	Semantics	• Describe objects, actions and events happening in child's visual field • 'Comments' work better than 'commands' • Instruct on 'what to do' than 'what not to do' • Stress on the words when introduced new and when expected to be spoken by the child • Can provide choices to name or ask for objects
Use	Pragmatics	• Provide opportunities to interact with multiple communication partners • Encourage peer interaction • Provide real time experience to communicate • Needs to be satisfied only when asked for
Parameters of Speech		**Tips to Facilitate Communication**
Fluency		• Encourage to speak fluently • Discourage yelling and shouting • Respond only when words are clear • Can teach how to place lips, tongue, teeth during production of a sound
Voice		
Articulation		

Alternative Modes of Communication

The use of alternative and augmentative mode of communication (AAC) to express needs and thoughts is often recommended to individuals who lack verbal expression of communication. The individuals who are recommended for AAC often have a severe medical etiology or co-exisiting disorders related to sensory or motor impairments. AAC is used by individuals with severe to profound retardation exhibited by close to nonverbal mode of communication or individuals with mild retardation whose speech is characterised by reduced intelligibility despite considerable amount of verbal output (Romski, Sevcik & Fonseca, 2003). AAC may reduce the occurrence of unacceptable behaviours such as temper tantrums which often arise due to challenges in communication, especially with respect to basic daily needs (Donnellan, Mirenda, Mesaros, & Fassbender, 1984; Doss & Reichle, 1991).

Introducing AAC in an individual with communication difficulty depends on a variety of factors such as history of long duration nonverbal mode of communication despite adequate stimulation for close to a year, basic receptive language, closer to V or VI Piagetian sensorimotor stage (Abbeduto et al., 2003). It is essential to select appropriate pictures which are of the individual's immediate needs with closer to typical representation while developing the AAC. However, AAC usage is not restricted to an alternative mode, but also to augment or initiate verbal expression. Assessing and recommending the use of AAC in individuals with intellectual disability require thorough assessment of candidacy and counselling the immediate communication partners. Choosing the appropriate type of AAC such as aided (using instruments or equipment) or unaided (without using any instruments or equipment) depends on a variety of factors such as cognitive level, language levels, motor skills, motor co-ordination, associated sensory or neurological issues and chronological age. Earliest form of AAC were predominantly through signing, gestures, pointing. Over the years, several other forms including picture boards/books, electronic devices and apps for using alternative modes for communication are commercially available. Several forms of AAC with hi tech support are being used in developed countries such as System for Augmenting Language (SAL). One such commonly used one in developing countries like India is AVAAZ which is a hi tech AAC with options for customisation. However, due to less awareness and acceptance, the usage of AAC is not extensive in these developing countries.

CRITICAL VIEW AND FUTURE DIRECTIONS

The chapter briefly described relationship between cognition and language, delay and deviant controversy of language development, specific characteristic features of various language and speech skills, assessment process and intervention approaches currently prevailing in clinical practice. Researches addressing the various aspects of communication in individuals with intellectual disability have been cited as examples to explain the current trends. Functional language assessment follows communication-first approach through spontaneous and generalised communication in natural setting. The interaction between the child and the communication partner becomes the medium for change. The communication partner who spends maximum time with the child is the child's caregiver. A speech pathologist often works with the caregivers to manipulate the linguistic and non-linguistic contexts. Functional language approach to intervention focuses on increasing the mean length of utterance, multiword utterance production, overall quantity and quality of spontaneous production, pragmatic skills, vocabulary growth, language complexity, receptive labelling and intelligibility, use of trained form in novel utterance in children with intellectual disability and other language disorders. The role of pragmatics in intervention is clearly depicted in functional approach to language intervention. Communication is often impaired because of challenges in pragmatics. Conversational partner should be aware of the preceding linguistic context, need and knowledge of the speaker and topic inorder to engage in a successful communication.

The earlier trainer-oriented models of intervention in 1970s focussed on the cognitive and intellectual readiness while giving less or no emphasis on the functional use of language. Intervention modules for individuals with special needs dealt with the processes of communication rather than a specific characteristic or concern of the individual. This lead to altering features such as echolalia and unusual language patterns as these were deemed inappropriate. While considering language interventions based on pragmatics and the processes underlying the communication act, child-oriented approaches than traditional approaches work towards improving the communication. The focus shifts from disorder to the child thereby increasing the functional usage in daily activities. This mandates the need for including family, teachers and other individuals whom the child spends quality time everyday and in those situations/environments too. It is also evident that the conversational constraint of communication partner may influence the structure and content (Owens, 2004). Thus, a functional approach ensures therapy that is bidirectional for learning, teaching and transfer of information.

Even while following a functional approach to language assessment and intervention, few components in language context require manipulation by the SLP. The dimensions involved in a language context include purpose, content, type and mode of discourse, participant characteristics, setting, activity and speech community. The SLP becomes a programmer by manipulating a child's environment to facilitate better communication. Adequate and appropriate cognitive, social, physical, linguistic and non-linguistic contexts facilitates better communication and thus is essential for the SLP to simulate such environment. Generalisation, i.e.carrying over learnt behaviour to non-clinical and natural setting (Fey, 1988; Halle, 1987; Hunt & Goetz, 1988; Warren, 1988) need to be considered. Various teaching contexts are considered while planning for generalisation. The goal of communication competence is achieved only when the leant behaviour is generalised to content, context and speaker. The SLP needs to address several questions while planning the therapy sessions. A few are: 'Will this behaviour be carried over to everyday environment?', 'Is the new behaviour that is taught through the therapy relevant to the child?', 'Are the methods used reflective enough in everyday context so that it is generalizable beyond the clinic?', etc. Evidence based practice and measurement of the intervention outcome is important. Pring (2004) states that 'the problem of choosing which treatment approach to adopt is daunting because, so far, there is only emerging evidence about which therapeutic approach should be used with specific types of disorder'. This opinion holds good even today, after a decade of researches in this area.

CONCLUSION

Parameters of language (form, content and use) and speech (fluency, voice, articulation and stress) need to be assessed thoroughly in individuals with intellectual disability in order to plan intervention and gauge progress. A variety of assessment methods such as formal standardized tests, informal observation, play based assessment, parental interview, etc. are followed by Speech Language Pathologists to evaluate communication skills in individuals with ID. Clinicians usually employ more than one assessment method to provide a complete and reliable results.

The next step after assessment is to plan intervention strategies for facilitating communication in these individuals. Clinicians report a variety of outcomes based on the approaches to language intervention such as child-oriented, clinician directed and hybrid therapies. However, there is no one single approach to therapy that works the best with specific degree or type of language disorder associated with intellectual disability. Combination of approaches to intervention of language disorders and getting the family involved along may provide better prognosis.

REFERENCES

Abbeduto, L. (1991). Development of verbal communication in persons with moderate to mild mental retardation. *International Review of Research in Mental Retardation*, *17*, 91–115. doi:10.1016/S0074-7750(08)60104-4

Abbeduto, L., Davies, B., Solesdy, S., & Furman, L. (1991). Indentifying the reference of spoken messages: The use of context and clarification requests by children with mental retardation and by nonretarded children. *American Journal of Mental Retardation*, *95*, 551–562. PMID:2043349

Abbeduto, L., Furman, L., & Davies, B. (1989). Relation between the receptive language and mental age of persons with mental retardation. *American Journal of Mental Retardation*, *93*, 535–545. PMID:2706121

Abbeduto, L., & Murphy, M. M. (2004). Language, social cognition, maladaptive behavior and communication in Down syndrome and Fragile X syndrome. In M. L. Rice & S. F. Warren (Eds.), *International Research in Developmental Disabilities,* (pp. 547–566).

Abbeduto, L., Murphy, M. M., Cawthon, S. W., Richmond, E. K., Weissman, M. D., Karadottir, S., & O'Brien, A. (2003). Receptive Language Skills of Adolescents and Young Adults With Down or Fragile X Syndrome. *American Journal of Mental Retardation*, *108*(3), 149–160. doi:10.1352/0895-8017(2003)108<0149:RLSOAA>2.0.CO;2 PMID:12691594

Abbeduto, L., Pavetto, M., Kesin, E., Weissman, M., Karadottir, S., O'Brient, A., & Cawthon, S. (2001). The linguistic and cognitive profile of Down syndrome: Evidence from a comparison with fragile X syndrome. *Down Syndrome Research and Practise, 7,* 9-16.

Abbeduto, L., & Rosenberg, S. (1980). The communicative competence of mildly retarded adults. *Applied Psycholinguistics*, *1*(04), 405–426. doi:10.1017/S0142716400009826

Alston, E., & St. James-Roberts, I. (2005). Home environments of 10-month-old infants selected by the WILSTAAR screen for pre-language difficulties. *International Journal of Language & Communication Disorders*, *40*(2), 123–136. doi:10.1080/13682820400006861 PMID:16101270

Bailoor, P., & SubbaRao, T.A. (2013). Semantic intentions and relations in children with intellectual disability (ID) in the mental age range of 4 to 7 years. *Journal of Advances in Life Science and Technology,* 13.

Bankson, N. W., & Bernthal, J. E. (1990). *Quick Screening of Phonology*. Chicago: Riverside Publishing.

Baroff, G. S. (1986). *Mental retardation: Nature, cause and management* (2nd ed.). Washington, DC: Hemisphere.

Bedrosian, J., & Prutting, C. A. (1978). Communicative performance of mentally retarded adults in four conversational settings. *Journal of Speech and Hearing Research*, *21*(1), 79–95. doi:10.1044/jshr.2101.79 PMID:642491

Beeghly, M., Jernberg, E., & Burrows, E. (1989). Validity of the Early Language Inventory (ELI) for use with 25-month-olds. *Journal of Child Language*, *23*(3), 515–528.

Belva, B. C., Matson, J. L., Sipes, M., & Bamburg, J. W. (2012). An examination of specific communication deficits in adults with profound intellectual disabilities. *Research in Developmental Disabilities*, *33*(2), 525–529. doi:10.1016/j.ridd.2011.10.019 PMID:22119701

Berger, J., & Cunningham, C. C. (1983). Development of early vocal behaviours and interactions in Down's syndrome and nonhandicapped infant-mother pairs. *Developmental Psychology*, *19*(3), 322–331. doi:10.1037/0012-1649.19.3.322

Bernthal, J. W., & Bankson, N. W. (2004). *Articulation & Phonological Disorders* (5th ed.). Boston, MA: Pearson Education, Inc./Allyn & Bacon.

Bharatraj, J. (1987). Speech and Hearing problems among the mentally retarded. *Indian Journal of Disability and Rehabilitation*, *1*, 5–8.

Bilsky, L. H. (1986). Comprehension and mental retardation. *International Review of Research in Mental Retardation*, *13*, 215–246. doi:10.1016/S0074-7750(08)60237-2

Bishop, D. V. (2006). *Children's Communication Checklist*. NCS Pearson, Inc.

Bohannon, J. N., & Bonvillian, J. D. (2005). Theoretical approaches to language acquisition. In *The development of language* (6th ed.; pp. 230–291). Boston: Allyn & Bacon.

Bondy, A. S., & Frost, L. A. (1994). The picture exchange communication system. *Focus on Autistic Behavior*, *9*, 1–19.

Brady, N. C., & Warren, S. F. (2003). Language intervention for children with mental retardation. *International Review of Research in Mental Retardation*, *27*, 231–254. doi:10.1016/S0074-7750(03)27007-5

Buntinx, W. H. E., & Schalock, R. L. (2010). Models of Disability, Quality of Life, and Individualized Supports: Implications for Professional Practice in Intellectual Disability. *Journal of Policy and Practice in Intellectual Disabilities*, *7*(4), 283–294. doi:10.1111/j.1741-1130.2010.00278.x

Calculator, S. N., & Dollaghan, C. (1982). The use of communication boards in a residential setting: An evaluation. *The Journal of Speech and Hearing Disorders*, *47*(3), 281–287. doi:10.1044/jshd.4703.281 PMID:6225904

Carrow-Woolfolk, F., & Lynch, J. (1982). *An approach to language disorders in children*. New York: Grune & Stratton.

Chomsky, N., & Skinner, B. F. (1959). Review of BF Skinner. Verbal Behavior. *Language*, *35*(1), 26–58. doi:10.2307/411334

Cole, K. N., Coggins, T. E., & Vanderstoep, C. (1999). The influence of language/Cognitive profile on discourse intervention outcome. *Language, Speech, and Hearing Services in Schools*, *30*(1), 61–67. doi:10.1044/0161-1461.3001.61

Craig, H. K. (1983). Applications of pragmatic language models for intervention. In T. Gallagher & C. Prutting (Eds.), Pragmatic assessment and intervention issues in language (pp. 101-127). San Diego, CA: College-Hill.

Crais, E. R. (1990). World knowledge to word knowledge. *Topics in Language Disorders*, *10*(3), 45–62. doi:10.1097/00011363-199006000-00006

Cromer, R. F. (1991). *Language and thought in normal and handicapped children*. Oxford, UK: Basil Blackwell.

Dale, P. S. (1991). The validity of parent report measure of vocabulary and syntax at 24 months. *Journal of Speech and Hearing Research*, *34*(3), 565–571. doi:10.1044/jshr.3403.565 PMID:2072681

Devenny, D. A., & Silverman, W. P. (1990). Speech dysfluency and manual specialisation in Down syndrome. *Journal of Mental Deficiency Research*, *34*, 253–260. PMID:2143231

Dewart, H. (1979). Language comprehension processes of mentally retarded children. *American Journal of Mental Deficiency*, *84*, 177–183. PMID:495665

Donnellan, A. M., Mirenda, P. L., Mesaros, R., & Fassbender, L. (1984). Analyzing the communicative functions of aberrant behavior. *The Journal of the Association for Persons with Severe Handicaps*, *9*, 210–222.

Doss, L. S., & Reichle, J. (1991). *Replacing excess behaviour with an initial communicative repertoire*. Baltimore, MD: Brooks Publishing Co.

Dunn, L. M., & Dunn, L. M. (1997). *PPVT-III: Peabody picture vocabulary test*. Circle Pines, MN: American Guidance Service.

Eheart, B. (1982). Mother-child interactions with non-retarded and mentally retarded preschoolers. *American Journal of Mental Deficiency*, *87*, 20–25. PMID:6181684

Fenson, L., Dale, P., Reznick, S., Thal, D., Bates, E., Hartung, J., & Reilly, J. et al. (1993). *McArthur Communication Inventories*. San Diego, CA: Singular Publishing.

Fey, M. E. (1986). *Language intervention with young children*. San Diego, CA: College-Hill.

Fey, M. E. (1988). Generalisation issues facing language interventionists: An introduction. *Language, Speech, and Hearing Services in Schools*, *19*(3), 272–281. doi:10.1044/0161-1461.1903.272

Finch-Williams, A. (1984). The developmental relationship between cognition and communication: Implications for assessment. *Topics in Language Disorders*, *5*(1), 1–13. doi:10.1097/00011363-198412000-00005

Fowler, A. E. (1990). Language abilities in children with Down syndrome: Evidence for a specific syntactic delay. In D. Cicchetti & M. Beeghley (Eds.), *Children with Down Syndrome: Developmental perspective* (pp. 302–328). Cambridge, UK: Cambridge University Press. doi:10.1017/CBO9780511581786.010

Fudala, J. B., & Reynolds, W. M. (2000). *Arizona Articulation Proficiency Scale*. Los Angeles, CA: Western Psychological Services.

Gathercole, S. E., & Baddeley, A. D. (1993). *Working memory and language*. Hillsdale, NJ: Erlbaum Associates.

Genesee, F., Paradis, J., & Crago, M. B. (2004). *Dual language development and disorders: A handbook on bilingualism and second language learners*. Baltimore, MD: Brookes Publishing Co.

Girolametto, L., Weitzman, E., & Clements-Baartman, J. (1998). Vocabulary intervention for children with Down syndrome: Parent training using focused stimulation. *Infant-Toddler Intervention: the Transdisciplinary Journal*, *8*(2), 109–125.

Goldstein, H., & Ferrell, D. (1987). Augmenting communicative interaction between handicapped and nonhandicapped preschool children. *The Journal of Speech and Hearing Disorders*, *52*(3), 200–211. doi:10.1044/jshd.5203.200 PMID:3455442

Grant, J., Karmiloff-Smidh, A., Gathercole, S. E., Paterson, S., Howlin, P., Davies, M., & Udwin, O. (1997). Phonological short-term memory and its relationship to language in Williams syndrome. *Cognitive Neuropsychiatry*, *2*(2), 81–99. doi:10.1080/135468097396342 PMID:25420198

Greenwald, C., & Leonard, L. (1979). Communicative and sensorimotor development of Down's syndrome children. *American Journal of Mental Deficiency*, *84*, 296–303. PMID:160755

Guralnick, N. J., & Paul-Brown, D. (1986). Communicative interactions of mildly delayed and normally developing preschool children: Effects of listener's developmental level. *Journal of Speech and Hearing Research*, *29*(1), 2–10. doi:10.1044/jshr.2901.02 PMID:3702375

Halle, J. W. (1987). Teaching language in the natural environment: An analysis of spontaneity. *The Journal of the Association for Persons with Severe Handicaps*, *12*, 28–37.

Henry, L. A., & Gudjonsson, G. G. (1999). Eyewitness memory and suggestibility in children with mental retardation. *American Journal of Mental Retardation*, *104*(6), 491–508. doi:10.1352/0895-8017(1999)104<0491:EMASIC>2.0.CO;2 PMID:10587731

Hunt, P., & Goetz, L. (1988). Teaching spontaneous communication in natural setting through interrupted behaviour chains. *Topics in Language Disorders*, *9*(1), 58–71. doi:10.1097/00011363-198812000-00006

Jarrold, C., Baddeley, A. D., & Phillips, C. E. (2002). Verbal short-term memory in Down syndrome: A problem of memory, audition, or speech? *Journal of Speech, Language, and Hearing Research: JSLHR*, *45*(3), 531–544. doi:10.1044/1092-4388(2002/042) PMID:12069005

Jeyachandran, P., & Vimala. (1983). *Madras Developmental Programming System* (3rd Ed.). Chennai, India: Vijay Human Services.

Jones, O. H. M. (1977). Mother-child communication with prelinguistic Down's syndrome and normal infants. In H. R. Schaffer (Ed.), *Studies in mother-infant interaction*. London: Academic Press.

Kahn, J. (1984). Cognitive training and initial use of referential speech. *Topics in Language Disorders*, *5*(1), 14–23. doi:10.1097/00011363-198412000-00006

Kail, R. (1992). General slowing of information-processing by persons with mental retardation. *American Journal of Mental Retardation*, *97*(30), 333–341. PMID:1449732

Kaiser, A. P., & Hancock, T. B. (2003). Teaching parents new skills to support their young children's development. *Infants and Young Children*, *16*(1), 9–21. doi:10.1097/00001163-200301000-00003

Kaiser, A. P., & Robert, M. Y. (2013). Parent-implemented enhanced milieu teaching with preschool children who have intellectual disabilities. *Journal of Speech, Language, and Hearing Research: JSLHR*, *56*(1), 295–309. doi:10.1044/1092-4388(2012/11-0231) PMID:22744141

Kamhi, A. G., & Johnston, J. R. (1982). Towards an understanding of retarded children's linguistic deficiencies. *Journal of Speech and Hearing Research*, *25*(3), 435–445. doi:10.1044/jshr.2503.435 PMID:7176618

Karanth, P. (1986). *Language proficiency test.* Mysore: All India Speech and Hearing Institute.

Karlin, I. W., & Strazzulla, M. (1952). Speech and language problems of mentally deficient children. *The Journal of Speech and Hearing Disorders*, *17*(3), 286–294. doi:10.1044/jshd.1703.286 PMID:13053550

Kay-Raining Bird, E., & Gaskell, A. (2000). Novel word acquisition in children with Down syndrome: Does modality make a difference? *Journal of Communication Disorders*, *33*(3), 241–266. doi:10.1016/S0021-9924(00)00022-8 PMID:10907718

Kelly, D., & Rice, M. (1986). A strategy for language assessment of young children: A combination of two approaches. *Language, Speech, and Hearing Services in Schools*, *17*(2), 83–94. doi:10.1044/0161-1461.1702.83

Kim, Y., & Lombardino, L. (1991). The efficacy of script contexts in language comprehension intervention with children who have mental retardation. *Journal of Speech and Hearing Research*, *34*(4), 845–857. doi:10.1044/jshr.3404.845 PMID:1956192

Klein, H. (1984). Procedure for maximizing phonological information from single-word responses. *Language, Speech, and Hearing Services in Schools*, *15*(4), 267–274. doi:10.1044/0161-1461.1504.267

Klein, H. B., & Moses, N. (1999). *Intervention planning for children with communication disorders: A guide for clinical practicum and professional practice* (2nd ed.). Boston: Allyn & Bacon.

Krupa, M., Perumal, R. C., & Kripa, S. (2009). *Semantic Intentions in normally developing children and children with Mental Retardation: A comparative study.* (Unpublished master's dissertation). Sri Ramachandra University, Chennai, India.

Kumin, L. (2006). Differential diagnosis and treatment of speech sound production problems in children with Down syndrome. *Down Syndrome Quarterly, 8,* 7-18.

Kumin, L. & Adams, J. (2000). Developmental apraxia of speech and intelligibility in children with Down syndrome. *Down Syndrome Quarterly, 5,* 1-6.

Kumin, L., Councill, C., & Goodman, M. (1994). A longitudinal study of the emergence of phonemes in children with Down syndrome. *Journal of Communication Disorders*, *27*(4), 265–275. doi:10.1016/0021-9924(94)90019-1 PMID:7876409

Kumin, M. (2014). Speech intelligibility helping children and adults develop and maintain understandable speech. *Down Syndrome News, 37*.

Kwiatkowski, J., & Shriberg, L. D. (1992). Intelligibility assessment in developmental phonological disorders: Accuracy of caregiver gloss. *Journal of Speech and Hearing Research*, *35*(5), 1095–1104. doi:10.1044/jshr.3505.1095 PMID:1280309

Lakanna, S., Venkatesh, K., & Bhat, J. S. (2008). *Assessment of Language Development*. Bakersfield, CA: Omni Therapy Services.

Lamberts, R., & Weener, P. (1976). Children's competence in processing negation. *American Journal of Mental Deficiency*, *81*, 181–186. PMID:970417

Leddy, M. (1999). The biological basis of speech in people with Down syndrome. In J. Miller, M. Leddy, & L. A. Leavitt (Eds.), *Improving the communication of people with Down syndrome* (pp. 61–80). Baltimore, MD: Paul H Brooks.

Lifter, K., & Bloom, L. (1989). Object knowledge and emergence of language. *Infant Behavior and Development*, *12*(4), 395–423. doi:10.1016/0163-6383(89)90023-4

Luria, A. R. (1961). *The Role of Speech in the regulation of normal and abnormal behaviour*. New York: Pergamon Press.

Luria, A. R. (1963). *The Mentally retarded child*. Oxford, UK: Pergamon Press.

Mahoney, G. J., & Snow, K. (1983). The Relationship of sensorimotor functioning to children's response to early language training. *Mental Retardation*, *21*, 248–254. PMID:6231449

Manolson, A. (1992). *It takes two to talk: A parent's guide to helping children communicate*. Toronto, Canada: The Hanen Centre.

Martin, H., McConkey, R., & Martin, S. (1984). From acquisition theories to intervention strategies: An experiment with mentally handicapped children. *The British Journal of Disorders of Communication*, *19*(1), 3–14. doi:10.3109/13682828409019832 PMID:6733030

McCauley, R., & Swisher, L. (1984b). Use and misuse of norm-referenced tests in clinical assessment: A hypothetical case. *The Journal of Speech and Hearing Disorders*, *49*, 338–348. doi:10.1044/jshd.4904.338 PMID:6389982

McDonald, E. (2000). *Deep Test of Articulation*. Pittsburg: Stanwix House.

McLeavy, B. C., Tomey, J. F., & Dempsey, P. J. R. (1982). Nonretarded and mentally retarded children's control over syntactic structures. *American Journal of Mental Deficiency*, *86*, 485–494. PMID:7124802

Merrill, E. C., & Mar, H. H. (1987). Differences between mentally retarded and non retarded persons' efficiency of auditory sentence processing. *American Journal of Mental Deficiency*, *86*, 485–494. PMID:3812610

Miller, J. (1981). *Assessing language production in children*. Needham Heights, MA: Allyn and Bacon.

Miller, J. F., & Yoder, D. (1974). An ontogenetic language teaching strategy for retarded children. In R. Schiefelbusch & L. Lloyd (Eds.), *Language perspectives-Acquisition, retardation and intervention*. Baltimore University Park Press.

Miller, L. (1984). Problem solving and language disorders. In G. P. Wallach & K. G. Butler (Eds.), *Language learning disabilities in school-age children* (pp. 199–229). Baltimore, MD: Williams & Wilkins.

Owens, R. E. (2004). *Language disorders: A functional approach to assessment and intervention* (4th ed.). Boston: Allyn & Bacon.

Owens, R. E. (2005). *Language development: An introduction* (6th ed.). Boston: Allyn & Bacon.

Owings, N. O., & McManus, M. D. (1980). An analysis of communication functions in the speech of deinstitutionalized adult mentally retarded client. *Mental Retardation*, *18*, 309–314. PMID:7253928

Paul, R., & Cohen, D. J. (1984). Responses to contingent queries in adults with mental retardation and pervasive developmental disorders. *Applied Psycholinguistics*, *5*(04), 349–357. doi:10.1017/S0142716400005221

Paul, R., & Norbury, C. F. (2012). *Language Disorders: From infancy through adolescence*. Missouri: Mosby-Yera Book.

Pena, E. D., Iglesias, A., & Lidz, C. S. (2001). Reducing test bias through dynami assessment of children's word learning ability. *American Journal of Speech-languag Pathology*, *10*, 138–154. doi:10.1044/1058-0360(2001/014)

Pena-Brooks, A., & Hegde, M. N. (2000). *Assessment & Treatment of Articulation and Phonological Disorders in Children*. Austin, TX: Pro-Ed.

Pendergast, K., Dickey, S. E., Selman, J. W., & Soder, A. (1990). *Photo Articulation Test*. Danville, IL: Interstate Printers and Publishers.

Plante, E. M., & Beason, P. M. (1999). *Communication and Communication Disorders: A clinical Introduction*. Needham, MA: Allyn & Bacon.

Pring, T. G. (2004). *Evidence-based practice*. Buckingham, UK: Open University Press.

Reed, V. A. (2005). *An introduction to children with language disorders* (3rd ed.). Boston: Pearson, Inc.

Rice, M. L., Warren, S. F., & Betz, S. K. (2005). Language symptoms of developmental language disorders: An overview of autism, Down syndrome, fragile X, specific language impairment, and Williams syndrome. *Applied Psycholinguistics*, *26*(1), 7–27. doi:10.1017/S0142716405050034

Roberts, M. Y., & Kaiser, A. P. (2011). The effectiveness of parent-implemented language interventions: A metaanalysis. *American Journal of Speech-Language Pathology*, *20*(3), 180–199. doi:10.1044/1058-0360(2011/10-0055) PMID:21478280

Romski, M. A., Sevcik, R., & Fonseca, A. (2003). Augmentative and alternative communication for persons with mental retardation. In L. Abbeduto (Ed.), *International review of research in mental retardation: Language and communication* (pp. 255–280). New York: Academic Press. doi:10.1016/S0074-7750(03)27008-7

Rondal, J. A., & Turnure, J. E. (1976). *Maternal speech to normal-hearing and down syndrome children matched for mean length of utterance.* Paper presented at the Annual meeting of the American Association on Mental Deficiency, Chicago, IL.

Roseberry-McKibbin, C. (2007). *Language disorders in children: A multicultural and case perspective.* Boston: Pearson Education, Inc.

Rosefeld-johnson, S. (1999). Oromotor exercise for speech clarity. Tucson, AZ: Innovative Therapists International.

Rosenberg, S. (1982). The language of the mentally retarded: Development, processes, and intervention. In S. Rosenberg (Ed.), Handbook of applied psycholinguistics: Major thrusts of research and theory (pp. 329-392). Hillsdale, NJ: Erlbaum.

Rosin, M., Siwft, E., Bless, D., & Vetter, D. K. (1988). Communication profile of adolescence with Down syndrome. *Journal of Childhood Communication Disorders, 12*(1), 49–64. doi:10.1177/152574018801200105

Rueda, R., & Chan, K. (1980). Referential communication skill levels of moderately mentally retarded adolescents. *American Journal of Mental Deficiency, 85*, 45–52. PMID:7446568

Salvador-Carulla, L., Reed, G., Vaez-Azizi, L., Cooper, S., Martinez-Leal, R., & Bertelli, M. et al.. (2011). Intellectual developmental disorders: Towards a new name, definition and framework for "mental retardation/intellectual disability" in ICD-11. *World Psychiatry; Official Journal of the World Psychiatric Association (WPA), 10*(3), 175–180. doi:10.1002/j.2051-5545.2011.tb00045.x PMID:21991267

Schalock, R. L. (2011, May 31). *Interview: Professor Robert Schalock.* Retrieved from http://enil.eu/2011/05/interview-professor-robert-schalock/

Silverstein, A., Pearson, L., Colbert, B., Cordeiro, W., Marwin, J., & Nakaji, M. (1982). Cognitive development of severely and profoundly mentally retarded individuals. *American Journal of Mental Deficiency, 87*, 347–349. PMID:7180897

Sinson, J., & Wetherick, N. (1982). Mutual gaze in preschool Down's and normal children. *Journal of Mental Deficiency Research, 26*, 123–129. PMID:6213781

Smith, K., Landry, S., & Swank, P. (2000). Does the content of mothers' verbal stimulation explain differences in children's development of verbal and nonverbal cognitive skills? *Journal of School Psychology, 38*(1), 27–49. doi:10.1016/S0022-4405(99)00035-7

Snyder, L. E., & Sherer, N. (2004). The development of symbolic play and language in toddlers in cleft palate. *American Journal of Speech-Language Pathology, 13*(1), 66–80. doi:10.1044/1058-0360(2004/008) PMID:15101815

Stoel-Gammon, C. (2000). Down syndrome phonology: Developmental patterns and intervention strategies. *Down's Syndrome: Research and Practice, 7*(3), 93–100. doi:10.3104/reviews.118 PMID:11721538

SubbaRao, T.A., & Srinivas, N.C. (1989). Speech and Language defects and mental retardation-A report on the analysis of 300 mentally retarded persons. *Indian Journal of Disability and Rehabilitation*, 31-43.

SubbaRao, T.A. (1992). *Manual on developing communication skills in mentally retarded persons.* Secundrabad: National Institute for the mentally handicapped.

SubbaRao. (1986). *Language Assessment Tool.* Author.

Swift, E., & Rosin, P. (1990). A remediation sequence to improve speech intelligibility for students with Down syndrome. *Language, Speech, and Hearing Services in Schools, 21*(3), 140–146. doi:10.1044/0161-1461.2103.140

Vyogotsky, L. (1962). *Thought and Language*. Cambridge, MA: MIT Press. doi:10.1037/11193-000

Wang, P. P., & Bellugi, U. (1994). Evidence from two genetic syndromes for a dissociation between verbal and visuo-spatial short-term memory. *Journal of Clinical and Experimental Neuropsychology, 2*(2), 317–322. doi:10.1080/01688639408402641 PMID:8021317

Warren, S. F. (1988). A behavioural approach to language generalization. *Language, Speech, and Hearing Services in Schools, 19*(3), 292–303. doi:10.1044/0161-1461.1903.292

Warren, S. F., & Brady, N. C. (2007). The role of maternal responsivity in the development of children with intellectual disabilities. *Mental Retardation and Developmental Disabilities Research Reviews, 13*(4), 330–338. doi:10.1002/mrdd.20177 PMID:17979201

Warren, S. F., Fey, M. E., Finestack, L. H., Brady, N. C., Bredin-Oja, S. L., & Fleming, K. K. (2008). A randomized trial of longitudinal effects of low-intensity responsivity education/ prelinguistic milieu teaching. *Journal of Speech, Language, and Hearing Research: JSLHR, 51*(2), 451–470. doi:10.1044/1092-4388(2008/033) PMID:18367689

Warren, S. F., Fey, M. E., & Yoder, P. J. (2007). Differential treatment intensity research: A missing link to creating optimally effective communication interventions. *Mental Retardation and Developmental Disabilities Research Reviews, 13*(1), 70–77. doi:10.1002/mrdd.20139 PMID:17326112

Weitzner-Lin, B. (2004). *Communication assessment and intervention with infants and toddlers.* St. Louis, MO: Butterworth Heinemann.

Weizman, Z. O., & Snow, C. E. (2001). Lexical Input as Related to Children's Vocabulary Acquisition: Effects of Sophisticated Exposure and Support for Meaning. *Developmental Psychology, 37*(2), 265–279. doi:10.1037/0012-1649.37.2.265 PMID:11269394

Westling, D., & Fox, L. (2000). *Teaching students with severe disabilities*. Upper Saddle River, NJ: Merrill.

Wethervy, A., & Prizant, B. (1993). *Communication and Symbolic Behaviour Scales.* Chicago, IL: Riverside Publishers.

Wiig, E., Secord, W., & Semel, E. (1992). *Clinical Evaluation of Language Fundamentals (CELF).* San Antonio, TX: Psychological Corporation.

World Health Organization. (2001). *International Classification of Functioning, Disability, and Health.* Geneva: Author.

World Health Organization. (2007). *International classification of functioning, disability and health: Children & youth version*. Geneva: Author.

Yoder, P., & Stone, W. L. (2006). A randomized comparison of the effect of two prelinguistic communication interventions on the acquisition of spoken communication in preschoolers with ASD. *Journal of Speech, Language, and Hearing Research: JSLHR*, *49*(4), 698–711. doi:10.1044/1092-4388(2006/051) PMID:16908870

Yoder, P., & Warren, S. (2001). Relative treatment effects of two prelinguistic communication interventions on language development in toddlers with developmental delays vary by maternal characteristics. *Journal of Speech, Language, and Hearing Research: JSLHR*, *44*(1), 224–237. doi:10.1044/1092-4388(2001/019) PMID:11218105

Yoder, P. J., & Warren, S. F. (1998). Maternal responsivity predicts the prelinguistic communication intervention that facilitates generalized intentional communication. *Journal of Speech, Language, and Hearing Research: JSLHR*, *41*(5), 1207–1219. doi:10.1044/jslhr.4105.1207 PMID:9771641

Yoder, P. J., & Warren, S. F. (2002). Effects of prelinguistic milieu teaching and parent responsivity education on dyads involving children with intellectual disabilities. *Journal of Speech, Language, and Hearing Research: JSLHR*, *45*(6), 1158–1174. doi:10.1044/1092-4388(2002/094) PMID:12546485

Zimmerman, I., Steiner, V. G., & Pond, R. (2011). *Preschool Language Scale – 5*. San Antonio, Tx: Psychological Corporation.

Chapter 10
Issues and Recent Trends in the Assessment and Management of ID in Childhood

Sumita Chowhan
Jain University, India

Plabita Patowary
Gujarat Forensic Sciences University, India

ABSTRACT

The Chapter begins with an attempt to understand disability aspect in general and assessment aspect extensively. This chapter would attempt to observe both classic and latest trends of assessment techniques. Since it was observed that the recent trends concentrate extensively on global concept, the present chapter would include assessment categories on different dimensions of ability, emotions and behaviors such as intelligence, achievement, adaptive, social behavior and emotional adjustment, communication/ language, sensory status, motor skills, and health status. The adaptivity skills will be emphasized more since it was observed adaptive skills plays a crucial role in the children with intellectual disability. in this current chapter a number of critical issues concerning the assessment of children with intellectual disabilities, including definitional problems, psychometric factors, and practical difficulties would be proposed to help students, counselors, teachers and psychologists.

INTRODUCTION

ID is characterized by deficits in general mental abilities and these deficits result in impairments of adaptive functioning, such that the individual fails to meet standards of personal independence and social-responsibility in one or more aspects of daily life, including communication, social participation, academic or occupational functioning, and personal independence at home or in community settings The DSM V included the construct of adaptive behaviour in terms of three domains conceptual, social and practical domains. The conceptual (academic) domain involves competence in memory, language, reading, writing, math reasoning etc. The social domain involves awareness of others' thoughts, feel-

DOI: 10.4018/978-1-5225-0089-6.ch010

ings, and experiences; empathy; interpersonal communication skills while the practical domain involves learning and self-management across life settings, including personal care, job responsibilities, money management, recreation, self-management of behavior, and school and work task organization, among others (DSM V, 2013).

1. PSYCHOLOGICAL ASSESSMENT

Psychological assessment in children is a process to evaluate and understand the child's problems in different areas, ones capabilities, strengths and limitations. Four important questions to be answered from assessment are:

- Where is the impairment in the functioning and how is the child functioning impaired?
- What are the consequences of the impairment and how it is impacting the normal functioning?
- What are the other factors (social, motivational,) that contributing in the maintain of the impairment?
- What intervention is best suited for the impairment?

The factors complicate the process of assessment with intellectual disable children in obtaining the legitimate estimate of intellectual performance, Presence of severe sensory impairment for example vision, auditory, presence of severe emotional and behavioral disturbance, medication interfere with cognitive neurological functioning. Henceforth it becomes so important that the factors needs to be addressed while assessing for intellectual assessment.

The continuous research on intellectual disability, emphasized that the assessment of intellectual functioning must be evaluated within the context of individual's age and in relation to peer's performance of the same age (Tasse et al., 2011). Assessment also should cater for:

- Accuracy in assessment also relies on cultural and linguistic diversity as well as differences in communication, sensory motor and behavioral factors.
- Assessment should also give a picture of strengths the child possesses.
- Assessment should also list out the problem behavior and desirable behavior (Luckasson et al., 2002, p. 1)

1.1 Principles of Assessment

Based on the different intellectual deficient research association, American Psychiatric Association (APA) and the American Association of Mental Retardation (AAMR) the following principles applied to the process of assessment in children with intellectual disability. Initially ruling out psychiatric and non-psychiatric causes for problems of concern, the medical problems (Epilepsy, psychotic illness, vision issues, hearing problem etc.,) and then understanding the problems in expectations and supports and emotional turmoil, the social and emotional problems (parenting issues, social skills deficits etc.,). After ruling out certain aspects as mentioned above, it work towards identifying the problem by seeking information on actual level of functioning in cognitive (intellectual level through assessment tools), adaptive (level of independence in daily activities), including communication for instance, receptive and expressive language issues, and the presence of any comorbidity like ADHD, autism. Lastly but crucial in identifying level of support, the American Association on Intellectual and Developmental Disabilities (AAIDD) emphasized so much on identify levels of support which helps to understand usual level of functioning in areas of: self-care, interest/involvement in school or work, play/leisure activity, social participation, taking initiative in participating in various activities and level of supervision required. Finally identifying behavioral issues (e.g., self-injurious behavior, stereotypies, obsessive thoughts, compulsive behaviours, fears, phobias) needs to consider. The entire the process of assessment and identification and diagnosis process discussed in detail in Figure 1.

1.1.2 Identification/Screening of Children with Intellectual Disability (ID)

The first step of identification of intellectual disability starts with taking case history, DSM and ICD criteria to assess then is to assess the delay in the milestones. However age range needs to be taken into consideration while screening the development delays in the milestone. During the process of taking the case history of the patient, first the chief complaints has to be noted down followed by the history of the illness. Family, social and developmental history should be also asked. To diagnose the case, MSE and appropriate assessments are also necessary (Ahuja, 2011).

To diagnose the intellectual developmental disorder, according to DSM V, three criteria that must be met are deficits in intellectual functions such as reasoning, problem solving etc, deficits in adaptive functioning which can result in failure to meet developmental and sociocultural standards for personal independence and onset of these deficits should be during the developmental period (DSM V, 2013). According to ICD, there should be reduced level of intellectual functioning resulting in diminished ability to adapt to demands of the normal social environment and they may have associated physical disorders like epilepsy or psychiatric problems (ICD 10, 1993)

1.1.3. Milestones

Growth and development of children follow a pattern. Universally every child passes through the stages of development/growth. These stages are called milestones of development. These milestones of development helps us to understand whether child have normal development or delayed development. The awareness of developmental milestones is important as it helps to identify children who show delayed development. Some of the normal milestones of development and its appropriate age range applicable

Figure 1. Step wise pattern for identification and management of intellectual disability
Based on NIMH Protocol (Madhavan, Kalyan, Naidu., Pashwarla, & Narayan, 1999).*

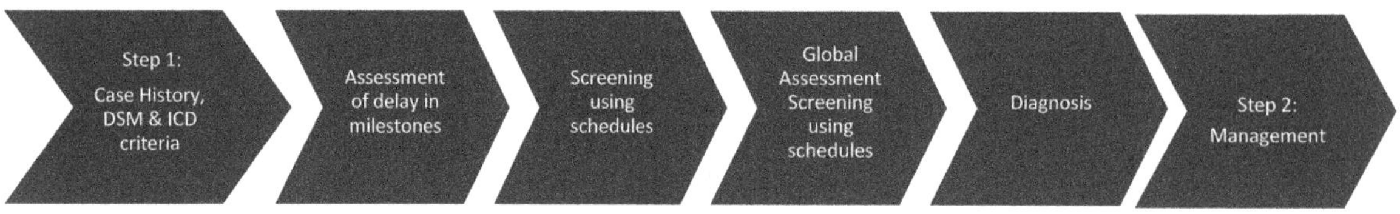

to Indian situation are given below. However some discrepancies in attaining milestones is very much common, some children may skip few of the stages.

Several studies showed that there is a normal pattern of the milestones of a child's development. A child can smile at others, can hold head erect and put objects into mouth at 4 months. The child can roll from back to stomach at 6 months while he can stand by holding on to an object and holds objects with thumb and index finger at 10 months. By 18 months, the child can tell his own name and can show body parts when named at 24 months. When the child is 30 months old, he can speak in small sentences. The child can give meaningful verbal answers to simple questions ad differentiate big from small things at 36 months and can combs hair at 48 months. (Madhavan, Kalyan, Naidu., Pashwarla, & Narayan (1999).

1.1.4. Assessment Tools

Secondly identification is made based on certain questionnaires or assessment schedules by screening out the child. The three schedules given by NIMH (1999), schedule 1 for the children below 3 years, second for the children between 3- 6 years of age. The third one is for those children age from 7 and above (NIMH, 1999).

According to the American Association of Mental Retardation (AAMR), the criteria for diagnosis intellectual functioning is to consider both difficulties in intellectual functioning and difficulties in adaptive behavior. The psychological assessment plays a crucial role in diagnosing the presence and severity of mental retardation. To assess intellectual disability it is always essential that more than one assessment tool is used for diagnosing the case rather than using a single one to have a reliable and fair diagnosis. It is also important to have information on the individual's level of functioning including cognitive, adaptive, physical sensations, levels of receptive understanding and expressive language, social involvement (Bradley, Burke, Drummond, Korossy, Lunsky, Morris, 2010).

Important areas of assessment to be considered for diagnosing the children with intellectual disability:

- The developmental milestones, developmental schedules.
- Assessment of overall Intellectual Functioning.
- Assessment of Adaptive behavior.
- Assessment of children's sensory & motor functioning, Language skills.
- Assessment of behavioral functioning.
- Assessment of children's strengths and weakness.

To develop a profile/case formulation, the importance of understanding the support needed based on the level of intellectual functioning needs to be emphasized, which helps to improve the global functioning of the children (Luckasson et al., 2002, p. 1).

Tools Frequently Used in the Area of Intellectual Disability

- **Developmental Screening Test:** The test was developed by Bharath Raj to measure mental development of children from birth to 15 years of age. It consists of 88 items. Larger number of items at early age levels permits assessment of very young children. Italicized items on the schedule cover the speech and language development. Items represent development in various areas like social, behavioral, motor skills etc. in this test, a caretaker have to be present to report their observation regarding the development of the child. This test provides for a brief and fairly dependable assessment without requiring the use of performance tests (J, Bharath Raj; 2004)

- **Gesell Developmental Schedule:** It is a drawing test which measures the "general" factor of intelligence. It helps in assessing the children's motor, adaptive, language and personal-social which helps to assess developmental disabilities, and to some extent intellectual disabilities. The child has to reproduce the geometrical drawings which are analyzed to give the percentile ranks to determine the intellectual functioning of the children (G, Arnold; 2011)
- **Seguin Form Board:** This test is based on a single factor theory of intelligence. It is devised by Seguin in 1907. Age group level is 3 to 15 years. It measures speed and accuracy by evaluating a child's eye-hand coordination, visual perception and cognitive ability. The child is asked to keep the ten geometrical shapes in their corresponding respective shapes in the wooden board.(J, Bharath Raj; 1971)
- **Coloured Progressive Matrices:** It is devised by J. C Raven in the year 1936 which assesses nonverbal abilities. It can be administered at 5 through 11 years. This test consists of 36 items divided into three series (A, Ab, B) each made up of 12 items. The items have the form of incomplete matrices, where the children have to identify the missing part from the available options.
- **Stanford Binet Intelligence Test:** SBIT was developed in 1916 revised by lewis M Terman from the Binet Simon scale and was later re revised in 1937, 1960 and 1986; 2003.it is a standardized test that measures the general intelligence of an individual. It can help to determine the level of intellectual functioning and the cognitive abilities and assist in the diagnosis of developmental delay, mental retardation etc. The test consists of 15 subtests and specific subtests are administered at different age level (2- 90 years). The subtests are grouped into 4 area scores: visual reasoning, verbal reasoning, quantitative reasoning and short term memory. The composite score evaluate the "general" intelligence score. Binet kamath test is the Indian adaptation of Standford Binet intelligence test. This test consist of both verbal and performance test.
- **Vineland Social Maturity Scale:** The Vineland social maturity scale consist of 89 items which assess social maturity and personal and social skills of an individual. It also helps in identifying the social deficits and assets which is good to locate the intellectual functioning of a growing child. It serves the purpose well as most of the clinical procedures of assessment and training are most often limited to the upper age limits of 15 years. It has 8 subscales which measure different skills in: general self-help ability, communication, locomotion, self-dressing abilities, self-eating abilities and socialization. It was originally devised by E.A Doll in 1935 and its Indian adapted version is devised by J Bharath Raj. This test is being used in many parts of the world and it proved itself to be uniquely useful instrument in measuring social maturity of children and young adults.
- **Bender Gestalt Test:** Bender gestalt is developed by Lauretta Bender in the year 1938. It is a brief test of visual motor and perception test which provide information about an individual's development and also assess of any presence of neurological damage. It is suitable for 3 years and older. It has three sub test which are copy and recall test, motor test and perception test. Copying figure requires fine motor skills, the ability to discriminate between visual stimuli, the capacity to integrate visual skills with motor skills.
- **Benton's Visual Perception Test:** It assesses visual perception, memory and visuoconstuctive abilities. This test is developed by Benton AL in 1998. It is used to assess children from 8 years and older. It is composed of 3 sets, or forms, of 10 designs which the individual is required to re-

produce. It can be administered in five different ways. This test helps in identifying g any cognitive distortions, possible learning disabilities, dementia, Alzheimer's disease etc.

- **Problem Behavior Checklist:** Children's behavior checklist is used to detect emotional and behavioral problems in children and adolescents. Information is gathered from parents or the primary care taker. It is to be used with children aged 6 to 18 years. It consists of 113 questions, scored on a three point likert scale (0= absent, 1= occurs sometimes, 2= occurs often). The responses should be based on the past 6 months experiences. It has eight syndrome scales: Anxious, Depressed, Somatic complaints, Social problems, thought problems, Attention problems, Aggressive behavior, and Rule breaking behaviour. For identifying psychopathology in children and adolescents with mental retardation, The Aberrant Behaviour Checklist, a screening assessment tool is used widely (Achenbach & Rescorla, 2000).

Intellectual assessment needs to be carried out using the age and culture appropriate instrument. The following tests are used based on levels of severity manifested in DSM V, ICD 10, screening tools of NIMH. The following tools would be administered based on levels of severity as indicated by screening tools, the diagnostic tools helps to understand the precise levels of functioning .The following diagnostic tools as shown in Table 1 would be selected based on age, education, culture, understanding of language and behavioral problems the child manifested. The Instruments helps to have a precise quotient of development (DQ), Intelligence (IQ), performance (PQ) social (SQ) and also the other sensation & motor issues and behavioral problems.

Table 1. Age wise classification of characteristics of adaptive functioning in children with intellectually disability

Severity	Mild	Moderate	Severe	Profound
Pre school (3-19 years)	Characteristics are not overt from those normal people until late age, very minimal retardation in sensory-motor areas.	Communication and motor development are intact. Slight difficulties are observed in social awareness and executing day to day tasks for living but it can be developed and rectified if proper training is provided.	Difficulty in self-help behavior and motor development. The individual also suffers from speech distortion and distorted communicative skills. Training does not provide a huge difference.	Needs help of caretaker in doing most of the tasks including activities of daily life. Distorted functioning in sensory motor areas is observed.
School age (6-20 years)	Appropriate social skills can be learned if training is provided and academic skills can be also acquired at least till 6th grade.	If proper training is provided to the individual, then appropriate social and occupational skills can be learned. Academic skills can be learned till 2nd grade. Child can also learn to travel to the familiar nearby places alone. For example: to a nearby shop or park.	Child can acquire the skills to communicate and can be trained in elementary skills.	Very limited self-help skills are acquired.
Adult (21 and over)	Individual can achieve social and vocational skills in adequate manner. Assistance is needed when under social and economic stress.	Self-help behavior can acquire properly after training is provided. Guidance is required when the individual is under mild social and economic stress.	Self-help behavior and self-help protection skills can be learned to a limited level in assisted environment.	Motor and speech development can be achieved. Self care needs can be achieved to a very limited level.

Source DSM V, 2013.

1.1.5. Global Assessment

Traditionally it was observed that only intellectual functioning is given importance. According to different diagnostic systems of classification, Mental retardation is defined as significantly subnormal intellectual ability that leads to deficits in functioning (DSM III, APA 1993). Later the construct of adaptive functioning is considered crucial. Recently the assessments not only look at intellectual deficit but also adaptive functioning and behavioral issues like appropriate & inappropriate behaviors are assessed in order to plan appropriate behavior modification programme. In the recent trends the assessment on desirable behaviors is also emphasized to concentrate on motivations levels of children with intellectual disability.

Tools for Measuring Adaptive Functions

The Intellectual disability encompasses impairments of general mental abilities which in turn impact adaptive functioning. The impairment in adaptive functioning seem to in three domains, or areas. These domains determine includes different day to day tasks and how well an individual copes with those daily tasks

- The conceptual domain denotes skills related to language, reading, writing, reasoning, solving maths problems, and Learning & memory, the ability to learn and remember.
- The social domain denotes interpersonal communication skills, the interpersonal ability the making and retaining friends, empathy, understanding others and social judgment.
- The practical domain refers to self-management in areas such as personal care, home activities money management, recreation, and consolidating school and work tasks and completing job responsibilities. (DSM V, 2013)

The assessment and diagnosis to be made with respect to one's education, appropriate behavior and environmental factors. Before diagnosing the case with mental retardation understanding the socio economic status and cultural criteria and environmental conditions of the children plays an important role. Therefore these aspects to be considered with caution for diagnosis the case with intellectual disability.

DSM V (2013) has classified the adaptive characteristics of intellectually disabled individuals based on the level of severity. The three domains that each level of severity is discussed are: conceptual, social and practical domain. In mild severity level, conceptually, differences are found in school children and adults related to learning skills with support needed in one or more areas to meet age related expectation. Executive functioning as well as STM is also impaired. In social domain, communication and language are more concrete or immature than expected for age. Individuals experience difficulties regulating emotions and behavior in age appropriate fashion. In practical domain, some individual may able to take responsibility of their own personal care even though they need support. Individual need support to perform a skilled vocation competently and to raise a family. In moderate level, conceptually, language and pre academic skills develop slowly. In social domain, individuals may not perceive or interpret social cues accurately. Social judgments are limited. In practical domain, extended period of training is required to make the individual learn to eat, dress, hygiene etc. in the severe level, little understanding is present of written language or of concepts involving numbers under conceptual domain. Socially and practically, spoken language is quite limited and speech comprises of single words or phrases and also requires support for daily living activities. Likewise, in the profound level, presence of motor and sensory impairments can prevent functional use of objects in the conceptual level. In social and practical domain, individual experience limited understanding of symbolic communication and gestures. He is dependent on others for all aspects in day to day activities.

Based on the different research, Both the American Psychiatric Association (APA) and the American Association on Intellectual and Developmental Disabilities (AAIDD) practice use of severity codes as shown in Table 2. These codes are used for diagnosis the case and categorizing intellectual disabilities into four levels mild, moderate, severe, profound. However, the meanings of the severity codes among two systems are seen differently. Previously APA used IQ scores to define severity. Recently these systems started concentrating on adaptive functioning to determine severity. However, the APA severity is based on categorizing levels of severity based on IQ and Adaptive functioning. In contrast, the AAIDD is based on the degree of support needed. This is called support intensity. The level of severity is assessed by the level of cognitive/intellectual functioning and the amount of support needed. The level of intellectual functioning is characterized by scores of approximately two standard deviations below the mean. The four levels of severity mild, moderate, severe and profound are classified as follows based on Intellectual functioning, support needed and mental age (Reynolds, Zupanick, Dombeck, 2013)

The recent trends follow the global functioning assessment process where in the developmental quotient (DQ), Intelligence quotient (IQ), performance quotient (PQ), social quotient (SQ), adaptive functioning) and also other sensory& motors kills, language & communication and also behavioral issues are assessed, both inappropriate and desirable behaviors are assessed to diagnose the case and to schedule the management plan (NIMH, 1990).

1.2 Issues in Assessments

Psychological assessment also should be viewed as sources of information and not as the endpoint of assessment. Different sources that can provide information which complements the psychological assessment process are: Clinical interview with the child, family and teacher, clinical & behavior observation of the child, school reports. Hence all the other sources of information needs to be considered rather than solely depending on psychological assessment especially when applies to children.

Since the child is in the developmental process, one should be extremely careful while interpreting the results. The examiner needs to be cautious and compassionate when analyzing and giving feedback to the parents. The examiner needs to be flexible in clinical analysis. For e.g., if the child is very shy and

Table 2. Different functioning and support needed in children with ID

Severity Level	Intellectual Functioning	Mental Age	Support Needed	Educational Functioning
Mild	55-69	8 -11 years	Intermittent (as needed basis)	Educable
Moderate	40-54	4-7 years	Limited(time limited training)	Trainable
Severe	25-39	2-3 years	Extensive (long term home living support)	Trainable to self help
Profound	Below 20	2 years	Pervasive (life sustaining support)	Custodial

Sources DSM, AAIDD.

non-compliant then special procedures of psychological assessment should be used. There are several factors that can affect the child's performance in assessment.

- Child's ability to communicate.
- Problems in comprehending the instructions.
- Child's physical and mental health problems.
- Low motivation levels.
- Anxieties about being tested.
- Difficulty level of the test items.
- The rapport between the child and the examiner.
- Individual differences.
- Latent possession of skills.

Enhance to the aforementioned points, the important point to be considered is the limitations of the test. Firstly, since it was always observed that the child performance can vary at different points, drawing conclusion solely based on testing can further complicate matters for the child. Secondly if assessments are used routinely, the significance of information is lost. Thirdly, the problem may not be based on test findings but on many factors in the child environment (Hirisave, Oommen, kapur 2002)

Hence the assessment results should not be taken as sole point of assessment but the alternative clinical information should be considered as a way of complementing the information obtained from other sources like by clinical interviews with the child and parents, and by naturalistic observation.

There are several problems observed specific to the assessment of children with intellectual disability such as

- The intellectual disability children have several motor and sensory impairment such as loss of vision, hearing impairment, and deficit in fine and gross motor functioning can leads to misinterpretation of results.
- Problems in expressive and receptive language because of which comprehending the instruction would become difficult and can also give rise to low score results.
- Cognitive problems like low attention and concentration and high distractibility hence shown difficulty in assessment
- Behavioral problem like hyperactivity, aggressive behavior and withdrawal, lack of motivation would cause difficulty in standardized psychological assessment.
- Social problem like shyness, scared to meet new people can also show discrepancies in assessment results.
- Even influence of socio-economic status, education, cultural issues influence the assessment of children with intellectual, these constructs should be taken as caution while diagnosis the case.

Hence forth it is always recommended to use more than one assessment tool and building up rapport is very crucial when assessing children with intellectual disability (Madhavan, Kalyan, Naidu., Pashwarla, & Narayan (1999)

In addition to deficit in intellectual ability and adaptive behavior, some intellectual disabilities have medical problems or associated handicaps. Some of the most common medical problems encountered in the intellectual disability are epilepsy, hyperkinesis, physical handicap, nutritional disorders and psychiatric problems such as autism, psychosis and neurotic disturbances:

- **Epilepsy:** About 40% of intellectual disabilities have convulsions of one type or other (Madhavan, Kalyan, Naidu., Pashwarla, & Narayan (1999)

Conditions mistaken for Intellectual disabilities:

1. Early infantile autism
2. Child with hearing impairment
3. Child with emotional disturbances
4. Cultural deprivation and lack of stimulation
5. Specific learning disabilities
6. Childhood psychosis
7. Child with visual handicap
8. Child with physical handicap

It is difficult to identify the intensity of each of the handicaps in a multiply handicapped person. It is also difficult to determine the ways in which the combinations of disabilities affect a person's behavior. Accurate assessment of the various handicaps is necessary in such children before a management plan is drawn out for them.

1.3 A Note on the Assessment Tool Used

Children with special need have selective motivation and attention towards tasks that they involved with deem desirable and enjoyable task and it is contextual too. Other tasks that don't fit that given descriptions yield low levels of motivation, low levels of attention, fatigability and lead to greater chances of an aggressive-explosive episode. It is the role of the individual assessing the child to keep such factors under control but at times it could also be due to the inherent nature of the tool used.

In the light of the above information it becomes important that the tools and materials used for the assessment be appealing, attractive and inviting to the child to ensure optimal performance. This can be ensured by turning each of the sub tests into a series of games that the child deems as fun and rewarding. Some of the sub-tests in the battery like the block design test, picture completion test, the visual motor free test and the colour cancellation test were those that the children enjoyed performing. The use of colors and animated figures in a way that doesn't compromise on the nature of the test would help yield better performance. It is a known fact that children with special needs show high levels of motivation and low levels of distraction when performing tasks on the touch screen, which means having assessment tools with software application format in turn could result in optimal performance of the child in during the course of the assessment (Sharma & Chowhan, 2014)

2. INTERVENTION/MANAGEMENT PLAN

The management plan of the child depends on the severity levels of intellectual disability (mild, moderate, severity and profound) and their adaptive functioning and also associated conditions sensory handicaps such as vision, hearing, epilepsy, hyper kinesis, autism and inappropriate behavioral problems and desirable behaviors they exhibit. Based on the level of severity and associated conditions the management plan varies from infant stimulation, training in daily living skills and functional academics to prevocational and vocational skills. Apart from this the help is needed in speech problems, locomotion, management of problematic behavior and management of medical problem.

The review of research describes the overview of behaviors commonly problematic in children population are sleep disturbances, agitated and aggressive behaviours, and self-injury behaviour. The general concepts which commonly applied to deal with the management of behaviour disorders seen in children and youth with an intellectual disability are seen as pharmacological form of treatment, however behavioral intervention is a more effective and better endured form of treatment, where the effect lasting longer (Ageranioti – Belanger, Brunet, D'Anjou and Gauthier, 2012). Similarly the results of the meta-analysis suggested that several risk markers could be identified for particular forms of challenging behaviour. Self-injury and stereotypy behaviour appeared to be more common amongst subjects with a severe/profound degree of ID. Self-injury behaviour (SIB) has been defined as a response that produces physical injury to the individual's own body. In children, it is most commonly reported in association with an ID (reported at rates ranging from 7% to 22%) (Berkson,.et. al, 2001). Mcclintock, Hall& Oliver (2003) propound that boys were considerably more likely to show aggression than girls. They also found that those with severe/profound degree of ID more likely to show self-injury and stereotypy behaviour than one with a mild/moderate degree of ID

Once the current level of functioning in all areas is obtained based on the level and severity of functioning the appropriated individualized management plan to be scheduled and executed. The systematic training and counseling session should to be planned to have structured programme to help children with intellectual disability to overcome their problems. Interventions for children and adolescents with ID focus primarily on either behavioral/ emotional issues or educational issues. To address problem behaviors, several techniques/programs are available across the developmental spectrum such as behavior chaining, secondary rewards, token economies (Handen, 1998).

Management Plan follows following steps:

- Systematic training of skills which they are lacking in.
- Behavior modification/Behaviour intervention.
- Occupational training.
- Parental Counseling.

2.1. Systematic Skills Training

The training follows systematic procedure of task analysis, the skills should be divided into small, sequential steps. The training activity should be divided into small steps. The process of breaking down the skills into small steps is called task analysis. The child is given repeated training in each activity. The training follows systematic approach with regularity. Each component should be clearly titled so that persons using them have clear idea of how to use it. There must be no ambiguity in the components. Even systematic record keeping method and regular follow-up are important factors for an intervention programme to be successful. Strict guidelines for maintaining record is followed to ensure accuracy and uniformity in recording. (Madhavan, Kalyan, Naidu., Pashwarla, & Narayan (1999)

2.2 Behavior Modification/Behavior Intervention

Behaviour Modification is the programme implemented to correct impairment in adaptive behavior. The problem exhibited in the children with intellectual disability as assessed by adaptive behavior checklist is divided broadly into two areas adaptive behavior (delay in motor development, self-help skills (NIMH, 1999) and secondly problem behaviors (tantrums, aggression, beating head bagging etc., (Ageranioti-Bélanger, Brunet, D'Anjou, Boivin, 2012). The impairment in adaptive behavior would be in behavior deficit and behavior excess. The first choice of behavioral modification is the selection of reinforcement and extinction-based strategies. For children with behavior deficits the different positive schedules of reinforcement work very well. For behavior excess/inappropriate behaviour, the negative schedules of reinforcement and punishment needs to be executed to correct the behavior pattern.

Behavioral intervention programs have been very successful in targeting and altering problematic social, emotional, and behavioral concerns. The success of the behavioral programs can be associated with the mechanisms of program like focus on breaking down problem behaviors into component parts (simplicity) and to systematically shaping behaviors into more socially adaptive skills through contingency programs of management. (Mather &Goldstein (2015)

Children with intellectual disabilities shows deficits in self-help skills like inability to eat, speech deficit, unable to attend to bowel and bladder needs, inability to have eye-eye contact. These are called bevioural deficit. Children with intellectual disability shows excessive aggression, temper tantrums, mood swings. These are called behavioral excess. To develop effective functioning the deficits and excess needs to corrected or learnt through proper training.

Behavior modification works on the use of basic learning techniques, such as conditioning, positive and negative reinforcement, or aversion therapy, to teach simple skills or alter undesirable and problem behavior. Behavior modification is used to alter the impairment in adaptive behavior. It works on altering absence of adaptive behavior (self-help skills, language delay, and motor skill) and the presence of undesirable behavior (head bagging, beating, showing aggression).

According to (Madhavan, Kalyan, Naidu., Pashwarla, & Narayan (1999)in India, five major steps executed to alter undesirable problem and deficit behavior are identification of the problem, defining target behavior, behavior recording, functional analysis and treatment. They are implemented to correct the impairments in the adaptive behaviour. There are five major steps:

1. Identification of the problems, the first task of the therapist is to obtain the list of problem behaviour by using a behaviour check list or through observations.
2. Defining target behaviours, based on the severity of the problem, selecting targets behaviour. The behaviours to be modified first are called target behaviours. Target one task at a time by having clear treatment plan.
3. Behaviour recording, recording of target behaviours should be done on the basis of frequency, duration and time interval. Maintaining behaviour records is essential as well as evaluating the effectiveness of ongoing therapy.
4. Functional analysis, is a strategy for the assessment and treatment of behaviour problem. Specifically, functional analysis is a set of procedures that attempts to identify important contextual variables such as history and environment that help to cause and/or maintain problematic behaviours or the interaction between behaviour-environment. The goal of functional analysis is to effectively identify targets of intervention that are alterable such that appropriate treatments may be rapidly implemented and evaluated through concentrated intervention efforts.

5. Treatment procedures, techniques used for decreasing Inappropriate behavior. According to Reynolds, Zupanick, & Dombeck, (2013), there are various strategies that can be used as effective tool for intellectual deficit children which are:
    a. One strategy is to break down one task into various small steps. Each sub task is introduced at a time. Once that sub test is mastered then the next step is introduced.
    b. A second strategy is to modify the teaching approach. Instead of lengthy verbal directions, it can teached by providing them performance task as the children learn more when the information is concrete and observed.
    c. Thirdly, visual aids can be used to enhance the learning process. The children with ID understand better of what is expected of them with the help of charts, drawings etc.
    d. The fourth strategy is to provide direct and immediate feedback. Individuals with ID require immediate feedback. This enables them to make a connection between their behavior and the teacher's response.

2.2.1 Behaviour Modification Techniques for Treating Undesirable /Inappropriate Behaviour (Carr, 2004)

- **Changing the Surroundings:** Challenging behavior can be diminished by altering the person's circumstances to make it less likely that the behavior will occur. For example: if a child cannot tolerate noisy public places, some soothing music can be provided to him and let him listen to the music in headphones.
- **Restructuring the Environment:** The occurrence of any behaviour is partly due to present or past antecedents. This is calls stimulus control. Eg. Child talking in class. Decreasing the behaviour by placing a screen around him
- **Extinction:** When behavior is followed by a reinforcer, it is strengthened or maintained. Without reinforcement, the behavior can eventually die out (extinguished). Initially, it can result in "extinction burst". When the person finds that the expected reinforcement is not coming, then he repeats the behavior number of time, expecting the occurrence of behavior. If the reinforcement is sternly withheld, no matter how repeatedly the behavior occurs, then the particular behavior lessens, slowly and gradually.
- **Punishment:** Consequences for a behaviour that reduces the future possibility of that behaviour. Common types of punishment are,
    - **Time-Out:** This means time-out from positive reinforcements. Mostly applied when behaviour are hazardous or self-injurious. Eg- the parents physically restrain the child when he/she beats others or punish by depriving him of positive reinforcements.
    - **Response Cost:** When undesirable behaviour occurs, a fixed numbers of tokens, stars or points are deducted from what the individual has already earned.
- **Time Out from Positive Reinforcement:** Time out from positive reinforcement is an option where the problem behavior happens when the person is already is in a reinforcing situation. Whenever the behavior occurs, the reinforcement is temporarily ceased. For example, earlier the child used to stay in her room alone aloof, without enjoying, so reinforcement is given every time she comes out of the room to play, interact and watch TV. But if the child started watching television excessively, a time out (for 5- 10 minutes) can be given when her favorite song or music appears in the TV.

- **Functional Communication Training:** Some children show problematic behavior which can be goal directed. It can be seen in them to gain attention or some tangible objects. These children can be taught the appropriate sign or the way to ask things and to express themselves. For example, if they want attention from the teacher to show their drawing, they can be trained to say "come here please" instead of exhibiting problematic behavior.
- **Stimulus Control:** Specific stimuli lead to specific associated response and this condition can be used to manage certain behavior. For example: a child has a habit of asking questions to his parents continuously and throw temper tantrums if not answered which create stress among the family. A sticker has been shown to the child and later the child has been trained not to ask questions until the sticker is not sticked to his shirt. Initially the sticker has been removed three times in one hour which gradually increased. It helped the child to be calm and wait for the appropriate time to ask questions.

2.2.2 Behaviour Modification Techniques for Increasing Appropriate Behavior (Madhavan, Kalyan, Naidu., Pashwarla, & Narayan (1999)

By using reinforcement techniques, the desirable appropriate behaviors are encouraged. Reinforcement is defined as a consequence that strengthens ones future behaviour and also frequency of occurrence of behavior.

- **Token Programme:** A token economy rewards good behavior with tokens that can be exchanged for something desired.
- **Shaping:** Refers to gradually moulding or training an organism to perform a specific response (behavior) by reinforcing any responses that are similar to the desired response.
- **Prompting:** Initially physically guided, to understand the desirable behaviour and then this is reinforced. It is effectively used in teaching self -help skills.
- **Cueing:** Gestural cues, visual cues are given and prompting is effectively used in language training.
- **Fading Programmes:** When the reinforcement techniques are achieved, it shouldn't end abruptly as child gets dependent which could worsen the case. So it could be stopped with irregular intervals. It can make the child less dependable on the reinforcement.
- Altering the environment and graded change.
- **Chaining:** The task is broken into a number of small steps and each steps is taught to the child. Forward chaining and backward chaining. It was observed that backward chaining is found to be creating wonders in training children with ID.
- Steps in implementing reinforcement programme:
    - **Specify the Goal:** Eg. the child will look at the therapist's face and have eye to eye contact when the therapist calls his name and talks to him.
    - **Identify the Reinforcer:** Four important aspects should be followed while presenting a reinforcement:
        - Contingency.
        - Immediacy.
        - Consistency.
        - Clarity.

- **Teach the Behaviour:** Eg. When the child looks at the therapist even for some few seconds while the therapist is talking give the child a chocolate.
- **Fade out the Reinforcement:** E.g. Once the child learns to look more and more steadily into the therapist's eyes gradually fade out the edible reinforcer and use praise as rein forcers.

2.3 Occupational Therapy (OT)

Occupational therapy work towards therapeutic practice of caring one self, ability to earn by doing some work, and entertainment activities to increase independent function, augment development, and prevent disability. Occupational therapy usually works towards accommodating any task or environment to achieve optimum independence and quality of life. Occupational Therapy includes assessment and treatment tasks to uphold the daily living and work skills of people with disability. These tasks can include grooming, bathing, toileting, dressing, eating, socializing, communicating, mobility, and sexual expression. Treatment begins by addressing the most basic self-care activities. Occupational therapy interventions focus on helping the client to adapt the environment, modify the task required through task analysis and by teaching the skill, and educating the client/family to increase participation in daily activities and performance of work activities among clients. (Hopkins & smith 1993 pp.04)

2.4 Parent Counselling

Initially, to impart the correct information of child with ID by being very professional and kind. The therapist should not hide anything. The counselling should help the parents to develop right attitude towards their child with ID, it happens that the parents either become overprotective or aggressive hence helping parents to develop right attitude is very crucial. The parents who accept the child's condition become overprotective and the parents who do not accept the child's condition become very critical. Finally, to create awareness to parents regarding their in training the child to become self-reliant(.

The major agenda and benefits of parental counselling in the present study are:

1. To provide psych education and awareness to the parents on mild level of intellectual disabilities in order help them better understand the problems of the child and provide appropriate assistance to them.
2. To provide support to the parents to deal with their emotional problems like frustrations, anxieties and hostilities so that they are better equipped to provide support to the child with Intellectual disability.

REFERENCES

Achenbach, T. M., & Rescorla, L. A. (2000). *Manual for the ASEBA Preschool Forms & Profiles*. Burlington, VT: University of Vermont, Research Center for Children, Youth, & Families.

Ageranioti-Bélanger, S., Brunet, S., D'Anjou, G., Tellier, G., Boivin, J., & Gauthier, M. (2012). Behaviour disorders in children with an intellectual disability. *Pediatric Child Health*, *17*(2), 84–88. PMID:23372399

Ahuja, N. (2011). *A Short Textbook of Psychiatry. VII 01*. JP Brothers. doi:10.5005/jp/books/11464

American Association on Intellectual and Developmental Disabilities. (2011). *What is the AAIDD definition of intellectual disability?* Retrieved from http://www.aaidd.org/IntellectualDisabilityBook/content_7473.cfm?navID=366

American Psychiatric Association. (2013). *Diagnostic and statistical manual of mental disorders* (5th ed.). Washington, DC: Author.

Berkson, G., Tupa, M., & Sherman, L. (2001). Early development of stereotyped and self-injurious behaviors: Incidence. *American Journal of Mental Retardation*, *106*(6), 539–547. doi:10.1352/0895-8017(2001)106<0539:EDOSAS>2.0.CO;2 PMID:11708939

Bharath Raj, J. (1971). AHSH Norms on seguin form board with Indian Children. *J. of AHSH*, *II*, 34–39.

Bharath Raj, J. (2004). *The developmental screening test manual*. Mysore: Swayamsiddha Prakashana.

Bradley, E., Burke, L., Drummond, C., Korossy, M., Lunsky, Y., & Morris, S. (2010). *Guidelines for managing the patient with developmental disability in the emergency room*. Retrieved from www.camh.net/Publications/Resources_for_Professionals/guidelines_manageclient_emerg2003.pdf

Carr, J. (2004). *Understanding intellectual disability and health*. Retrieved from http://www.intellectualdisability.info/mental-health/behaviour-management

Dhanesh, K. G., & Karthikeyan, S. (2012). *Gender difference in level of intelligence and social quotient among children with autism spectrum disorders*. International Journal of Scientific and Research Publications.

Disability Information. (2013). *Department of communities and social inclusion*. Government of South Australia.

Dumont, M., & Beaulieu, C. (2007). Light exposure in the natural environment: Relevance to mood and sleep disorders. *Sleep Medicine*, *8*(6), 557–565. doi:10.1016/j.sleep.2006.11.008 PMID:17383230

Hall, S., Oliver, C., & Murphy, G. (2001). Early development of self-injurious behavior: An empirical study. *American Journal of Mental Retardation*, *106*(2), 189–199. doi:10.1352/0895-8017(2001)106<0189:EDOSIB>2.0.CO;2 PMID:11321609

Handen, B. L., & Gilchrist, R. (2006). Practitioner review: Psychopharmacology in children and adolescents with mental retardation. *Journal of Child Psychology and Psychiatry, and Allied Disciplines*, *47*(9), 871–882. doi:10.1111/j.1469-7610.2006.01588.x PMID:16930381

Heather, S. (2013). Fighting the stigma caused by mental disorders: past perspectives, present activities, and future directions. World Psychiatric Association.

Hirisave, U., Oommen, A., & Kapur, M. (2002). Psychological assessment of children in the clinical setting - Introduction. In Psychological assessment of children in the clinical setting (pp 1-5) Bangalore: NIMHANS.

Hopkins, H. L., & Smith, H. D. (1993). Willard and Spackman's Occupational Therapy (8th ed.). Philadelphia: J.B. Lippincott. Retrieved from http://www.sgh.org.sa/Portals/0/Articles/International%20Handbook%20of%20Occupational%20Therapy%20Interventions.pdf

Jan, J.E., Owens, J.A., Weiss, M.D., Johnson, K.P., Wasdell, M.B., Freeman, R.D. (2008). Sleep hygiene for children with neurodevelopmental disabilities. *Ipsiroglu O.S Pediatrics, 122*(6), 1343-50.

Kahng, S., Iwata, B. A., & Lewin, A. B. (2002). Behavioral treatment of self-injury, 1964 to 2000. *American Journal of Mental Retardation, 107*(3), 212–221. doi:10.1352/0895-8017(2002)107<0212:BTOSIT>2.0.CO;2 PMID:11966334

Krutchzer, S., Deluca, J., & Caplan, B. (2012). Encyclopedia of neuropsychology. Academic Press.

Loewy, J., Hallan, C., Friedman, E., & Martinez, C. (2006). Sleep/sedation in children undergoing EEG testing: A comparison of chloral hydrate and music therapy. *American Journal of Electroneurodiagnostic Technology*, *46*, 343–355. PMID:17285817

Luckasson, R., Borthwick-Duffy, S., Buntinx, W. H. E., Coulter, D. L., Craig, E. M., Reeve, A., & Tasse´, M. J. et al. (2002). *Mental retardation: Definition, classification, and systems of supports* (10th ed.). Washington, DC: American Association on Mental Retardation.

Madhavan, T., Kalyan, M., Naidu, S., Pashwarla, R., & Narayan, J. (1999). *Mental retardation- a manual for psychologists*. Secunderabad, India: National Institute for the Mentally Handicapped.

Malin, A. J. (1949). Manual of Malin's Intelligence Scale for Indian Children. Lucknow: Indian Psychological Corporation.

Mather, N., & Goldstein, S. (2015). *Behaviour Modification in the classroom*. Retrieved from http://www.ldonline.org/article/6030/

Mindell, J. A., Kuhn, B., Lewin, D. S., Meltzer, L. J., & Sadeh, A. (2006). Behavioral treatment of bedtime problems and night wakings in infants and young children. *American Academy of Sleep Medicine Sleep.*, *29*(10), 1263–1276. PMID:17068979

Reynolds, T., & Zupanick, D.M. (2013). *Intellectual Disability and Severity Codes*. Retrieved from https://www.mentalhelp.net/articles/intellectual-disability-and-severity-codes/

Richdale, A., & Wiggs, L. (2005). Behavioural approaches to the treatment of sleep problems in children with developmental disorders. What is state of the art? *International Journal of Behavioral and Consultation Therapy*, *1*(3), 165–187. doi:10.1037/h0100743

Sharma, A., & Chowhan, S. (2014). *The Neuropsychological Components of Visual Processing and Learning in High and Low Functioning Children Exhibiting Autism Spectrum Disorder: A Comparative Study*. Unpublished manuscript.

Tassé, M. J., Schalock, R. L., Balboni, G., Bersani, H., & Sharon, A. (2012). The Construct of Adaptive Behavior: Its Conceptualization, Measurement, and Use in the Field of Intellectual Disability. *American Journal on Intellectual and Developmental Disabilities, 117*(4), 291–303. doi:10.1352/1944-7558-117.4.291 PMID:22809075

World Health Organization. (1992). *The ICD-10 classification of mental and behavioural disorders: Clinical descriptions and diagnostic guidelines*. Geneva: World Health Organization.

APPENDIX

Activities

- **Activity No. 1:** In order to form concepts of various objects and things, various catalogues from various stores that could be interesting for the child. These catalogues could range from clothes, toys hunting fishing etc. One can make a collage out of it. The child could learn from the catalogues or from the pictures about the features of the specific objects which could help in forming the concepts of the objects. One can work on sorting with so many of these pictures. One can instruct the child to cut out the things and sort things that have wheels and things that have wings or sort the pants from the shirts. One can also cut out a child from a magazine and have the child dress them. For example: ask the child to find a *purple shirt* or have them put a hat *on top of* the boy's head.
  - **Can Target:** Categories & Sorting-Vocabulary-Basic Concepts (colors, prepositions)-Life Skills.
- **Activity No. 2:** 'Backward chaining' is a technique that which can help the child to learn a new skill. In this technique, the trainer will complete all the steps of the task except the last step. The child needs to complete the task. This continues as the trainer complete one less step and the child does one more. Until he can do the whole task on their own. The child receives motivation and confidence along with success. For example: when a child is taught how to put their shoes and socks, the first task is to break it into small steps and making him learn.
  - Get shoes and socks from cupboard.
  - Bring socks and shoes over to chair.
  - Sit on chair.
  - Pull socks onto feet.
  - Slip shoes onto feet.

Chapter 11
Concerns for Individuals with Intellectual Disability in India

Priyanka Behrani
The Maharaja Sayajirao University, India

Dorothy Bhandari Deka
Gujarat Forensic Sciences University, India

ABSTRACT

Intellectual disability (intellectual developmental disorder) is characterized by deficits in general mental abilities, such as reasoning, problem solving, planning, abstract thinking judgment, academic learning, and learning from experience (DSM V). This neuro developmental disorder is one of the conditions with onset in the developmental period. This condition has been classified into four categories on the basis of the individual's IQ (Intelligence quotient). The objective of the present paper is to highlight some of the areas that are related to the concerns for the people with intellectual disability. The paper focuses on the following topics: 1) Legal services, 2) Challenges faced by parents, 3) Health issues, 4) Sexual knowledge, 5) Marriage, 6) Quality of life, 7) Old age, 8) Attitude of society towards the individual with intellectual disability, 9) Implications, management and prevention for future improvement for individuals with intellectual disability.

INTRODUCTION

Intellectual disability (intellectual developmental disorder) is a neuro developmental disorders is one of the conditions with an onset in the developmental period. This disability is characterized by inability to cope up with the mental abilities as per the child's chronological age (DSM V, 2015).

The common characteristics of intellectual disability are although uniqueness in every person, regardless of their IQ scores each individual has their own personality and areas of ability and difficulty. Generally a person with an intellectual disability has difficulty: learning and processing information as quickly as people without an intellectual disability. Grasping abstract concepts such as money and time, understanding the subtleties of interpersonal interactions, manipulating of the ideas and concepts is required for planning and organizing as compared to people without intellectual disability. The difficulties includes such as reasoning, problem solving, planning, abstract thinking judgment, academic

DOI: 10.4018/978-1-5225-0089-6.ch011

learning, and learning from experience. This inability results in impairments of adaptive functioning, such as the individual fails to meet the ideals of a person's independence and social responsibility in one or more aspects of daily life, that includes communication, social participation, academic or occupational functioning, and personal independence at home or in community settings. Diagnosis for intellectual disability includes an expected delay in developmental milestones that involves various areas of intellectual functioning (Ahuja, 2011).

Individual factors include personality, social and communication abilities, coping strategies and the presence of other disabilities (motor, social or sensory). The supports provided by family, friends and support staff are also crucial aspects of people's lives and have a profound influence on their confidence and function. Issues of access (including physical, social, communication, cognitive, financial access) to community based facilities and services also play a powerful role in either enabling or inhibiting opportunities for inclusion, participation and contribution and the ability of the individual to fulfill their community roles. (CDDH, 2015)

Presently, individuals with intellectual disability in India, majority of them are still excluded by the society irrespective of identified or unidentified. To fully understand the challenges that individuals with intellectual disability are facing within the Indian society, is by understanding that the barriers are primarily rooted in religious beliefs, cultural norms, and majorly lack of awareness regarding intellectual disability. India's rigid social structure within the society becomes a hurdle in inclusion and acceptance for individuals with intellectual disability.

LEGAL SERVICES PROVIDED FOR INDIVIDUALS WITH INTELLECTUAL DISABILITY

According to National Legal Services Authority (Legal Services to the Mentally Ill Persons and Persons with Mental Disabilities Schemes, 2010), there are 14 rights that are rendered to the individuals with intellectual disability. Rights provided to the individuals with intellectual disability such as, legal services to mentally retarded persons (MRs), appointment of guardians under the National Trust Act, 1999 for the their welfare in the society.

Matters to be considered while representing legal services to individuals with intellectual difficulty:

1. Individuals with Intellectual disability are not mentally ill individual.
2. Legal services to Individuals with Intellectual disability.
3. Legal services for ensuring the health care.
4. Legal services for ensuring the fundamental rights of individuals with intellectual disability.
5. Right to education.
6. Legal services for the benefits under PWD Act, 1995.
7. Prevention of exploitation and abuse of individuals with intellectual disability.
8. Legal services for individuals with intellectual disability for owing and inheriting properties and to have financial rights.
9. Appointment of guardians under the National Trust Act, 1999.
10. Need for setting up of a supported network.
11. Creating awareness campaigns amongst the other school children.
12. Awareness camps for educating the family members of individuals with intellectual disability.
13. Awareness programs for the general public.
14. Sensitization Program for Judicial Officers and Lawyers.

CHALLENGES FACED BY PARENTS AND THE INDIVIDUALS WITH INTELLECTUAL DISABILITY DURING THE EARLY AGE

Intellectual disability in India is a major challenge which not only limits the capacity of the afflicted individual but at the same time also leads to the parent's vulnerability to the stressors (Jena et al, 2013).

There are multiple problems in families having a mentally retarded child. It has been found that one of the overwhelming, problems of these parents is related to the feeling of social ridicule for possessing a child with intellectual disability. As a reaction to this attitude, the parents may prefer to keep these children socially isolated. They often feel guilty and. hold each other responsible (Ryckman & Handerson, 1965).Parental acceptance depends upon the knowledge and the awareness of the parents along with the strength and the readiness to face all the challenges that they have to welcome with the growing age of the child. The parent's resources and the support also play an important role in the acceptance of the child. There is considered evidence to suggest that parents of children with intellectual disability experience greater stress than caregivers of children without intellectual disability. This stress tends to be chronic in nature and therefore persists over substantial period of time. Caring for children with intellectual disabilities drains out parent's economic, physical, mental and psychological resources. Behavioral problems which are frequently associated with intellectual disabilities add to parental stress (Jena et. al, 2013).

Parenting stress and adaptation depend upon the type of disability; the family's coping resources and formal and informal supports in the community (Breslau et al, 1982). Here the stress for the parents is that no matter what level of disability the child has in intellectual functioning, the actual stress is that the child cannot be cured by medicine it is a condition that will remain with the child till the last day of their life. The fact of this condition is more stressful for the parents rather than providing them the treatment so that their child can be healthy but here the parents also have to live with the condition of their child.

The parents coping with the fact depends upon the resources and formal and informal supports that are available in the community. The coping resources include "faith in God, self-determination, attitude and perception towards the situation, and the available resources such as support from family members, relatives, friends, neighbours, professionals, community and governmental policies and programs" (Peshawaria et al, 1998). There are two types of social support systems one is formal social supports which include services provided by professionals such as school programmes, parent education specialists, therapists, and government and non- government agencies. Another is Informal social supports encompass relationships between family members, relatives, neighbours, friends, and community groups. Proximal support from spouse and immediate relatives has been found to promote family adaptation and reduce stress (Gupta et al., 2012).

Parental stress in the lower socioeconomic status of the family can be associated with more stress because of less resource availability. Shortage of resources, including food, medication, durable medical equipment, and apparel can add to the stress of raising children with disabilities (Gupta et al, 2012). Parents of children with intellectual disability face financial burden and also diminished quality of life in social aspect (Khare, 2015).

In conditions of poverty, a child with a disability is regarded as a burden, an evil spirit, and an object of charity without rights, rather than as an unfortunate child (Gupta et al., 2012). Parenting issues usually depends upon the severity, visibility, unpredictability, and number of invasive procedures such as surgeries, and overall type of disability - behavioral, developmental or medical – rather than the medical diagnosis (Breslau et al, 1982).

Parental expressed emotions play a very important role in the child's growing age. The expressed emotions need to be balanced towards the child so that the child has a positive attitude towards their life. High expressed emotion is said when the family has a negative attitude towards the patient, thinks that the disability or the disorder is controllable but the patient is not choosing to get better. In family having high expressed emotions the members in the family thinks that family's problems are due to the disabled individual's mental illness, the individual with intellectual disability is blamed for it that the disabled individual has trouble problem solving within the family. The attitude towards the individual with intellectual disability is hostile when the expressed emotion is high. Low expressed emotion is when the family members are more reserved with their criticism. Findings support the theory that low to moderate levels of negative expression may be less beneficial or detrimental for children with ID compared to children without intellectual disability (Green & Bake, 2011).

High or low expressed emotion makes the disabled individual feel trapped, out of control and dependent upon others, feels that because of their problem everyone is facing difficulty and everyone in the home is being affected and raising the stress level for everyone in family (Barker et al., 2012).

Children with intellectual disability in the early age initially are not able to understand the condition they are going through but as they start maturing slowly they start realizing the fact of their life usually in the case of mild moderate level of intellectual difficulty children. They realise that they are not similar to their age appropriate friends and they are not able to perform the way their age group friends does. This can be seen in their behavior as the child starts being irritable, aggressive, at times shows stubbornness and some children also might show sad moods. Their understanding regarding the difficulty also leads to additional behavioural, emotional and social problem that the parents as well as the child face it (Lemay et al., 2003).

The process of understanding that the young individual will be limited in his learning abilities would be a difficult task for any parent to face (Brown & Randel, 2007). Parents having children with intellectual disability can have issues in preparing the child to overcome the present and the future challenges. Childhood challenges that is faced by the child with intellectual disability which is an early life concern for the parents is for their child's education, vocation and secondly peer group and social acceptance. Education and vocational training is one very important aspect for children with intellectual disability as it helps the child develop his/ her self-esteem along with a reason for survival, if they are motivated and supported by their surroundings, especially parents because as in the later stage when the child starts realizing that it's a condition that is never ending might be a cause for the onset of other mental health issues.

Presently in India, we are passing through a phase in the area of rehabilitation wherein efforts are being made to spread services and training programs, to raise awareness levels related to mainstreaming and provision of equal rights and opportunity for the individuals with intellectual disability (Peshawaria et al, 1995)

VOCATIONAL TRAINING AND EMPLOYMENT FOR INDIVIDUALS WITH INTELLECTUAL DISABILITY

The ultimate aim of any education and training is for a gainful employment and it is one of the most critical aspects of independent living. This is true with every individual including the individuals with intellectual disability. Individual with intellectual disability are more likely to be unemployed and generally earn less than other disability areas even when they are employed. Individual with intellectual disability are rarely employed, probably due to the stigma attached to individual with intellectual disability (Abidi, 1999).

There are three major areas where the individuals with intellectual disability can be employed. One of them is Sheltered Employment, here the person with intellectual disability is trained in an occupation and employ him in the workshop itself. Another one are of employment is Open Employment, here the routine job is successfully performed by individuals with intellectual disability with initial support from the trainer. The individual with intellectual disability can work gainfully provided has developed social competence. The third area is Self Employment; it can be successful when the family of the individual with intellectual disability provide him with appropriate training and support (Narayan & Kurani, 1990).

Though individuals with intellectual disability are able to do complex tasks, if given a structured situation and adequate preparation (Gold,1972). But it needs the training for the same. The assumption of work roles in competitive or non -competitive work environment for the individuals with intellectual disability calls for three types of assistance: first is simplicity of environment so that they can respond promptly and efficiently, second formation of work personality through specific preparation for the tasks comprising the position where she /he is going to be employed. Third is development of supporting roles for them in the family and community (Narayan & Kurani, 1990).

Employment and income are also affected by the severity of disability .There is a 3 per cent quota for persons with disabilities (PWD act 1995). As such there is no separate quota out of the said 3 per cent for individuals with intellectual disability. The major issues identified in this area are:

1. **Identification of Jobs & Reservation Clause of The Disability Act:** The Disability Act 1995 provides for a 3% reservation in "identified posts" for people with disabilities in all categories of jobs. The posts were meant to have been identified soon after the Act coming into force and updated every 3 years. The initial identification of posts at the Central Government level was not completed until 2001 and no formal expansion of identified posts has been completed subsequently.
2. **Repeated Medical Examination of Disabled Employees:** Disabled employees get certain benefits like higher transport allowance; preference in the allotment of government accommodation etc. Every time a person applies for availing these benefits, she/he is asked to get a Medical Test done. The authorities do not accept the Disability Certificate, as an authentic proof of disability.
3. **Accessibility:** It is a major issue in Government offices there are not much facilities are for individuals to make the work environment more conducive to work.
4. **Discrimination:** An important legal right for persons with disabilities is the right to live free from discrimination in employment. Discrimination may normally take different forms. Some employers use pre-employment physicals to identify individuals with disabilities and to refuse their job applications. Some employers deny training, promotions and fringe benefits to employees with disabilities. Employees have been downgraded, discharged or harassed when an employer learns of the existence of a disability, or thinks that an employee is disabled (Employment of Persons with Disabilities in Public Sectors in India- Emerging Issues and Trends 2008).

Just as normal adults work to earn their livelihood, persons with intellectual disability also have the potential to work and earn if they are provided with the necessary training, placement and other supports. At present, many of them are idle, work in sheltered workshops or work for a few hours every week. Their earnings do not reflect their capabilities. To make employment a realistic option for people with intellectual disability, appropriate jobs from the open market need to be identified. Simple jobs that require minimum supervision needs to be selected for successful training and placement of individuals with intellectual disability. Vocational rehabilitation helps individual with intellectual disability to hold on to a job (Abidi, 1999).

HEALTH ISSUES IN INDIVIDUALS WITH INTELLECTUAL DISABILITIES

Individuals with intellectual disabilities are prone to a wide range of medical conditions that can affect the person physically as well as their mental health.

The most common physical health problems are epilepsy, mobility problems, and sensory problems. Health problems often occur in people with genetic syndromes. A small, general practice database study found that a quarter of people with intellectual disabilities and epilepsy were seizure-free and a third had poorly controlled seizures Oral health is often poor, and toothache may manifest as challenging behavior. Gastro-esophageal reflux disease often remains unnoticed (Henry et. al, 2008). Family members and care givers of individual with intellectual disability also come for receiving lifelong contraception or to have surgery to regulate fertility of the person with intellectual disability. The reproductive health, rights and contraceptive needs of women with intellectual disabilities have been the subject of extensive legal, ethical and health care deliberations in the United States (Paransky & Zurawin, 2003). The concerns of parents and care givers regarding pregnancy and menstrual management have in some cases led to women being surgically sterilized or undergoing hysterectomy. The women's capacity to make autonomous decisions and to care for children is not always clear, and the rights and wishes of the individual women have to be protected as far as possible (Diekema, 2003). Newer medical options, including hormonal implants, permit less invasive and reversible management of fertility and menstruation (Paransky & Zurawin, 2003).

Individuals with intellectual disability not just have physical health issues along with it there are also barriers present that hinders in their good health care such as missing out on health information in magazines, books and public health campaigns due to limited literacy. Cognitive difficulties might hinder in understanding the significance of maintaining the healthy diet, lifestyle choices, and disease screening. Social and communication difficulty in various circumstances may lead to hindrance in health monitoring. In order to improve the scenario of barrier for health issues among the individuals with intellectual disability strategies can be used. For fulfilling the purpose of the strategies very firstly the health professional and care givers need to be equipped with training and knowledge regarding their behaviour, exchange of response, comprehending capabilities, and how much the person with intellectual disability is able to do things on their own. People with intellectual disability often rely on health management and the barriers that prevent the identified health needs are being met with the help of support staff and healthcare staff (Tracy & McDonald, 2015).

SEXUAL KNOWLEDGE: FEELINGS AND NEEDS OF INDIVIDUAL WITH INTELLECTUAL DISABILITY

Important changes in public policies and attitudes have resulted in improved opportunities for people with mental disabilities. Unfortunately, societal attitudes have not changed much with regard to their sexual needs. Even today, society at large refuse to acknowledge that all people have sexual feelings, needs, and desires, regardless of their physical and/or mental abilities .Making good decisions about sexuality is a critical part of adulthood, but sometimes people with intellectual disabilities don't get the support or education they need to navigate this complex aspect of life (Walker–Hirrch, L. 2007). Sex education is a central issue for all the community integration of people with intellectual disability, yet they are greatly disadvantaged in this the nature of their disability as they are likely to experience difficulty when dealing with such subtle and complex issues. The development of appropriate sexual skills is easier said than done, because sex education is such a vexed topic, particularly in the area of disability. In order to avoid confronting sexual issues, some parents and care- givers deny that people with intellectual disabilities are sexual beings (Marita et al., 1996).

People with intellectual disability as mentioned may be denied as sexual being this may be true for individuals with severe or profound disability and is certainly not true for individuals with mild intellectual disability as people with intellectual disability might have less or no experience in sexual relationship unlike other individuals of their age but they might have positive feelings towards sexual needs and feeling (UNICEF, 2005). Consequently providing training for daily life and teaching them the basic life and social skills for their survival in is very important for the child to learn and adapt with the society and along with it sex education is also one of the very important aspects that the individuals with intellectual disability need to be know about as because adolescents with intellectual disability are the vulnerable ones. They are usually exploded not by strangers rather mostly by their own relatives or neighbours or friends. Therefore educating them right from the gender difference, puberty, their safety at home and at public places, unusual touch by relatives or strangers, knowledge about sex and its process and the appropriate age and social norms related to it would help the individual to have a better idea and reason to protect themselves. This will also help them in understanding the society in a more matured way so that they can lead a simple but a safe and secured life. As the WHO-UNFPA Guidance Note says, "The sexual and reproductive health of persons with disabilities is not a unique, complex, or highly specialized issue. It is, however, an issue that needs more attention and greater creativity, and it needs more attention now.

Marriage and Its Consequence for Individuals with Intellectual Disability

Global human rights laws grant all individuals with disabilities, including individuals with intellectual disabilities, the right to marry and have families. The key issue in marriage among individuals with intellectual disability is not the marriage itself, but the awareness and consent of the individual with disability to enter into the institution of marriage on their own free will. According to the laws, the disabled person have the right to go through the same marriage ceremony and celebration as the other young people in the family goes through and those in their social circles but the concern is that how much will they understand about the longer term implications of living within a new family structure, as well as the rights and responsibilities that marriage entails and the added responsibility of being sexually active and to have children. Therefore individuals with intellectual disability, in the middle age of their life; it is important for them to know about the institution of marriage and the responsibilities that come with it. It is the duty of the parents to make them aware of the process of marriage and its responsibilities as that will help the individual with intellectual disability to understand the overall picture of marriage and take a better decision by the individual for the their future (Groce et al., 2014).

The importance to educate the individual is important to make them aware of the responsibility so that if the parents are willing that their child should marry and start a new life with a partner, the individual with intellectual disability can give their own views and consent for their own future. Forcing the individual with intellectual disability to marry without consent will be an injustice for the individual as well as for the person with whom the individual will marry. It is difficult to answer the question as to why parents of adults with intellectual disability would encourage or force their children into marriages if their children are reluctant to wed or if they are frightened, confused or unable to understand the roles and responsibilities expected of them in marriage (Groce et al, 2014). But if given a thought the parents of individual with intellectual disability might think their child's marriage would secure their child's future and also probably someone who can look after their child after their parents grow old and weak to look after their child with the condition.

In case marriage takes place, it is important that the family and the partner are well aware of the condition of the disability of the individual before they marry. It is an illegal action if the parents of individual with intellectual disability do not inform the would be partner and their family about the condition and the marriage is taken place. Responsibility of parents increases as their child reaches the appropriate age of marriage, to educate them, help them take an insightful decision if they want to enter the institution of marriage and very importantly the whole process of marriage should be done in a lawful way rather than in deception (Nambi, 2005)

QUALITY OF LIFE OF INDIVIDUALS WITH INTELLECTUAL DISABILITY

Quality of life (QOL) in general terms is the overall well-being of an individual. It is basically the comfort experienced by an individual in their life. Quality of life has a wide range of contexts that include the fields of international development, healthcare, politics and employment. The standard indicators of the quality of life include not just wealth and employment it also includes the built environment, physical health and mental health both, education, recreation and leisure time, and social belongings.

Quality of Life is a universal concept as everybody has a quality of life and the quality of life of people with disabilities has the same components as the quality of life of people without disabilities (Interim report, 2003). The issue that the concept addresses is the lives of persons and ensuring that citizens with intellectual disability, experience the same human rights and a life of quality as any other member of society. To this end, the quality of life concept reflects the following four principles:

1. Quality of life is composed of the same factors and relationships for all people;
2. Quality of life is experienced when a person's needs are met and when the individual has the opportunity to pursue life enrichment in major life activity settings;
3. Quality of life has both subjective and objective components; and
4. Quality of life is a multidimensional construct, influenced by individual and environmental factors (Navas et al, 2012).

The field of intellectual disability is strongly influenced by the Quality of Life paradigm; the framework supports the equality of persons, which is reflected in concepts such as self-determination, liberation, inclusion, and empowerment. In daily practice the concepts are translated into tangible actions, professionals are often challenged with difficulties to apply the quality of life principles for individuals with intellectual difficulty.

The application of principles of quality of life, which should in ideal conditions should lead to positive outcomes with regard to social participation, independence, and well-being seems to be at risk, as accounts from professionals indicate that empowerment is sometimes replaced by actions solely aimed at "controlling," "dominating and excluding" clients with intellectual disability and co-occurring mental health problems (Morisse et al, 2013). In this respect, adequate support is a challenge and because of this complexity, the application of the QOL paradigm is not self-evident, although there seems to be consensus about the fact that the same domains are relevant for all persons, including this specific subpopulation. The policy of deinstitutionalization was based on the proposition that quality of life of individuals with intellectual disabilities will improve as a result of being moved from institutions to community-based care settings.

OLD AGE AND INDIVIDUALS WITH INTELLECTUAL DISABILITY

Ageing adults with intellectual disabilities are at particular disadvantage and risk. Older adults with severe and profound impairments are disregarded or institutionalized. Older adults with mild and moderate intellectual disability can be trained and educated so that they can look after themselves and lead a normal life like others but the same cannot be done with elderly person with severe and profound intellectual disability.

The highest priorities for the majority of people with intellectual disabilities in less developed countries generally include basic health care, adequate nutrition and housing, education, human rights, and political, social and economic stability (WHO, 2000).

In case of elderly individual housing is often inadequate and health provision is usually neglected. Nowadays the immediate family members are seen to ignore the older individuals with or without intellectual disability. Elderly people if kept in old age home or even at home can manage with their basic needs but elderly ones with intellectual disability if ignored by their family members they usually face a lot of problem. Communication and behavioral difficulties are generally observed. Speech and motor impairments may serve as barriers to communicate when no immediate family member is available with individuals with intellectual disability when need to deal with health services provision. Behavioral issues such as fear, confusion, and aggressiveness among adults with intellectual disabilities may have difficulty cooperating with health services provisions (Henny, 2008).

In both women and men, proper nutrition, exercise, and access to preventive health care can increase health and longevity. Women with intellectual disabilities generally receive less preventive health care than women generally, just as women receive less preventive health care than men. In developing countries, women with intellectual disability may be affected more frequently by malnutrition than are men. In many nations, older women with intellectual disabilities experience challenges that are particular to their sex. Their specific needs are often overlooked or dismissed. Older adults with co-morbid conditions experience particular problems and their compound physical and/or mental health conditions not addressed (WHO, 2000).

Older adults with impairments should be provided with rehabilitative services, vocational opportunities, and quality old-age services, which are not adequately provided. Government in developing countries should provide the disabled elderly people with adequate legal rights and also economical schemes can help them become independent. Shelter including food and stay along with basic skill training and adequate health and economic support from the government can make better changes in developing countries for older people with intellectual disability.

ATTITUDE OF SOCIETY TOWARDS THE INDIVIDUAL WITH INTELLECTUAL DISABILITY

The social system plays a major in the acceptance of the individuals with intellectual disability and the support from the society can actually bring changes to the lives of the children with intellectual disability. In country like India, although in most of the places in the country is aware of the conditions but still the acceptance and support is not available from the society. Government has provided immense support to the children with intellectual disability for the well fare of the child as well as for the family.

Social acceptance of the individual with intellectual disability is one major factor that can bring change to the social scenario and this can be a support to the immediate family and the child's mental health. Although deinstitutionalization and inclusive education, community integration has increased, still public attitudes continue to pose a potential barrier to the full social inclusion and equal rights of people with intellectual disability (Sheriden & Scior, 2013).

Society's attitude towards the individuals with intellectual disability might lead to socials comparison among the children with intellectual disability and the ones who do not have any disability. Such comparisons might affect the individual's attitude towards self. Individuals with intellectual disability might develop low self-esteem, lack of self-confidence which might later cultivate into social withdrawal behavior or depression in the individual.

IMPLICATIONS, MANAGEMENT AND PREVENTION FOR FUTURE IMPROVEMENT FOR INDIVIDUALS WITH INTELLECTUAL DISABILITY

Every individual is unique. Intellectual ability provides a guide as to how quickly a person is able to process new information grasp abstract concepts and manipulate ideas. The facts that will help understanding and managing people with intellectual disability could be majorly focused on their learning ability and information processing. It is required to understand that they are slow learners and the processing of information is slow as compared to others without intellectual disability. It is also important to understand that they have difficulty with abstract concepts such as money, time and the subtleties of interpersonal interactions (CDDH, 2015).

Individuals with intellectual disability require the kind of support and assistance is depended on their cognitive ability and the expectations on them in and within particular environments. We also need to be careful that whether they have other associated developmental disabilities such as cerebral palsy, autism or sensory impairments so that needs can be fulfilled accordingly for the individual with intellectual disability. Every one of us has areas of ability and other areas of function that we find difficult(CDDH, 2014) Subjective categories of mild, moderate, severe and profound levels of intellectual disability, defined on the basis of IQ 'scores', provide an escort to the level and types of support an individual might require.

Individuals with a mild intellectual disability that is according to ICD 10, 2007 individual with an IQ of 50- 69 may learn to read and write (depending on educational opportunities). Most people with mild intellectual disability have important relationships in their lives and participate in a variety of activities and do contribute to their families and their communities. Some of them live and travel independently while others require support and assistance in using public transport, managing money, and planning and organizing their lives. Most individuals with mild intellectual disability can work, and some of them can hold a job, with or without a level of personal or employment support. Many individuals do form intimate relationships and some do marry and raise children with various levels of social support such as from family, friends and the service system. People with mild intellectual disability do have trouble with academic learning and so reading, writing and numeral might remain at a basic level. Many people find the subtleties of interpersonal relationships and social rules difficult to comprehend (particularly as adolescents) and may unintentionally disobey social boundaries.

Individuals with a moderate intellectual disability, according to ICD 10, 2007 individual with an IQ of 35 – 49, do have important relationships in his/her life and will usually enjoy a variety of activities with families, friends and paid support workers and form valued and lasting friendships. With specific travel training many people learn to use public transport on familiar routes, but may have difficulty in management of money and issues while problem solving when unexpected events occur. Most people do learn to recognize some words in context (such as Ladies/Gents/Exit). People with adequate vision will benefit from visual prompts to clarify meaning, such as daily timetables and pictures used in communication systems. People with a moderate intellectual disability might need lifelong support in managing finances, and planning and organizing their lives and activities (CDDH, 2014) People with moderate level of intellectual disability, their ability to be independent in personal care tasks, such as toilet hygiene, dressing and bathing, will depend on what kind of opportunities do they get to learn and practice with these tasks also depends on their level of cognitive ability, and the presence or absence of other developmental disabilities such as cerebral palsy or any physical disability or any health issues.

According to ICD 10, 2007, individuals with a severe intellectual disability (IQ 20 – 35) or profound intellectual disability (IQ <20), usually recognizes familiar people and has strong relationships with key people in their lives. Most will have little or no speech and will rely on facial expression and body language and gestures to express their needs or feelings and those interacting with and supporting them must be active and keen observers in interpreting changes in a person's behavior. Communication systems for people with severe and profound level of disability generally rely on photographs or objects to facilitate understanding, example a picture of a cup, or the cup itself, may be used in conjunction with the spoken question, "Would you like a drink?" People with severe/profound disabilities will require lifelong assistance in personal care tasks, communication and support in accessing community facilities/services (CDDH, 2015).

For the management of individuals with intellectual disability expertise training is required in order to know how to manage such individuals. Training should be provided to the facilitators in hospitals, schools, rehabilitation centers in various areas in order to deal with the individuals with intellectual disability. Training in various areas such as:

- Understanding the person's needs and behavior.
- Being non-judgmental and empathetic with the person.
- Ways of communication with the person.
- How to understand their potential and channelized them accordingly.
- How to respond to their emotions.

Expert training can facilitate positive development in the area of intellectual disability. But along with the intensive training for the facilitators to manage people with intellectual disability, awareness about intellectual disability is also important. Providing education and awareness in various parts of our country might help parents to support their child with intellectual disability.

Rehabilitation is one very important spectrum that helps in progress of the individuals with intellectual disability. In a disability report by WHO, 2011, rehabilitation is defined as "a set of measures that assist individuals who experience, or are likely to experience, disability to achieve and maintain optimal functioning in interaction with their environments". Rehabilitation enhances the potential of the individuals with intellectual disability. Rehabilitation also helps in behavioral modification of the people. The enhancement in potential can lead the individual with intellectual disability develop a better picture of their own self in the society with increased self-confidence and an accepting self-image.

Along with managing individuals with intellectual disability, parental stress also needs to be managed so that children with intellectual disability are not hampered due to the stress bust out of parents. Parents having children with intellectual disability needs to be trained not only for how to look after and take care of their child with intellectual disability also for training is required for the parents so that they know how to manage their own stressors. Teaching parents to manage the stressors of their own is important so that their own physical health and mental health is in a good condition which will facilitate them to work for their own child with intellectual disability in a productive manner. On the other hand it will also help the parents not to blame or have stress outburst in front of their child which may lead to deterioration in the child's condition.

There are methods that can be taught to the parents regarding how they can manage their stress for their own good physical health and mental as well as their child's also. The techniques are: firstly for mothers having children with intellectual disability are taught self-help and language skill training. Secondly cognitive training such as cognitive restructuring or enhancing problem solving skills can be taught in order to deal with distortions, misconceptions and unrealistic expectation that contribute to the parental stress in children with intellectual disability. Thirdly relaxation can be taught for self-monitoring of stress and physiological reaction to self. Fourthly cognitive behavioral therapy can be used for parents in order to help them deal with and reduce issues such as self-blame and guilt in parents of children with intellectual disability. Cognitive behavioral techniques such as coping, communicating, problem solving skills can be taught. Such methods can help parents of children with intellectual disability in managing with the stressors and prevention in deteriorating the condition of their own physical and mental health as well as of their child. Singer et al. (2007) carried out a systematic review and meta-analysis of the impact of various interventions on parental distress (depression and related variables) even when the primary focus of the intervention may not have been stress reduction (i.e., behavioral parent training). Seventeen studies were included in the review, and results showed that cognitive behavioral interventions (CBT), behavioral parent training, and multi-component interventions all reduced parental distress. Larger reductions in distress were found for multi-component interventions (e.g., parent training, plus CBT, plus case management and/or respite care). However, only five studies included comparison against an active control intervention or an attention control condition. Given the lack of resources available to support families in several contexts (e.g., rural communities, low and middle income countries), parent-to-parent support models (parents trained to offer psychological/counseling support to other parents) are especially interesting. In a randomized waiting list control design effectiveness study (i.e., focused on support groups already established), Singer et al. (1999) found that those parents receiving support reported increased family strength and more progress towards meeting their current needs.

Teaching the care givers the ability to cope up with their stressors and awareness regarding the needs and basic understanding for the individuals can be done by arranging mental health programs in both urban and rural areas of the country, programs in schools and educational institute will also help develop understanding the concept and have a better outlook for the individuals with intellectual disability. Posters and useful advertisements regarding where and how facilities for the individuals with intellectual disability is available can help the parents as well as the individual for wellbeing in future. (WHO, 2003). Psychoeducation is one very important spectrum that the health care facilitators need to provide to the parents and caregivers of the person with intellectual disability. This will facilitate the parents and the caregivers to focus on every concern areas for the person with intellectual disability so as to have a smoother life ahead with the person and managing the issues related to the disability.

Education and awareness will not any facilitate the immediate members of the individual with intellectual disability but also will lead to change in attitude and mind set of the society towards the intellectual deficient people. The more understanding, acceptance and change in attitude will bring progress in our country as well.

CONCLUSION

In developing countries, for future improvement and development, individuals with intellectual disability should be provide with proper health and skill training facilities starting from the early age. Programs for educating intellectually disabled individual regarding the society and its needs and norms along with awareness about substance use and abuse and sexual exploitation should be arranged so that, this particular lot is not exploited and misused.

Awareness programs for parents and immediate family members should be provided regarding the issues and difficulties faced by the disabled person. Family members should also be educated regarding expressed emotions towards the individual with intellectual disability. Parents especially, should be trained to motivate and train individuals with intellectual disability for basic skill learning and if possible educate the disabled individuals till the grade they can cope up with.

Society also needs to be made aware about the issues and difficulties that the individuals with intellectual disability face so that the society can accept them socially. Societal acceptance could provide motivation and mental support to the individuals with intellectual disability.

People working in health, education and rehabilitation sector should be trained so that they know how to manage individuals with intellectual disability. Disabled individual usually have difficulty in communicating their needs and requirement and expressing their emotions in socially accepted way. Therefore training the people and parents in such areas would make the relation smoother between them.

Providing legal and economic rights to the individuals with intellectual disability gives them independence and free from exploitation and importantly provides support when family members are not present. Constitution provides them with rights to be the part of the society but the society either do not accept them or misuses the rights. Our aim should be to equip the individuals sufficiently so that they are able to survive along with the acceptance of the existing society

The issues concerned do come in various ranges on the basis of the categories but the responsibility doesn't just end here after discussing the concerned issues regarding the individuals with intellectual disability. India as a developing country needs to put immense effort for the individuals with intellectual disability. Future research should build on this foundation of the primary need from spreading awareness, where the care givers and family members are empowered to use the constitutional rights given to the people with mental retardation. A lot has been talked about their vocation needs but employment is still an issue future researches should emphasis on the available opportunities for people with mental retardation. India is a country where discussion of sexual needs is a taboo but it leads to the abuse of the people with mental retardation. Hence it is an important area which is worthy of future exploration in order to sustain their life with harmony.

REFERENCES

Abidi, J. (1999). Current status of employment of disabled people in Indian industries. Asia Pacific Disability Rehabilitation Journal, 10(2).

Ahuja, N. (2007). *Short Text Book of Psychiatry*. Academic Press.

American Psychological Association. (2015). Diagnostic and Statistical Manual of Mental Disorder, Publication manual of the American Psychological Association (5th ed.). Washington, DC: APA.

Barker, E. T., Greenberg, J. S., Seltzer, M. M., & Almeida, D. M. (2012). Daily Stress and Cortisol Patterns in Parents of Adult Children with a Serious Mental Illness. *Journal of Health Psychology*, *31*(1), 130–134. doi:10.1037/a0025325

Bhat, A.M., Sharma, V. & Jena, S.P. (2013). Managing stress in parents of children with intellectual disability. *Indian Journal of Health and Well-Being, 4*(9), 1790-1793.

Breslau, N., Staruch, K. S., & Mortimer, E. A. (1982). Psychological distress in mothers of disabled children. *American Journal of Diseases of Children, 136*, 682–686.

Brown & Randel., D. (1997). *The Individual with Intellectual Disabilities and Sex Education: Perspectives of Involved Adults*. Presented at the 7th Annual Meeting of the International Society for the Study of Human Subjectivity, Columbia.

Diekema, D. (2003). Involuntary sterilization of persons with mental retardation: Ethical analysis. *Mental Retardation and Developmental Disabilities Research Reviews*, *9*(1), 21–26. doi:10.1002/mrdd.10053

Employment of Persons with Disabilities in Public Sectors in India -Emerging Issues and Trends. (1995). *An Evaluation Study with Special Reference to Persons with Disabilities Act*. Commissioned by Planning Commission, Government of India.

Gold, M. W. (1972). stimulus factors in skill training of retarded adolescents on a complex assembly task: Acquisition, transfer, and relation. *American Journal of Mental Deficiency*, *76*, 517–526.

Green, S., & Bake, B. (2011). Parents emotion expression as a predictor of child's social competence: Children with or without intellectual disability. *Journal of Intellectual Disability Research*, *55*(3), 324–338. doi:10.1111/j.1365-2788.2010.01363.x

Groce, N., Gazizova, D., & Hassiotis, P. (2014). Forced Marriage among Persons with Intellectual Disability. *Journal of Intellectual Disabilities*.

Gupta, V.B., Mehrotra, P. &Mehrotra, N (2012). *Parental Stress in Raising a Child with Disabilities in India*. Academic Press.

Hassall, R., Rose, J., & McDonald, J. (2015). Parenting stress in mothers of children with an intellectual disability: The effects of parental cognitions in relation to child characteristics and family support. *Journal of Intellectual Disabilities*, *49*(6), 405–418. doi:10.1111/j.1365-2788.2005.00673.x

Henny, M. J., Schrojenstein, L. V., & Walsh, P. N. (2008). Managing Health Problems in People with Intellectual Disabilities. *British Medical Journal*, *337*, 1408–1412.

Khare,S. (2015). Impact of quality of life in parents of mentally retarded children: Research findings in a regional centre. *Innovation Journal of Nursing and Healthcare, 1*(3), 171 -178.

Lemay, J. F., Herbert, A. R., Dewey, D. M., & Micheil, A. I. (2003). A rational approach to the child with mental retardation for the paediatrician. *Journal of Paediatrics and Child Health*, *8*(6), 345–356.

Morisse, F., Vandemaele, E., Claes, C., Claes, L., & Vandevelde, S. (2013). Quality of Life in Persons with Intellectual Disabilities and Mental Health Problems: An Explorative Study. *The Scientific World Journal*.

Myers, J.S. (1962). Education and Rehabilitation. *The Journal of Education*, *145*(1), 3-34.

Nambi, S. (2005). Marriage, Mental health and the Indian legislation. *Indian Journal of Psychiatry*, *47*(1), 3–14. doi:10.4103/0019-5545.46067

Narayan, J. & Kurani, D.R. (1990). *Vocational training and employment of persons with mental retardation*. Academic Press.

National Legal Services Authority. (2010). *Legal services to the mentally ill persons and persons with mental disabilities: Scheme Sheet*. Author.

Navas, P., Verdugo, M. A., Gómez, L. E., & Schalock, R. L. (2012). The concept of quality of life and its role in enhancing human rights in the field of intellectual disability. *Journal of Intellectual Disability Research*, *56*(11), 1036–1045. doi:10.1111/j.1365-2788.2012.01585.x

Paransky, O., & Zurawin, R. (2003). Management of menstrual problems and contraception in adolescents with mental retardation: A medical, legal and ethical review with new suggested guidelines. *Journal of Pediatric and Adolescent Gynecology*, *16*(4), 223–235. doi:10.1016/S1083-3188(03)00125-6

Peshawaria, R., Menon D.K., Ganguly, R., Roy, S., RajanPillay, P.R.S., & Gupta, A. (1998). A study offacilitators and inhibitors that affect coping in parents of children with mental retardation in India. *Asia Pacific Disability Rehabilitation Journal, 9*(1).

Peshawaria, R., Menon, D.K., Ganguly, R., Roy, S., Rajan Pillay, P.R.S., Gupta, A., … Ayub, L. (1995). *Understanding Indian Families, having persons with mental retardation*. Academic Press.

Quality of life of young people with an intellect disability in Ireland: Interim Report. (2003). Retrieved from: https:// www.fedvol.ie

Ryckman, D. B., & Henderson, R. S. (1965). The meaning of a retarded child for his parents—A focus for counsellors. *Journal of Mental Retardation.*, *3*(4).

Sexuality and Disability in the Indian Context. (2010). TARSHI.

Sheridan, J., & Scior, K. (2013). Attitudes towards people with intellectual disabilities: A comparison of young people from British South Asian and White British backgrounds. *Research in Developmental Disabilities*, *34*(4), 1240–1247. doi:10.1016/j.ridd.2012.12.017

Singer, G. H. S., Ethridge, B. L., & Aldana, S. I. (2007). Primary and secondary effects of parenting and stress management interventions for parents of children with developmental disabilities: A meta-analysis. *Mental Retardation and Developmental Disabilities Research Reviews*, *13*(4), 357–367. doi:10.1002/mrdd.20175

Singer, G. H. S., Marquis, J., Powers, L. K., Blanchard, L., Divenere, N., Santelli, B., & Sharp, M. et al. (1999). A multi-site evaluation of Parent to Parent programs for parents of children with disabilities. *Journal of Early Intervention*, *22*, 217–229. doi:10.1177/105381519902200305

Siperstein, G. N., KeerthiSugumaran, D., Bardon, J.N., & Parker, R.C. (n.d.). *Attitudes of the Public in India towards People with Intellectual Disabilities*. Retrieved from: https://www.media.specialolympics.org

The Centre for Developmental Disability Health Victoria (CDDH). (2015). *Working with people with intellectual disabilities in healthcare settings: Fact Sheet*. Retrieved from: www.cddh.monash.org

Tracy, J., & McDonald, R. (2015). Health and Disability: Partnerships in Health care. *Journal of Applied Research in Intellectual Disabilities*, *28*(1), 22–32. doi:10.1111/jar.12135

Violence against Disabled Children: A summary report. (2005). UNICEF.

Walker-Hirsch, L. (2007). *The Facts of Life...and More Sexuality and Intimacy for People with Intellectual Disabilities*. Brookes Publishing Co.

World Health Organisation. (2003). *Caring for children and adolescents with mental disorders*. WHO.

World Health Organisation. (2007). International Classification Diseases (10th ed). Geneva: WHO.

World Health Organisation. (2009a). *Mental health aspects of women's reproductive health. A global review of literature*. WHO.

World Health Organisation. (2009b). *Promoting Sexual and Reproductive Health for People with Disabilities*. WHO.

World Health Organization. (2000). Ageing and Intellectual Disabilities - Improving Longevity and Promoting Healthy Ageing: Summative Report. Geneva, Switzerland: WHO.

World Health Organization. (2011). *Rehabilitation. World report on disability*. WHO.

Chapter 12
Intellectual Disability:
An Awareness towards Intervention

Jyoti Mishra Pandey
Former Assistant Professor CIP, Ranchi, India

Preeti Mishra
SMI Medical College and Hospital, India

ABSTRACT

Intellectual Disability is sub-average intellectual ability with impaired adaptive functioning, which starts before the age of 18. They have IQ below. There are many issues which require attention while dealing with ID like human resources, quality training of clinical psychologists in India, the conflicts among the team approach, acceptance in the family and society and many more. There are 1.5 million people with intellectual disability in India. However, experts working in the field of developmental disabilities feel that prevalence is much higher. The population with ID is increasing but the resources to deal with these issues are few. The mental health profession is a multidisciplinary one. The psychiatrist, the clinical psychologist and the psychiatric social worker all have their significant role in the management of ID. There is a long way to go. There are many things that can be offered but what we need is acceptance in our society of such people and Awareness towards Intervention.

INTRODUCTION

Being disabled should not mean being disqualified from having access to every aspect of life. – Emma Thompson

The World Health Organization defines Disability as "an umbrella term, covering impairments, activity limitations, and participation restrictions." Impairment is a problem in body function or structure; activity limitation is a difficulty encountered by an individual in executing a task or action; participation restriction is a problem experienced by an individual in involvement in life situations. Thus disability is a complex phenomenon, reflecting an interaction between features of a person's body and features of the society in which she or he lives. Intellectual disability (ID) means disability in the cognitive capacity of

DOI: 10.4018/978-1-5225-0089-6.ch012

an individual. In simple terms, whatever a mentally normal child can do within a particular frame of time the mentally sub-normal child is either unable to do or will take longer period of time to complete. The learning of particular skill will also depend upon the complexity of the task or on the rate of learning. The delay of learning also depends upon the severity of ID. The parents of developmentally disabled child often wonder about the future of their child, whether they will get a job, whether they will be accepted in the society and family, will they ever be able to live an independent life. These are the few questions which will haunt the society in general and the caregivers in particular and thus awareness towards intervention is imperative to provide a better future for this special population. This chapter will discuss awareness about ID in general with Indian scenario in particular.

Intellectual disability can be defined as impairments of general mental abilities that impact adaptive functioning in three domains. These domains determine how well an individual copes with everyday tasks:

- **The Conceptual Domain:** It includes skills in language, reading, writing, mathematics, reasoning, knowledge, and memory.
- **The Social Domain:** It refers to empathy, social judgment, interpersonal communication skills, the ability to make and retain friendships, and similar capacities.
- **The Practical Domain:** It centers on self-management in areas such as personal care, job responsibilities, money management, recreation, and organizing school and work tasks.

The various levels of severity are defined on the basis of adaptive functioning, and not IQ scores, because it is adaptive functioning that determines the level of supports required. Moreover, IQ measures are less valid in the lower end of the IQ range (DSM V).

It has been estimated that persons with ID comprise from 1% – 3% of populations around the world (WHO, 2001).The total number of disabled people in India are 26 million out of which 1.5 million have ID (Indian Census, 2011). This disability demarcates such people from the normal individuals of the society and because of discrimination and social stigma they face various problems throughout their life. They don't get proper education, they require supervision, they are unable to get a job and are isolated by the peer groups.

In the Medical model for definition of disability, individuals with certain physical, intellectual, psychological and mental impairments are defined as being disabled. According to this, disability lies in the individual as it is equated with restrictions of activity with the burden of adjusting with the environment through medications and rehabilitation. In contrast in the Social model the focus is on the society, which imposes undue restrictions on the behavior of persons with impairment. In this, disability does not lie in individuals, but in the interaction between individuals and the society. The transition from an individual, medical perspective to a structural, social perspective has been described as the shift from a "medical model" to a "social model". (WHO, 2011)

It is indeed unfortunate that the condition of the ID population is poor in India. Though the government has planed various schemes for this special population but majority of the population is unaware about these benefits and special schemes. An important area of concern is that, the benefits which can be availed by the ID population depend upon the level of severity of disability. To qualify for the benefits, the disability should be at least 40%.(The PWD Act of 1995). The question arises: What if the disability is less than 40%? Are they functionally maintaining so well that they are equivalent to normal population? They will face the same discrimination and isolation from society as other population of more than

40% disability faces. Also the people with ID must not be made to go from one office to another just to get a certificate of ID which they very rightfully deserve.

Overall, this population including all categories of intellectual disability requires special attention in all the aspects of their life from the family and society as a whole because their functional level also depends upon how others are responding to their disability. The fact cannot be denied that despite their limited intellectual capacity they have the ability to express their emotions, their needs and expectation from others. Notwithstanding the above facts our society becomes ignorant to them and to their existence. Thus apart from the behavioral management, it is also very important to be aware of other aspects of their life, be it education, parenting, life style, job perspectives and social life. The following paragraphs will throw light on various individuals, institutions and organizations that play significant role in the life of persons with intellectual disability, the obstacles that they are facing and the recommendations which can help improve their overall outcome.

AWARENESS

Awareness for Parents

A child is the most important part in parent's life. When parents come to know about the arrival of a new member in their life they start dreaming about the future and healthy life of the child. However this dream shatters when they become aware about the intellectual disability of the child. Initially there comes the phase of denial when it is very difficult for the parents to accept the bitter truth. They try to ignore the truth and convince themselves that it is not true and this just cannot happen to their children. However with time, they gradually come to terms with the condition of their child being intellectually disabled and then start asking themselves: Why me? Why my child? Then they start blaming themselves for being responsible for their child's mental condition. Slowly they accept the fact. The important part is whether the acceptance is positive or negative? If it is a positive acceptance than it becomes very healthy for the parents to cope with the unpleasant situation. However, if the acceptance is negative then the situation becomes very adverse. Traditional role of greater involvement of mothers in the care of children is universal. Sad part of the story is that fathers hardly play a role and mostly blame mothers for being responsible for the mental condition of their children. It is a fact that in psychiatry and psychology clinics the disabled child is accompanied mostly by mothers only. Everyone can be careless towards the ID child but a mother cannot. Greater maternal involvement has been associated with higher levels of maternal depression and anxiety (Lampert & Friedman, 1992). In a study published in the Journal Infant Behaviour and Development, mothers of developmentally delayed children reported that their infants presented substantial parenting difficulties, but at the same time, self-reports of stress associated with parenting were not different from normative levels (Moran, Pederson, Pettit, & Krupka, 1992). Many times both parents are equally worried and tensed about their child and take it as a joint responsibility. In a study it was seen that parents of children with developmental delays experienced greater levels of stress, and had children with higher maladaptive behaviour than children without delays. Despite differences in reported stress, parents of children with delays were using similar amounts and styles of coping as parents of children without delays (Lopez, Clifford, Minnes, & Kuntz, 2008).

A person with ID requires continuous training and supervision. Parents often lack patience, want immediate and permanent cure. When they fail to achieve the results they lose their patience and because of that they frequently change their doctors. At the end they lose hope. In such cases effective communication, reassurance, proper and planned management becomes very essential as parents are the most important participators in therapy as they hold the most knowledge about their child. They are the one who spend most of their time with the child, much more than a therapist can spend. Parents become the best doctor available for the child. Targeting them for the behavioural management can result in significant improvement in the child. With proper parental counseling the therapist should make them aware that though they can take second or multiple opinions, there is no need to frequently change doctors. Parents must be counseled that though it is not a completely reversible condition there is lot of scope of improvement. Proper awareness training program, psycho-education and parental counseling plays a very important role in management.

It is natural for parents to wonder what the future will hold for their child. Will the child be able to obtain a job and will she/he be able to live independently? In the early years of life, it is often impossible to answer these questions. It is important to remain optimistic about the child's progress, yet realistic when the problems are severe. This is often a difficult balance to achieve. All children, however, continue to learn and as adults they will also continue to develop new skills. Each new learned skill contributes to the growing child's scope for functionality and participation and contribution in society. It is very important to celebrate the child's achievements throughout their life. If the parents have any concerns, they must have authentic institutions/professionals with whom they can feel free to discuss core issues concerning the child's care. Parents often report feeling of loneliness and isolation and have a notion that others will not understand what they are going through. Families often find it very helpful if they find another family having a similarly affected member who are going through, or have been through, similar experiences. Parents report that other parents have been their best source of information and support.

Another important point while counseling of parents is that both the parents should be present in the session. The counselling should first focus on how to make the parents positively accept their child's mental condition. Only then would they work together towards the betterment of the child with optimistic state of mind. Sometimes it so happens that one parent gives up hope. This is the crucial period when the other parent becomes a strong and positive support and makes other more hopeful towards the child. In parenting sessions it is very important to tell the parents to have patience and to emphasize that there would be no dramatic sudden changes. The effort has to be continuous and sustained to see positive results. It is very important to know that parental counseling should not only be restricted to the parents of the affected child. At community level through the help of media, awareness should be spread among all families, even those who do not have affected children at their home. All this to reemphasize those children with ID have equal rights as their own children. They should not be discriminated on any ground and not treated as untouchables. The parents must also fight for their child's right. Parents can be the best doctor for their intellectually disabled child with the support of good professional guidance.

Awareness for Extended Family Members

The term extended family is frequently used to describe a household in which parents and children live with close relatives or with whom the family has regular contact. These individuals may include grandparents, uncles, aunts and cousins. India is a country where large number of people lives together as joint family. They share common rules, cultures and beliefs. The decision of the family related issues are taken together and mainly by the elders in the family and everyone is bound to follow the order or decision. In such families once the news of a child being mentally challenged is disclosed, there is huge emotional outburst. If grandparents and other members of the extended family show positive understanding and offer emotional support may positively impact the struggling mother and father. If grandparents and other members are negatively critical and non-responsive, they may add to the parents' suffering and worsen the already existing challenging situation. This becomes a very big burden on the family. They blame the already depressed parents. The other children of the family ignore the affected child and also avoid playing with them. It is very sad that the parents of the developmentally disabled child are often isolated by their own family members, the reason being social status, stigma and fear of social rejection. In a study it was seen that having a child with an intellectual disability can impose financial, social and physical stress on the family (Mak & Ho, 2007). Research also has shown that caregivers of children with disabilities experience greater stress than caregivers of children without disabilities (Hassall, Rose, & McDonald, 2005). If these initial obstacles are so difficult to overcome then it would be difficult to expect positive growth in the affected child. Thus the role of extended family and their impact becomes an important issue to deal with. It is difficult to expect all the members of the extended family to be there in the therapy sessions. In such cases, the head of the family should come for few sessions with the treating specialist so that she/he is made aware about the child's condition and make the significant and positive changes in the family in favour of ID child. The extended family may perform many parental roles/duties. Cousins may be as close as siblings. Sometimes the proximity of the extended family may create problem for parents. For example, presence of extended family puts pressure on the other members to compare themselves to their relatives. The mother of the child with a disability who is surrounded by sisters, sister-in-law, mother-in-law and cousins whose children do not have disabilities may become upset by the constant reminder of her child being different from others. They sometimes intrude significantly in their personal affairs. Many children with ID live with their grandparents who are their primary caregivers. These grandparents struggle with many of the same issues and challenges as other parents, including, depression, stress and other financial issues.

Proper awareness and training must be imparted to the extended members of the family. An endeavor must be made by the immediate family members to provide support, involvement, creating non discriminative environment and avoiding the feeling that the condition is a social stigma and against their social status. They should understand that this can happen to anyone. They may also provide financial support to the parents in terms of their child's special need and long term support. On the positive note, grandparents and other family members may contribute a great deal to the primary family unit and can increase its overall happiness.

Awareness for Society

Human being is a social animal. Society has particular rules and norms and any deviance from that makes a human different from others and the society labels her/him as abnormal or insane. In this case it becomes very challenging for both the family as well as the ID individuals to live as per their expectations. Families of ID population face various problems in their day to day activities no matter it is social, professional or personal life. No school is ready to take their children for education. Either no or very few number of organizations are there for their training. Even if they exist, teach for very few hours and charge enormous amount of money. The ID children are ignored by their peer groups and often bullied and looked down upon by the so called "normal people". In such situations those children who are towards the higher functioning spectrum of the ID category feel inferior. Even in educated societies social marginalization and exclusion of the ID children's families from social gathering is very common. They think that letting their children play with the ID children will affect their own children adversely. This fear of acceptance in the society puts the families and care takers of ID population under immense pressure and it become a social stigma. Even the siblings of the ID people have difficulty in getting married because of the social stigma attached with being a member of an affected family. Many families sometimes hide the fact that they have ID member in their family. They do not let the child go out from home and often they chain them in the home because of the social pressure. A study in four districts of Gujarat found that people with disabilities were discouraged from attending weddings (UNNATI, 2004). Another study by Mohapatra and Mohanty (2004) in Orissa found that only 27 percent of women with intellectual disabilities leave their homes and 19 percent take part in social activities. Furthermore, only about one-third of women and girls interviewed had ever attended school prior to being admitted to institutions. Such negative attitudes towards women sideline them, preventing them from performing any of their societal roles to their full capacity and send them to social invisibility. If this would continue to be the condition of the developmentally disabled population then the future of this special population definitely looks very gloomy.

Even in today's modern day society, because of the lack of understanding of intellectual disability and many misconceptions associated with such people, especially in rural areas, many people believe that intellectual disabilities are a result of past sins, a curse, or possession by a spirit. Worst part of the story is that many a times even the parents think that they would have done something bad in the past. In India, many parents of affected children come to the doctor as a last resort for their child's treatment. For them the role of the faith healers is more important than the mental health professionals because in India religion plays a very important role and it has a very significant impact on the thinking process of people.(Bathla, Chandna, Bathla & Kaloiya, 2015) Interestingly, many of the faith healers are aware of the illness and retardation but they don't refer the case to the doctors. So, there should be a liaison between the faith healers/religious teachers and mental health professionals. Proper awareness should be given to the faith healers about symptoms and identification of the intellectual disability, so that they refer the cases directly to the professionals. For each proper timely referral they may be paid some remuneration or honorarium.

The society plays a very important role in an individual's life. Social awareness of ID is very essential. This can be done through organisation of plays and making the people, especially the youth of the country aware about ID. Acceptance of ID population as an inseparable part of the society will itself solve a lot many problems and will ease out much pressure from the families of children affected with ID.

Awareness for School Management

School is a primary institution of education. It gives hope and direction to the future of the students and the nation. However, providing education to intellectually disabled population in Indian society becomes difficult where social exclusion, stigma and discrimination of this affected population is very significant. Despite its importance, educational outcomes for children and adults with intellectual disabilities remain very poor. The current methods for getting admissions in schools show a very sad state of affairs. There is cut throat competition even at nursery level. There is a huge struggle among students for percentage. In this race somewhere the ID child is nowhere to be seen and is neglected. Neither can they vouch for higher percentages nor in most cases are the parents rich enough to give donations or huge admission charges. Though as per the government law disabled population have the right to get education in normal schools but no school is ready to take the intellectually disabled child in their schools. The head of such institutions think that having such children will affect other children in a negative manner. This discrimination for education makes the ID child more disabled and more dependent on their family.

Education is recognized as a basic human right. The negligence shown by the schools towards ID children gave rise to the NGO's to start special education program for disabled population. The knowledge and process of educating the disabled children or 'special education' as it is known now, came to India in the last two decades of the 19th century. Special education enables the teachers to focus on the needs of disabled children and these special schools are equipped with the resources that are required as per the needs of the disabled children. However, the major problems of these special schools are that they are very less in numbers in comparison to the intellectually disabled population. In addition to that, the resources such as funding for such organisations and special educators are also very few in numbers.

Another concern for parents is regarding the level of severity of intellectual disability. In the special school, the entire ID category (mild, moderate, severe and profound mental retardation) study and get training together. Often grouping the categories together creates chaos in the training process. The ID children have different abilities and strengths as per the level of severity. The training module for mild ID category should differ from the other ID category and it is also very difficult for the special educators to manage all the categories together. This is a genuine concern of the parents. Every special school should have different sections as per the level of severity and as per the level of learning. Making individual category for all the four levels of severity will result in better outcomes in the overall development of affected children. It will also become easy for special educators to handle them without difficulty and make a specific plan for each category separately.

Discriminating children on the basis of intellectual capability for imparting education is a crime. School is a place where all the race, religion and caste come together under a single roof without any bias or partiality. The school also should not discriminate children on the basis of their intellectual capabilities. Providing place in the school to the special population will give hope to the parents. The responsibility of the intellectually disabled population is not only of their caretakers and the government; it should be taken by all the members of the society specially the schools because education improves self esteem and makes the life of an individual more independent. The school authority should take this as an opportunity to provide education to intellectually disabled population. Another important step contributing in a big way could be by conducting surveys of school going children to identify children with disabilities to ascertain their specific needs and associated co-morbidities and to look for the extent to which these are being addressed.

Managing school on the administration level and making the classroom free from prejudice and discrimination can open new vistas in planning the intellectually disabled children's future.

Awareness for Education

A person with intellectual disabilities faces social stigma, bias and unable to exercise their fundamental human rights. Discrimination against people with intellectual disability is intensely rooted, widespread and creating obstacles in the way of positive change in intellectually disabled population. Without adequate education the intellectually disabled person will not be able to secure meaningful employment. If the person is unaware about this fundamental right of getting education, their life will be dependent on others, social exclusion will be there. All this put together will start the never ending vicious cycle of poverty and will add to the woes of already stigmatised and marginalised section of our society.

Education of children with disabilities has been a part of policy development in India for the past few decades. The Persons with Disabilities Act, 1995 and the Right to Education Act, 2009 have given a new thrust to the education of children with disabilities, as without including those the objectives of universalization of elementary education cannot be achieved. There are various other plans for supporting education for ID population in India. They are as follows

1. Kothari Commission 1964-66,
2. National Policy on Education (NPE) 1986,
3. Centrally Sponsored Scheme of Integrated Education of Disabled Children (IEDC) 1974,
4. Plan of Action (POA) 1992,
5. Rehabilitation Council of India Act (RCI) 1992,
6. Salamanca statement and framework for action 1994,
7. Person with Disability (equal opportunity, production of right and full participation Act) 1995,
8. National Trust Act for the Welfare of persons with autism, cerebral palsy, mental retardation and multiple disability 1999,
9. SarvaShikshaAbhiyaan 2000,
10. Comprehensive action plan for inclusion in education of children 2005,
11. National Policy Persons with Disabilities Act 2006,
12. Right of Children to Free and Compulsory Education Act 2009.

The Government of India's appreciation of the need to integrate children with disabilities came in 1974 when the Union Ministry of Welfare launched the centrally sponsored scheme of Integrated Education of Disabled Children (IEDC). All these acts were made to support education for special population. In 1992 Parliament of India enacted the Rehabilitation Council of India (RCI) Act, subsequently amended in 2000, to establish standardizing courses for the training of 16 categories of professionals required in the field of special education and rehabilitation of persons with disability. Training of special educators and resource teachers that can offer support services to children with disabilities in regular schools is the responsibility of RCI. Even Plan of Action (POA) 1992 postulated that a child with disability who can be educated in a general school should be educated in a general school only and not in a special school. Even those children who are initially admitted to special schools for training in skills should be transferred to general schools once they acquire daily living skills, communication skills and basic academic skills. It provides educational opportunities for the disabled children in common schools, to facilitate their retention in the school system after they acquire the communication and the daily living skills at the functional level (Mondal & Mete, 2013).

There is a false notion in society that intellectually disabled population cannot get education because of their poor intellectual capability. The fact is that based on the level of adaptive functioning in three domains: social, conceptual, and practical skills this population has been divided into four categories (American Psychiatric Association, 2013);

1. Mild ID,
2. Moderate ID,
3. Severe ID,
4. Profound ID.

Children with mild ID have the ability to get primary education. Children falling in the category of moderate ID can be trained in specific tasks like working in grocery stores, ration stores, stationery shops for helping the main shopkeeper, various housekeeping tasks like cleaning rooms, looking after hygiene and sanitation of an institute under someone's supervision. Their services can be utilised at airports and railway stations for helping passengers in loading and unloading of luggage. Children with severe ID can do some work by prompting and supervision. Only children with profound ID need lifelong support and care, however with some behaviour modification training and self help skill training they can learn few things about their day to day activities.

The issue of concern is, are there enough number of institutions at place for providing basic education and training to this group of people in India? The intellectually disabled population are spread all across the country be it rural, semi-urban or urban but the special schools who teach these children are minuscule in number and that too only present in the metros. They charge huge money from the caretakers. It is a very sad state of affairs that only a very limited portion of population of intellectual disabled are fortunate enough to get these educational facilities. It is indeed very difficult to start special schools and vocational training centres for these specially abled children in each and every village and city of India. However all endeavors must be made that such children who require special education and training must be found out and not just left to be looked after by their parents who do not have any idea about what best can be done to improve the condition and functional level of their children. All efforts must be put to give them their fundamental right i.e., the right for education.

The majority of families and care takers of intellectually disabled population don't think that it is important for their children to go to school. To top it up, most belong to very poor socio economic background. They do not have money for even basic needs of food, clothes and shelter. Thus the core issue here is that this special population should not be just left to their families to be supported by. It should be the responsibility of the state or country at large to give them their basic human rights. Thus the government must formulate plans and programs to promote education for this special population. Government has started mid-day meal plan to catch attention of parents to send their children for education. Such policies should also be extended for the intellectually disabled population. Another policy can be integrating the ID children within all schools at each level. Every school has sections for every class. For example, standard one will have various sections like section-A, section-B etc. Adding one more section to particular standard for special children and placing one special educator can do wonders in providing education to majority of special population children. As all the schools have particular syllabus for particular class, the same can be done for ID children. For example, standard one, section-E (ID children group) will follow a particular syllabus that can include basic education, self-help skill training etc. The International Community has become increasingly aware about the various models of special education. The three basic models are segregated, integrated and inclusive special education. Great amount of support is being shown by human rights activists and governments in favour of inclusive special education as the most beneficial type of education for people of all ability levels.

Segregated education is one in which students with disabilities learn completely separate from their peers. Integrated education places students in a mainstream classroom with "some adaptations and resources." Inclusive education is a process involving strengthening the education system to reach out to each learner. It requires restructuring the policies and practices in the schools so that they can attend to and respond to the diversity of students. For an educational instituition to be inclusive, the attitudes of every member in the institute, including administrators, teachers, and other students, should be positive towards students with ID. It implies that all students, regardless of their ability level, are included in mainstream classes. It means that students of all intellectual levels are taught as equals, and teachers adjust their curriculum and teaching methods to benefit all students. Studies show that truly inclusive institutes have less drop-out rates and higher average levels of achievement, compared to institutes that are not inclusive. (The Salamanca Statement and Framework for Action on Special Needs Education, 1994). Governments or organizations who believe in inclusive education believe that every child is capable of learning and has full potential to grow. (National University of Educational Planning and Administration. "Status of Education in Indian National Report." Ministry of Human Resource Development, Government of India, 2012).

Thus awareness among society regarding ID children's right for education can give a lot of hope to the parents. Inclusion of ID children in the mainstream school (with modified curriculum) can make the parents of ID children feel one with the society.

Awareness for Government

The Government of India (GOI) has implemented various rehabilitation programs and schemes for ID population. There are various other government schemes and programs like schemes offered by the national trust and other central government schemes like rail travel concession, income tax concessions etc. These acts and schemes offer equality of opportunity regarding education, employment, freedom, right to property, right to enforce fundamental rights, right to live independently as others in the society and right to justice. The government has also focused on various aspects in terms of trained teachers/ special educators, therapeutic services, special programs, providing learning material and promotion of non-government organizations (NGOs). Though the government has various plans and scheme in favor of intellectually disabled population but hindrances are still there in its full implementation. Majority of the population, guardians and caretakers of disabled person is unaware about the government facilities. The mental health professionals must be aware about the various schemes of the Government so that they can guide the caregivers correctly. The government should take steps to make the society aware about the available services by the use of media like the news papers and television. Among all the resources media is a very powerful resource for spreading awareness among society. Apart from media, special team of social workers specially prepared for the awareness campaigns for the intellectually disabled population can also do wonders to make people aware about the services by home visits and role plays.

The government, despite of various strict laws, is still facing various problems like dumping of patients in the government institutions, unawareness about the resources and government facilities, social discrimination, stigma and abuse of the ID population. Shockingly, various incidents of sexual, emotional and physical abuse in the institutions are reported. It is very depressing that this special population are either ignorant of these abuses or even if they are aware of these assaults they don't know where and to whom to report or complain. Even if they complain these assaults to the police with someone's help, the police will not consider the statement of the victim because of their mental condition. Many a times the institution tries to hide these incidents because the reputation of the institute is at stake. Generally it is said that the home is the safest place for a person but it cannot be denied that most of the times this vulnerable ID population are abused at home by close family members and relatives and cases are never even reported. Even if the child or the abuse victim reports those incidents to the parents, then, she/he tries to hide the incidents because of the fear of social outcast and shame even if the fault is not theirs.

Another important point of concern about ID population is there is a mismatch between demand and supply of special institutions for these children, be it health care, educational support or vocational rehabilitation centers. Even if there are hospitals, they are in very limited numbers and out of them only few provide quality care. Parents of such children have to travel long distances to reach such hospitals, and after reaching the hospital they get only limited personal attention by the doctor in busy clinics. The point is simple: both the quality and quantity of such institutions need to be improved. The endeavor of the government should be to provide care at the doorstep. From each village a volunteer can be chosen who can identify population with intellectual disability and guide the family members on how to proceed about the care of the child, where to go for expert help, how to avail the government facilities. The volunteer can ensure regular follow up of the ID persons at nearest health care centre.

The programs that already exist have various drawbacks, for example: lack of resources, have a very limited staff and absence of monitoring. The parents and caretakers of the disabled population lack information about the disabilities their child has and they do not know about the community services for their assistance. Due to the absence of the accessibility to services, the families and caretakers find it difficult to cope with the demands of the intellectually disabled person. They have no guidelines to follow for their affected child, so they find it easy to admit their child in the hospital or institution for the intellectually disabled or they abandon the patient because they see them as a burden on their family. Facilitating the person with intellectual disability by providing health care services, rehabilitation, equal opportunity, accessible schools, acceptance in the society, independent living services will go a long way in improving their quality of living. There should be strict laws against those who sexually exploit or emotionally and physically abuse those affected with intellectual disability.The policies and schemes for the intellectually disabled population require more attention and awareness among society. The laws should be strictly followed in terms of the protection offered by them to target population.

Awareness for Mental Health Professionals

The role of mental health professionals in the field of intellectual disability is of utmost importance. They are the one who are at the core of the matter. They have authentic scientific knowledge about the mental illnesses and can contribute most by spreading more and more awareness about this much less talked about issue of concern in our society that is Intellectual Disability. As per 2011 Census, there are 26 million people with disabilities in India who constitute 2.7% of the total population. However, experts working in the field of developmental disabilities feel that prevalence of mental disability is much higher (Cavan & Rozatkar, 2013). The population affected is increasing but the resources to deal with these problems are very less.

In India the professionals working in the field of mental health are very few in numbers in comparison to the affected population. There is a huge demand supply mismatch. Perhaps, the reasons could be many like less number of institutions for training, less awareness about the courses running mainly in the area of psychology and psychiatric social work. Graduates and post graduate students are not aware about the possibilities available if they take up mental health as their subject. Thus less awareness can be a major reason for less numbers of clinical psychologists and psychiatric social workers.

Mental health professionals while dealing with the intellectually disabled people and their family members must be very sensitive to their emotions. Involvement of family members in the treatment sessions is very important along with proper therapeutic plan and its implementation. The information that is provided to the parents and care takers should not be vague. If there is no visible improvement in the condition of the child then they should be referred to higher centres for more detailed evaluation and opinion of specialists. There may be associated co morbidities which might require further investigations at higher centres. A very major issue is many professionals only prefer giving medicines and do not believe in behavioural/psychological management. This can hamper the proper management of the patients apart from being unethical.

Under section 19 of the Mental Health Act, family members and friends have the right to admit affected members in mental hospitals. Many a time these laws are misused by the family members just to get rid of from the responsibilities of mentally disabled person. In that case it becomes very important for mental health professionals to take the most appropriate decisions which might influence the management of the patient. While admitting the patients the doctor should make sure that whether the admission is required or not and if yes then make sure about the address they are giving and verify that address and phone number also in case if the doctor suspects that the patient might be dumped by the family members.

The mental health profession is a multidisciplinary one. We should work as a team in the management of intellectual disability. In the field of mental health profession; the psychiatrist, the clinical psychologist and the psychiatric social worker all have their significant role in the management of intellectual disability. Researchers have shown that in dealing with mental illness, medicine and psychotherapy goes hand in hand. For proper management and outcome the role of both medicine and therapy cannot be overemphasised. Apart from the role of clinical psychologist in the behavioural management, the role of psychiatric social worker also takes an important place because they work at the community level. They play a very important role in terms of primary intervention. Awareness training program on the community level, family psycho-education, making the family members aware about the plans and available resources of government and home visits are the activities that does wonders in terms of management and acceptance in the society. All the mental health professionals should work as a team in managing intellectual disability keeping the prejudices aside.

Awareness for Therapeutic Aspect

Managing a case of intellectual disability is a very challenging job and requires lots of patience. A very common issue which the mental health professional face in clinical practice is to answer the questions of the parents and caretakers of the intellectually disabled children. The parents often ask this question that whether their children ever live an independent life? Parents come to experts with lots of hope and expectations. Proper guidance and counseling to the parents and caretakers is very essential. The purpose of the clinical psychologist is first to set realistic goals in front of the parents. The expectations must never be too high and professionals should never put false claims of magical improvement. Parents must be explained that rather than striving for curing the disability our endeavor must be how to make the child more functional. For this the clinical psychologist should convince the parents and caretakers to understand that they themselves are the real doctor of their children and having patience is of prime importance because the improvement of the ID children is very slow. Therefore, while dealing with this special population, the professionals should have proper management plan beforehand. However, the question arises that what should be the first step towards management. Every child has some qualities and strength in them. A clinician should explore those abilities in them and use them as a tool to make them more functional. These strengths and abilities can be assessed by using standard tools or a very good and reliable source of information could be parents and caretakers of the intellectually disabled children. While keeping this in mind we can start with the assessment and management plan for individuals.

There are many behavioural interventions in intellectual disability. In the mental health profession there are multiple levels at which one can intervene. It can be primary, secondary and tertiary intervention.

Talking about primary intervention in the area of intellectual disability, the mental health professionals must identify what are the causes of ID and how can the causes itself be prevented from occurring. The best way would be doing various programs on the community level to prevent ID, for example awareness towards predisposing factors causing intellectual disability like "fetal alcohol syndrome". Alcohol consumption in female is common not only in urban areas but also it is very common in the rural areas. The focus of psycho-education and awareness should be more towards women and their mental & physical health in term of intellectual disability. We must identify other predisposing factors leading to intellectual disability so that we can stop them before its occurrence. Identifying chromosomal anomalies which are associated with mental retardation can be an important step towards primary prevention. Hypothyroidism is an important preventable cause of intellectual disability and all efforts must be made towards early identification of hypothyroidism. Neonatal screening for congenital hypothyroidism can go a long way in preventing intellectual disability in a large number of children, as also food fortification with iodine can help in prevention of acquired hypothyroidism. Secondary intervention means early identification of ID and appropriate intervention because the earlier the identification and intervention the better the prognosis. The other medical specialties should be an integral part of this prevention. As soon as they come across a child with intellectual disability they should refer such patients to the mental health professionals and pediatricians so that they can start early assessment and intervention. Tertiary intervention means intervening at a stage where the focus is not on cure but to make the individual as functional as possible. It is very important to educate the parents that there is no permanent cure in intellectual disability but there is an immense scope of improvement. With proper management they can be made more functional and can also be lead independent life after some vocational training. A therapist can even offer information, advice and support to parents and caretakers of a child with additional support through phone helpline services. So, proper therapeutic module and required changes at appropriate time can make a long term positive effect and result in good prognosis for this special population.

Awareness for Job Perspective

Intellectual disability makes a person disabled in many aspects of life. Throughout their life they are dependent on their family members or care takers for their basic needs. This dependency puts a lot of psychological and economical burden on the family members. Social stigma, no acceptance from schools for education, peer and social neglect and ignorance give rise to depressive symptoms in parents and care takers. Various NGO's are working in this field by making them independent and helping them to earn for themselves. They train them in making candles, cards, bags and many more such objects but very limited population is able to avail this training facility. If the government and private companies take the step to provide jobs for this special population as per their abilities then every disabled individual will be able to earn bread for themselves and not be felt as a burden on family members.

A step by National Institute for the Mentally Handicapped (NIMH) in the Department of Adult Independent Living (DAIL) is working towards improving quality of life of person with intellectual disability through vocational training and placement services. As part of these services, the adult persons with intellectual disability are trained to acquire vocational and independent living skills. Independent living means living like anyone else with same limitations and same opportunities. Persons with intellectual disability also observe the same style of living like other individuals of their society. The ability of Persons with intellectual disability to be productive was linked to social behaviour and practice and bore very little relationship to their intelligence (Cornelius, 2009). The role of Occupational Therapy is significant and cannot be overemphasized. The Comprehensive rehabilitation services based on life cycle approach are required to enhance quality of life of persons with intellectual disability. Adult living skills enables individual to establish her/his identity in the community. Vocational training is offered by nearly 60% of the 736 special schools in the country (Rao, Govinda, Shivakumar, 2003). The training strategies evolved are sheltered workshops, supported employment training; home based training and competitive employment training (Sivakumar & Kumar, 2004). Development and implementation of strategic partnership between occupational therapy and Human Resource (HR) Professionals/ agencies will promote inclusive employment. Trained persons with intellectual disability can perform specific tasks independently. Human resource professionals develop and implement policies. Appropriate understanding by HR professionals about employability of persons with intellectual disability is essential for inclusive employment (Berry & Kymar, 2012). So, a step towards job of the intellectually disabled population can make their future bright and independent and then no disabled person will be a burden on their family and caretakers.

RECOMMENDATIONS

Intellectual disability in a child is of concern for the parents, society and nation. Neglect, discrimination, avoidance, stigma and shame are the few words that have been used for the intellectually disabled person and for their families by the society. A society is so strong and powerful that it can make or break a family. Proper management, free and independent life, education and empowerment, space in the society are the few requirements of the intellectually disabled population. There are few recommendations for all those who are working for the intellectually disabled children and care for them and their families:

- Treat the ID population as a member of the society. They have the same right to live in the society as other normal individual has.
- Reduce the stigma and discrimination in the society against ID.
- Get authentic and detailed information about ID and spread correct knowledge and awareness in society.
- Every ID person is different. They have different abilities and strengths. The plan of management should be as per the abilities of the individuals. An umbrella approach will not work. Proper management chart should be prepared and changes in the process should be done if required in the process of management.
- Improving the condition and the environment of the institutions and NGO's in terms of infrastructure, living conditions, sufficient supply of water, food, clothes and medicine.
- Abuses against ID persons are very common. Ensure proper security at required locations like schools, colleges, institutions, mental health hospitals and places of work. Even places where ID persons are admitted and cared for can have people who take advantage of vulnerability of ID children. Thus special care needs to be taken at such places where emotional, physical and sexual abuses in the institutions may actually be a common thing not being disclosed by the institutions themselves. If any such case is reported, immediate legal step must be taken against the person committing the crime. There should be a confidential complaint box, where the crime can be reported.

- Proper awareness training programs or campaign of schemes and services to not only the affected individual's families and care takers but also to the other members of the society. It will help to spread awareness regarding available government services to all those affected families who are unaware and unable to reach to the available services.
- It is also very important for the mental health professionals to be aware about the available government schemes and services and the related updates. It is a responsibility of all professionals working in the field of mental health to give correct and authentic information to the families and caretakers of the ID individual.
- The government should provide adequate resources and funding to the institutions and NGO's working in the area of ID. To strike a balance of demand and supple, train more doctors, paramedical staff including psychiatrist, clinical psychologist, psychiatric social workers, counsellors and psychiatric nurses for better output.
- There should be help lines established for proper guidelines and detailed information regarding ID and even confidential complains against any misdeed.
- Forced treatment and any kind of violence against ID person should be strongly prohibited and stringent laws must be in place to prevent any crime against ID persons.
- Prohibit discriminative practices and marginalization against ID population and their families in the society. There should not be any discrimination and non-acceptance in the school. The door of education should be open to all the students disregarding caste, race and intellectual capacity. To employ trained teachers who are qualified in special education to facilitate training of special children will go a long way.
- Apart from the work in the sheltered workshops, they should have other job opportunities. Not only the government but all the private companies should provide jobs to the ID population as per their abilities and in which they are vocationally trained.
- The schools for this special population should have separate sections as per the level of ID of the child. This will help in preparing proper management plan as per the level of their intellectual capacity.
- We should remember that there is space for everyone. We just need to find the right space for the right person.

CONCLUSION

To conclude, intellectual disability is an important health issue about which more needs to be spoken about. Persons with ID should be never discriminated on any ground. To create a society free of discrimination there has to be comprehensive shifts in the manner in which our institutions and legal system works, however it is the attitude of the society towards these specially abled children and families which needs to be changed the most. Children with ID are just like others with the only difference that they take more time than the so called "normal" people to complete or do any task. They have same emotions like others. Equal rights for children with ID requires not only provision of legal acts but also requires our society to change their thinking, attitude and perception towards the differently abled population. Awareness should be given to everyone in the society regarding their right for education, right for equality and the right to live a discrimination free life. Ensuring good job perspectives after education and to live their life as per their own wish and comfort should be the aim. There is a long way to go. There are many things that can be offered for individuals with ID in terms of management but what we need is acceptance in our society of people with ID and *Awareness towards Intervention.*

The best way is always through. – Robert Frost

REFERENCES

American Psychiatric Association. (2013). *Diagnostic and statistical manual of mental disorders* (5th ed.). Retrieved from http://www.dsm5.org/Pages/Default.aspx

Berry, B. S., & Kymar, K. R. (2012). Human resource professionals' perception on disability related barriers to employment of persons with intellectual disability. *The Indian Journal of Occupational Therapy*, *44*(2).

Census of India. (2011). *Central Statistics Office Ministry of Statistics & Programme Implementation Government of India*. Retrieved from:http://mospi.nic.in/Mospi_New/site/home.aspx

Chavan, B. S., & Rozatkar, A. S. (2014). Intellectual disability in India: Charity to right based. *Indian Journal of Psychiatry*, *56*(2), 113–116. doi:10.4103/0019-5545.130477 PMID:24891695

Cornelius, D. J. K. (2009). *Vocational Training and Employment for Persons with mental retardation to meet the needs of 21st Century*. Report of the National Seminar - Planning for Comprehensive Rehabilitation of Persons with mental retardation, Chennai, India.

Disabled Persons in India. (2002). *National sample survey 58th round: Ministry of statistics and programme implementation*. New Delhi: Govt. of India.

Hassall, R., Rose, J., & McDonald, J. (2005). Parenting stress in mothers of children with an intellectual disability: The effects of parental cognitions in relation to child characteristics and family support. *Journal of Intellectual Disability Research*, *49*(6), 405–418. doi:10.1111/j.1365-2788.2005.00673.x PMID:15882391

ICD 10. (1992). *Classification of mental and behavioural disorder: Diagnostic criteria for Research*. Author.

Lampert, A., & Friedman, A. (1992). Sex differences in vulnerability and maladjustment as a function of parental investment: An evolutionary approach. *Social Biology*, *39*, 65–81. PMID:1514125

Lopez, V., Clifford, T., Minnes, P., & Kuntz, H. O. (2008). Parental stress and coping in families of children with and without developmental delays. *Journal on Developmental Disabilities*, *14*(2).

Mak, W. S., & Ho, S. M. (2007). Care giving perceptions of Chinese mothers of children with intellectual disability in Hong Kong. *Journal of Applied Research in Intellectual Disabilities*, *20*(2), 145–156. doi:10.1111/j.1468-3148.2006.00309.x

Mohapatra, S., & Mohanty, M. (2004). *Abuse and Activity Limitation: A Study on Domestic Violence Against Disabled Women in Orissa, India*. Retrieved: http://swabhiman.org/userfiles/file/Abuse%20and%20Activity%20Limitation%20Study.pdf,10-11

Mondal, A., & Mete, J. (2013). Education of children with disabilities in India.*Indian. The Journal of Educational Research*, *2*, 56–67.

Moran, G., Pederson, D. R., Pettit, P., & Krupka, A. (1992). Maternal sensitivity and infant-mother attachment in a developmentally delayed sample. *Journal of Infant Behavior and Development*, *15*(4), 427–442. doi:10.1016/0163-6383(92)80011-I

National University of Educational Planning and Administration. (2012). *Status of Education in India National Report*. Department of Higher Education, Ministry of Human Resource Development, Government of India.

Rao, L., Govinda, &Sivakumar, T.C. (2003). Vocational Training of the mentally retarded. *EDUTRACTS, 2*(10).

Sivakumar, T. C., & Kumar, R. (2009). *Selection and Training to develop adult independent living skills in the Indian context across socio cultural and economic levels*. Report of the National Seminar - Planning for Comprehensive Rehabilitation of Persons with mental retardation, Chennai, India.

UNNATI. (2004). *Understanding Disability: Attitude and Behaviour Change for Social Inclusion*. Retrieved from http://www.unnati.org/pdfs/books/research-eng.pdf

WHO. (2011). *World Report on Disability*. Retrieved from: http://www.who.int/whosis/whostat/2011/en/

World Health Organization. (2001). *The World Health Report 2001- Mental Health: New Understanding, New Hope*. Retrieved from http://www.who.int/whr/2001/en/

Chapter 13
Attitude towards People with Intellectual Disabilities (PWID)

Mythili Hazarika
Gauhati Medical College Hospital, India

Sandamita Choudhury
Gujarat Forensic Sciences University, India

ABSTRACT

History on PWID indicates influence of various psycho-social, biological, religious and educational factors for the existence of stereotypical attitudes towards PWID. Across the world until the mid-80's they were a marginalized group of people who were discriminated from others' who considered themselves as "normal". But since the early part of the 21st century significant efforts have been reported across countries in integrating and mainstreaming the PWID in the community at large. To attain this challenging milestone attitude plays a very significant role. Families of PWID undergo high levels of stress and emotional reactions resulting from daily care demands, emotional distress, interpersonal difficulties (family discord), financial hardships as well as social isolation which call for intervention not just for the intellectually disabled but also with the family members. Positive attitude among the health and all professionals with humane qualities such as empathy, genuineness, unconditional positive regard towards the PWID leads to positive expectation and better outcome. Interestingly in developing countries stereotypes are based on ignorance and families find it extremely difficult to disclose the presence of Intellectual Disability (ID) as it is considered to be a 'loss of face'' and is believed to tarnish the family reputation. Hence, families often adopt strategies to hide the existence of a disability, which in turn delays the treatment, and rehabilitation of PWID. Along with parents and family members other stakeholders like siblings and relatives, teachers, educationists, health professionals and general public's attitudes towards them are highly influential factors for their rehabilitation and integration in the mainstream community. Hence, this chapter is an attempt to focus on the importance of attitude that determines the course towards acceptance of PWID. The authors' focus is on the various perceptions towards intellectual disability and the implications of the favorable and unfavorable attitudes towards PWID since the Egyptian era in developed and developing nations. Further, the recommendations provided are for the policymakers and stakeholders to design intervention programs to alter people's attitude towards acceptance and compassion towards PWID. This is believed to help in their rehabilitation, and integration into the society at all levels and thereby reduces the prejudice and discrimination towards them.

DOI: 10.4018/978-1-5225-0089-6.ch013

BACKGROUND

Intellectual disability (ID) is one of the most common disabilities across countries. Braddock and Parish (2002) have defined disability as socially determined interpretation of impairment by others. Therefore the whole concept of ID or how to define or categorize people with ID (PWID) has been always affected by how people in different places, cultures at different periods of time have defined it and perceived it. Rehabilitation of PWID has largely been affected by changing concepts and attitudes. Attitudes are learned pre-dispositions to respond in a favorable or unfavorable manner to a particular person, behavior, event, thing, belief or situation in a direct or discreet manner. According to Charles Osgood, an attitude has three dimensions i.e. Moral (good or bad), potency (strong or weak) and activity (active or passive). These dimensions classify people's attitude towards ID. As relationships with significant others as well society are important determinants for the quality of life of individuals with ID our chapter is focused on attitudes towards them and their various dimensions of life which are significant factors for their adaptation and assimilation in the society.

The authors would focus on attitude towards persons with intellectual disabilities (PWID) worldwide and the review of literature will give an overall insight about this population. The terms mental retardation (MR) and intellectually disabled (ID) is used interchangeably in this chapter.

ATTITUDES TOWARDS PEOPLE WITH INTELLECTUAL DISABILITIES (PWID) IN THE EARLIEST CENTURIES

Egyptian Papyrus of Thebes in 1552 B.C. (Harris 2006) was the first to refer to ID. Attitudes in the earlier times were delimited by religious and spiritual explanations. The ancient Greeks and Romans before 18th century believed children with ID are the cause of curse by god who were allowed to die while some societies in Rome did allow some form of protection to children with ID who were born to the wealthy, by allowing them with right to property and also to have guardians (Beirne-Smith et al. 2006; Harris, 2006). Traditionally, in Indian context mental retardation (MR) or intellectual disabilities (ID) has been referred by Charaka and Susruta in Ayurvedaas as 'manasmandyam' (weak head) caused by genetic, nutritional and environmental factors and is influenced by 'Graha' (planetary influences). In the current scenario the past, present and future are attributed to supernatural powers and there is a strong belief in 'karma'. Hence, disabilities have been considered punishments for sins committed in a previous life by the individual or their family members (Schlossar, 2004). Interestingly before the 18th century, societies differed in conceptualization of intellectual disability. Those with mild ID who were socially competent never received special identification or treatment, and those with more severe conditions received protective care from their families or in monasteries while few societies believed people with more severe ID to be capable of receiving divine revelation (Beirne-Smith et al. 2006; Harris 2006).

Jean-Marc Itard in 1799, first developed systematic and documented program of intervention for ID in France. Seguin elaborated on Itard's methods and formulated a systematic program to educate the "feebleminded" at Salpetrière Hospital in Paris. Henceforth, the stakeholders in Europe worked towards educating PWID which received recognition and subsequently began to spread to other developed and developing countries. In the U.S., and other developed countries there was an initial optimism about rehabilitating, training, and reintegrating PWID into "normal" life. Positive attitudes prevailed and reformers like Dorthea Dix advocated improving treatment of people who were living in asylums, poorhouses, country homes, and almshouses in the mid-1800s. Samuel Howe in 1848 established the first public training facility in the U.S. for PWID and in the same year Hervey Wilbur established in his home the first private institution for PWID (Beirne-Smith et al. 2006) at Massachusetts. There were favorable attitudes during those times towards the PWID as mainstream education was the goal.

However, in the latter half of the 1800s US population became more urbanized and the early optimism about the curability of ID waned. It became highly apparent that people with more severe ID were less able than those without ID to adapt to a developing nation where employment depended on intellectual ability and less so on physical ability in most cases. Furthermore, the ideal of training, rehabilitation, and reintegration of PWID proved to be an illusion as with time it was noticed that people although learned skills but failed to attain "normalcy" as they couldn't pace themselves with the progressive society. Hence, eventually residential institutions were established after the systematic programs were not found to be quite effective. People's attitude towards ID became less favorable and they were called "feebleminded," and were blamed for the poverty, illness, and crime that accompanied urbanization creating a fearful and hostile attitude toward PWID. In those days again the anti-social behaviors and ID, as well as mental or psychiatric illness, tuberculosis, prostitution, and poverty were thought to be heritable. Negative attitudes prevailed to such an extent that great attention was focused on eliminating the possibilities for PWID and others to reproduce so as to control the undesirable heritable traits from passing on to their offspring (Beirne-Smith et al. 2006; Radford 1991; Reilly 1987).

The Eugenics movement started with the publication of the first book on *Hereditary Genius* in 1869 by Sir Francis Galton, a cousin of Charles Darwin, which established a theoretical basis for the heritability of ID (Beirne-Smith et al. 2006). The eugenists rightly concluded that only nature (not characteristics of nurture, like socio-economic status, education, nutrition) determined personality and intellect, so breeding had to be brought under supervision to prevent the degeneration of the human species (Radford 1991; Bachrach 2004). This social myth of heritability and ID was reinforced by the publication of two popular books in 1877 namely The Jukes: A Study in Crime, Pauperism, Disease and Heredity by Richard Louis Dugdale, and The Kallikak Family: A Study in the Heredity of Feeble-Mindedness in 1912 by Henry Goddard. Moreover, Goddard published from his research that many of the immigrants to the US were "*feebleminded*" (Beirne-Smith et al. 2006). Heritability factors in ID dominated the attitude towards them which was not favorable. This led to the belief among the supporters of the eugenics movement that medicine interfered with Darwinian natural selection and kept the weak alive and that people with MR and mental illnesses reproduced faster than intellectual and productive people (Bachrach, 2004).

ATTITUDES TOWARDS PEOPLE WITH INTELLECTUAL DISABILITIES (PWID) IN THE 20TH CENTURY

Following the Eugenics movement of the 19th century, US states like Indiana, Virginia, North Carolina, Georgia, and California enacted sterilization laws (Sofair and Kaldijian 2000). Indiana passed the nation's first sterilization law in 1907 for the "imbeciles" and they have been diagnosed as "unimproveable" (Reilly 1987). Between 1907-1944, more than 42,000 people in US and 22,000 people in 27 states were sterilized in an attempt to eliminate the presumed genetic sources of diseases including ID (Radford, 1991; Sofair and Kaldijian, 2000).In the UK, the Mental Deficiency Act of 1913 emphasized segregation of males and females over sterilization which was active till 1959. Unlike in the U.S., British practitioners preferred to implement educational programs for PWID and used a social definition of mental deficiency as "those individuals who could not fit in to the modern world" (Radford 1991; Reilly 1987). In Germany, compulsory sterilization law was passed during 1933, under which people with "congenital feeblemindedness" which was a very subjective diagnosis could be forcibly sterilized (Bachrach, 2004; Sofair & Kaldijian, 2000).

Further, the most common method of controlling reproduction by PWID was segregation in the U.S., Canada, and Great Britain, through limitations on marriage, immigration controls, sterilization, and, most importantly, custodial institutionalization (Joseph 2005; Radford 1991; Reilly 1987). The reason for the segregation was to protect the so-called "normal" people from the PWID and also to control their reproductive lives. "Custodial institutions were the means by which the feebleminded were removed from a society in which they were perceived as a genetic threat and they were placed in isolated environments, completely segregated by gender" (Radford 1991). Within institutions "feebleminded" men and women were kept strictly apart from each other and lot of them was forcefully sterilized. Medical literature supported sterilization in the 20th century. Unfortunately "euthanasia" of "idiot" children was advocated by some professionals in the US so as to avoid passing on their genes and thereby to reduce the burden on the society (Joseph 2005; Reilly 1987).

ATTITUDES TOWARDS PEOPLE WITH INTELLECTUAL DISABILITIES (PWID) IN THE PRESENT CONTEXT

The 20th century marks the beginning for the search of the cause and cure of PWID in a scientific manner for which the psychological tests were developed leading to early identification of PWID. Tests identified mild intellectually disabled who were otherwise not been given a diagnosis (Beirne-Smith et al., 2006). Although there has been a positive transformation with the development of qualitative methods in social sciences in Britain and in the U.S. but institutionalizing them still continued (Radford, 1991).

Favorable attitudes towards PWID prevailed slowly when heritability as the only cause was refuted in 1928 by Penrose and contemporaries, when they revealed multiple etiologies for ID (Radford 1991). Various non-genetic factors such as metabolic disturbances or PKU (phenylketonuria) and environmental factors, such as infection, trauma, and endocrine disturbance, were recognized as having an association with ID. Though there were mixed reports about genes vs environment on the development of feeblemindedness still social policies reflected deterministic and largely inaccurate hereditarianism views of mental deficiency until after World War II (Radford 1991). Eugenic sterilization in Germany and in the U.S. was opposed by the Catholic churches and the Holocaust discredited eugenics practices (Bachrach 2004; Sofair and Kaldijian 2000; Reilly 1987).

By the early 1960s most state sterilization programs had ended in the developed countries (Reilly 1987).Legal rights, protection and services for PWID revolutionized the attitudes towards them in developed as well as in underdeveloped countries. In 1911, first time New Jersey mandated that education be provided for students with intellectual disabilities (Beirne-Smith et al., 2006).

With the formation of The National Association of Parents and Friends of Mentally Retarded Children in 1950 in US there was the transformation towards tolerance and compassion among the children and families with ID, along with the availability of financial support and formulation of new legislations and community services.

The world has undergone tremendous alterations in attitudes towards PWID in the last four decades with an increased focus on early intervention, community-based rehabilitation (CBR), definition and diagnosis, human rights, and legislation, with particular stress on deinstitutionalization leading to better quality of life and improved choice making (Beadle-Brown et al. 2007). The institutionalized ID population has declined at a significant rate in England, Canada, and Norway, and there is no report of anyone living in an institution in Sweden. Scandinavia was the first country to introduce the concept of "normalization" in 1950s, and suggested access to supports to ID so that they can experience patterns and conditions of everyday life that are as similar to those in the mainstream society (Beirne-Smith et al. 2006). In the US there has been an increase in the trend for individuals with ID to live in inclusive community settings, with appropriate supports to facilitate their experience. Since the 1980s the number of children diagnosed as intellectually disabled has dropped, partly as a result of increased early intervention, and also because of a more cautious professional outlook on definition and diagnosis (Beirne-Smith et al. 2006). The rate of institutions had declined in Australia and Ireland though both countries still have substantial portions of their PWID housed in institutions (Beadle-Brown et al. 2007). Though in Germany, Spain, the Netherlands, Greece, and Belgium deinstitutionalizing was but institutional care continued to dominate. Reports suggests that deinstitutionalization has just begun in countries like France, Poland, Romania, Hungary, and the Czech Republic while many PWID live in poor quality group settings (Beadle-Brown et al. 2007). Argentina continues to institutionalize a large proportion of its people with mental disabilities including ID (MDRI 2007) though mental health care providers are present unlike some developing countries like India where the mental health service providers for PWID in some states are absent.

Interestingly, according to a survey conducted by the World Health Organization's Atlas on 2007 among ID reported that institutional settings still continue to be prevalent in the middle income countries .It is insightful that though education, health, disability, and social welfare were the key governmental sectors involved in programs and policies related to ID, but the availability or the accessibility of such services were more widespread in high income countries with almost 90% reported of having high levels of access compared to only 10% of similar levels of access among low income countries. Special judicial laws for offenders with ID were prevalent in only half of the countries indicating under-development in many of the sectors

Though taxes accounted for the largest source of finances for services of the PWID but only 60% of such services were covered in low income countries compared to 90% in high income countries. Hence, the financial burden incurred for PWID is quite high in the societies of low income countries due to out of pocket expenditure with no favorable returns from PWID.

Across the world there has been a relentless effort for community care of the individuals with ID. Worldwide voluntary disability organizations have been providing community-based supports and services for decade, which are now evolving as 'mainstream disability specialists'. The intrinsic features which make the organizations a vital community resource include: they are naturally person-centered; they have specialist knowledge and skills; they can innovate and adapt to change; and they have forged strong connections both within communities and beyond (National disability survey, 2006). Social inclusion in the community requires active support to establish and maintain connections with family, friends, carers and community members. Successful campaigns carried out in Scotland and New Zealand influenced public attitudes towards PWID which involved a combination of strategies, like information, training and media portrayal (NSW Consumer Advisory Group). While in India and other developing countries the concept of community care needs a very different conceptualization because informal support is the norm and support by untrained non-professionals in non-institutional settings without any responsibility and accountability is apparent. The major program of the United Nations Development Programs (UNDP) is the community–based rehabilitation (CBR).In a very short time CBR has become very popular among the masses in India and integration of the people with ID into the societal mainstream has been the main focus. The goals of CBR would be fulfilled if people with disabilities, their families, and the local community join in this program and work together for realization of the goals (Dalal, 1998) but the efforts would fail if the attitude towards individual with intellectual disability is not favorable.

There has been a "strong awakening of interest in humane treatment of the mentally retarded" (Anastasi, 1982) in the 19th century in developing countries like but the common perception exists that intellectually disabled children are social outcasts, due to the stigmatizing consequences of the process of labeling (Parekh and Jackson, 1997). Throughout the 1990's, the government of India has been developing acts and strategies, amendments and laws to cater to the various needs of the disabled people. Apart from the government, the Non-governmental organizations (NGO) too play a major role in supporting the inclusion of individuals with ID in various educational and occupational institutes. Though they have established orphanages, vocational training programs, parental organizations, half way homes, day care centers etc. to increase awareness and to empower individuals with ID there is still a huge gap between needs and services available for them.

The Multinational Study of Attitudes (2003) conducted in Brazil, China, Egypt, Germany, Ireland, Japan, Nigeria, Russia and USA showed cultural differences in the perception and attitudes toward PWID. Worldwide, the public perceives individuals with intellectual disabilities as more capable of engaging in simple activities such as sustaining friendships and washing and dressing, but less capable of complex activities such as understanding a national news event or handling emergencies. Across these countries, the public notion is that ID should "live with their family." In those countries that do not favor placement with the family, they believe that ID should live either in supervised apartments or independently.

Worldwide (more than 60% in the countries) people believe there are significant obstacles to the inclusion of individuals with intellectual disabilities in society. In particular, the public believes the lack of available supports (e.g., the lack of community services, job training and school resources), the negative attitudes of others and the negative attitudes of the media as major obstacles to inclusion (Siperstein et al., 2005).

In developing countries people perceive disability differently. In some studies they are considered as an object of pity, sympathy, and are isolated or rejected in the family and other social institutions while in others they have been looked as special people in need of love and affection. Interestingly in a few cases families regard their children with ID as "cursed" and a burden that they must deal with, which at times leads to their neglect, abuse and rejection; and often the child is hidden from the community as the family fears social rejection (Girimaji et al. 2001;Census Bureau, 2001). This leads to social isolation for which the community care fails to reach them. Despite advances in public policy and legislation, significant barriers towards people with ID exists while attitudes held by general public as well significant care givers especially parents are often cited as an important component of the "handicapping" environment by various researchers from time to time. The rigid social structure in India makes it extremely difficult to include individuals with ID into various occupations and institutes as they are perceived as fundamentally "flawed" having diminished capabilities, thereby placing them at the bottom of the social structure (Ghai, 2002).

Detection and identification of mild intellectual disabilities is not simply recognized and the benefits too do not reach them easily because unlike individuals who have genetic disabilities, those with mild

ID, is often caused by environmental factors such as malnutrition and under stimulation, and they may have no anomalies in their physical features similarly with individuals with no disability (Reschly, 1996)

In conclusion there is not much change in the perception and acceptance of individuals with ID from earlier to modern times as the stereotypes are based on ignorance and families find it extremely difficult to disclose the presence of disability as they believe disability to be a 'loss of face'' which tarnish the family reputation. Hence, families often adopt strategies to hide the existence of a disability, which could be a source of delay in treatment and rehabilitation services and many times due to lack of knowledge about intellectual disability they do not seek for treatment services as well.

GENERAL PUBLIC ATTITUDE TOWARDS INDIVIDUALS WITH ID

Every individual with or without ID is a part and product of his social environment so one's relationship, attitude and behavior patterns are vitally affected by the nature and extent of the harmony or disharmony of relationship with the family members, relatives, friends, community members, workplace colleagues and employers etc. Tragically enough, the persons with disabilities are comparatively less handicapped by their own disability than by the attitude of the society towards them (Silver, 1957; Shrivastava, 1970).

Moreover, they are not accepted by the society because people's attention is more focused on his/her disabilities rather than on his/her abilities and they are further victimized by the peculiar and irrational prejudice of the society. It has been a well-established fact that the able-bodied people tend to avoid interacting with people with disabilities, because they are uncertain about how to behave in their presence (Yamamoto, 1971; Thompson, 1982). Hence, the common attitudes towards individuals with ID range from curiosity, pity, mild dislike or embarrassment, repugnance, indifference, fear or sympathy.

There has been interesting facts from developing countries where services for ID are lacking. In 2003, Gary N. Siperstein et al. assessed the attitudes of the public in India towards PWID which included questions about perceptions of people with ID, knowledge of Special Olympics (SO) and beliefs about inclusion. Findings indicated that people in urban India were aware of ID as more than 70% had some type of contact with a person with ID like any other countries in the world. Also that people in India interacted with disabled people but majority i.e. more than 54% didn't have any knowledge about SO. United States and Ireland was estimated to have high levels of awareness and involvement with SO but India and all other countries lacked knowledge and were less involved in SO. Indians underestimated the capabilities of the people with ID and viewed them as severely impaired not only in complex independent living skills but also in simple self-help skills. This reinforced the stereotype that exists among the Indian public that individuals with ID as less capable than their non-disabled peers and are categorized as problematic comparable to other children (Ghai, 2002). Whereas in a few studies (Hazarika et al., 2014) it was seen that training in special schools helps in the development of self-help skills and social skills in children with ID like any other children without ID.

The importance of language in disability is very significant and so labeling disabled people with negative terms reflect negatively which is detrimental (Gorden & Rosenblum, 2001). Hence, the language used by general public to describe about disability and impairment affects the way society views them. Inappropriate language prove to be disempowering, humiliating and rude and often terms like victim, abnormal, defective, infirm, invalid, idiot, unsound expresses perceptions of helplessness and dependency on other individuals.

FAMILIES AND PARENTS' ATTITUDE TOWARDS THEIR CHILDREN WITH ID

Some people in the neighborhood hate him. They never let their children to play with my son. Even if he tries to play with them their parents stop them. Others are kind, and tell me these children are blessings from God – Father of a 12 year old boy with intellectual disability in a study (Hamdani et al., 2014).

The attitude towards PWID is mixed but more towards negativity. Every child is special to a parent while some children have special needs and others do not and this determines the parental care and treatment services in the developmental stages of life (Ravindranadan, 2007). No parent would like his or her child to have any deficits in intellectual functioning. Intellectual disability typically reflects a misfit between the capabilities of an individual and the structure and expectations of the environment. All prospective parents look forward to a baby free from flaws, deformity and disability, but the birth of a intellectually disabled child comes as a traumatic experience involving strong negative reactions. Often terms such as " disabled", " impaired" or "abnormal" are interchangeably used for the child which itself profoundly influences the parent's opinions and attitudes towards their own children with intellectual disability. It has been noted that mothers undergo a more intense psychological trauma or emotional state as it involves adjustment of the notion of so called "perfect child" and the "death" of the child of parental expectation.

When a child is diagnosed to have ID the early parental reactions include ambivalence, anger, confusion, denial, self-pity, blame, feelings of helplessness, depression, disappointment, grief, guilt, mourning, rejection, shock, impulses to kill the child and suicidal impulses (McConachie, 1986; Mary, 1990; Ntombela, 1991). Parental reactions vary from experience of a state of shock at the initial disclosure with being unable to register or understand the news and thus withdraw. This is usually followed by a reaction stage, during which sudden emotions of denial, sadness, anger evolves and gradually parents enter an adaptation stage when they start inquiring and asking questions about what could be done for the future and finally enters a stage of reorganization when they would seek help and begin to plan ahead. But during all these stages love and sorrow, guilt, high expressed emotions of hostility, criticality, and over-protectiveness were reported. So the people working with individuals with ID need to know at which stage of adaptation the parents of ID are in for adequate treatment and rehabilitation of the child.

In a study by Hazarika et al., 2015 (in press) it was seen that though the parents of children with ID had love and acceptance towards their children but frustration, disappointment and overprotectiveness were significantly high which were considered to be deterrent factors in their growth and adaptive functioning in the society. Hence, the father of attachment theory (Bowlby, 1988) had rightly mentioned that the greatest loss and negative consequences of an ID child is lack of adequate nurturing relationship with parents. When parents are critical towards the child's immediate environment it negatively hampers the process of development. The way parents' react to a child with special needs partly depends on how they perceive it and the practical implications the disability or illness has on them (Chaturvedi, 1984). This in turn determines their attitude. Findings have been consistent about families experiencing high levels of stress and research has focused on parental dynamics. One view suggests that the presence of a child with special needs causes a crisis in the family. Hence, the environment in which a child is born and brought up has a huge impact on a child's psychological and physical well-being.

One very significant finding suggests that disability increases stress and negative emotions due to the manner by which they are informed of the child's disability that strongly influences initial reactions by parents (McConachie, 1986). Cunningham & Davis argued that parents who were informed 'well' reported feelings of sadness rather than of anger (as cited in McConachie, 1986). If there is a delay in the news about disability and is told in an impersonal manner than they are unlikely to accept the status easily (Ntombela, 1991).Though "there is no good way of letting parents know that their child is mentally handicapped, but there must be ways of not making a bad situation worse" (Hannam, 1975) and this is to be always kept in mind while dealing with children with ID and their parents for comprehensive management.

It has been suggested that negative reactions hampers ones emotionality with more of pessimistic and self -blaming attitude leading to family disharmony. Positive reaction combined with valued support, love, acceptance and contentment with one's own situation increases ones coping efforts. Problem focused coping strategies such as gathering information to deal with the underlying problem, planning, making decisions, resolving conflicts and making realistic goals acts as a booster to the psychological and physical resources during stress. Adverse consequences of stress further deteriorates the child's growth and development. (Gupta & Singhal, 2004)

In a study done by Lakhan & Sharma (2010) among 55,366 people on knowledge, attitudes and practices related to intellectual disability among families in Barwani, India it was found that a large number lacked knowledge and information about ID for which misconceptions and misperceptions were evident. Parents believed that birth of these children has taken place only due to sins of their previous life and not because of poor nutrition, improper delivery, or other birth related problems. This was reinforced by Persha and colleagues study in 2007 where in parents were convinced that their offspring could be cured if they could remove the effects of "God's punishment" by prayers. They paid money to faith healers to conduct worship rituals. However, many of these faith healers used practices like beating, burning on stomach, and not giving food for days in the name of treatment. In some studies the community believed that the intellectual disability is contagious, and can infect other children (Madhavan & Menon, 1988). Another belief was that marriage cures disability so many respondents wanted their disabled children to get married early in life (Peshawaria, 1994)

Grebler (1952) believes that the parent's attitude towards their child impacts greatly on the child's sense of self while Govender (1984) further mentioned the development of positive self-concept in disabled children if they are defined positively by their "significant others" and vice-versa. Thus the role of parents and siblings is of vital importance, especially for the mentally retarded child whose inter-personal experiences are mainly within the family context. Grebler mentioned in his study that the parents are immensely frustrated due to the elements present in the child's condition and external limitations as reported in most studies. Parent's personality determines the level of frustration and anxiety too. Parental reactions are interrelated to the attitude hence, if parents have feeling of guilt then ambivalence is mostly seen towards the child and if they condemn the external world for the child's status then they reject the child, and parents who don't blame anyone for the child's ID accept the child as he or she is. Parental unfavorable attitude cause behavior problems in these children which in turn prevent them from using their limited capacities. According to Ntombela (1991) emotional stress of parents is unavoidable due to the constant physical care, financial demands, restrictions placed lifestyles, the disappointment of having a handicapped child, the guilt feelings arising from their anger and rejection of the child and concerns about his/her. Another common attitude of parents i.e. Hyperpaedophilia,is reported in many studies which is the pathological over-attachment to the child. When this happens the parents love for the handicapped child develops into a grossly exaggerated devotion and over-protectiveness which negatively affects the life and needs of other members of the family as well as for adequate adaptation of the child to the mainstream society.

ATTITUDES OF SIBLINGS AND RELATIVES TOWARDS INDIVIDUALS WITH ID

System theory suggests the importance of sibling sub-system as important determining factor for family homeostasis. Sibling relationships make up a child's first social network and are the basis for his or her interactions with people outside the family (Powell & Ogle, 1985). A child's temperament plays an important role in their response toward a sibling, including one with an ID. Although both positive and negative feelings exist in all sibling relationships, McHale and Gamble (1987) states "for school-age children and young adolescents, these relationships tend to be more positive than negative in their feeling tone. It is an interesting insight that children with disabled siblings appear to have more positive and fewer negative behavioral interactions than in those with non-disabled siblings". The positive aspects include higher levels of empathy and altruism, increased tolerance for differences, increased sense of maturity and responsibility, and pride in the sibling's accomplishments (Powell & Ogle, 1985). The attitudes of siblings are greatly influenced by the attitude of parents so if parental attitudes are positive then positive feelings in siblings follow and this is a very important observation to be aware of while giving psycho-education to parents of ID.

According to Ntombela (1991) siblings experience emotions range from jealousy, shame, guilt, to frustration. And it gets exacerbated by the material deprivation they experience due to the increased financial responsibilities towards the disabled child. Studies report shame leading to social isolation as they feel that they cannot invite their friend's home.

The siblings may feel victimized and feel frustrated due to the parent's restrictions concerning the kind of games and outings in which their disabled child and his/her siblings may be involved, so as to protect the child from social discrimination. The chores and responsibilities assigned to the siblings as a result of parent's involvement with the child with ID are matters of concern.

ATTITUDES OF TEACHERS AND STUDENTS TOWARDS INDIVIDUALS WITH ID

The educational experience of any student is influenced by teachers' attitude so if the attitude is negative then the impact is profound. Children with ID spend most of their time with teachers in schools and vocational institutes so their attitude matters a lot. Studies report mixed messages regarding the teacher's attitude.

Though the legal mandates declare children with ID to be included in the regular classrooms, but they don't ensure their acceptance or fair treatment in schools (Marks, 1997) and some studies also indicates that inclusion can fail to result in positive outcomes in these children (Genesi, 2000; Cook et al, 2000) if social comparison is upward and discrimination persists.

A study conducted by Efron & Efron (1967) revealed that special education class teachers expressed more favorable attitudes to the intellectually disabled than do teachers of ordinary children (Rawlins, 1983). But only a small minority of teachers is in favor of integrating the intellectually disabled-into regular classes (Gotlieb, 1975; Rawlins, 1983). Studies by Scruggs et al., (1996) gives an insight into the social desirability factor indicating that although in the educational fields teachers agreed with inclusive programs for children with ID, but in practice they expressed hesitancy. Intellectually disabled children were the most rejected children in twenty regular classes for their behavior in the classrooms, playground and outside the school environment and they were very seldom chosen as 'a best friend', irrespective of the organizational or integrated settings (Johnson, 1950; Rawlins, 1983). Several studies show that specific Inclusive Education (IE) training courses improve future teachers' attitudes and self-confidence (Glumbic, Kaljaca, & Brojcin, 2004; Stella, Forlin, & Lan, 2007), as well as their abilities and self-awareness regarding abilities of ID thus creating a more positive attitude (Cologon, 2012).

Davis, Tang, Oliver and Wu (2000) found that compared to a sample of Irish children, the Chinese children were more positive towards school integration and were more willing to have social interactions and form social relationships with people who were intellectually disabled.-While in Japan, a study (SO, 2004) among middle school students indicated underestimating the intellectually disabled and even hesitation to interact with them but North American students expressed their willingness to interact and had better perception of the competencies of the intellectually disabled. (Norins-Bardon et al., 2005). While, more than 516 studies stated that more the contact with people with intellectual disability, less was the prejudice. (Pettigrew et al., 2000; Hewstone, 2003) .

Students with higher marks or higher qualifications show better attitudes towards people with disabilities than those with lower marks and qualifications (Sharma, Forlin, Loreman, & Earle, 2006; Forlin et al., 2009).

PEOPLE'S ATTITUDE ABOUT THEIR EDUCATION AND INCLUSION IN THE MAINSTREAM.

Education is the right of every child because it equips him to meet the challenges of life.

Inclusive Education (IE) or Mainstreaming as a type of education ensures the exercising of the right to a complete, and quality education for all, maximizing integration of the society and promoting diversity in knowledge sharing and experience (EADSNE, 2011). According to statistical data, Spain is one of the EU countries with the highest levels of IE. Only 0.4% of Spanish students with special educational needs (SEN) attend specific educational institutions (EADSNE, 2011; Chiner & Cardona, 2012) in contrast to 4% in Belgium, Denmark, Germany or Switzerland.

Some significant milestones in the field of education of the disabled are the Salamanca Statement and Framework for Action on Special Needs Education (UNESCO, 1994); the Declaration of Madrid in 2002; the UN Convention on the Rights of Persons with Disabilities (UN, 2006), which was signed by 147 countries and ratified by 97; and the 48th Session of the International Conference on Education "Inclusive Education: the way of the future" (UNESCO, 2008).

The policies of the government of India towards the education of children with disabilities have been reflected in the enactments, schemes and through institutions established for various relevant activities. According to the NSS 58th round (Jul.–Dec. 2008), 19.68% children with ID were enrolled in grades between 1st-5th, 8.62% were enrolled in grades between 6th-8th. Some of the major policies and legislature framework in India for education of the disabled in order to alter people's mind set and reduce discrimination are the constitutional safeguards provided by the Constitution (86th Amendment) Act 2002 declaring education as a fundamental right of all children in the age group of 6–14 years, adoption of the National Policy on Education (NPE) in 1986 whose objectives include integrating the physically and mentally handicapped with the general community as equal partners, to prepare them for normal growth and to enable them to face life with courage and confidence. Concept of special education, teacher's training to deal with ID, and importance of vocational enrolment was bought up in this policy. Policies like the Integrated Education of Disabled Children (IEDC) which is the centrally sponsored scheme of Integrated Education of the Disabled Children providing educational opportunities for the disabled children in common schools, to facilitate their retention in the school system, and also to place the children in special school to common schools after they acquire the communication and the daily living skills at the functional level. Another policy developed in 1992 is the Plan of Action (POA) which postulates that a child with disability who can be educated in a general school should be educated in a general school only and not in a special school. Even those children who are initially admitted to special schools for training in plus curriculum skills should be transferred to general schools once they acquire daily living skills, communication skills and basic academic skills. The Parliament of India enacted the Rehabilitation Council of India Act (RCI Act –1992) which was subsequently amended in 2000, to establish a statutory mechanism for monitoring and standardizing courses for the training of 16 categories of professionals required in the field of special education and rehabilitation of persons with disability. Persons with Disabilities (Equal Opportunities, Protection of Rights & Full Participation) Act, 1995: The most landmark legislation in the history of special education in India is the Persons with Disabilities (Equal opportunities, protection of rights & full participation) Act, 1995 involved with providing free education up to 15 years, integrating of disabled children with regular children and setting of special school in public and private sector and providing vocational training facilities. It is welcoming to note in the developing country like India that the Sarva Shiksha Abhiyan (SSA) has been operational since 2000-01 in partnership with state governments to achieve the goal of universalization of elementary education. This adopts a ZERO rejection policy and it covers the following components under education for children with disability. They are early detection and identification, functional and formal assessment, education placement, aids and appliances, support services, teacher training, resource support, Individual Educational Plan (IEP), parental training and community mobilization, planning and management, strengthening of special schools, removal of architectural barriers, research, monitoring and evaluation of females with disability.

Across the world the right of every child to education is proclaimed in the Universal Declaration of Human Rights (1948) and was strongly reaffirmed by the World Declaration on Education for All (1990). The UN Standard Rules on the Equalisation of Opportunities for Persons with Disabilities (1993) was an important resolution for improving the educational conditions of persons with disabilities which affirms, 'Those with special educational needs must have access to regular schools which should accommodate them within a child centered pedagogy capable of meeting these needs".

Though the mentioned legal policies and laws with few other policies have been mandatary in developed and developing nations but still there is a growing fear among parents and educationists that the children with ID would create discipline problems and decrease the growth and productivity of fellow students as a result cause hindrance to overall progress of the society. Hence, it is better to put them in separate special schools. This mind-set causes obstacles to the integrated education system. In a study among regular school teachers of Nigeria regarding inclusion of children with ID revealed that 57.4% teachers could not cope with the children with ID because of their learning difficulties. Teachers with higher years of teaching experience were found to be more favorable to exclusion (Tolu.et al, 2014)

Moreover, just bringing a child into a mainstream classroom does not indicate integration if no other supports is in place. There are children who are integrated but very lonely as nobody plays with the child. These may lead to social exclusion, isolation and psychological problems in him/her. There is a lack of community resources like health and transportation, job training programs, lack of special teachers, and special learning aids to provide the supports necessary for their success in the inclusive workplace or schools. Need for social services is high but services are less and inclusion in the work and school environments has been extremely difficult due to the diversity that exists within some countries.

Four variables like general demographics, educational background, teaching experience and perceived competence to teach the disabled affect regular classroom teacher's (RCT) attitude towards mainstreaming. Teacher's cultural background, knowledge regarding intellectual disabilities that have been gained either with one's own personal experience or formal studies seems to be the factor towards building up of positive attitude. Perceived competence i.e. the RCT's perceptions of their ability to meet the academic and social needs of the disabled children, personality characteristics such as openness to experience, empathizing, conscientiousness, intuitive, good power of observation, even tempered and having received in service training appears to have a significant positive impact on attitude towards mainstreaming.

ATTITUDES OF EMPLOYERS TOWARDS INDIVIDUALS WITH ID AND THEIR INCLUSION IN WORK

People with disabilities would be benefitted if they were employed in various skilled and unskilled tasks as it helps in skill development, increase income, decrease social isolation and leads to life satisfaction. But they face many challenges when integrating into the work force. Overcoming co-workers and employers' negative attitudes and perceptions is one such challenge. The employment rate of people with disabilities remains low despite efforts, legislation, and identified benefits of hiring people with disabilities (Stokes, 1990,Geng-qing & Qu, 2003; Ruggeri-Stevens & Goodwin, 2007;).

Despite rules and laws only 44% of intellectually disabled adults are in the labor force, either employed or looking for work, while just 34 percent are actually working, according to a survey by Special Olympics and conducted by Gallup and the University of Massachusetts at Boston. Studies by Rimrnerman, 1998 have shown that the attitudes of employers play a major role in determining the success of employing workers who have been labeled with mild and moderate intellectual disability. Employing such people reduces support and treatment costs of caring for these individuals, and allows them to pay taxes and improve their level of self-confidence and independence. Levy, Jones-Jessop, Rimrnerman & Levy reported that larger companies have been found to be more positive in their attitudes towards hiring persons with disabilities than small companies (in Rimrnerman, 1998, p.246.)

People from the work-force who had prior experience with ID are positive towards their recruitment and less educated corporate executives place less emphasis on the educational accomplishments of persons with disabilities and are more favorable towards hiring them. People with ID who have vocational and social skills, had greater chance of employment while executives in many companies avoid hiring persons whose ID raises concerns about their ability to integrate into thc workplace. But in another study coworkers of people with disabilities mentioned contagious excitement about the job as a positive experience while working with people with disabilities (Ruggeri-Stevens & Goodwin, 2007). It is also possible that public's underestimation is the result of the strongly held stereotype that exists among some people that individuals with ID are less capable than their non-disabled peers (Ghai, 2002).

In the United States, of the 43 million people classified as having disabilities, 56% are employed compared to 88% of people without disabilities (U.S. Census Bureau, 2007). Hence, discrimination against individuals with disabilities appears to continue as a serious problem all over the world. Many intellectually disabled people work in fast food joints, and retail chains such as Walgreens, Best Buy and Safeway have stepped up to hire them. Sheltered workshop is another platform which inculcates high self-esteem and sense of purpose in life, where about 30% of ID work but they face segregation from non-disabled workers in the basic task and outcome they perform. They can legally be paid less than the minimum wage under a 1938 federal law that allows wages to be based on comparing their productivity level with that of a non-disabled worker. But disability rights groups won a victory when President Obama signed an executive order raising the minimum wage to $10.10 an hour for federal contract workers. The order includes several thousand disabled workers at sheltered workshops run by federal contractors. In comparison to other countries surveyed, India is most comparable to South Africa in terms of where they believe individuals with ID should not work but countries like Japan, Ireland and the United States were extremely positive indicating that individuals with ID could work in skilled or unskilled work set-up.

In Columbia, the Rehabilitation Services Administration (RSA) is responsible for empowering individuals with disabilities to "maximize employment, economic self-sufficiency, independence, and inclusion and integration into society". By law, the local RSA would conduct a review and assess to determine eligibility and priority for services. Provision for supported employment, on-the-job training, and other experiences using supports and realistic work settings are also reported to be available and no individual is denied individual services based on disability. Once the local RSA determines that an individual is eligible for Vocational rehabilitation (VR) services, the VR specialist develops an Individual Plan for Employment (IPE). The IPE generally include among other things, the individual's employment goals and means to achieve them. (University Legal services report, Washington, 2010)

Some of the common barriers identified in inclusion of ID to employment are the perception that individual with ID lack the necessary skills to work in a competitive employment, belief that inclusion will have a negative consequence on the environment, such as lower the productivity of other workers and create safety problem for the individual himself and others, and the presence of external obstacles such as lack of services which prevent inclusion from happening and finally, inclusion is hindered by negative attitude harbored by many individuals.

ATTITUDES OF HEALTH PROFESSIONALS TOWARDS INDIVIDUALS WITH ID

Never discourage anyone who continually makes progress, no matter how slow. – Plato

The trend towards deinstitutionalization and the movement towards community rehabilitation programs imply that more physicians are caring for mentally retarded patients in their daily practices. Medical students have positive attitudes towards people with intellectually disabled (Rutledge and Scatt, 1997) .A study on the systematic review on health care professionals and students attitude towards disability in New York indicated that one's experience with a person with disability, ones background with disability influences in becoming more comfortable with a challenging rehabilitation situation. Female health care students and professionals are found to be showing more positive attitude towards patients with disabilities then do their male colleagues (Satchidanand et al., 2009). Attitude of the medical students holds importance as they are the future professionals who would provide their service to the disabled. In a study conducted by Karl et al. (2013) to assess the effects of a clinical experience that involved caring for people with ID indicated favorable attitude among the medical students and they wanted to learn more about this group. A similar study by Khandelwal and Workneh (1986) to understand medical students' perceptions of, and attitudes towards, mental illnesses and ID, before the start of a 6-week psychiatric attachment indicated 92% regarded ID as an illness; 62% regarded it as very serious; 78% stated that they would have some problem in their family life.

Rose (1996) revealed that families are enormously affected by the perception of their health professionals' lack of information, support system and dissatisfaction with the services. In United States, a study by Doornbos (2002) suggested that 85% of the caregivers regarded communication problems with mental health professionals as the most non supportive aspect of a mental health care system, indicating that there lies incongruence between the collaboration and partnership between the two parties increasing iatrogenic burden for families. "Iatrogenic burden" was the term coined by Lefley (1996) to describe the stress felt by families from a system that most of the times reacts to them with indifference. Therefore, it is essential to generate collaboration between the health professionals and the families as often family is regarded as liability for the condition of the intellectually disabled, not that the population is unique and deserves special services themselves.

Mental health professionals clinical training programs should focus more on family coping, adaptation, and competence rather than family pathology (Mohr, Lafuze, & Mohr, 2000).Some of the barriers that prevent one from collaboration with the families include lack of insight about family stress, limited outreach to families, the lack of awareness of the needs of families, and continued exposure to a pathology.

A step was taken by National Association of the Mentally Ill (NAMI), Professional Provider Family Education Course (PPFEC) in United States which is a 10 week course developed for the purposes of educating, encouraging, and helping professional mental health providers to better understand the family's responses to mental illness and involve the family in the delivery of care, Physician's negative attitude towards individuals with ID will have deep detrimental effect on the delivery and outcomes of medical services and may influence the beliefs and attitudes of others who assist in this health care so the issue needs sensitive handling and management.

ATTITUDE TOWARDS SEXUALITY OF INDIVIDUALS WITH ID

The world worries about disabilities more than disabled people do. – Warwick Davis

Sexuality is an innate part of each and every individual. Sexual behavior develops on three levels, biological, social and psychological (McLeod, 2008). Children and young people develop physically, mentally, emotionally and sexually through exploration, observation and processing the information gathered. Sexual development is not only physiological but also changes in sexual knowledge and behaviors.

Sexual needs or rather sexual health often becomes a neglected aspect of people with intellectual disability, although the biological needs that arises among human beings tends to be the same. Individuals with intellectual disabilities are no different in this respect, and express the need and desire to form relationships, engage in sexual contact, and acquire sexual knowledge (Kelly, Crowley, & Hamilton, 2009; Konstantareas & Lunsky, 1997; McCabe, 1999; Siebelink et. al, 2006).

Some of the essential skills in which PWID may require specific educative and/or medical management are in maintenance of hygiene, general gynecological care compliance, sexually transmitted infections (STI), abuse and knowledge about prevention of unwanted pregnancies

An efficacious way of protecting child's sexuality mostly during adolescents involves education in sexuality and gender mainstreaming. This could be provided by parents, teachers and friends. They could be taught in a disabled friendly language about the distinction between proper and improper touch, knowledge about private and public behavior, age appropriate sexual issues and teaching the importance of fulfilling sex life. Studies report that both males and females with ID react differently to the experience of sexual abuse. Findings suggest that females become passive in their later sexual relationships, make poor relational decisions and submit to physical, sexual and emotional abuse easily, while males are unable to understand the act and in turn internalize the action and become aggressive in their own relationship with others (Alplott, 1999; Block, 2000 ; Jobling et al.,2000 ; Griffth et. al., 2000; Trigler & Pfeiffer, 2001). The emotional impact of engaging in sexually inappropriate behaviors and/or being charged can include shame, guilt, fear, rejection, blame, stress, loss of trust and confusion. The physical impact can include bullying, isolation, STIs, pregnancy, a loss of job/home/money/freedom, risk of harm and injury. Inappropriate sexual (ISB) behavior at the earliest stage warrant redirection and depending on the behavior, age and impact to self or others can escalate to a situation whereby professional intervention is required

Education is the mechanism to promote the decision making abilities and empower the individuals with intellectual disability, thus reducing vulnerability and inappropriate sexual expression (Aylott, 2000; Black, 2000; Lumley & Scotti, 2001 ;Nirji,1972; Ward, et al.,2001).Vulnerability to abuse among intellectually disabled can be reduced by adequate social skills training, appropriate judgment skills, and provision of practical knowledge based training in formal sex education programs(Sobsey,1988;Sobsey &Varnhagen, 1988; Watson, 1984). Differentiating appropriate sexual behavior from inappropriate sexual behavior, relation to sexuality and protective behavior to individuals was addressed in a training program in People 1st Program (PIP), a project of Family Planning Western Australia (2009) which had favorable outcome.

ATTITUDE OF THE MEDIA TOWARDS INDIVIDUALS WITH ID

The role of media in promoting prevention, detection and rehabilitation of intellectual disabilities has been grim. There has been a noticeable lack of coordination between media professionals and those working for the disabled. There is a lack of moral responsibility to help in policy formulation and implementation by the media so there are very few media efforts to address disability needs and to promote disability awareness. There is general indifference to the cause of integration of people with disabilities into mainstream society by the media. Many times in various movies individuals with ID are projected with a touch of humor and sympathy which is both unethical and immoral while few of the films have also sought to enhance the sensitivity of society towards the needs, rights, sensibilities and potential of people with disabilities.

Although, there are few television and radio programs which telecast programs to promote assistive devices available for persons with disabilities as well as on integration of children with disabilities in normal schools but the main emphasis on early intervention in the management of disabled children is not often seen as the right target. Since stigma due to negative media coverage impedes the recovery process, triggers discrimination and prejudice, and creates barriers to seeking and finding decent housing, employment, and education, it is essential to make use of appropriate advertisement, share success stories and circulate appropriate facts about the condition to remove the stigma and dogmatization that lies among the population at large to create an aura of positivity and compassion towards PWID.

CONCLUSION

Special children are the god's gift in its purest form, brimmed with innocence, nonjudgmental and generous attitude within them. They are not odd or weird; all they want is to be accepted.

The general approach towards the care and rehabilitation of the individuals with ID reflects the confused state of mind of a person who wants to be emancipated and modern while preserving age-old traditions and cultural values. Though the Government policies, legislative actions, schemes and provisions, programs for the disabled give the impression of commitment to human rights and equal opportunities across countries but the ground reality is quite different in most of the developing countries.

There is not much work done to create awareness about disability in many countries so most people continue to believe that disability is either an irreversible medical condition or an act of fate. And in both the cases the onus of care rests with the family of the disabled and not on the community at large. Though various schemes have been offered for the welfare of this population, due to lack of adequate information among the stakeholders, the PWID, their families and organizations that work for them are either unaware or cannot avail of the provisions therein and many times it is seen that the process of availing the benefits of these schemes are very cumbersome as well as time-consuming.

There are significant myths and misconceptions about disability causing the disabled to be discriminated, isolated and marginalized. The legal definitions in many countries view disability strictly from the medical and/or psychometric perspectives that reinforce a medical model of intervention rather than the much-needed community-based rehabilitation. Very interestingly though the rehabilitation programs have received recognition but they are funded because of their activities rather than achievements and in reality they are not need based but fund driven so are very cost-intensive, lacking in real goal or long-term viability. Hence, these programs become counterproductive to the cause of development of rehabilitation services in the long run.

Overall, it is apparent that the general public of many countries lacks an appreciation of the range of capabilities of individuals with intellectual disabilities, and therefore has low expectations of what they can do. The world still believes that individuals with intellectual disabilities should work and learn in separate settings, apart from people without disabilities. The family is seen as the most appropriate living environment for individuals with intellectual disabilities, a function of both cultural values and availability of services. In thinking about the barriers to inclusion, there is unanimous recognition that the lack of resources and services in the community, employment and school are the major obstacles to inclusion. In addition, the world sees the negative attitudes of others, including the media, as standing in the way of inclusion.

People who perceive individuals with intellectual disabilities as more capable support inclusion in work and school, and believe that the existence of obstacles are not too large and expect few negative outcomes of inclusion.

The direct and indirect efforts made in many jurisdictions needs to be monitored on a continuous basis. These include efforts to ensure the substantive equality of people with disabilities in the field of employment, education, independent living and full societal participation. Hence, more research on this population is essential in all socio-economic levels for planning and program implementation. Also it is essential to translate research evidence into practice to bring about the change.

Recommendation

- Awareness and education programs are needed to educate the public about the capabilities of individuals with ID, and, that there is great variability that exists among people with ID. Further, it needs to be made clear that not all people with ID fall into the moderate to severely disabled category and that most people with ID are not physically distinguishable from their non-disabled peers.
- If education of the ID is to become a reality all over the World then the training of teachers has to become a top priority. The teachers need to be provided with intensive training to work with various disabilities. In-service teachers also need continued training to update their skills and knowledge of inclusive education strategies.
- It is important for the health professionals to focus more in the capabilities instead of the inadequacies in the assessment process in order to promote smooth functioning of the IEP that are to be maintained for the children .Also, ensuring that one's practice, clinic or hospital is open and welcoming to persons with intellectual disabilities, educating oneself and colleagues about the needs of individuals with intellectual disabilities, holding high health expectations for persons with intellectual disabilities and including them as partners in making decisions about their health are some steps towards a progressive mind-set.
- Specific organizations working for specific disability should develop advocacy program to sensitize the community and the administration to the needs of people with disability as a whole and not be involved in one or two specific disabilities only.
- Families and other stakeholders should be provided the necessary insight about their views and their attitudes towards their own children with ID.As families become more knowledgeable about the capabilities of their children with ID, they will begin to expect more from the community and take part in the community rehabilitation programs.
- A strong school and family partnership would ensure good planning taking into consideration of the student's needs and the school division's resources and policies. An effective way to attain that is to introduce self-help group of parents with intellectually disabled child. Thus parents with positive perception can help the other parents in the early stages of adjustment to develop positive and realistic expectation.
- There is a clear need to provide effective, timely, ongoing training for people responsible for the health and wellbeing of PWID. Provision of training to help parents, care givers and disability workers better identify inappropriate sexual behavior at its earliest stage may reduce the escalation, severity and repeated occurrence of behaviors that adversely impact lifestyle and opportunities of the PWID.
- In low income countries, disability is strongly linked to poverty so improving the quality of life of people with disabilities and their families should be the focus of the health care services as this would benefit a large disadvantaged section of the society.
- For the success of community based rehabilitation services, it is crucial that professionals learn from success in the developed countries, as well as from failures so need based programs should be initiated which would be viable in the long run. The activities, mission and vision of any rehabilitation program should be clearly laid down and reviewed from time to time.
- Another strategy for promoting change in attitudes could be programs such as Unified Sports which provide a dynamic model for inclusion in the community by creating the opportunity for

individuals with and without ID to participate in sports side-by-side in an effort to break down existing stereotypes.

- The current societal attitudes towards people with ID partially dictate the importance the government places on the issue. There is a need for legitimization of rights of the ID with acquiring of their basic services protesting against discrimination and injustice and acknowledging their richness and the diversity.
- Role of the media is crucial in changing the myths and superstitions about PWID and giving appropriate knowledge, responsible reporting, information about care, opportunities and rehabilitation of PWID to reduce prejudice and discrimination is the need of the hour

Hindsight: *There is no doubt that the dream for discrimination free and equal education for the people with intellectual disability may require a comprehensive change in the institutional arrangements and legal provisions but the most important change has to come in our mindset, in our thinking and attitude towards the disabled to bring about the larger change.*

REFERENCES

Alderson, E. (2013). *Supporting People with Intellectual Disability to Express Appropriate Sexual Behaviors*. Retrieved from http://www.ndis.gov.au/sites/default/files/documents/5_Supporting_People_with_Intellectual_Disability_to_Express_Appropriate.docx

Arendt, S. W., & Paez, P. (2014). Managers' Attitudes Towards Employees with Disabilities in the Hospitality Industry. *International Journal of Hospitality & Tourism Administration*, *15*(2), 172–190. doi:10.1080/15256480.2014.901065

Bachrach, S. (2004). In the name of public health – Nazi racial hygiene. *The New England Journal of Medicine*, *351*(5), 417–420. doi:10.1056/NEJMp048136 PMID:15282346

Beirne, S. M., Patton, J. R., & Kim, S. H. (2006). *Mental retardation: An introduction to intellectual disabilities*. Upper Saddle River, NJ: Pearson Merrill Prentice Hall.

Block, P. (2000). Sexuality, fertility and danger: Twentieth-century images of women with cognitive disabilities. *Sexuality and Disability*, *18*(4), 239–254. doi:10.1023/A:1005642226413

Bowlby, J. (1988). A secure base: Parent-child attachment and healthy human development. New York: Basic Books. Retrieved from http://www.psychology.sunysb.edu/attachment/online/inge_origins.pdf

Braddock, D., & Parish, S. L. (2002). *An institutional history of disability*. Washington, DC: American Association of Mental Retardation.

Braithwaite, D. O., & Thompson, T. L. (1999). *Handbook of Communication and People With Disabilities: Research and Application*. Retrieved from https://books.google.co.in/books?isbn=1135675805

Brown, B. J., Mansell, J., & Kozma, A. (2007). Deinstitutionalization in intellectual disabilities. *Current Opinion in Psychiatry*, *20*(5), 437–442. doi:10.1097/YCO.0b013e32827b14ab PMID:17762584

Chaturvedi, S. K., & Malhotra, S. (1984). A follow up study of mental retardation focussing parental attitudes. *Indian Journal of Psychiatry*, *26*(4), 370–376.

Chiner, E., & Cardona, M. C. (2012). Inclusive education in Spain: How do skills, resources, and supports affect regular education teachers' perceptions of inclusion? *International Journal of Inclusive Education*, *17*(5), 526-541. Retrieved from10.1080/13603116.2012.689864

Cologon, K. (2012). Confidence in their own ability: Postgraduate early childhood students examining their attitudes towards inclusive education. *International Journal of Inclusive Education*, *16*(11), 1155–1173. doi:10.1080/13603116.2010.548106

Cook, B. G., Tankersley, M., Cook, L., & Landrum, T. (2000). Abstract of Teachers' Attitudes toward their included students with disabilities. *Exceptional Children*, *67*(1), 115–135.

Dalal, A. (1998). CBR in Action - Some Reflections from the Sirathu Project. *Asia Pacific Disability Rehabilitation Journal*, *9*(1), 29–31.

Davis, C., Oliver, C., Tang, C. S., & Wu, A. (2000). Chinese children's attitudes towards mental retardation. *Journal of Developmental and Physical Disabilities*, *12*.

Doornbos, M. M. (2002). Predicting family health in families of young adults with severe mental illness. *Journal of Family Nursing*, *8*(3), 241–263. doi:10.1177/107484070200800306

European Agency for Development in Special Needs Education. (2011). *Mapping the implementation of policy for inclusive education - An exploration of challenges and opportunities for developing indicators*. Retrieved from http://www.european-agency.org/publications/flyers/mipie/MIPIE-summary-of-proposalsEN.pdf/view

Forlin, C., Loreman, T., Sharma, U., & Earle, C. (2009). Demographic differences in changing pre-service teachers' attitudes, sentiments and concerns about inclusive education. *International Journal of Inclusive Education*, *13*(2), 195–209. doi:10.1080/13603110701365356

Frey, G. C., & Temple, V. A. (2008). Health promotions for Latin Americans with intellectual disabilities. *Salud Pública de México*, *2*, 167–177. doi:10.1590/S0036-36342008000800010 PMID:18470345

Genesi, D. (2000). *Disability Discrimination against students in the classroom*. Retrieved from http://www.cedarville.edu/academics/education/classes/edsp202/examples/literature_review_genesi.htm

Geng-qing, C., & Qu, H. (2003). Integrating persons with disabilities into the workforce: A study on employment of people with disabilities in foodservice industry. *International Journal of Hospitality & Tourism Administration*, *4*, 59–83. doi:10.1300/J149v04n04_04

Ghai, A. (2002). Disabled Women: An excluded agenda of Indian feminism. *Hypatia*, *17*(3), 49–66. doi:10.1111/j.1527-2001.2002.tb00941.x

Girimaji, S., Zahman, S., Wijetunja, P. M., Pejarasangharn, U., & Nagpal, J. (2001). *Mental Retardation: From Knowledge to Action*. Retrieved June 24, 2005 from http://whqlibdoc.who.int/searo/2001/SEA_Ment_119.pdf

Glumbic, N., Kaljaca, S., & Brojcin, B. (2004). The attitude of future special educators towards inclusive education of children with mild intellectual disability. *Journal of Intellectual Disability Research*, *48*, 505–505.

Gordon, B. O., & Rosenblum, K. E. (2001). Bringing Disability into the Sociological Frame: A comparison of disability with race, sex, and sexual orientation statuses. *Disability & Society*, *16*(1), 23–44.

Govender, N., (2002). *Attitudes of Parents towards their Mentally Retarded Children: A Rural area Examination*. Academic Press.

Grebler, A. M. (1952). Parental attitudes towards mentally retarded children. *American Journal of Mental Deficiency*, *56*, 475–483. PMID:14902885

Gupta, A., & Singhal, N. (2004). Positive Perceptions in Parents of Children with Disabilities. *Asia Pacific Disability Rehabilitation Journal*, *15*(1). Retrieved from http://english.aifo.it/disability/apdrj/apdrj104/positive-perceptions.pdf

Hamdani, S., Atif, N., Tariq, M., Minhas, F., Iqbal, Z., & Rahman, A. (2014). Family networks to improve outcomes in children with intellectual and developmental disorders: a qualitative study. *International Journal of Mental Health Systems*. doi:10.1186/1752-4458-8-7

Hannam, C. (1975). *Parents and Mentally Handicapped Children*. London: Penguin.

Harbour, C. K., & Maulik, P. K. (2010) History of Intellectual Disability. *International Encyclopedia of Rehabilitation*. Retrieved from http://cirrie.buffalo.edu/encyclopedia/en/article/143/

Harris, J. C. (2006). *Intellectual disability: understanding its development, causes, classification, evaluation and treatment*. New York: Oxford University Press.

Hewstone, M. (2003). Inter-group contact: Panacea for prejudice? *The Psychologist*, *12*(7), 352–355.

International Labour Office. (2003). *Employment of People with Disabilities: The impact of Legislation.* India Country Profile. Retrieved March, 17, 2005 from http://www.ilo.org/publi/english/employment/skills/disability/download/ cpindia.pdf

Jacobson, J. W., Mulick, J. A., & Rojahn, J. (2007). *Handbook of Intellectual and Developmental Disabilities*. doi:10.1007/0-387-32931-5

Jobling, A., Moni, K., & Nolan, A. (2000). Understanding friendship: Young adults with Down syndrome explore relationships. *Journal of Intellectual & Developmental Disability*, *25*, 235–245. doi:10.1080/13269780050144299

Joseph, J. (2005). The 1942 'euthanasia' debate in the American Journal of Psychiatry. *History of Psychiatry*, *16*(2), 171–179. doi:10.1177/0957154X05047004 PMID:16013119

Karl, R., McGuigan, D., Withiam-Leitch, M. L., Akl, E. A., & Symons, A. B. (2013). Reflective impressions of a precepted clinical experience caring for people with disabilities. *Intellectual and Developmental Disabilities*, *51*(4), 237–245. doi:10.1352/1934-9556-51.4.237 PMID:23909585

Kelly, G., Crowley, H., & Hamilton, C. (2009). Rights, sexuality, and relationships in Ireland: "It'd be nice to be kind of trusted. *British Journal of Learning Disabilities*, *37*(4), 308–315. doi:10.1111/j.1468-3156.2009.00587.x

Kelly, G., & Parry, A. (2008). Managing Challenging Behaviour of People with Acquired Brain Injury in Community Settings: The first 7 years of specialist clinical service. *Brain Impairment*, *9*(3), 293–304. doi:10.1375/brim.9.3.293

Khandelwal, S. K., & Workneh, F. (1986). Perception of mental illness by medical students Indian. *Journal of Psychological Medicine*, *9*, 26–32.

Konstantareas, M. M., & Lunsky, Y. J. (1997). Socio-sexual knowledge, experience, attitudes, and interests of individuals with autistic disorder and developmental delay. *Journal of Autism and Developmental Disorders*, *27*(4), 397–413. doi:10.1023/A:1025805405188 PMID:9261666

Lakhan, R., & Sharma, M., (2010). A study of Knowledge, Attitudes and Practices (KAP) Survey of Families towards their Children with Intellectual Disability in Barwani, India. *Asia Pacific Disability Rehabilitation Journal,* 21.

Madhavan, T., Menon, D. K., & Kalyan, M. (1988). *Mental Retardation: A Manual for Village Rehabilitation Workers*. National Institute for the Mentally Handicapped.

Mary, N. L. (1990). Reactions of black, hispanic, and white mothers to having a child with handicaps. *Mental Retardation*, *28*(1), 1–5. PMID:2308509

McCabe, M. P. (1999). Sexual knowledge, experience, and feelings among people with disability. *Sexuality and Disability*, *17*(2), 157–170. doi:10.1023/A:1021476418440

McConachie, H. (1986). *Parents & Young mentally handicapped children: a review of research issues*. London: Croom Helm.

McHale, S. M., & Gamble, W. C. (1987). Sibling relationships and adjustment of children with disabled brothers and sisters. In F. Fuchs Schachter & R. K. Stine (Eds.), Practical concerns about siblings: Bridging the research-practice gap (pp. 131-158). New York: Haworth Press.

McLeod, S. A. (2008). *Erik Erikson/Psychological Stages*. Retrieved from www.simplypsychology.org/Erik-Erikson.html

Mencap. (2007). *Death by indifference*. Mencap.

Mental Disability Rights International (MDRI). (2007). *Ruined Lives: Segregation from Society in Argentina's Psychiatric Asylums*. Washington, DC: Mental Disability Rights International.

Mondal, A., Mete, J., (2011). *Education of Children with Disabilities in India: Concern and Policy Perspective*. Academic Press.

Morris, J. (2005). *Citizenship and disabled People, Disability Rights Commission*. London: DRC.

Norins-Bardon, Matsumoto, & Siperstein. (2005). *US students attitudes to students with intellectual disabilities at the Global Youth Summit, Nagano, Japan, February 2005*. Available at www.specialolympics.org

Nowicki, E. A. (2006). A cross-sectional multivariate analysis of children's attitudes towards disability. *Journal of Intellectual Disability Research*, *50*(5), 335–348. doi:10.1111/j.1365-2788.2005.00781.x PMID:16629927

Ntombela, T. (1991). *The family of a mentally retarded child* (Vol. I). Social Work Practise.

Persha, A., Arya, S., & Nagar, R. K. et al.. (2007). Biological and Psychological Predictors of Developmental Delay in Persons with Intellectual Disability: Retrospective Case- File Study. *Asia Pacific Disability Rehabilitation Journal*, *18*(1), 93–100.

Peshawaria, R., Menon, D. K., Ganguly, R., Roy, S., Pillay, R.P.R.S., & Gupta, A. (1995). *Understanding the Indian Families Having Persons with Mental Retardation.* NIMH, Secundrabad. Retrieved from http://nimhindia.gov.in/Understanding%20Indian%20Families.pdf

Pettigrew, T. F., & Tropp, L. R. (2000). Reducing prejudice and discrimination. *The Claremont Symposium on Applied Social Psychology.*

Powell, T. H., & Ogle, P. A. (1985). *Brothers & sisters: A special part of exceptional families*. Baltimore, MD: Paul H. Brookes Publishing.

Radford, J. P. (1991). Sterilization versus segregation: Control of the 'feebleminded', 1900-1938. *Social Science & Medicine*, *33*(4), 449–458. doi:10.1016/0277-9536(91)90327-9 PMID:1948159

Ravindranodan, S., & Raju, V. (2007). Attitudes of parents of children with mental retardation. *Journal of the Indian Academy of Applied Psychology*, *1*, 137–141.

Rawlins, R. C. A. (1983). *Attitudes to Mental retardation: a cross cultural study.* (MA Counseling Psychology Thesis). University of Natal.

Reilly, P. R. (1987). Involuntary sterilization in the United States: A surgical solution. *The Quarterly Review of Biology*, *62*(2), 153–170. doi:10.1086/415404 PMID:3299450

Reschly, D. J. (1996). Identification and Assessment of Students with Disabilities. *The Future of Children Special Education for Students with Disabilities*, *6*(1). Retrieved from https://www.princeton.edu/futureofchildren/publications/docs/06_01_02.pdf

Rimmerman, A. (1998). Factors relating to attitudes of Israeli corporate executives towards the employability of persons with intellectual disability. *Journal of Intellectual & Developmental Disability*, *23*(3), 245–254. doi:10.1080/13668259800033731

Ruggeri-Stevens, G., & Goodwin, S. (2007). "Learning to work" in small businesses: Learning and training for young adults with learning disabilities. *Education + Training*, *49*(8/9), 745–755. doi:10.1108/00400910710834139

Rutledge, M. S., & Scott, M. H. (1997). Students' attitudes towards people with mental retardation. *Academic Medicine*, *72*(4).

Satchidanand, N., Gunukula, S. K., Lam, W. Y., McGuigan, D., New, I., Symons, A. B., & Akl, E. A. et al. (2012). Attitudes of healthcare students and professionals toward patients with physical disability: A systematic review. *American Journal of Physical Medicine & Rehabilitation*, *91*(6), 533–545. doi:10.1097/PHM.0b013e3182555ea4 PMID:22596075

Schlossar, S. (2004). *Opening Doors*. Multicultural Disability Advocacy Association of NSW. Retrieved on June. 13.2015 from http://www.mdaa.org.au/publications/ethnicity/indian/IndianOpenDoors.pdf

Scott, M. H., & Rutledge, C. M. (1997). Students' attitudes toward people with mental retardation. *Academic Medicine*, *72*(4), 246–247. doi:10.1097/00001888-199704000-00005 PMID:9125936

Scruggs, T. E., & Mastropieri, M. A. (1996). Teacher perceptions of inclusion/ mainstreaming, 1958-1995: A research synthesis. *Exceptional Children*, *1996*, 59–74. Retrieved from http://ecx.sagepub.com/content/63/1/59

Shrivastava, S. P. (Ed.). (1970). Social Work and the Rehabilitation of the Physically Handicapped. *The Journal of Rehabilitation in Asia*, *11*(1).

Siebelink, E. M., de Jong, M. D. T., Taal, E., & Roelvink, L. (2006). Sexuality and people with intellectual disabilities: Assessment of knowledge, attitudes, experiences, and needs. *Mental Retardation*, *44*(4), 283–294. doi:10.1352/0047-6765(2006)44[283:SAPWID]2.0.CO;2 PMID:16834465

Silver, H. (1957). *The Physically Handicapped*. Social Work Year Book.

Singal, N. (2009). *Education of children with disabilities in India*. Retrieved from http://unesdoc.unesco.org/images/0018/001866/186611e.pdf

Siperstein, G. N., Hardman, M. L., Wappett, M. T., & Clary, L. (2001). *National Evaluation of the Special Olympics Unified Sports Program (Final Report for Special Olympics, Incorporated)*. Boston: University of Massachusetts, Center for Social Development and Education.

Siperstein, G. N., Sugumaran, K., Bardon, J. N., & Parker, R. S. (2001). *Attitudes of the Public in India towards People with Intellectual Disabilities*. Retrieved from www.specialolympics.org/uploadedfiles/.../india_full%20report.pdf

Sofair, A. N., & Kaldijian, L. C. (2000). Eugenic sterilization and a qualified Nazi analogy: The United States and Germany, 1930-1945. *Annals of Internal Medicine*, *132*(4), 312–319. doi:10.7326/0003-4819-132-4-200002150-00010 PMID:10681287

Special Olympics. (2004). *A Study of Youth Attitudes about Intellectual Disabilities*. Retrieved from http://www.specialolympics.org

Special Olympics. (2005). *Multinational Study of Attitudes towards Individuals with Intellectual Disabilities*. Retrieved from www.specialolympics.org/...Studies.../Multinational_Attitudes_Study.asp

Stella, C. S. C., Forlin, C., & Lan, A. M. (2007). The influence of an inclusive education course on attitude change of pre-service secondary teachers in Hong Kong. *Asia-Pacific Journal of Teacher Education*, *35*(2), 161–179. doi:10.1080/13598660701268585

Stokes, S. (1990). Restaurant supervisors: Don't discount the disabled. *The Cornell Hotel and Restaurant Administration Quarterly*, *30*(4), 14–17. doi:10.1177/001088049003000405

Tervo, R. C., Azuma, S., Palmer, G., & Redinius, P. (2002). Medical students' attitudes toward persons with disability: A comparative study. *Archives of Physical Medicine and Rehabilitation*, *83*(11), 1537–1542. doi:10.1053/apmr.2002.34620 PMID:12422321

Tolu, E.A., Temitayo, & Kofoworola, A. (2014). Exclusion of Children with Intellectual Disabilities from Regular Classroom: Nigeria Perspective. *African Journal for the Psychological Study of Social Issues*, *17*, 99-109. Retrieved from http://ajpssi.org/index.php/ajpssi/article/view/94/pdf_65

United Nations Educational, Scientific and Cultural Organization. (1994). *The Salamanca Statement and framework for action on special needs education*. Paris: Author.

United Nations Educational, Scientific and Cultural Organization. (2008a). *Inclusive education: The way of the future. 48th session of the International Conference on Education*. Genova: Author.

United Nations Educational, Scientific and Cultural Organization. (2008b). *Defining an Inclusive Education agenda: Reflection around the 48th session the International Conference on Education*. Retrieved from www.ibe.unesco.org/.../48th.../Defining_Inclusive_Education_Agenda_2

University Legal Services. (2012. *The Work Option for Individuals with Intellectual Disabilities: The Obstacles and the Possibilities*. Retrieved from www.ulsdc.org/Employment%20Report_FINAL.pdf

U.S. Census Bureau. (2007). *American with disabilities act: July 26*. Retrieved February 25, 2008 from the World Wide Web: vikaspedia.in/health/...disabilities/legal-rights-of-the-disabled-in-india

Werner, D. (2006). *Disabled Village Children: A Guide for Community Health Workers, Rehabilitation Workers, and Families*. Berkeley, CA: Hesperian Foundation.

Williams, J. R., & Algozzine, B. (1979). Teachers' Attitudes toward Mainstreaming. *The Elementary School Journal*, *80*(2), 63–67. doi:10.1086/461173

Wilson, A. S. (2007). *Caregiver Attitude of Sexuality of the Intellectually Disabled Population*. Proquest Theses & Dissertation.

World Health Organization. (2007). *Atlas: global resources for persons with intellectual disabilities*. Geneva: World Health Organization. Retrieved from http://www.who.int/mental_health/evidence/atlas_id_2007.pdf

Chapter 14
Psychosocial Interventions for Individuals with Intellectual Disability

Rajesh Sharma
Sunrise Behavioural Health Pty Ltd, Australia

Aditi Lohan
The University of Queensland, Australia

ABSTRACT

In the recent years, there has been an increased interest and focus on improving the quality of life of individuals with disabilities. In the year 2006, the United Nations drafted the Convention on the Rights of the Persons with Disabilities (CRPD) aimed at securing and protecting the human rights of persons with disabilities. As of November 2015, 160 countries have become signatories of this convention and many countries are working towards making legislations consistent with the CRPD to protect the human rights of individuals with disabilities (UN Convention on the Rights of the Persons with Disabilities, 2015). Individuals with intellectual disabilities often face increased challenges in self-care, emotional regulation and decision making due to their cognitive and adaptive skill limitations, which further impacts on their quality of life (Emerson, 2001a). A large proportion of population with intellectual disability display several forms of challenging behaviours including aggressive behaviours, self-harm, stereotypical behaviours and sexual misconducts (Crocker, Mercier, Lachapelle, Brunet, Morin & Roy 2006; Emerson et al., 2001b; Poppes, Putten, & Vlaskamp, 2010). Poppes et al. (2010) found a prevalence of self-harm and stereotypical behaviour in 82% of their participants with Profound Intellectual and Multiple Disabilities (PIMD) and 45% of their study participants displayed aggressive and destructive behaviours. Challenging behaviour appears to be a central theme in intellectual disability and its treatment. This chapter provides a discussion of the principles of Applied Behaviour Analysis (ABA) in prevention and treatment of challenging behaviours as well as improving the adaptive behaviours of individuals with intellectual disability.

DOI: 10.4018/978-1-5225-0089-6.ch014

INTRODUCTION: APPLIED BEHAVIOUR ANALYSIS AND CHALLENGING BEHAVIOURS

Cooper, Heron and Heward (2007) defined ABA as, ''Applied behaviour analysis is a scientific approach for discovering environmental variable that reliably influence socially significant behaviours and for developing a technology of behaviour change that takes practical advantage of those discoveries". In a nutshell, the ABA practitioners are interested in discovering the functional relationships between behaviour and environmental variables rather than searching for causes of challenging behaviours in intra-psychic or other abstract mental concepts such as, mental conflict, ego, unconscious forces, self-concept or self-esteem. Baer, Wolf, and Risley (1968) proposed seven dimensions of ABA i.e. applied, behavioural, analytic, technological, conceptually systematic, effective, and generalization of behaviour change. These seven dimensions are considered as the defining features of ABA. The 'applied' dimension of ABA refers to commitment of the discipline of ABA to improve the socially significant behaviours to enhance the quality of life of people. 'Behavioural' dimension seeks to stay focused on what the individual does rather what he or she thinks or feels. Behaviours are seen as physical or environmental events that can be measured in terms of frequency, duration, latency, and intensity or other physical measurement. 'Analytic' dimension seeks to establish a predictive and functional relationship between independent and dependent variable; presence or absence of independent variable reliably determines the changes in dependent variables. 'Technological' dimension of ABA requires that all interventional procedures are to be identified and described with optimal details to facilitate an easy use or replication of the intervention procedures by readers or other practitioners and get the same or similar results when intervention procedures are implemented with integrity. 'Conceptually systematic' dimension asserts that ABA interventions are not merely a set of tricks; rather the intervention strategies are derived from decades of applied research and behavioural principles. 'Effective' dimension asserts that an intervention is considered effective only when it produces a socially significant behavioural change of practical value. 'Generality' dimension seeks to extend the behavioural change beyond the original treatment setting to other settings, and untargeted related behaviours (Cooper et al., 2007).

In addition to these seven characteristic dimensions of ABA, Wolf (1978) added the eighth dimension of ABA i.e., Social Validity. Wolf (1978) emphasized that the behavioural change outcome must be socially valid / socially valued, and methods of behavioural change must not be viewed as punitive or restrictive but rather viewed as socially acceptable positive strategies of behaviour change by society. These characteristic dimensions are worth emulating for behaviour analysts and other related practitioners of helping professions in their practice to deliver effective treatment for clients (Baer et al., 1968). As evident in the research literature the treatment strategies derived from the ABA have demonstrated effectiveness in reducing the various forms of challenging behaviours in individuals with disabilities (LaVagina & Willis, 2012; Tarbox, Wallace, Tarbox, Landaburu, & William, 2004; Britton, Carr, Kellum, Dozier, & Weil, 2000; Jones, Drew, & Weber, 2000; Fisher, Adelinis, Thompson, Worsdell, & Zarcone 1998; Didden, Duker, & Korzilius, 1997; Hanley, Piazza, & Fisher, 1997; Lalli, Casey, & Kates, 1997; Grace, Thompson, & Fisher 1996; Homer, & Day, 1991; Piazza, Hanley, & Fisher, 1996; Iwata, Pace, Cowdery, & Miltenberger 1994).

FUNCTIONAL BEHAVIOUR ASSESSMENT

Identifying functions of challenging behaviours is a critical component of a sound behavioural intervention. Functional behaviour assessment (FBA) is a systematic approach that identifies the type and sources of reinforcers or reinforcing events maintaining the challenging behaviours. The reinforcers could be positive or negative, automatic, or tangible items. Challenging behaviours often attract more and quicker attention than non-problematic behaviours often in the form of social or positive reinforcement such as smile, attempts to soothe or calm, attempts to distract, advice or suggestion, reprimands, and tangible reinforcers such as access to preferred items. Similarly, many individuals engage in challenging behaviours such as self-harm, aggression, tantrums, non-compliance to delay or escape the non-preferred demands, requests, or activities, these behaviours are understood to have been getting negative reinforcement or social negative reinforcement. All problem behaviours are not necessarily maintained by the positive, negative or tangible reinforcements. Some of the behaviours are maintained simply because those behaviours produce their own reinforcing value or reinforcement. The FBA helps to generate the hypothesis about the functions of challenging behaviours; the hypothesis can be tested using Functional Analysis Methodology (Cooper et al., 2007 pp 501-504). O'Neill, Horner, Albins, Sprague, Storey and Newton (1997) have delineated three stages of functional behaviour assessment, (1) Indirect assessment: includes conducting interviews with family members and caregivers, and gathering information about the problem behaviours using questionnaires, scales, and checklists; (2) Direct Observation: involves observing the client's naturally occurring behaviours in his / her natural environment or context. Usually clinicians use A-B-C event / narrative recording or A-B-C checklists, and scatterplots to assist with direct observations; and (3) Functional / Experimental /Analysis: involves intentionally manipulating the independent variable (such as attention or escape which is hypothesized to maintain or reinforce the problem behaviour) and to examine its reinforcing value or strength on the target challenging behaviour.

Functional behaviour assessment often begins with interviewing client's family members and other caregivers to identify the behaviours of concern and the circumstances under which the client engage in those behaviours such as where, when, with whom, how long, how often. It is equally important to review the files of client's reports such as diagnostic assessment, past treatments including medical and non-medical interventions, school records, behavioural incident reports, and behavioural data. File reviews and interviewing provides broad-based information about the problem behaviours. However, information gleaned may be incomplete and inaccurate or partially accurate (Feenley & Jones, 2006). Many authors have developed rating scales, questionnaires and checklists to identify the functions of behaviours. For example, Motivation Assessment Scale (Durand & Crimmins, 1988), Functional Analysis Screening Tool (Iwata & DeLeon, 1996), Functional Analysis Interview Form (O'Neil, Horner, Albin, Storey, & Sprague, 1990), Problem Behaviour Questionnaire (Lewis, Scott, & Sugai, 1994), Functional Assessment Checklist for Teachers and Staff (March et al, 2002), Functional Assessment Informant Record for Teachers-Preschool version (Dufrene, Doggett, Henington, & Watson, 2007), Questions About Problem Behavioural Function (Matson & Vollmer, 1995). Most of these assessment tools require minimum amount of training to administer them. In Author's knowledge most of these rating scales, questionnaires and checklists are freely available on the internet. These rating scales, questionnaires, and checklists are often useful in identifying the maintaining factors associated with challenging behaviours. However, the responses captured by these rating scales, questionnaires and checklists could be misleading and not revealing the true functions of the problem or target behaviour. Therefore, it is important to include direct observational assessment such as, collecting Antecedent-Behaviour-Consequence (A-B-C) data to gain further understanding of the challenging behaviour (Mayer, Sulzer-Azaroff & Wallace, 2014 p.p. 187-188).

The A-B-C event recording was originally developed by Bijou, Peterson, and Ault (1968). The A-B-C event recording also known as ABC narrative recording is a direct observational method used most often in clinical settings. Observation of client's behaviour is made in his or her natural setting and real-time data is recorded. The A-B-C data recording is completed only when the target behaviour occurs. The data collector or observer uses a form containing five columns i.e. date, time (duration of the behaviour), antecedent, behaviour, and consequences. The observer is required to note down the date of observation, day, time (how long the target behaviour lasted), precisely write down what preceded the target behaviour (antecedent), and what happen immediately after the occurrence of the target behaviour (consequence). Each occurrence of the behaviour of concern (target behaviour) is recorded and analysed in the A-B-C format (Kozlowski & Matson, 2012). Clinicians often modify or adapt the existing A-B-C recording form to capture the target behavioural event to suit their own research or clinical needs. One of authors of this chapter has also developed a data collection tool to meet the clinical needs of his clients, refer to Appendix A & B. ABC Narrative Recording often helps to operationalise the definition of target behaviour and assists in developing hypothesis about the functions of problem behaviour (Lanovaz, Argumedes, Roy, & Duquette, 2013). A-B-C event recording form can also be used for continuous recording of naturally occurring events. A-B-C narrative recording can potentially help identify several antecedent stimuli and their predictive relations to the target problem behaviours as well as commonly occurring consequences to the problem behaviours. Lalli, Browder, Mace and Brown (1993) have identified and coded antecedent stimuli and its behavioural responses and similarly codified the consequences as a part of their descriptive assessment during classroom activities. In A-B-C continuous recording, the natural occurring behaviours are documented for an extended period of time in the A-B-C format irrespective of the occurrence of target problem behaviours. A-B-C continuous recording conducted in natural settings often suggests a predictive relation between antecedent event and the target problem behaviour as well as problem behaviour and its consequences (i.e. escape form demand). A-B-C continuous recording is often time consuming whereas, ABC Narrative Recording is less time consuming because the data is documented only when the target problem behaviour occurs (Cooper et al., 2007 pp. 506-509). It is important for clinicians to exercise caution while interpreting the A-B-C recordings. Thompson and Iwata (2007) noted in their study that descriptive assessment (A-B-C recording) overestimated the attention as a reinforcing or maintaining factor of problem behaviour.

Scatterplots

Scatterplot recording is also one of the descriptive (direct) functional behaviour assessment tools to identify the time segment associated with the presence and absence of problem behaviours. Scatterplot is a data collection sheet containing time intervals ranging from 5 minutes to 30 minutes and these intervals are blocked within and across successive days depending upon the frequency and duration of the target behaviours. Touchette, McDonal and Langer (1985) divided the observation day into a series of 30 minutes time intervals and used designated symbols to mark the low and high frequency of problem behaviour on the scatterplot sheet. Often information gathered from the scatterplot is useful in planning and conducting further A-B-C analysis during the time periods associated with the higher frequency problem behaviours (Cooper et al., 2007 pp 509).

FUNCTIONAL ANALYSIS

Functional Analysis is a standard assessment methodology in ABA. The term 'functional' is frequently used. As Mayer, Sulzer-Azaroff and Wallace (2014) suggest, "Technically the term functional implies the lawful manner in which the rate, form, or other pattern with which the behaviour is repeatedly relates to how the consequences of that behaviour have influenced it previously". Functional analysis enables the clinicians to determine the functional relations between the problematic behaviours and environmental events. Iwata, Dorsey, Slifer, Bauman, and Richman (1994;1982) & Hanley (2012). had initially developed the procedures for conducting functional analysis involving test conditions of Alone, Contingent, Attention and Escape from Demands, to pinpoint the source of reinforcement such as social positive reinforcement (e.g., attention), social negative reinforcement (e.g., escape from demand), and automatic reinforcement (e.g. sensory stimulations) maintaining the challenging behaviour. Hagopian, Wilson and Wilder (2001) determined in their study that their research participant's challenging behaviours such as aggressive, disruptive and self-harming behaviours were maintained by an access to tangible item. Tangible items were not included as test conditions in the studies by Iwata et al. (1994; 1982) standard procedures. A 'Tangible Condition' was later included in the functional analysis designed to test the socially mediated positive reinforcement. Vollmer, Marcus, Ringdahl, & Roane (1995) were among the first few researchers using the standardized tangible condition in their studies. Hanley, Iwata and McCord (2003) noted in their review on functional analysis of problem behaviours that functional analysis procedures are varied and often have been adapted to meet the clinical assessment needs of the clients or contexts. However, most of the functional analyses continue to share the characteristics as pioneered by Iwata et al. (1994; 1982).

Clinicians often choose the relevant test conditions for experimental or functional analysis based on the descriptive assessment results. The functional analysis is conducted either in an analogue condition (resembling the natural setting) or during the naturally occurring events such as, regular ongoing instruction in the classroom (trial based functional analysis). Generally 'Alone' condition examines whether the problematic behaviour is maintained by automatic reinforcement such as self-stimulations. Under this condition, the client is left alone in a room, and observer records the frequency of the target behaviours occurring most often, without having been seen by the clients directly. The purpose of the 'Attention' test condition is to examine whether the problematic behaviour is maintained by the attention. The clinician actively ignores the client's appropriate behaviours to gain attention, by appearing busy in some task and waits for the occurrence of the problematic behaviour, once the target behaviour is displayed, the clinician or experimenter immediately provides contingent attention in the form of reprimand, request or suggestion relevant to the problematic behaviour such as, 'Don't hit yourself', 'You are hurting yourself, it is painful'. The frequency of the target behaviour (self-injurious behaviours) is documented. 'Demand Condition' aims to test whether the problematic behaviour is escape maintained. The client is presented with an age appropriate task of moderate difficulty level depending upon the skills level of the client. If the client engages in the target problem behaviour then the client is allowed to escape or leave the situation briefly for about thirty seconds. The experimenter or clinician notes down the frequency of the occurrence of the target problem behaviour on the data sheet. Finally, the client is placed in the 'Control' condition. The 'Control' (play) condition provides an engaging and enriching environment for the client. The clinician or experimenter does not provide any consequences for engaging in problematic behaviour, however, the experimenter redirects the client and counts the frequency of target problem behaviour.

The client is offered attention at least every thirty seconds. The data from this condition (play) serves as a baseline score for comparison purposes for all test conditions. The test conditions are alternated over a number of days and data is collected using a frequency measure. Each test condition must last at least 10 minutes in length. Data is often plotted on a graph for visual analysis to identify a causal link between the test conditions (such as attention, demand, alone) and the problematic behaviours. Functions of behaviours are determined by the elevation of the frequency of problem behaviour on the graph. For example, if elevated problem behaviour is observed under the 'attention' condition, this suggests that the problematic behaviour is maintained by social positive reinforcement such as attention. Similarly, elevated problematic behaviours under the 'demand' condition indicate that the target behaviour is escape maintained. It is often observed that under control / play condition, problem behaviour may not surface altogether or might occur in low frequencies. It is possible that the problematic behaviour might occur in higher frequencies in more than one test condition such as, 'attention' and 'demand'. However, the functional analysis is considered inconclusive or invalid if the frequency of problem behaviour is higher across all conditions including 'control/ play' condition (Mayer et al., 2014 pp 197; Cooper et al., 2007 pp 504-505; Iwata et al., 1994; 1982)

TREATMENT STRATEGIES

Applied Behaviour Analysis as a discipline has a major contribution in the treatment of challenging behaviours in individuals with intellectual disability (Matson & Coe, 1992). Didden et al. (2007) noted that the treatment based on identified functions of behaviours consists of strategies to modify the motivating operations, modifying antecedents, changing or removing the reinforcing or consequent events, and teaching replacement behaviours; adaptive and functional skills.

Modifying Motivating Operations

Motivating operations (MO) is a term used for establishing operations (EO). Keller and Schoenfeld (1950) introduced the term EO. Jack Michael reintroduced the term in 1982 with its current meaning, i.e. an environment or events that change the value of a stimulus as a reinforcer as well as frequency of behaviour that has been maintained or reinforced by that stimulus (Cooper et al., 2007; Michael, 2000; 1982).

Hagopian et al. (2001) found in their study that the research participant's challenging behaviour was maintained by escape and tangible item. The researchers could ameliorate the challenging behaviour providing the identified tangible item non-contingently frequently, using Non-Contingent Reinforcement procedure (NCR) and teaching the research participant to request for break when needed. The researchers noted a decrease of 96% in the challenging behaviours.

Simó-Pinatella, Font-Roura, Planella-Morató, McGill, Alomar-Kurz, & Giné, (2013) conducted a systematic research literature review of modification of MOs and their impact on challenging behaviours. Their review included 31 published research articles from eight leading behavioural and special education research journals. The research participants (fifty-five) in these selected studies were school children with intellectual disability. Simó-Pinatella et al. (2013) concluded that modification of MO (either increasing or decreasing the value of reinforcers by temporary deprivation or satiation) usually has treatment effect on the challenging behaviours.

Modifying Antecedents

Antecedent based strategies aim to alter or modify the stimuli just before the individual engages in a challenging behaviour (Kern, Choutka & Sokol, 2002). This involves identifying the antecedents of disruptive behaviour through functional behaviour assessment and then working actively to change them prior to a challenging behaviour. Feeley and Jones (2006) outlined 4 antecedent-based strategies: Offering choices; Using high probability requests (with which the individual is more likely to comply) paired with reinforcement, and followed by a low probability request; Collaboration and Using preferred item as a distractor.

Horner et al. (1991) conducted two studies to investigate the effect of high probability requests on aggression and self-injury of participants whose behaviour was maintained by escape/ avoidance. Results from both studies indicated that high probability interspersed requests were effective in reducing aggression and self-injury and increasing participants' responsiveness to instructions.

Changing or Removing the Reinforcing or Consequent Events

Reinforcers and consequences are used in ABA to facilitate the learning of the desired behaviour and decrease undesirable and challenging behaviour. The reinforcing and consequent events can be altered through the use of various differential reinforcement procedures such as, DRO (differential reinforcement of other behaviour), DRA (differential reinforcement of alternative behaviour), and DRI (differential reinforcement of incompatible behaviour) and extinction.

When using DRO, the therapist delivers a reinforcer when the problem behaviour has not occurred during specific times, i.e. reinforcement is contingent on problem behaviour not occurring. In DRA, delivery of reinforcement is contingent on an appropriate alternative to the inappropriate response. The alternative response to be reinforced should be functional for the individual. For example, if the function of engaging in aggressive behaviour for a client is to get attention, s/he can be taught to raise their hand instead by reinforcing that behaviour. DRI is used to deliver reinforcement upon the occurrence of a behaviour that is incompatible with the behaviour selected for reduction (Deitz & Repp, 1983). For example, sitting still and rocking back and forth are incompatible behaviours. The two cannot be performed simultaneously. The desired behaviour is reinforced (sitting still) and not the other behaviour (rocking back and forth).

These differential reinforcement procedures are often used in conjunction with the extinction procedure. Extinction involves withholding reinforcement for a previously reinforced behaviour following the occurrence of challenging behaviour (Lerman & Iwata, 1996). Consistency is very important in the use of extinction. Inconsistent extinction may actually maintain behaviour and make the behaviour resistant to extinction. The appropriate behaviours should also be reinforced consistently. Repp and Karsh (1994) used DRA and extinction in dealing with participants with developmental disabilities using tantrums to get attention. The challenging behaviour decreased substantially post-intervention and the results were maintained at one-year follow-up.

Teaching Replacement Behaviours

Teaching communicative behaviours that replace the disruptive and challenging behaviour is very helpful for individuals with disability as it provides them an avenue to communicate their needs and express themselves in a socially appropriate manner. Functional communication training (FCT) is a replacement strategy, used to teach the individual an appropriate communicative response that serves the same function as the problem behaviour (Carr et al., 1994). For example, for children who run away to escape a task can be taught to raise their hand to excuse themselves from the task. FCT is a specific type of DRA (Fisher, Kuhn, & Thompson, 1998). It has been used extensively with positive outcomes for individuals with disability (Brooks, Todd, Tofflemoyer & Horner, 2003; Carr et al., 1999; Hagopian, Fisher, Sullivan, Acquisto, & LeBlanc, 1998; Derby et al., 1997; Didden, Duker, & Korzilius, 1997; Hall, Neuharth-Pritchet and Belfiore, 1997).

TEACHING FUNCTIONAL SKILLS TO INDIVIDUALS WITH INTELLECTUAL DISABILITY

Functional skills are skills that are vital for an individual to function in society (Lerner, 2003). These include daily living and self-care skills, such as self-hygiene, toileting, reading, cooking, communication skills, academic skills and community participation skills (Mesibov, Shea, & Schopler, 2004). Individuals with disability are often limited in their ability to carry out tasks related to everyday living. Teaching functional skills to individuals with intellectual disability is thus very important to help them increase their ability to live as autonomously as possible.

ABA based strategies such as Imitation, shaping and chaining are often utilized to help individuals with disabilities to acquire new skills and behaviours (Mayer, Sulzer-Azaroff & Wallace, 2014 p.p. 248-294). Similarly, Cooper et al., 2007 (Pp 413) have emphasized the significance of imitative skills to help acquire social and communication skills quickly as well as develop other new behaviours and skills. Some young children with developmental disabilities particularly individuals with autism spectrum disorders fail to acquire the imitative repertoire (Rogers, Hepburn, Stackhouse, Wehner, 2003). Therefore, these individuals need to be taught the imitation skills first. Holth 2003, has provided a detailed behavioural analytic description of the term 'Imitation' that description has been further precisely refined by Cooper et al., 2007 (Pp 413), they have defined imitation as a 'behaviour-environment relations' and physical movement are considered to have predictive value to function as a model for imitation. Model as an antecedent stimulus is capable of evoking imitative behaviours. The model must control the occurrence of the imitative behaviour. The definition has an emphasis on the immediacy of the initiation of behaviour of the organism (the imitative behaviour must be initiated within 3 to 5 seconds following the presentation of model). It is important that the imitative behaviour and the model resemble each other and share the same sense mode i.e. auditory, visual, tactile etc. (Holth, 2003)

Cooper et al., 2007 (Pp 415) have suggested some pre-requisite skills imitation training such as learner's capacity to stay seated and hands in lap, orienting his/ her attention on the model / teacher or object etc. For implementing the imitation skill training, Cooper et al., 2007 (Pp 417), have recommended some guidelines such as an emphasis on active and brief training sessions, reinforcing both prompted and imitative behaviours initially and gradually fading out the prompts and eventually reinforcing only those imitative behaviour occurring within 3 to 5 seconds of the presentation of the model and without prompts. Cooper et al., 2007 (Pp 417) have also suggested to combine verbal praise, attention with tangible reinforcers, as the client makes progress clinician can slowly fade out the edible reinforcers and strengthen the verbal praise and attention. However, if the data does not show continuous progress or displays deterioration in skill acquisition, the clinician may re-consider the prompting hierarchy, ratio and variety of reinforcers or other contextual variables such as difficulty task or other environmental distractions.

Imitation and modelling have their origin in social learning theory (Bandura, 1977), which suggests that people learn through observing other people's behaviour and outcomes of those behaviours. New behaviour can be learnt more rapidly by observational learning than by shaping alone (Bandura, 1969). Attention and motivation are of utmost important for observational learning to take place. Modeling refers to learning that occurs after the observation of the behavior of a model. It is a type of learning that occurs as a result of observing and retaining behavior of others. For learning to take place, observer merely needs to watch the behavior of the model and does not need to engage in overt responses or receive any consequences. Imitation, on the other hand involves learning by copying or replicating the behavior exhibited by the model. For example, imitation can be used to teach children to tie shoelaces by copying exact steps of a model doing the same. This can also be used in conjunction with chaining and reinforcement.

Models are usually individuals that are observed, but they can also be symbolic (presented via TV, books, movies and videos). Video modeling (i.e. demonstration of desired behavior through video) is very popular and has been found to be effective in teaching a range of self-care, social- communication and daily living skills to children with disabilities (Kellems & Edwards, 2015; Allen, Wallace, Renes, Bowen & Burke, 2010; Cihak, Fahrenkrog, Ayres & Smith,2009; Bellini & Akullian, 2007; Delano, 2007; Keen, Brannigan & Cuskelly, 2007; Shipley-Benamou, Lutzker & Taubman, 2002; Wert & Neisworth, 2003).

Shaping is another technique that is used to teach new skills or develop a new behaviours that are not yet present in a person's behavioural repertoire. It is a systematic process of reinforcing successive approximations of target behaviour. Each time an approximate desired behaviour occurs it is reinforced, whereas other behaviours that are not approximations of target behaviour are not reinforced. Responses that resemble the target response or that include components of that response are reinforced (Kazdin, 2012). For example, to teach a child to eat food (target behaviour), any response related to eating such as, sitting on the table, being near the plate, touching food etc. will be reinforced. When using shaping it is very important to define the target behaviour and to know when to deliver and withhold reinforcement (Wolfgang, 2001). Many researchers have used shaping successfully to teach self-help skills to individuals with developmental disabilities (Azrin & Foxx, 1971; Watson, 1968; Bensberg, Colwell & Cassel, 1965).

Chaining procedures can be used to teach functional skills to individuals with intellectual disability. Chaining is a technique used in ABA to teach complex tasks to individuals with a disability by breaking them down into discrete and simple steps. The chain/task is broken down into links/steps, using task analysis. Three types of chaining procedures are used (Cooper et al., 2007): Forward chaining is a chaining procedure in which the teaching progresses from the first task in the chain to the next and so on. The behaviour is taught in its naturally occurring order. Each step in the chain must be mastered before progressing to the next step. For example, to teach a child to wash hands, the task first needs to be broken down into steps (task analysis)-Turn on water, wash hands, put soap on hands, rub palms together, rinse hands, turn off water, take towel, dry hands, and put towel down. The forward chaining of this task will begin with the first step, i.e. turning on water, and move to the next step with the mastery of each step. A backward chaining procedure is the reverse of the forward chaining procedure, in that the teaching process moves from the last step in the chain to the first step. In the washing hands example, the teaching will begin with the last step, i.e. putting towel down and move to the first step, turning on water, after all the steps in between are mastered. Backward chaining is used when the individual can complete most steps at the end of the chain. It provides immediate satisfaction to the learner, and can operate as a natural reinforcer. In total task chaining, the individual is taught entire behaviour chain at each presentation. Unlike forward and backward chaining procedures, total task chaining does not require the learner to master steps before progressing to the next one. Total task training is often used when the learner knows many of the tasks but needs to learn how to do them in sequence. Using the example above, the child will be given prompts and assistance as needed to wash hands in the natural order.

Chaining procedures can also be taught through the use of videos, pictures and computer-based multimedia. Video and computer-based teaching procedures have been found to be effective in teaching self-care (Norman, Collins, & Schuster, 2001;Tiong, Blampied, & Le Grice, 1992), and daily living skills (Kagohara et al., 2013; Graves, Collins, Schuster, & Kleinert, 2005; Mechling, Gast, & Barthold, 2003; Rehfeldt, Dahman, Young, Cherry, & Davis, 2003) to individuals with disability.

PROGRAMS FOR PARENTS AND FAMILIES

Families of individuals with disability play a crucial role in their care and management. Parents and caregivers of individuals with disability often report feelings of stress, anxiety and depression (Blacher, Neece, & Paczkowski, 2005). At the same time, families report less time and opportunity for recreational and leisure activities (Mactavish & Schleien, 2004). Parenting and family factors have been associated with child behaviour and wellbeing in children with intellectual disabilities. For example, better parent psychological and marital adjustment is related to better child functioning (Friedman, Holmbeck, Jandasek, Zukerman, & Abad, 2004), while factors such as lack of parental attention and inactivity have been linked to increased behaviour problems in children (Passey & Feldman, 2004).

In the recent years, many different programs and interventions have been designed to help parents and families in their caregiving roles, thus optimising outcomes for parents, children and families. Mindfulness-based stress reduction (MBSR) training is one such program that has been effectively used with parents and caregivers of individuals with developmental disabilities to reduce parent stress and depression, improve life satisfaction and happiness and decrease behaviour problems in children (Neece, 2014; Singh et al., 2014; Bazzano et al., 2013; Singh et al., 2010; Singh et al., 2007; Singh et al., 2006).

A number of parent training programs have also been developed to help parents deal more effectively with their child behaviour and build positive parent-child relationships. Stepping Stones Triple P (SSTP) is a variant of the Triple P-Positive Parenting Program, designed specifically for parents of children with disabilities (Sanders, Mazzucchelli & Studman, 2003). The program aims to improve the knowledge, skills, and confidence of parents to deal with a range of child behavioural and developmental issues (Sanders, Mazzucchelli & Studman, 2004). SSTP is based on the Triple P model of multi-level intervention, with five different levels of intensity, where parents can choose a level more appropriate to their needs (Sanders et al., 2004). The program has been found to be effective in improving child behaviour, parenting styles, parenting satisfaction and efficacy, parental adjustment, and parental relationships (Roux, Sofronoff, & Sanders, 2013; Tellegen & Sanders, 2013; Sofronoff, Jahnel & Sanders, 2011; Whittingham, Sofronoff, Sheffield & Sanders, 2009; Plant & Sanders, 2007).

The Incredible Years Parent Training Program (IYPT; Webster-Stratton, 2001; 2000) is another popular parent training program designed for typically developing children with behaviour problems. The program includes training parents in use of strategies such as praise, limit setting, and reinforcement to teach acceptable social behaviour and treat challenging behaviours in children (Reid, Webster-Stratton

& Hammond, 2007). McIntyre (2008) adapted the IYTP for parents of children with developmental delays. The intervention consisted of 12-weekly 2.5-hour group sessions, including topics such as, play, praise, rewards, limit setting, and handling challenging behaviour. The researcher concluded that the program was effective in reducing negative parenting and child maladaptive behaviour. Parents also reported high program satisfaction.

Parent-Child Interaction Therapy (PCIT; Eyberg, Boggs & Algina, 1995) has also been used successfully with families of children with disabilities. Like other parent training programs mentioned above, the PCIT also aims to teach skills that parents can use to build a nurturing and positive relationship with their child and deal effectively with their child's behaviour. The therapy involves two phases- Child-Directed Interaction phase and Parent-Directed Interaction phase. In both these phases, therapists provide active coaching to parents to help them master the parent-child interaction skills. The program has demonstrated positive outcomes on parent-child interactions, child behaviour, parenting stress and parent perceptions of child behaviour (Solomon, Ono, Timmer & Goodlin-Jones, 2008; Bagner & Eyberg, 2007).

CONCLUSION

Applied Behaviour Analysis and Intellectual Disability share a long term relationship with each other. The development of the discipline of applied behaviour analysis (ABA) had led to better treatment outcomes and improved quality of life measures for individuals with developmental disabilities (Remington 1998). More than forty years of cumulative applied behaviour analytic peer reviewed scientific research has been constantly refining the behavioural technologies. Today ABA enjoys the reputation of being the most research evidence-based approach in the disability sector particularly for treating the challenging behaviours and improving the quality of life by teaching self-help, communication, pre-vocational, vocational, academic, social skills etc. Positive Behaviour Support approach has become a preferred approach to support people with developmental disabilities such intellectual disability and autism spectrum disorders presenting challenging behaviours (Emerson & Einfeld 2011). However, there is a severe shortage of professionals trained in ABA partly due to a fewer universities offering the undergraduate and post graduate programmes in ABA (Rethink Autism Provides Distance BCBA Supervision…., 2010). Dillengburger (2012) argued for an extensive use of ABA technologies for teaching children with intellectual disabilities both academic and non-academic skills rather than wasting time in developing a newer teaching methodology. Dissemination of knowledge and skills of ABA among helping professionals such as teachers, psychologists, social workers, nurses, and people employed in the disability sector may need to be prioritized over other treatment and teaching methodologies. A systematic supervision by credentialed behaviour analysts can potentially offer better learning opportunities for the supervisees and an assurance of quality behavioural services to the public. It is equally important that more institutions of higher learning such as colleges and universities should offer programmes in behavioural psychology or applied behaviour analysis. It may also be helpful to include courses in ABA in the general education as well as in the special education programmes to prepare well-trained education professionals who would be able to support these students in the least restrictive environments by providing them high quality educational and behavioural services.

Applied Behaviour Analysis is a rapidly growing discipline, and it still needs to catch up with several issues. Remington (1998) noted that almost half of studies published in Journal of Applied Behaviour Analysis (a flagship journal of ABA) were focused on treatment of severe problematic behaviours, aggression, stereotypy, and language / communication. Other important areas of intellectual disability such as self-care/ daily living skills, leisure skills etc remained under represented. Most behaviour analysts or behaviour specialists take a consultative role. Data collection and treatment implementation is generally carried out by others such as teacher aid, disability support staff etc. Most of ABA programme implementers have limited college / university educational experience in ABA. Many concepts and procedures in ABA look deceptively easy without a working knowledge of ABA and work experience. The A-B-C analysis often gets misinterpreted and at times inappropriate behaviours do get reinforced unintentionally by less experienced staff. The treatment outcome most often depends on how well the procedural and treatment integrity were maintained. The success of behavioural interventions often requires a strong commitment from parents, care givers and disability support staff. At times parents/ carers fail in their commitment or drop out of the programme prematurely due to funding issues or other concerns. It is recognized that parenting or caring for an individual with intellectual disability or other developmental disability brings in considerable amount of psychological distress to the family members (Yamaoka, Tamiya, Moriyama, Felipe Alfonso Sandoval Garrido, Sumazaki & Noguchi (2015). Psychological counseling support to the parents / carers of children with developmental disabilities may help parents to stay motivated and resilient. Recently, Positive Parenting Program (Triple P) has gained some popularity and acceptance in Australia. The programme is built around empowering families, carers, and professionals in using evidence-based parenting practices (Triple P is giving.., 2015). It appears that Triple P provides a generic parenting advice and recommendations for parents and carers to follow through whereas applied behaviour analytic approach goes beyond the recommendations to the actual implementation of the intervention strategies based on the rigorous behavioural assessment. In case, Triple P fails (general parenting advice) to deliver the desired results, it is recommended that Applied Behaviour Analytic approach must become a default option for further intervention.

REFERENCES

Allen, K. D., Wallace, D. P., Renes, D., Bowen, S. L., & Burke, R. V. (2010). Use of video modeling to teach vocational skills to adolescents and young adults with autism spectrum disorders. *Education & Treatment of Children*, *33*(3), 339–349. doi:10.1353/etc.0.0101

Azrin, N. H., & Foxx, R. M. (1971). A rapid method of toilet training the institutionalized retarded. *Journal of Applied Behavior Analysis*, *4*(2), 89–99. doi:10.1901/jaba.1971.4-89 PMID:16795291

Baer, D. M., Wolf, M. M., & Risley, T. R. (1968). Some current dimensions of applied behavior analysis. *Journal of Applied Behavior Analysis*, *1*(1), 91–97. doi:10.1901/jaba.1968.1-91 PMID:16795165

Bagner, D. M., & Eyberg, S. M. (2007). Parent–child interaction therapy for disruptive behavior in children with mental retardation: A randomized controlled trial. *Journal of Clinical Child and Adolescent Psychology*, *36*(3), 418–429. doi:10.1080/15374410701448448 PMID:17658985

Bandura, A. (1969). *Principles of Behavior Modification*. New York: Holt, Rinehart and Winston.

Bandura, A. (1977). *Social learning theory*. Englewood Cliffs, NJ: Prentice Hall.

Bazzano, A., Wolfe, C., Zylowska, L., Wang, S., Schuster, E., Barrett, C., & Lehrer, D. (2013). Mindfulness based stress reduction (MBSR) for parents and caregivers of individuals with developmental disabilities: A community-based approach. *Journal of Child and Family Studies*, *24*(2), 298–308. doi:10.1007/s10826-013-9836-9

Beavers, G. A., Iwata, B. A., & Lerman, D. C. (2013). Thirty years of research on the functional analysis of problem behavior. *Journal of Applied Behavior Analysis*, *46*(1), 1–21. doi:10.1002/jaba.30 PMID:24114081

Bellini, S., & Akullian, J. (2007). A meta-analysis of video modeling and video self-modeling interventions for children and adolescents with autism spectrum disorders. *Exceptional Children*, *73*(3), 264–287. doi:10.1177/001440290707300301

Bensberg, G. J., Colwell, C. N., & Cassel, R. (1965). Teaching the profoundly retarded self-help activities by behavior shaping techniques. *American Journal of Mental Deficiency*, *69*, 674–679. PMID:14286827

Bijou, S. W., Peterson, R. F., & Ault, M. H. (1968). A method to integrate descriptive and experimental field studies at the level of data and empirical concepts. *Journal of Applied Behavior Analysis*, *1*(2), 175–191. doi:10.1901/jaba.1968.1-175 PMID:16795175

Blacher, J., Neece, C. L., & Paczkowski, E. (2005). Families and intellectual disability. *Current Opinion in Psychiatry*, *18*(5), 507–513. doi:10.1097/01.yco.0000179488.92885.e8 PMID:16639109

Britton, L. N., Carr, J. E., Kellum, K. K., Dozier, C. L., & Weil, T. M. (2000). A variation of noncontingent reinforcement in the treatment of aberrant behavior. *Research in Developmental Disabilities*, *21*(6), 425–435. doi:10.1016/S0891-4222(00)00056-1 PMID:11153827

Brooks, A., Todd, A. W., Tofflemoyer, S., & Horner, R. H. (2003). Use of functional assessment and a self-management system to increase academic engagement and work completion. *Journal of Positive Behavior Interventions*, *5*(3), 144–152. doi:10.1177/10983007030050030301

Carr, E., Horner, R., Turnbull, A., Marquis, J., McLaughlin, D., & McAtee, M. et al.. (1999). *Positive behavior support for people with developmental disabilities: A research synthesis*. Washington, DC: American Association on Mental Retardation.

Carr, E., Levin, L., McConnachie, G., Carlson, J., Kemp, D., & Smith, C. (1994). *Communication-based intervention for problem behavior*. Baltimore: Paul H. Brookes.

Cihak, D., Fahrenkrog, C., Ayres, K. M., & Smith, C. (2009). The use of video modeling via a video iPod and a system of least prompts to improve transitional behaviors for students with autism spectrum disorders in the general education classroom. *Journal of Positive Behavior Interventions*. doi:10.1177/1098300709332346

Cooper, J. O., Heron, T. E., & Heward, W. L. (2007). *Applied Behavior Analysis* (2nd ed.). Upper Saddle River, NJ: Pearson.

Crocker, A. G., Mercier, C., Allaire, J., & Roy, M. (2007). Profiles and correlates of aggressive behaviour among adults with intellectual disabilities. *Journal of Intellectual Disability Research: JIDR*, *51*(Pt 10), 786–801. doi:10.1111/j.1365-2788.2007.00953.x PMID:17803497

Crocker, A. G., Mercier, C., Lachapelle, Y., Brunet, A., Morin, D., & Roy, M. (2006). Prevalence and types of aggressive behaviour among adults with intellectual disabilities. *Journal of Intellectual Disability Research*, *50*(9), 652–661. doi:10.1111/j.1365-2788.2006.00815.x PMID:16901292

Deitz, D. E., & Repp, A. C. (1983). Reducing Behavior through Reinforcement. *Exceptional Education Quarterly*, *3*(4), 34–46.

Delano, M. E. (2007). Video modeling interventions for individuals with autism. *Remedial and Special Education*, *28*(1), 33–42. doi:10.1177/07419325070280010401

Derby, K., Wacker, D., DeRaad, A., Ulrich, S., Asmus, J., & Harding, J. et al.. (1997). The long-term effects of functional communication training in home settings. *Journal of Applied Behavior Analysis*, *30*(3), 507–531. doi:10.1901/jaba.1997.30-507 PMID:9316262

Didden, R. (2007). Functional analysis methodology in developmental disabilities. In P. Strumey (Ed.), *Functional analysis in clinical treatment: Practical resources for mental health professional* (pp. 65–86). San Diego, CA: Elsevier Academic Press. doi:10.1016/B978-012372544-8/50005-7

Didden, R., Duker, P. C., & Korzilius, H. (1997). Meta-analytic study on treatment effectiveness for problem behaviors with individuals who have mental retardation. *American Journal of Mental Retardation*, *101*(4), 387–399. PMID:9017085

Didden, R., Korzilius, H., van Oorsouw, W., & Strumey, P. (2006). Behavioural treatment of challenging behaviours in individuals with mild mental retardation: Meta-analysis of single- subject research. *American Journal of Mental Retardation*, *111*(4), 290–298. doi:10.1352/0895-8017(2006)111[290:BTOCBI]2.0.CO;2 PMID:16792430

Dillenburger, K. (2012). Why reinvent the wheel? A behaviour analyst's reflections on pedagogy for inclusion for students with intellectual and developmental disability. *Journal of Intellectual & Developmental Disability*, *37*(2), 169–180. doi:10.3109/13668250.2012.685705 PMID:22563693

Dufrene, B. A., Doggett, R. A., Henington, C., & Watson, T. S. (2007). Functional assessment and intervention for disruptive classroom behaviors in preschool and head start classrooms. *Journal of Behavioral Education*, *16*(4), 368–388. doi:10.1007/s10864-007-9048-8

Durand, V. M., & Carr, E. G. (1991). Functional communication training to reduce challenging behavior: Maintenance and application in new settings. *Journal of Applied Behavior Analysis*, *24*(2), 251–264. doi:10.1901/jaba.1991.24-251 PMID:1890046

Durand, V. M., & Crimmins, D. B. (1988). Identifying the variables maintaining self-injurious behavior. *Journal of Autism and Developmental Disorders*, *18*(1), 99–117. doi:10.1007/BF02211821 PMID:3372462

Emerson, E. (2001). *Challenging behaviour: Analysis and intervention in people with severe learning disabilities* (2nd ed.). Cambridge, New York: Cambridge University Press. doi:10.1017/CBO9780511543739

Emerson, E., & Einfeld, S. (2011). *Challenging Behaviour*. Cambridge: Cambridge University Press. doi:10.1017/CBO9780511861178

Emerson, E., Kiernan, C., Alborz, A., Reeves, D., Mason, L., Mason, H., & Hatton, C. (2001). The prevalence of challenging behaviors: A total population study. *Research in Developmental Disabilities*, *22*(1), 77–93. doi:10.1016/S0891-4222(00)00061-5 PMID:11263632

Eyberg, S. M., Boggs, S. R., & Algina, J. (1995). Parent–child interaction therapy: A psychosocial model for the treatment of young children with conduct problem behavior and their families. *Psychopharmacology Bulletin*, *31*(1), 83–91. PMID:7675994

Feeley, K., & Jones, E. (2006). Addressing challenging behaviour in children with Down syndrome: The use of applied behaviour analysis for assessment and intervention. *Down's Syndrome: Research and Practice*, *11*(2), 64–77. doi:10.3104/perspectives.316 PMID:17048800

Fisher, W. W., Adelinis, J. D., Thompson, R. H., Worsdell, A. S., & Zarcone, J. R. (1998). Functional analysis and treatment of destructive behavior maintained by termination of "don't" (and symmetrical "do") requests. *Journal of Applied Behavior Analysis*, *31*(3), 339–356. doi:10.1901/jaba.1998.31-339 PMID:9757579

Fisher, W. W., Kuhn, D. E., & Thompson, R. H. (1998). Establishing discriminative control of responding using functional and alternative reinforcers during functional communication training. *Journal of Applied Behavior Analysis*, *31*(4), 543–560. doi:10.1901/jaba.1998.31-543 PMID:9891393

Friedman, D., Holmbeck, G. N., Jandasek, B., Zukerman, J., & Abad, M. (2004). Parent functioning in families of preadolescents with spina bifida: Longitudinal implications for child adjustment. *Journal of Family Psychology*, *18*(4), 609–619. doi:10.1037/0893-3200.18.4.609 PMID:15598166

Grace, N. C., Thompson, R., & Fisher, W. W. (1996). The treatment of covert self-injury through contingencies on response products. *Journal of Applied Behavior Analysis*, *29*(2), 239–242. doi:10.1901/jaba.1996.29-239 PMID:8682739

Graves, T. B., Collins, B. C., Schuster, J. W., & Kleinert, H. (2005). Using video prompting to teach cooking skills to secondary students with moderate disabilities. *Education and Training in Developmental Disabilities*, *40*, 34–46.

Hagopian, L., Fisher, W., Sullivan, M., Acquisto, J., & LeBlanc, L. (1998). Effectiveness of functional communication training with and without extinction and punishment: A summary of 21 inpatient cases. *Journal of Applied Behavior Analysis*, *30*, 229–237. PMID:9652101

Hagopian, L. P., Wilson, D. M., & Wilder, D. A. (2001). Assessment and treatment of problem behavior maintained by escape from attention and access to tangible items. *Journal of Applied Behavior Analysis*, *34*(2), 229–232. doi:10.1901/jaba.2001.34-229 PMID:11421317

Hall, A. M., Neuharth-Pritchett, S., & Belfiore, P. J. (1997). Reduction of aggressive behaviors with changes in activity: Linking descriptive and experimental analysis. *Education and Training in Mental Retardation and Developmental Disabilities*, *32*, 331–339.

Hanley, G. P. (2012). Functional assessment of problem behavior: Dispelling myths, overcoming implementation obstacles, and developing new lore. *Behavior Analysis in Practice*, *5*(1), 54. PMID:23326630

Hanley, G. P., Iwata, B. A., & McCord, B. E. (2003). Functional analysis of problem behavior: A review. *Journal of Applied Behavior Analysis*, *36*(2), 147–186. doi:10.1901/jaba.2003.36-147 PMID:12858983

Hanley, G. P., Piazza, C. C., & Fisher, W. W. (1997). Noncontingent presentation of attention and alternative stimuli in the treatment of attention-maintained destructive behavior. *Journal of Applied Behavior Analysis*, *30*(2), 229–237. doi:10.1901/jaba.1997.30-229 PMID:9210303

Holth, P. *(2003).* Generalized imitation and generalized matching to sample. *The Behavior Analyst / MABA, 26*(1), 155-158.

Horner, R. H., Day, H. M., Sprague, J. R., O'Brien, M., & Heathfield, L. T. (1991). Interspersed requests: A nonaversive procedure for reducing aggression and self-injury during instruction. *Journal of Applied Behavior Analysis*, *24*(2), 265–278. doi:10.1901/jaba.1991.24-265 PMID:1890047

Iwata, B., Dorsey, M., Slifer, K., Bauman, K., & Richman, G. (1994). Toward a functional analysis of self-injury. *Journal of Applied Behavior Analysis, 27*, 197-209.

Iwata, B. A., & DeLeon, I. (1996) The functional analysis screening tool. Gainesville, FL: The Florida Centre on Self-Injury, The University of Florida.

Iwata, B. A., & Dozier, C. L. (2008). Clinical application of functional analysis methodology. *Behavior Analysis in Practice*, *1*(1), 3–9. PMID:22477673

Iwata, B. A., Pace, G. M., Cowdery, G. E., & Miltenberger, R. G. (1994). What makes extinction work: An analysis of procedural form and function. *Journal of Applied Behavior Analysis*, *27*(1), 131–144. doi:10.1901/jaba.1994.27-131 PMID:8188555

Jones, K. M., Drew, H. A., & Weber, N. L. (2000). Noncontingent peer attention as treatment for disruptive classroom behavior. *Journal of Applied Behavior Analysis*, *33*(3), 343–346. doi:10.1901/jaba.2000.33-343 PMID:11051579

Kagohara, D. M., van der Meer, L., Ramdoss, S., O'Reilly, M. F., Lancioni, G. E., Davis, T. N., & Sigafoos, J. et al. (2013). Using iPods® and iPads® in teaching programs for individuals with developmental disabilities: A systematic review. *Research in Developmental Disabilities*, *34*(1), 147–156. doi:10.1016/j.ridd.2012.07.027 PMID:22940168

Kahng, S., Iwata, B. A., Fischer, S. M., Page, T. J., Treadwell, K. R., Williams, D. E., & Smith, R. G. (1998). Temporal distributions of problem behavior based on scatter plot analysis. *Journal of Applied Behavior Analysis*, *31*(4), 593–604. doi:10.1901/jaba.1998.31-593 PMID:9891396

Kazdin, A. E. (2012). *Behavior modification in applied settings*. Waveland Press.

Keen, D., Brannigan, K. L., & Cuskelly, M. (2007). Toilet training for children with autism: The effects of video modeling. *Journal of Developmental and Physical Disabilities*, *19*(4), 291–303. doi:10.1007/s10882-007-9044-x

Kellems, R. O., & Edwards, S. (2015). Using Video Modeling and Video Prompting to Teach Core Academic Content to Students With Learning Disabilities. *Preventing School Failure: Alternative Education for Children and Youth*, 1-8.

Keller, F. S., & Schoenfeld, W. N. (1950). *Principles of psychology: A systematic text in the science of behavior*. New York: Appleton-Century-Crofts. doi:10.1037/11293-000

Kern, L., Choutka, C. M., & Sokol, N. G. (2002). Assessment-based interventions used in natural settings to reduce challenging behaviors: A review of the literature. *Education & Treatment of Children*, *25*, 113–134.

Kozlowski, A. M., & Matson, J. L. (2012). Interview and observation methods in functional assessment. In J. L. Matson (Ed.), *Functional assessment for challenging behaviour* (pp. 105–124). New York, NY: Springer New York; doi:10.1007/978-1-4614-3037-7_7

Lalli, J. S., Browder, D. M., Mace, F. C., & Brown, D. K. (1993). Teacher use of descriptive analysis data to implement interventions to decrease students' problem behaviors. *Journal of Applied Behavior Analysis*, *26*(2), 227–238. doi:10.1901/jaba.1993.26-227 PMID:8331019

Lalli, J. S., Casey, S. D., & Kates, K. (1997). noncontingent reinforcement as treatment for severe problem behavior: Some procedural variations. *Journal of Applied Behavior Analysis*, *30*(1), 127–137. doi:10.1901/jaba.1997.30-127 PMID:9103988

Lanovaz, M. J., Argumedes, M., Roy, D., Duquette, J. R., & Watkins, N. (2013). Using ABC narrative recording to identify the function of problem behavior: A pilot study. *Research in Developmental Disabilities*, *34*(9), 2734–2742. doi:10.1016/j.ridd.2013.05.038 PMID:23787117

LaVigna, G. W., & Willis, T. J. (2012). The efficacy of positive behavioural support with the most challenging behaviour: The evidence and its implications. *Journal of Intellectual & Developmental Disability*, *37*(3), 185–195. doi:10.3109/13668250.2012.696597 PMID:22774760

Lerman, D., & Iwata, B. (1996). Developing a technology for the use of operant extinction in clinical settings: An examination of basic and applied research. *Journal of Applied Behavior Analysis*, *29*(3), 345–382. doi:10.1901/jaba.1996.29-345 PMID:8926226

Lerner, J. (2003). *Learning disabilities: Theories, diagnosis, and teaching practices* (9th ed.). Boston, MA: Houghton Mifflin Company.

Lewis, T., Scott, T., & Sugai, G. (1994). The problem behaviour questionnaire: A teacher-based instrument to develop functional hypotheses of problem behaviour in general education classroom. *Diagnostique*, *19*, 103–115.

Lowe, K., Allen, D., Jones, E., Brophy, S., Moore, K., & James, W. (2007). Challenging behaviours: Prevalence and topographies. *Journal of Intellectual Disability Research*, *51*(8), 625–636. doi:10.1111/j.1365-2788.2006.00948.x PMID:17598876

Mactavish, J. B., & Schleien, S. J. (2004). Re-injecting spontaneity and balance in family life: Parents' perspectives on recreation in families that include children with developmental disability. *Journal of Intellectual Disability Research*, *48*(2), 123–141. doi:10.1111/j.1365-2788.2004.00502.x PMID:14723655

March, R. E., Horner, R. H., Lewis-Palmer, T., Brown, D., Crone, D., & Todd, A. W. et al.. (2000). *Functional Assessment Checklist: Teachers and Staff (FACTS)*. Eugene, OR: Educational and Community Supports.

Matson, J. L. (2012). Functional assessment for challenging behaviors. New York, NY: Springer. doi:10.1007/978-1-4614-3037-7

Matson, J. L., & Coe, D. A. (1992). Applied Behaviour Analysis: Its impact on the treatment of mentally retarded emotionally disturbed people. *Research in Developmental Disabilities*, *13*(2), 171–189. doi:10.1016/0891-4222(92)90023-Y PMID:1574625

Matson, J. L., & Vollmer, T. R. (1995). *User's guide: Questions About Behavioral Function (QABF)*. Baron Rouge, LA: Scientific Publishers, Inc.

Mayer, G. R., Sulzer-Azaroff, B., & Wallace, M. (2014). *Behavior analysis for lasting change* (3rd ed.). Cornwall-on-Hudson, NY: Sloan Publishing.

McIntyre, L. L. (2008). Adapting Webster-Stratton's incredible years parent training for children with developmental delay: Findings from a treatment group only study. *Journal of Intellectual Disability Research*, *52*(12), 1176–1192. doi:10.1111/j.1365-2788.2008.01108.x PMID:18671808

Mechling, L. C., Gast, D. L., & Barthold, S. (2003). Multimedia computer-based instruction to teach students with moderate intellectual disabilities to use a debit card to make purchases. *Exceptionality*, *11*(4), 239–254. doi:10.1207/S15327035EX1104_4

Mesibov, G. B., Shea, V., & Schopler, E. (2004). *The TEACCH approach to autism spectrum disorders*. Springer Science & Business Media. doi:10.1007/978-0-306-48647-0

Michael, J. (1982). Distinguishing between discriminative and motivational functions of stimuli. *Journal of the Experimental Analysis of Behavior*, *37*(1), 149–155. doi:10.1901/jeab.1982.37-149 PMID:7057126

Michael, J. (2000). Implications and refinements of the establishing operation concept. *Journal of Applied Behavior Analysis*, *33*(4), 401–410. doi:10.1901/jaba.2000.33-401 PMID:11214018

Neece, C. L. (2014). Mindfulness-based stress reduction for parents of young children with developmental delays: Implications for parental mental health and child behaviour problems. *Journal of Applied Research in Intellectual Disabilities*, *27*(2), 174–186. doi:10.1111/jar.12064 PMID:23813562

Norman, J. M., Collins, B. C., & Schuster, J. W. (2001). Using an instructional package including video technology to teach self-help skills to elementary students with mental deficiency. *Journal of Special Education Technology*, *16*, 5–18.

O'Neill, R. E., Horner, R. H., Albin, R. W., Sprague, J. R., Storey, K., & Newton, J. S. (1997). *Functional Assessment and Program Development for Problem Behavior* (2nd ed.). Pacific Grove, CA: Brooks/Cole.

O'Neill, R. E., Horner, R. H., Albin, R. W., Storey, K., & Sprague, J. R. (1990). *Functional Analysis of Problem Behavior: A Practical Assessment Guide*. Sycamore, IL: Sycamore Publishing.

Passey, J., & Feldman, M. (2004). Descriptive analysis of parent–child interactions in young children with or at risk for developmental delay. *Behavioral Interventions*, *19*(4), 233–246. doi:10.1002/bin.164

Piazza, C. C., Hanley, G. P., & Fisher, W. W. (1996). Functional analysis and treatment of cigarette pica. *Journal of Applied Behavior Analysis*, *29*(4), 437–450. doi:10.1901/jaba.1996.29-437 PMID:8995829

Plant, K. M., & Sanders, M. R. (2007). Reducing problem behavior during care-giving in families of preschool-aged children with developmental disabilities. *Research in Developmental Disabilities*, *28*(4), 362–385. doi:10.1016/j.ridd.2006.02.009 PMID:16781115

Poppes, P., van der Putten, A. J. J., & Vlaskamp, C. (2010). Frequency and severity of challenging behaviour in people with profound intellectual and multiple disabilities. *Research in Developmental Disabilities*, *31*(6), 1269–1275. doi:10.1016/j.ridd.2010.07.017 PMID:20728304

Rehfeldt, R. A., Dahman, D., Young, A., Cherry, H., & Davis, P. (2003). Teaching a simple meal preparation skill to adults with moderate and severe mental retardation using video modeling. *Behavioral Interventions*, *18*(3), 209–218. doi:10.1002/bin.139

Reid, M. J., Webster-Stratton, C., & Hammond, M. (2007). Enhancing a classroom social competence and problem-solving curriculum by offering parent training to families of moderate-to-high-risk elementary school children. *Journal of Clinical Child and Adolescent Psychology*, *36*(4), 605–620. doi:10.1080/15374410701662741 PMID:18088218

Remington, B. (1998). Applied behaviour analysis and intellectual disability: A long-term relationship?1. *Journal of Intellectual & Developmental Disability*, *23*(2), 121–135. doi:10.1080/13668259800033631

Repp, A. C., & Karsh, D. (1994). A hypothesis-based interventions for tantrum behavior of person with developmental disabilities in school settings. *Journal of Applied Behavior Analysis*, *27*(1), 21–31. doi:10.1901/jaba.1994.27-21 PMID:8188561

Rethink autism provides distance BCBA supervision to candidates seeking certification in behavior analysis. (2010). PR Newswire.

Rogers, S. J., Hepburn, S. L., Stackhouse, T., & Wehner, E. (2003). Imitation performance in toddlers with autism and those with other developmental disorders. *Journal of Child Psychology and Psychiatry, and Allied Disciplines*, *44*(5), 763–781. doi:10.1111/1469-7610.00162 PMID:12831120

Roux, G., Sofronoff, K., & Sanders, M. R. (2013). A Randomized Controlled Trial of Group Stepping Stones Triple P: A Mixed-Disability Trial. *Family Process*, *52*(3), 411–424. doi:10.1111/famp.12016 PMID:24033239

Sanders, M. R., Mazzucchelli, T. G., & Studman, L. J. (2003). *Practitioner's manual for standard Stepping Stones Triple P*. Brisbane: Triple P International Pty. Ltd.

Sanders, M. R., Mazzucchelli, T. G., & Studman, L. J. (2004). Stepping Stones Triple P: The theoretical basis and development of an evidence-based positive parenting program for families with a child who has a disability. *Journal of Intellectual & Developmental Disability*, *29*(3), 265–283. doi:10.1080/13668250412331285127

Shipley-Benamou, R., Lutzker, J. R., & Taubman, M. (2002). Teaching daily living skills to children with autism through instructional video modeling. *Journal of Positive Behavior Interventions*, *4*(3), 165–175. doi:10.1177/109830070200400305 01

Singh, N. N., Lancioni, G. E., Winton, A. S., Fisher, B. C., Wahler, R. G., Mcaleavey, K., & Sabaawi, M. et al. (2006). Mindful parenting decreases aggression, noncompliance, and self-injury in children with autism. *Journal of Emotional and Behavioral Disorders*, *14*(3), 169–177. doi:10.1177/10634266060140030401

Singh, N. N., Lancioni, G. E., Winton, A. S., Karazsia, B. T., Myers, R. E., Latham, L. L., & Singh, J. (2014). Mindfulness-Based Positive Behavior Support (MBPBS) for mothers of adolescents with autism spectrum disorder: Effects on adolescents' behavior and parental stress. *Mindfulness*, *5*(6), 646–657. doi:10.1007/s12671-014-0321-3

Singh, N. N., Lancioni, G. E., Winton, A. S., Singh, J., Curtis, W. J., Wahler, R. G., & McAleavey, K. M. (2007). Mindful parenting decreases aggression and increases social behavior in children with developmental disabilities. *Behavior Modification*, *31*(6), 749–771. doi:10.1177/0145445507300924 PMID:17932234

Singh, N. N., Lancioni, G. E., Winton, A. S., Singh, J., Singh, A. N., Adkins, A. D., & Wahler, R. G. (2010). Training in mindful caregiving transfers to parent–child interactions. *Journal of Child and Family Studies*, *19*(2), 167–174. doi:10.1007/s10826-009-9267-9

Sofronoff, K., Jahnel, D., & Sanders, M. R. (2011). Stepping Stones Triple P seminars for parents of a child with a disability: A randomized controlled trial. *Research in Developmental Disabilities*, *32*(6), 2253–2262. doi:10.1016/j.ridd.2011.07.046 PMID:21871779

Solomon, M., Ono, M., Timmer, S., & Goodlin-Jones, B. (2008). The effectiveness of parent–child interaction therapy for families of children on the autism spectrum. *Journal of Autism and Developmental Disorders*, *38*(9), 1767–1776. doi:10.1007/s10803-008-0567-5 PMID:18401693

Sturmey, P. (2011). Functional analysis in clinical treatment. Amsterdam: Academic Press.

Tarbox, J., Wallace, M. D., Tarbox, R. S. F., Landaburu, H. J., & Williams, W. L. (2004). Functional analysis and treatment of low rate problem behavior in individuals with developmental disabilities. *Behavioral Interventions*, *19*(3), 187–204. doi:10.1002/bin.158

Tellegen, C. L., & Sanders, M. R. (2013). Stepping Stones Triple P-Positive Parenting Program for children with disability: A systematic review and meta-analysis. *Research in Developmental Disabilities*, *34*(5), 1556–1571. doi:10.1016/j.ridd.2013.01.022 PMID:23475006

Thompson, R. H., & Iwata, B. A. (2007). A comparison of outcomes from descriptive and functional analyses of problem behavior. *Journal of Applied Behavior Analysis*, *40*(2), 333–338. doi:10.1901/jaba.2007.56-06 PMID:17624074

Tiong, S. J., Blampied, N. M., & Le Grice, B. (1992). Training community-living, intellectually handicapped people in fire safety using video prompting. *Behaviour Change*, *9*, 65–72.

Touchette, P. E., MacDonald, R. F., & Langer, S. N. (1985). A scatter plot for identifying stimulus control of problem behavior. *Journal of Applied Behavior Analysis*, *18*(4), 343–351. doi:10.1901/jaba.1985.18-343 PMID:4086416

Triple P is giving our parents help. (2015). *The Newcastle Herald (Newcastle, Australia).*

United Nations. (n.d.). Conventions on the Rights of the Persons with Disabilities. *Treaty Series*. Retrieved November 17, 2015, from UN Treaty Collection website: https://treaties.un.org/Pages/ViewDetails.aspx?src=TREATY&mtdsg_no=IV-15&chapter=4&lang=en

Van Houten, R., Axelrod, S., Bailey, J. S., Favell, J. E., Foxx, R. M., Iwata, B. A., & Lovaas, O. I. (1988). The right to effective behavioral treatment. *Journal of Applied Behavior Analysis*, *21*(4), 381–384. doi:10.1901/jaba.1988.21-381 PMID:3225255

Vollmer, T. R., Marcus, B. A., Ringdahl, J. E., & Roane, H. S. (1995). Progressing from brief assessments to extended experimental analyses in the evaluation of aberrant behavior. *Journal of Applied Behavior Analysis*, *28*(4), 561–576. doi:10.1901/jaba.1995.28-561 PMID:16795882

Watson, L. S. Jr. (1968). Application of behaviour-shaping devices to training severely and profoundly mentally retarded children in an institutional setting. *Mental Retardation*, *6*, 21–23. PMID:5705586

Webster-Stratton, C. (2000). The Incredible Years Training series. Office of Juvenile Justice and Delinquency Prevention Bulletin Review, 1–24.

Webster-Stratton, C. (2001). *The Incredible Years: Parents, teachers, and children training series, leader's guide*. Seattle, WA: Author.

Wert, B. Y., & Neisworth, J. T. (2003). Effects of video self-modeling on spontaneous requesting in children with autism. *Journal of Positive Behavior Interventions*, *5*(1), 30–34. doi:10.1177/10983007030050010501

Whittingham, K., Sofronoff, K., Sheffield, J., & Sanders, M. R. (2009). Stepping Stones Triple P: An RCT of a parenting program with parents of a child diagnosed with an autism spectrum disorder. *Journal of Abnormal Child Psychology*, *37*(4), 469–480. doi:10.1007/s10802-008-9285-x PMID:19023654

Wolf, M. M. (1978). Social validity: The case for subjective measurement or how applied behavior analysis is finding its heart. *Journal of Applied Behavior Analysis*, *11*(2), 203–214. doi:10.1901/jaba.1978.11-203 PMID:16795590

Wolfgang, C. H. (2001). *Solving discipline and classroom management programs: Methods and models for today's teachers*. New York: John Wiley.

Yamaoka, Y., Tamiya, N., Moriyama, Y., Sandoval Garrido, F. A., Sumazaki, R., & Noguchi, H. (2015). Mental health of parents as caregivers of children with disabilities: Based on Japanese nationwide survey: E0145200. *PLoS ONE*, *10*(12), e0145200. doi:10.1371/journal.pone.0145200 PMID:26692344

Chapter 15
Recent Trends and Issues in Vocational Rehabilitation of People with ID

Bijoy Kumar Dehuri
Exservicemen Contributory Health Scheme, India

Bhavna Mukund
Gujarat Forensic Sciences University, India

ABSTRACT

Employment has many advantages for people. Besides earning an income, work provides opportunities for social interaction, a means of structuring and occupying time, enjoyable activity and involvement, and a sense of personal achievement. Work is considered therapeutic and essential for both the physiological survival and psychological well-being of people in contemporary societies and hence it's importance in people with intellectual disability. The rights of people with disabilities have been given new attention with the entry into force of the United Nations Convention on the Rights of Persons with Disabilities (CRPD) in May 2008. The various policies, issues and trends in vocational rehabilitation of people with intellectual disabilities in existence in different countries need to be examined along with different models in existence to develop appropriate executable models whereby such rehabilitation services could be made available early in life to such individuals and after training they could be provided with supported employment or integrated employment as the case may be.

INTRODUCTION

Vocation or employment is central to human existence. It enables an individual to possess a valued social position and identity that has a significant influence on self-concept and relationships with others. As an important aspect of life in today's society, work has a substantial effect on our fundamental aspects of personality and is a major contributing factor to our levels of self-esteem. Besides earning an income, work provides opportunities for social interaction, a means of structuring and occupying time, enjoyable activity and involvement, and a sense of personal achievement. In addition, work provides an opportunity for improving skills while also providing income and financial security. Employment as a

DOI: 10.4018/978-1-5225-0089-6.ch015

basic right of citizenship is often taken for granted. Yet, many people with intellectual disability through the non-availability of evidence-based services are excluded from this basic right. Work is considered therapeutic and essential for both the physiological survival and psychological well-being of people in contemporary societies. Conversely, unemployment can produce high levels of stress, anxiety, and depression; low levels of self-worth; and decrease opportunities for self-development, autonomy, and social contact. The shift from being employed to unemployed is significantly associated with not only an increased risk of depression, alcohol dependence, anxiety states, and psychosomatic reactions, but also stigma, aimlessness, and poverty, which combine to trigger or amplify mental health problems. Recognizing the importance of work, vocational rehabilitation professionals such as rehabilitation counselors, have consistently advocated for work as a fundamental human right of people with disabilities. (Rubin &Roessler, 1995; Wright, 1980).

The rights of people with disabilities have been given new attention with the entry into force of the United Nations Convention on the Rights of Persons with Disabilities (CRPD) in May 2008. The provisions of the CRPD contribute to other international standards concerning persons with disabilities, signaling a dramatic shift in international policy terms. In relation to training and employment, for example, states are called on to provide opportunities for disabled people alongside non-disabled people.

People with intellectual disabilities are entitled to benefit from the provisions of the CRPD and ILO Convention concerning the Vocational Rehabilitation and Employment (Disabled Persons), ACT 159 in 1983 as well as people with other kinds of disabilities. Yet, they are frequently not well placed to gain from this changed emphasis on inclusion. In many developing countries, in particular, they are often excluded from school and deprived of opportunities to acquire relevant vocational skills at all, presenting further disadvantages when it comes to seeking jobs. Yet, experience in many countries shows that, with the right training, support in the workplace as required, and the right opportunities, they can make valued contributions in the workplace and to a country's economy (ILO,2008).

Research has shown that people with intellectual disabilities often have multiple secondary impairments, including complex physical and mental health problems (Beange et al., 1999; Einfeld et al., 2006; Hofer et al., 2009). These co-existing disabilities are particularly likely to be problems of agility, mobility, speech and language; and emotional problems including anger control, anxiety and depression. They are also more likely to experience loneliness and lack of friends (McVilly et al., 2004).

It is acknowledged that people with all categories of disabilities have experienced discrimination and stigmatization throughout the centuries. Yet, an intact intellect has historically been highly valued and often seen as the essential characteristic of being fully human (Parmenter, 2001), and people with intellectual disabilities are often the last within the community of disabled persons to receive attention. In the not-too-distant past a person with an intellectual disability "was viewed not as a second-class citizen, but rather as one who possessed no citizenship" (Stevens, 1967).

In the planning and delivery of educational and vocational programs for people with intellectual disabilities, a support needs approach to classification has significant benefits in contrast to the earlier practice of classification based on IQ levels (mild, moderate, severe and profound). Areas of functioning important to employment, where people with intellectual disabilities may need specific supports, include (ILO,2011)

- Literacy and numeracy;
- Comprehension of instructions and information;
- Interpreting non-verbal language;

- Short-term and long-term memory;
- Attention span and concentration;
- Motivation;
- Problem-solving and decision-making skills;
- Making choices;
- Following instructions;
- Time telling/management and organization;
- Ability to travel and/or live independently;
- Appropriate behaviors and social skills;
- Grooming and self-care.

The degree of difficulty and the extent of support required will vary from person to person.

Undoubtedly the early work of Gold and Tizard was a catalyst for change in promoting a deeper understanding of the learning potential of people with even the highest level of cognitive impairment. Later research focused on a more systems-based approach where emphasis has been placed on adaptations and accommodations in a person's environment, in addition to effective skills training (Parmenter, Trevor R.,2011)

Research helped to lead the development of the "place and train" model of employment support services, in contrast to the more traditional rehabilitation approach of "train and then place". Experience has shown that, to be effective, teaching and training of people with intellectual disabilities should take place using real work in practical situations to the extent possible. Support staff should also be aware that making modifications to the person's environment may be an alternative way to assist individuals in handling the requirements of a job. Therefore, support staff should be encouraged to target both their learning needs and adjustments to the workplace. In addition to a good knowledge of work practices, support staff require training in the basic teaching procedures and principles used by special educators (Parmenter, Trevor R., 2011).

Evidence indicates that, irrespective of the culture or the economic circumstances of a country, the employment circumstances for persons with intellectual disabilities are equally alarming, if not worse (Dempsey and Ford, 2009; Department of Health, 2009). Just as they have been denied education, they have been denied access to jobs. This dismal state of affairs has come about largely through ignorance and superstition (Parmenter, 2001).

In Canada, for example, a survey reported by Staintonet. al. (2006) in a survey found that people with disabilities that are working, work only half as many weeks per year as people who do not have a disability; are unemployed longer; and spend three times as long outside the labour force. People with intellectual disabilities were found to experience even lower rates of employment, with only 27 per cent being employed at the time of the survey, while 40 per cent had never worked. In terms of income, nearly 50 per cent of people with intellectual disabilities had incomes below the Statistics Canada low-income cut-off, a widely used measure of poverty.

In Australia, people with intellectual disabilities made up 41 per cent of those served in government funded employment services in 2010, with more males than females benefitting (64 per cent vs. 36 per cent). They represented 27 per cent of all participants with disabilities n open employment, but 73 per cent of those in segregated business enterprises, formerly called sheltered workshops. There has been a gradual decline in the proportion of people with intellectual disabilities accessing inclusive employment services. And finally, there is evidence of 'creaming'—that is, providing services to people who have relatively low support needs and are easier to place in employment - by providers of both employment options, leading to increasing numbers of people with high support needs being referred to state/territory day option programmes. Parmenter, 2011).

In European Union countries, the unemployment rate for people with intellectual disabilities was found to approach almost 100 per cent (Greve, 2009). The vast majority who do work are found in sheltered workshops and those with high support needs are generally directed to day activity centres. A similar picture was reported by Verdonschot et al. (2009), who found from a systematic review of the literature that people with intellectual disabilities were three to four times less likely to be employed than people without intellectual disabilities. In Northern Finland a follow-up of those born with intellectual disability in 1966 had revealed a similar position (Taanila et al., 2005). As per Strategic Social Report Finland 2015, there are 25 000 people with intellectual disabilities of working age in Finland, 13 000 people with intellectual disabilities are engaged in sheltered work or day activities in activity centers.

Employment options for people with disabilities, and those with intellectual disabilities in particular, can be broadly distinguished as those in which people with disabilities work in a segregated environment of only workers with disabilities; and those in which they work in an integrated or inclusive environment of workers largely without disabilities. Employment models under these headings, currently accessed by people with intellectual disabilities in countries around the world, are described below. (Kregel & Dean, 2002).

EMPLOYMENT MODELS/OPTIONS

- **Day Programmes/Centres:** Traditional day centres were initially based on the principles of occupational therapy and were created as respite for family members caring for their adult children or siblings with disabilities. This is slowly changing, however, as programmes offered become more skills-based and focused on increasing independence. For instance, in New South Wales, Australia, one of the post school options initiatives for school leavers classified as not being ready for open employment, is the "transition to work" programme. Since the programme's inception in 2004, Jobsupport, the most successful agency delivering the programme, placed 60 per cent of the 179 school leavers it supported into paid open employment. This agency specifically targets young people with intellectual disabilities who have been classified as having moderate support needs, referred to under the older classification system as "moderately intellectually disabled"(Trevor R. Parmenter, 2011).

Under a medical model of service delivery, people with intellectual disabilities who were assessed or deemed to be unsuitable for employment were catered for in "activity therapy centre" programmes, where one of the goals was to prepare them for employment options. Typically, only a very small number "graduate" to sheltered employment. In practice, these centres in the past became the life-long option for people assessed as not being suitable for employment. Some of the constraints to moving to other employment options may arise from the reluctance of persons with intellectual disabilities themselves to move from a day centre where they have built up friendships over many years. This reluctance acts as a barrier to change, unless opportunities are open to maintain friendships outside of work. This pattern has been highlighted in the UK context by Beyer et al. (2004), who also found that people with intellectual disabilities in day centres were considered to have had restricted lives, leading to a poor attitude to employment, low desire to work, and little self-confidence, in combination with the lack of the experience to make a judgement about what work they might want to do.

- **Sheltered Workshops:** Sheltered workshops, initially established by parent groups, were essentially segregated facilities established for people considered unable or unlikely to obtain or retain a job in the open labour market. The majority of those employed have tended to have intellectual disabilities. The workshops engage in remunerative work to cover some of their costs. Workers are often paid a training allowance in addition to any welfare payments they might be entitled to, and very minimal or no wages - sometimes in the form of a bonus if production targets are met. In many countries, these facilities are described as rehabilitation and training facilities, but very few workers ever graduate to the general employment market, even when financial incentives are offered. In fact, there was a major disincentive to progress the more skilled workers to real jobs in the open labour market, as their productivity was crucial for the financial viability of the organization (Murphy & Rogan, 1995; Parmenter, 1980).

Given the results of research studies, in combination with the realization that a real job in the community gives people a strong sense of identity, it came to be recognized that segregated settings send a message to people with disabilities, and to the population at large, that they are different from the rest of society, and that alternatives were needed to allow them to have the same conditions of life as everyone else (Nirje, 1985). This gave rise to a debate about sheltered workshops that continues to the present.

Arguments have been put forward in favour of sheltered employment. These include the avoidance of perceived physical risks in the outside world (Dudley and Schatz 1985; Migliore et al. 2008); the high complexity of jobs in outside employment being beyond the skills range and psychological capacity of people with intellectual disabilities (McConkey and Mezza 2001; Visier, 1998); that sheltered workshops provide greater opportunities for the development of friendships than outside jobs (Dudley and Schatz 1985; Weikle 2008); and that sheltered employment tends to provide surety of employment across the person's life span without affecting disability benefits. Sheltered workshops are also seen to provide an option for people who fail to secure or maintain employment in the open labour market.

Yet it is widely recognized that change was and continues to be required. In recent years, for example, high-income countries, such as Australia, have re-badged sheltered workshops as "Australian Disability Enterprises" where a much greater emphasis has been placed on good business practices and productivity. Wages and working conditions for the disabled employees have improved, in some cases as a result of Trade Union support. In New Zealand, legislation has ensured workers receive the minimum wage unless an exemption is granted in individual cases, based on assessed productivity rates. In Australia, wages are linked to assessed productivity of the individual employee, compared to the normal industrial award. (Hedger S., 2012).

The rate of successful transition of people with disabilities from sheltered workshops to the open labour market has been minimal, ranging from under one per cent to about five per cent (Beyer et al., 2002; US Government Accountability Office, 2001). However, Cimera (2011) found that two matched cohorts of employees—one in which employees had previously worked in sheltered workshops and the other in which they had not had prior sheltered workshop placement—were equally likely to be employed in the open labour market. There was a difference in the rates of pay with the non-sheltered workshop cohort earning significantly more than those from the sheltered workshops. The former group also worked more hours per week and cost less to support.

Studies conducted in Northern Ireland, Spain and the US have shown that people working in sheltered workshops would like the opportunity to work in outside employment (McConkey and Mezza, 2001; Migliore et al., 2007; Verdugo et al., 2009).

In the US, a network of 23 state developmental disabilities agencies have developed policies under the umbrella of Employment First which has led states and providers to adopt service delivery strategies for persons with disabilities, including those with the most significant disabilities, that embrace the principle of integrated competitive employment (Kiernan et al., 2011). This initiative is strongly supported by self-advocates (Walker, 2011).

There are increasing signs that many sheltered workshops are transitioning to community employment options. In Australia, Greenacres, a large employment agency for people with intellectual and other disabilities, conducts an open employment programme in parallel with its sheltered workshop. It has a policy of actively seeking to move its employees into the competitive employment labour market7. In the US, Rogan and Rinne (2011) have described the processes followed by ten organizations that have shifted their service delivery from sheltered to community employment.

- **Supported Employment:** Alternatives to sheltered employment and day activity centres emerged in the early 1970s. In the US, in addition to the factors described above, the establishment of the President's Panel on Mental Retardation (now 'The President's Committee for Intellectual Disabilities') in 1961, and the subsequent research agenda under the auspices of the newly created National Institute on Child Health and Human Development (NICHD), saw the development of energetic research teams which targeted the post-school options for this population. These influences led to the establishment of an Employment Initiative for Persons with Developmental Disabilities, which promoted the concept of supported employment (SE) to business leaders, community groups, and journals, and to the enactment of two public laws that provided a mandate for the national development of SE: The Developmental Disabilities Assistance and Bill of Rights Act of 1984 (P.L. 98-527), and the Rehabilitation Amendments of 1986 (P.L. 99-506).

Researchers working with people with very high support needs developed four alternative pathways, all of which were characterized as 'supported employment' (Mank et al., 1986). The first was called the 'supported jobs' model, which later became the SE model described above. Other alternatives were the 'enclave' model, the 'mobile crew' model and the 'benchwork' model. Each of these models specifically targeted people with intellectual disabilities who had high support needs.

- **Supported Jobs Model:** The 'supported jobs' employment model involves a 'place and train' approach, rather than the practice in rehabilitation facilities where the model is 'train and then place'. Therefore, to provide employment, a job is required at the outset of the service, and not at its completion. The 'place, train and support' model for SE usually involves job coaches working with the potential employee to identify interests and skills. This is followed by job seeking, matching and placement. The employer might also be encouraged to make adaptations (i.e. accommodations) to a specific job in order to match it with the abilities and skills of the employee with an intellectual disability. In many cases the job coach might learn to do the job first, in order to subsequently teach the employee with the disability. In other circumstances, the employer might prefer for a regular staff member to teach the skill. This person may subsequently become a 'mentor' to the person with the disability, thus becoming part of the natural support for the person within the workplace (ILO, 2010).

- **Enclave Model:** The enclave model consists of a group of people with disabilities who are trained and supervised among workers who do not have a disability, usually in an industrial or commercial environment. In its original design, the workers were to be paid at a level commensurate to the non-disabled workers, often adjusted according to their relative productivity. This meant that wages for the person with a disability continued to be paid by the sheltered workshop, at the sheltered workshop rates. Storey and Horner (1991) found that individual and enclave job sites were more likely to involve interactions between disabled and non-disabled workers. However, the authors suggested that it could possibly be the features of specific job sites rather than the employment model in itself that result in positive interactions.
- **Mobile Crew Model:** This model is a combination of service and business. It may consist of a crew of five people with disabilities working from a van, rather than a building, performing service jobs in community settings. Examples of work carried out may include lawn cutting, window cleaning, and general ground maintenance. In its original conception, a mobile crew is set up as a small, single-purpose business, rather than as an extension of a large organization. (Parmenter,2011), (ILO, 2011)

Kregel, Wehman and Banks (1989) reported that group settings such as enclaves and mobile work crews provided significantly fewer opportunities for both physical and social interactions. They also found that people with very high-support needs were more likely to be placed in enclaves than any other supported work placements.

- **Benchwork Model:** This model was developed in the early 1970s by the Specialized Training Programme at the University of Oregon, US, as an alternative to day-activity programmes to provide long-term employment to people previously denied access to any vocational services. This model operates as a small, single purpose, not-for-profit commercial operation providing a range of goods or services. The model requires a number of highly qualified staff skilled in instructional technology with no more than a 1:5 staff-to-worker ratio. The size of the business was limited to 20 workers and they were located in close proximity to stores, restaurants, and other community venues that can provide opportunities for integration and participation into the regular community activities during lunch breaks as well as before and after work. At first the model was faithfully replicated in five states of the US and in Australia. The costs of operating the facilities were no more than those incurred in the day-activity centres, but employees received wages based on their productivity for the first time in their lives. Follow-up studies showed that some opportunities for community participation were realized, especially during meal breaks when employees could access local shopping centers. CNS Precision Assembly is an Australian example of a bench work model. Although designed for people with very high support needs, who would not normally be employed in a sheltered workshop because of their supposed low productivity, the bench work model shares many characteristics and constraints with traditional sheltered workshops. (Fletcher-Janzen,Reynolds,2007)

The four models described above have undergone some transformations since their original conception. Supported Employment has expanded and has become the preferred option internationally, particularly as it embraces the core values of the UN Standard Rules on the Equalization of Opportunities for Persons with Disabilities, and the more recent UN CRPD, which advocates employment options in inclusive work settings for all people with disabilities, irrespective of their level of support needs. Even in high-income countries, however, the penetration of SE has not been sufficient to encompass all people with intellectual disabilities wishing to work. This has resulted in an increased emphasis on job matching and making adjustments to jobs, so that all or part of a job can be performed by people with a range of disabilities, including intellectual disabilities. This has led to a modified version of SE developed in US called "Customized employment", a term first defined by the Office of Disability Employment Policy in 2001, (ILO, 2001)

- **Customized Employment (CE):** This model embraces a 'person-centred' approach, beginning with the person's needs, aspirations, talents and skills. This profile serves as a basis for contacting potential employers (Inge, 2006; 2008). It also emphasizes the person's choices, strengths and abilities. It is employed in One-Stop Service Delivery Systems (Blanck et al., 2009; Inge, 2008) where workforce investment, education, and other human service programmes work together to optimize access to services and long-term employment outcomes. Similar principles are used by Jobsupport Inc., one of Australia's most successful SE programmes, in its transition from school to work initiative (Tuckerman, 2008a).

Beyer and Robinson (2009) reported on a 2005 study conducted for the US Department of Labor, which found that CE had been used successfully with people with high support needs. In the first round of the study 345 people had been placed in competitive employment. The majority had found highquality jobs, with 95 per cent earning the minimum wage or above, and over 50 per cent placed in jobs with the potential for career advancement. A second round of data collection on 536 randomly selected individuals yielded similar results. Approximately 42 per cent of the sample disclosed a psychiatric or emotional disability, with 20 per cent reporting an intellectual disability. In essence, the major contribution of the CE model to the SE model has been the recognition that a person's job choices play a crucial role in achieving a successful job match. It is another example of the application of the social model of disability, in that environmental adjustments may be more important than trying to change the person.

- **Self-Employment, Self-Directed Employment, Microenterprises:** Neufeldt and Albright (1998, p. 6) defined self-directed employment as:

Income-generating work where disabled people, to a significant degree, have a prime decision-making role in the kind of work that is done, how time is allocated, what kinds of investment in time and money should be made, and how to allocate revenue generated.

Duce and Biersdorff (2002) suggested that business considerations for people with intellectual disabilities are little different from those for people who do not have a disability. In the case of the former, it is usual for someone to perform duties not dissimilar to the role of a job coach. Sometimes this is a family member. They proposed five major steps in the process of establishing a business: i) developing a business plan; ii) obtaining the required skills; iii) securing start-up capital; iv) implementing the business plan; and v) expanding the business. Again, the skills necessary to support self employment will be very similar to those for SE, and may include job analysis, skills training and on-going provision of support. It is also possible for the support worker to initiate contacts with natural supports such as unpaid volunteers and mentors who have experience as entrepreneurs who can act as an on-going resource.

This model has also been described as a micro-enterprise: a small business created around one person. Beyer and Robinson (2009, p. 65-66) reported that the main strengths of the model for people with intellectual disabilities are that:

- It respects the capacity and the assets of people with intellectual disabilities, by focusing on people's interests and strengths, and can be more flexible than mainstream employment and working conditions;
- It pursues equality by opening up the self-employment sector of the labour market, where people with intellectual disabilities are not represented;
- It reflects aspects of governmental thinking on increasing employment for disadvantaged groups, and on developing services to meet individual needs;
- It is for some people a way of gaining income from a hobby or an interest, with support and funding through person-centered planning, direct payments and individualized budgets; and
- It provides another way for a person with intellectual disability to move from being a client to being a citizen.

A review by Neufeldt and Albright (1998) of over 120 self-employment projects across low-, middle- and high-income countries found that there was considerably more experience in low- to middle-income countries in supporting entrepreneurship for people with disabilities than in high-income countries. In the context of people with intellectual disabilities, the small amount of research conducted on this model has addressed the best practice processes involved, rather than outcomes (Okahashi, 2001).

Despite it being a popular option for people with other disabilities, self employment was not considered a viable option for people with intellectual disabilities during a recent technical cooperation project in Zambia, on the grounds that they lacked business skills (Koistenen, 2008). While family-based businesses were seen as an option suited to those with higher support needs, involving support to the well-being of the family as a whole, they provided only limited opportunities for social integration and, in some cases; the people with intellectual disabilities were not receiving wages for their work efforts.

- **Social Firms:** Social firms are a type of social enterprise initially developed in the European context for people with psychosocial disabilities following the closure of the large 'mental asylums'. The specific social purpose of social firms is to create jobs for people who find it hardest to get them. (Sayce, June 2011).

Sheltered workshops have sometimes established small businesses which are labelled as 'social enterprises'. In Singapore, for example, MINDS (Movement for the Intellectually Disabled of Singapore*)*, an organization which provides sheltered employment for people with intellectual disabilities in Singapore, has established a car-wash business in a regular community setting. In this case, all of the workers are people with intellectual disabilities with limited opportunities to engage in regular work related or social activities within the general community. (Tay Tiong Beng & Aaron, 2003)

There is limited research information on the outcomes achieved by social firms for workers with intellectual disabilities. In a comparison of 40 people with intellectual disabilities working in a social enterprise and 40 others attending day centres, Forester-Jones et al. (2010) found that people in the social enterprise scored significantly higher on measures of life experience, self-esteem and satisfaction than those in day centres. They concluded, however, that while social enterprises represented better training settings for future employment compared to the day centres, social inclusion was still inadequate.

EMPLOYMENT MODELS/OPTIONS: DIFFERENT COUNTRIES

Recent decades have seen growing recognition of the working capacity of persons with intellectual disabilities in many countries around the world and a flourishing of initiatives to provide them with opportunities to perform meaningful, productive work in ordinary workplaces. Supported Employment has been the main approach adopted, in a variety of forms reflecting the different levels of support required by different persons with intellectual disabilities.It must be recognized, though, that the SE model was developed in high-income countries with well-established formal services. In low-income countries, the informal economy, especially in rural and less developed areas, is the major source of employment. People with intellectual disabilities are often employed in village-based industries, including farm work, similar to the patter in western countries in the pre-industrial era.(Parmenter, Trevor R.,2011) (ILO, 2011).

- **United States:** A feature of the SE programmes in the US, not always present in other countries, is the legislative base supporting inclusive employment options for people with disabilities in general. This strong legislation supported the initial growth of SE programmes across the country. At the same time, the strong support the US Federal Government gave to research and to research centres specializing in the study of intellectual disability was another significant factor in the growth and support of SE programmes. Legislation and subsequent funding initiatives led to better educational services for this population, including an emphasis on the transition of students with disabilities from school to work and further study.

Despite this enabling environment, there is consistent evidence that there has not been a parallel diminution in the number of people with intellectual disabilities in segregated sheltered employment settings (Braddock et al., 2008). And the latest State of the States in Developmental Disabilities, conducted by David Braddock and associates at the University of Colorado, reported that the proportion of Supported Employment workers among recipients of day/work programmes declined from a high of 24 per cent to 21 per cent in the period 2000 to 2006. The report also indicated that there is approximately a 3:1 ratio of non-competitive to competitive work outcomes for people served in day work, and sheltered employment programmes (Braddock et al., 2008).

Experience in the US indicates that the anti-discrimination provisions in the Americans with Disabilities Act (ADA) of 1990 appear not to have stimulated effective employment outcomes for people with intellectual disabilities. Therefore, it is assumed that there is still a strong belief that a person with cognitive limitations is incapable of gaining an integrated employment outcome, despite evidence that even those with high support needs are capable of learning complex tasks with adequate training and support (Bellamy et al., 1988; Gold, 1972, 1975; Horner et al., 1988).

- **Australia:** The development of employment services for people with intellectual disabilities in Australia has followed a similar trajectory to that of the US. In the early 1970s, the Australian

Association for the Mentally Retarded (now the National Council on Intellectual Disability, or NCID) expressed concern about the high numbers of people with mild intellectual disabilities entering sheltered workshops rather than open employment (Rigby, 1973). The Australian Federal Government, through the Commonwealth Rehabilitation Service subsequently established seven Work Preparation Centres for school leavers with mild intellectual disabilities in a number of state capital cities. After 12 to 18 months of intensive job skills and social skills training, trainees obtained permanent employment in the open labour market, generally in manufacturing industries, which were the major employers in those years in Australia (Parmenter et al., 1977; Ward et al., 1978). During their ten years of programme development, the Work Preparation Centres commenced trials of SE models, based on the research work being conducted in the US.

In order to stimulate the development of paid employment in integrated settings, the Australian Government sponsored several open employment demonstration pilot projects, a number of which concentrated on supporting people with high support needs. One of these, Jobsupport, has continued since its inception in 1986 and has achieved one of the best records in the country for supporting people with intellectual disabilities and high support needs (Tuckerman, 2008a; Tuckerman, et al., 1999).

The overall picture currently for integrated employment in Australia is not dissimilar to that in other countries. There has been no reduction in the numbers of people with disabilities employed in segregated settings. In fact the Commonwealth Government, despite earlier attempts to limit funds to this area of employment, has given way to the strong lobby groups including parents and service organizations by accepting segregated options as a viable employment alternative. This is also in spite of strong anti-discrimination legislation and a formal commitment to the various United Nations Declarations and Conventions.

- **Canada:** Neufeldt et al., (2000) found that the SE model was fairly well established in the four provinces of Nova Scotia, Ontario, Manitoba and Alberta. Canadian SE programmes are funded by the federal government under the Opportunities Fund, some Labour Market Development Agreements and by provincial/territorial governments, or by cost-sharing with the federal government.

In Canada, as in other countries, there is a pattern of SE agencies rejecting applicants with complex needs, such as those with intellectual disabilities. Stainton et al. (2006) have suggested that the increasing market competition in service provision and the emergence of for-profit organizations into the disability 'industry' have increased the 'commodification' of disability (in other words people with intellectual disabilities become commodities from which to make a profit), resulting in competition among agencies for clients who are easier to support. Special incentives may have to be built into the funding systems to counter the trend towards 'creaming' practices.

- **Finland:** With Finland's entry into the European Union (EU) in 1995, the country could access the Community Initiative Programmes of the EU Social Fund (ESF) to start several pilot projects on SE for people with intellectual disabilities. Regular surveys of the state of SE in Finland have been conducted since 1998 (Saloviita and Pirttimaa, 2007).

It is concluded that since the introduction of SE programmes in 1995, no more than 100 people had been supported. Clear changes in the composition of the people being supported changed markedly during the period 2001–2003. There was a major increase in the proportion of people with mental illness and a similar decrease in the proportion of those with intellectual disabilities being supported. The original concept of SE appears to have been distorted to be used to facilitate employment of people from different marginalized groups and, in the process, people with significant intellectual disabilities have found themselves barred, with sheltered employment and day care centres being the main options (Saloviita and Pirttimaa, 2007, p. 233). It clearly indicates that there are differing moral, political and economic value systems operating when the question of how best to support people with intellectual disabilities is considered, in contrast to other marginalized groups in a society.

- **Ireland:** Ireland has also been at the forefront in pilot-testing SE, the first programme being introduced in the late 1980s when a not-for-profit organization, St Michael's House, set up the "Open Road" demonstration project designed to provide job coaches for adults with moderate to severe intellectual disabilities to support them finding regular entry-level jobs. Soon after, several other similar programmes were initiated by other not-for-profit organizations, including St John of God's STEP Enterprises, Sunbeam House's Dargle Employment Centre and KARE's Employment Assist Bureau. At a conference Disability and Employment - What the Research tells Us, sponsored by the National Disability Authority, McCormick and McRae (2005) cited the 1996 RISE evaluation study by Lynch, McCormack, Pierce and Kelly into the status of SE in Ireland which found that 388 individuals in 30 agencies were in part-time employment, using the individual Supported Employment model, increasing to 449 by 1999. By 2005, McCormick and McRae reported that almost all agencies supporting people with intellectual disabilities offered supported employment to at least some of their service users.

In their paper McCormick and McRae (2005) highlighted that many people with intellectual disabilities who were working in Dublin supermarkets did not progress beyond entry-level jobs and did not get opportunities to move onto jobs of their choice. They emphasized the need for job development and career enhancement through additional on-the-job training. They also raised the possibility that low expectations of employers were placing a ceiling on the potential of people with intellectual disabilities. Kelly, Craig and Kelly (2010) reported that in 2009, 951 persons with intellectual disabilities were in some form of SE, whereas a group four-fold in size attended sheltered workshops. Still, questions remain as to whether the extension of the SE model to people with other impairments, such as those with mental health disabilities, has led to discrimination against people with intellectual disabilities who have higher support needs; the very population for which it was originally designed.

- **The Netherlands:** In the Netherlands, in addition to special secondary schools, there are two options for students with intellectual disabilities within the mainstream system - the 'supported learning route' and the 'practical education' route. The former is more appropriate to students who will graduate with a diploma, provided they receive special needs support. The pre-vocational practical education route is for students with higher support needs who would not qualify for a diploma even with additional support as reported in (The Netherlands Monitoring Report, 2005). The situation for people with intellectual disabilities in the Netherlands is not dissimilar to other countries with a history of welfare provisions for people with disabilities. Likewise, its extensive legal and policy framework establishes an approach that supports active independent living and access to employment for this population. The Netherlands is attempting, as are other high-income countries, to rein in burgeoning numbers of people who are in receipt of unemployment and disability welfare payments. This policy is having a negative effect on open employment opportunities for people with intellectual disabilities, as government initiatives to increase the employment participation rate of people with disabilities tend to target people with lower support needs. Despite some strong attempts to increase numbers of people with intellectual disabilities accessing SE, sheltered employment appears the preferred option for this population for the majority of parents and government. (Trevor Parmenter, 2011).

- **New Zealand:** The repeal of the 1960 Disabled Persons Employment Promotion Act and the adoption of the Minimum Wage Amendment Act in 2007 ensured that people with intellectual disabilities are guaranteed the same employment rights as other workers, including the payment of the minimum wage to people employed in sheltered workshops, unless an individual work has an exemption.

A partnership between IHC New Zealand and Tokanui Psychiatric Hospital led to the development in 1990 of the Teawamutu Gracelands Trust to support patients moving out into the community. The Graceland Group of Services has expanded its services across New Zealand, supporting people with disabilities (including intellectual disabilities) in inclusive employment opportunities and helping them to live independently or semi-independently. In the early 1990s a small group of people who had been pioneering SE in New Zealand set up the Association for Supported Employment New Zealand (ASENZ). ASENZ has developed and refined a set of principles of SE which are universally applicable. These are now accepted as the core principles and are central to all aspects of SE in New Zealand. The Association has given significant attention to training and development for people who work in SE. To date, New Zealand has not developed a significant research profile in SE. Thus, data on SE outcomes are unavailable. However, ASENZ has a considerable number of association and individual members, indicating that SE is seen by government and service providers as a strongly viable employment option. (Annual Report, New Zealand Disability Support Network, Annual General Meeting, 25 September 2014).

- **United Kingdom:** Supported Employment had its early beginnings in the United Kingdom (UK) around 1985, about the same time as pilot programmes were being sponsored in Australia and Ireland (Beyer et al., 1999). The term 'supported employment' in the UK at that time was used by the UK Government's Employment Service, responsible for vocational rehabilitation of people with disabilities, to describe sheltered workshops and a wage subsidy scheme that operates largely without job coach support. This is similar to the way the terminology is currently used in Australia.

Three important UK Government initiatives provided a useful framework in which to examine the penetration of SE in improving the life quality of people with intellectual disabilities. The first is the Disability Discrimination Act (UKDDA), which was passed in 1995. The UKDDA defines a person with a disability as someone who has a physical or mental impairment that has a substantial and long-term adverse effect on his or her ability to carry out normal day-to-day activities. The Act seeks to prevent discrimination on the grounds of disability in employment and other areas. The second important initiative was the release in 2001 of "Valuing people: A New Strategy for Learning Disability for the 21st Century", which identified significant difficulties in the coordination and delivery of services to people with intellectual disabilities in the UK (Department of Health, 2001). In recognition of the slow progress being made in achieving objectives in employment for people with intellectual disabilities, the UK Government has recently released Valuing Employment Now – Real Jobs for People with Learning Disabilities (Department of Health, 2009). This strategy sets out an ambitious goal to radically increase the number of people with intellectual disabilities in employment by 2025. The strategy will focus on people with moderate and severe intellectual disabilities, because they have benefited least from previous initiatives. This was a major landmark policy event in the UK, being the first Government White Paper in 30 years dedicated to people with intellectual disabilities (UK,Department of Health, 2009).

REMPLOY, the leading UK provider of specialist employment services for people facing complex barriers to employment, offers a combination of supports to placement in mainstream employment along with work opportunities in businesses which it runs in different parts of the country, catering solely to persons with disabilities. Following a review of its future business options in 2006, to enable it to support more disabled people into open employment in a cost effective manner, REMPLOY has taken steps to expand its network of tailored employment support services ('Interwork'). While people with intellectual disabilities (called 'learning disabilities' in the UK) are acknowledged to have high support requirements when it comes to mainstream employment, Interwork reports considerable success in its placement rates for job-seekers with this type of disability (see: http://www.remploy.co.uk).

- **Other European Countries:** The unemployment rate for people with intellectual disabilities in Eastern European countries was found to approach almost 100 per cent (Open Society, 2006). The vast majority who do work are found in sheltered workshops, and those with high support needs are generally directed to day activity centres. However, there was evidence of attempts to increase the participation of people with intellectual disabilities in SE. In a comparative study of Supported Employment in ten countries of Europe, undertaken in 2006-2007, it was found that over a third of users of SE services (35.3 per cent) were people with intellectual disabilities (Jordan de Urries, Beyer and Verdugo, 2007).

The European Union of Supported Employment (EUSE), established in 1993 and now with 19 national associations for SE, is a driving force in the endeavor to increase employment opportunities for their clients. EUSE conducts regular conferences and training workshops across Europe. It recently received support from the European Union Leonardo Partnership to develop a European Supported Employment Toolkit which was completed in mid-2010. This toolkit consists of a range of position papers and 'How To' guides, and has been designed to increase the knowledge and skills of professionals responsible for the delivery of Supported Employment services. To increase the replication of good models at the national and international levels will require strong government support. (EUSE Toolkit 2010)

- **Singapore:** Educational and employment services for the majority of people with intellectual disabilities are provided by two large voluntary agencies: the Association for Persons with Special Needs (APSN), which conducts schools and employment services for those with 'mild' intellectual disabilities; and the Movement for the Intellectually Disabled of Singapore (MINDS), which conducts schools, employment services, day activity programmes and residential living for those in the 'moderate' to 'severe' range. Both organizations conduct traditional sheltered workshops and programmes known as 'social enterprises'. Examples of social enterprises in Singapore are a car wash 'crew' which works in a regular community setting, and a 'thrift shop' that sells recycled clothing. While in some cases, these enterprises are located in regular community settings, they tend to project a welfare impression, rather than a regular commercial image. (Parmenter, Trevor R., 2011)

- **Japan:** In 1966, Japan adopted a voluntary employment quota policy to benefit workers with disabilities. Since 1976, under amendments to the Law for Employment Promotion for Persons with Disabilities, the quota is now a legal obligation, initially relating to persons with physical disabilities only. In 1998, amendments to the Law extended its provisions to people with intellectual disabilities. Two hundred and forty two such companies existed, employing 7,700 persons with disabilities. Over 40 per cent of these employees were persons with intellectual disabilities. (Parmenter, Trevor R., 2011)

The Japan Association for the Employment of the Elderly and Persons with Disabilities (JEED) plays a major role in implementing the nation's policies for people with disabilities. As part of its role, JEED conducts research into employment support methods for various disability groups, including those with intellectual and other developmental disabilities.Through its network of Local Vocational Centres for Persons with Disabilities, JEED provides support to people with intellectual disabilities in work experience and job coaching in order to facilitate a smooth transition to work opportunities. JEED also provides extensive support services to employers, including general information, counselling services, employment management support and technical advice.

The Japan International Cooperation Agency (JICA) has been active in assisting the development of SE and the training of job coaches in the Asia Pacific region. (Parmenter, Trevor R.,2011)

- **Malaysia:** In July 2008, the Malaysian Government passed the Persons with Disabilities Act, marking a shift from the former charity model to a rights based approach for people with disabilities in Malaysia. This Act stresses the importance of accessibility, equal opportunities and protection and assistance from the government, private sector and NGOs to ensure the full participation of disabled people in society. The National Council for Persons with Disabilities was subsequently established and a National Action Plan for Disabled Persons 2007-12 was developed.

The Joy Workshop in Melaka was founded in 1999 to improve the quality of life of persons with learning disabilities through integration into society through employment opportunities and enhanced community living skills. Its INTOWORK programme supports the transition of workers from the sheltered workshop environment into SE. Inspiration for this initiative was the work of the late Marc Gold and his "Try Another Way" approach to training people with intellectual disabilities. The approach starts from the underlying conviction that everyone can learn. It involves a planning process with the individuals with disabilities, their families and employers; proposed job matches, based on the requirements of jobs and individuals; actual job match based on job analysis; commencement of work, with on-site assistance, fading and transfer; and on-going support where needed (Warner, G. 2010)

- **South America:** Centro Ann Sullivan del Peru (CASP) was inaugurated in 1979 by DrLiliana Mayo with the help of her parents and colleagues, teaching eight children with different abilities in the garage of her parents' home located in the district of La Punta, Callao, Peru. Since 1985, Dr Judith M. LeBlanc, from the Schiefelbusch Institute for Research in Life Span Studies of the University of Kansas, joined the CASP as principal consultant. With Dr LeBlanc's specialist education input, CASP has turned into an international model centre where a series of unique teaching procedures have been developed into what is known as the Functional-Natural Curriculum. (Mayo,LeBlanc,2000).

The CASP SE programme is aimed at youths and adults with different abilities (such as autism, Down syndrome, cerebral palsy or developmental delay) of 16 or more years of age, who have the skills to be included full-time or part-time paid work in a real workplace. For example, student workers of the SE programme started working at the Ministry of Health (MINSA) in February, 2011. Tasks such as putting codes on documents, filing and other clerical duties have been assigned to them. They have become the first young people with different abilities who work for public institutions in Peru. An agreement reached between CASP and MINSA in October 2010 made possible this important hiring. It is part of a plan for promoting inclusion for people with different abilities into the Ministry of Health, a policy the present administration strongly supports. The CASP SE programme follows the principles first established by researchers in the US, including job coaches and on-going support in real jobs in the community. (Parmenter, 2011)

- **India:** The prevalence of intellectual disability is 94 out of 1,000,000 population (NSSO 2002). There is a paradigm shift in the approach to disability rehabilitation from charity mode to right based. However, Persons with intellectual disability have been proving their skills in specific jobs. Department of Adult Independent Living (DAIL) of National Institute for the Mentally Handicapped (NIMH) strives towards improving quality of life of Persons with Intellectual Disability through vocational training and placement services. As part of these services, the Adult persons with intellectual disability are trained to acquire vocational and independent living skills. Independent living means living like anyone else with same limitations and same opportunities. Persons with intellectual disability also observe the same style of living like other individuals of their society. The ability of Persons with intellectual disability to be productive was linked to social behaviour and practice and bore very little relationship to their intelligence (Cornelius D.J.K, 2009).

The Government of India has set up the Vocational Rehabilitation Centre for disabled at Bangalore and the same has been functioning from 1991. The Centre is providing vocational training in Computers, Carpentry, Welding, Fitter, Electrical, Embroidery, Book Binding and Tailoring etc. The Vocational Rehabilitation Centre has provided 100% placement for all the trainees who have undergone training. The Vocational Training Centre also provides counselling services for children/ persons with intellectual disabilities. The Government also has a scheme to provide incentive employers. for providing employment to persons with disabilities in the private sector. The Rehabilitation Council of India (RCI) was set up as a registered society in 1986. On September, 1992 the RCI Act was enacted by Parliament and it became a Statutory Body on 22 June 1993. The Act was amended by Parliament in 2000 to make it more broad based. The mandate given to RCI is to regulate and monitor services given to persons with disability. There is a need to study on the prevalence of employed persons with intellectual disability. Further more studies need to be done involving more number of HR professionals in different locations of the country. These efforts will enhance awareness creation among HR professionals regarding vocational potential of persons with intellectual disability. This in turn boosts inclusive employment of persons with intellectual disability in Govt. and Corporate sectors. HR policies may be developed and implemented to recruit the persons with intellectual disability. Data bases of trained persons with intellectual disability potential for employment need to be developed by the Govt. agencies in collaboration with all organizations working for empowerment of persons with intellectual disability. Employment exchanges need to register potential candidates and enable providing suitable employment (Bino S. Berry and K. Ravi Kymar).

- **Low-Income Countries - Examples from Africa:** There is a dearth of examples of SE in Africa for people with disabilities in general, and those with intellectual disabilities in particular. This is not surprising, given the degree to which this section of the community has been discriminated against for a variety of complex reasons; a major factor being general community negative attitudes toward this population (Mung'omba, 2008). Even in countries where SE has been an employment option for several decades, the take-up has been difficult. One of the reasons for this is the lack of government initiatives to ensure the long-term sustainability of programmes for people with high support needs, despite the cost benefits that can be achieved. There also remains a tension between the welfare and human rights approaches to support for people with disabilities.
- **South Africa:** The Living Link, a non-profit organization, founded in 2000 in Johannesburg, South Africa, supports the inclusion of people with intellectual disabilities in society and facilitates their transition from school to work to independent living. Students at the Living Link complete an Adult Integration Programme aimed at integrating them into society and into the community. The programme is life-skills based and focuses on practical components of daily living that are essential. After students have graduated from the programme, the Living Link assists in placing their members in suitable positions in the open labour market using a SE approach. Adults are placed in ordinary working environments, doing regular work where salaries and benefits are realistic and reflect work performance. Supports are provided to the employers and employers, in a mutually beneficially way. (Julia, Ingrid, 2000).

The Ntiro Project for Supported and Inclusive Employment, founded in 2000 in the Tschwane South District of the Guateng province of South Africa, targets the multiple barriers that people with intellectual disabilities face in the areas of education and work. Of particular significance is the Ntiro Project's emphasis on changing attitudes and building integrated community-based support. It gives strong focus to providing information and skills to district officials, NGOs and community organizations, and to building partnerships among them. The inclusive model has proved extremely successful, serving to progressively replace older segregationist models throughout the district. The project gives concrete expression to the new vision of inclusive education in South Africa and to the call for more inter-sectoral approaches. (Permenter, 2011).

- **Zambia:** The concept of Supported Employment for people with intellectual disabilities has been introduced in Zambia through a project funded by the Government of Finland. Implemented by the Finnish Association on Intellectual and Developmental Disabilities (FAIDD), in association with the Zambia Association on Employment for Persons with Disabilities (ZAEPD), the project focused on examining the relative benefits of an SE model in formal and informal economies, small business ventures and self-employment (Koistinen, 2008). Through this project, which ended in 2005, more than a hundred graduates were placed in employment either in the formal economy (as kitchen assistants, agricultural workers, office orderlies, cleaners, tailors and weavers) and in the informal economy (as housemaids, gardeners and poultry workers) which absorbs up to 70 per cent of the Zambian labour force. This project is an excellent example of collaboration between a high income country with experience in SE policies and practices, and a low income country. The issue remaining to be addressed, however, is how to ensure the sustainability of such initiatives, especially job retention, when the foreign aid programme concludes. (Koistinen, 2008).

CHARACTERISTICS OF SUCCESSFUL PROGRAMMES

- **Commitment of Stakeholders:** Programmes in which all the stakeholders, including government, employers, service providers and families, were committed to the principle of equity for people with intellectual disabilities led to successful and sustainable integrated employment outcomes (Mills, 2006; Wehman et al., 2006).
- **Programme Size:** Programme size appears to play a role in the type and range of day and/or employment services offered. In a national survey of rehabilitation agencies in US, Kiernan, Gilmore and Butterworth (1997) reported that smaller agencies, providing support to 50 people or fewer, were found to be more likely to provide integrated employment exclusively than larger organizations. In the current globalized climate of business amalgamations, based on the principle of economies of scale, the loss of a personalized service militates against the delivery of effective outcomes for individual beneficiaries.
- **Support Needs Assessment:** A comprehensive support needs assessment of the person with intellectual disabilities has been shown to be important, not only for the purposes of employment, but also for other life activities, including community living and leisure activities (Riches et al., 2009a, 2009b; Thompson, et al., 2004). It has been shown that work cannot be dealt with in isolation from other life activities (Halpern, et al., 1986). In terms of the sustainability of integrated employment, there is overwhelming evidence that people with intellectual disabilities tend to lose jobs, not because of their inability to perform the job tasks, but because of negative social behaviours (Chadsey et al., 1999; Knox and Parmenter, 1993). On the other hand, Chadsey et al. (1997) warned against too much emphasis being placed on a 'deficit-remedial model', rather than emphasizing the congruence or 'ecological fit' between the person and his/her environment. It may be more efficacious to find the right environment, rather than changing a particular social behaviour. This principle is especially relevant for people with intellectual disabilities and high support needs.
- **Person-Centred Planning:** Person-centred planning puts the person with the disability at the centre of the decision-making processes, taking into account the person's wishes and desires (Coyle and Moloney, 1999; Wiese and Parmenter, 2009). In the employment area, strong motivation on the part of the person seeking a job has been shown to be a significant predictor of a satisfactory outcome. Whilst more work remains to be done on assessing the impact of person-centred planning on client outcomes and satisfaction, research to date has shown promising results (Robertson, et al., 2006). In the pilot SE project in Zambia, Koistinen (2008) found, that good job matches were made when job-seekers' preferences and needs were recognized, leading to better long-term outcomes.
- **On-Job Support:** The 'place, train and support' model for SE usually involves job coaches working with the potential employee to identify interests and skills. This is followed by job seeking,

matching and placement. The employer might also be encouraged to make adaptations (i.e. accommodations) to a specific job in order to match it with the abilities and skills of the employee with an intellectual disability. In many cases the job coach might learn to do the job first, in order to subsequently teach the employee with the disability. In other circumstances, the employer might prefer for a regular staff member to teach the skill. This person may subsequently become a 'mentor' to the person with the disability. Another role for the job coach is as support to families who may initially have negative attitudes to their son/daughter working in a regular work environment, because of fears that they may be victimized. Parents of children with a disability are frequently over-protective. For others, cultural factors may encourage them to persist in hiding their child with a disability because of negative community prejudices (Mung'omba, 2008).

- **Parental Support:** Griffin et al. (2008) and Lindstrom et al. (2007) stressed the importance of families' attitudes toward their adult children's capabilities as being a critical determinant in their support for community-based employment options. Since the first point of contact in the diagnostic process is the medical and allied health professions, limited expectations are often entrenched in the child's early years. Lack of career choice was highlighted in a study of attitudes of parents and primary caregivers of people with high support needs towards SE (Ford et al., 1995). This study also emphasized the need for greater communication between the service providers and families. Donelly et al. (2010) have shown the importance of family networks to the person with intellectual disabilities achieving satisfactory employment outcomes. Koistinen (2008) concluded that parental support was important, though often lacking in Zambia, especially at the vocational training, job-seeking and placement levels.

CONCLUSION

Since its inception in the 1970s, SE has provided inclusive employment options for people with intellectual disabilities across several continents. The personal stories of what having a job means to people with intellectual disabilities is testimony to how important this issue is in terms of social justice and human dignity. A key factor in the growth of initiatives has been a clear policy commitment by governments to support such initiatives. However, experience from both high- and low-income countries indicates that on-going support is required for these initiatives to be sustainable. Low-income countries, given their rural nature and severe fiscal constraints, may be in a better position to test a number of the alternative models described above. For instance, self-employment, small business enterprises, and, at a regional level, CED, may be viable options, but these have not as yet been critically analysed. The evidence from a study conducted in Zambia questioned the viability of the small business enterprise model for people with intellectual disabilities, as it was suggested they lack the necessary business skills (Koistinen 2008, p. 32). An alternative would be to employ a person with business experience and a strong commitment to assisting people with intellectual disabilities, as the manager. The SE principles, including the important 'place and train' and on-going support features, can be used in each of these approaches. A positive feature is the growth of national SE organizations which provide advocacy and training support to their constituents. As these organizations gain strength, they may be in a position to mentor initiatives in low-income countries.

Two phenomena are emerging in countries where SE has a longer history. First, there is a natural tendency to extend SE to other disability groups; for instance, to people with mental health disabilities.

This has had the effect of lessening the take-up for people with intellectual disabilities. The second, and related, issue is the tendency for agencies supporting SE to select easier-to-place people for SE programmes. To further complicate the matter, the exponential growth of people receiving welfare benefits has led governments in many parts of the world to tighten the criteria and the assessment processes in an attempt to rein in welfare expenditures. However, a contrary position has been taken by Heath (2010), whose analysis suggest that welfare benefits to people with disabilities reduces poverty, but does not necessarily discourage employment.

Various countries have clear policies concerning employment for people with disabilities in general, which affirm the goal of community integration and support for individual choice. Despite this, however, the reviews highlight the reality that the vast majority of people with intellectual disabilities still do not have access to integrated employment; and in many cases, no access to any meaningful day activities.

At National level, Governments in consultation and collaboration with civil society and social partners bear responsibility for promoting opportunities for people with intellectual disabilities to take part in their communities and the broader society. They have to conduct a systems analysis of current situations, develop a set of goals and objectives to guide the implementation of SE initiatives and develop a national policy on integrated employment for people with intellectual disabilities. They have to develop a national implementation strategy and have in place an effective data collection system designed to track progress. Further they have to communicate the results of programmes to assist the process of attitudinal change among social partners in the community and widely disseminate positive results of pilot projects through all available media, since success stories can stimulate further successes. Also they must involve social partners and community leaders to act as 'champions' who can assist this process.(Parmenter T.,2011)

At Regional level it would be of value to develop a Regional Association of Supported Employment. To assist in the sharing of information and technical assistance, consideration may be given to the establishment of a regional support organization modelled along the lines of the European Union for Supported Employment (EUSE) or the World Association for Supported Employment (WASE), which would have Links with the EUSE and similar national associations for supported employment would give access to training materials and other technical assistance. These would subsequently organize workshops and training programmes at regional and/or national levels.

Despite enormous challenges, including extreme poverty and difficulties faced from attitudinal and policy perspectives in the provision of support to people with disabilities in general, and those with intellectual disabilities in particular, there are some positive trends. Of special significance is that the majority of countries around the world have subscribed to the various contemporary human rights principles relating to people with disabilities. What remains is the need for a genuine commitment to ensuring these principles are not only incorporated into national disability policies, but are put into practice and monitored to the best level possible in terms of the socio-economic conditions prevailing. Most countries have signed and ratified the UN Convention on the Rights of Persons with Disabilities. Article 27 of the Convention states:

States parties recognize the right of persons with disabilities to work on an equal basis with others; this includes the right to the opportunity to gain a living by work freely chosen or accepted in a labour market and work environment that is open, inclusive and accessible to persons with disabilities. States parties shall safeguard and promote the realization of the right to work.

This statement provides a compelling reason to explore how a country, even with limited resources, might embark on a programme to assist one of the most disadvantaged groups in its society to become engaged in work 'that is open, inclusive and accessible'. The fact that countries around the world have enacted specific disability legislation is a positive feature, but as noted throughout this chapter, people with intellectual disabilities are often left until last in the provision of support.

REFERENCES

Arnold, S. R. C., Riches, V. C., Parmenter, T. R., & Stancliffe, R. J. (2009). The I-CAN: Using e-health to get people the support they need. Electronic Journal of Health Informatics, 4(1), e4.

Beange, H., Lennox, N., & Parmenter, T. R. (1999). Health targets for people with an intellectual disability. *Journal of Intellectual & Developmental Disability*, *24*(4), 283–297. doi:10.1080/13668259900034051

Bellamy, G. T., Rhodes, L. E., Mank, D. M., & Albin, J. M. (1988). *Supported employment: A community implementation guide*. Baltimore, MD: Paul H. Brookes.

Berry & Kymar. (2012). Human Resource professionals' perception on disability relatedbarriers to employment of Persons with intellectual disability. *Indian Journal of Occupational Therapy*, *44*(2).

Beyer, S., Grove, B., Schneider, J., Simons, K., Williams, V., & Heyman, A. (2004). *Working lives: The role of day centres in supporting people with learning disabilities into employment*. Leeds, UK: Department of Work and Pensions.

Beyer, S., Hedebouw, G., Morgan, C., Van Regenmortel, T., & Samoy, E. (2002). *Inter-national reflections: An interim report on effective approaches to vocational training and employment for people with learning disabilities*. Academic Press.

Beyer, S., Kilsby, M., & Shearn, J. (1999). The organisation and outcomes of supported employment in Britain. *Journal of Vocational Rehabilitation*, *12*, 137–146.

Beyer, S., & Robinson, C. (2009). A review of research literature on supported employment: A report for the cross-government learning disability employment strategy team. London: Cabinet Office.

Blanck, P., Hill, E., Siegal, C., & Waterstone, M. (2009). Disability civil rights law and policy (2nd ed.). Thomson/West Publishers.

Braddock, D., Hemp, R., & Rizzolo, M. (2008). The state of the states in developmental disabilities. Washington, DC: American Association on Intellectual and Developmental Disabilities (AAIDD).

Chadsey, J.G., Linneman, D., Rusch, F.R., & Cimera, R.E. (1997). The impact of social integration interventions and job coaches in work settings. *Journal of Education and Training in Mental Retardation and Developmental Disabilities, 32,* 281–292.

Chadsey, J. G., Shelden, D. L., Horn, J. R., Bardeleben, D., & Cimera, R. E. (1999). Description of variables impacting successful and unsuccessful cases of social integration involving co-workers. *Journal of Vocational Rehabilitation*, *12*, 103–112.

Cimera, R. (2011). Does being in sheltered workshops improve the employment outcomes of supported employees with intellectual disabilities? *Journal of Vocational Rehabilitation*, *35*, 21–27.

Cornelius, D. J. K. (2009). *Vocational Training and Employment for Persons with mental retardation to meet the needs of 21st Century*. Report of the National Seminar - Planning for Comprehensive Rehabilitation of Persons with mental retardation, Chennai, India.

Coyle, K., & Moloney, K. (1999). The introduction of person-centred planning in an Irish agency for people with intellectual disabilities: An introductory study. *Journal of Vocational Rehabilitation*, *12*, 175–180.

de Urries, Beyer, & Verdugo. (2007). *A comparative study of the situation of Supported Employment in Europe*. Universities of Salamanca and Cardiff, in collaboration with EUSE.

Dempsey, I., & Ford, J. (2009). Employment for people with an intellectual disability in Australia and the United Kingdom. *Journal of Disability Policy Studies*, *19*(4), 233–243. doi:10.1177/1044207308314946

Department of Health (UK). (2009). *Valuing employment now – Real jobs for people with learning disabilities*. Available at: http://www.dh.gov.uk/en/Publicationsandstatistics/ Publications/Publications Policy And Guidance/DH_101401

Donelly, M., Hillman, A., Stancliffe, R. J., Knox, M., Whitaker, L., & Parmenter, T. (2010). The role of informal networks in providing effective work opportunities for people with intellectual disability. *Work (Reading, Mass.)*, *36*, 227–237. PMID:20634616

Duce, J., & Biersdoff, K. (2002).Supporting self-employment. Rehabilitation Review, 13(8).

Dudley, J. R., & Schatz, M. S. (1985). The missing link in evaluating sheltered workshop programs: The clients' input. *Mental Retardation*, *23*, 235–240. PMID:4069003

Einfeld, S. L., Piccinin, A. M., McKinnon, A., Hofer, S. M., Taffe, J., Gray, K. M., & Tonge, B. J. et al. (2006). Psychopathology in young people with intellectual disability. *Journal of the American Medical Association*, *296*(16), 1981–1989. doi:10.1001/jama.296.16.1981 PMID:17062861

Fletcher-Janzen, E., & Reynolds, C. R. (2007). Encyclopedia of Special Education (3rd ed.; Vol. 1). Academic Press.

Gold, M. W. (1972). Stimulus factors in skill training of the retarded on a complex assembly task: Acquisition, transfer and retention. *American Journal of Mental Deficiency*, *76*, 517–526. PMID:5012132

Gold, M. W. (1975). Vocational training. In J. Wortis (Ed.), Mental retardation and developmental disabilities. An annual review (Vol. 7, pp. 254–264). Academic Press.

Greve, B. (2009). *The labour market situation of disabled people in European countries and implementation of employment policies: A summary of evidence from country reports and research studies. Report prepared for the Academic Network of European Disability Experts (ANED)*. University of Leeds.

Griffin, C. C., Hammis, D., & Geary, T. (2007). *The job developer's handbook.Practical tactics for customized employment*. Baltimore, MD: Paul H. Brookes.

Halpern, A. S., Close, D. W., & Nelson, D. J. (1986). *On my own. The impact of semi-independent living programs for adults with mental retardation*. Baltimore, MD: Paul H. Brookes.

Hofer, S. M., Gray, K. M., Piccinin, A. M., Mackinnon, A., Bontempo, D. E., Einfeld, S. L., & Tonge, B. J. et al. (2009). Correlated and coupled within-person change in emotional and behavior disturbance in individuals with intellectual disability: Results from the Australian Child to Adult Development (ACAD) study. *American Journal on Intellectual and Developmental Disabilities*, *114*(5), 307–321. doi:10.1352/1944-7558-114.5.307 PMID:19928014

Horner, R. H., Dunlap, G., & Koegel, R. L. (1988). *Generalization and maintenance. Life-style changes in applied settings*. Baltimore, MD: Paul H. Brookes.

ILO. (2001). Influencing self-employment success for people with developmental disabilities. *Rehabilitation Review*, *12*, 75–85.

Inge, K. (2006). Customized employment: A growing strategy for facilitating inclusive employment. *Journal of Vocational Rehabilitation*, *24*, 191–193.

Inge, K. (2008). Choice and customized employment: A critical component. *Journal of Vocational Rehabilitation*, *28*, 67–70.

Kelly, C., Craig, S., & Kelly, F. (2010). *Annual Report of the National Intellectual Disability Database Committee 2009*. Dublin: HRB.

Kiernan, W. E., Gilmore, D., & Butterworth, J. (1997). Provider perspectives and challenges in integrated employment. In W. E. Kiernan & R. L. Schalock (Eds.), *Integrated employment. Current status andfuture directions* (pp. 97–105). Washington, DC: American Association on Mental Retardation.

Kiernan, W. E., Hoff, D., Freeze, S., & Mank, D. M. (2011). Employment first: A beginning not an end. *Journal of Intellectual & Developmental Disability*, *49*(4), 300–3004. doi:10.1352/1934-9556-49.4.300 PMID:21721982

Knox, M., & Parmenter, T. R. (1993). Social networks and support mechanisms for people with mild intellectual disability in competitive employment. *International Journal of Rehabilitation Research. Internationale Zeitschrift fur Rehabilitationsforschung. Revue Internationale de Recherches de Readaptation*, *16*(1), 1–12. doi:10.1097/00004356-199303000-00001 PMID:8486438

Koistinen, M. (2008). *Understanding experiences of vocational training and employment for persons with learning disabilities in Zambia: Lessons for the future*. Helsinki: FAIDD Finnish Association in Developmental Disabilities.

Kregel, J., & Dean, D. H. (2002). Sheltered vs. supported employment: A direct comparison of long-term earnings outcomes for individuals with cognitive disabilities. In J. Kregel, D.H. Dean, & P. Wehman (Eds.), *Achievements and challenges in employment services for people with disabilities: The longitudinal impact of workplace supports monograph*. Available at: http://www.worksupport.com/ resources/ viewContent.cfm/151

Kregel, J., Wehman, P., & Banks, P. D. (1989). The effects of consumer characteristics and type of employment model on individual outcomes in supported employment. *Journal of Applied Behavior Analysis*, *22*(4), 407–415. doi:10.1901/jaba.1989.22-407 PMID:2533194

Lee. (2004). *Vocational Rehabilitation for People with Disabilities*. Department of Counseling, School and Educational Psychology, University at Buffalo.

Lindstrom, L., Doren, B., Metheny, J., Johnson, P., & Zane, C. (2007). Transition to Employment: Role of the Family in Career Development. *Council for Exceptional Children, 73*, 348–366.

Mank, D. M., Rhodes, L. E., & Bellamy, G. T. (1986). Four supported employment alternatives. In W. E. Kiernan & J. A. Stark (Eds.), *Pathways to employment for adults with developmental disabilities*. Baltimore, MD: Paul H. Brookes.

McConkey, R., & Mezza, F. (2001). Employment aspirations of people with learning disabilities attending day centres. *Journal of Learning Disabilities*, *5*, 309–310.

McCormick, R., & McRae, J. (2005). *Job development in supported employment: A study of Dublin supermarkets*. National Disability Authority (NDA) Disability Research Conference, Dublin, Ireland.

McVilly, K. R., Parmenter, T. R., Stancliffe, R. J., & Burton-Smith, R. M. (2004). Friendship experiences and aspirations of adults with intellectual disability (ID). *Journal of Intellectual Disability Research*, *48*, 428.

Migliore, A., Grossie, T., & Rogan, P. (2008). Why do adults with intellectual disabilities work in sheltered workshops? *Journal of Vocational Rehabilitation*, *28*, 29–12.

Migliore, A., Mank, D., Grossi, T., & Rogan, P. (2007). Integrated employment or sheltered workshops: Preferences of adults with intellectual disabilities, their families, and staff. *Journal of Vocational Rehabilitation*, *26*, 5–19.

Mills, L. A. (2006). *Revitalizing integrated employment: A study of nationwide best practices for increasing integrated employment outcomes among people with developmental disabilities*. Madison, WI: Wisconsin Department of Health and Family Services/Pathways to Independence.

Mung'omba, J. (2008). Comparative policy brief: Status of intellectual disabilities in the Republic of Zambia. *Journal of Policy and Practice in Intellectual Disabilities*, *5*(2), 142–144. doi:10.1111/j.1741-1130.2008.00163.x

Murphy, S. T., & Rogan, P. M. (1995). *Closing the shop: Conversion from sheltered to integrated work*. Baltimore, MD: Paul H. Brookes.

National Sample Survey Organization (NSSO) Ministry of Statistics and Programme Implementation Government of India. (2003). *Disabled Persons in India, NSS 58th round (July - December 2002) Report No. 485 (58/26/1)*. Available from: http://www.domain.b.com/economy/general/ 2005/pdf/Disability_in_India.pdf

Neufeldt, A., & Albright, A. (1998). *Disability and self-directed employment. Business development models*. Concord, Canada: Captus Press.

Neufeldt, A., Sandys, J., Fuchs, P., & Logan, P. (2000). Economic integration and disability: A baseline benefits and costs study of supported and self-directed employment initiatives in Canada. *International Journal of Practical Approaches to Disability*, *23*, 24–36.

Nirje, B. (1985). "The basis and logic of the normalization principle", in Australia & New Zealand. *Journal on Developmental Disabilities*, *11*, 65–68.

Office of Disability Employment Policy. (2001). Customized employment. In *Applying practical solutions for employment success* (Vol. 2). Washington, DC: United States Department of Labor.

Okahashi, P. (2001). Self-employment for people with disabilities. *Rehabilitation Record*, *12*, 1–2.

Parmenter, T. R. (1980). *Vocational training for independent living*. New York: World Rehabilitation Fund Inc.

Parmenter, T. R. (2001). Intellectual disabilities. Quo vadis? In G. Albrecht, K. D. Seelman, & M. Bury (Eds.), *Handbook of Disability Studies* (pp. 267–296). New York: Sage. doi:10.4135/9781412976251.n11

Riches, V. C., Parmenter, T. R., Llewellyn, G., Hindmarsh, G., & Chan, J. (2009a). I-CAN: A new instrument to classify support needs for people with disability: Part I. *Journal of Applied Research in Intellectual Disabilities*, *22*(4), 326–339. doi:10.1111/j.1468-3148.2008.00466.x

Riches, V. C., Parmenter, T. R., Llewellyn, G., Hindmarsh, G., & Chan, J. (2009b). The reliability, validity and practical utility of measuring supports using the I-CAN Instrument: Part II. *Journal of Applied Research in Intellectual Disabilities*, *22*(4), 340–353. doi:10.1111/j.1468-3148.2008.00467.x

Rigby, N. (Ed.). (1973). *The retarded: Pensions or progress?* Canberra: Australian Association on the Mentally Retarded.

Robertson, L., Emerson, E., Hatton, C., Elliot, J., McIntosh, B., & Swift, P. et al.. (2006). Longitudinal analysis of the impact and cost of person centered planning for people with intellectual disabilities in England. *American Journal of Mental Retardation*, *111*(6), 400–416. doi:10.1352/0895-8017(2006)111[400:LAOTIA]2.0.CO;2 PMID:17029498

Rogan, P., & Rinne, S. (2011). National call for organizational change from sheltered to integrated employment. Journal of Intellectual and Developmental Disabilities, 49, 248-260. doi:10.1352/1934-9556-49.4.248

Rubin, S. E., & Roessler, R. T. (1995). *Foundations of the vocational rehabilitation process* (4th ed.). Austin, TX: Pro-Ed.

Saloviita, T., & Pirttimaa, R. (2007). Surveying supported employment in Finland: A follow-up. *Journal of Policy and Practice in Intellectual Disabilities*, *4*(4), 229–234. doi:10.1111/j.1741-1130.2007.00126.x

Sayce. (2011). *Getting in, staying in and getting on: Disability employment support fit for the future*. Presented to Parliament by the Secretary of State for Work and Pensions by Command of Her Majesty.

Stainton, T., Hole, R., Charles, G., Yodanis, C., Powell, S., & Crawford, C. (2006). Non-residential supports and intellectual disability: A review of the literature on best practices, alternatives and economic impacts. Vancouver: Community Living Research Project, University of British Columbia.

Stainton, T., Hole, R., Charles, G., Yodanis, C., Powell, S., Crawford, C., & Wilson, L. (2006, October). *Non-residential Supports and Intellectual Disability: A Review of the Literature on Best Practices, Alternatives and Economic Impacts*. Community Living Research Project School of Social Work and Family Studies, University of British Columbia

Stevens, H. (1967). Mental deficiency in an international perspective. In B.W. Richards (Ed.), *Proceedings of the First Congress of the International Association for the Scientific Study of Mental Deficiency*.

Storey, K., & Horner, R. H. (1991). Social interactions in three supported employment options: A comparative analysis. *Journal of Applied Behavior Analysis*, *24*(2), 349–360. doi:10.1901/jaba.1991.24-349 PMID:1890051

Taanila, A., Rantakallio, P., Koiranen, M., von Wendt, L., & Jarvelin, M. R. (2005). How do persons with intellectual disability manage in the open labour market? A follow-up of the Northern Finland 1966 Birth Cohort. *Journal of Intellectual Disability Research*, *49*(3), 218–227. doi:10.1111/j.1365-2788.2005.00648.x PMID:15713197

Thompson, J. R., Bryant, B., Campbell, E. M., Craig, E. M., Hughes, C., & Rotholz, D. A. et al.. (2004). *Support needs intensity scale (SIS)*. Washington, DC: American Association on Mental Retardation.

Tizard, J., & Loos, F. M. (1954). The learning of spatial relations by adult imbeciles. *American Journal of Mental Deficiency*, *59*, 85–90.

Tuckerman, P. (2008a). Job support: a demonstration of what is possible. *Interaction, 21*, 6-10.

US Government Accountability Office. (2001). *Centers offer employment and support services to workers with disabilities, but Labor should improve oversight*. Washington, DC: United States General Accounting Office.

Verdonschot, M. M., deWitte, L. P., Reichrath, E., Buntinx, W. H., & Curfs, L. M. (2009). Community participation of people with an intellectual disability: A review of empirical findings. *Journal of Intellectual Disability Research*, *53*(4), 303–318. doi:10.1111/j.1365-2788.2008.01144.x PMID:19087215

Verdugo, M. A., Martín-Ingelmo, R., Jordán de Urríes, F. B., & Vicent, C. et al.. (2009). Impact on quality of life and self-determination of a national program for increasing supported employment in Europe. *Journal of Vocational Rehabilitation*, *31*, 55–64.

Visier, L. (1998). Sheltered employment for persons with disabilities. *International Labour Review*, *137*, 347–365.

ILO Vocational Rehabilitation and Employment (Disabled Persons) Convention (No. 159) and Recommendation (No. 168). (2008). *United Nations Convention on the Rights of Persons with Disabilities / International Labour Office*. Geneva: ILO.

Walker, A. (2011). CHECKMATE! A self-advocate's journey through the world of employment. *Intellectual and Developmental Disabilities*, *49*(4), 310–312. doi:10.1352/1934-9556-49.4.310

Ward, J., Parmenter, T. R., Riches, V., & Hauritz, M. (1978). Adjustment to work: A follow-up of mildly handicapped adolescents who have undergone training in a Work Preparation Centre. National Rehabilitation Digest, 2(3-4).

Warner, G. (2010). *Good practices in economic empowerment programme for people with disabilities*. Paper presented to 3rd Malaysian Conference on Rehabilitation (MCR), Kuala Lumpur, Malaysia.

Wehman, P., Inge, K. J., Revell, W. G., & Brooke, V. A. (Eds.). (2006). *Real work for real pay.Inclusive employment for people with disabilities*. Baltimore, MD: Paul H. Brookes.

Weikle, D. W. J. Jr. (2008). Achieving community membership through CRPs: A reaction to Metzel et al. *Journal of Intellectual & Developmental Disability*, *46*(1), 58–63. doi:10.1352/0047-6765(2008)46[58:ACMTCA]2.0.CO;2 PMID:18271613

Wright, G. N. (1980). *Total rehabilitation*. Boston: Little Brown.

Chapter 16
Vocational Rehabilitation:
Recent Trends and Issues in Vocational Rehabilitation of People with ID

Neerajana Ghosh
Central Institute of Psychiatry, India

Vinod Kumar Sinha
Central Institute of Psychiatry, India

Shuvabrata Poddar
Central Institute of Psychiatry, India

ABSTRACT

The chapter summarizes key issues in vocational rehabilitation for individuals with intellectual disability, nature of vocational rehabilitation in in mild, moderate and severe intellectual disability, principles of rehabilitation for individuals with intellectual disability, assessment of intellectual disability and it's limitations. Then the chapter reviews the need for vocational rehabilitation, assessment required for rehabilitation and barriers of vocational rehabilitation for individuals with intellectual disability. the chapter then covers vocational rehabilitation process and preparation of the individual for rehabilitation. The chapter ends with social skills training and newer trends in rehabilitation like use of virtual reality and sensory integration.

INTRODUCTION: RECENT TRENDS AND ISSUES IN VOCATIONAL REHABILITATION OF PEOPLE WITH ID

Intellectual disability as the DSM-5 defines is characterized by deficits in general mental abilities. The mental abilities include planning, problem solving, reasoning, abstract thinking, and judgment, academic learning and learning from experience. All these abilities are essential for optimal adjustment for the individual. Inability to perform these functions results in deficits in adaptive functioning, so that the individual fails to meet criteria for personal responsibility or social and occupational independence.

DOI: 10.4018/978-1-5225-0089-6.ch016

There is marked deficits in communication, general self help skills, academic skills, activities of daily living and participation in society.

Intellectual disability or intellectual developmental disorder has its onset in the developmental years of the child, marked by deficits in conceptual, social and practical domains (DSM-5) (American Psychological Association (APA), 2013)

Criteria for the diagnosis of intellectual disability according to DSM-5 (American Psychological Association (APA), 2013):

1. Deficits in intellectual functions, such as reasoning, problem solving, planning, abstract thinking, judgment, academic learning, and learning from experiences, confirmed by both clinical assessment and individualized, standardized intelligence testing.
2. Deficits in adaptive functioning that result in failure to meet developmental and socio-cultural standards for personal independence and social responsibility. Without ongoing support, the adaptive deficits limit functioning in one or more activities of daily life, such as communication, social participation, and independent living, across multiple environments, such as home, school, work, and community.
3. Onset of intellectual and adaptive deficits during the developmental period.
    a. ICD-10 still uses the term 'Mental Retardation' to indicate intellectual disability. ICD-10 (World HealthOrganization [WHO], 1993) defines mental retardation as "a condition of arrested or incomplete development of the mind, which is especially characterized by impairment of skills manifested during the developmental period, which contribute to the overall level of intelligence, i.e. cognitive, language, motor, and social abilities. Retardation can occur with or without any other mental or physical disorder."

The definitions share some common factors, such as:

- Difficulty in learning.
- Difficulty or marked retardation in age appropriate cognitive tasks.
- Deficits in adaptive functioning.
- Deficits manifested during the developmental years.

Intellectual disability is further sub-divided into mild, moderate, severe and profound; the division is based on the level of functioning in conceptual, social and practical domain (Table 1).

Vocational rehabilitation or work rehabilitation or occupational rehabilitation aims at empowerment of the individual through employment. Vocational rehabilitation may be defined as an active, individualized process that is directed towards individual empowerment through assessing the individual's current level of functioning and use it effectively to engage the individual in a vocation suited to his or her needs. The core idea is to 'return to work' and 'stay at work'.

VOCATIONAL TRAINING AND REHABILITATION

Intervention and rehabilitation should always be planned and implemented based on the level of the individual's current functioning. To plan vocational training, functional assessment should be done. It is

Table 1. Level of intellectual disability and functioning

Level of Intellectual Disability	Conceptual Domain	Social Domain	Practical Domain
Mild	Preschool children may not show any conceptual differences. School-age children and adults often show difficulties and differences in academic skills like learning, arithmetic, writing etc. With support is able to do age appropriate tasks. Have concrete approach to problems. They show deficits in executive functioning and short term memory.	Appear to be socially immature compared to their age and may not be able to appropriately perceive the social cues and show deficits in social interaction. Conversation is less mature and may have difficulty in regulating emotions.	May able to perform age appropriate functions in personal care however need assistance in complex tasks.
Moderate	Lag markedly in conceptual skills. Academic achievement is limited to elementary level.	There is marked difference in social interaction. Spoken language is less complex than children of same age, may not be able to interpret social cue accurately	Can take care of basic personal needs and often participate in basic household tasks. Can perform independent job if under supervision.
Severe	Conceptual skills are limited. No or very little understanding of concepts and symbols.	Language in limited in respect of grammer and vocabulary. They are able to understand simple speech and gestural communications.	Require support for daily activities and continuous supervision. They are not able to make responsible decisions. They require training for skill development. Maladaptive behavior may be present
Profound	Conceptual skills involve physical materials; symbolic representations may not be available.	Very limited understanding of symbolic communication and gestures. Difficulty in understanding simple instructions.	Dependent on others for daily living

Adapted from DSM-5.

a wide spectrum of assessment that will help the therapist and the client to understand the level of functioning, difficulty, problems in personal and social life and range of activities of daily living. Vocational counseling may be implemented to assess the individual's aptitude, interest, level of intelligence etc. A vocational counselor usually focuses on interests, ability and skill level; here the assessment of the level of intellectual functioning is crucial. For the vocational rehabilitation of an individual with mental retardation understanding the adaptive functioning, interest and level of intellectual functioning is important, as this determines how far a person can be trained and adapts eventually to gain self-sufficiency and economic independence. After assessment the interest of the individual, suitable positions, requirements and other limiting factors are determined and the individual is trained.

Vocational rehabilitation has emerged as a mainstream intervention for individuals with intellectual disability and plays an important role in their empowerment.

Issues in Vocational Rehabilitation of People with ID

Intellectual disability is often accompanied by motor, perceptual and emotional difficulties. A child's behavior gives insight of the underlying emotional tone and is very important for planning rehabilitation and treatment.

Grigal and Hart (2001) found students with intellectual disability were less likely to have post secondary education or competitive employment goals; they are more likely to have supported or sheltered employment. Yamaki and Fujiura (2002) in their study found out that adults with developmental disabilities have limited economic resources irrespective to the fact that they had income support from government or were employed. Only a minor group earn higher than previous estimate, the majority is usually unemployed.

Verdonschot et al (2009) delineated several environmental factors that positively affect vocational participation like:

- Opportunities to make choices.
- Variety and stimulation of the environment of facilities.
- Opportunities for resident involvement in policy making.
- Small residential facilities.
- Opportunities for autonomy.
- Vocational services.
- Social support.
- Family involvement.
- Assistive technology.
- Positive staff attitudes.

There are other factors that negatively affect participation like lack of transport and feeling of not being accepted. Environmental factors are essential for rehabilitation at the community level, as optimal rehabilitation aims at making the individual as fully functioning as possible in personal and social sphere based on his or her ability. Therefore, while planning vocational rehabilitation, these factors should be considered.

- **Vocational Rehabilitation for Mild Intellectual Disability:** Individuals with mild mental retardation are apparently identical to the individuals in general population; however they are often not able to profit from the prevalent academic setting. They were previously called the educable mentally retarded, in a sense that the can gain from primary education. They are well able to be trained in skilled and semi-skilled tasks and be independent. So rehabilitation often involves training and eventual employment.
- **Vocational rehabilitation for Moderate Intellectual Disability:** Individuals with moderate intellectual disability is not able to profit much from school training and the focus of rehabilitation is usually to make them self-sufficient in managing daily activities, learn self care skills. With individuals with moderate intellectual disability, prompting and behavioral interventions have appeared to be effective.
- **Vocational Rehabilitation for Severe Intellectual Disability:** For vocational training and rehabilitation, the task is usually to make the individual enough self sufficient to manage specific activities of daily living. Fetko et al studied the effectiveness of instructional procedure (simultaneous prompting) which included providing task direction and controlling prompt at the same time form teaching simple tasks like closing locker door to young adults with severe intellectual disability and found that it is effective in teaching the task and the behavior generalized as well. Hence prompting, providing cues is effective in rehabilitation of individuals with intellectual disability.

Definitions of important terms to consider in Rehabilitation:

- **Mental Health:** Mental health is not just the absence of mental disorder. It is a state of well-being in which every individual realizes his or her own potential, can cope with the normal stresses of life, can work productively and fruitfully, and is able to make a contribution to his or her community (WHO, 2009)
- **Impairment:** Any loss or abnormality of psychological, physiological or anatomical structure or functioning resulting from underlying pathology (Anthony & Liberman, 1986)
- **Disability:** Any restriction or lack resulting from an impairment of ability to perform an activity in the manner or within the range considered normal for a human being (Anthony & Liberman, 1986)
- **Handicap:** A disadvantage for a given individual resulting from impairment or a disability that limits or prevents the fulfillment of a role that is normal depending on age, sex, social and cultural factors for that individual (Anthony & Liberman, 1986)

Principles of Rehabilitation for Individuals with Intellectual Disability

The International Association of Psychosocial Rehabilitation Services (IAPRSA), USA lays down the principles of psychosocial rehabilitation. According to the IAPRSA, USA, the therapist at the time of planning rehabilitation and throughout the process to the patients should adhere to the principles (Hughes, 1994):

- The ultimate goal of psychosocial rehabilitation is recovery. The process of rehabilitation should facilitate the recovery.
- The goal is to re-establishing normal roles in the community and integration of the individual with disability in the community.
- The goal of psychosocial rehabilitation is to facilitate and develop the individual's personal support.
- Psychosocial rehabilitation should facilitate improvement in the quality of life of the individual receiving the rehabilitation services.
- It is based on the principle that all individuals have the capacity to learn and grow.
- All individual must be treated with dignity and respect in the process.
- There are conscious and consistent efforts from the part of psychosocial and vocational rehabilitation practitioners to eliminate bias, labeling and discrimination practiced against the individuals with psychiatric or any other disability.
- Culture and ethnicity play an important role in the integration of the disabled individual in the community and improvement in their quality of life. They act as sources of strength and enrichment for the person with disability.
- The psychosocial rehabilitation program is to be based on the individual's strengths and weaknesses. So each rehabilitation process is unique and tailor made for the individual.
- The services provided in the process of psychosocial rehabilitation should be accessible, continuous, coordinated and available as long as there is necessity.

- The services in rehabilitation are to be designed based on the individual's unique need. The design must be consistent with the individual's capacities, and consistent with his or her cultural values and norms.
- The task is to integrate the individual with disability in the community and aim for his or her involvement as much as it is possible. The vocational or psychosocial rehabilitation practices should encourage the person's involvement in normal community activities such as school, work, participation in various community services, family occasions etc. in the process of rehabilitation.
- For the psychosocial rehabilitation to be a success, the active collaboration and cooperation between the therapist, the family or the care givers and the individual seeking the services are essential in the process of rehabilitation and fast recovery.
- The psychosocial rehabilitation practitioners should always strive to improvise the services they provide.

Keeping in line with the above laid down principles; the vocational rehabilitation for individuals with intellectual disability should target to facilitate:

- The process of adjustment to their environment. Adjustment is not limited to family but is expanded to the community.
- Enable self sufficiency. Often an individual with intellectual disability is scarred by social bias, discrimination, neglect and humiliation, they feel that they are different from others but are not able to comprehend the reason or difference. This discrimination against these individuals is often practiced by their own family. Vocational rehabilitation should aim in establish the individual's self sufficiency, self esteem and make them independent.
- Establish a role in the community. Role in community can be established by giving the individuals tasks that are suited for the individual but this should not overwhelm them.
- Vocational rehabilitation should aim to build personal support this in turn will give them a feeling of empowerment.
- Enhance quality of life, to improve self esteem and self sufficiency.
- Individuals with intellectual disability receiving the services should be treated with dignity. The society is often biased against the individuals with disability especially with intellectual sub normality, these individuals at times might have difficulty in completely and aptly perceiving social situations but they are sensitive to emotional tones and cues. Care must be taken to be sensitive to their emotion and they must not feel inferior despite of their limitations.
- They have the right to select their own areas of services. While planning the process of vocational rehabilitation the family and culture plays an important role in determining the process and targets of rehabilitation but the opinion of the individual should be taken into consideration.
- Services should be designed considering the age, needs and cultural demands of the individual.
- The rehabilitation process should target to incorporate the family in the intervention. The family and the care givers should be actively involve in the process as involvement of the care givers in any therapy or intervention facilitates faster recovery.
- The process of vocational rehabilitation is an active process. The therapist has to be in constant touch with the family and the individual receiving the treatment to assess the progress.
- Vocational rehabilitation for individuals with intellectual disability should be based on the interest of the concerned individual. While planning a vocation, the feasibility is crucial but the interest of

the individual should not be ignored. Often individuals with intellectual disability have difficulty in regulating emotions and have difficulty in motivating themselves, hence the plan must interest them so they remain motivated

- Reinforcement can also be used in the rehabilitation process. Improvement in self sufficiency, self esteem is a continuous, ongoing process and perhaps takes time to be effective and experienced by the individual receiving the rehabilitation service. So it is necessary to keep them motivated throughout the process of vocational rehabilitation. Based on the intellectual functioning the reinforcement can be chosen, both primary and secondary reinforcement can be used. The schedules for the reinforcements can be planned based on task demands and individual needs.

ASSESSMENT OF INTELLECTUAL DISABILITY

The lack of a universally applicable test poses a particular problem in research on groups of children. – Gould (1981)

Assessment of disability is necessary to assess current functioning and area of strengths and deficits; however, there is a lack of universally accepted test to assess intellectual disability. There are a number of tests, batteries and rating scale s are available but there are none that can give us a holistic picture of abilities and functioning of the individual. The vocational therapist or the psychologist has to make a choice of tests to be administered based on the age, and pattern of deficits of the individual. So while choosing tests or group of tests, there are few factors one has to be attentive to:

- The age of the child or individual.
- The testing procedure should not be so lengthy that the child becomes disinterested.
- Areas to be investigated, other than interview to plan intervention.
- Social adaptability of the individual.
- Test must be culture fair.

Gould (1981), states that there are two separate but important aspects to be assessed in cognitive skills in children with severe mental retardation, these are the assessment of overall intellectual functioning and exploration of the child's abilities and impairment. This is in fact mandatory in assessment of functioning in any individual suspected of intellectual sub normality. However there are many difficulties that arise while testing an individual with intellectual disability described by Gould:

- A single numerical index is not sufficient to give an indication of the individual's level of intellectual functioning, it is perhaps an over simplification of the level of ability of the individual. Many a times, assessment of children shows a marked difference in test results. There may be discrepancy in findings with scores varying from different skills to skills.
- Handicaps like motor, vision or hearing and other co-morbidities also adversely affect the test scores. So intelligence testing alone does not suffice for assessment of disability. Hence while planning intervention these findings and co-morbidities should be incorporated in treatment plan.
- Intellectual disability is often accompanied by behavioural problems. Also individuals with intellectual disability often find it difficult to motivate themselves or to carry out tasks. Lack of motivation and behavioural problems can at times give lower IQ scores.

So while the task at hand is vocational rehabilitation of individuals with intellectual disability it is essential to be aware of the limitations of intelligence tests as the scores are often colored by confounding variables (Table 2).

Need For Vocational Rehabilitation

Cooper, Smiley and Morrison (2007) studied the prevalence of mental ill health in adults with intellectual disabilities and investigated factors associated with poor mental health in these individuals. In their study point prevalence of mental ill health was found to be 40.9% (clinical diagnoses), with problem behaviour being the most prominent type. Further investigations indicated that mental ill health was associated with gender, females being more prone to mental ill health, life events, type of support available.

For the 1023 participants the major factors that were found to be associated with mental ill health were intellectual disability, experience of higher number of life events, smoking, high number of consultations with general medical professionals, living with paid support, etc.

Mental ill-health is found to be common in adults with intellectual disabilities. In their study they found that more than a third of their participants had mental ill health.

Intellectual disability is a lifelong condition, these individuals often experience a life time of discrimination, inequalities compared to general population, shorter life expectancy along with other health needs (Cooper et al, 2004; NHS Health Scotland, 2004)

Table 2.

Tests for Intellectual Development	Author
The Bayley Infant Scales of Menatl and Motor Developmeny	Francis Williams and Yule, 1967;Bayley, 1969
The Merrill-Palmer Scale of Mental Tests	Stutsman, 1931
The Weschler Tests	
Raven's Progressive Matrices	Raven, 1956;1960
The Columbia Mental Maturity Scale	Burgemeister, Hollander, Blum and Lorge, 1972
The Leiter International Performance Scale	Leiter, 1952
Scales for Social Development	
The Vineland Social Maturity Scale	Doll, 1953
The Gunzburg Progress Assessment Chart	Gunzburg, 1974
The American Association on Mental Deficiency (A.A.M.D.) Adaptive Behaviour Scale	Nihira et al., 1969, 1974
The MRC Handicaps, Behaviour and Skills (HBS) schedule	Wing and Gould, 1978
Tests of Language Development	
The Peabody Picture Vocabulary Test	Dunn, 1959
The Reynell Developmental Language Scale	Reynell, 1969
The Illionis Test of Psycholinguistic Abilities	Kirk, McCarthy and Kirk, 1968
Tests for Symbolic Development	
Mary Scheridan Technique	Mary Scheridan
The Symbolic Play Test	Lowe and Costello, 1976

Compiled from: Assessing the Handicaps and Needs of Mentally Retarded Children, edited by Brian Cooper

ASSESSMENT OF REHABILITATION

Before planning vocational rehabilitation, it is necessary to have a outlook of what is expected from the rehabilitation. As rehabilitation involves wide areas hence effective assessment is crucial. Assessment in vocational rehabilitation is a complex process and involves delving into vast areas of functioning.

Assessment of rehabilitation is of immense importance as it involves wide areas and functioning of the individual. An effective evaluation is essential to assess the requirements of an individual and have an understanding of the unique challenges each individual face. It is essential to establish the goals of rehabilitation and prioritize those goals.

The important objectives for tha assessment of functioning and disability should revolve around the following:

- **Identification of Needs:** The needs of the individual seeking vocational rehabilitation if ofcourse of crucial importance, but one should consider the needs of the needs and requirements of the individual's family. It should not be felt that the objectives of rehabilitation are imposed on both the individual and his or her family. They too must have an equal say in this matter.
- **Assessment of the Key Factors:** To plan vocational rehabilitation, it is essential to assess the strengths and weaknesses of the individual, the aim is to use the areas of strength effectively and to improvise the areas of weaknesses. The areas to be assessed along with others while considering the strengths and weaknesses of an individual may include but is not exclusive to the individual's family supports, expressed emotions in the famiy, social and economic status.
- **Development of a Plan:** The plan for vocational rehabilitation must be formulated based on the weakness, need and strengths of the individual. It also must be cost effective at the same time, appppropriate and keeping the background, degree of disability, social and cultural background and the resources that are available in view. The plan for vocational rehbilitation should always be individualized.
- **Individualized Plan:** The plan for occupational rehabilitation should always be individualized. There in no rule of thumb in planning vocational rehabilitation. Each individual is unique, presenting himself or herself with different challenges to the vocational therapist or mental health professional. So the plan should be based on the culture, social and economic background, family support, resources etc. Also along with it, the individual's and the family's attitude towards is or her disability must also be assessed as these factors predict the outcome of rehabilitation.
- **Follow-Up:** regular monitoring of the indivdual in the vocational rehabilitation process must be monitored. Vocational rehabilitation is a process, it is gradual and takes time and requires active involvement of the individual seeking rehabilitation, family members and care givers and the therapist. Regular follow up is necesssary to monitor the developments and progress. It is also essential to assess any other difficulty faced by the individaul in the process of rehabilitation or any other factors that ight cause hinderance to the process. The therapist can also monitor the emotional well being, self esteem and emotions of the individual to assess progress.

Domains of assessment for planning vocational rehabilitation for individuals with intellctual disability:

- Diagnosis and severity of disability.
- Gender.

- Present level of functioning.
- Performance of Activities of Daily Living (ADL).
- Self care skills.
- Quality of life.
- Behavior problems.
- Any other co-morbidities.

Assessment Tools/Instruments in Rehabilitation

Assessment is necessary for planning and implementation of the rehabilitation plan, the basic objectives of assessment are

- Assessment of the needs of the patient and his or her family.
- Assessment of strength and weakness of the patient and the family.
- To assess motivation and adherence to the treatment of the patient and his family.
- Present socio-adaptive functioning .
- To assess the role of family in intervention.
- To evaluate the progress of rehabilitation and areas of improvement.

Scales available for psychosocial rehabilitation are:

- Social Adjustment Scale.
- Katz Adjustment Scale-Relative Report Form (KAS-R).
- Independent Living Scale (Revheim & Medelia, 2004).
- UCSD Performance Based Skills Assessment (UPSA) Patterson et al, 2001.
- Independent Living Skills Survey (ILSS) (Wallace et al, 2000).
- The Social Occupational Functioning Scale (Mundt et al, 2002).
- Instrumental Activities of Daily Living (IDAL) (Lawton & Brody, 1969).
- Activities of Daily Living (Katz et al, 1963).

BARRIERS FOR VOCATIONAL REHABILITATION

Our work defines us. It is a medium through which we contribute to the community, it gives us an identity, a social identity, influences our self esteem, defines us and has a therapeutic value. Studies have revealed that engaging self fosters a better mental health. However important it is, vocation for an individual with intellectual disability is accompanied by barriers, both intrinsic and extrinsic:

- **The Narrow and Ever Shrinking Job Market:** Individuals with intellectual disability are always faced with the problem of a narrow job market. There are very few areas where they can apply. With each day the society is being dependent more and more on specialized work and computer technology. Also when an individual with intellectual disability seeks job assistance he or she is competing with all other work force who are perhaps well equipped than they are.

- **Impact of Stigma:** The society has moved away from how it used to perceive the 'mentally feeble' but there is stigma attached to individuals with disability. This prejudice is harbored by family, often care givers, employers and society. This adversely effects the individual's adjustment. Work or vocation itself pose as a huge adjustment challenge for an individual with intellectual disability who has difficulty in executive functioning and perceiving social cues appropriately. Bias and discrimination from others complicate the problem.

Often the vocational trainers do not maintain biases against individuals with disabilities; they often convey faulty and biased ideas about disability to the care givers and the individual seeking help. They expect that the clients will conform to a more dependent role and often employ them to unskilled jobs.

- **Poor Infrastructure:** Often vocational rehabilitation is difficult to implement as even after proper screening, planning and assessment, there is problem of poor infrastructure in many countries. There are many governments that have special services and reservations for individuals with intellectual disability or individuals with chronic mental illness but many times the recipients are often unaware of the services or the infrastructure flawed. There is often no or poor liaison between the psychiatric professional, psychologist and the vocational rehabilitation professional. Services are also at times overlapping, "unnecessarily replicated", time consuming and not economic. At the same time, many vocational rehabilitation services are poorly funded, lacking qualified professionals (Swart, 2007) (1)
- **Barriers Particular to the Individual:** Individuals with intellectual disability may have difficulty in screening out environmental stimuli and in turn interferes with their ability to concentrate which may be manifested as restlessness, forgetfulness, difficulty in attending to a task for long, remembering details of tasks. There may be difficulty in motivating one self, the tasks often may seem too monotonous at the same time, and they may have difficulty in learning new tasks. This is often accompanied by difficulty in interacting in social situation, handling negative feedback and critical comments, relating to superiors and co-workers which interrupts the individual's adjustment.

VOCATIONAL REHABILITATION PROCESS

Vocational rehabilitation is a multi-disciplinary process and requires collaboration between medical team, social workers, psychologists and administrators.

According to International Labour Organization (1981) vocational counseling is "assistance to individuals in developing a career or vocation plan. It involves helping the individual in clarifying his values, establishing vocational goals, identifying alternatives, formulating and implementing a career plan and periodically reviewing and revising such a plan on the basics of new information, goals and progress made." Vocational counseling plays an important role in the process of rehabilitation as it makes the goals of rehabilitation clearer for the individual at the same time identifying alternatives and formulating a plan for intervention. The International Labour Organization includes the following services in the process of vocational rehabilitation:

1. Vocational assessment.
2. Vocational counseling.

3. Work preparation and training.
4. Selective placement.
5. Follow-up.

Vocational rehabilitation for individuals with psychosocial disabilities can be implemented in various settings like sheltered workshops, supported employment, specific vocational rehabilitation facilities, community centers, hospital based, and employer based etc. Throughout the process interaction between the medical team, mental health professionals, employers and vocational therapist remains of immense importance.

Vocational Assessment

According to Jacobs, (1993), vocational rehabilitation assessment comprises of

1. Initial interview,
2. General medical (psychiatric) examination, and
3. Evaluation (Swart, 2007)

So assessment of vocational rehabilitation for individuals with intellectual disability must comprise of an initial interview which should focus on establishment to a therapeutic relationship with the individual.

Focus must be on assessment of the level of functioning of the individual i.e. intelligence quotient, social functioning, adaptability, ability to acquire skill and clarify the objectives and goals of vocational rehabilitation with the family or care givers and if possible with the individual with disability. It should also include observations of the client's communication, both verbal and non-verbal, interaction with family members and others and attitude towards engaging oneself in work (Swart, 2007)

Jacobs (1993) states that vocational assessment includes the following:

1. **Initial Interview:** The initial interview focuses primarily on establishing rapport with the individual. The interview may be structured or semi-structured. In the initial stage information is gathered, assessment of intellectual functioning, motivation, interests can be assessed and other medical history is clarified.
2. **Medical Examination:** It may involve any necessary psychiatric evaluation or other medical investigations.
3. **Evaluation:** At this stage for vocational rehabilitation for individuals with intellectual disability, the evaluation aims at investigating the general intellectual functioning, ability to attain skill, support available etc.

Randall (2002) puts down components of vocational rehabilitation of people with psychosocial disabilities:

1. **Work Motivation:** Work motivation assesses the individual's perception of his or her condition or whether the individual is able to comprehend any existing disability. Vocational therapist focuses on assessing the motivation of the individual, also must be careful to inculcate motivation in the individual seeking help. Individuals with mild to moderate intellectual functioning are able to

take responsibility and plan with the help of therapist short and long-term goals. Motivating and demotivating factors may be both intrinsic and extrinsic. The vocational therapist has to assess the motivating and demotivating factors that will affect adjustment to the rehabilitation process and performance.

2. **Work Endurance:** Work endurance involves compliance to treatment, attendance, current level of functioning. These factors determine the competence of the individual in vocational rehabilitation.
3. **Basic Work Habits:** Basic work habits are indicated by awareness of self, communication skills attitude, these factors determine the individual's adjustment with others in the work environment. Factors such as ability to concentrate, motivate one-self, correction of errors, task concept are essential in performance but are often deficit in an individual with intellectual disability hence these has to be objectively analyzed to be later included in intervention plan and skill training.
4. **Work Related Skills and Knowledge:** Individuals with mild intellectual disability are able to learn skilled or semi-skilled tasks. Hence before planning vocational assessment the skill or ability to acquire any new skill, prior work experience, prior experience, job seeking skills are to be assessed.
5. **Productivity:** Productivity includes work speed, quality of work and consistency in performance.

Techniques of evaluation: Botterbusch (1992) categorized techniques for work performance evaluation into psychological measurements, work samples work simulation or situational assessment and On the job evaluation.

1. **Psychological Assessments:** Rating scales, intelligence tests can be used as a starting point in evaluation of ability and to predict skill attainment and work performance. Psychological assessments may include measurement of interests, aptitude, intelligence, behavior and attitudes related to work and disability. However the psychological tests have to be administered and interpreted in great caution. The test results are to be used along with other techniques such as observation etc. to assess competency and plan vocational rehabilitation.
2. **Work Samples:** Rosenberg (1973) defined work sample as "A well defined work activity involving tasks, materials and tools which are identical or similar to those in actual job or cluster of jobs."Work samples have specific advantages; it is application based and practical. The vocational therapist creates a work situation similar to that of real situation and observes the individual based on specific criteria. It enables the therapist to assess the individual on his productivity in a time frame. Since the work sample resembles actual work performance, the vocational therapist has the advantage to assess the basic work habits of the individual, motivation, ability to motivate oneself, productivity in a time frame, skills required for the particular task as well as the area of deficits. Training can be given to improvise skill areas and to provide skill training in areas that require improvement.
3. **Work Simulation:** Swart (2007) defines work simulation as " placing the person into a realistic work situation where environmental, interpersonal, task, tool and other such demands are met. Work simulation can be set up in the vocational rehabilitation facility, or on-site at the workplace….a good understanding of the process of job analysis is necessary in order to set up a meaningful job simulation." Work simulation provides an opportunity to alter the important variables like level and extent of supervision, work speed, duration of work, tasks and other stress factors that affect the

individual's performance. It gives the opportunity to observe the stress tolerance of the individual and plan the task and duration of work accordingly.

4. **On the Job Evaluation:** The individual is observed and evaluated in the "on-site competitive work situation" (Swart, 2007). Since the observation is made on-site, all the criteria of the job and work situation are taken into consideration. It is often advised that the occupational therapist take the assistance of those who are well accustomed to the job, for example the employees to assist in the process of evaluation of work performance especially if the work is of skilled nature. On-the-site evaluation is usually recommended at the end of rehabilitation process when the client starts to show competence in work.
5. **Interpretation of Standardized Tests and Observations:** The process of assessment and evaluation is a continuous and ongoing process. The individual's performance is continuously evaluated to determine work performance, competence and placement suitability. Objective test findings should be corroborated with observations in work setting to plan vocational rehabilitation. Also the data for assessing work performance should not be based on the observations made in a single setting. There are many limiting factors that play an important role like motivation, physical discomfort, nervousness, environmental stresses, mood or other medical condition that might significantly affect the work performance.

Vocational Counseling

Vocational counseling while planning vocational rehabilitation for individuals with intellectual disability is conducted in a one-to-one session with the individual, the individual's family or immediate care givers. Counseling involves imparting information and helping the individual and family make the best choices. The vocational counselor considers the intrinsic and extrinsic factors influencing work performance and productivity while planning the rehabilitation. The goals of the rehabilitation and its feasibility are decided upon keeping in mind the client's interest and motivation. The vocational therapist provides the family of the individual seeking rehabilitation provide information regarding vocational opportunities and training and helps them to have a rational expectation from the rehabilitation process. The therapist also assists the client and the family to formulate short term and long term goal.

Work Preparation and Training

Work preparation and training involves preparing the individual for the task. After evaluation of goals, preference and work competence the next logical step is to prepare the individual for the work. The training may involve 1) pre vocational intervention; 2) work hardening programs; 3) transitional work programs; 4) case management; and 5) formal training (Swart, 2007) depending on the work and competency of the individual.

Selective Placement in Vocational Rehabilitation for Individuals with Intellectual Disability

The International Labour Organization (1981) defines selective placement as "the process aimed at placing the disabled people in employment suited to their age, experience, qualifications and physical and mental capacities. It should make use of all the normal resettlements services and provisions, in the light of the known and carefully assessed needs of each disabled person. This is the final stage of rehabilitation and includes three distinct processes: 1) knowing the worker; 2) knowing the job; and 3) matching the worker to the job."

There are various placement options available, a placement option can be chosen depending on the potential, need and work abilities of the individual.

Sheltered employment: Individuals with intellectual disability are often not able to work in real life competitive working conditions. Sheltered employment provides the option to work under special condition like sheltered workshops or home. This facility is provided by government, community or social aid bodies. In sheltered environments the workers enjoy a "quasi worker status" and the work environments also provide a therapeutic value.

However there are several disadvantages of sheltered employments (Swart, 2007):

- There is segregation from the mainstream.
- Remuneration is often inadequate and minimal.
- There is limited vocational development.
- The individual rarely enjoy a status of an employee, hence do not enjoy the allowances a full term employee enjoys.

Supported employment: Supported employment is way of enabling those who are capable of full time employment so as to enable them social and economic so as to enable them social and economic benefits. On-the-job support is provided by a professional or a para-professional to help achieve independence in real work settings. Researches indicate that supportive employment help in work performance, enhance financial situation, well-being and social involvement (Riddell, 2002)

Social Skill Training

Intellectual disability is often accompanied by deficits in social skills that mate vocational adjustments difficult. Social skill training is an important part of psychosocial rehabilitation and is defined by Liberman et al, 1989 as "behavioral techniques or learning activities that enable people to establish or restore practical skills in domains required to meet the interpersonal, self-care and coping demands of community living".

Social skill training can be divided into but not restricted to, the following stages (WHO, 1996; Bellack, 2004; Kopelowicz et al 2006):

- **Problem Definition:** This stage targets to enable the individual to identify and accept the deficits in social functioning.
- **Inventory of Assets:** Focusing and identifying the strengths.
- **Establishing a Reinforcing Therapeutic Alliance:** Improves the patient's self image, establish rapport with the patient so the patient is aware of the therapist's concern and is accepting.
- **Goal Setting:** It requires an open communication between the therapist and the patient to help set goals.
- **Behavioral Rehearsal:** Rehearsal of the learned behavior, through role playing or other techniques.
- **Shaping:** It involves building a sequence of socially appropriate behavior, and reinforcing the patient in every step.

- **Prompting:** Prompting or cuing can be used by the therapist to rehearse learned behavior.
- **Modeling:** Demonstrating the patient appropriate behavior.
- **Homework and Follow Up:** Regular homework can be assigned to maintain compliance to the therapeutic sessions and acquisition of required skill.

NEWER TRENDS IN VOCATIONAL REHABILITATION OF INDIVIDUALS WITH INTELLECTUAL DISABILITY

Virtual Reality

Virtual reality can be defined as a technological medium that consists of technological advances like hardware and computers, a high end interface that involving simulations and interactions from the user's end.

Virtual reality can be used for both assessment and intervention of intellectual disability. It provides a safe setting for teaching skills that may be cumbersome or risky in real world. It does not have any limitations of a real therapist or trainer like no time constraint, is patient and most importantly convenient. It also can be manipulated in ways which is not possible for the real world. Standen and Brown (2005) state that it can be used for rehabilitative interventions like improving social skills, improving skills required for independent living and enhancing cognitive performance. They reviewed five group of studies that used virtual reality to promote independent living skills like preparing food, shopping, road safety etc. It supported that the skills learned through virtual help can be generalized and applied to the real world. These findings can help in promoting other specific behaviors through virtual reality.

Kagohara, van der Meer, Ramdoss, O'Reilly, Lancioni, Davis & Green conducted a review of studies that involved electronic gadgets like the iPods®, iPads®, and related devices that were used to teach individuals with developmental disabilities. The studies covered the domains of:

1. Academic,
2. Communication,
3. Employment,
4. Leisure, and
5. Transitioning across school settings.

The individuals' age ranged from 4 to 27 years and the diagnosis was of autism spectrum disorder (ASD) and/or intellectual disability. Findings indicated that these gadgets proved to be useful technological aids for individuals with developmental disabilities.

Findings also suggest the effectiveness of computer based video instruction used to teach reading and task recognition, like reading names on grocery store aisle and finding corresponding location in individuals with moderate intellectual disability as these training sessions also provided "life-like" video recordings (Mechling, Gast, & Langone, 2002). There are more and more researches that indicate virtual reality training and assistive technology proves to be useful in teaching individuals with intellectual disability daily life skills (Tam, Man, Chan, Sze & Wong, 2005: Mechling, 2007). Video modeling can also be used to teach social skills to children with intellectual disability and results in improved interactions (Avcloglu, 2013).

Sensory Integration and Rehabilitation

Individuals who are intellectually disabled have difficulty in processing and integrating sensations from the environment. Sensory Integration (SI for short) refers to how our senses work together to organize and process incoming sensory information from the environment around us. Sensory integration is mediated by the central nervous system, made up of the brain and spinal cord. When our sensory system works together, we are able to interact with the environment in purposeful and meaningful ways. Research suggests that use of multisensory approach in occupational therapy for individuals with intellectual disability is beneficial.

The theory of sensory integration is based on the assumptions (Jaarsveld, 2007):

1. **Neural Plasticity:** The brain is able to change and modify.
2. **Developmental Sequence:** The ability to integrate the sensations develop in a sequence which is a result of the brain maturation, active interaction between brain mechanism and sensory experiences that leads to accumulation of sensory experiences.
3. **Integrated Brain Function:** The different structures of the brain are dependent on each other for its function. The different areas work together to result in integrated and meaningful behavior.
4. **Brain orgaNization and Adaptive Behavior:** Integration of the sensory information results to organized and meaningful behavior, this adaptive behavior in turn has impact on the brain.
5. **Inner Drive:** Every individual has the need to participate in activities that engages the sensorimotor systems and engage in sensory integrative activities.

Significance of Sensory Integration

According to Ayres (1983) theory of sensory integration, the various senses are always active and interacting with other, the tactile, vestibular, auditory and visual systems combine the continuous stimulation from the environment, make it meaningful for us and help us make a meaningful motor response. If the pathology restricts integration of the senses this leaves the individual dysfunctional and unable to perform the activities of daily living. Hence, Sensory Integration Therapy can effectively be used as an approach in the rehabilitation.

Integration of Senses and Intellectual Disability

Literature suggests a dichotomy in effectiveness of sensory integration, but there are case studies that indicate positive effect of sensory integration in individuals with intellectual disability. Wuang, Wang, Huang and Su (2008), studied sensorimotor profile and any possible association between cognitive and motor functions in children with mild intellectual disability (ID). They examined 233 children aging from 7 to 8 years of age with mild intellectual disability. The results indicated deficits in fine motor skills and mild impairment in sensory integration. They concluded that sensorimotor dysfunction was found to be frequent in children with mild intellectual deficiency. This indicates need for early intervention in children, focusing on fine motor skills and tasks that require sensory integration.

Jaarsveld (2007) is of the opinion that sensory integration can be used as a model of practice: "a child's development is dependent on many important experiences and one of these experiences is sensory, especially touch and movement. If a child is deprived of these because of cognitive, motor and dispositional restrictions, then there is no reason why they could not be provided to them through therapeutic environment".

The children with intellectual disability are not cognitively competent to incorporate all the information from the environment and respond to them meaningfully; often intellectual disability is accompanied by sensory seeking and self stimulating behavior, self injurious behavior, drooling, hyperactivity, seizures etc. sensory integration therapy can be used effectively along with other behavior modification strategies if necessary as an intervention process.

CONCLUSION

Vocational rehabilitation for individuals with intellectual disability is a challenging and ongoing process, rehabilitation procedures which are applicable to other individuals with psychiatric disorders are not applicable to them. The techniques have to be trimmed according to the ability and requirements. Vocational rehabilitation can be provided both in community as well as individual level but there are other factors that have an important role like prejudices and discrimination practiced against the individuals with intellectual disability by the family and community. The government also can take measures to provide them with rehabilitation and improvise the infrastructure. These individuals are part of our society and it is up to us to provide them with an environment suited to their abilities to enable a holistic development.

REFERENCES

American Psychiatric Association. (2013). *Diagnostic and Statistical Manual of Mental Disorders* (5th ed.). American Psychiatric Publishing.

Anthony, W. A., & Liberman, R. P. (1986). The practice of psychiatric rehabilitation: Historical, conceptual, and research base. *Schizophrenia Bulletin*, *12*(4), 542–559. doi:10.1093/schbul/12.4.542 PMID:3810064

Avcioglu, H. (2013). Effectiveness of video modelling in training students with intellectual disabilities to greet people when they meet. *Educational Sciences: Theory and Practice*, *13*(1).

Ayres, A. J. (1983). *Sensory integration and learning disorders* (8th ed.). Los Angeles, CA: Western Psychological Services.

Bellack, A. S. (2004). Skills training for people with severe mental illness. *Psychiatric Rehabilitation Journal*, *27*(4), 375–391. doi:10.2975/27.2004.375.391 PMID:15222149

Botterbusch, K. F. (1982). *A Comparison of Commercial Vocational Evaluation Systems*. Academic Press.

Cooper, B. (1981). *Assessing the handicaps and needs of mentally retarded children*. Academic Press Inc.

Cooper, S. A., Melville, C. A., & Morrison, J. (2004). People with intellectual disabilities. Their health needs People with intellectual disabilities. *BMJ (Clinical Research Ed.)*, *329*(7463), 414–415. doi:10.1136/bmj.329.7463.414 PMID:15321883

Cooper, S. A., Smiley, E., Morrison, J., Williamson, A., & Allan, L. (2007). Mental ill-health in adults with intellectual disabilities: Prevalence and associated factors. *The British Journal of Psychiatry*, *190*(1), 27–35. doi:10.1192/bjp.bp.106.022483 PMID:17197653

Fetko, K. S., Schuster, J. W., Harley, D. A., & Collins, B. C. (1999). Using simultaneous prompting to teach a chained vocational task to young adults with severe intellectual disabilities. *Education and Training in Mental Retardation and Developmental Disabilities*, 318–329.

Grigal, M., Hart, D., & Migliore, A. (2011). Comparing transition planning, postsecondary education, and employment outcomes of students with intellectual and other disabilities. *Career Development for Exceptional Individuals*.

Health Scotland, N. H. S. (2004). *Health Needs Assessment Report*. People with Learning Disabilities in Scotland. NHS Health Scotland.

Hughes, R. (1994). Psychiatric rehabilitation: An essential health service for people with serious and persistent mental illness. In An Introduction to Psychiatric Rehabilitation. Academic Press.

International Labour Organization (ILO). (1981). *Vocational rehabilitation and the employment of the disabled: A glossary*. Geneva: ILO.

Jaarsveld, A. V. (2007). Sensory Integration in mental retardation and pervasive developmental disorders. In R. Crouch & V. Alers (Eds.), *Occupational therapy in psychiatry and mental health* (pp. 369–391). Whurr Publishers.

Jacobs, K. (1993). Work assessments and programming. Willard and Spackman's Occupational Therapy, 7, 272-299.

Kagohara, D. M., van der Meer, L., Ramdoss, S., O'Reilly, M. F., Lancioni, G. E., Davis, T. N., & Green, V. A. et al. (2013). Using iPods® and iPads® in teaching programs for individuals with developmental disabilities: A systematic review. *Research in Developmental Disabilities*, *34*(1), 147–156. doi:10.1016/j.ridd.2012.07.027 PMID:22940168

Katz, M. M., & Warren, W. L. (1999). *Katz Adjustment Scales relative report form (KAS-R) manual*. Academic Press.

Katz, S., Ford, A. B., Moskowitz, R. W., Jackson, B. A., & Jaffe, M. W. (1963). Studies of illness in the aged: the index of ADL: a standardized measure of biological and psychosocial function. *Journal of the American Medical Association*, *185*(12), 914–919. doi:10.1001/jama.1963.03060120024016 PMID:14044222

Kopelowicz, A., Liberman, R. P., & Zarate, R. (2006). Recent advances in social skills training for schizophrenia. *Schizophrenia Bulletin*, *32*(suppl 1), S12–S23. doi:10.1093/schbul/sbl023 PMID:16885207

Lawton, M., & Brody, E. (1969). Assessment of older people: Self maintaining and instrumental activities of daily living. *The Gerontologist*, *9*(3 Part 1), 179–186. doi:10.1093/geront/9.3_Part_1.179 PMID:5349366

Liberman, R. P., Corrigan, P. W., & Schade, M. L. (1989). The interaction of drug and psychosocial treatment. *International Review of Psychiatry (Abingdon, England)*, *1*, 289–294. doi:10.3109/09540268909110419

Mechling, L. C., Gast, D. L., & Langone, J. (2002). Computer-based video instruction to teach persons with moderate intellectual disabilities to read grocery aisle signs and locate items. *The Journal of Special Education, 35*(4), 224–240. doi:10.1177/002246690203500404

Mundt, J. C., Marks, I. M., Shear, M. K., & Greist, J. M. (2002). The Work and Social Adjustment Scale: A simple measure of impairment in functioning. *The British Journal of Psychiatry, 180*(5), 461–464. doi:10.1192/bjp.180.5.461 PMID:11983645

Patterson, T. L., Goldman, S., McKibbin, C. L., Hughs, T., & Jeste, D. V. (2001). UCSD Performance-Based Skills Assessment: Development of a new measure of everyday functioning for severely mentally ill adults. *Schizophrenia Bulletin, 27*(2), 235–245. doi:10.1093/oxfordjournals.schbul.a006870 PMID:11354591

Randall, L. (2002). *Psychosocial aspects of functional capacity evaluations.* Paper presented at Vocational Rehabilitation Workshop, Pretoria, South Africa.

Revheim, N., & Medalia, A. (2004). The independent living scales as a measure of functional outcome for schizophrenia. *Psychiatric Services (Washington, D.C.), 55*(9), 1052–1054. doi:10.1176/appi.ps.55.9.1052 PMID:15345767

Riddell, S. (2002). Work preparation and vocational rehabilitation: a literature review. Book Work Preparation and Vocational Rehabilitation: A literature. *RE:view.*

Rosenberg, B. (1973). *The work sample approach to vocational evaluation.Vocational evaluation for rehabilitation services.* Springfield, IL: Charles C Thomas.

Standen, P. J., & Brown, D. J. (2005). Virtual reality in the rehabilitation of people with intellectual disabilities [review]. *Cyberpsychology & Behavior, 8*(3), 272–282. doi:10.1089/cpb.2005.8.272 PMID:15971976

Swart, L. (2007). Vocational Rehabilitation in psychiatry and mental health. In R. Crouch & V. Alers (Eds.), *Occupational therapy in psychiatry and mental health* (pp. 208–229). Whurr Publishers.

Tam, S. F., Man, D. W. K., Chan, Y. P., Sze, P. C., & Wong, C. M. (2005). Evaluation of a Computer-Assisted, 2-D Virtual Reality System for Training People With Intellectual Disabilities on How to Shop. *Rehabilitation Psychology, 50*(3), 285–291. doi:10.1037/0090-5550.50.3.285

Verdonschot, M. M., De Witte, L. P., Reichrath, E., Buntinx, W. H. E., & Curfs, L. M. G. (2009). Impact of environmental factors on community participation of persons with an intellectual disability: A systematic review. *Journal of Intellectual Disability Research, 53*(1), 54–64. doi:10.1111/j.1365-2788.2008.01128.x PMID:19093982

Wallace, C. J., Liberman, R. P., Tauber, R., & Wallace, J. (2000). The Independent Living Skills Survey: A comprehensive measure of the community functioning of severely and persistently mentally ill individuals. *Schizophrenia Bulletin, 26*(3), 631–658. doi:10.1093/oxfordjournals.schbul.a033483 PMID:10993403

Weissman, M. M., & Bothwell, S. (1976). Assessment of social adjustment by patient self-report. *Archives of General Psychiatry, 33*(9), 1111. doi:10.1001/archpsyc.1976.01770090101010 PMID:962494

World Health Organization. (1996). *Psychosocial rehabilitation: A consensus statement.* Geneva: World Health Organization.

World Health Organization. (1993). *The ICD-10 Classification of Mental and Behavioural Disorders* (10th ed.). Geneva: World Health Organization.

Wuang, Y. P., Wang, C. C., Huang, M. H., & Su, C. Y. (2008). Profiles and cognitive predictors of motor functions among early school-age children with mild intellectual disabilities. *Journal of Intellectual Disability Research*, *52*(12), 1048–1060. doi:10.1111/j.1365-2788.2008.01096.x PMID:18557969

Yamaki, K., & Fujiura, G. T. (2002). Employment and income status of adults with developmental disabilities living in the community. *Mental Retardation*, *40*(2), 132–141. doi:10.1352/0047-6765(2002)040<0132:EAISOA>2.0.CO;2 PMID:11925267

Chapter 17
Use of Assistive Technology to Empower Persons with Intellectual Disabilities

Sanjeev Kumar Gupta
All India Institute of Speech and Hearing, India

ABSTRACT

This chapter focuses on the use of assistive technology in persons with Intellectual Disabilities (IDs). Persons with IDs have significant limitations, both in intellectual functioning and in adaptive behaviors. The use of assistive technology is essential to help persons with IDs and make them independent in all spheres of life. Assistive technology devices and services can be used to teach, train, rehabilitate, and empower persons in a variety of daily activities viz. new learning, home living, employment, health and safety, communication, social activities, protection and leisure. Empirical studies suggest that assistive technology is effective in improving the quality of life of persons with IDs and make them less dependent on others. This chapter investigates the available research evidence on the use of assistive technology in IDs, discusses utilizations, impediments/barriers, implications and suggests recommendations for future research.

INTRODUCTION

In today's world, technology has become an integral part of human life impacting every sphere of daily living. For example, people are purchasing everything from cookies to clothes, movie tickets to flight tickets online; using elevator and escalators, using smart phones to send instant group messages, photos, videos, and files; to name a few. Technology has also become an integral part of the advancement of medical diagnostic assessment and treatment. Telemedicine has reached remote areas of villages. But, there is a common concern that persons with disabilities in general, are among the most excluded ones in the process of development of the country. Technology has changed and continues to change the way people manage things in both, their personal as well as professional lives. So, the natural extension of that is to see the impact and the integration of technology in the empowerment of persons with disabilities in the same way as it has been in other areas of life (Alnahdi, 2014).

DOI: 10.4018/978-1-5225-0089-6.ch017

The focus on technology being used by people with intellectual disabilities (IDs) is a fairly recent phenomenon (Wehmeyer & Smith, 2004). The American Association on Intellectual and Developmental Disabilities (2009), defined Intellectual disability as a "disability characterized by significant limitations, both in intellectual functioning (reasoning, learning, problem solving) and in adaptive behavior, which covers a range of everyday social and practical skills. This disability originates before the age of 18". Technology has the potential to contribute to a better quality of life for persons with IDs, which is more than just a matter of convenience (Wehmeyer, Palmer, Smith, Davies, & Stock, 2008). Use of technology is indispensable in persons with IDs, particularly in the area of early disability detection, prevention, identification, assessment and rehabilitation.

According to the Census of India 2011, there are 26.81 million persons with disabilities in India who constitute 2.21% of the total population. Out of the total persons with disabilities, 1.5 million (5.61%) are mentally retarded or intellectually disabled in India. The distribution of the population suffering from mental retardation is shown in Table 1 (Census of India, 2013). However, estimates vary across sources. A new World Bank Report (O'Keefe, 2009) on disabled persons in India, has observed that there is growing evidence that people with disabilities comprise between 5 and 8 per cent of the Indian population (around 55-90 million individuals). The prevalence of IDs is calculated to be 1 to 3% in developed countries (Petterson, Bourke, Leonard, Jacoby, & Bower, 2007). Millions of people worldwide are affected by IDs which burdens not only the people who suffer from it, but also the family and society as a group (Katz & Lazcano-Ponce, 2008). The development of assistive technology devices and equipments has made significant contributions towards improving lives of people with IDs and reducing the burden on their families and society (Table 1).

The term "assistive technology" (AT) refers to a variety of tools, devices, equipments or instruments that help persons with IDs to educate, empower, improve, rehabilitate, train and adjust within their daily context and achieve a superior quality of life. AT includes many resources, which are expected to create positive and vital behavioral as well as social profits for the users by reducing the negative impact of their problems and related difficulties (Bauer, Elsaesser, & Arthanat, 2011; Reichle, 2011). AT can be a device or a service. An *assistive technology device* is any item, piece of equipment, or product system that is used to increase, maintain, or improve functional capabilities of persons with IDs, whereas an *assistive technology service* refers to any service that helps an individual with IDs to select, acquire, or use an assistive technology device (P.L. 103-218: The Tech Act amendments in 1994). AT devices and services can be used in a variety of daily activities viz. education, new learning, home living, employment, health and safety, communication, social activities, protection, sports, recreation and leisure, and in medical services. Persons with IDs should receive AT that is best suited to their characteristics, tasks, and environments (Bauer et al., 2011; Borg, Larson, & Östegren, 2011).

The mere use of AT may not be sufficient to guarantee a positive outcome. Such an outcome is more likely to occur if one adds, to the provision of technology, an explicit and carefully designed intervention

Table 1. Population suffering from mental retardation

Gender	Total	Rural	Urban
Persons	15,05,624	10,25,560	4,80,064
Males	8,70,708	5,91,408	2,79,300
Females	6,34,916	4,34,152	2,00,764

Census of India, 2013.

aimed at ensuring that the persons learn how to use it effectively (Lancioni, Sigafoos, O'reilly, & Singh, 2013). When one thinks of issues pertaining to technology and IDs, it is within the context of a class of high-and-low tech devices that fall under the category of *assistive technology* (Wehmeyer, Smith, Palmer, Davies, & Stock, 2004). This chapter aims to serve as a general review on the use of assistive technology to empower persons with intellectual disabilities. Especially, this chapter aims to:

1. Identify key assistive technology services for persons with intellectual disabilities,
2. Identify key assistive technology devices for persons with intellectual disabilities,
3. Compiling recent studies on assistive technology and intellectual disabilities,
4. Discuss impediments, and
5. Recommend directions for future research.

ASSISTIVE TECHNOLOGY SERVICES FOR PERSONS WITH INTELLECTUAL DISABILITIES

The Tech Act defines the term assistive technology service as any service that directly assists an individual with a disability in the selection, acquisition, or use of assistive technology devices. The term includes:

1. Evaluating the needs of an individual in the individual's customary environment.
2. Purchasing, leasing, or otherwise providing for the acquisition of AT devices by individuals with disabilities.
3. Selecting, designing, fitting, customizing, adapting, applying, maintaining, repairing, or replacing assistive technology devices.
4. Coordinating and using other therapies, interventions, or services with assistive technology devices, such as those associated with existing education and rehabilitation plans and programs.
5. Training or technical assistance for an individual with disabilities or, where appropriate, the family.
6. Training or technical assistance for professionals, employers, or other individuals who provide employment services or are involved in the major life functions of individuals with IDs.

ASSISTIVE TECHNOLOGY DEVICES FOR PERSONS WITH INTELLECTUAL DISABILITIES

AT devices enables an individual to perform functions that can be achieved by no other means. These devices help to access for participation in programs or activities which otherwise would be closed to the individuals with IDs. There are many AT devices that can be useful for persons with IDs. Few devices/ technology have been discussed here:

1. **Computer-Aided Instruction:** Okolo, Bahr, and Reith (1993) have defined Computer-Aided Instruction (CAI) as "the use of a computer or other associated technology with the intention of improving students' skills, knowledge, or academic performance". CAI devices aimed at providing verbal or pictorial cues to support persons through the performance of multistep activities (Sigafoos et al., 2009). Traditional CAI programs are mostly presented in a linear format, involving text or

still pictures, and give little control of the process to students. Whereas, contemporary CAI programs are different from traditional ones, in the way they involve sound, video or animation, and also allow a range of interaction. With the help of CAI, young children with disabilities can learn word recognition and transfer acquired skills to functional materials (Lee & Vail, 2005).

2. **Microswitches and Microswitch Clusters:** Microswitch devices can be activated with minimal responses and are used in combination with an electronic control system and basic software (Lancioni, O'Reilly, & Basili, 2001). Microswitches have been used among people with severe/profound intellectual or multiple disabilities to help reduce isolation and increase their interaction with the surrounding world such as obtaining environmental stimulation independently or requesting for it efficiently (Lancioni et al., 2001). Microswitches aimed at allowing the persons to access environmental stimulation with minimal responses. Microswitch clusters devices are useful to strengthen adaptive responses and inhibit problematic behaviour (Lancioni et al., 2008).
3. **Portable Electronic Devices:** Portable electronic devices (PEDs) are a type of electronic device having the capacity to record, store, and transmit text, video or audio data. PEDs include iPad, iPhone, iPod, cellular/smartphones, digital watches, portable digital assistant, laptops, media players with audio playback, and handheld video players. Use of PEDs by persons with IDs is gaining increasing research attention. These devices and apps clearly have a role within the spectrum of augmentative and alternative communication devices currently available. They may have some distinct advantages in cost, ease of use and acceptability, but more research into their use is needed (Mechling, 2011). Thus, the proper use of PEDs can be helpful for persons with IDs or multiple disabilities.
4. **Mobile Technology:** Recent developments in mobile technology (m-technology), including the introduction of the iPad and other smartphone and tablet devices, have provided important new tools for communication (McNaughton & Light, 2013). The m-technology revolution has had dramatic effects on the lives of many individuals with complex communication needs, including those with developmental disabilities (Flores et al., 2012). The use of technology-based interventions for persons with IDs is evident by the support of various studies (Goldsmith & LeBlanc, 2004; Mechling, 2011). Hernández, Zorrilla, and Zapirain (2012) presented a technological solution to promote independent living for persons with IDs and used Android Smartphones to support them for daily tasks and found that it meets the needs of persons with IDs perfectly. Mobile-learning can bring the learning experience to a whole new level if used wisely and appropriately. Indeed, with the proliferation of m-technologies, such as cellphones/smartphones, personal digital assistants and tablets, or mobile applications, many on-the-go services are now offered (Metcalf & Marco, 2006).
5. **Speech Generating Devices:** Speech-generating devices (SGDs), also known as voice output communication aids, are programmable digital devices that provide voice output in the form of digitized or synthesized speech when activated (Trottier, Kamp, & Mirenda, 2011). SGD are aimed at allowing the persons to translate their simple motor responses into the production/utterance or verbal message (Rispoli, Franco, van der Meer, Lang, & Camargo, 2010; Sigafoos et al., 2009) and vary greatly in terms of features, cost, and appearance (Sigafoos, Didden, & O'Reilly, 2003).
6. **Spatial Orientation System:** These devices are aimed at helping the persons navigate when they are indoors by the use of auditory or visual direction cues or through corrective feedback (Lancioni et al., 2007).

Assistive Technology devices can further be divided into two- low tech and high tech devices (Franklin, 1991). Examples of low and high tech devices that might be useful for persons with IDs have been listed in Table 2.

RECENT INVESTIGATIONS ON ASSISTIVE TECHNOLOGY AND INTELLECTUAL DISABILITIES

The main objectives of recent studies on assistive technology and IDs is to compile the evidenced-based studies and use the finding to empower and enable persons with IDs. In one study, Lancioni, Oliva, and Bracalente (1995) assessed the effectiveness of an orientation system, consisting of a programmable control device linked to acoustic and light sources, for facilitating independent indoor navigation and activity in two persons with profound intellectual disability and blindness respectively. The control device was programmed to activate the acoustic or light sources that led the persons to their desired destination automatically (i.e., after a preset time was arrived at from previous trials of the persons reaching the destinations successfully). One person was exposed to two baseline phases without the system being alternated between two orientation phases; the other person received only one baseline and one orientation phase. Results showed that during the orientation phases, both persons benefited from the use of the system and could reach the destinations successfully and carry out the activities.

Derer, Polsgrove, and Rieth (1996) investigated the use of AT in classrooms through surveying teachers who worked with students with IDs. The results of the study indicated that 10% to 23% of the students with IDs were using AT, and 34% students were using some form of AT. The researcher identified six barriers to technology use for students with IDs, including locating and procuring equipments; lack of time for training students and teachers to use the equipment as well as time to obtain and prepare equipment for use; high cost of devices and the lack of funds to access devices or services, and teacher's knowledge about and training in the area of AT. Lesar (1998) conducted a study that aimed at providing state-of-the-art descriptive information regarding preparation needs, concerns, and perceived barriers to the use of assistive technology for young children with disabilities. Surveys were completed by 62 early childhood special education professionals in 2 south eastern states. The findings indicated that respondents had frequent and significant concerns about their knowledge and utilization of AT.

Table 2. Examples of low and high tech devices

Low Tech	High Tech
Note-taking voice recorders or Audionote	Optical character recognition
Pencil grips	Talking Calculator
Non-Carbon paper/Copy machine	Electronic spell and grammar checker
Simple switches	Word prediction
Head pointers	Voice recognition
Picture boards	Speech synthesizers
Taped instructions	Augmentative communication devices (e.g. Liberator)
Workbooks	Alternative keyboards (e.g. Portable, Touch window, PowerPad, intellikeys)

Mechling, Gast, and Barthold (2003) studied the effectiveness of a multimedia program (interactive computer program, video captions, and still photographs) to teach 3 students with moderate IDs to make purchases using a debit card and an automated payment machine (APM). A multiple probe design across participants was used to evaluate the effectiveness of the multimedia program. All instructional sessions occurred through simulations using video captions and still photographs replicating operation of the APM. Generalization of skills was assessed through purchasing at community stores. Results showed that the multimedia program alone was effective in teaching generalized operation of APMs with a debit card.

Holburn, Nguyen, and Vietze (2004) conducted a study on five adults with profound physical and intellectual disabilities, in which they were taught to respond to photographs of preferences embedded in Microsoft PowerPoint presentations by operating microswitches that functioned as mouse clicks. Rate of responding was generally correlated with changes in types of presentation, although variability in rate was often high, and session durations were quite short. Two participants showed substantial increases in responding when fitted with switches that were easier to manipulate. This exploratory study demonstrates that people with extremely limited physical and cognitive abilities can be taught to operate switches that produce changes in visual arrays on a computer screen.

Today's electronic technologies, including computers, cell phones, Internet, and electronic organizers, hold great promise for individuals with IDs, yet little research has been conducted to explore patterns of use among this population. Drawing upon a survey of 83 adults with IDs, Carey, Friedman, and Bryen (2005) examined factors affecting use of three key electronic technologies: computer, Internet, and electronic organizers. Forty-one percent of participants used a computer; 25%, the Internet; and 11%, electronic organizers. Primary barriers reported by participants included lack of access, training and support, and expense of technologies. Interest in using such technologies was high, and participants offered suggestions for improved accessibility.

Hoppestad (2007) conducted an online comprehensive search of literature pertaining to computer access for persons with severe and multiple disabilities to provide a review of the contemporary literature regarding computer access for persons with severe and multiple disabilities using AT. The study depicts the evolution from a 'medical model' to a 'social model' in rendering AT services for these individuals. Prescribing the proper device to enable computer access to persons with severe disabilities is a complex undertaking, and services have been inadequate. Technological advances that enable access to computers for persons with disabilities have not reached those persons that need it most, particularly those with severe disabilities, for a number of reasons. The literature is replete with explanations for the underutilization of AT for computer access including prejudicial views towards persons with disabilities, inadequate assessments, lack of a person-centered approach, and methods for practice that are not evidence based.

Rai (2008) investigated the effectiveness of a treatment package that included video technology (e.g., video modelling and video prompting) to teach three self-help skills (e.g., cleaning sunglasses, putting on a wrist watch, and zipping a jacket) to three elementary school students with mental disabilities in a small group setting. Using a constant time delay procedure, observers measured the percentage of steps of the task analysis performed correctly before and after a video model prompt. A multiple probe design across behaviors, replicated across participants, demonstrated experimental control. The results indicate that an instructional package that includes video technology can be an effective method for teaching self-help skills to students with mental disabilities.

Selecting an appropriate mode of communication is an important clinical decision when beginning an AAC intervention. In the present study, Cannella-Malone, DeBar, and Sigafoos (2009) investigated whether two boys with significant IDs would show a preference for using one of the three AAC devices. Initially, the boys were taught to use three AAC devices (i.e., Cyrano CommunicatorTM, Mini-MessageMateTM, and a Picture Communication Board) using a multiple-probe-across-devices design. One participant was successful with only one device, while the other was successful in acquiring basic use of all three devices (i.e., making a request using the device and demonstrating correspondence between the picture icon and the item requested). The child who acquired basic use of all three devices participated in the second phase. A choice assessment was conducted using a free operant paradigm to determine which of the three devices he preferred. In the final phase, the most preferred device was targeted for more specific instruction (i.e., retrieving the device from a distance, turning the device on, approaching a communication partner, getting the communication partner's attention, and using the device to make a request), using a changing criterion design. Results for this participant indicated that he had a clear preference for one device and was able to learn how to use it in a more functional manner.

Many people with IDs also have physical difficulties which prevent them from using standard computer control devices. Custom made alternative devices for those with special needs can be expensive and the low unit turnover makes the prospect unattractive to potential manufacturers. One solution is to explore the potential of devices used in contemporary gaming technology, such as the Nintendo Wii. This study evaluated the feasibility of using the Nunchuk by comparing its performance as a switch with the participant's usual switch. Twenty-three volunteers aged between 17 and 21 years with intellectual and physical disabilities completed a single switch performance test using the new device and their familiar device. For most functions of the switch, there was no significant difference between the participants' performance using the Nunchuck and their familiar device. Additional analysis found that some participants' performance did improve whilst using the Nunchuck, but this was not significantly related to physical or cognitive ability. Those whose performance was better with the Nunchuk were more likely to hold it in the conventional way than were those who had better performance with their familiar device. This merits it being offered as a possible alternative to currently available switches for those with physical difficulties affecting their grip (Standen, Camm, Battersby, Brown, & Harrison, 2011)

Davidson (2012) studied the application of collaborative action research to the use of iPods by a small group of adults with IDs. The study was aimed at developing abilities to become autonomous using videos with mobile computing devices. Davidson produced instructional videos, which uploaded onto iPods. The iPods were lent to the young adults with IDs for a period of ten weeks, to try to develop abilities needed for autonomous living such as cooking, using a stove, using a washing machine and keeping oneself safe. The results of focus groups conducted at the end of the collaborative action research during which participants voiced their opinion about the project and revealed their true interests with regards to mobile technologies.

Computer and computer-aided instruction can be used as a high tech device to teach mathematics for persons with IDs, as demonstrated by Singh and Agarwal (2013). In their study wherein, they investigated whether computer games help in teaching mathematics to children with IDs and whether computer games help both boys and girls equally. The quasi-experimental two-group pre & post test design was used for the study. The results obtained through ANCOVA were in favour of Computer games for both boys and girls. However, boys seemed to benefit more from computer games.

UTILIZATION OF ASSISTIVE TECHNOLOGY FOR PERSONS WITH INTELLECTUAL DISABILITIES

AT can be used as device and service in many ways, such as in communication, learning and education, employment, home living, health and medical services, mobility and sports and recreation.

- **Communication:** Augmentative and alternative communication (AAC) includes methods of communication for those with difficulty on the production or comprehension of spoken and written language. AAC systems are extremely varied and dependent on the capabilities of the individual. They may be as basic as pictures on a board that are used to request eatables, beverages or other needs; or they can be advanced speech generating devices, which are based on speech synthesis, that are capable of storing hundreds of phrases and words. Thus, AAC ranges from low technology message boards to computerized voice output communication aids and synthesized speech for those who cannot use vocal communication.
- **Learning and Education:** Education is the most effective vehicle of socio-economic empowerment. Computer-aided instruction can help in many areas, including word recognition, mathematics, spelling and even social skills for individuals with IDs. Portable electronic devices have been found to promote social interaction with peers/friends.

Assistive technology for cognition is the use of technology to augment and assist cognitive processes such as attention, memory, self-regulation, navigation, emotional recognition and management, planning, and sequencing activity. Systematic reviews of the studies have found that the development and use of assistive technology for cognition is growing rapidly. It was also found that a lot of scope still exists in the development of new assistive technology for cognition, specifically, in the areas of memory and planning, such as NeuroPage which prompts users about meetings.

- **Employment:** Video-aided instruction/training can be used for job training and job skill development and to teach higher order functioning and complex skills for appropriate job behavior and social interaction. Prompting systems like voice recorders and computer-based prompting devices have been used to help individuals stay on task, and manage their time in scheduling job activities respectively.
- **Home Living:** AT is helping persons with IDs to successfully complete day to day tasks of self-care. For instance, automated and computerized dining devices allow an individual to eat more independently. Audio prompting devices may be used to assist a person with memory difficulties in completing a task or to follow a certain sequence of steps from start to finish. Video-based instructional materials can help people learn functional life skills such as cooking food, grocery shopping, writing a cheque, paying the bills or using the ATM machine (Jeyachandran, Gadkari, & Mishra, 2009).
- **Health and Medical Services:** Recent advances in medical technology are revolutionizing services to persons with IDs and have focused on cost reduction. Medical technology may broadly include medical devices, information technology and healthcare services. Advances in mapping techniques have allowed good progress toward the specific goals of the Human Genome Project and are also providing strong corollary benefits throughout biomedical research (Olsen, 1993).

Developments of affordable, cost-effective and user friendly assistive and augmentative devices need to be undertaken such as the Hawking Communicator.

- **Mobility:** Wheelchairs are devices that include a seating system and are designed to be a substitute for the normal mobility of individuals with disabilities or those in their old age. These devices allow individuals to perform activities of daily living that require mobility, such as feeding, toileting, dressing, grooming and bathing. The device comes in a number of variations where they can be handled manually or by motors wherein, the user uses electrical controls to manage motors and seating control actuators through a joystick, sip-and-puff control, or other input devices. Often there are handles behind the seat for someone else to manually handle the device or input devices for caregivers.
- **Sports and Recreation:** Toys can be fitted with switches and other technologies to facilitate play among children with IDs. Computer or video games help children learn cognitive and visual-motor coordination skills. Specially designed software can help people with IDs access the World Wide Web. Exercise and physical fitness can be supported by audio and video-based technology. Bailey (1994) suggested that toys using switches and other technologies encourage young children to play, motivate and support cause-effect learning. Switches are simple, intuitive and can be mastered with low physical and mental effort.

An increasing number of people with disabilities are participating in sports, leading to the development of new assistive technology. Use of assistive technology can be found in sports ranging from local community recreation to the elite Paralympics Games.

IMPEDIMENTS

Copley and Ziviani (2004) reviewed the literature on AT in order to identify current barriers to its effective integration within schools for children with multiple disabilities. These barriers were lack of appropriate staff training and support, negative staff attitudes, inadequate assessment and planning processes, insufficient funding, difficulties procuring and managing equipment and time constraints. Wehmeyer (1999) found that the main impediments or barriers about the devices are lack of information on the availability of AT devices, cost and complexity of the devices, training assessment and limited training in their use.

FUTURE RESEARCH DIRECTIONS

At present, the use of technology is associated with intervention and in learning/education as aids for persons with IDs which will become wider in scope and more encompassing in its dimensions. Future research studies can assess the efficacy and impact of various types of available assistive technologies for enhancing the adaptive behaviour, abilities and overall quality of life of persons with IDs. Some research areas that have been identified are as follows:

1. Effect of the level of cognitive development in the understanding of working with the portable electronic devices among children.

2. The most appropriate age, and the best way to introduce portable electronic devices into the learning and educational process.
3. Developing cost-effective and easy to use portable electronic devices for better communication, leisure activity, social and occupational life of persons with IDs or multiple disabilities.
4. Developing new and better computer-aided instruction materials.
5. Developing new technology approaches and solutions.

Research on adaptive technology that focuses on enhancing personal mobility, verbal/non-verbal communication, design changes in articles of every day usage, etc., with a view to develop cost effective, user-friendly and durable aids & appliances is the need of the hour. Appropriate hardware and software suitable for persons with IDs to ensure access to information technologies have to be developed.

CONCLUSION

In Conclusion, AT can be useful for persons with IDs if it is provided as per their learning and working ability, need, characteristics, and environments. The use of AT in persons with IDs would help them to lead an independent life to some extent and also reduce the caregiver's burden. However, further research studies can examine the impact, efficacy and effectiveness of various types of available AT devices and services for enhancing the abilities and overall quality of life of persons with IDs and their family as a whole.

REFERENCES

Alnahdi, G. (2014). Assistive Technology in Special Education and the Universal Design for Learning. *The Turkish Online Journal of Educational Technology*, *13*(2), 18–23.

American Association on Intellectual and Developmental Disabilities. (2009). *Frequently Asked Question on intellectual disability*. Retrieved from http://www.aamr.org/content_104.cfm

Bailey, D. M. (1994). Technology for adults with multiple impairments: A trilogy of case reports. *The American Journal of Occupational Therapy*, *48*(4), 341–345. doi:10.5014/ajot.48.4.341 PMID:8059867

Bauer, S. M., Elsaesser, L. J., & Arthanat, S. (2011). Assistive technology device classification based upon the World Health Organization's, International Classification of Functioning, Disability and Health (ICF). *Disability and Rehabilitation: Assistive Technology*, *6*(3), 243–259. doi:10.3109/17483107.2010.529631 PMID:21446850

Borg, J., Larsson, S., & Östergren, P. O. (2011). The right to assistive technology: For whom, for what, and by whom? *Disability & Society*, *26*(2), 151–167. doi:10.1080/09687599.2011.543862

Cannella-Malone, H. I., DeBar, R. M., & Sigafoos, J. (2009). An examination of preference for augmentative and alternative communication devices with two boys with significant intellectual disabilities. *Augmentative and Alternative Communication*, *25*(4), 262–273. doi:10.3109/07434610903384511 PMID:19883289

Carey, A. C., Friedman, M. G., & Bryen, D. N., S. J. (2005). Use of Electronic Technologies by People with Intellectual Disabilities. [PubMed]. *Mental Retardation*, *43*(5), 322–333.

Census of India. (2013). *Disabled population by type of Disability, age, and sex*. Office of the Registrar General & Census Commissioner.

Copley, J., & Ziviani, J. (2004). Barriers to the use of assistive technology for children with multiple disabilities. [PubMed]. *Occupational Therapy International*, *11*(4), 229–243. doi:10.1002/oti.213

Davidson, A. L. (2012). Use of Mobile Technologies by Young Adults Living with an Intellectual Disability: A Collaborative Action Research Study. *Journal on Developmental Disabilities*, *18*(3), 21–32.

Derer, K., Polsgrove, L., & Rieth, H. (1996). A survey of assistive technology applications in schools and recommendations for practice. *Journal of Special Education Technology*, *13*, 62–80.

Flores, M., Musgrove, K., Renner, S., Hinton, V., Strozier, S., Franklin, S., & Hil, D. (2012). A comparison of communication using the Apple iPad and a picture-based system. *Augmentative and Alternative Communication*, *28*(2), 74–84. doi:10.3109/07434618.2011.644579 PMID:22263895

Franklin, K. S. (1991). Supposed employment and assistive technology-a powerful partnership. In L. Griffin & W. G. Revell (Eds.), *Rehabilitation counselor desktop guide supported employment*. Richmond, VA: Virginia Commonwealth University, Rehabilitation Research and Training Center on Supported Employment.

Goldsmith, T. R., & LeBlanc, L. A. (2004). Use of technology in interventions for children with autism. *Journal of Early and Intensive Behavior Intervention*, *1*(2), 166–178. doi:10.1037/h0100287

Hernández, F. J., Zorrilla, A. M., & Zapirain, B. G. (2012). Management Platform to Support Intellectually Disabled People Daily Tasks Using Android Smartphones. In *Ambient Intelligence-Software and Applications* (pp. 119–128). Springer Berlin Heidelberg. doi:10.1007/978-3-642-28783-1_15

Holburn, S., Nguyen, D., & Vietze, P. M. (2004). Computer-assisted learning for adults with profound multiple disabilities. *Behavioral Interventions*, *19*(1), 25–37. doi:10.1002/bin.147

Hoppestad, B. S. (2007). Inadequacies in computer access using assistive technology devices in profoundly disabled individuals: An overview of the current literature. *Disability and Rehabilitation: Assistive Technology*, *2*(4), 189–199. doi:10.1080/17483100701249540 PMID:19263537

Jeyachandran, P., Gadkari, J. P., & Mishra, S. K. (2009). Mental Retardation, Status of Disability in India-2007. New Delhi: Rehabilitation Council of India. Retrieved from http://www.rehabcouncil.nic.in/writereaddata/mr.pdf

Katz, G., & Lazcano-Ponce, E. (2008). Intellectual disability: Definition, etiological factors, classification, diagnosis, treatment and prognosis. *Salud Pública de México*, *50*, s132–s141. doi:10.1590/S0036-36342008000800005 PMID:18470340

Lancioni, G. E., O'Reilly, M. F., & Basili, G. (2001). Use of microswitches and speech output systems with people with severe/profound intellectual or multiple disabilities: A literature review. *Research in Developmental Disabilities*, *22*(1), 21–40. doi:10.1016/S0891-4222(00)00064-0 PMID:11263629

Lancioni, G. E., O'Reilly, M. F., Singh, N. N., Sigafoos, J., Oliva, D., Antonucci, M., & Basili, G. et al. (2008). Microswitch-based programs for persons with multiple disabilities: An overview of some recent developments. *Perceptual and Motor Skills*, *106*(2), 355–370. doi:10.2466/pms.106.2.355-370 PMID:18556894

Lancioni, G. E., O'Reilly, M. F., Singh, N. N., Sigafoos, J., Oliva, D., Bracalente, S., & Montironi, G. (2007). Orientation systems to support indoor travel by persons with multiple disabilities: Technical aspects and applicability issues. *Technology and Disability*, *19*(1), 1–6.

Lancioni, G. E., Oliva, D., & Bracalente, S. (1995). An acoustic orientation system to promote independent indoor travel in blind persons with severe mental retardation. *Perceptual and Motor Skills*, *80*(3), 747–754. doi:10.2466/pms.1995.80.3.747 PMID:7567392

Lancioni, G. E., Sigafoos, J., O'reilly, M. F., & Singh, N. N. (2013). *Assistive technology: Interventions for individuals with severe/profound and multiple disabilities*. New York: Springer. doi:10.1007/978-1-4614-4229-5

Lee, Y., & Vail, C. O. (2005). Computer-based reading instruction for young children with disabilities. *Journal of Special Education Technology*, *20*(1), 5–18.

Lesar, S. (1998). Use of Assistive Technology with Young Children with Disabilities Current Status and Training Needs. *Journal of Early Intervention*, *21*(2), 146–159. doi:10.1177/105381519802100207

McNaughton, D., & Light, J. (2013). The iPad and mobile technology revolution: Benefits and challenges for individuals who require augmentative and alternative communication. *Augmentative and Alternative Communication*, *29*(2), 107–116. doi:10.3109/07434618.2013.784930 PMID:23705813

Mechling, L. C. (2011). Review of twenty-first century portable electronic devices for persons with moderate intellectual disabilities and autism spectrum disorders. *Education and Training in Autism and Developmental Disabilities*, 479-498.

Mechling, L. C., Gast, D. L., & Barthold, S. (2003). Multimedia computer-based instruction to teach students with moderate intellectual disabilities to use a debit card to make purchases. *Exceptionality*, *11*(4), 239–254. doi:10.1207/S15327035EX1104_4

Metcalf, D. S., & De Marco, J. M. (2006). mLearning: Mobile learning and performance in the palm of your hand. Amherst, MA: HRD Press.

O'Keefe, P. (2009). *People with disabilities in India: from commitments to outcomes. Human Development Unit, South Asia Region*. The World Bank.

OkoloC. M.BahrC. M.RiethH. J. (1993). A retrospective view of computer-based instruction. *Journal of Special Education Technology*, 12(1), 1-27.

Olson, M. V. (1993). The human genome project. *Proceedings of the National Academy of Sciences of the United States of America*, *90*(10), 4338–4344. doi:10.1073/pnas.90.10.4338 PMID:8506271

Petterson, B., Bourke, J., Leonard, H., Jacoby, P., & Bower, C. (2007). Co-occurrence of birth defects and intellectual disability. *Paediatric and Perinatal Epidemiology*, *21*(1), 65–75. doi:10.1111/j.1365-3016.2007.00774.x PMID:17239182

P.L. 103-218. (1994). *Technology-related Assistance for Individuals with Disabilities Act Amendments of 1994*. Author.

Rai, K. (2008). Technology to teach self-help skills to elementary students with mental disabilities. *Journal of the Indian Academy of Applied Psychology*, *34*(2), 201–214.

Reichle, J. (2011). Evaluating assistive technology in the education of persons with severe disabilities. *Journal of Behavioral Education*, *20*(1), 77–85. doi:10.1007/s10864-011-9121-1

Rispoli, M. J., Franco, J. H., van der Meer, L., Lang, R., & Camargo, S. P. (2010). The use of speech generating devices in communication interventions for individuals with developmental disabilities: A review of the literature. *Developmental Neurorehabilitation*, *13*(4), 276–293. doi:10.3109/17518421003636794 PMID:20629594

Sigafoos, J., Didden, R., & O'Reilly, M. (2003). Effects of speech output on maintenance of requesting and frequency of vocalizations in three children with developmental disabilities. *Augmentative and Alternative Communication*, *19*(1), 37–47. doi:10.1080/0743461032000056487

Sigafoos, J., Green, V. A., Payne, D., Son, S. H., O'Reilly, M., & Lancioni, G. E. (2009). A comparison of picture exchange and speech-generating devices: Acquisition, preference, and effects on social interaction. *Augmentative and Alternative Communication*, *25*(2), 99–109. doi:10.1080/07434610902739959 PMID:19444681

Singh, Y. P., & Agarwal, A. (2013). Teaching Mathematics to Children with Mental Retardation using Computer Games. *Educationia Confab*, *2*(1), 44–58.

Standen, P. J., Camm, C., Battersby, S., Brown, D. J., & Harrison, M. (2011). An evaluation of the Wii Nunchuk as an alternative assistive device for people with intellectual and physical disabilities using switch controlled software. *Computers & Education*, *56*(1), 2–10. doi:10.1016/j.compedu.2010.06.003

Trottier, N., Kamp, L., & Mirenda, P. (2011). Effects of peer-mediated instruction to teach use of speech-generating devices to students with autism in social game routines. *Augmentative and Alternative Communication*, *27*(1), 26–39. doi:10.3109/07434618.2010.546810 PMID:21284561

Wehmeyer, M. L. (1999). Assistive technology and students with mental retardation: Utilization and barriers. *Journal of Special Education Technology*, *14*, 50–60.

Wehmeyer, M. L., Palmer, S. B., Smith, S. J., Davies, D. K., & Stock, S. (2008). The efficacy of technology use by people with intellectual disability: A single-subject design meta-analysis. *Journal of Special Education Technology*, *23*, 21–30.

Wehmeyer, M. L., & Smith, S. J. (2004). Introduction to the special issue on technology use by students with intellectual disabilities. *Journal of Special Education Technology*, *19*(4), 5–6.

Wehmeyer, M. L., Smith, S. J., Palmer, S. B., Davies, D. K., & Stock, S. E. (2004). Technology use and people with mental retardation. In L. M. Glidden (Ed.), *International review of research in mental retardation*. Elsevier Academic Press. doi:10.1016/S0074-7750(04)29009-7

KEY TERMS AND DEFINITIONS

Assistive Technology Device: An object or a machine designed for a special purpose to increase, maintain or improve activities of daily living of individuals with disabilities.

Assistive Technology Services: It helps individuals with disabilities to use a set of articles or devices to help them in the area of daily living, education, etc.

Disability: A sensory, physical or mental condition and may be present from birth, or occur during person's lifetime.

Empowerment: To equip persons with qualities or abilities and essential skills so they can take initiative and make decisions to solve problems and improve performance in personal and professional life.

Independent Living: The ability or skill to live and cope up independently in the social system.

Quality of Life: The general well-being or the standard of health, comfort, and happiness experienced by an individual or group.

Technology: The application of the knowledge and usage of tools or device and techniques to control one's environment.

APPENDIX: LIST OF ASSISTIVE TECHNOLOGY VENDORS

The following list provides the name of vendors with websites/URLs that carry assistive technology products. Listing the vendors name does not recommend an endorsement by the author or publisher.

- **AbleNet, Inc.**
  - **Website:** https://www.ablenetinc.com/
  - AbleNet, Inc. provides a wide range of products such as switches, speech generating devices, accessible toys, and apps and software. AbleNet also conduct webinars and onsite training programs for professionals and parents.
- **Adaptivation, Inc.**
  - **Website:** http://www.adaptivation.com/
  - Adaptivation, Inc. is the producer of electronic communication aids, environmental controls, switches and other assistive technology for individuals with special needs.
- **Barrier Break**
  - **Website:** http://barrierbreak.com/
  - Barrier Break provides a variety of assistive technology products for visual, hearing, learning and mobility, and for elderly. These products are helpful to users for daily living skills or other routine task.
- **Boundless**
  - **Website:** http://www.boundlessat.com/
  - Boundless Assistive Technology offers with over 3,000 products, complete PC and Mac systems, and bundled tablets, access solutions meet the needs of virtually any ability.
- **EnableMart**
  - **Website:** https://www.enablemart.com/
  - EnableMart is provider of products for people with special needs and providing solutions in learning curriculum, adaptive equipment, and therapy products. EnableMart is also conduct free webinar covering a variety of products and brands related to special education, speech therapy and assistive technology.
- **Prentke Romich Company**
  - **Website:** http://www.prentrom.com/
  - Prentke Romich Company (PRC) is a member of a consortium of companies that are pioneers in the field of assistive technology and augmentative communication. The mission of PRC is to help people with disabilities achieve their potential in educational, vocational, and personal pursuits. Products include augmentative communication devices, computer access technology and switches. PRC provides practical and clinically sound product training and AAC implementation classes based on years of client support.
- **Vitasta India**
  - **Website:** http://vitastaindia.com/
  - Vitasta India (originally known as Vitasta Healthcare International) is involved in marketing and selling of Tobii eye tracking Technology Devices for analytical and assistive use. It also provides alternative and augmentative communication devices, products for Child Therapy of Timocco to increase children's motivation for physical, cognitive and social activities and medical devices for healthcare professional's safety.

Chapter 18
Crime and Legal Issues among Intellectually Disabled Individuals

Vaitsa Giannouli
Aristotle University of Thessaloniki, Greece

ABSTRACT

Intellectual Disability (ID) can be caused by a variety of factors, which may lead to a variety of signs and symptoms. Individuals with ID are living in societies where during the past decade there is a steady increase in the amount of research focused on civil law, criminal law and mental health. In this chapter, there will be a theoretical presentation of the research on ID regarding criminal law and the different forms of aggressive behavior such as sexual violence, homicide, theft, arson and alcohol-drug abuse. There will be information on research regarding civil law and the most common problems for individuals with ID, such as financial capacity and capacity for medical consent. Finally, there will be a section for the most important issues regarding the trial and conviction for individuals with ID and a presentation of a recent research on attitudes toward ID and legal issues. The above will be examined through the prism of current neuropsychological data, while cross-cultural restrictions will be discussed.

INTRODUCTION

The mission of the proposed chapter is to give an outline of the background information regarding crime and legal issues among individuals with Intellectual Disability (ID). Although there is a lot of information generally on ID, which follows the widespread adoption of a changed construct and of a new term, which replaces mental retardation by renaming it in DSM 5 (Schalock, Luckasson & Shogren, 2007), there is scarce information on the significance of ID for a number of legal issues. As scientific literature indicates the theme of legal issues turns out to be particularly salient for ID worldwide. Current texts regarding psychology and law (legal psychology and forensic psychology) begin to include extensive sections concerning individuals with ID, who may play the role of suspect or victim according to the criminal law, or the role of the person who claims civil capacities according to the civil law. So, this

DOI: 10.4018/978-1-5225-0089-6.ch018

chapter will be an in-depth introduction, which will be focused on a variety of relevant themes, which are selected in order to include key terms and information on law and ID.

CRIMINAL LAW AND INDIVIDUALS WITH ID

In western societies, there is a general tendency to consider individuals with ID as a group of people who are more likely to commit a crime (New South Wales. Law Reform Commission, 1994). Individuals with ID may be over-represented in the criminal justice system (Baroff, Gunn & Hayes, 2004; Hayes, 1996; Holland, Clare, & Mukhopadhyay, 2002; Jones, 2007; Søndenaa, Rasmussen, Palmstierna, & Nøttestad, 2008), given the intellectual and other psychosocial disadvantages which they experience and their incapacity to evade arrest, but the level of offending behavior in this group is found to be strikingly low (Holland et al., 2002), because much criminal activity of individuals with ID goes undetected or unreported, and as a result scientific research can only investigate data and individuals who are already involved with the criminal justice process. Individuals with ID are not overrepresented in prisons in most western countries (Murphy & Mason, 2014). For example, the likelihood of conviction for a man with ID in Sweden is as high as for a man without disability (Hodgins, 1992). It is of special interest that in a research from Denmark convicted individuals with ID, who had been admitted to psychiatric hospitals were found to have an increased risk of committing various kinds of crimes in comparison with individuals with ID without a previous admission history (Hodgins et al., 1996).

Individuals with ID are usually seen as potential suspects for crimes worldwide and this is due to a general misunderstanding and bias of different societies and communities (Lyal, Holland & Collins, 1996; McNulty et al., 1995; Vaughan, Pullen & Kely, 2000). Studies using IQ as a continuous variable indicate that significantly below-average intellectual ability is an independent predictor of future offending (Holland et al., 2002), but the studies which adopt an IQ-based concept of ID show lower rates of offending than those which use wider definitions (e.g. attendance at special schools). There is also evidence coming from a systematic review by Simpson and Hogg (2001) for believing specifically that the prevalence of arson and sexual offences may be higher relative to other kinds of crimes for individuals with ID than for other offenders (Barron, Hassiotis & Bannes, 2002; Simpson & Hogg, 2001), but there exist contradictory evidence for that (Murphy & Mason, 2014). In addition to this, intellectually disabled offenders start offending at an early age [ID youth, aged under 18 may demonstrate delinquent behavior as other individuals who are not of legal age, and who commit acts considered to be rule violations, which according to legal definitions, include such acts as robbery, assault, property damage, drug possession, and other similar crimes (Salkind, 2002)], and these same young offenders usually have a history of multiple offences. Offenders with ID are considered to be a group with complex needs who may pose a recurrent risk to the public (Barron, Hassiotis & Bannes, 2002). Individuals with ID and forensic involvement are those who also have a diagnosis of borderline to mild IQ and psychopathology-psychotic disorder, and are also more likely to have previously used drugs or alcohol and have significantly longer prior lengths of stay in psychiatric hospitals (Raina & Lunsky, 2010).

Violence and Crime among Individuals with ID

Over half of the ID population according to a review engages in some form of aggression, but only a small number is responsible for frequent or severe acts with serious legal implications, although ID is associated with psychosocial adversities and psychiatric comorbidities (Benson & Brooks, 2008; Gopalan, Sharma & Unnikrishnan, 2014). The relative prevalence of aggressive behavior is found to be higher among institutionalized persons compared to those living in group homes or other community-based facilities (as data from Australia indicate: Sjigafoos et al., 1994). In the same study of institutionalized individuals with ID and aggressive behavior, a higher percentage of males were described as functioning in the severe/profound or moderate range of intellectual disability with one-third having no intelligible speech capacity (Sjigafoos et al., 1994). The current aggression levels for an individual can be predicted by many factors such as gender, level of mental retardation, and history of previous institutional placement, and the strongest predictor is proposed to be the personal history of aggression (Davidson et al., 1994), but without evidence or research until now supporting the possible link between adult criminality and testosterone levels in ID.

The aggressive behavior may take many forms, with the most frequent in order: property damage, verbal, self-oriented and physical aggression, and sexually aggressive behavior, most of which is characterized as mild in severity. Of course, there is only a minority of individuals displaying aggressive behavior leading to injury of the victim and there are few or none recorded gender differences (Crocker et al., 2006). In contrast to the above, a possible rapid increase in arrests during adolescence in tandem with a relatively rapid decline during adulthood, which is called the 'age-crime curve', has not yet been empirically proven to be true for the ID population mainly due to the lack of existing research. Finally, it is claimed, based on empirical evidence, that the relationship between moral reasoning and illegal behavior may be curvilinear, such that lower moral reasoning and higher moral reasoning relates to lower rates of illegal behavior and possible inappropriate conduct. It seems that individuals with ID are reasoning at a lower moral stage than their peers, and it is proposed that some people with intellectual disabilities may actually be less likely to engage in illegal behavior, because they are reasoning at an earlier moral stage. Individuals with 'borderline' intelligence would be more likely to engage in illegal behavior, something that suggests that the relationship between moral reasoning and illegal behavior is moderated by intelligence (Langton Clare & Murphy, 2011).

Sexual Violence and ID

Sexual violence refers to any sexual act or attempt with the aim of abusing by violence or coercion someone else or even a group of others. Research on forensic issues and ID come mainly from the USA and UK, and as a result conclusions have to be confined to these countries only (Søndenaa, Rasmussen & Nøttestad, 2008). There is an old tendency in the scientific literature that rapists tend to be of low intelligence (Day, 1994), while other researchers claim that low IQ is not more frequent in sexual violence, and is equally found in individuals who commit aggressive non-sexual crimes (Vera, Barnard & Holzer, 1979; Ruff et al., 1976). Although attitudes toward sexuality and ID are not well investigated in different countries (Cuskelly & Bryde, 2004), it seems that children with disabilities are 3.4 times more likely to be maltreated than their nondisabled peers (Sullivan & Knutson, 2000). Sexual abuse is proven to be a significant variable in the history of future sexual offenders, while physical abuse seems a significant variable only in the life history of nonsexual offenders (Lindsay et al., 2001). One major cognitive factor contributing to sexual violence demonstrated by individuals with ID is the problem of understanding the laws relating to sexuality (O'Callaghan & Murphy, 2007). About the sex of sexual offenders with ID, it seems that female offenders show similar characteristics to their male offenders with ID, but there are higher levels of mental illness, higher levels of prior sexual abuse and lower levels of re-offending for the female sexual offenders (Lindsay et al., 2004). For the male sexual offenders a high prevalence of family psychopathology, psychiatric illness, minor physical disabilities, sexual experience, impaired relationship skills and sexual recidivism are found (Day, 1994). Among individuals with intellectual disabilities, women are more likely to have a diagnosis of mood disorder and sexual abuse history, while men are more likely to have a substance abuse diagnosis, legal issues, and documented past destructive behavior (Lunsky et al., 2009).

Homicide and ID

Given the frequency of mentally retarded defendants, there is little systematic attention on murders, which are the most well-known non-suicidal dangerous behavior among individuals with ID (Day, 1993). Typically 0.5 – 1.5% of prisoners worldwide are diagnosed with intellectual disabilities (range 0% to 2.8% across studies), something that makes the number of prisoners with ID considerable and this condition as one with important implications for policy and practice (Fazel, Xenitidis & Powell, 2008). A question that is still not answered is: Are all murderers mentally ill? Some researchers claim that ID murderers are not as common as murderers coming from the general population, but female murder defendants are more likely to receive a diagnosis of ID (Dwyer & Frierson, 2006). There may be a link between the severity of ID and violent behaviors toward third parties. According to self-report measures, individuals who reported low self-concept also reported high levels of depression, but mildly mentally retarded individuals were more likely to report anger against others than severe/moderately retarded persons (Benson & Ivis, 1992).

Theft and ID

The taking of another person's property without that person's permission or consent may be an act that can be prosecuted as a crime for individuals with ID. They may commit such an act, because they may not understand what these acts really are (their legal consequences), and they may not identify themselves as illegal or 'bad' when committing this sort of crime. According to the general literature, there are many forms of theft (burglary, embezzlement, larceny, looting, robbery, shoplifting, library theft, and fraud), but there is no research on the characteristics of the persons who commit these acts or the factors that may lead an individual with ID to such acts (Parry & Drogin, 2007).

Arson and ID

Fire-setting behavior in individuals with ID may be expressed as arson attempts. Although there is evidence that the prevalence of arson may be higher relative to other kinds of crimes for people with ID in UK (Simpson & Hogg, 2001) and these individuals are over-represented according to data in the criminal justice system in Australia (Curtis, McVilly & Day, 2014), there are no large-scale systematic research on the characteristics of the individuals with ID and this type of behavior. A study from UK supports that the most common reasons for setting fires for individuals with ID were the feeling of being angry, wanting revenge and excitement around fires. External factors that may play an important role is a precipitating argument or wanting to move to different accommodation (Orchard, 2013). In addition to that according to another study from the UK the most common reason for arson is revenge, closely followed by suggestibility, while the majority of offenders with ID have an associated diagnosis of personality disorders along with an Axis I psychiatric diagnosis. Other factors include large family size, history of childhood psychiatric disorders, abuse, homelessness, unemployment and relationship difficulties (Devapriam et al., 2007). Finally, fire setting is claimed to be associated with significant psychopathology (e.g. psychosis and personality disorders), but not all of the convicted individuals with ID have a formal arson conviction. Fire setters according to that are more likely to have a violence conviction, and criminal sections/restriction orders (Alexander et al., 2015).

Alcohol-Drugs Abuse and ID

Individuals with mild ID who are involved with the criminal justice system regularly consume alcohol and use illicit drugs (Lindsay, Tinsley & Emara, 2012), and this implies that there may be a possible link between substance abuse and offending behavior in this population. Although they may be just (ab)users of illegal substances, they may participate in groups of dealers as well. Individuals who had offended reported greater use of both legal and illicit drugs than their non-offending counterparts and many reported that they had been under the influence of alcohol or illicit drugs at the time of committing the offence (McGillivray & Moore, 2001). Alcohol and cannabis are the commonest drugs of abuse in the English ID population, while cocaine, stimulants and opiates are abused by a small, but significant number of ID offenders (Plant et al., 2011). The history of alcohol abuse for individuals with ID is associated with alcohol-related offences and theft and there are higher rates of alcohol problem history which are associated with histories of a number of offences, psychiatric disturbance in adulthood, psychiatric disturbance in childhood, and experiences of childhood adversity (Lindsay et al., 2013). Drug-involved inmates with high intellectual abilities are less motivated to enter substance abuse treatment compared to those with average and low intellectual abilities-characterized as individuals with ID (Vandevelde et al., 2005). The risk of reoffending, that is the recidivist rate for individuals with ID is related with the variables of unemployment, substance abuse and a psychiatric history (Klimecki, Jenkinson & Wilson, 1994), but there are no relevant studies focusing on individuals with ID and illegal acts that are committed prior to and for drug and alcohol use.

Crime and Individuals with ID: Are There Any Other Variables Involved?

In the relationship between different forms of crime and ID, we may hypothesize the existence of a series of confounding variables, such as the socioeconomic status, the gender, and the educational qualification of the individual with ID. In Norway, for example, research support that the socio-economic status does have a relationship with ID, since parents of children with severe mental retardation seem to have a higher socioeconomic level than parents of children with mild mental retardation, something that holds true only for the identification of the children and only for this specific country and sample of participants (Strømme, & Magnus, 2000). More specifically, when examining adolescents and adults with ID and anti-social behavior, a lower socio-economic status and the existence of mental health problems are claimed to be associated with the actual expression of any form of anti-social behavior (Dickson et al., 2005; Lund, 1990; Timms & Goreczny, 2002). Although sexual crimes are claimed not to be overrepresented among ID individuals, there are more reported cases of individuals with ID who are men and who are charged with sexual offenses, rather than women. This does not really give us a clear picture, because much criminal offending goes undetected and/or unreported, and because of that studies can only investigate and include in the counting of individuals those already involved with the criminal justice process (Holland et al., 2002). So, the data usually come from subjects who are already in prison for their offenses, and ending up in prison may be related to the fact that men with mild ID and a history of sexual offending have significantly lower expressed general empathy for their own and other victims something that may involve them in similar illegal activities and exposure to the police (Hockley & Langdon, 2015). Finally, no research as far has clear results on the relationship concerning the type and the duration of previous education for ID offenders and the type and/or severity of the committed crime.

CIVIL LAW: LEGAL ISSUES RELATED TO FINANCIAL MATTERS AND MEDICAL CONSENT FOR INDIVIDUALS WITH ID

Civil law means non-criminal law and it includes a wide array of issues concerning capacity for medical consent, capacity for sexual consent, financial capacity, testamentary capacity, driving capacity, and capacity for independent living (American Psychological Association, 2005; 2006). Individuals with ID may not have the capacity to decide for actions with legal implications, such as their own wedding (Reed, 1997). So, legislation in European countries and USA is clear, when capacity is in doubt, it might be necessary for the individual to be referred to a competency hearing or/and may need the appointment of a guardian. Within the context of current legislation (mainly in western countries) relating to mental capacity in adults, elders is the most examined group, but individuals with ID should also come to the center of attention (Carey, 2010; Demakis, 2011). Although in the United States the capacity to make legal/financial decisions is considered through legal surrogate decision-making processes, until now little has been done for this new and at the same time old medico-legal topic in Europe, with the exception of the introduction of the Mental Capacity Act in the UK. Two forms of legal capacity are presented below: financial capacity and capacity for medical consent.

Financial Capacity

Individuals with even mild ID have problems in financial capacity and more specifically in decision making for everyday financial issues (Suto et al., 2005). Individuals with ID as all other cognitively impaired groups of patients face difficulties regarding the decision making process, since they have problems in identifying the decision to be made, gathering relevant information, identifying alternatives, weighing evidence, choosing among alternatives, describing verbally how to take relevant action and reviewing decision and consequences (Giannouli & Tsolaki, 2011; 2015). Any difficulty even in one of the above steps of the decision making process may lead the individual to decisions that are harmful to himself/herself or others and to actions that are considered by contemporaries as illegal (e.g. receiving or giving goods-property that is acquired in an illegal way, participating in illegal activities and fraud etc.).

Capacity for Medical Consent and ID

Consent for medical treatments and procedures may result to serious legal outcomes. Individuals with mild or moderate ID are characterized as incapable to provide informed consent to hypothetical treatment scenarios-vignettes (Morris, Niederbuhl & Mahr, 1993). While adults with mental retardation as a group show consent deficits, many may attain consent capacity scores comparable to those of 'normals' (Fisher et al., 2006). Most adults with mild and no mental retardation and almost half of adults with moderate mental retardation in a study were characterized as able to make and justify treatment choices and fully or partially understand treatment information. Most adults without mental retardation, 50% with mild, and 18% with moderate mental retardation are able to partially appreciate relevance of treatment choice to patient's situation and weigh treatment risks against benefit (Cea & Fisher, 2005). As a conclusion, clinicians and legal experts should always consider the wide range of individual differences.

TRIAL AND CONVICTION OF INDIVIDUALS WITH ID: MORE QUESTIONS THAN ANSWERS

There are some basic questions for trial and conviction: Should offenders with ID be treated and held accountable-responsible for their actions in the same way as nondisabled citizens? (Glaser & Deane, 1999). ID does not necessary eliminate that someone has the ability to appreciate right from wrong, but this condition causes some unique difficulties for the person. Individuals with ID according to their families are significantly disadvantaged when they come into contact with the justice system and more specifically with the criminal justice system personnel and jurors who are likely to fail to identify defendants with ID, and for this reason it is argued that offenders with ID must be supported by legal representation from the earliest stages of the legal process (Cockram, Jackson & Underwood, 1998), and be dealt with differently from the general population (Jones, 2007). As a consequence, several states in the USA have laws that exempt persons who have ID from the death penalty and other severe sentences under the criminal code (Borromeo, 2001; Olvera, Dever & Earnest, 2000).

Another question to be answered: Should individuals with ID who have been victims or witnesses or even responsible themselves of a crime be given limited access to the criminal justice system, often on the basis of assumptions about their incapacity to be interviewed by the police, and to give evidence in court? (Gudjonsson, Murphy & Clare, 2000). In general, the trial of a person with or without ID is the same as for 'normal' individuals regardless of country or legal system, but there is a tendency to consider individuals with ID as people who face barriers, due their cognitive-emotional-behavioral problems such as possible difficulties in oral language development, deficits in memory skills, difficulty in learning social rules, difficulty with problem solving skills, delays in the development of adaptive behaviors, such as self-help or self-care skills and lack of social inhibitors, which determine the way they get involved with the legal system (Daily, Ardinger & Holmes, 2000). The above deficits can also be exacerbated by an ignorance of the current law.

Do the cognitive deficits of individuals with ID influence the procedures in civil and criminal law matters? Individuals with ID may have problems during criminal proceedings with the confession and waiver, proceeding to trial and functioning at trial (Appelbaum & Appelbaum, 1994). They are found to be less able to comprehend their rights in legal procedures, they are significantly more likely to respond to suggestive questioning, confabulate more and change more frequently their answers than normal individuals (Clare & Gudjonsson, 1993; Everington & Fulero, 1999; Perske 2008; 2011; Ridley, Gabbert & La Rooy, 2012). Interrogative suggestibility may have higher rates in children and adults with ID than in normal children and adults, because of their much poorer memory, but differences in suggestibility are only partly explained by poorer memory scores. Age may play a significant role alongside the existence of ID, since children with ID are more susceptible to altering their answers under pressure than are adults with ID (Beail, 2002; Gudjonsson & Henry, 2003). Individuals with ID in the USA face special problems in the process of interrogation and confession, particularly with regard to the understanding of the information of the Miranda rights or also called Miranda warning (Fulero & Everington, 1995), and by being suggestible and acquiescent on interviews and making 'unwise' decisions (Murphy & Mason, 2014). Individuals with ID are thought to be incompetent witnesses in courts, although a relevant research claims that there is available evidence that they can provide accurate accounts of witnessed events. Of course, the accounts are usually less complete than those provided by the general 'normal' population and are greatly influenced by the methods of questioning. The available evidence suggests that cross-examination methods may lead to memory distortion, and that the use of closed, complex, and leading questions and the absence of aids to recall may have a particularly adverse effect on people with mental retardation (Kebbell & Hatton, 1999).

So, individuals with ID may be arrested and accused of crimes for which they often receive discriminatory treatment, are falsely convicted and punished (even with serious punishments, such as death penalty in the USA) (Lorenzo, 1991). Although experts raise doubts concerning the death penalty, which is characterized as a cruel and unusual punishment [Atkins v. Virginia, 536 U.S. 304 (2002)], still each American state and court has the responsibility to define who is mentally retarded or as we now call Intellectually Disabled. Police and other criminal justice personnel often misunderstand the responses that people with ID make to them. Their main characteristics often include an inordinate desire to please authority figures, an inability to abstract from concrete thoughts, observation of interrogators for clues regarding responses, a longing for friends, a pleasant facade, abhorrence of the term "mental retardation", memory gaps, impaired judgment, and problems with receptive and expressive language skills. In addition, they often lack understanding of rights, court proceedings, and/or punishment. Therefore, they may confess to crimes they did not actually commit and receive sentences of capital punishment (Perske, 1991; Perske, 2005), but we have to keep in mind that the above lack of competence may not be true for every individual with ID (Bonnie, 1990).

AN INTRODUCTION TO FORENSIC NEUROPSYCHOLOGICAL ASSESSMENT

The last questions to be answered are: What information do the lawyers and the court need? and How information which will serve as proof of limited intellectual functioning in ID are gathered and examined by mental health experts and presented to legal experts?

Following the tendency in modern criminology, we have moved from the study of the clues (19th century Scotland Yard approach) to a focus on the specific crime to the study of the person-criminal. Because of that, court-ordered and independent forensic neuropsychological examinations are necessary and in our days there is a growing number of cases when criminal offendants at some point of the legal procedure are claiming ID or civil cases for which a neuropsychologist's opinion and consultation is required for clarifying the above (Heilbronner, 2004; Larrabee, 2005; Sweet et al., 2002). This rapidly increasing need for neuropsychological expert witness' input in both civil and criminal legal proceedings is due to the vital question of the current capacity to stand trial and/ or the capacity to form criminal intent at the time of the offense (insanity) and/or the risk for future dangerous acts related to violence and re-offending, which can only be thoroughly assessed by forensic neuropsychologists by examining not only the cognitive capacities, but also the case of malingering-feigned ID (Boone, 2007). Since brain damage is not itself an adequate basis for legal decision making, the scope of neuropsychological assessment and investigation is the systematic and objective exposition of the nature, extent, and course of the individual's brain dysfunction and an explanation of its behavioral consequences relative to the psychological issue at hand (Martell, 1992). The diagnosis of a lifelong condition affecting cognitive and social development needs many sources of information and each neuropsychological evaluation may not only focus on the diagnosis and recording of deficits, but also on the future rehabilitation planning (Jakab, 1990).

The forensic neuropsychologist determines the procedure(s) which are required to answer the question(s) posed by the retaining party. A request may be made by the retaining party to administer certain tests, but the neuropsychologist is obliged to explain and support scientifically if different or additional measures-tests should be used (Bush, 2005). There are a variety of neuropsychological tests which could be used for the assessment in civil and criminal settings. More specifically, the classic standardized neuropsychological tests are widely used for the examination of civil capacities (Giannouli & Tsolaki, 2011), and there are a lot of areas to be addressed with caution during a neuropsychological examination: language, current intellectual level-IQ, verbal and visuospatial memory, attention/concentration, executive functioning, and emotional adjustment (McKinlay & McGowan, 2003). The decision making capacity seems to be really important for all civil cases and there are is a variety of new specific tests for that in different cultural and legal settings (Giannouli, 2014; Giannouli & Tsolaki, 2015), but neuropsychological information regarding competence follow the continuous paradigm of variation in degrees and by function, unlike the civil proceedings for which an absolute value of yes or no (competent-incompetent) must be answered (Schoenberg & Scott, 2011). Another frequent question in civil courts is whether the individual understands what he has done in cases of civil law (e.g., making a will and excluding his/her family members or making decisions with direct and indirect financial/legal consequences). In this respect the collected data during the evaluation may be used during the proceedings, by changing for example the way that the verbal material is presented.

The above findings for possible deficits could be included in medico-legal reports along with data from the individual/relatives interviews, and information coming from records on their functional capacity in various social settings and their health background. The forensic neuropsychologist must then answer the specific question at hand, for example in the case of criminal acts, whether the individual was before the commission, at the time and now (in)capable of doing a criminal act. In this case the forensic neuropsychologist can do that by providing a complete assessment of dangerousness based on all different sources for that person (self-reports, collaborative sources-e.g. family and evaluative collaborative sources-e.g. neuropsychological test data, medical and neurological examination and neuroimaging) (Denney & Wynkoop, 2000). The information obtained by the neuropsychological assessment will also be important for the future treatment of the individual by the judge, the jurors, and other people who work for the judicial system in prisons, in psychiatric hospitals or even when these individuals with ID return back to the community. Although the main focus of using these information in the legal system is unfortunately the management of prisoners with ID, rather than the rehabilitation planning, there is evidence for example that cognitive deficits may largely contribute to the lower completion rate of alcohol and drug treatment programmes for individuals with ID (McGillivray et al., 2015), a clue that could be used in order to improve the goals and structure of rehabilitation programmes and in order to overcome possible obstacles that relate to the different cognitive profiles (Lindsay, Taylor & Sturney, 2004). In addition to that, there is a need to educate people with ID about the civil and criminal laws, and here comes the importance not only of classic cognitive-behavioral treatments, but also of the attitudes-public opinion regarding ID and law. These attitudes can shape the role that families, caregivers and society as a whole can play for the future therapeutic treatments and interventions (Lindsay, 2002).

A STUDY OF ATTITUDES TOWARD ID AND LAW

Research Rationale

Intellectual Disability is related to major obstacles toward social, educational, and vocational integration. In modern western societies, although many things have changed from the past toward a more positive approach of the public for individuals with ID (Morin et al., 2013; Yazbeck, McVilly & Parmenter, 2004) with the de-institutionalisation movement in the direction of the 'normalisation principle', that is by trying to make the living environment of the individuals with ID to resemble as much as possible to the independent living conditions of the 'normals' (Louhiala, 2004), still the implicit and explicit negative perceptions and attitudes lead to discrimination and stigma not only in everyday life, but also in all areas of law (Wilson & Scior, 2015). This is supported by a cross-cultural study which reveals that the general population in ten examined countries lack an appreciation of the range of capabilities of individuals with ID and report low expectations of how much people with ID can achieve in their lives. This large-scale study also revealed that the public still believes that individuals with ID should work and learn in separate settings, apart from people without disabilities (Siperstein, 2003).

Research Objective

In this study new data are presented for the attitudes toward individuals with ID, and more specifically toward a neglected topic: ID and the Greek law.

Participants-Procedure

One hundred twenty-three healthy adults were examined. They all came from Northern Greece. The males were 45 and the females were 78. Their age varied between 22 and 62 years old. The mean age was 38 years old (SD = 8). They were divided into three age groups: from 21 to 35 years old (N = 48), from 36 to 50 years old (N = 61), and above 50 years old (N = 14). The participants had different family statuses: 32 were married, 42 were single, 13 were divorced, 12 were widowed, and 24 cohabitated. Most of them graduated from university (N = 64). A big part had secondary education (N = 44), and only a minority had a basic education (N = 15). All participants were native Greek speakers and participated in the research voluntarily. No participant had a relative with ID or a close friend with ID. They were all given a short new questionnaire to complete by themselves, which included the following questions:

Question 1: Do individuals with ID experience more frequently legal problems than individuals without ID?

Question 2: Do you believe that individuals with ID have problems in Greek courts more frequently regarding civil cases or criminal cases?

Question 3: Why do you believe that individuals with ID get involved with the law?

Question 4: What kind of crimes do you expect an individual with ID to commit in Greece?

Question 5: What can we do in order to avoid possible future involvement with the criminal-civil law for individuals with ID?

Question 6: Is the Greek legal system protecting or treating individuals with ID in a special way? Is this positive or negative?

Question 7: Is this treatment characterized by you as fair? Why? Why not?

Results

The results of the present study revealed for Question 1 that Greeks believe that individuals with ID engage more frequently with the law (89 participants responded that they believe this to be true). For Question 2, 56 participants responded that they believe that the civil law cases to be more frequent and 67 that criminal cases as more frequent in Greece. For Question 3, there were a variety of recorded reasons for the involvement of individuals with ID with the law: the most common reason is the fact that they do not understand what they are doing and what others are doing (70), the second reason is that they do not know what the law says (22), and the third was that they come from or end up in environments were illegal behavior is the norm (31). For Question 4, three were the most reported crimes that respondents believe that individuals with ID commit in Greece: theft (78), sexual assault (30), and homicide (15). For Question 5, there was a clear pattern in the responses of the participants of what we can do in order to change the current situation: the state must create treatment programs or institutions for this group of people to attend, where they can be controlled and educated on these issues of legal matters, but also on social behavior (101), the remaining respondents (22) did not have a clear view and did not propose anything, either because they do not believe that there is a problem, or because they could not think of anything to propose. For Question 6, respondents believe that the Greek Civil Code is giving to incapable adults and minors a different positive and protective treatment (110). For Question 7, the respondents believe that this treatment is fair (95), because according to their opinion when you have to deal with incapacitated individuals you have to change the way you are approaching him/her (94). The rest of the respondents (28) who believe that the treatment to be unfair, explain their view mainly on the basis of the fact that everyone knows what is good and what is bad in general, something that constitutes the foundation of any legal system (26). Finally, there were no statistically significant differences in the responses that the participants gave when categorized according to their age, sex, educational and family status groups in the present sample.

DISCUSSION AND CONCLUSION

The above results yield useful information to target public awareness on law and ID. Unfortunately, there are no studies on the socio-demographic characteristics of individuals with ID in Greece, which could give as more information in order to compare the opinions of the participants in this sample with the documented legal reality. But Greeks according to this research, do have a clear view on this unique population and it seems that a change of attitudes is necessary, with future initiatives aiming at collecting data on this topic not only locally, but also worldwide.

ID, Attitudes, and Legal Issues in Non-Western Societies

The relationship between mental retardation and criminality is complex especially if the cultural factor is included and examined. The cultural factor is considered to be very important, because it plays a significant role in stigma for mental illness, which seems to be less evident for example in Asian and African countries (Fabrega, 1991). In addition to that, while attitudes toward mental illness vary among non-Western cultures, the stigma of mental illness may be less severe than in Western cultures, because of the lack of differentiation between psychiatric and non-psychiatric illness in the three great non-Western medical traditions (Dols, 1987; Ng, 1997). Unfortunately, the cross-cultural studies in the western world concerning different aspects of ID and law are scarce (McAfee et al., 2001), and the existing replication studies come all from western societies (Hayes, 1996), where in general an individual's age, educational attainment and prior contact with someone with an ID may predict attitudes (Scior, 2011), while in other studies again conducted in western societies (e.g. Canada) only gender and age categories serve as predictive factors for the attitudes toward ID (Morin et al., 2014). We must keep in mind that there is always an additional influence of the culture where the individual comes from as a study with North Indian Hindu immigrants living in the mid-Western United States demonstrate on the ways in which immigrants think and talk about mental retardation even in another cultural context (Gabel, 2004). Although crime and legal issues among ID individuals in other countries besides western societies is recognized to be a little investigated topic (Kuo, 1983), there is still no adequate scientific literature on that. The main problem for this lack of information is not the existence of different legal systems, but the lack of research initiatives on this field.

Of course, there are some recent cross-cultural studies such as the Scior et al. (2010), which examine and compare the attitudes among the Hong Kong Chinese public and the British public toward intellectual disability. This study found that the Chinese were less favorable than the British sample, who were less opposed to the exclusion of people with intellectual disabilities, less likely to view them as similar to themselves and more in favor of sheltering such individuals. In Taiwan, the general attitudes of employees toward individuals with ID and their affective reactions toward their coworkers with ID are reported to be positive (Hsu et al., 2015). In India, a relevant research revealed that cultural and religious beliefs perpetuate negative attitudes towards disability (Edwardraj et al., 2010). Raw data from India indicate that ID is mainly associated with male gender, poor socio-economic status, pre-natal, peri-natal and post-natal complications, family history of ID, mental illness, and increased maternal age (Gopalan et al., 2014). High rates of comorbidity with psychiatric disorders, especially with externalizing disorders and psychosis followed by bipolar affective disorders are found in India, and ID is claimed to be associated with psychosocial adversities and psychiatric comorbidities (Gopalan et al., 2014; Kishore et al., 2004), a finding that is in line with the general trend in the western studies that offenders regardless of their IQ have in large part psychiatric comorbidities.

Another recent non-western study from China revealed that the majority of mentally retarded offenders were men, with an IQ which characterized them as mildly mentally retarded, with an additional psychiatric comorbidity for nearly half of the sample and a repeated history of offenses. The offenders had committed crimes against property, while the property offenses, especially petty theft and arson were frequently seen, but there was no noteworthy above average reported frequency of sexual offenses (Su et al., 2000). Another study from China found a high percentage of individuals diagnosed with ID who are convicted of murder (Wenhua, 2005). Finally, research from Africa revealed the high vulnerability of women with learning disabilities in the mild or moderate categories for sexual abuse (Calitz, 2011; Dickman & Roux, 2005) and a similar finding is supported for a sample of women from India (Mohaparta & Mohanty, 2004).

All the above findings may change as developing countries adopt western style consumer-driven economies, and in the future there might be an imitative tendency for the general public of these countries that will follow the same western trajectory of exclusion, which will impose the culture of "otherness" for the individuals with ID whose contribution to the society will be subsequently further devalued (Parmenter, 2008).

Based on this lack of basic relevant information on the way that the general public form different cultural environments perceive ID and legal issues and on how ID individuals react in their cultural environment, it is almost impossible to propose certain steps taken in different countries towards negating stigma and discriminatory treatment of people with ID. At the same time, no recipe can be proposed concerning strategies that must be followed in every country in order to improve the way(s) the society(ies) view(s) people with ID and reduce the disadvantages faced by the people with ID and their family members in the way the legal systems conduct trial and conviction. We must keep in mind that the socially constructed phenomenon of mental retardation varies cross-culturally in important respects (Manion & Bersani, 1987), which have to be further investigated by collecting data following identical research protocols not only on what the public believes, but also on what is the 'reality' of the legal reality in terms of descriptive statistics for each country in an effort to overcome relativism (Jenkins & Angrosino, 1998).

QUO VADIS: FUTURE RESEARCH DIRECTIONS

There are more questions on issues regarding ID and law, than there are answers. Future research should move from simple prevalence and descriptive studies of the excluded individuals with ID, to attempts of investigating identification of ID and the psychological and social processes, which determine how an individual with ID gets in and out of the justice system. Of course, research until now has given little attention to the fact that there are different societies-cultures and as a consequence different attitudes toward ID and that there is no clear answer to autonomy questions (Wilker, 1979). Methodological issues from previous research should be taken into consideration since there is not one single population with ID, but numerous with different forms of ID, different levels of severity of ID, concerning the two different sexes, and different social environments. So, it will be necessary to have research from the field of civil and criminal law focusing on the different demographics of ID, the different countries and these data should have only one aim, to be used for the improvement of the assessment and treatment approaches for clinicians and for the improvement of the legal process for legal experts (Lambrick & Glaser, 2004). In addition to large-scale research cross-cultural projects, research should be conducted on public protection. Based on these empirical evidence, proposals should be made to governments for mental health legislation and new models of care should be put under discussion for these different groups of individuals who fall under the umbrella of ID.

REFERENCES

Alexander, R. T., Chester, V., Green, F. N., Gunaratna, I., & Hoare, S. (2015). Arson or fire setting in offenders with intellectual disability: Clinical characteristics, forensic histories, and treatment outcomes. *Journal of Intellectual & Developmental Disability*, *40*(2), 1–9. doi:10.3109/13668250.2014.998182

American Psychological Association, (2005). *Assessment of older adults with diminished capacity. A handbook for lawyers.* American Bar Association Commission on Law and Aging – American Psychological Association.

American Psychological Association, (2006). *Assessment of older adults with diminished capacity. A handbook for psychologists*. American Bar Association Commission on Law and Aging – American Psychological Association.

Appelbaum, K. L., & Appelbaum, P. S. (1994). Criminal-justice-related competencies in defendants with mental retardation. *The Journal of Psychiatry & Law*, *22*, 483.

Baroff, G. S., Gunn, M., & Hayes, S. (2004). Legal issues. In W. Lindsay, J. Taylor, & P. Sturmey (Eds.), *Offenders with developmental disabilities* (pp. 37–65). West Sussex, UK: Wiley. doi:10.1002/9780470713440.ch3

Barron, P., Hassiotis, A., & Banes, J. (2002). Offenders with intellectual disability: The size of the problem and therapeutic outcomes. *Journal of Intellectual Disability Research*, *46*(6), 454–463. doi:10.1046/j.1365-2788.2002.00432.x PMID:12354316

Beail, N. (2002). Interrogative suggestibility, memory and intellectual disability. *Journal of Applied Research in Intellectual Disabilities*, *15*(2), 129–137. doi:10.1046/j.1468-3148.2002.00108.x

Benson, B. A., & Brooks, W. T. (2008). Aggressive challenging behaviour and intellectual disability. *Current Opinion in Psychiatry*, *21*(5), 454–458. doi:10.1097/YCO.0b013e328306a090 PMID:18650686

Benson, B. A., & Ivins, J. (1992). Anger, depression and self-concept in adults with mental retardation. *Journal of Intellectual Disability Research*, *36*(2), 169–175. doi:10.1111/j.1365-2788.1992.tb00492.x PMID:1591500

Bonnie, R. J. (1990). The competence of criminal defendants with mental retardation to participate in their own defense. *The Journal of Criminal Law & Criminology*, *81*(3), 419–446. doi:10.2307/1143845

Boone, K. B. (Ed.). (2007). *Assessment of feigned cognitive impairment: A neuropsychological perspective*. New York: Guilford Press.

Borromeo, A. D. (2001). Mental retardation and the death penalty. *Loyola Journal of Public Interest Law*, *3*, 175.

Bush, S. S.Planning Committee. (2005). Independent and court-ordered forensic neuropsychological examinations: Official statement of the National Academy of Neuropsychology. *Archives of Clinical Neuropsychology*, *20*(8), 997–1007. doi:10.1016/j.acn.2005.06.003 PMID:16076547

Calitz, F. J. (2011). Psycho-legal challenges facing the mentally retarded rape victim. *South African Journal of Psychiatry*, *17*(3), 66–72.

Carey, A. C. (2010). *On the margins of citizenship: Intellectual disability and civil rights in twentieth-century America*. Philadelphia, PA: Temple University Press.

Cea, C. D., & Fisher, C. B. (2003). Health care decision-making by adults with mental retardation. *Journal Information*, *41*(2). PMID:12622524

Clare, I. C. H., & Gudjonsson, G. H. (1993). Interrogative suggestibility, confabulation, and acquiescence in people with mild learning disabilities (mental handicap): Implications for reliability during police interview. *The British Journal of Clinical Psychology*, *32*(3), 295–301. doi:10.1111/j.2044-8260.1993.tb01059.x PMID:8251959

Clare, I. C. H., & Gudjonsson, G. H. (1995). The vulnerability of suspects with intellectual disabilities during police interviews: A review and experimental study of decision-making. *Mental Handicap Research*, *8*(2), 110–128. doi:10.1111/j.1468-3148.1995.tb00149.x

Cockram, J., Jackson, R., & Underwood, R. (1998). People with an intellectual disability and the criminal justice system: The family perspective. *Journal of Intellectual & Developmental Disability*, *23*(1), 41–56. doi:10.1080/13668259800033571

Crocker, A. G., Mercier, C., Lachapelle, Y., Brunet, A., Morin, D., & Roy, M. E. (2006). Prevalence and types of aggressive behaviour among adults with intellectual disabilities. *Journal of Intellectual Disability Research*, *50*(9), 652–661. doi:10.1111/j.1365-2788.2006.00815.x PMID:16901292

Curtis, A., McVilly, K., & Day, A. (2014). Sentencing offenders with mental impairment: The case of arsonists with intellectual disability. *Journal of Intellectual Disabilities and Offending Behaviour*, *5*(2), 78–87. doi:10.1108/JIDOB-05-2014-0005

Cuskelly, M., & Bryde, R. (2004). Attitudes towards the sexuality of adults with an intellectual disability: Parents, support staff, and a community sample. *Journal of Intellectual & Developmental Disability*, *29*(3), 255–264. doi:10.1080/13668250412331285136

Daily, D. K., Ardinger, H. H., & Holmes, G. E. (2000). Identification and evaluation of mental retardation. *American Family Physician*, *61*(4), 1059–1067. PMID:10706158

Davidson, P. W., Cain, N. N., Sloane-Reeves, J. E., & Van Speybroech, A. (1994). Characteristics of community-based individuals with mental retardation and aggressive behavioral disorders. *American Journal of Mental Retardation*, *98*(6), 704–716. PMID:8054199

Day, K. (1993). Crime and mental retardation: A review. *Clinical Approaches to the Mentally Disordered Offender*, 111-44.

Day, K. (1994). Male mentally handicapped sex offenders. *The British Journal of Psychiatry*, *165*(5), 630–639. doi:10.1192/bjp.165.5.630 PMID:7866678

Demakis, G. J. (Ed.). (2011). *Civil capacities in clinical neuropsychology: Research findings and practical applications*. New York: Oxford University Press.

Denney, R. L., & Wynkoop, T. F. (2000). Clinical neuropsychology in the criminal forensic setting. *The Journal of Head Trauma Rehabilitation*, *15*(2), 804–828. doi:10.1097/00001199-200004000-00005 PMID:10739969

Devapriam, J., Raju, L., Singh, N., Collacott, R., & Bhaumik, S. (2007). Arson: Characteristics and predisposing factors in offenders with intellectual disabilities. *British Journal of Forensic Practice*, *9*(4), 23–27. doi:10.1108/14636646200700023

Dickman, B. J., & Roux, A. J. (2005). Complainants with learning disabilities in sexual abuse cases: A 10-year review of a psycho-legal project in Cape Town, South Africa. *British Journal of Learning Disabilities*, *33*(3), 138–144. doi:10.1111/j.1468-3156.2005.00355.x

Dickson, K., Emerson, E., & Hatton, C. (2005). Self-reported anti-social behaviour: Prevalence and risk factors amongst adolescents with and without intellectual disability. *Journal of Intellectual Disability Research*, *49*(11), 820–826. doi:10.1111/j.1365-2788.2005.00727.x PMID:16207279

Dols, M. W. (1987). Insanity and its treatment in Islamic society. *Medical History*, *31*(1), 1–14. doi:10.1017/S0025727300046287 PMID:3543559

Dwyer, R. G., & Frierson, R. L. (2006). The presence of low IQ and mental retardation among murder defendants referred for pretrial evaluation. *Journal of Forensic Sciences*, *51*(3), 678–682. doi:10.1111/j.1556-4029.2006.00115.x PMID:16696721

Edwardraj, S., Mumtaj, K., Prasad, J. H., Kuruvilla, A., & Jacob, K. S. (2010). Perceptions about intellectual disability: A qualitative study from Vellore, South India. *Journal of Intellectual Disability Research*, *54*(8), 736–748. doi:10.1111/j.1365-2788.2010.01301.x PMID:20633202

Everington, C., & Fulero, S. M. (1999). Competence to confess: Measuring understanding and suggestibility of defendants with mental retardation. *Mental Retardation*, *37*(3), 212–220. doi:10.1352/0047-6765(1999)037<0212:CTCMUA>2.0.CO;2 PMID:10473340

Fabrega, H. Jr. (1991). Psychiatric stigma in non-Western societies. *Comprehensive Psychiatry*, *32*(6), 534–551. doi:10.1016/0010-440X(91)90033-9 PMID:1778081

Fazel, S., Xenitidis, K., & Powell, J. (2008). The prevalence of intellectual disabilities among 12000 prisoners - A systematic review. *International Journal of Law and Psychiatry*, *31*(4), 369–373. doi:10.1016/j.ijlp.2008.06.001 PMID:18644624

Fisher, C., Cea, C., Davidson, P., & Fried, A. (2006). Capacity of persons with mental retardation to consent to participate in randomized clinical trials. *The American Journal of Psychiatry*, *163*(10), 1813–1820. doi:10.1176/ajp.2006.163.10.1813 PMID:17012694

Fulero, S. M., & Everington, C. (1995). Assessing competency to waive Miranda rights in defendants with mental retardation. *Law and Human Behavior*, *19*(5), 533–543. doi:10.1007/BF01499342

Gabel, S. (2004). South Asian Indian cultural orientations toward mental retardation. *Journal Information*, *42*(1), 12–25. PMID:14720098

Giannouli, V. (2014). What do Greeks believe about elders and mental? *Agora International Journal of Juridical Sciences*, *8*(3), 1–5.

Giannouli, V., & Tsolaki, M. (2011). Competency and dementia: A challenge of today. [in Greek]. *Neurology*, *20*(6), 12–19.

Giannouli, V., & Tsolaki, M. (2015). A neglected drama for elders: Discrepancy between self-perception and objective performance regarding financial capacity in patients with cognitive deficits. *Psychological Thought*, *8*(2), 142–147. doi:10.5964/psyct.v8i2.130

Glaser, W., & Deane, K. (1999). Normalisation in an abnormal world: A study of prisoners with an intellectual disability. *International Journal of Offender Therapy and Comparative Criminology*, *43*(3), 338–356. doi:10.1177/0306624X99433007

Gopalan, R. T., Sharma, R., & Unnikrishnan, M. P. (2014). Socio-demographic and clinical features of children with intellectual disability and their parents - An Indian study. *International Neuropsychiatric Disease Journal*, *2*(6), 2321–7235. doi:10.9734/INDJ/2014/10610

Gudjonsson, G. H., & Henry, L. (2003). Child and adult witnesses with intellectual disability: The importance of suggestibility. *Legal and Criminological Psychology*, *8*(2), 241–252. doi:10.1348/135532503322363013

Gudjonsson, G. H., Murphy, G. H., & Clare, I. C. H. (2000). Assessing the capacity of people with intellectual disabilities to be witnesses in court. *Psychological Medicine*, *30*(2), 307–314. doi:10.1017/S003329179900149X PMID:10824651

Hayes, S. (1996). Recent research on offenders with learning disabilities. *Tizard Learning Disability Review*, *1*(3), 7–15. doi:10.1108/13595474199600003

Heilbronner, R. (2004). A status report on the practice of forensic neuropsychology. *The Clinical Neuropsychologist*, *18*(2), 312–326. doi:10.1080/13854040490501574 PMID:15587677

Hockley, O. J., & Langdon, P. E. (2015). Men with intellectual disabilities with a history of sexual offending: Empathy for victims of sexual and non-sexual crimes. *Journal of Intellectual Disability Research*, *59*(4), 332–341. doi:10.1111/jir.12137 PMID:24761788

Hodgins, S. (1992). Mental disorder, intellectual deficiency, and crime: Evidence from a birth cohort. *Archives of General Psychiatry*, *49*(6), 476–483. doi:10.1001/archpsyc.1992.01820060056009 PMID:1599373

Hodgins, S., Mednick, S. A., Brennan, P. A., Schulsinger, F., & Engberg, M. (1996). Mental disorder and crime: Evidence from a Danish birth cohort. *Archives of General Psychiatry*, *53*(6), 489–496. doi:10.1001/archpsyc.1996.01830060031004 PMID:8639031

Holland, T., Clare, I. C. H., & Mukhopadhyay, T. (2002). Prevalence of 'criminal offending' by men and women with intellectual disability and the characteristics of 'offenders': Implications for research and service development. *Journal of Intellectual Disability Research*, *46*(s1), 6–20. doi:10.1046/j.1365-2788.2002.00001.x PMID:12061335

Hsu, T. H., Huang, Y. T., Liu, Y. H., Ososkie, J., Fried, J., & Bezyak, J. (2015). Taiwanese attitudes and affective reactions toward individuals and coworkers who have intellectual disabilities. *American Journal on Intellectual and Developmental Disabilities*, *120*(2), 110–124. doi:10.1352/1944-7558-120.2.110 PMID:25715181

Jakab, I. (1990). Neuropsychological evaluation and rehabilitation in mental retardation. *Neuropsychology Review*, *1*(2), 137–164. doi:10.1007/BF01108715 PMID:2152529

Jenkins, R., & Angrosino, M. V. (1998). *Questions of competence: Culture, classification and intellectual disability*. Cambridge, UK: Cambridge University Press.

Jones, J. (2007). Persons with intellectual disabilities in the criminal justice system: Review of issues. *International Journal of Offender Therapy and Comparative Criminology*, *51*(6), 723–733. doi:10.1177/0306624X07299343 PMID:17636203

Kebbell, M. R., & Hatton, C. (1999). People with mental retardation as witnesses in court: A review. *Mental Retardation*, *37*(3), 179–187. doi:10.1352/0047-6765(1999)037<0179:PWMRAW>2.0.CO;2 PMID:10473337

Kishore, M. T., Nizamie, A., Nizamie, S. H., & Jahan, M. (2004). Psychiatric diagnosis in persons with intellectual disability in India. *Journal of Intellectual Disability Research*, *48*(1), 19–24. doi:10.1111/j.1365-2788.2004.00579.x PMID:14675227

Klimecki, M. R., Jenkinson, J., & Wilson, L. (1994). A study of recidivism among offenders with an intellectual disability. *Journal of Intellectual & Developmental Disability*, *19*(3), 209–219. doi:10.1080/07263869400035241

Kuo, S. H. (1993). Forensic psychiatry in Taiwan. *International Journal of Law and Psychiatry*, *6*(3-4), 457–472. doi:10.1016/0160-2527(83)90032-8 PMID:6679535

Lambrick, F., & Glaser, W. (2004). Sex offenders with an intellectual disability. *Sexual Abuse*, *16*(4), 381–392. PMID:15560418

Langdon, P. E., Clare, I. C., & Murphy, G. H. (2011). Moral reasoning theory and illegal behaviour by adults with intellectual disabilities. *Psychology, Crime & Law*, *17*(2), 101–115. doi:10.1080/10683160903392384

Larrabee, G. J. (2005). *Forensic neuropsychology: A scientific approach*. New York: Oxford University Press.

Lindsay, W. R. (2002). Integration of recent reviews on offenders with intellectual disabilities. *Journal of Applied Research in Intellectual Disabilities*, *15*(2), 111–119. doi:10.1046/j.1468-3148.2002.00112.x

Lindsay, W. R., Carson, D., Holland, A. J., Taylor, J. L., O'Brien, G., Wheeler, J. R., & Steptoe, L. (2013). Alcohol and its relationship to offence variables in a cohort of offenders with intellectual disability. *Journal of Intellectual & Developmental Disability*, *38*(4), 325–331. doi:10.3109/13668250.2013.837154 PMID:24279785

Lindsay, W. R., Law, J., Quinn, K., Smart, N., & Smith, A. H. (2001). A comparison of physical and sexual abuse: Histories of sexual and non-sexual offenders with intellectual disability. *Child Abuse & Neglect*, *25*(7), 989–995. doi:10.1016/S0145-2134(01)00251-4 PMID:11523873

Lindsay, W. R., Smith, A. H., Quinn, K., Anderson, A., Smith, A., Allan, R., & Law, J. (2004). Women with intellectual disability who have offended: Characteristics and outcome. *Journal of Intellectual Disability Research*, *48*(6), 580–590. doi:10.1111/j.1365-2788.2004.00627.x PMID:15312059

Lindsay, W. R., Taylor, J. L., & Sturmey, P. (Eds.). (2004). *Offenders with developmental disabilities*. Chichester, UK: John Wiley & Sons. doi:10.1002/9780470713440

Lindsay, W. R., Tinsley, S., & Emara, M. (2012). Alcohol use and offending in people with intellectual disability. *Alcohol-Related Violence. Prevention & Treatment*, 285–302.

Lorenzo, L. A. (1991). Societal prejudice reflected in our courts: The unfavorable treatment of the mentally retarded. *Seton Hall Const. LJ*, *2*, 771.

Louhiala. (2004). *Preventing intellectual disability. Ethical and clinical issues.* Cambridge, UK: Cambridge University Press.

Lund, J. (1990). Mentally retarded criminal offenders in Denmark. *The British Journal of Psychiatry*, *156*(5), 726–731. doi:10.1192/bjp.156.5.726 PMID:2095951

Lunsky, Y., Bradley, E. A., Gracey, C. D., Durbin, J., & Koegl, C. (2009). Gender differences in psychiatric diagnoses among inpatients with and without intellectual disabilities. *Journal Information*, *114*(1). PMID:19143463

Lyall, I., Holland, A. J., & Collins, S. (1995). Offending by adults with learning disabilities and the attitudes of staff to offending behaviour: Implications for service development. *Journal of Intellectual Disability Research*, *39*(6), 501–508. doi:10.1111/j.1365-2788.1995.tb00570.x PMID:8746737

Manion, M. L., & Bersani, H. A. (1987). Mental retardation as a Western sociological construct: A cross-cultural analysis. *Disability, Handicap & Society*, *2*(3), 231–245. doi:10.1080/02674648766780301

Martell, D. A. (1992). Forensic neuropsychology and the criminal law. *Law and Human Behavior*, *16*(3), 313–336. doi:10.1007/BF01044772

McAfee, J. K., Cockram, J., & Wolfe, P. S. (2001). Police reactions to crimes involving people with mental retardation: A cross-cultural experimental study. *Education and Training in Mental Retardation and Developmental Disabilities*, 160–171.

McGillivray, J. A., Gaskin, C. J., Newton, D. C., & Richardson, B. A. (in press). Substance Use, Offending, and Participation in Alcohol and Drug Treatment Programmes: A Comparison of Prisoners with and without Intellectual Disabilities. *Journal of Applied Research in Intellectual Disabilities*. PMID:25754684

McGillivray, J. A., & Moore, M. R. (2001). Substance use by offenders with mild intellectual disability. *Journal of Intellectual & Developmental Disability*, *26*(4), 297–310. doi:10.1080/13668250120087317

McKinlay & McGowan. (2003). Forensic issues in neuropsychology. In P. W. Halligan, U. Kischka, & J. C. Marshall (Eds.), *Handbook of clinical neuropsychology* (pp. 676–693). New York: Oxford University Press.

McNulty, C., Kissi-Deborah, R., & Newsom-Davies, I. (1995). Police involvement with clients having intellectual disabilities: A pilot study in South London. *Mental Handicap Research*, *8*(2), 129–136. doi:10.1111/j.1468-3148.1995.tb00150.x

Mohapatra, S., & Mohanty, M. (2004). *Abuse and activity limitation: a study on domestic violence against disabled women in Orissa, India*. Bhubaneswar, Orissa: Swabhiman.

Morin, D., Rivard, M., Boursier, C. P., Crocker, A. G., & Caron, J. (2015). Norms of the Attitudes Toward Intellectual Disability Questionnaire. *Journal of Intellectual Disability Research*, *59*(5), 462–467. doi:10.1111/jir.12146 PMID:25041088

Morin, D., Rivard, M., Crocker, A. G., Boursier, C. P., & Caron, J. (2013). Public attitudes towards intellectual disability: A multidimensional perspective. *Journal of Intellectual Disability Research*, *57*(3), 279–292. doi:10.1111/jir.12008 PMID:23279318

Morris, C. D., Niederbuhl, J. M., & Mahr, J. M. (1993). Determining the capability of individuals with mental retardation to give informed consent. *American Journal of Mental Retardation*, *98*(2), 263–272. PMID:8398085

Murphy, G., & Mason, J. (2014). Forensic and offending behaviours. In E. Tsakanikos & J. McCarthy (Eds.), Handbook of psychopathology in intellectual disability (pp. 281-303). New York: Springer. doi:10.1007/978-1-4614-8250-5_18

Neuwirth, G. S., Heisler, P. A., & Goldrich, K. S. (1974). Capacity, competence, consent: Voluntary sterilization of the mentally retarded. *Columbia Human Rights Law Review*, *6*, 447. PMID:11663600

New South Wales. Law Reform Commission. (1994). *People with an intellectual disability and the criminal justice system: Courts and sentencing issues* (Vol. 35). The Commission.

Ng, C. H. (1997). The stigma of mental illness in Asian cultures. *The Australian and New Zealand Journal of Psychiatry*, *31*(3), 382–390. doi:10.3109/00048679709073848 PMID:9226084

O'Callaghan, A. C., & Murphy, G. H. (2007). Sexual relationships in adults with intellectual disabilities: Understanding the law. *Journal of Intellectual Disability Research*, *51*(3), 197–206. doi:10.1111/j.1365-2788.2006.00857.x PMID:17300415

Olvera, D. R., Dever, R. B., & Earnest, M. A. (2000). Mental retardation and sentences for murder: Comparison of two recent court cases. *Mental Retardation*, *38*(3), 228–233. doi:10.1352/0047-6765(2000)038<0228:MRASFM>2.0.CO;2 PMID:10900930

Orchard, A. (2013) *The burning issue: Why do people with intellectual disability commit arson?* (MSc dissertation). University of Portsmouth.

Parmenter, T. R. (2008). The present, past and future of the study of intellectual disability: Challenges in developing countries. *Salud Pública de México*, *50*, s124–s131. doi:10.1590/S0036-36342008000800004 PMID:18470339

Parry, J., & Drogin, E. Y. (2007). *Mental disability law, evidence, and testimony: A comprehensive reference manual for lawyers, judges, and mental disability professionals*. American Bar Association.

Perske, R. (1991). *Unequal justice?: What can happen when persons with retardation or other developmental disabilities encounter the criminal justice system*. Nashville, TN: Abingdon Press.

Perske, R. (2005). Search for persons with intellectual disabilities who confessed to serious crimes they did not commit. *Journal Information*, *43*(1), 58–65. PMID:15628935

Perske, R. (2008). False confessions from 53 persons with intellectual disabilities: The list keeps growing. *Intellectual and Developmental Disabilities*, *46*(6), 468–479. doi:10.1352/2008.46:468-479 PMID:19006433

Perske, R. (2011). Perske's list: False confessions from 75 persons with intellectual disability. *Intellectual and Developmental Disabilities*, *49*(5), 365–373. doi:10.1352/1934-9556-49.5.365 PMID:21905830

Plant, A., McDermott, E., Chester, V., & Alexander, R. T. (2011). Substance misuse among offenders in a forensic intellectual disability service. *Journal of Learning Disabilities and Offending Behaviour*, *2*(3), 127–135. doi:10.1108/20420921111186589

Raina, P., & Lunsky, Y. (2010). A comparison study of adults with intellectual disability and psychiatric disorder with and without forensic involvement. *Research in Developmental Disabilities*, *31*(1), 218–223. doi:10.1016/j.ridd.2009.09.008 PMID:19854026

Reed, E. J. (1997). Criminal law and the capacity of mentally retarded persons to consent to sexual activity. *Virginia Law Review*, *83*(4), 799–827. doi:10.2307/1073749

Ridley, A. M., Gabbert, F., & La Rooy, D. J. (2012). *Suggestibility in legal contexts: psychological research and forensic implications*. Chichester, UK: John Wiley & Sons.

Ruff, C. F., Templer, D. I., & Ayers, J. L. (1976). The intelligence of rapists. *Archives of Sexual Behavior*, *5*(4), 327–329. doi:10.1007/BF01542085 PMID:952615

Salkind, N. J. (2002). *Child development*. New York: Macmillan Reference USA.

Schalock, R. L., Luckasson, R. A., & Shogren, K. A. (2007). The renaming of mental retardation: Understanding the change to the term intellectual disability. *Journal Information*, *45*(2). PMID:17428134

Schoenberg, M. R., & Scott, J. G. (2011). *The little black book of neuropsychology: a syndrome-based approach*. New York: Springer Science & Business Media. doi:10.1007/978-0-387-76978-3

Scior, K. (2011). Public awareness, attitudes and beliefs regarding intellectual disability: A systematic review. *Research in Developmental Disabilities*, *32*(6), 2164–2182. doi:10.1016/j.ridd.2011.07.005 PMID:21798712

Scior, K., Kan, K. Y., McLoughlin, A., & Sheridan, J. (2010). Public attitudes toward people with intellectual disabilities: A cross-cultural study. *Intellectual and Developmental Disabilities*, *48*(4), 278–289. doi:10.1352/1934-9556-48.4.278 PMID:20722478

Simpson, M. K., & Hogg, J. (2001). Patterns of offending among people with intellectual disability: A systematic review. Part I: Methodology and prevalence data. *Journal of Intellectual Disability Research*, *45*(5), 384–396. doi:10.1046/j.1365-2788.2001.00345.x PMID:11679044

Siperstein, G. N. (2003). *Multinational study of attitudes towards individuals with intellectual disabilities: General findings and calls to action*. Special Olympics.

Sjgafoos, J., Elkins, J., Kerr, M., & Attwood, T. (1994). A survey of aggressive behaviour among a population of persons with intellectual disability in Queensland. *Journal of Intellectual Disability Research*, *38*(4), 369–381. doi:10.1111/j.1365-2788.1994.tb00417.x PMID:7949789

Søndenaa, E., Rasmussen, K., & Nøttestad, J. A. (2008). Forensic issues in intellectual disability. *Current Opinion in Psychiatry*, *21*(5), 449–453. doi:10.1097/YCO.0b013e328305e5e9 PMID:18650685

Søndenaa, E., Rasmussen, K., Palmstierna, T., & Nøttestad, J. A. (2008). The prevalence and nature of intellectual disability in Norwegian prisons. *Journal of Intellectual Disability Research*, *52*(12), 1129–1137. doi:10.1111/j.1365-2788.2008.01072.x PMID:18498332

Strømme, P., & Magnus, P. (2000). Correlations between socioeconomic status, IQ and aetiology in mental retardation: A population-based study of Norwegian children. *Social Psychiatry and Psychiatric Epidemiology*, *35*(1), 12–18. doi:10.1007/s001270050003 PMID:10741531

Su, K. P., Yu, J. M., Yang, T. W., Tsai, S. Y., & Chen, C. C. (2000). Characteristics of mentally retarded criminal offenders in Northern Taiwan. *Journal of Forensic Sciences*, *45*(6), 1207–1209. doi:10.1520/JFS14869J PMID:11110172

Sullivan, P. M., & Knutson, J. F. (2000). Maltreatment and disabilities: A population-based epidemiological study. *Child Abuse & Neglect*, *24*(10), 1257–1273. doi:10.1016/S0145-2134(00)00190-3 PMID:11075694

Suto, W. M. I., Clare, I. C. H., Holland, A. J., & Watson, P. C. (2005). Capacity to make financial decisions among people with mild intellectual disabilities. *Journal of Intellectual Disability Research*, *49*(3), 199–209. doi:10.1111/j.1365-2788.2005.00635.x PMID:15713195

Sweet, J. J., King, J. H., Malina, A. C., Bergman, M. A., & Simmons, A. (2002). Documenting the prominence of forensic neuropsychology at national meetings and in relevant professional journals from 1990 to 2000. *The Clinical Neuropsychologist*, *16*(4), 481–494. doi:10.1076/clin.16.4.481.13914 PMID:12822057

Timms, S., & Goreczny, A. J. (2002). Adolescent sex offenders with mental retardation: Literature review and assessment considerations. *Aggression and Violent Behavior*, *7*(1), 1–19. doi:10.1016/S1359-1789(00)00031-8

Vandevelde, S., Broekaert, E., Schuyten, G., & Van Hove, G. (2005). Intellectual abilities and motivation toward substance abuse treatment in drug-involved offenders: A pilot study in the Belgian criminal justice system. *International Journal of Offender Therapy and Comparative Criminology*, *49*(3), 277–297. doi:10.1177/0306624X04270779 PMID:15851508

Vaughan, P. J., Pullen, N., & Kelly, M. (2000). Services for mentally disordered offenders in community psychiatry teams. *Journal of Forensic Psychiatry*, *11*(3), 571–586. doi:10.1080/09585180010004829

Vera, H., Barnard, G. W., & Holzer, C. (1979). The intelligence of rapists: New data. *Archives of Sexual Behavior*, *8*(4), 375–377. doi:10.1007/BF01541880 PMID:475583

Wenhua, L. (2005). Analysis of 294 cases of murder in forensic psychiatric expertise. *Journal of Clinical Psychosomatic Diseases, 4,* 25.

Wikler, D. (1979). Paternalism and the mildly retarded. *Philosophy & Public Affairs*, 377–392.

Wilson, M. C., & Scior, K. (2015). Implicit attitudes towards people with intellectual disabilities: Their relationship with explicit attitudes, social distance, emotions and contact. *PLoS ONE*, *10*(9), e0137902. PMID:26366575

Yazbeck, M., McVilly, K., & Parmenter, T. R. (2004). Attitudes toward people with intellectual disabilities an Australian perspective. *Journal of Disability Policy Studies*, *15*(2), 97–111. doi:10.1177/10442073040150020401

ADDITIONAL READING

Boone, K. B. (2012). *Clinical practice of forensic neuropsychology: An evidence-based approach*. New York: Guilford Press.

Conley, R. W., Luckasson, R., & Bouthilet, G. N. (Eds.), *The criminal justice system and mental retardation*. Baltimore, MD: Paul H. Brookes.

Demakis, G. J. (Ed.). (2011). *Civil capacities in clinical neuropsychology: Research findings and practical applications*. New York: Oxford University Press.

Denney, R. L., & Sullivan, J. P. (Eds.). (2008). *Clinical neuropsychology in the criminal forensic setting*. New York: Guilford Press.

Horton, A. M., & Hartlage, L. C. (Eds.). (2010). *Handbook of forensic neuropsychology*. New York: Springer Publishing Company.

Larrabee, G. J. (Ed.). (2011). *Forensic neuropsychology: A scientific approach*. New York: Oxford University Press.

Morgan, J. E., & Sweet, J. J. (Eds.). (2010). *Neuropsychology of malingering casebook*. New York: Psychology Press.

Parckard, W. B. (2013). *Intellectual disability and the criminal justice system: Solutions through collaboration*. Create Space Independent Publishing Platform.

Søndenaa, E. (2009). *Intellectual disabilities in the criminal justice system*. Norwegian University of Science and Technology.

Towl, G. J., & Crighton, D. A. (2010). *Forensic psychology*. London: BPS Blackwell.

Wehmeyer, M. L. (2013). *The story of intellectual disability: An evolution of meaning, understanding, and public perception*. Baltimore: Paul H. Brookes Publishing.

Young, S., Kopelman, M., & Gudjonsson, G. (Eds.). (2009). *Forensic neuropsychology in practice: A guide to assessment and legal processes*. New York: Oxford University Press. doi:10.1093/med/9780198566830.001.0001

KEY TERMS AND DEFINITIONS

Civil Law: Civil Law consists a branch of law, which consists of non-criminal law.

Crime: This general term denotes an unlawful act punishable by the state.

Criminal Law: Criminal Law consists a branch of law, which relates to crime.

Financial Capacity: The capacity of an individual to manage his/her own money-financial affairs and make relevant decisions while keeping in mind all possible financial-legal consequences of his/her acts.

Forensic Neuropsychological Assessment: The evaluation of performance on various areas of functioning, which is based on the use of standardized testing methods focusing on cognitive, behavioral and emotional functioning which aim at clarifying issues for legal decision-making.

Intellectual Disability: A new term used for disability characterized by significant limitations in both intellectual functioning and inadaptive behavior, which covers many everyday social and practical skills and refers to individuals who are under 18 years of age. Intellectual Disability has replaced the term mental retardation.

Miranda Rights or Miranda Warning: Warning given by the police in the USA to criminal suspects in police custody or in a custodial interrogation stating that: You have the right to remain silent. Anything you say or do can or will be used against you in a court of law. You have the right to an attorney. If you cannot afford an attorney, one will be appointed to you. Do you understand these rights as they have been read to you?

Sexual Abuse: Any form of forced-undesired sexual behavior by one person upon another.

Chapter 19
Intellectual Disability in the Family Context:
Parents with Intellectual Disability

Swarnima Bhargava
Independent Researcher, India

Daanesh Marazban Umrigar
Independent Researcher, India

ABSTRACT

Literature with regard to parents with intellectual disability is scant. On one hand, parents with intellectual disability engage in the valued social role of raising children; on the other, their parenting attracts (typically negative) attention based on an expectation of their limited capacities to parent. Available research primarily addresses the question of whether or not individuals with intellectual disability can be adequate parents or reports on methods for improving their parenting skills. There has been relatively negligible work in the Indian context with regard to parents with intellectual disability. This paper attempts to review literature on the current data available about parents and parenting with intellectual disability in the Indian context concentrating on directions for future research.

INTRODUCTION

Intellectual disability has been defined in several ways in literature. It can be described as a neurodevelopmental disorder, which has onset in childhood and leads to impaired development of one or more human capacities (Girimaji, 2015). Intellectual disability is characterized by limitations in intellectual functioning and resulting in the need for extraordinary supports for the person to participate in activities involved with typical human functioning (Wehmeyer et al., 2008). Intellectual disability, then, is a disability in which impairments to the brain (e.g., body functions and structures) result in activity limitations and participation restrictions, specifically limitations in intellectual functioning. Intellectual functioning is defined in the American Association on Intellectual and Developmental Disabilities (AAIDD) Manual (2002) on Definition, Classification, and Support Systems in Mental Retardation, as

DOI: 10.4018/978-1-5225-0089-6.ch019

referring to a general mental ability that includes reasoning, planning, problem solving, abstract thinking, comprehending complex ideas, learning quickly, and learning from experience (Luckasson et al., 2002). In the past internationally and in India the term "mental retardation" was widely applied and defined as "a condition of arrested or incomplete development of mind of a person which is specially characterized by sub-normality of intelligence" according to The National Trust For Welfare Of Persons With Autism, Cerebral Palsy, Mental Retardation And Multiple Disabilities Act, 1999. However, a more comprehensive definition takes into consideration the lower IQ scores on standard intelligence tests, as well as difficulties in social and adaptive functioning, occurring before the age of eighteen years. The latest mental health diagnostic publication, the Diagnostic and Statistical Manual -5 (DSM-5), replaces the term "mental retardation" and defines intellectual (developmental) disability as "a disorder with onset during the developmental period that includes both intellectual and adaptive functioning deficits in conceptual, social, and practical domains." These revisions bring DSM into alignment with terminology used by the World Health Organization's International Classification of Diseases (ICD-10), other professional disciplines and organizations, such as the American Association on Intellectual and Developmental Disabilities, and the U.S. Department of Education. While suggesting that the term intellectual disability "covers the same population of individuals who were diagnosed previously with mental retardation in number, kind, level, type and duration of the disability and the need of people with this disability for individualized services and supports" Schalock and colleagues also recognized that the term "intellectual disability" more effectively "reflects the changed construct of disability proposed by AAIDD and the WHO" (Schalock et al., 2007). Contemporary literature uses the term "learning disability" or "learning difficulty" while discussing the same condition.

A break up of the ICD definition is as follows:

- *Deficits in intellectual functions such as reasoning, problem-solving, planning, abstract thinking, judgment, academic learning and learning from experience, and practical understanding confirmed by both clinical assessment and individualized, standardized intelligence testing.*
- *Deficits in adaptive functioning that result in failure to meet developmental and sociocultural standards for personal independence and social responsibility. Without ongoing support, the adaptive deficits limit functioning in one or more activities of daily life, such as communication, social participation, and independent living, and across multiple environments, such as home, school work and school, work, and recreation.*
- *Onset of intellectual and adaptive deficits during the developmental period. (DSM – 5, pg. 33).*

Thus one observes that individuals with Intellectual Disabilities (ID) face challenges throughout their life with regard to scholastic performance as well as in the realm of day-to-day life.

Looking at the etiology and manifestation of intellectual disability, we can regard it as one of a set of disabilities that can result from impairment to the central nervous system that manifest in limitations to general cognitive functioning. Cognition refers to the processes of knowing, including attending, remembering, and reasoning; also the content of the processes, such as concepts and memories (Gerrig et al., 2002). Other cognitive disabilities include traumatic brain injury, learning disability, and dementia associated with Alzheimer's disease. Intellectual disability is set apart from other cognitive disabilities by factors such as scope of impairment (e.g., global) and age of onset (e.g., prior to age 18). Because intellectual disability must be manifested in the developmental period (e.g., prior to age 18), it is also a developmental disability. Developmental disability is a non-diagnostic category that refers to people with both cognitive and physical disabilities, whose disability: originates in childhood (the developmental period from birth to 18), constitutes a significant challenge to typical functioning, and is expected to continue indefinitely (Thompson & Wehmeyer, 2008).

ID and Children

Prevalence of intellectual disability (ID) was established to range between 1 per 1,000 to 32 per 1,000 in an analysis by Girimaji and Srinath, (2010). Given the population of India, the numbers can be projected to be significant. When one talks about intellectual disabilities, the first image that springs to mind is a child, or an adolescent, with an intellectual disability. In literature as well as in common parlance one tends to infantilize the individual with ID and view them as childlike and in need of parental supervision. It is challenging to view such individuals as being parents themselves. Literature abounds on parenting a child with intellectual disability (Seshadri, 1983; Wig et al., 1985; Narayan et al., 1993; Dhar, 2009). Literature has also centered on children and adolescents with intellectual disabilities or on the parents of children with these disabilities. However, a miniscule amount of research deals with individuals with ID, who have become parents.

The current chapter is an inquiry with regard to parents with ID and the manner in which their needs are represented in academic literature and in the broader rhetoric of mental health. The authors have endeavoured to review available literature in an attempt to direct attention beyond the predominant narrative of parenting individuals with ID and move towards looking at the possible needs of parents with ID and propose how present mental health infrastructure may be mobilized to best serve them.

PARENTING WITH INTELLECTUAL DISABILITY

Morrison (1978) defined parenting as "the process of developing and utilising the knowledge and skills appropriate to planning for, creating, giving birth to, rearing and/or providing care for offspring". The Cambridge Dictionary of Psychology (2009) defines parenting as "All aspects of behaviour by adults with children intended to protect, nurture, teach, discipline, and guide them." These definitions imply that parenting involves not just bringing up the children but also providing care and a nurturing environment for them. Questions about the adequacy of parenting by a person with ID have been raised in both a legal (Hayman, 1990) and a clinical framework (Tymchuk, 1990), with the primary concerns revolving around the child's physical and emotional health and safety. At first, persons with intellectual disabilities may seem ill-equipped for this demanding role when, by definition, they demonstrate low general cognitive ability and a significant deficit in at least one of the three adaptive behaviour domains: conceptual, social and practical (Luckasson et al. 2002). Parenting is influenced by cultural and subcultural expectations of what is expected of the children, and what is considered appropriate for parents (Lynch & Hanson, 1992).

In the past, socio-political discourse has even raised the question of eugenics and whether individuals with ID "should be permitted" to exercise their sexual and reproductive rights and bear children. The first paper in scientific literature on the topic of parents with intellectual disabilities appeared in the 51st volume of the American Journal of Mental Deficiency in 1947. The author, Phyllis Mickelson, reflecting the times, set out to understand "methods of control of feeble-minded parents": institutionalization, sterilization, and community supervision". It is now increasingly recognized that people with an ID have the same rights as everybody else to pursue valued social roles. Recent legislation and guidance indicates that parents with a learning disability have a right to support that enables them to have a normal family life (Human Rights Act 1998, Disability Discrimination Act 2005, DH 2009).

Most of the literature available on parents with intellectual disability is from studies conducted in the 80's and 90's. And a lot of them have focused on the negative impact having parents with ID may have on their children (Seagull & Scheurer, 1986; Schilling et al., 1982; Mørch, Skår, & Andersgård, 1997; Accardo, & Whitman, 1990). The term – "parents with intellectual disability" – also needs further clarification. Despite this term being frequently used most studies include only mothers with ID under this rubric. There are several themes that emerge in the literature that pertains to parents with intellectual disability. The first addresses the question of whether people with intellectual disability can provide "good enough" parenting. The second theme relates to concerns about the well-being of the children of parents with intellectual disability, including the impact of impoverished home and social environments, child neglect and abuse, and delayed development or disability. The third focuses attention on interventions designed to increase parenting skills and, more recently, social supports.

INDIVIDUALS WITH INTELLECTUAL DISABILITY: "GOOD ENOUGH" PARENTS?

Parents with intellectual disabilities (i.e., IQs less than 80) are considered to be at-risk for child maltreatment (Feldman, 1997, 1998; Tymchuk & Feldman, 1991). Parents with intellectual disabilities (i.e., IQ < 80; mental retardation) are overrepresented in child maltreatment cases and have a variety of parenting skill deficits. Their children are at risk for neglect, developmental delay, and behavioural disorders. Feldman (1997) reviewed parenting education interventions for such parents and identified 20 published studies with adequate outcome data. A total of 190 such parents (188 mothers, 2 fathers), with IQs ranging from 50 to 79 were involved. Children of parents with intellectual disabilities are found to be at-risk for developmental delay, psychosocial retardation, and behavioural disorders (Collings & Llewellyn, 2012; Feldman, 1998; Feldman & Walton-Allen, 1997). Collings and Llewellyn identified two groups of studies. The first investigated an association between parental intellectual disability and child outcomes, where there were significant disadvantages. Some findings suggested that low parental intellectual capacity could negatively impact child outcomes, but others indicated that child development approached population norms. A second, group of studies explored the narrative accounts of childhood, of children of parents with ID, and found that social exclusion, bullying, and stigma were commonplace. Removal from parental care emerged as a significant risk for this group of children. Based on their review, the researchers concluded that studies that focused on child development represented 85% of the literature but reached no consensus about the likely developmental or behavioural outcomes. Children studied usually came from clinical populations or other high-risk groups, and were typically young children.

Most parenting stress research has been conducted with mothers because they are typically their children's primary or exclusive caregivers. Faureholm, (2010), provided a longitudinal perspective of growing up with a mother with ID. 23 children were interviewed first at ages ranging from 8 – 12-years, and then the same individuals were interviewed as young adults, a decade later. They tried to reflect their upbringing and relationship with their mothers. All the children under study lived with their mothers until they started school. They reported that they became aware that their mothers were different, while they were in school. A lot of them reported that comparatively poor hygiene levels and difficulty getting their mothers to help with homework triggered this line of thinking. Social ostracism also clued them to their mother's differences. Social stigma and peer rejection often followed recognition of the mother as "Different". Adolescent children would often question their upbringing and their social ostracism. Through all this, the children reported that they received unconditional love from their mothers, and this provided them with support even in the face of rejection. During the study it was very rare to find a child talking negatively of their mothers; however, the adolescents would report that their extended families were unsupportive and condescending. Perkins et al. (2002) found a more secure style of attachment in those children, whose mothers were perceived to be warm and caring, which is similar to the results of children without ID parents. They also found that these children, would in turn be less likely to perceive their ID mothers as stigmatized, and their self-esteem was better since they were able to see themselves fulfilling various life roles. From all these studies, we understand the importance of the parent–child relationship and how it affects children of parents with intellectual disabilities. All it does is adds support to the inclusion of intervention strategies aimed specifically to enhance parental warmth and sensitivity and to help encourage children of parents with ID to adopt a number of different roles, which can help boost their self-esteem, and in turn their general level of life satisfaction.

Influences on Parenting

Some adults with intellectual disability give accounts of abusing or neglectful parenting in their own childhoods (Seagull & Scheurer, 1986; Schilling & Schinke, 1984; Andron & Tymchuk, 1987). Westbrook and Legge (1993) wrote that family attitudes toward the cause and meaning of a disability, as well as toward appropriate responses, will be indirectly communicated to the child, and will affect the experiences that are provided and the life roles that the child is expected to achieve. The authors compared parents' attitudes and expectations regarding children with disabilities across six ethnic communities in Australia. They drew on Triandis's (1990) distinction between cultures that are individualistic (valuing independence and self-reliance) and collectivist (valuing dependence on and sacrifice for in-groups), classifying the Anglo and German families in the former, and Chinese, Italian, Greek, and Arabic families in the latter. The philosophy of inclusion is consistent with individualistic values and they found that in the individualistic communities' attitudes toward disabilities were more positive (Westbrook, Legge & Pennay, 1993), and children were more likely to be integrated into family and community activities (Westbrook & Legge, 1993). In the collectivist communities there was less expectation that children with disabilities should behave like other children, be included in family outings, or play with neighbourhood children. The disability was more likely to be considered shameful for the family and to be: kept secret. In adulthood, their lack of intellectual competence may result in limited social opportunities as well as negative reactions from others, exacerbating their low self-esteem and poor interpersonal skills (Whitman et al., 1989; Budd & Greenspan, 1984). These studies aptly illustrate that the impact of a child with intellectual disability in the family and also the subsequent parenting adaptations to disability are shaped by a multitude of influences that are often invisible to the service provider.

The person-context engagement model suggests that successful human functioning results from the engagement between capacity—emphasizing personal strengths—and the context, emphasizing supports defined as strategies, resources and activities that enhance human functioning. This model presumes that limitations in personal strengths can be at least partially offset by supports, and that poor functioning may result from of lack of supports or limited opportunities for participation. Mental health outcomes may be related to a range of risk factors, for example: nutritional intake, maternal weight, smoking, use of medications, lack of social support, poorer access to appropriate antenatal care, or mental health problems such as stress, anxiety and depression (McConnell, 2008). Research has shown that intellectual disability per se is an unreliable predictor of parenting performance: some parents with intellectual disability demonstrate adequate parenting skills, while others require training and support (Feldman, 1994; Hur, 1997; Aunos et al., 2003). Complementing the varying characteristics and history of a parent's disability are the characteristics of the child -- that is, the age and temperament of the child as well as whether or not the child also has a disability (whether similar to the parent's disability, or not). Many routine parenting tasks are age-specific (e.g., diapering an infant, modelling language or motor skills, assisting with a child's homework) -- and a parent's intellectual disability may affect a particular age-related parenting task. Raising a developmentally delayed child is likely to be stressful for any parent and parents with ID are especially vulnerable (Abramson et al., 1988; Schilling & Schinke, 1984). As children progress beyond the pre-school stage, the demands placed upon parents grow. Parents with ID faced with the emotional demands of middle childhood or adolescence find it substantially more difficult to cope (Accardo & Whitman, 1990s). As children enter the world of school and begin to demonstrate emotional and behavioural difficulties, parents with ID have been found to be less likely to seek and use professional help than parents of average ability (Accardo & Whitman, 1990; Whitman et al., 1989). Several studies place great emphasis on the ability of individuals with ID for parenting, consequences for children and evaluation of such individuals as parents with regard to the legal context (Tymchuk, 1990; Feldman, 1997, 1998).

Several parents' reports show a remarkable extent of normality (Pixa-Kettner, 1999). Individuals with ID have the recognized right to reproduction and to fulfil the roles of spouse and parents. There are a number of factors that can affect parental capacity for people with an intellectual disability. Parents with ID are more likely to face specific problems that make the task of child rearing more difficult. These include: poor physical health, poverty, unemployment, inadequate housing, unsafe neighbourhoods, relationship difficulties, high stress, poor treatment throughout life, depression, low self-esteem, difficulties in decision making and little exposure to positive parenting role models. Those are wide-spread problems and it would not be correct to attribute them to the parents' intellectual disabilities. While parents without disabilities often receive support and ideas from other parents, those with ID typically are unable to obtain and/or are provided less opportunities to develop such relationships that provide natural support. Other supports provided through government programs or non-profit agencies are also scarce. No single factor, such as IQ, has been proven determinative or predictive of actual fitness or unfitness to parent. More generally, there is no proven causal correlation between a person's level of intelligence and the ability to parent adequately.

Parenting is greatly influenced by forces beyond the child and family, such as day care and school programs, workplace practices, religious practices, governmental laws, and cultural and sub cultural expectations (Lynch & Hanson, 1992). Many contextual factors can affect parenting skills, for example: parental history and experience, health, stress, social support, financial status, access to services or health inequality (Feldman 1998, Feldman et al 2002). Sterling (1998) tested the relationships between depression, parenting stress, satisfaction with social support and parenting abilities in mothers with ID. Results from this study suggested that those parents who were more socially isolated and more depressed displayed poorer parenting ability.

What is clear — and sobering — is that the children of parents with ID are as likely as not to be raised by someone other than their parent with ID (McConnell, Feldman, Aunos, & Prasad, 2010). This increases the urgency for a critical review of research on the lives of children of parents with ID to differentiate influences that may stem from parental ID from contextual factors related to, for instance, the significant socioeconomic disadvantage and social exclusion experienced by people with ID (Emerson, 2007).

Contrary to prevalent discourse, people with intellectual disabilities can be good parents (Field & Sanchez, 1999; Hur 1997; Aunos et al. 2003). Wade et al. (2008) point out that parents with a learning disability are 'a heterogeneous group, demonstrating variability in parenting skills and living circumstances' (pp. 352). It is important to consider that contextual factors – a range of personal, social and environmental factors – will affect parenting skills. These include: parental history and experience, health status, stress, social support, financial status and access to services (Feldman, 1998; Feldman et al., 2002). Grayson (2000) reviewed studies attempting to identify factors contributing to successful parenting. These factors include: higher IQ (greater than 50 or 60), being married or living with the child's grandparents or daily support from a high functioning adult, having fewer children or only one, adequate motivation and willingness to accept support from service providers or informal sources, training in the home to enhance generalization, appropriate parent models during childhood, good physical and mental health, adequate finances and low stress and adequate education and reading skills.

Supporting Parents with Intellectual Disability: Training and Intervention

The next wave of literature speaks of training and intervention in order to better support parenting efforts in individuals with ID (Grayson, 2000). Studies relating to teaching parents with intellectual disability new skills, especially parenting skills has been ongoing since the late 80's. Feldman (1994) has consistently pointed out that these parents can be trained in better social as well as parenting skills, when the training is more performance based, with adequate feedback and praise. Feedback indicated that parents preferred interactive and practical learning to verbal learning. They liked having pictorial aids, achievable, individualized plans for their home with regard to safety improvements, material matched to their child's needs and age and lessons that were not too long. Rewards, also improved attendance as well as rapid acquisition as well as maintenance of information. Commonly, parent training services were only offered on an out-of-home basis, thus leading to difficulties for parents with intellectual disabilities to generalize what they learn to the home setting (Bakken et al. 1993). Feldman (1994) has added that if training is provided out-of-home, then the training environment should be as home like as possible, so as to ensure that the parenting skills are actually utilized in the home as well as elsewhere, and that programs should be flexible enough to be adaptable to providing training in environments where the skills are really needed. No matter the context, actual parent-child positive interactions only improved when performance-based training was provided. The most recent studies reveal that specialized training programs have enabled persons with ID to improve their parenting skills and experience.

One of the frequently cited reasons for undertaking parenting interventions is the assumption that the children of parents with ID will inevitably be at risk of poor developmental outcomes or maltreatment (Booth & Booth, 2000; Wade, Llewellyn, & Matthews, 2008). Parenting interventions are typically conducted with families headed by parents with ID who have come to the attention of welfare and family support services, meaning they already exhibit parenting difficulties and a host of parental vulnerabilities (Feldman, 2002; Hewitt, 2007).

McConnell, Llewellyn and Bye (1997) surveyed service providers and identified principles associated with effective services to parents with ID such as providing individualized, long-term care that caters to the whole family and assists parents in becoming part of their community.

Although there is limited research into the needs and experiences of parents with a learning disability (Booth & Booth 2006), a consistent finding of the available research is that mothers with a learning disability learn parenting skills when education and support are individually tailored to their own particular circumstances and learning needs (Feldman, 1994; Ray et al., 1994, Llewellyn et al., 2003). Such a consistent finding offers tremendous potential to all health and social care staff involved in supporting this group of parents.

Feldman (1994) reviewed parenting education interventions from 20 published studies and noted that the most common instructional approach was behavioural (e.g., task analysis, modelling, feedback, reinforcement). Overall, initial training, follow-up, and social validity results were encouraging. A need for further research was identified to (a) identify variables associated with responsiveness to intervention, and (b) develop and compare innovative programs that teach parents with ID the necessary generalized skills to demonstrate long-term beneficial effects on their children. Feldman (2002) proposes a model of parenting for parents with a learning disability that takes account of child, family, parent and social variables. This model assumes 'accumulated risk' – that parenting abilities and parental health are the accumulated product of a range of psychosocial and environmental factors. The more risk factors present, the larger the potential negative impact on parenting ability (Aunos & Feldman 2007).

Pixa-Kettner (1999) proposed the following requirements for professional support for parents with ID:

- Parents should take part in deciding how much support they need and who should give it. Equal focus should be provided to the development of the father's competencies as a parent.
- In order to avoid overdependence that puts parents into the role of child, the person giving support in parental tasks should not give support in financial and other affairs, as well.
- Parents should be encouraged to carry parental responsibility and receive appreciation for doing so. One goal should be to strengthen their self-confidence and through this to affirm them in their parental role.
- Parents should have the chance to develop their own style of education and everyday life, even if this may provide less stimulation for the child than the caretakers' own style would, provide. The right of parents to self-determine and structure the parenting role based on their strengths and vulnerabilities should be supported by caregivers.
- Every life is subject to change. Caretakers should not overestimate their influence upon and their responsibility for the course of parents' lives and their personal decisions.

FUTURE DIRECTIONS FOR RESEARCH IN THE INDIAN CONTEXT

The nation of India currently has four different laws that pertain to people with disabilities. These laws include: The Mental Health Act of 1987, The Persons with Disabilities Act, The Rehabilitation Council of India Act, The National Trust for Welfare of Persons with Autism, Cerebral Palsy, Mental Retardation, and Multiple Disabilities Act of 1999. The majority of the legislation in India related to people with disabilities is based on the medical model of disability; it adopts a welfare attitude, looking at physical impairments of people and labelling them as, 'disabilities.' The UN Convention on the Rights of People with Disabilities defines, 'disability,' as an evolving concept. The Convention believes that, 'disability,' results from the interaction of impairments with various barriers which hinder full and active participation in society on an equal basis with others.

Literature in India is silent with regard to parenting by individuals with ID. Our lay observation has been in keeping with the assertions of Westbrook and Legge (1993) that in collectivist communities there was less expectation that children with ID should behave like other children, or have experiences shared by other children such as family outings, or playing with neighborhood children. The disability was more likely to be considered shameful for the family and was to be kept secret. Myths and misconceptions also abound in India with regard to ID such as marriage and sexual fulfilment can "cure" ID or that when individuals have the responsibility of marriage and family they will automatically develop the skills to meet them. No Indian law or policy has a clear-cut statement that prohibits discrimination against persons with disabilities on matters relating to marriage, family, parenthood and relationships on an equal basis with others.

Family often provides a lot of the help and support. Parents with intellectual disability often need training in basic child care, health and safety, child behaviour management, parent–child interactions, social skills, problem solving or decision making, managing transitions, and stress management (Tymchuk & Feldman, 1991; Tymchuk, 1992). Specialized parent education programs that offer intensive interventions are still rare and rarer still in India; although many practitioners and researchers now believe that a substantial number of parents with mild intellectual disabilities do, or could learn to, provide adequate child-care (Feldman, 1994; Feldman, 1997).

Research on ID and family experiences focuses on parents of children with ID and their concerns and challenges they face. Research focusing on parents who have ID and their experiences and parenting practices is few and far between. Indian literature on the subject is also skewed toward evaluating experiences of parenting a child with ID. There is no doubt that more widespread, more efficient, and more comprehensive services and support systems from a life-span perspective have to be developed to ensure adequate quality of life for individuals with ID and their families. With regard to the Indian context, we need awareness with regard to adulthood and associated roles of spouse and parent in individuals with ID and to develop programs and interventions that meet the needs of these individuals.

In India we need more research into this area and that it should also be included in the rehabilitation of parents with ID. The government and NGOs that work in this field need to identify and meet the needs of this segment. No separate laws or mental health guidelines in India currently address the needs and rights of this group of individuals and as a result there is no infrastructure that individuals with ID can access that can support them in evolving their roles as parents.

For practitioners, the implications are clear about areas of focus in working with parents with intellectual disability. The first is the need to address parental social skills, relationships and networks to reduce social isolation and increase social support. A carry over effect could be anticipated as there is good evidence from social support interventions more broadly that social participation is associated with better mental health in parents. A specific focus on the mental health needs of mothers would also be beneficial. A further benefit in attending to maternal mental health is the "protective" feature of better parental mental health and good social support for the well-being of children.

CONCLUSION

It is not possible to capture all of the aspects of intellectual disability, the strengths and support needs of people with intellectual disability, or the experience of parenting with an intellectual disability in this chapter. In conclusion, the authors would like to restate the unmet need for individuals with intellectual disability who become parents to have recognition and support at the family, societal, government/ NGO and policy level and in the mental health community and in literature. The authors would like to encourage researchers to focus on individuals with intellectual disability as adults, particularly in the role of parents and help identify their needs and work toward creating an infrastructure that accommodates their concerns.

REFERENCES

Accardo, P. (1990). Children of Mentally Retarded Parents. *Archives of Pediatrics & Adolescent Medicine*, *144*(1), 69. doi:10.1001/archpedi.1990.02150250079036 PMID:2403750

Accardo, P. J., & Whitman, B. Y. (1990). Children of mentally retarded parents. *American Journal of Diseases of Children*, *144*(1), 69–70. PMID:2403750

Aunos, M., Feldman, M., & Goupil, G. (2008). Mothering with Intellectual Disabilities: Relationship Between Social Support, Health and Well-Being, Parenting and Child Behaviour Outcomes. *Journal of Applied Research In Intellectual Disabilities, 21*(4), 320-330. doi:.00447.x10.1111/j.1468-3148.2008

Aunos, M., Goupil, G., & Feldman, M. (2003). Mothers with intellectual disabilities who do or do not have custody of their children. *Journal on Developmental Disabilities*, *10*(2), 65–80.

Australian Bureau of Statistics. (1998). 1996 Census of population *and housing: Socio-economic indexes for areas (information paper). Cat. no. 2039.0.* Canberra, ACT: Author.

Bakken, J., Miltenberger, R., & Schauss, S. (1993). Teaching parents with mental retardation: Knowledge versus skills. *American Journal of Mental Retardation*, *97*, 405–417. PMID:8427695

Bayley, N. (1969). *Bayley scales of infant development: Birth to two years*. New York, NY: Psychological Corporation.

Belsky, J., Lerner, R. M., & Spanier, G. B. (1984). *The child in the family*. Reading, Massachusetts: Addison-Wesley.

Booth, T., & Booth, W. (1994). *Parenting under pressure: Mothers and fathers with learning difficulties*. Buckingham, UK: Open University Press.

Booth, T., & Booth, W. (1998). *Growing up with parents who have learning difficulties*. London, UK: Routledge.

Booth, T., & Booth, W. (2000). Against the odds: Growing up with parents who have learning difficulties. *Mental Retardation*, *38*(1), 1–14. doi:10.1352/0047-6765(2000)038<0001:ATOGUW>2.0.CO;2 PMID:10703213

Booth, T., Booth, W., & McConnell, D. (2005). The prevalence and outcomes of care proceedings involving parents with intellectual disabilities in the family courts. *Journal of Applied Research in Intellectual Disabilities, 18*, 7–17. doi:. 00204.x10.1111/ j.1468-3148.2004

Bowling, M., & Keltner, B. (1996). Primary health care for children of mothers with intellectual limitations. *Pediatric Nursing*, *22*, 312–319. PMID:8852110

Cleaver, H., & Nicholson, D. (2007). *Parental learning disability and children's needs: Family experiences and effective practice*. London, UK: Kingsley.

Collings, S., & Llewellyn, G. (2012). Children of parents with intellectual disability: Facing poor outcomes or faring okay? *Journal of Intellectual & Developmental Disability*, *37*(1), 65–82. doi:10.3109/13668250.2011.648610 PMID:22300240

Coren, E., Hutchfield, J., Thomae, M., & Gustafsson, C. (2010). Parent training support for intellectually disabled parents. *Campbell Systematic Reviews*, *3*, 1–60. PMID:20556787

Crittenden, P. M., & Bonvillian, J. D. (1984). The relationship between maternal risk status and maternal sensitivity. *American Orthopsychiatric Association*, *54*(2), 250–262. doi:10.1111/j.1939-0025.1984.tb01492.x PMID:6731591

Dowdney, L., & Skuse, D. (1993). Parenting provided by adults with mental retardation. *Journal of Child Psychology and Psychiatry*, *34*, 5–47. doi:. 1993.tb00966.x10.1111/j.1469-7610

Edgerton, R. B. (1967). The cloak of competence: Stigma in the lives of the mentally retarded. Berkeley, CA: University of California Press.

Emerson, E. (2007). Poverty and people with intellectual disabilities. *Mental Retardation and Developmental Disabilities Research Reviews*, *13*(2), 107–113. doi:10.1002/mrdd.20144 PMID:17563898

Emerson, E., Malam, S., Spencer, I., & Spencer, K. (2005). *Adults With Learning Difficulties in England 2003/4. Full Report, Health and Social Care Information Centre.* Retrieved 4th April 2015, from http://www.lancs.ac.uk/staff/emersone/FASSWeb/Emerson 05_ALDE_Main.pdf

Faureholm, J. (2010). Children and their life experiences. In G. Llewellyn, R. Traustadóttir, D. McConnell, & H. B. Sigurjónsdóttir (Eds.), *Parents with intellectual disabilities: Past, present and futures* (pp. 63–78). West Sussex, UK: Wiley-Blackwell; doi:10.1002/9780470660393.ch4

Feldman, M. (1994). Parenting education for parents with intellectual disabilities: A review of outcome studies. *Research in Developmental Disabilities*, *15*(4), 299–332. doi:10.1016/0891-4222(94)90009-4 PMID:7972968

Feldman, M., Case, L., Rincover, A., Towns, F., & Betel, J. (1989). Parent education project. III: Increasing affection and responsivity in developmentally handicapped mothers: component analysis, generalization, and effects on child language. *Journal of Applied Behavior Analysis*, *22*(2), 211–222. doi:10.1901/jaba.1989.22-211 PMID:2745240

Feldman, M., Sparks, B., & Case, L. (1993). Effectiveness of home-based early intervention on the language development of children of mothers with mental retardation. *Research in Developmental Disabilities*, *14*(5), 387–408. doi:10.1016/0891-4222(93)90010-H PMID:8234958

Feldman, M., Towns, F., Betel, J., Case, L., Rincover, A., & Rubino, C. (1986). Parent education project II. Increasing stimulating interactions of developmentally handicapped mothers. *Journal of Applied Behavior Analysis*, *19*(1), 23–37. doi:10.1901/jaba.1986.19-23 PMID:3710945

Feldman, M., & Walton-Allen, N. (1997). Effects of maternal mental retardation and poverty on intellectual, academic and behavioural status of school-age children. *American Journal of Mental Retardation*, *101*, 352–364. PMID:9017082

Feldman, M. A. (1986). Research of parenting by mentally retarded persons. *The Psychiatric Clinics of North America*, *9*, 777–796. PMID:3543895

Feldman, M. A. (2002). Children of parents with intellectual disabilities. In R. J. McMahon & R. DeV. Peters. (Eds.), The effects of parental dysfunction on children (pp. 205–223). New York, NY: Kluwer Academic/Plenum. doi:10.1007/978-1-4615-1739-9_10

Feldman, M. A., Gase, L., Towns, F., & Betel, J. (1985). Parent education project I: Development and nurturance of children of mentally retarded parents. *American Journal of Mental Deficiency*, *90*, 253–258. PMID:2417482

Feldman, M. A., Towns, F., Betel, J., Gase, L., Rincover, A., & Rubino, G. A. (1686). Parent education project II: Increasing stimulating interactions of developmentally handicapped mothers. *Journal of Applied Behavior Analysis*, *19*(1), 23–37. doi:10.1901/jaba.1986.19-23 PMID:3710945

Garber, H. (1988). *The Milwaukee project: Preventing mental retardation in children at risk*. Washington, DC: American Association on Mental Retardation.

Garber, H. L., & Hodge, J. D. (1989). Risk for deceleration in the rate of mental development. *Developmental Review*, *9*(3), 259–300. doi:10.1016/0273-2297(89)90031-2

Gillberg, C., & Geijer-Karlsson, M. (1983). Children born to mentally retarded women: A 1–21-year follow-up study of 41 cases. *Psychological Medicine*, *13*(04), 891. doi:10.1017/S003329170005162X PMID:6665104

Glaun, D. E., & Brown, P. F. (1999). Motherhood, intellectual disability and child protection: Characteristics of a court sample. *Journal of Intellectual & Developmental Disability*, *24*(1), 95–105. doi:10.1080/13668259900033901

Grayson, J. (Ed.). (2000). *Parents with mental retardation* (Vol. 57). Virginia Child Protection Newsletter.

Hayman, R. L. (1990). Presumptions of justice: Law, politics, and the mentally retarded parent. *Harvard Law Review*, 103.

Hewitt, O. (2007). What is the effect on a child of having a parent with a learning disability? *Tizard Learning Disability Review*, *12*(2), 33–44. doi:10.1108/13595474200700015

Hur, J. (1997). Review of research on parent training for parents with intellectual disability: Methodological issues. *International Journal of Disability Development and Education*, *44*(2), 147–162. doi:10.1080/0156655970440206

IASSID Special Interest Research Group on Parents and Parenting with Intellectual Disabilities. (2008). Parents labelled with intellectual disability: Position of the IASSID SIRG on parents and parenting with intellectual disabilities. *Journal of Applied Research in Intellectual Disabilities, 21*, 296–307. doi:. 00435.x10.1111/j.1468-3148.2008

Keltner, B., Finn, D., & Schearer, D. (1995). Effects of family intervention on maternal-child interaction for mothers with developmental disabilities. *Family & Community Health*, *17*(4), 35–49. doi:10.1097/00003727-199501000-00006

Keltner, B., Wise, L., & Taylor, G. (1999). Mothers with intellectual limitations and their 2-year-old children's developmental outcomes. *Journal of Intellectual & Developmental Disability*, *24*(1), 45–57. doi:10.1080/13668259900033871

Llewellyn, G., McConnell, D., & Ferronato, L. (2003). Prevalence and outcomes for parents with disabilities and their children in an Australian court sample. *Child Abuse & Neglect*, *27*(3), 235–251. doi:10.1016/S0145-2134(03)00004-8 PMID:12654323

Luckasson, R., Borthwick-Duffy, S., Buntinx, W. H. E., Coulter, D. L., Craig, E. M., Reeve, A., & Tassé, M. J. et al. (2002). *Mental retardation: Definition, classification, and systems of supports* (10th ed.). Washington, DC: American Association on Mental Retardation.

Luckasson, R., & Reeve, A. (2001). Naming, defining, and classifying in mental retardation. *Mental Retardation*, *39*(1), 47–52. doi:10.1352/0047-6765(2001)039<0047:NDACIM>2.0.CO;2 PMID:11270213

Maccoby, E., & Martin, J. (1983). Socialization in the context of the family: parent-child interaction. In E. M. Hetherington (Ed.), Socialization, personality and social development. New York: Wiley.

Martin, S. L., Ramey, C. T., & Ramey, S. (1990). The prevention of intellectual impairment in children of impoverished families: Findings of a randomized trial of educational day care. *American Journal of Public Health*, *80*(7), 844–847. doi:10.2105/AJPH.80.7.844 PMID:2356909

Mayes, R., Llewellyn, G., & McConnell, D. (2006). Misconception: The Experience of Pregnancy for Women with Intellectual Disabilities. *Scandinavian Journal Of Disability Research*, *8*(2-3), 120–131. doi:10.1080/15017410600774178

McConnell, D. (2008). Parents labelled with intellectual disability: Position of the IASSID SIRG on Parents and Parenting with Intellectual Disabilities. *Journal of Applied Research in Intellectual Disabilities*, *21*(4), 296–307. doi:10.1111/j.1468-3148.2008.00435.x

McConnell, D., Feldman, M., Aunos, M., Prasad, N., & Westad, C. (2010). *Child welfare process and outcomes: Caregiver cognitive impairment*. Edmonton, Alberta: University of Alberta Press.

McConnell, D., & Llewellyn, G. (2000). Disability and Discrimination in Statutory Child Protection Proceedings. *Disability & Society*, *15*(6), 883–895. doi:10.1080/713662015

McConnell, D., Llewellyn, G., Mayes, R., Russo, D., & Honey, A. (2003). Developmental profiles of children born to mothers with intellectual disability. *Journal of Intellectual & Developmental Disability*, *28*(2), 122–134. doi:10.1080/1366825031000147067

McConnell, D., Mayes, R., & Llewellyn, G. (2008). Women with intellectual disability at risk of adverse pregnancy and birth outcomes. *Journal of Intellectual Disability Research*, *52*, 529–535. doi:.01061.x10.1111/j.1365-2788.2008

McGaw, S. (2004) Parenting exceptional children. In Handbook of Parenting. Theory and Research for Practice. Sage Publications. doi:10.4135/9781848608160.n14

McGaw, S., Shaw, T., & Beckley, K. (2007). Prevalence of Psychopathology Across a Service Population of Parents With Intellectual Disabilities and Their Children. *Journal Of Policy And Practice In Intellectual Disabilities, 4*(1), 11-22. doi:. 00093.x10.1111/j.1741-1130.2006

Mercer, J. (1973). *Labelling the mentally retarded.* Berkeley, CA: University of California Press.

Mickelson, P. (1947). The feeble-minded parent: A study of 90 family cases. *American Journal of Mental Deficiency, 51*, 644–653. PMID:20267775

Mørch, W. T., Skår, J., & Andersgård, A. B. (1997). Mentally retarded persons as parents: Prevalence and the situation of their children. *Scandinavian Journal of Psychology, 38*(4), 343–348. doi:10.1111/1467-9450.00044 PMID:9449195

Nichols, M. L. (1989). *The self-esteem of normal children of mothers with mental retardation: An exploratory study.* (Unpublished doctoral dissertation). University of Oregon, Portland, OR.

O'Neill, A. M. (1985). Normal and bright children of mentally retarded parents: The Huck Finn syndrome. *Child Psychiatry and Human Development, 15*(4), 255–268. doi:10.1007/BF00706369 PMID:4042738

Perkins, T., Holburn, S., Deaux, K., Flory, M., & Vietze, P. (2002). Children of Mothers with Intellectual Disability: Stigma, Mother-Child Relationship and Self-esteem. *Journal Of Applied Research In Intellectual Disabilities, 15*(4), 297-313. doi:.00140.x10.1046/j.1468-3148.2002

Peterson, S., Robinson, E., & Littman, I. (1983). Parent-child interaction training for parents with a history of mental retardation. *Applied Research in Mental Retardation, 4*(4), 329–342. doi:10.1016/0270-3092(83)90033-4 PMID:6670870

Pixa-Kettner, U. (1998). Parents with Intellectual Disability in Germany: Results of a Nation-wide Study. *Journal of Applied Research in Intellectual Disabilities, 11*(4), 355-364. doi:.1998.tb00043.x10.1111/j.1468-3148

Pixa-Kettner, U. (1999). Follow-up study on parenting with intellectual disability in Germany. *Journal of Intellectual & Developmental Disability, 24*(1), 75–93. doi:10.1080/13668259900033891

Pixa-Kettner, U. (2008). Parenting with Intellectual Disability in Germany: Results of a New Nationwide Study. *Journal Of Applied Research In Intellectual Disabilities, 21*(4), 315-319. doi:.00446.x10.1111/j.1468-3148.2008

Ramey, C., & Campbell, F. (1984). Preventive education for high-risk children: Cognitive consequences of the Carolina Abecedarian Project. *American Journal of Mental Deficiency, 88*, 515–523. PMID:6731489

Ramey, C., & Campbell, F. (1987). The Carolina Abecedarian Project: An educational experiment concerning human malleability. In J. Gallagher & C. Ramey (Eds.), *The malleability of children* (pp. 127–139). Baltimore, MD: Brookes.

Ramey, C. T., & Ramey, S. L. (2004). Early learning and school readiness: Can early intervention make a difference? *Merrill-Palmer Quarterly, 50*(4), 471–491. doi:10.1353/mpq.2004.0034

Ray, N. K., Rubenstein, H., & Russo, N. J. (1994). Understanding the parents who are mentally retarded: Guidelines for family preservation programmes. *Child Welfare League of America, 73*, 725–743. PMID:7988279

Ronai, C. R. (1997). On loving and hating my mentally retarded mother. *Mental Retardation, 35*, 417–432. doi:<0417:OLAHMM>2.0.CO;210.1352/0047-6765(1997)035

Schalock, R. L., Luckasson, R. A., Shogren, K. A., Borthwick-Duffy, S., Bradley, B., Buntinx, W. H. E., & Yeager, M. H. et al. (2007). The renaming of Mental Retardation: Understanding the change to the term Intellectual Disability. *Intellectual and Developmental Disabilities*, *45*(2), 116–124. doi:10.1352/1934-9556(2007)45[116:TROMRU]2.0.CO;2 PMID:17428134

Schilling, R., Schinke, S., Blythe, B., & Barth, R. (1982). Child maltreatment and mentally retarded parents: Is there a relationship? *Mental Retardation*, *20*(5), 201–209. PMID:6757649

Seagull, E., & Scheurer, S. (1986). Neglected and abused children of mentally retarded parents. *Child Abuse & Neglect*, *10*(4), 493–500. doi:10.1016/0145-2134(86)90054-2 PMID:3791026

Seligman, M. (1975). *Helplessness. On Depression, Development and Death*. San Francisco: W.H. Freeman.

Taylor, C., Norman, D., Murphy, J., Jellinek, M., Quinn, D., Poitrast, F., & Goshko, M. (1991). Diagnosed intellectual and emotional impairment among parents who seriously mistreat their children: Prevalence, type, and outcome in a court sample. *Child Abuse & Neglect*, *15*(4), 389–401. doi:10.1016/0145-2134(91)90023-7 PMID:1959072

Traustadóttir, R., & Sigurjónsdóttir, H. B. (2005). Adult children of mothers with intellectual disabilities: Three life histories. In A. Gustavsson, J. Sandrin, R. Traustadóttir, & J. Tøssebro (Eds.), *Resistance, reflections and change: Nordic disability research* (pp. 147–161). Lund, Sweden: Studentlitteratur.

Tymchuk, A. (2001). Family life: Experiences of people with mild cognitive limitations. In A. J. Tymchuk, K. C. Lakin, & R. Luckasson (Eds.), *The forgotten generation: The status and challenges of adults with mild cognitive limitations* (pp. 249–274). Baltimore, MD: Brookes.

Tymchuk, A. J., & Andron, L. (1990). Mothers with mental retardation who do or do not abuse or neglect their children. *Child Abuse & Neglect*, *13*(3), 313–323. doi:10.1016/0145-2134(90)90003-C PMID:2207800

Wade, C., Llewellyn, G., & Matthews, J. (2008). Review of parent training interventions for parents with intellectual disability. *Journal of Applied Research in Intellectual Disabilities*, *21*, 351–366. doi:.00449.x10.1111/j.1468-3148.2008

Ward, L., & Tarleton, B. (2007). Sinking or swimming? Supporting parents with learning disabilities and their children. *Tizard Learning Disability Review*, *12*(2), 22–32. doi:10.1108/13595474200700014

Wehmeyer, M. L., Buntix, W. H. E., Lachapelle, Y., Luckasson, R. A., Verdugo, M. A., Borthwick-Duffy, S., & Yeager, M. H. et al. (2008). The intellectual disability construct and its relation to human functioning. *Intellectual and Developmental Disabilities*, *46*(4), 48–55. doi:10.1352/1934-9556(2008)46[311:TIDCAI]2.0.CO;2 PMID:18671445

Weikart, D. P., Deloria, D., Lawser, S., & Wegerink, R. (1970). *Longitudinal results of the Ypsilanti Perry Preschool Project*. Ypsilanti, MI: HighScope Educational Research Foundation.

Whitman, B. Y., Graves, B., & Accardo, P. J. (1989). Training in parenting skills for adults with mental retardation. *Social Work*, *34*, 431–434.

World Health Organization. (2001). *International classification of functioning, disability, and health (ICF)*. Geneva: Author.

Zigler, E., & Hodapp, R. M. (1986). *Understanding mental retardation*. Cambridge, UK: Cambridge University Press.

Chapter 20
Sexuality, Parenting Skills, and Related Issues in Persons with Intellectual Disability

Rejani Thudalikunnil Gopalan
Gujarat Forensic Sciences University, India

Prathibha Agustus
Gujarat Forensic Sciences University, India

ABSTRACT

Sexuality begins from the moment of birth and has an active role in the development, evolution, emotional balance and affective stability of the individual. It has a significant role in interpersonal and couple's relationships. As intellectually disabled person approach puberty their control of behaviour and expression of sexuality may manifest in unacceptable ways. Persons with intellectual disabilities are at increased risk for physical, sexual and emotional abuse. The chapter focused on the issues related to sexual feelings and its expression among intellectually disabled people and the risk for sexual abuse. The necessity of sex education and components of sex education for different group also explained in detail. The chapter also addressed the parenting skills and problems related with parenthood among individuals with intellectual disability.

INTRODUCTION

Sexuality begins from the moment of birth and has an active role in the development, evolution, emotional balance and affective stability of the individual. It has a significant role in interpersonal and couple's relationships. The primary objective of sexuality is pleasure hence human beings tend to focus their minds on obtaining and giving pleasure and relate to one another. This could be found in persons with intellectual disability also (Clarke & O'toole, 2007). Given the complexity of intellectual disability, the development of socially appropriate sexual attitudes and behaviours in intellectually disabled persons is challenging and depends on the participation of parents, teachers and society as a whole. This is important

DOI: 10.4018/978-1-5225-0089-6.ch020

to get adequately integrated into society as it would help them to interact appropriately in social, work and family domains (Rademakers, Mouthaan & deNeef, 2005).

As intellectually disabled person approach puberty their control of behaviour and expression of sexuality may manifest in unacceptable ways. Aberrant or delinquent behaviour can be seen in adolescence and adult age (McDonald, Keys & Balcazar, 2007).Affective dimensions along with intellectual disability increases the likelihood of being sexually abused (Steptoe, Lindsay, Forrest & Power, 2006). This point out the need for sex education and counselling from an early age. From infancy onwards persons with intellectual disability should receive continuous sexual guidance in such concepts as intellectual deficiency limits their capacity to learn from role models or experiences in life which in turns affects generalization processes (Piaget, 1977).

Intellectual disability may not interfere with healthy display of sexuality in all cases. Their needs are often stigmatized when identified with inability to express age appropriate sexual development. With training such people can be helped to express their sexuality with respect and in accordance with the norms (Carrier, 2007). Presence of weak self esteem due to continuous reflection from society or inability to control impulses due to cerebral damage which accompanies intellectual disability are some of the factors that should be considered while looking into sexuality issues in persons with intellectual disability (Katz & Lazcano- Ponce, 2008).

SEXUAL ABUSE IN PERSONS WITH INTELLECTUAL DISABILITY

Persons with intellectual disabilities are at increased risk for physical, sexual and emotional abuse. With regard to sexual abuse an incidence rate of 50% is seen among such individuals (Van Dyke, McBrien & Sherbondy, 1995). It has been found that about 90 percent of people with developmental disabilities will experience sexual abuse at some point in their lives. Mostly, females are victims of sexual abuse and those with borderline to mild mental retardation. The incidence of abuse tend to decrease as the level of disability become severe (Schor, 1987).

In a study conducted in Australia it was found that persons with developmental disabilities (intellectual disabitlity, autism, cerebral palsy, epilepsy and learning disabilities) were sexually assaulted 10.7 times more than the rate of nondisabled persons. Though studies consistently report high prevalence of sexual abuse in intellectually disabled individuals, only 3% of such cases involving people with developmental disabilities get reported (Valenti-Hein & Schwartz, 1995). There are a multitude of factors which predispose these individuals to sexual abuse. Social isolation, communication skill deficits, cognitive problems like diminished ability to protect oneself due to lack of instruction and/or resources and impaired judgment (the inability to detect who is safe to be around). Some researchers have suggested that people with mental retardation are more likely to give and receive affection (Kempton & Gochros, 1986; Schor, 1987). Since intellectually disabled individuals feel lonely, they would be grateful for any form of attention. Their desire to be normal and the anxiety to please others predispose the individual to abuse (Heaton, 1995) The living arrangements like institutional setting, such as residential and group homes where there are multiple and transient care takers also increases the risk for abuse (Sobsey & Mansell, 1990). Mostly abusers (97%) are known and trusted by the victim who has developmental disability. This include family members and acquaintances which could be residential care staff, transportation providers and personal care attendants (Baladerian, 1991).

The effects of sexual abuse are manifold. Pregnancy, sexually transmitted diseases, bruises, lacerations and other physical abuse are issues which often follow sexual abuse. Psychosomatic symptoms such as stomach aches, headaches, seizures and problems with sleeping manifest. Low self-esteem, shame and guilt, irrational fear, depression and loss of trust are the psychological symptoms that follow sexual abuse. Behavioural symptoms include withdrawal, as well as noncompliant, aggressive, self-injurious and sexually inappropriate behaviour (Sobsey, 1994).

This scenario calls for comprehensive training programs which include sex education, training in personal and emotional safety as well as relationship issues that should be part any educational or rehabilitative work with population of intellectual disability .

SEX EDUCATION IN CHILDHOOD, ADOLESCENCE AND ADULTHOOD IN PERSONS WITH INTELLECTUAL DISABILITY

Sex Education in Childhood

In their early years children show their feelings through behaviour and which depends on the emotional development level of each person. They notice that their behaviour elicit certain reactions in parents and others. Gradually, as they mature they realize that their behaviour affects people and society as a whole. This leads to the formation of behaviour in children and the incorporation of norms and rules of the society. In children with intellectual disability emotional development does not follow the same way and they lack the ability to generalize or assimilate norms and rules. Therefore, they require a specific way for handling such behaviour.

Children with intellectual disability tend to search for gratification through pleasant sensations because of poor impulse control, low tolerance of frustration and limited comprehension. As a response to such behaviour authority figures try to exercise control these sensations which in turn the child interprets as the person`s effort to impede their experiencing pleasure. They require more time to understand this exercise of control is to prevent them from injury or abuse. Authority figures in collaboration with a counselor should therefore create a system of cause and effect marked by consistency, firmness, clarity and should not impart double messages and not use physical or verbal aggression. Intellectually disabled children should be made aware of public and private conducts. Public conducts are those that do not offend or hurt anyone and are accepted by the society. Examples are greeting someone, sitting with legs together when wearing a dress, being quiet, not lowering pants except in bathroom, not yelling among others. Private conducts, though easy for normal children, are abstractions for children with intellectual disability. They should be counselled not to burp in public, pass gases, pick the nose, touch their genitals, masturbate or take off clothes in public. When children assimilate the concept of public and private, they are able to differentiate from sexual behaviour from predominant social behaviour. When improvement is evident and new behaviour appear the repertoire of behaviours can be broadened. It is important to deal with behaviours that are related to how and when behaviour occurs rather than why behaviour occurs. Children should be trained to develop responsibility for impulse control. The formation of moral judgement should be facilitated which would help them to respect their body and that of others. It is important for the counsellor to work together with parents and other family members as they spend more time with the child and majority of inappropriate behaviour occurs at home. Guidance imparted to parents is equally important. They should be counselled about the general ways of dealing with behaviour and breaking the generalised taboos of the society Parents should also be helped to overcome the feelings of denial, rejection and grief (Walter, 2002).

Sex Education in Adolescence

The arrival of puberty is marked by changes in physical and mental aspects of a normal adolescent. The development of secondary sexual traits transforms the body of the child which provoke a state of anxiety about how their body will look in the end. At the cognitive level, stage of formal operations begins, which help them to understand the experiences they face. However, the emerging sexuality overwhelms them and the adolescent is preoccupied with doubt, uncertainty and insecurity. This does not seem to be the process in an adolescent with intellectual disability. Their sexual development is late when compared to that of adolescents with normal development. The average age at which disabled females attain menarche is 14 and the first wet dream experience among men with intellectual disability occurs at the age of 15. It is rarely that a premature sexual development is observed among such people (Kijak, 2011).

Adolescents with intellectual disability unaware about the development of secondary sexual characteristics and they conceptualize gender through their external experience (image). At the cognitive level, they never reach the stage of formal operations and sexual impulses are not questioned in conceptual terms. They do not acquire self-control and therefore impulses are acted upon without repression or guilt. This scenario calls for sex education starting from early childhood (Berman et al., 1999). If sexual education is imparted during childhood without affecting the child's need to display sexual curiosity and expression of sexual tension, then the individual is equipped to deal with the sexual processes that appear in adolescence. If this has not been imparted or achieved then the process becomes more complicated and requires greater effort. In this context before beginning the sexual counselling that is appropriate for this (adolescence) stage of development, it is necessary for the individual to be trained to control sexual impulses ideally through a humanistic-behavioural therapeutic program. Incorporation of the social concept of public and private conduct with regard to control of sexual impulses is the primary aim of this program. Once this is achieved, the adolescent is ready to receive sexual education. The main components of sexual education include the following:

1. **Anatomy and Physiology of the Reproductive Apparatus:** Adolescents with intellectual disability often believe that there is no difference between both genders. Therefore, it is necessary to provide them the basic information about sexual organs and their functions. Different methods are to be used to allow these individuals to explore the difference between men and women. The concepts that have to be emphasized include: 1.The same sex organs always exist for each gender and 2. They vary in terms of shape, size and certain characteristics. Adolescents should be explained that genitals are intimate parts and has to be dealt privately. They should be also helped to broaden their vocabulary and use appropriate terms (Angelopoulou et al., 1999).
2. **Maturation and Changes in Physical Appearance:** This includes the use of coloured drawings or anatomically suitable dolls to explain the process of maturation of body. Adolescent should be helped to identify his or her gender, recognize what his or her body is like at that moment, what it was like during childhood, and how it will transform in future. Questions from adolescents should be encouraged and clarified. Self-care methods can be taught using this method. For girls menstrual hygiene, use of deodorants, genital cleanliness, what to do with vaginal secretions removal of axillary and leg hair are described. Boys are taught skills such as shaving, combing their hair,

use of deodorants, genital cleanliness and information about erections and night ejaculations are provided.

3. **Public and Private Conduct:** This include situations typically found in adolescence. The areas addressed in public conduct include development of skills with regard to social adaptation, maturation of friendship relationships within groups of belonging and identification of all non-sexual behaviour. This is a complex task due to its abstract nature as the individuals have to develop attitudes with regard to respect for other people in general and create a place in the world for belonging. The counsellor can develop a moral code of public and private conduct which incorporates the norms of the society and culture. At this point it is necessary to take care not to neglect the difficulty in carrying out any kind of behavioural control in adolescence. Adolescents are taught about normal behaviour in social situations such as going to the movies, gatherings etc so as to differentiate what behaviours are acceptable at particular places. The purpose of this is to help the person generalize appropriate behaviours regardless of the place involved and to identify places suitable for carrying out public or private conduct.
4. **Masturbation:** It is a resource that an adolescent with intellectual disability frequently use for sexual gratification. Individuals should be helped to recognize that manipulation of genitals is a private conduct and doing it appropriately is a normal process in adolescence and should not cause guilt. They should be made aware about how prevent from hurting themselves, especially when using sharp objects. Individuals should be encouraged to express the feelings associated with masturbation and control the negative sensations that accompany this practice. With those who engage in masturbation excessively, help should be offered to deal with anxiety constructively. For individuals who do not engage in this practice or do not want to talk about it or causes conflict, it need to be respected (Scott, 1998).
5. **Taking Responsibility for Sexual Behaviour:** This area should be considered with utmost care as it involves ethical and moral issues surrounding intellectual disability. The counsellor works with the individual on the consequences of sexual behaviour. At first the individuals are provided information to fill in gaps in their knowledge so that they form a functional pattern of appropriate sexual behaviour. Parents, teachers, family members and others are counselled so that they reinforce appropriate social behaviour when they occur. This would help the person to build self-esteem. It is also important to notify the counselor about any inappropriate behaviour. Secondly, role playing is employed to correct inappropriate behaviour and their consequences. The counselor recreates the scene where the behaviour occurred and through discussion offer alternative possibilities. Consistent display of appropriate sexual behaviour by an adolescent who is intellectually disabled depends on sexual education and counselling. Only by this they can be prepared to begin a sexual life appropriate to their age and establish relationships for a successful marriage .

Sex Education During Adulthood

Adults with intellectual disability display appropriate sexual behaviour if sexual education and counselling is imparted in childhood or adolescence. If an individual is untrained with regard to what is socially appropriate sexual behaviour for that age, training programs could include the following components:

1. **Taking Responsibility for Sexual Behaviour:** It involves efforts to make the behaviour of all intellectually disabled persons to be similar to adults without intellectual disability. The counselor

should always remember that the maximum mental age that persons with intellectual disability attain is 12 years which means that they lack the ability to evaluate the risk associated with relationships motivated by sexual gratification. Hence, they should be assisted to make decisions and delineate behaviours determined by conventional societal values.

2. **Sexual Activity with Same and Opposite Gender:** Due to affective deficiency in persons with intellectual disability they constantly seek sexual pleasure. Parents often deny the sexuality aspect of such persons which leads the individual to engage in sexual activity with same gender. In such cases it is difficult to discuss about homosexual tendencies as it may be due to the inability to relate with persons of opposite gender or a comparative choice over past unsatisfactory sexual relationships.
3. **Birth Control:** Programs should teach about different contraceptive methods to avoid unwanted pregnancy. It is also important to evaluate the use of sterilization techniques for men and women as permanent birth control alternative.
4. **Marriage and Parenthood:** Individuals with mild intellectual disability has the ability to fully experience sexuality and have stable relationship with a partner through marriage. Some of the difficulties faced by such persons include lack of economic support from families and presence of children. Due to high social vulnerability and low frustration tolerance individuals tend to regress in stressful conditions and act impulsively. The decision to have children would be due to lack of knowledge regarding what it means to have a child. Sexual counselling programs should assist the individual to understand their limitations to assume the role of a parent and take responsibility for choosing a birth control method which ensures marriage without children.
5. **Sexually Transmitted Infections and Their Prevention:** Individuals should be provided adequate information regarding risks of sexually transmitted diseases and how to protect themselves. They should be helped to identify the symptoms of diseases, use of condoms or abstinence in view of possible infection. The counselor should make sure that the subjects have comprehended the information and they are equipped to prevent any type of infection.
6. **Unacceptable or Criminal Conducts:** This comes under the purview of private conducts and the norms of society regarding conventionally acceptable sexual behaviour. Intellectually disabled adults should be made aware about unacceptable behaviours like incest, sexual abuse or violation. The incorporation of norms is carried out through cause and effect relationships and identification of behaviours with their consequences. Moral and legal implications of unacceptable behaviours are looked into to behave as per the norms of the society (Katz & Lazcano-Ponce, 2008).

FUTURE DIRECTIONS

In order for persons with intellectual disability to express their sexuality in accordance with their developmental stage and societal norms and also to safeguard them from any form of sexual abuse the following factors could be considered:

- Primary prevention involving prevention programs to identify high risk factors, personal factors, and cultural factors associated with sexual abuse.
- Secondary prevention involving identification of vulnerable sub groups in this population and deliver services promptly.

- Tertiary care which includes well structured, personalised, well responsive sytems to act effectively when intellectually disabled individuals are harmed through sexual abuse.
- Education and training programs to provide information about sexuality and sexual health to enhance personal and emotional safety.
- Training programmes for multitude of professionals who are associated with service delivery to this population in preventing as well as handling sexuality related issues.
- Meaningful and well-articulated government policies to safeguard the rights of persons with intellectual disability.
- Research work intended to study sexuality related issues in people with intellectual disability across cultural, familial, institutional,legal and personal paradigms.

PARENTHOOD AND INTELLECTUAL DISABILITY

The ability of persons with intellectual disability to take the role of parent is a matter of great concern as it involves moral, financial, technical, medical and legal implications. These individuals, like others, have feelings and want relationships and are able to have children. Over time the attitudes of society has undergone change and factors now focused involve how these individuals can be trained and supported to carry out their role as parents adequately instead of heredity and fertility issues (Kandel, Morad, Vardi & Merrick, 2005). The prevalence rate of parents with intellectual disability is not known fully. Literature suggest a possible prevalence rate of less than 1 per cent in Australia i. e 0.99 per cent of the general population has intellectual disability (stereo). Another study conducted in New Zealand ascertained a prevalence figure of 0.25 per cent. Though information regarding the prevalence rates lacks clarity, there is general consensus in the literature that more people with intellectual disability become parents as opportunities for community living expand (Mc Connel & Llewellyn, 2002). As there is no clear definitions regarding adequate parenting and parental competence, assessing minimal parental competence remains significant issue in this area. This become even more complex when intellectually disabled parents are concerned (Lamont & Bromfield, 2009). They are considered to be unable to provide adequate care for their children. It is likely that parents with intellectual disability may neglect their child, subject them to physical and sexual abuse or witness violence (James, 2004; Booth & Booth, 1998).

There are certain factors which are identified to be associated with maltreatment of children by parents who are intellectually disabled. They include the following: social isolation, parental stress, parents with past histories of being abused or neglected as children, „ demographic characteristics such as parental income, education, and employment status, parental physical and mental health problems, children with physical or mental health problems, behavioural problems or disability, parental substance abuse; and domestic/family violence (Cleaver, Unell, & Aldgate, 1999; Feldman et al., 2002).

Records of data from the U. S, U. K and Australia reveals that parents with intellectual disability is less likely to have received support in their parenting. They are over-represented in child care proceedings and are at greater risk to have their parental responsibility terminated. They are likely to be judged against a stricter criteria and are more likely to have their children removed. They are also less likely to receive support in correcting the condition (Kandel, Morad, Verdi &Merrick, 2005)

Providing Support Services

Early provision of support services should be ensured where intellectual disability of the parent is affecting the welfare of the child. Research in this area suggests that support programs are effective if they are family-centred, provided over the long-term, focused on strengths rather than deficits, home based, feature participatory rather than relational elements of practice and performance rather than knowledge based (Lamont & Bromfield, 2009).

CONCLUSION

Like any other individual a person with intellectual disability possess the biological ability to conceive and bear offspring. They enjoy the legal right to raise a family. But these individuals are faced with multitude of issues related to personal and societal factors. If support services are organised and delivered promptly and systematically to handle such issues they will be able to ensure the welfare of their children. Collborative services by governmental, medical, legal, familial, educational and community level agencies can provide these individuals with the necessary support and prevent from compromising the welfare of the child.

REFERENCES

Angelopoulou, N., Souftas, V., Sakadamis, A., Matziari, C., Papameletiou, V., & Mandroukas, K. (1999). Gonadal function in young women with Down syndrome. *International Journal of Gynaecology and Obstetrics: the Official Organ of the International Federation of Gynaecology and Obstetrics*, *67*(1), 15–21. doi:10.1016/S0020-7292(99)00123-X PMID:10576235

Balderian, N. (1991). Sexual abuse of people with developmental disabilities. *Sexuality and Disability*, *9*(4), 323–335. doi:10.1007/BF01102020

Berman, H., Harris, D., Enright, R., Gilpin, M., Cathers, T., & Bukovy, G. (1999). Sexuality and the adolescent with a physical disability: Understandings and misunderstandings. *Issues in Comprehensive Pediatric Nursing*, *22*(4), 183–196. doi:10.1080/014608699265275 PMID:10827606

Booth, T., & Booth, W. (1998). *Growing up with parents who have learning difficulties*. London: Routlege.

Carrier, S. (2007). Understanding social and professional integration as an adjustment process: Contribution to a theory of coadaptation. *Intellectual and Developmental Disabilities*, *45*(1), 10–22. doi:10.1352/1934-9556(2007)45[10:USAPIA]2.0.CO;2 PMID:17428122

Clark, L. I., & O'toole, M. S. (2007). Intellectual impairment and sexual health: Information needs. *British Journal of Nursing (Mark Allen Publishing)*, *16*(3), 154–156. doi:10.12968/bjon.2007.16.3.22968 PMID:17363881

Cleaver, H., Unell, I., & Aldgate, J. (1999). *Children's needs, parenting capacity: The impact of parental mental illness, problem alcohol and drug use and domestic violence on children's development*. London: Department of Health, Stationary Office.

Feldman, M., Varhese, J., Ramsay, J., & Rajska, D. (2002). Relationships between social support, stress and mother–child interactions in mothers with intellectual disabilities. *Journal of Applied Research in Intellectual Disabilities*, *15*(4), 314–323. doi:10.1046/j.1468-3148.2002.00132.x

James, H. (2004). Promoting effective working with parents with learning disabilities. *Child Abuse Review*, *13*(1), 31–41. doi:10.1002/car.823

Kandel, I., Morad, M., Vardi, G., & Merrick, J. (2005). Intellectual disability and parenthood. *TheScientificWorldJournal*, *5*, 50–57. doi:10.1100/tsw.2005.12 PMID:15674450

Katz, G., & Lazcano-Ponce, E. (2008). Sexuality in subjects with intellectual disability: An educational intervention proposal for parents and counsellors in developing countries. *Salud Pública de México*, *2*, 239–254. doi:10.1590/S0036-36342008000800018

Kempton, W., & Gochros, J. (1986). The developmentally disabled. In H. L. Gochros, J. S. Gochros, & J. Fisher (Eds.), *Helping the sexually oppressed* (pp. 224–237). Englewood Cliffs, NJ: Prentice-Hall.

Kijak, R. J. (2011). Desire for love: Considerations on sexuality and sex education of people with intellectual disability in Poland. *Sexuality and Disability*, *29*(1), 65–74. doi:10.1007/s11195-010-9184-2 PMID:21423325

Lamont, A., & Bromfield, L. (2009). Parental intellectual disability and child protection: Key issues. National Child Protection Clearing house. *Issues (National Council of State Boards of Nursing (U.S.))*, *31*. Retrieved from http://www. aifs. gov

Mc Connel, D., & Llewllyn, G. (2002). Stereotypes, parents with intellectual disability and child protection. *Journal of Social Welfare and Family*, *24*(3), 297–317. doi:10.1080/09649060210161294

McDonald, K. E., Keys, C. B., & Balcazar, F. E. (2007). Disability, race/ethnicity and gender: Themes of cultural oppression, acts of individual resistance. *American Journal of Community Psychology*, *39*(1-2), 145–161. doi:10.1007/s10464-007-9094-3 PMID:17294120

Piaget, J. (1997). The essential Piaget. In R. E. Gruber & J. J. Voneche (Eds.), *The language and thought of the child* (p. 85). New York: Basic Books, Inc. Publishers.

Rademakers, J., Mouthaan, I., & de Neef, M. (2005). Diversity in sexual health: Problems and dilemmas. *The European Journal of Contraception & Reproductive Health Care*, *10*(4), 207–211. doi:10.1080/13625180500279847 PMID:16448946

Schor, D. P. (1987). Sex and sexual abuse in developmentally disabled adolescents. *Seminars in Adolescent Medicine*, *3*, 1–7. PMID:2955493

Scott, H. (1998). Helping clients in their sexual expression. *British Journal of Nursing (Mark Allen Publishing)*, *7*(10), 568. doi:10.12968/bjon.1998.7.10.5678 PMID:9775763

Sobsey, D. (1994). *Violence and abuse in the lives of people with disabilities: The end of silent acceptance?* Baltimore: Paul H. Brookes Publishing Co.

Sobsey, D., & Mansell, S. (1990). The prevention of sexual abuse and assault: Sexual exploitation of people with disabilities. *Sexuality and Disability*, *9*, 243–259. doi:10.1007/BF01102395

Steptoe, L., Lindsay, W. R., Forrest, D., & Power, M. (2006). Quality of life and relationships in sex offenders with intellectual disability. *Journal of Intellectual & Developmental Disability*, *31*(1), 13–19. doi:10.1080/13668250500488652 PMID:16766318

Tower, C. (1989). *Understanding child abuse and neglect*. Boston: Allyn and Bacon.

Van Dyke, D. E., Mc Brien, D. M., & Sherbondy, A. (1995). Issues of sexuality in Down Syndrome. *Down's Syndrome: Research and Practice*, *3*(2), 65–69. doi:10.3104/reviews.53

Walter, J. (n.d.). From taboo to self-actualization–acceptance problems and learning processes in working with mentally handicapped patients. *Praxis der Kinderpsychologie und Kinderpsychiatrie*, *51*(8), 587–597. PMID:12425228

Compilation of References

Abbeduto, L., Pavetto, M., Kesin, E., Weissman, M., Karadottir, S., O'Brient, A., & Cawthon, S. (2001). The linguistic and cognitive profile of Down syndrome: Evidence from a comparison with fragile X syndrome. *Down Syndrome Research and Practise, 7,* 9-16.

Abbeduto, L. (1991). Development of verbal communication in persons with moderate to mild mental retardation. *International Review of Research in Mental Retardation, 17,* 91–115. doi:10.1016/S0074-7750(08)60104-4

Abbeduto, L., Davies, B., Solesdy, S., & Furman, L. (1991). Indentifying the reference of spoken messages: The use of context and clarification requests by children with mental retardation and by nonretarded children. *American Journal of Mental Retardation, 95,* 551–562. PMID:2043349

Abbeduto, L., Furman, L., & Davies, B. (1989). Relation between the receptive language and mental age of persons with mental retardation. *American Journal of Mental Retardation, 93,* 535–543. PMID:2706121

Abbeduto, L., Krauss, M. W., Murphy, M. M., Orsmond, G., Seltzer, M. M., & Shattuck, P. (2004). Psychological well-being and coping in mothers of youths with autism, Down syndrome, or fragile X syndrome. *American Journal of Mental Retardation, 109*(3), 237–254. doi:10.1352/0895-8017(2004)109<237:PWACIM>2.0.CO;2 PMID:15072518

Abbeduto, L., & Murphy, M. M. (2004). Language, social cognition, maladaptive behavior and communication in Down syndrome and Fragile X syndrome. In M. L. Rice & S. F. Warren (Eds.), *International Research in Developmental Disabilities,* (pp. 547–566).

Abbeduto, L., Murphy, M. M., Cawthon, S. W., Richmond, E. K., Weissman, M. D., Karadottir, S., & O'Brien, A. (2003). Receptive Language Skills of Adolescents and Young Adults With Down or Fragile X Syndrome. *American Journal of Mental Retardation, 108*(3), 149–160. doi:10.1352/0895-8017(2003)108<0149:RLSOAA>2.0.CO;2 PMID:12691594

Abbeduto, L., & Rosenberg, S. (1980). The communicative competence of mildly retarded adults. *Applied Psycholinguistics, 1*(04), 405–426. doi:10.1017/S0142716400009826

Abbeduto, L., Seltzer, M. M., Shattuck, P., Krauss, M. W., Orsmond, G., & Murphy, M. M. (2004). Psychological well-being and coping in mothers of youths with Autism, Down Syndrome, or Fragile X Syndrome. *Journal Information, 109*(3). PMID:15072518

Abberley, P. (1987). The concept of oppression and the development of a social theory of disability. *Disability, Handicap & Society, 2*(1), 5–19. doi:10.1080/02674648766780021

Abbey, A., & Andrews, F. M. (1986). Modeling the psychological determinants of life quality. In F. M. Andrews (Ed.), *Research on the quality of life.* Ann Arbor, MI: Institute for Social Research, University of Michigan.

Abbott, D. A., & Meredith, W. H. (1986). Strengths of parents with retarded children. *Family Relations, 35*(3), 371–375. doi:10.2307/584363

Abidi, J. (1999). Current status of employment of disabled people in Indian industries. Asia Pacific Disability Rehabilitation Journal, 10(2).

Accardo, P. (1990). Children of Mentally Retarded Parents. *Archives of Pediatrics & Adolescent Medicine*, *144*(1), 69. doi:10.1001/archpedi.1990.02150250079036 PMID:2403750

Accardo, P. J., & Whitman, B. Y. (1990). Children of mentally retarded parents. *American Journal of Diseases of Children*, *144*(1), 69–70. PMID:2403750

Achenbach, T. M., & Edelbrock, C. (1983). *Manual for the child behavior checklist and revised child behaviour profile*. Burlington, VT: Queen City Printers.

Achenbach, T. M., & Rescorla, L. A. (2000). *Manual for the ASEBA Preschool Forms & Profiles*. Burlington, VT: University of Vermont, Research Center for Children, Youth, & Families.

Ageranioti-Bélanger, S., Brunet, S., D'Anjou, G., Tellier, G., Boivin, J., & Gauthier, M. (2012). Behaviour disorders in children with an intellectual disability. *Pediatric Child Health*, *17*(2), 84–88. PMID:23372399

Ahmedani, B. K., & Hock, R. (2012). Parent perceptions of autism severity: Exploring social ecological context. *Disability and Health Journal*, *5*(4), 298–304. doi:10.1016/j.dhjo.2012.06.002 PMID:23021742

Ahuja, N. (2007). *Short Text Book of Psychiatry*. Academic Press.

Ahuja, N. (2011). *A Short Textbook of Psychiatry. VII 01*. JP Brothers. doi:10.5005/jp/books/11464

Aicardi, J. (1998). The etiology of developmental delay. *Seminars in Pediatric Neurology*, *5*(1), 15–20. doi:10.1016/S1071-9091(98)80013-2 PMID:9548636

Ainsworth, M. D. (1985). Attachments across the life span. *Bulletin of the New York Academy of Medicine*, *61*, 792–812. PMID:3864511

Ainsworth, M. S., Blehar, M. C., & Everett Waters, E. et al.. (1978). *Patterns of attachment: A psychological study of the strange situation*. New York: Lawrence Erlbaum.

Alderson, E. (2013). *Supporting People with Intellectual Disability to Express Appropriate Sexual Behaviors*. Retrieved from http://www.ndis.gov.au/sites/default/files/documents/5_Supporting_People_with_Intellectual_Disability_to_Express_Appropriate.docx

Alexander, R. T., Chester, V., Green, F. N., Gunaratna, I., & Hoare, S. (2015). Arson or fire setting in offenders with intellectual disability: Clinical characteristics, forensic histories, and treatment outcomes. *Journal of Intellectual & Developmental Disability*, *40*(2), 1–9. doi:10.3109/13668250.2014.998182

Ali, A., Hassiotis, A., Strydom, A., & King, M. (2012). Self stigma in people with intellectual disabilities and courtesy stigma in family carers: A systematic review. *Research in Developmental Disabilities*, *33*(6), 2122–2140. doi:10.1016/j.ridd.2012.06.013 PMID:22784823

Alimovic, S. (2013). Emotional and behavioural problems in children with visual impairment, intellectual and multiple disabilities. *Journal of Intellectual Disability Research*, *57*(2), 153–160. doi:10.1111/j.1365-2788.2012.01562.x PMID:22563696

Al-Krenawi, A., Graham, J. R., & Al Gharaibeh, F. (2011). The impact of intellectual disability, caregiver burden, family functioning, marital quality, and sense of coherence. *Disability & Society*, *26*(2), 139–150. doi:10.1080/09687599.2011.543861

Allen, D. (2008). The relationship between challenging behaviour and mental ill-health in people with intellectual disabilities: A review of current theories and evidence. *Journal of Intellectual Disabilities*, *12*(4), 267–294. doi:10.1177/1744629508100494 PMID:19074934

Allen, K. D., Wallace, D. P., Renes, D., Bowen, S. L., & Burke, R. V. (2010). Use of video modeling to teach vocational skills to adolescents and young adults with autism spectrum disorders. *Education & Treatment of Children*, *33*(3), 339–349. doi:10.1353/etc.0.0101

Alnahdi, G. (2014). Assistive Technology in Special Education and the Universal Design for Learning. *The Turkish Online Journal of Educational Technology*, *13*(2), 18–23.

Alston, E., & St. James-Roberts, I. (2005). Home environments of 10-month-old infants selected by the WILSTAAR screen for pre-language difficulties. *International Journal of Language & Communication Disorders*, *40*(2), 123–136. doi:10.1080/13682820400006861 PMID:16101270

American Association on Intellectual & Developmental Disabilities. (2012). *Definition of Intellectual Disability*. Author.

American Association on Intellectual and Developmental Disabilities. (2009). *Frequently Asked Question on intellectual disability*. Retrieved from http://www.aamr.org/content_104.cfm

American Association on Intellectual and Developmental Disabilities. (2011). *What is the AAIDD definition of intellectual disability?* Retrieved from http://www.aaidd.org/IntellectualDisabilityBook/content_7473.cfm?navID=366

American Psychiatric Association. (1994). *Diagnostic and Statistical Manual of mental disorders: DSM-IV*. Washington: D.C. American Psychiatric Association.

American Psychiatric Association. (2013). *Diagnostic and Statistical Manual of Mental Disorders* (5th ed.). American Psychiatric Publishing.

American Psychiatric Association. (2013). *Diagnostic and statistical manual of mental disorders* (5th ed.). Retrieved from http://www.dsm5.org/Pages/Default.aspx

American Psychiatric Association. (2013). *Diagnostic and statistical manual of mental disorders* (5th ed.). Washington, DC: Author.

American Psychiatric Association. (2013). *Diagnostic and Statistical Manual of Mental Disorders: DSM-V*. American Psychiatric Publishing, Incorporated.

American Psychological Association, (2005). *Assessment of older adults with diminished capacity. A handbook for lawyers*. American Bar Association Commission on Law and Aging – American Psychological Association.

American Psychological Association, (2006). *Assessment of older adults with diminished capacity. A handbook for psychologists*. American Bar Association Commission on Law and Aging – American Psychological Association.

American Psychological Association. (2015). Diagnostic and Statistical Manual of Mental Disorder, Publication manual of the American Psychological Association (5th ed.). Washington, DC: APA.

Anderson, D. J., Lakin, K. C., Hill, B. K., & Chen, T. (1992). Social integration of older persons with mental retardation in residential facilities. *American Journal of Mental Retardation*. PMID:1562307

Andreou, E., Didaskalou, E., & Vlachou, A. (2013). Bully/victim problems among Greek pupils with special educational needs: Associations with loneliness and self-efficacy for peer interactions. *Journal of Research in Special Educational Needs*.

Andrews, G., Henderson, S., & Hall, W. (2001). *Prevalence, comorbidity, disability and service utilisation* (Vol. 178). Academic Press.

Andrews, F. M. (1974). Social indicators of perceived life quality. *Social Indicators Research*, *1*(3), 279–299. doi:10.1007/BF00303860

Angelopoulou, N., Souftas, V., Sakadamis, A., Matziari, C., Papameletiou, V., & Mandroukas, K. (1999). Gonadal function in young women with Down syndrome. *International Journal of Gynaecology and Obstetrics: the Official Organ of the International Federation of Gynaecology and Obstetrics*, *67*(1), 15–21. doi:10.1016/S0020-7292(99)00123-X PMID:10576235

Anthony, W. A., & Liberman, R. P. (1986). The practice of psychiatric rehabilitation: Historical, conceptual, and research base. *Schizophrenia Bulletin*, *12*(4), 542–559. doi:10.1093/schbul/12.4.542 PMID:3810064

APA. (2013). Diagnostic and Statistical Manual of Mental Disorders - Fifth Edition (DSM-5). Washington, DC: American Psychiatric Publishing.

Appelbaum, K. L., & Appelbaum, P. S. (1994). Criminal-justice-related competencies in defendants with mental retardation. *The Journal of Psychiatry & Law*, *22*, 483.

Arendt, S. W., & Paez, P. (2014). Managers' Attitudes Towards Employees with Disabilities in the Hospitality Industry. *International Journal of Hospitality & Tourism Administration*, *15*(2), 172–190. doi:10.1080/15256480.2014.901065

Armatas, V. (2009). Mental retardation: Definitions, etiology, epidemiology and diagnosis. *Journal of Sport and Health Research.*, *1*(2), 112–122.

Arnold, S. R. C., Riches, V. C., Parmenter, T. R., & Stancliffe, R. J. (2009). The I-CAN: Using e-health to get people the support they need. Electronic Journal of Health Informatics, 4(1), e4.

Arthur, M. (1998). *Socio-communicative variables and behaviour states in students with the most severe and multiple disabilities: An observational study.* (Unpublished PhD dissertation). Macquarie University, Sydney, Australia.

Atik, G., & Guneri, O. Y. (2013). Bullying and victimization: Predictive role of individual, parental, and academic factors. *School Psychology International*, *34*(6), 658–673. doi:10.1177/0143034313479699

Aunos, M., Feldman, M., & Goupil, G. (2008). Mothering with Intellectual Disabilities: Relationship Between Social Support, Health and Well-Being, Parenting and Child Behaviour Outcomes. *Journal of Applied Research In Intellectual Disabilities*, *21*(4), 320-330. doi:.00447.x10.1111/j.1468-3148.2008

Aunos, M., Goupil, G., & Feldman, M. (2003). Mothers with intellectual disabilities who do or do not have custody of their children. *Journal on Developmental Disabilities*, *10*(2), 65–80.

Australian Bureau of Statistics. (1998). 1996 Census of population *and housing: Socio-economic indexes for areas (information paper). Cat. no. 2039.0.* Canberra, ACT: Author.

Avcioglu, H. (2013). Effectiveness of video modelling in training students with intellectual disabilities to greet people when they meet. *Educational Sciences: Theory and Practice*, *13*(1).

Ayres, A. J. (1983). *Sensory integration and learning disorders* (8th ed.). Los Angeles, CA: Western Psychological Services.

Azad, G., Blacher, J., & Marcoulides, G. A. (2013). Mothers of children with developmental disabilities: Stress in early and middle childhood. *Research in Developmental Disabilities*, *34*(10), 3449–3459. doi:10.1016/j.ridd.2013.07.009 PMID:23920028

Azar, M., & Badr, L. K. (2010). Predictors of coping in parents of children with an intellectual disability: Comparison between Lebanese mothers and fathers. *Journal of Pediatric Nursing*, *25*(1), 46–56. doi:10.1016/j.pedn.2008.11.001 PMID:20117676

Azeem MW, Dogar IA, Shah S, et al. (2013) Anxiety and Depression among Parents of Children with Intellectual Disability in Pakistan. *Journal of the Canadian Academy of Child and Adolescent Psychiatry, 22*(4), 290-296.

Azrin, N. H., & Foxx, R. M. (1971). A rapid method of toilet training the institutionalized retarded. *Journal of Applied Behavior Analysis*, *4*(2), 89–99. doi:10.1901/jaba.1971.4-89 PMID:16795291

Bachrach, S. (2004). In the name of public health – Nazi racial hygiene. *The New England Journal of Medicine*, *351*(5), 417–420. doi:10.1056/NEJMp048136 PMID:15282346

Baer, D. M., Wolf, M. M., & Risley, T. R. (1968). Some current dimensions of applied behavior analysis. *Journal of Applied Behavior Analysis*, *1*(1), 91–97. doi:10.1901/jaba.1968.1-91 PMID:16795165

Bagner, D. M., & Eyberg, S. M. (2007). Parent–child interaction therapy for disruptive behavior in children with mental retardation: A randomized controlled trial. *Journal of Clinical Child and Adolescent Psychology*, *36*(3), 418–429. doi:10.1080/15374410701448448 PMID:17658985

Bailey, D. M. (1994). Technology for adults with multiple impairments: A trilogy of case reports. *The American Journal of Occupational Therapy*, *48*(4), 341–345. doi:10.5014/ajot.48.4.341 PMID:8059867

Bailoor, P., & SubbaRao, T.A. (2013). Semantic intentions and relations in children with intellectual disability (ID) in the mental age range of 4 to 7 years. *Journal of Advances in Life Science and Technology,* 13.

Baker, B. L., Blacher, J., Crnic, K. A., & Edelbrock, C. (2002). Behavior problems and parenting stress in families of three-year-old children with and without developmental delays. *American Journal of Mental Retardation*, *107*(6), 433–444. doi:10.1352/0895-8017(2002)107<0433:BPAPSI>2.0.CO;2 PMID:12323068

Baker, B. L., Blacher, J., & Olsson, M. B. (2005). Preschool children with and without developmental delay: Behaviour problems, parents' optimism and well-being. *Journal of Intellectual Disability Research*, *49*(8), 575–590. doi:10.1111/j.1365-2788.2005.00691.x PMID:16011551

Baker, B. L., Landen, S. J., & Kashima, K. J. (1991). Effects of parent training on families of children with mental retardation: Increased burden or generalized benefit? *American Journal of Mental Retardation*. PMID:1930946

Baker, B. L., McIntyre, L. L., Blacher, J., Crnic, K., Edelbrock, C., & Low, C. (2003). Pre-school children with and without developmental delay: Behaviour problems and parenting stress over time. *Journal of Intellectual Disability Research*, *47*(4-5), 217–230. doi:10.1046/j.1365-2788.2003.00484.x PMID:12787154

Baker, B. L., Neece, C. L., Fenning, R. M., Crnic, K. A., & Blacher, J. (2010). Mental disorders in five-year-old children with or without developmental delay: Focus on ADHD. *Journal of Clinical Child and Adolescent Psychology*, *39*(4), 492–505. doi:10.1080/15374416.2010.486321 PMID:20589561

Bakken, J., Miltenberger, R., & Schauss, S. (1993). Teaching parents with mental retardation: Knowledge versus skills. *American Journal of Mental Retardation*, *97*, 405–417. PMID:8427695

Bakken, T. L., Helverschou, S. B., Eilertsen, D. E., Heggelund, T., Myrbakk, E., & Martinsen, H. (2010). Psychiatric disorders in adolescents and adults with autism and intellectual disability: A representative study in one county in Norway. *Research in Developmental Disabilities*, *31*(6), 1669–1677. doi:10.1016/j.ridd.2010.04.009 PMID:20493660

Balderian, N. (1991). Sexual abuse of people with developmental disabilities. *Sexuality and Disability*, *9*(4), 323–335. doi:10.1007/BF01102020

Baldry, A. C., & Farrington, D. (2000). Bullies and delinquents: Personal characteristics and parental styles. *Journal of Community & Applied Social Psychology*, *10*(1), 17–31. doi:10.1002/(SICI)1099-1298(200001/02)10:1<17::AID-CASP526>3.0.CO;2-M

Bandura, A. (1969). *Principles of Behavior Modification*. New York: Holt, Rinehart and Winston.

Bandura, A. (1977). *Social learning theory*. Englewood Cliffs, NJ: Prentice Hall.

Bandura, A. (1991). Social cognitive theory of self-regulation. *Theories of Cognitive Self-Regulation*, *50*, 248–287.

Bankson, N. W., & Bernthal, J. E. (1990). *Quick Screening of Phonology*. Chicago: Riverside Publishing.

Banks, R. (1997). *Bullying in Schools*. Washington, DC: U.S. Government Printing Office.

Barak-Levy, Y., & Atzaba-Poria, N. (2013). Paternal versus maternal coping styles with child diagnosis of developmental delay. *Research in Developmental Disabilities*, *34*(6), 2040–2046. doi:10.1016/j.ridd.2013.02.026 PMID:23584184

Barker, E. T., Greenberg, J. S., Seltzer, M. M., & Almeida, D. M. (2012). Daily Stress and Cortisol Patterns in Parents of Adult Children with a Serious Mental Illness. *Journal of Health Psychology*, *31*(1), 130–134. doi:10.1037/a0025325

Baroff & Olley. (2012). Mental Retardation: Nature, Cause and Management. Routledge.

Baroff, G. S. (1986). *Mental retardation: Nature, cause and management* (2nd ed.). Washington, DC: Hemisphere.

Baroff, G. S., Gunn, M., & Hayes, S. (2004). Legal issues. In W. Lindsay, J. Taylor, & P. Sturmey (Eds.), *Offenders with developmental disabilities* (pp. 37–65). West Sussex, UK: Wiley. doi:10.1002/9780470713440.ch3

Barr, J., & McLeod, S. (2010). They never see how hard it is to be me: Siblings' observations of strangers, peers and family. *International Journal of Speech-Language Pathology*, *12*(2), 162–171. doi:10.3109/17549500903434133 PMID:20420357

Barron, P., Hassiotis, A., & Banes, J. (2002). Offenders with intellectual disability: The size of the problem and therapeutic outcomes. *Journal of Intellectual Disability Research*, *46*(6), 454–463. doi:10.1046/j.1365-2788.2002.00432.x PMID:12354316

Bauer, S. M., Elsaesser, L. J., & Arthanat, S. (2011). Assistive technology device classification based upon the World Health Organization's, International Classification of Functioning, Disability and Health (ICF). *Disability and Rehabilitation: Assistive Technology*, *6*(3), 243–259. doi:10.3109/17483107.2010.529631 PMID:21446850

Bauman, S. (2004). Parents of children with Mental Retardation: Coping Mechanisms and Support needs, Greenberg, Krauss, Osmond, Seltzer; 1999, Siblings of Adults with Mental Illness or Mental Retardation: Current Involvement and Future Caregiving.*Psychiatric Services (Washington, D.C.)*, *50*, 1214–1219.

Bauminger, N., Solomon, M., & Rogers, S. J. (2010). Externalizing and internalizing behaviors in ASD. *Autism Research*, *3*(3), 101–112. doi:10.1002/aur.131 PMID:20575109

Bayley, N. (1969). *Bayley scales of infant development: Birth to two years*. New York, NY: Psychological Corporation.

Bazzano, A., Wolfe, C., Zylowska, L., Wang, S., Schuster, E., Barrett, C., & Lehrer, D. (2015). Mindfulness Based Stress Reduction (MBSR) for parents and caregivers of individuals with developmental disabilities: A community-based approach. *Journal of Child and Family Studies*, *24*(2), 298–308. doi:10.1007/s10826-013-9836-9

Beail, N. (2002). Interrogative suggestibility, memory and intellectual disability. *Journal of Applied Research in Intellectual Disabilities*, *15*(2), 129–137. doi:10.1046/j.1468-3148.2002.00108.x

Beange, H., Lennox, N., & Parmenter, T. R. (1999). Health targets for people with an intellectual disability. *Journal of Intellectual & Developmental Disability*, *24*(4), 283–297. doi:10.1080/13668259900034051

Bear, G. G., Mantz, L. S., Glutting, J. J., Yang, C., & Boyer, D. E. (2015). Differences in bullying victimization between students with and without disabilities. *School Psychology Review*, *44*(1), 98–116. doi:10.17105/SPR44-1.98-116

Beavers, G. A., Iwata, B. A., & Lerman, D. C. (2013). Thirty years of research on the functional analysis of problem behavior. *Journal of Applied Behavior Analysis*, *46*(1), 1–21. doi:10.1002/jaba.30 PMID:24114081

Beckman, P. J. (1991). Comparison of mothers' and fathers' perceptions of the effect of young children with and without disabilities. *American Journal of Mental Retardation*, *95*, 585–595. PMID:2043351

Bedrosian, J., & Prutting, C. A. (1978). Communicative performance of mentally retarded adults in four conversational settings. *Journal of Speech and Hearing Research*, *21*(1), 79–95. doi:10.1044/jshr.2101.79 PMID:642491

Beeghly, M., Jernberg, E., & Burrows, E. (1989). Validity of the Early Language Inventory (ELI) for use with 25-month-olds. *Journal of Child Language*, *23*(3), 515–528.

Begab, M. J., & Richardson, S. A. (1975). *The mentally retarded and society: A social Perspective*. London University Press.

Begg, S., Vos, T., Barker, B., Stevenson, C., Stanley, L., & Lopez, A. (2007). *Burden of disease and injury in Australia, 2003*. Australian Institute of Health and Welfare AIHW.

Beirne, S. M., Patton, J. R., & Kim, S. H. (2006). *Mental retardation: An introduction to intellectual disabilities*. Upper Saddle River, NJ: Pearson Merrill Prentice Hall.

Bellack, A. S. (2004). Skills training for people with severe mental illness. *Psychiatric Rehabilitation Journal*, *27*(4), 375–391. doi:10.2975/27.2004.375.391 PMID:15222149

Bellamy, G. T., Rhodes, L. E., Mank, D. M., & Albin, J. M. (1988). *Supported employment: A community implementation guide*. Baltimore, MD: Paul H. Brookes.

Bellini, S., & Akullian, J. (2007). A meta-analysis of video modeling and video self-modeling interventions for children and adolescents with autism spectrum disorders. *Exceptional Children*, *73*(3), 264–287. doi:10.1177/001440290707300301

Belsky, J., Lerner, R. M., & Spanier, G. B. (1984). *The child in the family*. Reading, Massachusetts: Addison-Wesley.

Belva, B. C., Matson, J. L., Sipes, M., & Bamburg, J. W. (2012). An examination of specific communication deficits in adults with profound intellectual disabilities. *Research in Developmental Disabilities*, *33*(2), 525–529. doi:10.1016/j.ridd.2011.10.019 PMID:22119701

Bensberg, G. J., Colwell, C. N., & Cassel, R. (1965). Teaching the profoundly retarded self-help activities by behavior shaping techniques. *American Journal of Mental Deficiency*, *69*, 674–679. PMID:14286827

Benson, B. A., & Brooks, W. T. (2008). Aggressive challenging behaviour and intellectual disability. *Current Opinion in Psychiatry*, *21*(5), 454–458. doi:10.1097/YCO.0b013e328306a090 PMID:18650686

Benson, B. A., & Ivins, J. (1992). Anger, depression and self-concept in adults with mental retardation. *Journal of Intellectual Disability Research*, *36*(2), 169–175. doi:10.1111/j.1365-2788.1992.tb00492.x PMID:1591500

Benson, P., & Karlof, K. L. (2009). Anger, stress proliferation, and depressed mood among parents of children with ASD: A longitudinal replication. *Journal of Autism and Developmental Disorders*, *39*(2), 350–362. doi:10.1007/s10803-008-0632-0 PMID:18709548

Berger, J., & Cunningham, C. C. (1983). Development of early vocal behaviours and interactions in Down's syndrome and nonhandicapped infant-mother pairs. *Developmental Psychology*, *19*(3), 322–331. doi:10.1037/0012-1649.19.3.322

Berk, L. E. (2006). *Child development* (7th ed.). Boston: Allyn & Bacon.

Berkson, G., Tupa, M., & Sherman, L. (2001). Early development of stereotyped and self-injurious behaviors: Incidence. *American Journal of Mental Retardation*, *106*(6), 539–547. doi:10.1352/0895-8017(2001)106<0539:EDOSAS>2.0.CO;2 PMID:11708939

Berman, H., Harris, D., Enright, R., Gilpin, M., Cathers, T., & Bukovy, G. (1999). Sexuality and the adolescent with a physical disability: Understandings and misunderstandings. *Issues in Comprehensive Pediatric Nursing*, *22*(4), 183–196. doi:10.1080/014608699265275 PMID:10827606

Bernard, S. H. (2009). Mental health and behavioural problems in children and adolescents with learning disabilities. *Psychiatry*, *8*(10), 387–390. doi:10.1016/j.mppsy.2009.06.017

Bernthal, J. W., & Bankson, N. W. (2004). *Articulation & Phonological Disorders* (5th ed.). Boston, MA: Pearson Education, Inc./Allyn & Bacon.

Berry & Kymar. (2012). Human Resource professionals' perception on disability relatedbarriers to employment of Persons with intellectual disability. *Indian Journal of Occupational Therapy*, *44*(2).

Berry, B. S., & Kymar, K. R. (2012). Human resource professionals' perception on disability related barriers to employment of persons with intellectual disability. *The Indian Journal of Occupational Therapy*, *44*(2).

Berry, P. B. (1972). Comprehension of possessive and present continuous sentences by nonretarded, mildly retarded, and severely retarded children. *American Journal of Mental Deficiency*, *76*, 540–544. PMID:5012135

Berthold, K., & Hoover, J. (2000). Correlates of bullying and victimization among intermediate students in Midwestern USA. *School Psychology International*, *21*(1), 65–79. doi:10.1177/0143034300211005

Besser, S. (1998). The positive impact of children with an intellectual disability on the family. Journal of intellectual & Developmental Disability, 23(1), 57-70.

Beyer, S., & Robinson, C. (2009). A review of research literature on supported employment: A report for the cross-government learning disability employment strategy team. London: Cabinet Office.

Beyer, S., Hedebouw, G., Morgan, C., Van Regenmortel, T., & Samoy, E. (2002). *Inter-national reflections: An interim report on effective approaches to vocational training and employment for people with learning disabilities*. Academic Press.

Beyer, S., Grove, B., Schneider, J., Simons, K., Williams, V., & Heyman, A. (2004). *Working lives: The role of day centres in supporting people with learning disabilities into employment*. Leeds, UK: Department of Work and Pensions.

Beyer, S., Kilsby, M., & Shearn, J. (1999). The organisation and outcomes of supported employment in Britain. *Journal of Vocational Rehabilitation*, *12*, 137–146.

Bharath Raj, J. (1971). AHSH Norms on seguin form board with Indian Children. *J. of AHSH*, *II*, 34–39.

Bharath Raj, J. (2004). *The developmental screening test manual*. Mysore: Swayamsiddha Prakashana.

Bharatraj, J. (1987). Speech and Hearing problems among the mentally retarded. *Indian Journal of Disability and Rehabilitation*, *1*, 5–8.

Bhat, A.M., Sharma, V. & Jena, S.P. (2013). Managing stress in parents of children with intellectual disability. *Indian Journal of Health and Well-Being*, *4*(9), 1790-1793.

Bickenbach, J. E. (1993). *Physical disability and social policy*. Toronto: University of Toronto Press.

Bigby, C. (1997). Parental substitutes? The role of siblings in the lives of older people with intellectual disability. *Journal of Gerontological Social Work*, *29*(1), 3–21. doi:10.1300/J083v29n01_02

Bigby, C. (2004). *Ageing with a Lifelong Disability: A Guide to Practice, Program and Policy Issues for Human Services Professionals*. London: Jessica Kingsley.

Bigby, C., & Balandin, S. (2004). Issues in researching the ageing of people with intellectual disability. In E. Emerson, C. Hatton, T. Thompson, & T. R. Parmenter (Eds.), *The International Handbook of Applied Research in Intellectual Disabilities* (pp. 221–236). West Sussex, UK: Wiley. doi:10.1002/9780470713198.ch10

Bijou, S. W., Peterson, R. F., & Ault, M. H. (1968). A method to integrate descriptive and experimental field studies at the level of data and empirical concepts. *Journal of Applied Behavior Analysis*, *1*(2), 175–191. doi:10.1901/jaba.1968.1-175 PMID:16795175

Bilsky, L. H. (1986). Comprehension and mental retardation. *International Review of Research in Mental Retardation*, *13*, 215–246. doi:10.1016/S0074-7750(08)60237-2

Bischoff, L. B., & Tingstrom, D. H. (1991). Siblings of children with disabilities: Psychological and behavioral characteristics. *Counselling Psychology Quarterly*, *4*(4), 311–321. doi:10.1080/09515079108254439

Bishop, D. V. (2006). *Children's Communication Checklist*. NCS Pearson, Inc.

Blacher, J. (1984). Sequential stages of parental adjustment to the birth of a child with handicaps: Fact or artifact? *Mental Retardation*, *22*, 55–68. PMID:6234448

Blacher, J., Baker, B. L., & Eisenhower, A. S. (2009). Student–teacher relationship stability across early school years for children with intellectual disability or typical development. *American Journal on Intellectual and Developmental Disabilities*, *114*(5), 322–339. doi:10.1352/1944-7558-114.5.322 PMID:19928015

Blacher, J., Baker, B. L., & MacLean, W. E. Jr. (2007, September). Positive Impact of Intellectual Disability on Families. *American Journal of Mental Retardation*, *112*(5), 330–348. doi:10.1352/0895-8017(2007)112[0330:PIOIDO]2.0.CO;2 PMID:17676958

Blacher, J., & Bromley, B. E. (1990). Correlates of out-of-home placement of handicapped children: Who places and why? *Journal of Children in Contemporary Society*, *21*, 3–41. doi:10.1300/J274v21n03_02

Blacher, J., Neece, C. L., & Paczkowski, E. (2005). Families and intellectual disability. *Current Opinion in Psychiatry*, *18*(5), 507–513. doi:10.1097/01.yco.0000179488.92885.e8 PMID:16639109

Blake, J. J., Lund, E. M., Zhou, Q., Kwok, O., & Benz, M. (2012). National prevalence rates of bully victimization among students with disabilities in the United States. *School Psychology Quarterly*, *27*(4), 2100–2222. doi:10.1037/spq0000008 PMID:23294235

Blanck, P., Hill, E., Siegal, C., & Waterstone, M. (2009). Disability civil rights law and policy (2nd ed.). Thomson/West Publishers.

Block, P. (2000). Sexuality, fertility and danger: Twentieth-century images of women with cognitive disabilities. *Sexuality and Disability*, *18*(4), 239–254. doi:10.1023/A:1005642226413

Blumberg, E. R., Horner, R. H., Irvin, L. K., Laverty, R., Lucyshyn, J. M., & Sprague, J. R. (2004). Validating the construct of coercion in family routines: Expanding the unit of analysis in behavioral assessment with families of children with developmental disabilities. *Research and Practice for Persons with Severe Disabilities*, *29*(2), 104–121. doi:10.2511/rpsd.29.2.104 PMID:26321883

Bohannon, J. N., & Bonvillian, J. D. (2005). Theoretical approaches to language acquisition. In *The development of language* (6th ed.; pp. 230–291). Boston: Allyn & Bacon.

Bondy, A. S., & Frost, L. A. (1994). The picture exchange communication system. *Focus on Autistic Behavior*, *9*, 1–19.

Bonham, G. S., Basehart, S., Schalock, R. L., Marchand, C. B., Kirchner, N., & Rumenap, J. M. (2004). Consumer-based quality of life assessment: The Maryland Ask Me! Project. *Mental Retardation*, *42*(5), 338–355. doi:10.1352/0047-6765(2004)42<338:CQOLAT>2.0.CO;2 PMID:15335259

Bonnie, R. J. (1990). The competence of criminal defendants with mental retardation to participate in their own defense. *The Journal of Criminal Law & Criminology*, *81*(3), 419–446. doi:10.2307/1143845

Boone, K. B. (Ed.). (2007). *Assessment of feigned cognitive impairment: A neuropsychological perspective*. New York: Guilford Press.

Booth, T., Booth, W., & McConnell, D. (2005). The prevalence and outcomes of care proceedings involving parents with intellectual disabilities in the family courts. *Journal of Applied Research in Intellectual Disabilities*, *18*, 7–17. doi:. 00204.x10.1111/ j.1468-3148.2004

Booth, T., & Booth, W. (1994). *Parenting under pressure: Mothers and fathers with learning difficulties*. Buckingham, UK: Open University Press.

Booth, T., & Booth, W. (1998). *Growing up with parents who have learning difficulties*. London, UK: Routledge.

Booth, T., & Booth, W. (2000). Against the odds: Growing up with parents who have learning difficulties. *Mental Retardation*, *38*(1), 1–14. doi:10.1352/0047-6765(2000)038<0001:ATOGUW>2.0.CO;2 PMID:10703213

Borg, J., Larsson, S., & Östergren, P. O. (2011). The right to assistive technology: For whom, for what, and by whom? *Disability & Society*, *26*(2), 151–167. doi:10.1080/09687599.2011.543862

Borromeo, A. D. (2001). Mental retardation and the death penalty. *Loyola Journal of Public Interest Law*, *3*, 175.

Borthwick-Duffy, S. A., & Eyman, R. K. (1990). Who are the dually diagnosed? *American Journal of Mental Retardation*. PMID:2340136

Bos, A. E. R., Muris, P., Mulkens, S., & Schaalma, H. P. (2006). Changing self-esteem in children and adolescents: A roadmap for future interventions. *Netherlands Journal of Psychology*, *62*(1), 26–33. doi:10.1007/BF03061048

Botterbusch, K. F. (1982). *A Comparison of Commercial Vocational Evaluation Systems*. Academic Press.

Bouras, N. (2011). Mental health problems and related issues for people with developmental and intellectual disability. *Current Opinion in Psychiatry*, *24*(5), 365–366. doi:10.1097/YCO.0b013e328349d249 PMID:21778881

Bourke, J., Ricciardo, B., Bebbington, A., Aiberti, K., Jacoby, P., Dyke, P., . . . Leonard, H. (2008). Physical and mental health in mothers of children with Down syndrome. *The Journal of Pediatrics, 153*(3), 320-326.

Bourke-Taylor, H., Law, M., Howie, L., & Pallant, J. F. (2010). Development of the Child's Challenging Behaviour Scale (CCBS) for mothers of school-aged children with disabilities. *Child: Care, Health and Development*, *36*(4), 491–498. doi:10.1111/j.1365-2214.2009.01055.x PMID:20047597

Bourke-Taylor, H., Pallant, J. F., Law, M., & Howie, L. (2012). Predicting mental health among mothers of school-aged children with developmental disabilities: The relative contribution of child, maternal and environmental factors. *Research in Developmental Disabilities*, *32*(6), 1732–1740. doi:10.1016/j.ridd.2012.04.011 PMID:22699247

Bowe, F. (1978). *Handicapping America: Barriers to Disabled People*. New York: Harper and Row.

Bowen, M. (1978). *Family therapy in clinical practice*. New York: Aronson.

Bowlby, J. (1988). A secure base: Parent-child attachment and healthy human development. New York: Basic Books. Retrieved from http://www.psychology.sunysb.edu/attachment/online/inge_origins.pdf

Bowlby, J. (1988a). *A secure base: clinical applications of attachment theory*. Hove, New York: Brunner-Routledge, Taylor & Francis Group.

Bowlby, J. (1988b). *A secure base: Parent-child attachment and healthy human development*. New York: Basic Books.

Bowlby, J. (1989). *The Making and Breaking of Affectional Bonds*. New York: Routledge, Taylor and Francis Group.

Bowling, M., & Keltner, B. (1996). Primary health care for children of mothers with intellectual limitations. *Pediatric Nursing*, *22*, 312–319. PMID:8852110

Boyes, M. E., Bowes, L., Cluver, L. C., Ward, C. L., & Badcock, N. A. (2014). Bullying victimization, internalizing symptoms, and conduct problems in South African children and adolescents: A longitudinal investigation. *Journal of Abnormal Child Psychology*, *42*(8), 1313–1324. doi:10.1007/s10802-014-9888-3 PMID:24882504

Braddock, D., Hemp, R., & Rizzolo, M. (2008). The state of the states in developmental disabilities. Washington, DC: American Association on Intellectual and Developmental Disabilities (AAIDD).

Braddock, D., & Parish, S. L. (2002). *An institutional history of disability*. Washington, DC: American Association of Mental Retardation.

Bradley, E., Burke, L., Drummond, C., Korossy, M., Lunsky, Y., & Morris, S. (2010). *Guidelines for managing the patient with developmental disability in the emergency room*. Retrieved from www.camh.net/Publications/Resources_for_Professionals/guidelines_manageclient_emerg2003.pdf

Bradley, R. H., Corwyn, R. F., Burchinal, M., McAdoo, H. P., & Garcia Coll, C. (2001). The home environments of children in the United States Part II: Relations with behavioral development through age thirteen. *Child Development*, *72*(6), 1868–1886. doi:10.1111/1467-8624.t01-1-00383 PMID:11768150

Bradshaw, C. P., Stuart, E. A., & Zablotsky, B. (2013). The association between mental health, stress and coping supports in mothers of children with autism spectrum disorders. *Journal of Autism and Developmental Disorders*, *43*(6), 1380–1393. doi:10.1007/s10803-012-1693-7 PMID:23100053

Bradshaw, C. P., Waasdorp, T. E., & Johnson, S. L. (2015). Overlapping verbal, relational, physical, and electronic forms of bullying in adolescence: Influence of school context. *Journal of Clinical Child and Adolescent Psychology*, *44*(3), 494–508. doi:10.1080/15374416.2014.893516 PMID:24738548

Brady, N. C., & Warren, S. F. (2003). Language intervention for children with mental retardation. *International Review of Research in Mental Retardation*, *27*, 231–254. doi:10.1016/S0074-7750(03)27007-5

Braithwaite, D. O., & Thompson, T. L. (1999). *Handbook of Communication and People With Disabilities: Research and Application*. Retrieved from https://books.google.co.in/books?isbn=1135675805

Bray, N. W. (1997). Article. *International Review of Research in Mental Retardation*, *20*(111), 112.

Brehaut, J. C., Kohen, D. E., Raina, P., Walter, S. D., Russell, D. J., Swinton, M., & Rosenbaum, P. et al. (2004). The health of primary caregivers of children with cerebral palsy: How does it compare with that of other Canadian caregivers? *Pediatrics*, *4*(2), e182–e191. doi:10.1542/peds.114.2.e182 PMID:15286255

Breslau, N., Staruch, K. S., & Mortimer, E. A. (1982). Psychological distress in mothers of disabled children. *American Journal of Diseases of Children*, *136*, 682–686.

Brighi, A., Guarini, A., Melotti, G., Galli, S., & Genta, M. L. (2012). Predictors of victimization across direct bullying, indirect bullying and cyberbullying. *Emotional & Behavioural Difficulties*, *17*(3-4), 375–388. doi:10.1080/13632752.2012.704684

Brinker, R. P., Seifer, R., & Smeroff, A. J. (1994). Relations among maternal stress, cognitive development, and early intervention in middle and low SEC infants with developmental disabilities. (I*). American Journal of Mental Retardation*, *98*, 463–480. PMID:8148123

Bristol, M. M., & Schopler, E. (1984). A Developmental Perspective on Stress and Coping in Families of Autistic Children. *Journal of Educational and Social Research.*

Britton, L. N., Carr, J. E., Kellum, K. K., Dozier, C. L., & Weil, T. M. (2000). A variation of noncontingent reinforcement in the treatment of aberrant behavior. *Research in Developmental Disabilities*, *21*(6), 425–435. doi:10.1016/S0891-4222(00)00056-1 PMID:11153827

Brody, G. (2004). Siblings' direct and indirect contributions to child development. *Current Directions in Psychological Science*, *13*(3), 124–126. doi:10.1111/j.0963-7214.2004.00289.x

Brooks, A., Todd, A. W., Tofflemoyer, S., & Horner, R. H. (2003). Use of functional assessment and a self-management system to increase academic engagement and work completion. *Journal of Positive Behavior Interventions*, *5*(3), 144–152. doi:10.1177/10983007030050030301

Brown & Randel., D. (1997). *The Individual with Intellectual Disabilities and Sex Education: Perspectives of Involved Adults.* Presented at the 7th Annual Meeting of the International Society for the Study of Human Subjectivity, Columbia.

Brown, I., & Brown, R. I. (2009). Choice as an aspect of quality of life for people with intellectual disabilities. *Journal of Policy and Practice in Intellectual Disabilities, 6*, 10-17.

Brown, R. I. (1998). *Conceptualisation of quality of life: An overview.* Paper presented at the 1998 Australian Society for the Study of Intellectual Disability (ASSID) Conference: Conceptualisation of quality of life workshop, Flinders University of South Australia, Adelaide, Australia.

Brown, B. J., Mansell, J., & Kozma, A. (2007). Deinstitutionalization in intellectual disabilities. *Current Opinion in Psychiatry*, *20*(5), 437–442. doi:10.1097/YCO.0b013e32827b14ab PMID:17762584

Browne, G., & Bramston, P. (1998). Stress and the quality of life in the parents of young people with intellectual disabilities. *Journal of Psychiatric and Mental Health Nursing*, *5*(5), 415–421. PMID:10067490

Brown, I. (2006). *Family Quality of Life Survey: Main caregivers of people with intellectual or developmental disabilities.* Toronto: Surrey Place Centre.

Brown, I., & Brown, R. I. (2003). *Quality of Life and Disability: An Approach for Community Practitioners.* London, UK: Jessica Kingsley.

Brown, N., McLinden, M., & Porter, J. (1998). Sensory needs. In P. Lacey & C. Ouvry (Eds.), *People with profound and multiple learning disabilities: A collaborative approach to meeting complex needs* (pp. 29–38). London: David Fulton.

Brown, R. I. (1995). Measuring new dimensions through quality of life: The personal equation. *Evaluation Journal of Australasia*, *7*(1), 14–23.

Brown, R. I., Bayer, M. B., & MacFarlane, C. (1989). *Rehabilitation programs: Performance and Quality of Life of adults with developmental handicaps*. Toronto: Lugus Productions.

Brown, R. I., & Brown, I. (2005). The application of quality of life. *Journal of Intellectual Disability Research*, *49*(10), 718–727. doi:10.1111/j.1365-2788.2005.00740.x PMID:16162116

Brown, R. T., & Pacini, J. N. (1989). Perceived family functioning, marital status, and depression in parents of boys with attention deficit disorder. *Journal of Learning Disabilities*, *22*(9), 581–587. doi:10.1177/002221948902200911 PMID:2809411

Bruce, E. J., Schultz, C. L., Smyrnios, K. X., & Schultz, N. C. (1994). Grieving related to development: A preliminary comparison of three age cohorts of parents of children with intellectual disability. *The British Journal of Medical Psychology*, *67*(1), 37–52. doi:10.1111/j.2044-8341.1994.tb01769.x PMID:7515655

Bruininks, R. H., Hill, B. K., & Morreau, L. E. (1988). *Prevalence and implications of maladaptive behaviors and dual diagnosis in residential and other service programs. In Mental retardation and mental health* (pp. 3–29). Springer.

Buckley, S., Bird, G., Sacks, B., & Archer, T. (2002). A comparison of mainstream and special school education for teenagers with Down syndrome: Effects of social and academic development. *Down's Syndrome: Research and Practice*, *2*(2), 46–54.

Buntinx, W. H. E., & Schalock, R. L. (2010). Models of Disability, Quality of Life, and Individualized Supports: Implications for Professional Practice in Intellectual Disability. *Journal of Policy and Practice in Intellectual Disabilities*, *7*(4), 283–294. doi:10.1111/j.1741-1130.2010.00278.x

Burack, Hodapp, & Zigler. (1988). Handbook of Mental Retardation and Development. Cambridge University Press.

Bush, S. S.Planning Committee. (2005). Independent and court-ordered forensic neuropsychological examinations: Official statement of the National Academy of Neuropsychology. *Archives of Clinical Neuropsychology*, *20*(8), 997–1007. doi:10.1016/j.acn.2005.06.003 PMID:16076547

Butterfield, N., Arthur, M., & Linfoot, K. (1992). Meeting communication needs in communication programming for students with severe intellectual disability: The creating communicative contexts manual. *Special Education Perspectives*, *1*(1), 35–43.

Calculator, S. N., & Dollaghan, C. (1982). The use of communication boards in a residential setting: An evaluation. *The Journal of Speech and Hearing Disorders*, *47*(3), 281–287. doi:10.1044/jshd.4703.281 PMID:6225904

Calitz, F. J. (2011). Psycho-legal challenges facing the mentally retarded rape victim. *South African Journal of Psychiatry*, *17*(3), 66–72.

Caltabiano, M. L., Sarafino, E. P., Byrne, D., & Martin, P. R. (2002). *Health Psychology: Biopsychosocial Interactions*. Milton: John Wiley & Sons.

Cannella-Malone, H. I., DeBar, R. M., & Sigafoos, J. (2009). An examination of preference for augmentative and alternative communication devices with two boys with significant intellectual disabilities. *Augmentative and Alternative Communication*, *25*(4), 262–273. doi:10.3109/07434610903384511 PMID:19883289

Cant, R., Gething, L., Kendig, H., Llewellyn, G., & McConnell, D. (2010). Health status and coping strategies among older parent-carers of adults with intellectual disabilities in an Australian sample. *Research in Developmental Disabilities: A Multidisciplinary Journal, 31*(6), 1176-1186.

Cantwell, J., Muldoon, O. T., & Gallagher, S. (2014). Social support and mastery influence the association between stress and poor physical health in parents caring for children with developmental disabilities. *Research in Developmental Disabilities*, *35*(9), 2215–2223. doi:10.1016/j.ridd.2014.05.012 PMID:24927515

Caplan, B., Neece, C. L., & Baker, B. L. (2015). Developmental level and psychopathology: Comparing children with developmental delays to chronological and mental age matched controls. *Research in Developmental Disabilities*, *37*, 143–151. doi:10.1016/j.ridd.2014.10.045 PMID:25498740

Cappadocia, M. C., Weiss, J. A., & Pepler, D. (2012). Bullying experiences among children and youth with autism spectrum disorders. *Journal of Autism and Developmental Disorders*, *42*(2), 266–277. doi:10.1007/s10803-011-1241-x PMID:21499672

Carbone-Lopez, K., Esbensen, F. A., & Brick, B. T. (2010). Correlates and consequences of peer victimization: Gender differences in direct and indirect forms of bullying. *Youth Violence and Juvenile Justice*, *8*(4), 332–350. doi:10.1177/1541204010362954

Card, N. A., & Hodges, E. V. E. (2008). Peer victimization among schoolchildren: Correlations, causes, consequences, and considerations in assessment and intervention. *School Psychology Quarterly*, *23*(4), 451–461. doi:10.1037/a0012769

Carey, A. C. (2010). *On the margins of citizenship: Intellectual disability and civil rights in twentieth-century America*. Philadelphia, PA: Temple University Press.

Carey, A. C., Friedman, M. G., & Bryen, D. N., S. J. (2005). Use of Electronic Technologies by People with Intellectual Disabilities.[PubMed]. *Mental Retardation*, *43*(5), 322–333.

Carlesimo, G. A., Marotta, L., & Vicari, S. (1997). Long-term memory in mental retardation: Evidence for a specific impairment in subjects with Down's syndrome. *Neuropsychologia*, *35*(1), 71–79. doi:10.1016/S0028-3932(96)00055-3 PMID:8981379

Carlson, I. W., & Cornell, D. W. (2008). Differences between persistent and desistent middle school bullies. *School Psychology International*, *29*(4), 442–451. doi:10.1177/0143034308096433

Carney, A., & Merrell, K. (2001). Bullying in schools: Perspectives on understanding and preventing an international problem. *School Psychology International*, *21*(3), 364–382. doi:10.1177/0143034301223011

Carr, J. (2004). *Understanding intellectual disability and health*. Retrieved from http://www.intellectualdisability.info/mental-health/behaviour-management

Carr, E., Horner, R., Turnbull, A., Marquis, J., McLaughlin, D., & McAtee, M. et al.. (1999). *Positive behavior support for people with developmental disabilities: A research synthesis*. Washington, DC: American Association on Mental Retardation.

Carr, E., Levin, L., McConnachie, G., Carlson, J., Kemp, D., & Smith, C. (1994). *Communication-based intervention for problem behavior*. Baltimore: Paul H. Brookes.

Carrier, S. (2007). Understanding social and professional integration as an adjustment process: Contribution to a theory of coadaptation. *Intellectual and Developmental Disabilities*, *45*(1), 10–22. doi:10.1352/1934-9556(2007)45[10:USAPIA]2.0.CO;2 PMID:17428122

Carrow-Woolfolk, F., & Lynch, J. (1982). *An approach to language disorders in children*. New York: Grune & Stratton.

Carter, B. B., & Spencer, V. G. (2006). The Fear Factor: Bullying and Students with Disabilities. George Mason University. *International Journal of Special Education*, *21*(1). Retrieved from http://www.forockids.org/PDF Docs/Bullying.pdf

Carter, M., & Hook, J. (1998). Communication programming for students with high support needs: A model for deciding what to teach. *Special Education Perspectives*, *7*(1), 42–55.

Carulla, L. S., Reed, G. M., Vaezazizi, L. M., Cooper, S. N., Leal, R. M., Bertelli, M., & Saxena, S. et al. (2011). Intellectual developmental disorders: Towards a new name, definition and framework for "mental retardation/intellectual disability" in ICD-11. *World Psychiatry; Official Journal of the World Psychiatric Association (WPA), 10*(3), 175–180. doi:10.1002/j.2051-5545.2011.tb00045.x PMID:21991267

Cascella, P. W. (2004). *Receptive communication abilities among adults with significant intellectual disability*. Taylor & Francis Ltd.

Cascella, P. W. (2006). Standardised speech-language tests and students with intellectual disability: A review of normative data. *Journal of Intellectual & Developmental Disability, 31*(2), 120–124. doi:10.1080/13668250600681503 PMID:16782597

Cassidy, S. B., & Morris, C. A. (2001). Behavioral phenotypes in genetic syndromes: Genetic clues to human behavior. *Advances in Pediatrics, 49*, 59–86. PMID:12214780

Cea, C. D., & Fisher, C. B. (2003). Health care decision-making by adults with mental retardation. *Journal Information, 41*(2). PMID:12622524

Census of India. (2011). *Central Statistics Office Ministry of Statistics & Programme Implementation Government of India*. Retrieved from:http://mospi.nic.in/Mospi_New/site/home.aspx

Census of India. (2013). *Disabled population by type of Disability, age, and sex*. Office of the Registrar General & Census Commissioner.

Cermak, S. A., & Aberson, J. R. (1998). Social skills in children with learning disabilities. *Occupational Therapy in Mental Health, 13*(4), 1–24. doi:10.1300/J004v13n04_01

Chadsey, J.G., Linneman, D., Rusch, F.R., & Cimera, R.E. (1997). The impact of social integration interventions and job coaches in work settings. *Journal of Education and Training in Mental Retardation and Developmental Disabilities, 32,* 281–292.

Chadsey, J. G., Shelden, D. L., Horn, J. R., Bardeleben, D., & Cimera, R. E. (1999). Description of variables impacting successful and unsuccessful cases of social integration involving co-workers. *Journal of Vocational Rehabilitation, 12*, 103–112.

Chadwick, O., Kusel, Y., Cuddy, M., & Taylor, E. (2005). Psychiatric diagnoses and behaviour problems from childhood to early adolescence in young people with severe intellectual disabilities. *Psychological Medicine, 35*(05), 751–760. doi:10.1017/S0033291704003733 PMID:15918352

Chandramuki, K. S., & Vranda, M. N. (2012). Attitudes of parents towards children with specific learning disabilities. *Disability, CBR and Inclusive Development, 23*(1), 63-69.

Chan, J. B., & Sigafoos, J. (2001). Does respite care reduce parental stress in families with developmentally disabled children? *Child and Youth Care Forum, 30*(5), 253–263. doi:10.1023/A:1014467226528

Charach, A., Pepler, D., & Ziegler, S. (1995). Bullying at school. *Education Canada, 37*, 12–18.

Chaturvedi, S. K., & Malhotra, S. (1984). A follow up study of mental retardation focussing parental attitudes. *Indian Journal of Psychiatry, 26*(4), 370–376.

Chavan, B. S., & Rozatkar, A. S. (2014). Intellectual disability in India: Charity to right based. *Indian Journal of Psychiatry, 56*(2), 113–116. doi:10.4103/0019-5545.130477 PMID:24891695

Cheslock, M. A., Barton-Hulsey, A., Romski, M., & Sevcik, R. A. (2008). Using a speech-generating device to enhance communicative abilities for an adult with moderate intellectual disability. *Intellectual and Developmental Disabilities, 46*(5), 376–386. doi:10.1352/2008.46:376-386 PMID:19090639

Chiner, E., & Cardona, M. C. (2012). Inclusive education in Spain: How do skills, resources, and supports affect regular education teachers' perceptions of inclusion? *International Journal of Inclusive Education, 17*(5), 526-541. Retrieved from10.1080/13603116.2012.689864

Chiu, M. Y., Yang, X., Wong, H. T., & Li, J. H. (2014). The mediating effect of affective stigma between face concern and general mental health - The case of Chinese caregivers of children with intellectual disability. *Research in Developmental Disabilities, 36C*, 437–446.

Chomsky, N., & Skinner, B. F. (1959). Review of BF Skinner. Verbal Behavior. *Language, 35*(1), 26–58. doi:10.2307/411334

Christensen, H., Calear, A., Tait, R., Gosling, J., Griffiths, K., & Murray, K. (2011). *School based intervention programs and shared care collaborative models targeting the prevention of or early intervention in child and adolescent mental health problems: An Evidence Check rapid review*. NSW Ministry of Health.

Christensen, L., Fraynt, B., Neece, C. L., & Baker, B. L. (2012). Bullying adolescents with intellectual disability. *Journal of Mental Health Research in Intellectual Disability, 5*(1), 49–65. doi:10.1080/19315864.2011.637660

Cihak, D., Fahrenkrog, C., Ayres, K. M., & Smith, C. (2009). The use of video modeling via a video iPod and a system of least prompts to improve transitional behaviors for students with autism spectrum disorders in the general education classroom. *Journal of Positive Behavior Interventions*. doi:10.1177/1098300709332346

Cimera, R. (2011). Does being in sheltered workshops improve the employment outcomes of supported employees with intellectual disabilities? *Journal of Vocational Rehabilitation, 35*, 21–27.

Cirrin, F. M., & Rowland, C. M. (1985). Communicative assessment of non-verbal youths with severe/profound mental retardation. *Mental Retardation, 23*(2), 52–62. PMID:3990553

Clare, I. C. H., & Gudjonsson, G. H. (1993). Interrogative suggestibility, confabulation, and acquiescence in people with mild learning disabilities (mental handicap): Implications for reliability during police interview. *The British Journal of Clinical Psychology, 32*(3), 295–301. doi:10.1111/j.2044-8260.1993.tb01059.x PMID:8251959

Clare, I. C. H., & Gudjonsson, G. H. (1995). The vulnerability of suspects with intellectual disabilities during police interviews: A review and experimental study of decision-making. *Mental Handicap Research, 8*(2), 110–128. doi:10.1111/j.1468-3148.1995.tb00149.x

Clarke, D. J., Littlejohns, C. S., Corbett, J. A., & Joseph, S. (1989). Pervasive developmental disorders and psychoses in adult life. *The British Journal of Psychiatry, 155*(5), 692–699. PMID:2611600

Clark, K. E., & Ladd, G. W. (2000). Connectedness and autonomy support in parent–child relationships: Links to children's socioemotional orientation and peer relationships. *Developmental Psychology, 36*(4), 485–498. doi:10.1037/0012-1649.36.4.485 PMID:10902700

Clark, L. I., & O'toole, M. S. (2007). Intellectual impairment and sexual health: Information needs. *British Journal of Nursing (Mark Allen Publishing), 16*(3), 154–156. doi:10.12968/bjon.2007.16.3.22968 PMID:17363881

Cleaver, H., & Nicholson, D. (2007). *Parental learning disability and children's needs: Family experiences and effective practice*. London, UK: Kingsley.

Cleaver, H., Unell, I., & Aldgate, J. (1999). *Children's needs, parenting capacity: The impact of parental mental illness, problem alcohol and drug use and domestic violence on children's development*. London: Department of Health, Stationary Office.

Cleveland, D. S., & Miller, N. B. (1977). Attitudes and life commitments of older siblings of mentally retarded adults: An exploratory study. *Mental Retardation*, *15*, 38–41. PMID:875727

Cockram, J., Jackson, R., & Underwood, R. (1998). People with an intellectual disability and the criminal justice system: The family perspective. *Journal of Intellectual & Developmental Disability*, *23*(1), 41–56. doi:10.1080/13668259800033571

Cohen, S. R., Holloway, S. D., Domínguez-Pareto, I., & Kuppermann, M. (2015, January). Support and Self-Efficacy Among Latino and White Parents of Children With ID. *American Journal on Intellectual and Developmental Disabilities*, *120*(1), 16–31. doi:10.1352/1944-7558-120.1.16 PMID:25551264

Cole, K. N., Coggins, T. E., & Vanderstoep, C. (1999). The influence of language/Cognitive profile on discourse intervention outcome. *Language, Speech, and Hearing Services in Schools*, *30*(1), 61–67. doi:10.1044/0161-1461.3001.61

Collings, S., & Llewellyn, G. (2012). Children of parents with intellectual disability: Facing poor outcomes or faring okay? *Journal of Intellectual & Developmental Disability*, *37*(1), 65–82. doi:10.3109/13668250.2011.648610 PMID:22300240

Cologon, K. (2012). Confidence in their own ability: Postgraduate early childhood students examining their attitudes towards inclusive education. *International Journal of Inclusive Education*, *16*(11), 1155–1173. doi:10.1080/13603116.2010.548106

Conger, R., Patterson, G. R., & Ge, X. (1995). It takes two to replicate: A mediational model for the impact of parents' stress on adolescent adjustment. *Child Development*, *66*(1), 80–97. doi:10.2307/1131192 PMID:7497831

Cook, B. G., Tankersley, M., Cook, L., & Landrum, T. (2000). Abstract of Teachers' Attitudes toward their included students with disabilities. *Exceptional Children*, *67*(1), 115–135.

Cooper, B. (1981). *Assessing the handicaps and needs of mentally retarded children*. Academic Press Inc.

Cooper, J. O., Heron, T. E., & Heward, W. L. (2007). *Applied Behavior Analysis* (2nd ed.). Upper Saddle River, NJ: Pearson.

Cooper, S. A. (1997). Psychiatry of elderly compared to younger adults with intellectual disabilities. *Journal of Applied Research in Intellectual Disabilities*, *10*(4), 303–311. doi:10.1111/j.1468-3148.1997.tb00025.x

Cooper, S. A., Melville, C. A., & Morrison, J. (2004). People with intellectual disabilities. Their health needs People with intellectual disabilities. *BMJ (Clinical Research Ed.)*, *329*(7463), 414–415. doi:10.1136/bmj.329.7463.414 PMID:15321883

Cooper, S. A., Smiley, E., Morrison, J., Williamson, A., & Allan, L. (2007). Mental ill-health in adults with intellectual disabilities: Prevalence and associated factors. *The British Journal of Psychiatry*, *190*(1), 27–35. doi:10.1192/bjp.bp.106.022483 PMID:17197653

Copley, J., & Ziviani, J. (2004). Barriers to the use of assistive technology for children with multiple disabilities.[PubMed]. *Occupational Therapy International*, *11*(4), 229–243. doi:10.1002/oti.213

Corbett, J. A. (1979). Psychiatric morbidity and mental retardation. In F. E. James & R. P. Snaith (Eds.), *Psychiatric illness and mental handicap* (pp. 11–25). London: Royal College of Psychiatry, Gaskell.

Coren, E., Hutchfield, J., Thomae, M., & Gustafsson, C. (2010). Parent training support for intellectually disabled parents. *Campbell Systematic Reviews*, *3*, 1–60. PMID:20556787

Cornelius, D. J. K. (2009). *Vocational Training and Employment for Persons with mental retardation to meet the needs of 21st Century*. Report of the National Seminar - Planning for Comprehensive Rehabilitation of Persons with mental retardation, Chennai, India.

Costeff, H., Cohen, B. E., Weller, L., & Kleckner, H. (1981). Pathogenic factors in idiopathic mental retardation. *Developmental Medicine and Child Neurology*, *23*(5), 484–493. doi:10.1111/j.1469-8749.1981.tb02022.x PMID:7196853

Costello, H., & Bouras, N. (2006). Assessment of mental health problems in people with intellectual disabilities. *The Israel Journal of Psychiatry and Related Sciences*, *43*(4), 241. PMID:17338443

Coyle, K., & Moloney, K. (1999). The introduction of person-centred planning in an Irish agency for people with intellectual disabilities: An introductory study. *Journal of Vocational Rehabilitation*, *12*, 175–180.

Craig, H. K. (1983). Applications of pragmatic language models for intervention. In T. Gallagher & C. Prutting (Eds.), Pragmatic assessment and intervention issues in language (pp. 101-127). San Diego, CA: College-Hill.

Craig, W. M., & Pepler, D. J. (1995). Peer processes in bullying and victimization: An observational study. *Exceptionality Education Canada*, *5*, 81–95.

Crais, E. R. (1990). World knowledge to word knowledge. *Topics in Language Disorders*, *10*(3), 45–62. doi:10.1097/00011363-199006000-00006

Cramm, J. M., & Nieboer, A. P. (2011). Psychological well-being of caregivers of children with intellectual disabilities: Using parental stress as a mediating factor. *Journal of Intellectual Disabilities*, *15*(2), 101–113. doi:10.1177/1744629511410922 PMID:21750213

Crick, N. R., & Grotpeter, J. K. (1995). Relational aggression, gender, and social-psychological adjustment. *Child Development*, *66*(3), 710–722. doi:10.2307/1131945 PMID:7789197

Crittenden, P. M., & Bonvillian, J. D. (1984). The relationship between maternal risk status and maternal sensitivity. *American Orthopsychiatric Association*, *54*(2), 250–262. doi:10.1111/j.1939-0025.1984.tb01492.x PMID:6731591

Crnic, K., Hoffman, C., Gaze, C., & Edelbrock, C. (2004). Understanding the emergence of behavior problems in young children with developmental delays. *Infants and Young Children*, *17*(3), 223–235. doi:10.1097/00001163-200407000-00004

Crocker, A. G., Mercier, C., Allaire, J., & Roy, M. (2007). Profiles and correlates of aggressive behaviour among adults with intellectual disabilities. *Journal of Intellectual Disability Research: JIDR*, *51*(Pt 10), 786–801. doi:10.1111/j.1365-2788.2007.00953.x PMID:17803497

Crocker, A. G., Mercier, C., Lachapelle, Y., Brunet, A., Morin, D., & Roy, M. (2006). Prevalence and types of aggressive behaviour among adults with intellectual disabilities. *Journal of Intellectual Disability Research*, *50*(9), 652–661. doi:10.1111/j.1365-2788.2006.00815.x PMID:16901292

Croen, L. A., Grether, J. K., & Selvin, S. (2001). The epidemiology of mental retardation of unknown cause. *Pediatrics*, *107*(6), e86–e86. doi:10.1542/peds.107.6.e86 PMID:11389284

Cromer, R. F. (1991). *Language and thought in normal and handicapped children*. Oxford, UK: Basil Blackwell.

Crowe, T. K., Cunningham-Sabo, L. D., Helitzer, D. L., & Vanleit, B. (2002). Perceived changes in self image and coping strategies of mothers of children with disabilities. *The Occupational Therapy Journal of Research*, *22*(1), 25–33. doi:10.1046/j.0045-0766.2001.00276.x

Cummings, J., Pepler, D. J., Mishna, F., & Craig, W. M. (2006). Bullying and victimization among children with exceptionalities. *Exceptionality Education Canada*, *16*, 193–222.

Cummings, S. T. (1976). The impact of the child's deficiency on the father: A study of fathers of mentally retarded and chronically ill children. *The American Journal of Orthopsychiatry*, *46*(2), 246–255. doi:10.1111/j.1939-0025.1976.tb00925.x PMID:1266948

Cummins, R.A. (1996). The domains of life satisfaction: An attempt to order chaos. *Social Indicators Research, 38*, 303-28.

Cummins, R. A. (1996). Assessing quality of life. In R. L. Schalock (Ed.), *Quality of life. Volume Conceptualization and measurement*. Washington, DC: American Association on Mental Retardation.

Cummins, R. A. (2005). Moving from the quality of life concept to a theory. *Journal of Intellectual Disability Research*, *49*(10), 699–706. doi:10.1111/j.1365-2788.2005.00738.x PMID:16162114

Cunningham, C. E., Clark, M. L., Heaven, R. K., Durrant, J., & Cunningham, L. H. (1989). The effects of coping-modelling problem solving and contingency management procedures on the positive and negative interactions of learning disabled and attention deficit disordered children with an autistic peer. *Child & Family Behavior Therapy*, *11*(3-4), 89–106. doi:10.1300/J019v11n03_06

Curtis, A., McVilly, K., & Day, A. (2014). Sentencing offenders with mental impairment: The case of arsonists with intellectual disability. *Journal of Intellectual Disabilities and Offending Behaviour*, *5*(2), 78–87. doi:10.1108/JIDOB-05-2014-0005

Cuskelly, M., & Bryde, R. (2004). Attitudes towards the sexuality of adults with an intellectual disability: Parents, support staff, and a community sample. *Journal of Intellectual & Developmental Disability*, *29*(3), 255–264. doi:10.1080/13668250412331285136

Cuskelly, M., & Dadds, M. (1992). Behaviour problems in children with Down syndrome and their siblings. *Journal of Child Psychology and Psychiatry, and Allied Disciplines*, *33*(4), 749–761. doi:10.1111/j.1469-7610.1992.tb00910.x PMID:1534811

Dabrowska, A., & Pisula, E. (2010). Parenting stress and coping styles in mothers and fathers of pre-school children with autism and Down syndrome. *Journal of Intellectual Disability Research*, *54*(3), 266–280. doi:10.1111/j.1365-2788.2010.01258.x PMID:20146741

Daily, D. K., Ardinger, H. H., & Holmes, G. E. (2000). Identification and evaluation of mental retardation. *American Family Physician*, *61*(4), 1059–1067. PMID:10706158

Daily, D. K., Ardinger, H. H., & Holmes, G. E. (2000, February). Identification and evaluation of mental retardation. *American Family Physician*, *61*(4), 1059–1067, 1070. PMID:10706158

Dalal, A. (1998). CBR in Action - Some Reflections from the Sirathu Project. *Asia Pacific Disability Rehabilitation Journal*, *9*(1), 29–31.

Dale, P. S. (1991). The validity of parent report measure of vocabulary and syntax at 24 months. *Journal of Speech and Hearing Research*, *34*(3), 565–571. doi:10.1044/jshr.3403.565 PMID:2072681

Davidson, A. L. (2012). Use of Mobile Technologies by Young Adults Living with an Intellectual Disability: A Collaborative Action Research Study. *Journal on Developmental Disabilities*, *18*(3), 21–32.

Davidson, P. W., Cain, N. N., Sloane-Reeves, J. E., & Van Speybroech, A. (1994). Characteristics of community-based individuals with mental retardation and aggressive behavioral disorders. *American Journal of Mental Retardation*, *98*(6), 704–716. PMID:8054199

Davis, S., & Nixon, C. (2010). *The youth voice research project: Victimization and strategies*. Retrieved from: http://njbullying.org/documents/YVPMarch2010.pdf

Davis, B. (1990). Loneliness in children and adolescents. *Issues in Comprehensive Pediatric Nursing*, *13*(1), 59–69. doi:10.3109/01460869009009745 PMID:2391259

Davis, C., Oliver, C., Tang, C. S., & Wu, A. (2000). Chinese children's attitudes towards mental retardation. *Journal of Developmental and Physical Disabilities, 12.*

Davis, H. (1985). Counselling parents of children who have intellectual disabilities. *Early Child Development and Care*, *22*(1), 19–35. doi:10.1080/0300443850220102

Davis, K., & Gavidia-Payne, S. (2009). The impact of child, family, and professional support characteristics on the quality of life in families of young children with disabilities. *Journal of Intellectual & Developmental Disability*, *34*(2), 153–162. doi:10.1080/13668250902874608 PMID:19404836

Davis, P. B., & May, J. E. (1991). Involving fathers in early intervention and family support programs: *Issues and strategies. Children's Health Care*, *20*(2), 87–92. doi:10.1207/s15326888chc2002_3

Dawkins, J. L. (1996). Bullying, physical disability and the pediatric patient. *Developmental Medicine and Child Neurology*, *38*(7), 603–612. doi:10.1111/j.1469-8749.1996.tb12125.x PMID:8674911

Day, K. (1993). Crime and mental retardation: A review. *Clinical Approaches to the Mentally Disordered Offender*, 111-44.

Day, K. (1994). Male mentally handicapped sex offenders. *The British Journal of Psychiatry*, *165*(5), 630–639. doi:10.1192/bjp.165.5.630 PMID:7866678

De Caroli, M. E., & Sagone, E. (2013). Siblings and disability: A study on social attitudes toward disabled brothers and sisters. *Procedia: Social and Behavioral Sciences*, *93*, 1217–1223. doi:10.1016/j.sbspro.2013.10.018

de Urries, Beyer, & Verdugo. (2007). *A comparative study of the situation of Supported Employment in Europe*. Universities of Salamanca and Cardiff, in collaboration with EUSE.

Deater-Deckard, K. (2005). Parenting stress and children's development: Introduction to the special issue. *Infant and Child Development*, *13*(2), 111–115. doi:10.1002/icd.383

Deb, S., Thomas, M., & Bright, C. (2001). Mental disorder in adults with intellectual disability. 1: Prevalence of functional psychiatric illness among a community-based population aged between 16 and 64 years. *Journal of Intellectual Disability Research*, *45*(6), 495–505. doi:10.1046/j.1365-2788.2001.00374.x PMID:11737536

Deitz, D. E., & Repp, A. C. (1983). Reducing Behavior through Reinforcement. *Exceptional Education Quarterly*, *3*(4), 34–46.

Dekker, M. C., & Koot, H. M. (2003a). DSM-IV disorders in children with borderline to moderate intellectual disability. I: Prevalence and impact. *Journal of the American Academy of Child and Adolescent Psychiatry*, *42*(8), 915–922. doi:10.1097/01.CHI.0000046892.27264.1A PMID:12874493

Dekker, M. C., & Koot, H. M. (2003b). DSM-IV Disorders in Children With Borderline to Moderate Intellectual Disability. II: Child and Family Predictors. *Journal of the American Academy of Child and Adolescent Psychiatry*, *42*(8), 923–931. doi:10.1097/01.CHI.0000046891.27264.C1 PMID:12874494

Dekker, M. C., Koot, H. M., & van der Ende, J. et al.. (2002). Emotional and behavioral problems in children and adolescents with and without intellectual disability. *Journal of Child Psychology and Psychiatry, and Allied Disciplines*, *43*(8), 1087–1098. doi:10.1111/1469-7610.00235 PMID:12455929

DeLambo, D., Chung, W., & Huang, W. (2011). Stress and age: A comparison of Asian American and Non-Asian American parents of children with developmental disabilities. *Journal of Developmental and Physical Disabilities*, *23*(2), 129–141. doi:10.1007/s10882-010-9211-3

Delano, M. E. (2007). Video modeling interventions for individuals with autism. *Remedial and Special Education*, *28*(1), 33–42. doi:10.1177/07419325070280010401

Demakis, G. J. (Ed.). (2011). *Civil capacities in clinical neuropsychology: Research findings and practical applications*. New York: Oxford University Press.

Dempsey, I., & Ford, J. (2009). Employment for people with an intellectual disability in Australia and the United Kingdom. *Journal of Disability Policy Studies*, *19*(4), 233–243. doi:10.1177/1044207308314946

Denney, R. L., & Wynkoop, T. F. (2000). Clinical neuropsychology in the criminal forensic setting. *The Journal of Head Trauma Rehabilitation*, *15*(2), 804–828. doi:10.1097/00001199-200004000-00005 PMID:10739969

Department of Health (UK). (2009). *Valuing employment now – Real jobs for people with learning disabilities*. Available at: http://www.dh.gov.uk/en/Publicationsandstatistics/ Publications/Publications Policy And Guidance/DH_101401

Derby, K., Wacker, D., DeRaad, A., Ulrich, S., Asmus, J., & Harding, J. et al.. (1997). The long-term effects of functional communication training in home settings. *Journal of Applied Behavior Analysis*, *30*(3), 507–531. doi:10.1901/jaba.1997.30-507 PMID:9316262

Derer, K., Polsgrove, L., & Rieth, H. (1996). A survey of assistive technology applications in schools and recommendations for practice. *Journal of Special Education Technology*, *13*, 62–80.

Devapriam, J., Raju, L., Singh, N., Collacott, R., & Bhaumik, S. (2007). Arson: Characteristics and predisposing factors in offenders with intellectual disabilities. *British Journal of Forensic Practice*, *9*(4), 23–27. doi:10.1108/14636646200700023

Devenny, D. A., & Silverman, W. P. (1990). Speech dysfluency and manual specialisation in Down syndrome. *Journal of Mental Deficiency Research*, *34*, 253–260. PMID:2143231

Dew, A., Llewellyn, G., & Balandin, S. (2004). Post-parental care: A new generation of siblingcarers. *Journal of Intellectual & Developmental Disability*, *29*(2), 176–179. doi:10.1080/13668250410001709520

Dewart, H. (1979). Language comprehension processes of mentally retarded children. *American Journal of Mental Deficiency*, *84*, 177–183. PMID:495665

DeWeaver, K. L., & Kropf, N. P. (1992). Persons with mental retardation: A forgotten minority in education. *Journal of Social Work Education*, *28*, 36–46.

Dhanesh, K. G., & Karthikeyan, S. (2012). *Gender difference in level of intelligence and social quotient among children with autism spectrum disorders*. International Journal of Scientific and Research Publications.

Di Nuovo, S. F., & Buono, S. (2007). Psychiatric syndromes comorbid with mental retardation: Differences in cognitive and adaptive skills. *Journal of Psychiatric Research*, *41*(9), 795–800. doi:10.1016/j.jpsychires.2006.02.011 PMID:16697412

Dickerson Mayes, S., Baweja, R., Calhoun, S. L., Syed, E., Mahr, F., & Siddiqui, F. (2014). Suicide ideation and attempts and bullying in children and adolescents: Psychiatric and general population samples. *Crisis*, *35*(5), 301–309. doi:10.1027/0227-5910/a000264 PMID:25115491

Dickman, B. J., & Roux, A. J. (2005). Complainants with learning disabilities in sexual abuse cases: A 10-year review of a psycho-legal project in Cape Town, South Africa. *British Journal of Learning Disabilities*, *33*(3), 138–144. doi:10.1111/j.1468-3156.2005.00355.x

Dickson, K., Emerson, E., & Hatton, C. (2005). Self-reported anti-social behaviour: Prevalence and risk factors amongst adolescents with and without intellectual disability. *Journal of Intellectual Disability Research*, *49*(11), 820–826. doi:10.1111/j.1365-2788.2005.00727.x PMID:16207279

Didden, R. (2007). Functional analysis methodology in developmental disabilities. In P. Strumey (Ed.), *Functional analysis in clinical treatment: Practical resources for mental health professional* (pp. 65–86). San Diego, CA: Elsevier Academic Press. doi:10.1016/B978-012372544-8/50005-7

Didden, R., Duker, P. C., & Korzilius, H. (1997). Meta-analytic study on treatment effectiveness for problem behaviors with individuals who have mental retardation. *American Journal of Mental Retardation*, *101*(4), 387–399. PMID:9017085

Didden, R., Korzilius, H., van Oorsouw, W., & Strumey, P. (2006). Behavioural treatment of challenging behaviours in individuals with mild mental retardation: Meta-analysis of single- subject research. *American Journal of Mental Retardation*, *111*(4), 290–298. doi:10.1352/0895-8017(2006)111[290:BTOCBI]2.0.CO;2 PMID:16792430

Didden, R., Scholte, R. H. J., Korzilius, H., De Moor, J. M. H., Vermeulen, A., O'Reilly, M., & Lancioni, G. E. et al. (2009). Cyberbullying among students with intellectual and developmental disability in special education settings. *Developmental Neurorehabilitation*, *12*(3), 146–151. doi:10.1080/17518420902971356 PMID:19466622

Diekema, D. (2003). Involuntary sterilization of persons with mental retardation: Ethical analysis. *Mental Retardation and Developmental Disabilities Research Reviews*, *9*(1), 21–26. doi:10.1002/mrdd.10053

Diez Roux, A. V. (2004). The Study of Group-Level Factors in Epidemiology: Rethinking Variables, Study Designs, and Analytical Approaches. *Epidemiologic Reviews*, *26*(1), 104–111. doi:10.1093/epirev/mxh006 PMID:15234951

Dillenburger, K. (2012). Why reinvent the wheel? A behaviour analyst's reflections on pedagogy for inclusion for students with intellectual and developmental disability. *Journal of Intellectual & Developmental Disability*, *37*(2), 169–180. doi:10.3109/13668250.2012.685705 PMID:22563693

Dinkes, R., Kemp, J., Baum, K., & Snyder, T. (2009). *Indicators of school crime and safety: 2009 (NCES 2010–012/NCJ 228478)*. Washington, DC: National Center for Education Statistics, Institute of Education Sciences, U.S. Department of Education, and Bureau of Justice Statistics, Office of Justice Programs, U.S. Department of Justice.

Disability Information. (2013). *Department of communities and social inclusion*. Government of South Australia.

Disabled Persons in India. (2002). *National sample survey 58th round: Ministry of statistics and programme implementation*. New Delhi: Govt. of India.

Dishion, T. J., & Stormshak, E. (2007). Intervening in children's lives: An ecological, family- centered approach to mental health care. Washington, DC: Academic Press.

Dols, M. W. (1987). Insanity and its treatment in Islamic society. *Medical History*, *31*(1), 1–14. doi:10.1017/S0025727300046287 PMID:3543559

Donelly, M., Hillman, A., Stancliffe, R. J., Knox, M., Whitaker, L., & Parmenter, T. (2010). The role of informal networks in providing effective work opportunities for people with intellectual disability. *Work (Reading, Mass.)*, *36*, 227–237. PMID:20634616

Donnellan, A. M., Mirenda, P. L., Mesaros, R., & Fassbender, L. (1984). Analyzing the communicative functions of aberrant behavior. *The Journal of the Association for Persons with Severe Handicaps*, *9*, 210–222.

Doornbos, M. M. (2002). Predicting family health in families of young adults with severe mental illness. *Journal of Family Nursing*, *8*(3), 241–263. doi:10.1177/107484070200800306

Doran, C. M., Einfeld, S. L., Madden, R. H., Otim, M., Horstead, S. K., Ellis, L. A., & Emerson, E. (2012). How much does intellectual disability really cost? First estimates for Australia. *Journal of Intellectual & Developmental Disability*, *37*(1), 42–49. doi:10.3109/13668250.2011.648609 PMID:22339044

Doren, B., Bullis, M., & Benz, M. R. (1996). Predictors of victimization: Experiences of adolescents with disabilities in transition. *Exceptional Children*, *63*, 7–18.

Dosen, A. (2007). Integrative treatment in persons with intellectual disability and mental health problems. *Journal of Intellectual Disability Research*, *51*(1), 66–74. doi:10.1111/j.1365-2788.2006.00868.x PMID:17181604

Doss, L. S., & Reichle, J. (1991). *Replacing excess behaviour with an initial communicative repertoire*. Baltimore, MD: Brooks Publishing Co.

Dowdney, L., & Skuse, D. (1993). Parenting provided by adults with mental retardation. *Journal of Child Psychology and Psychiatry, 34*, 5–47. doi:. 1993.tb00966.x10.1111/j.1469-7610

Duce, J., & Biersdoff, K. (2002).Supporting self-employment. Rehabilitation Review, 13(8).

Dudley, J. R., & Schatz, M. S. (1985). The missing link in evaluating sheltered workshop programs: The clients' input. *Mental Retardation*, *23*, 235–240. PMID:4069003

Dufrene, B. A., Doggett, R. A., Henington, C., & Watson, T. S. (2007). Functional assessment and intervention for disruptive classroom behaviors in preschool and head start classrooms. *Journal of Behavioral Education*, *16*(4), 368–388. doi:10.1007/s10864-007-9048-8

Dumont, M., & Beaulieu, C. (2007). Light exposure in the natural environment: Relevance to mood and sleep disorders. *Sleep Medicine*, *8*(6), 557–565. doi:10.1016/j.sleep.2006.11.008 PMID:17383230

Duncan, N. (1999). *Sexual bullying: Gender conflict and pupil culture in secondary schools*. New York, NY: Routledge.

Dunn, L. M., & Dunn, L. M. (1997). *PPVT-III: Peabody picture vocabulary test*. Circle Pines, MN: American Guidance Service.

Durand, V. M., & Carr, E. G. (1991). Functional communication training to reduce challenging behavior: Maintenance and application in new settings. *Journal of Applied Behavior Analysis*, *24*(2), 251–264. doi:10.1901/jaba.1991.24-251 PMID:1890046

Durand, V. M., & Crimmins, D. B. (1988). Identifying the variables maintaining self-injurious behavior. *Journal of Autism and Developmental Disorders*, *18*(1), 99–117. doi:10.1007/BF02211821 PMID:3372462

Dwyer, R. G., & Frierson, R. L. (2006). The presence of low IQ and mental retardation among murder defendants referred for pretrial evaluation. *Journal of Forensic Sciences*, *51*(3), 678–682. doi:10.1111/j.1556-4029.2006.00115.x PMID:16696721

Dyken, E. M. (2005). Happiness, well-being, and character strengths: Outcomes for families and siblings of persons with mental retardation. *American Association on Mental Retardation*, *43*, 360–364. PMID:16131234

Dyson, L. (2010). Unanticipated effects of children with learning disabilities on their families. *Learning Disability Quarterly*, *33*(1), 43–55. doi:10.1177/073194871003300104

Dyson, L. L. (1991). Families of young children with handicaps: Parental stress and family functioning. *American Journal of Mental Retardation*, *95*, 623–629. PMID:1829374

Dyson, L. L. (1997). Fathers and mothers of school-age children with developmental disabilities: Parental stress, family functioning, and social support. *American Journal of Mental Retardation, 102*(3), 267–279. doi:10.1352/0895-8017(1997)102<0267:FAMOSC>2.0.CO;2 PMID:9394135

Dyson, L. L. (1999). The psychosocial functioning of school-age children who have siblings with developmental disabilities: Change and stability over time. *Journal of Applied Developmental Psychology*, *20*(2), 253–271. doi:10.1016/S0193-3973(99)00016-7

Eakes, G. G. (1995). Chronic sorrow: The lived experience of parents of chronically mentally ill individuals. *Archives of Psychiatric Nursing*, *9*(2), 77–84. doi:10.1016/S0883-9417(95)80004-2 PMID:7755411

Eakes, G. G., Burke, M. L., & Hainsworth, M. A. (1998). Middle range theory of chronic sorrow. *Journal of Nursing Scholarship*, *30*(2), 179–184. doi:10.1111/j.1547-5069.1998.tb01276.x PMID:9775562

Eapen, V., & Jairam, R. (2009). Integration of child mental health services to primary care: challenges and opportunities. *Mental Health in Family Medicine, 6*(1), 43.

Eapen, V. (2014). Developmental and mental health disorders: Two sides of the same coin. *Asian Journal of Psychiatry*, *8*, 7–11. doi:10.1016/j.ajp.2013.10.007 PMID:24655619

Eapen, V., Al-Gazali, L. I., Bin-Othman, S., & Pramathan, T. (1998). Learning disorders in school-going children–detection and diagnosis. *Journal of Tropical Pediatrics*, *44*(4), 192–193. doi:10.1093/tropej/44.4.192 PMID:9718902

Edelstein, T. M., & Glenwick, D. S. (1977). Referral reasons for psychological services for adults with mental retardation. *Research in Developmental Disabilities*, *18*(1), 45–59. doi:10.1016/S0891-4222(96)00037-6 PMID:9085429

Edgerton, R. B. (1967). The cloak of competence: Stigma in the lives of the mentally retarded. Berkeley, CA: University of California Press.

Edwardraj, S., Mumtaj, K., Prasad, J. H., Kuruvilla, A., & Jacob, K. S. (2010). Perceptions about intellectual disability: A qualitative study from Vellore, South India. *Journal of Intellectual Disability Research*, *54*(8), 736–748. doi:10.1111/j.1365-2788.2010.01301.x PMID:20633202

Eheart, B. (1982). Mother-child interactions with non-retarded and mentally retarded preschoolers. *American Journal of Mental Deficiency*, *87*, 20–25. PMID:6181684

Einfeld, S. L., Ellis, L. A., & Emerson, E. (2011). Comorbidity of intellectual disability and mental disorder in children and adolescents: A systematic review. *Journal of Intellectual & Developmental Disability*, *36*(2), 137–143. doi:10.1080/13668250.2011.572548 PMID:21609299

Einfeld, S. L., Piccinin, A., Mackinnon, A., Hofer, S., Taffe, J., Gray, K., & Tonge, B. et al. (2006). Psychopathology in young people with intellectual disability. *Journal of the American Medical Association*, *296*(16), 1981–1989. doi:10.1001/jama.296.16.1981 PMID:17062861

Einfeld, S. L., & Tonge, B. (1999). Observations on the use of the ICD-10 Guide for Mental Retardation. *Journal of Intellectual Disability Research*, *43*(5), 408–412. doi:10.1046/j.1365-2788.1999.043005408.x PMID:10546965

Einfeld, S. L., & Tonge, B. J. (1996). Population prevalence of psychopathology in children and adolescents with intellectual disability: II epidemiological findings. *Journal of Intellectual Disability Research*, *40*(2), 99–109. doi:10.1111/j.1365-2788.1996.tb00611.x PMID:8731467

Einfeld, S. L., & Tonge, B. J. (1996a). Population prevalence of psychopathology in children and adolescents with intellectual disability: I rationale and methods. *Journal of Intellectual Disability Research*, *40*(2), 91–98. doi:10.1111/j.1365-2788.1996.tb00610.x PMID:8731466

Eisenberg, L. (1957). The fathers of autistic children. *The American Journal of Orthopsychiatry*, *27*(4), 715–724. doi:10.1111/j.1939-0025.1957.tb05539.x PMID:13470021

Eisenhower, A. S., Baker, B. L., & Blacher, J. (2007). Early student–teacher relationships of children with and without intellectual disability: Contributions of behavioral, social, and self-regulatory competence. *Journal of School Psychology*, *45*(4), 363–383. doi:10.1016/j.jsp.2006.10.002 PMID:21490876

Eisenhower, A., Blacher, J., & Baker, B. L. (2013). Mothers' perceived physical health during early and middle childhood: Relations with child developmental delay and behavior problems. *Research in Developmental Disabilities*, *34*(3), 1059–1068. doi:10.1016/j.ridd.2012.12.002 PMID:23306002

Elliott, S. N., & Gresham, F. M. (1993). Social skills interventions for children. *Behavior Modification*, *17*(3), 287–313. doi:10.1177/01454455930173004 PMID:8343100

Emerson, E., Malam, S., Spencer, I., & Spencer, K. (2005). *Adults With Learning Difficulties in England 2003/4. Full Report, Health and Social Care Information Centre.* Retrieved 4th April 2015, from http://www.lancs.ac.uk/staff/emersone/FASSWeb/Emerson 05_ALDE_Main.pdf

Emerson, E. (2001). *Challenging behaviour: Analysis and intervention in people with severe learning disabilities* (2nd ed.). Cambridge, New York: Cambridge University Press. doi:10.1017/CBO9780511543739

Emerson, E. (2003). Mothers of children and adolescents with intellectual disability: Social and economic situation, mental health status, and the self-assessed social and psychological impact of the child's difficulties. *Journal of Intellectual Disability Research*, *47*(4-5), 385–399. doi:10.1046/j.1365-2788.2003.00498.x PMID:12787168

Emerson, E. (2003). Prevalence of psychiatric disorders in children and adolescents with and without intellectual disability. *Journal of Intellectual Disability Research*, *47*(1), 51–58. doi:10.1046/j.1365-2788.2003.00464.x PMID:12558695

Emerson, E. (2004). Poverty and children with intellectual disabilities in the world's richer countries. *Journal of Intellectual & Developmental Disability*, *29*(4), 319–337. doi:10.1080/13668250400014491

Emerson, E. (2007). Poverty and people with intellectual disabilities. *Mental Retardation and Developmental Disabilities Research Reviews*, *13*(2), 107–113. doi:10.1002/mrdd.20144 PMID:17563898

Emerson, E. (2010). Self-reported exposure to disablism is associated with poorer self-reported health and well-being among adults with intellectual disabilities in England: A cross-sectional survey. *Public Health*, *124*(12), 682–689. doi:10.1016/j.puhe.2010.08.020 PMID:21035153

Emerson, E. (2012). Deprivation, ethnicity and the prevalence of intellectual and developmental disabilities. *Journal of Epidemiology and Community Health*, *66*(3), 218–224. doi:10.1136/jech.2010.111773 PMID:20889590

Emerson, E., Blacher, J., Einfeld, S., Hatton, C., Robertson, J., & Stancliffe, R. J. (2014). Environmental risk factors associated with the persistence of conduct difficulties in children with intellectual disabilities and autistic spectrum disorders. *Research in Developmental Disabilities*, *35*(12), 3508–3517. doi:10.1016/j.ridd.2014.08.039 PMID:25238636

Emerson, E., & Einfeld, S. (2011). *Challenging Behaviour*. Cambridge: Cambridge University Press. doi:10.1017/CBO9780511861178

Emerson, E., & Hatton, C. (2007). The socio-economic circumstances of children at risk of disability in Britain. *Disability & Society*, *22*(6), 563–580. doi:10.1080/09687590701560154

Emerson, E., & Hatton, C. (2007a). Contribution of socioeconomic position to health inequalities of British children and adolescents with intellectual disabilities. *Journal Information*, *112*(2). PMID:17295554

Emerson, E., & Hatton, C. (2007b). Mental health of children and adolescents with intellectual disabilities in Britain. *The British Journal of Psychiatry*, *191*(6), 493–499. doi:10.1192/bjp.bp.107.038729 PMID:18055952

Emerson, E., & Hatton, C. (2008). Poverty, socio-economic position, social capital and the health children with intellectual disability. *Journal of Intellectual Disability Research.*

Emerson, E., Kiernan, C., Alborz, A., Reeves, D., Mason, L., Mason, H., & Hatton, C. (2001). The prevalence of challenging behaviors: A total population study. *Research in Developmental Disabilities*, *22*(1), 77–93. doi:10.1016/S0891-4222(00)00061-5 PMID:11263632

Employment of Persons with Disabilities in Public Sectors in India -Emerging Issues and Trends. (1995). *An Evaluation Study with Special Reference to Persons with Disabilities Act.* Commissioned by Planning Commission, Government of India.

Ericson, N. (2001). *Addressing the problem of juvenile bullying.* Washington, DC: U.S. Government Printing Office. doi:10.1037/e317892004-001

Esbensen, A. J. (2011). Families of individuals with intellectual disability and comorbid mental health problems. *Journal of Mental Health Research in Intellectual Disabilities*, *4*(3), 140–157. doi:10.1080/19315864.2011.597018

Espelage, D. L., Low, S. K., & Jimerson, S. R. (2014). Understanding school climate, aggression, peer victimization, and bully perpetration: Contemporary science, practice, and policy. *School Psychology Quarterly*, *29*(3), 233–237. doi:10.1037/spq0000090 PMID:25198615

Espelage, D. L., & Swearer, S. M. (2003). Research on school bullying and victimization: What have we learned and where do we go from here? *School Psychology Review*, *32*, 365–383.

Essex, E., Seltzer, M., & Krauss, M. (1999). Differences in coping effectiveness and well-being among aging Mothers and Fathers of Adults with Mental Retardation. *American Journal of Mental Retardation*, *104*(6), 545–563. doi:10.1352/0895-8017(1999)104<0545:DICEAW>2.0.CO;2 PMID:10587735

Estell, D. B., Farmer, T. W., Irvin, M. J., Crowther, A., Akos, P., & Boudah, D. J. (2009). Students with exceptionalities and the peer group context of bullying and victimization in late elementary school. *Journal of Child and Family Studies*, *18*(2), 136–150. doi:10.1007/s10826-008-9214-1

European Agency for Development in Special Needs Education. (2011). *Mapping the implementation of policy for inclusive education - An exploration of challenges and opportunities for developing indicators.* Retrieved from http://www.european-agency.org/publications/flyers/mipie/MIPIE-summary-of-proposalsEN.pdf/view

Evans, D. R. (1994). Enhancing quality of life in the population at large. *Social Indicators Research*, *33*(1-3), 47–88. doi:10.1007/BF01078958

Everington, C., & Fulero, S. M. (1999). Competence to confess: Measuring understanding and suggestibility of defendants with mental retardation. *Mental Retardation*, *37*(3), 212–220. doi:10.1352/0047-6765(1999)037<0212:CTCMUA>2.0.CO;2 PMID:10473340

Eyberg, S. M., Boggs, S. R., & Algina, J. (1995). Parent–child interaction therapy: A psychosocial model for the treatment of young children with conduct problem behavior and their families. *Psychopharmacology Bulletin*, *31*(1), 83–91. PMID:7675994

Fabian, E. S. (1991). Using quality-of-life indicators in rehabilitation program evaluation. *Rehabilitation Counseling Bulletin*, *34*(4), 344–356.

Fabrega, H. Jr. (1991). Psychiatric stigma in non-Western societies. *Comprehensive Psychiatry*, *32*(6), 534–551. doi:10.1016/0010-440X(91)90033-9 PMID:1778081

Fairthorne, J., Jacoby, P., Bourke, J., de Klerk, N., & Leonard, H. (2015). Onset of maternal psychiatric disorders after the birth of a child with intellectual disability: A retrospective cohort study. *Journal of Psychiatric Research*, *61*, 223–230. doi:10.1016/j.jpsychires.2014.11.011 PMID:25499469

Farber, B., & Kirk, S. A. (1959). Effects of a severely retarded child on family integration. *Monographs of the Society for Research in Child Development*, *24*(2), 1–112. doi:10.2307/1165597

Farmer, T. W., Irvin, M. J., Motoca, L. M., Leung, M., Hutchins, B. C., Brooks, D. S., & Hall, C. M. (2015). Externalizing and internalizing behavior problems, peer affiliations, and bullying involvement across the transition to middle school. *Journal of Emotional and Behavioral Disorders*, *23*(1), 3–16. doi:10.1177/1063426613491286

Farmer, T. W., Petrin, R., Brooks, D. S., Hamm, J. V., Lambert, K., & Gravelle, M. (2012). Bullying involvement and the school adjustment of rural students with and without disabilities. *Journal of Emotional and Behavioral Disorders*, *20*(1), 19–37. doi:10.1177/1063426610392039

Faureholm, J. (2010). Children and their life experiences. In G. Llewellyn, R. Traustadóttir, D. McConnell, & H. B. Sigurjónsdóttir (Eds.), *Parents with intellectual disabilities: Past, present and futures* (pp. 63–78). West Sussex, UK: Wiley-Blackwell; doi:10.1002/9780470660393.ch4

Faux, S. A. (1993). Siblings of children with chronic physical and cognitive disabilities. *Journal of Pediatric Nursing*, *8*, 305–317. Retrieved from http://www.sciencedirect.com.ezproxy.lib.rmit.edu.au/science/journal/08825963 PMID:8271152

Fazel, S., Xenitidis, K., & Powell, J. (2008). The prevalence of intellectual disabilities among 12000 prisoners - A systematic review. *International Journal of Law and Psychiatry*, *31*(4), 369–373. doi:10.1016/j.ijlp.2008.06.001 PMID:18644624

Feeley, K., & Jones, E. (2006). Addressing challenging behaviour in children with Down syndrome: The use of applied behaviour analysis for assessment and intervention. *Down's Syndrome: Research and Practice*, *11*(2), 64–77. doi:10.3104/perspectives.316 PMID:17048800

Feil, N. (1993). *The validation breakthrough*. Sydney: McLennan & Petty.

Felce, D., & Perry, J. (1996). Exploring current conceptions of quality of life. In R. Renwick, I. Brown, & M. Nagler (Eds.), *Quality of life in health promotion and rehabilitation: Conceptual approaches, issues, and applications* (pp. 51–62). Thousand Oaks, CA: Sage Publications.

Feldman, M. A. (2002). Children of parents with intellectual disabilities. In R. J. McMahon & R. DeV. Peters. (Eds.), The effects of parental dysfunction on children (pp. 205–223). New York, NY: Kluwer Academic/Plenum. doi:10.1007/978-1-4615-1739-9_10

Feldman, M. (1994). Parenting education for parents with intellectual disabilities: A review of outcome studies. *Research in Developmental Disabilities*, *15*(4), 299–332. doi:10.1016/0891-4222(94)90009-4 PMID:7972968

Feldman, M. A. (1986). Research of parenting by mentally retarded persons. *The Psychiatric Clinics of North America*, *9*, 777–796. PMID:3543895

Feldman, M. A., Gase, L., Towns, F., & Betel, J. (1985). Parent education project I: Development and nurturance of children of mentally retarded parents. *American Journal of Mental Deficiency*, *90*, 253–258. PMID:2417482

Feldman, M. A., & Werner, S. E. (2002). Collateral effects of behavioral parent training on families of children with developmental disabilities and behavior disorders. *Behavioral Interventions*, *17*(2), 75–83. doi:10.1002/bin.111

Feldman, M., Case, L., Rincover, A., Towns, F., & Betel, J. (1989). Parent education project. III: Increasing affection and responsivity in developmentally handicapped mothers: component analysis, generalization, and effects on child language. *Journal of Applied Behavior Analysis*, *22*(2), 211–222. doi:10.1901/jaba.1989.22-211 PMID:2745240

Feldman, M., Sparks, B., & Case, L. (1993). Effectiveness of home-based early intervention on the language development of children of mothers with mental retardation. *Research in Developmental Disabilities*, *14*(5), 387–408. doi:10.1016/0891-4222(93)90010-H PMID:8234958

Feldman, M., Towns, F., Betel, J., Case, L., Rincover, A., & Rubino, C. (1986). Parent education project II. Increasing stimulating interactions of developmentally handicapped mothers. *Journal of Applied Behavior Analysis*, *19*(1), 23–37. doi:10.1901/jaba.1986.19-23 PMID:3710945

Feldman, M., Varhese, J., Ramsay, J., & Rajska, D. (2002). Relationships between social support, stress and mother–child interactions in mothers with intellectual disabilities. *Journal of Applied Research in Intellectual Disabilities*, *15*(4), 314–323. doi:10.1046/j.1468-3148.2002.00132.x

Feldman, M., & Walton-Allen, N. (1997). Effects of maternal mental retardation and poverty on intellectual, academic and behavioural status of school-age children. *American Journal of Mental Retardation*, *101*, 352–364. PMID:9017082

Feniger-Schaal, R., & Oppenheim, D. (2013). Resolution of the diagnosis and maternal sensitivity among mothers of children with Intellectual Disability. *Research in Developmental Disabilities*, *34*(1), 306–313. doi:10.1016/j.ridd.2012.08.007 PMID:22983017

Fenning, R. M., Baker, J. K., & Bruce, L. et al.. (2014). Parent-child interaction over time in families of young children with borderline intellectual functioning. *Journal of Family Psychology*, *28*(3), 326–335. doi:10.1037/a0036537 PMID:24707801

Fenson, L., Dale, P., Reznick, S., Thal, D., Bates, E., Hartung, J., & Reilly, J. et al. (1993). *McArthur Communication Inventories*. San Diego, CA: Singular Publishing.

Ferraioli, S. J., & Harris, S. L. (2010). The impact of autism on siblings. *Social Work in Mental Health*, *8*(1), 41–53. doi:10.1080/15332980902932409

Fetko, K. S., Schuster, J. W., Harley, D. A., & Collins, B. C. (1999). Using simultaneous prompting to teach a chained vocational task to young adults with severe intellectual disabilities. *Education and Training in Mental Retardation and Developmental Disabilities*, 318–329.

Fey, M. E. (1986). *Language intervention with young children*. San Diego, CA: College-Hill.

Fey, M. E. (1988). Generalisation issues facing language interventionists: An introduction. *Language, Speech, and Hearing Services in Schools*, *19*(3), 272–281. doi:10.1044/0161-1461.1903.272

Fiese, B., Tomcho, T., Douglas, M., Josephs, K., Poltrock, S., & Baker, T. (2002). A review of 50 years of research on naturally occurring family routines and rituals: Cause for celebration? *Journal of Family Psychology*, *16*(4), 381–390. doi:10.1037/0893-3200.16.4.381 PMID:12561283

Finch-Williams, A. (1984). The developmental relationship between cognition and communication: Implications for assessment. *Topics in Language Disorders*, *5*(1), 1–13. doi:10.1097/00011363-198412000-00005

Findler, L. (2014, February). The Experience of Stress and Personal Growth Among Grandparents of Children With and Without Intellectual Disability. *Intellectual and Developmental Disabilities*, *52*(1), 32–48. doi:10.1352/1934-9556-52.1.32 PMID:24635690

Findler, L., Vardi, A., & Taylor, S. J. (2009, February). Psychological Growth Among Siblings of Children With and Without Intellectual Disabilities. *Intellectual and Developmental Disabilities*, *47*(1), 1–12. doi:10.1352/2009.47:1-12 PMID:19170414

Fisher, C., Cea, C., Davidson, P., & Fried, A. (2006). Capacity of persons with mental retardation to consent to participate in randomized clinical trials. *The American Journal of Psychiatry*, *163*(10), 1813–1820. doi:10.1176/ajp.2006.163.10.1813 PMID:17012694

Fisher, W. W., Adelinis, J. D., Thompson, R. H., Worsdell, A. S., & Zarcone, J. R. (1998). Functional analysis and treatment of destructive behavior maintained by termination of "don't" (and symmetrical "do") requests. *Journal of Applied Behavior Analysis*, *31*(3), 339–356. doi:10.1901/jaba.1998.31-339 PMID:9757579

Fisher, W. W., Kuhn, D. E., & Thompson, R. H. (1998). Establishing discriminative control of responding using functional and alternative reinforcers during functional communication training. *Journal of Applied Behavior Analysis*, *31*(4), 543–560. doi:10.1901/jaba.1998.31-543 PMID:9891393

Fisman, S., Wolf, L., Ellison, D., & Freeman, T. (2000). A longitudinal study of children with chronic disabilities. *Canadian Journal of Psychiatry*, *45*, 369–375. PMID:10813071

Flander, G. B., Stimac, D., Bagaric, E. S., & Vinscak, M. (2014). Patterns of and copying with cyberbullying in Croatia. *The International Journal of Person Centered Medicine.*

Fletcher-Janzen, E., & Reynolds, C. R. (2007). Encyclopedia of Special Education (3rd ed.; Vol. 1). Academic Press.

Flores, M., Musgrove, K., Renner, S., Hinton, V., Strozier, S., Franklin, S., & Hil, D. (2012). A comparison of communication using the Apple iPad and a picture-based system. *Augmentative and Alternative Communication*, *28*(2), 74–84. doi:10.3109/07434618.2011.644579 PMID:22263895

Floyd, F. J., & Gallagher, E. M. (1997). Parental stress, care demands, and use of support services for school-age children with disabilities and behavior problems. *Family Relations*, *46*(4), 359–371. doi:10.2307/585096

Floyd, F. J., Greenberg, J. S., Hong, J., Pettee, Y., & Seltzer, M. M. (2001). Life course impacts of parenting a child with a disability. *American Journal of Mental Retardation*, *106*(3), 265–286. doi:10.1352/0895-8017(2001)106<0265:LCIOPA>2.0.CO;2 PMID:11389667

Floyd, F. J., & Phillippe, K. A. (1993). Parental interactions with children with and without mental retardation: Behavior management, coerciveness, and positive exchange. *American Journal of Mental Retardation*, *97*, 673–684. PMID:7686014

Floyd, F. J., & Zmich, D. E. (1991). Marriage and the parenting partnership: Perceptions and interactions of parents with mentally retarded and typically developing children. *Child Development*, *62*(6), 1434–1448. doi:10.2307/1130817 PMID:1786726

Flynt, S. W., & Morton, R. C. (2007). Bullying prevention and students with disabilities. *National Forum of Special Education Journal, 19*(1), 1-6.

Forlin, C., Loreman, T., Sharma, U., & Earle, C. (2009). Demographic differences in changing pre-service teachers' attitudes, sentiments and concerns about inclusive education. *International Journal of Inclusive Education*, *13*(2), 195–209. doi:10.1080/13603110701365356

Fowler, A. E. (1990). Language abilities in children with Down syndrome: Evidence for a specific syntactic delay. In D. Cicchetti & M. Beeghley (Eds.), *Children with Down Syndrome: Developmental perspective* (pp. 302–328). Cambridge, UK: Cambridge University Press. doi:10.1017/CBO9780511581786.010

Fox, C. L. (1989). Peer acceptance of learning disabled children in the regular classroom. *Exceptional Children*, *56*(1), 50–59.

Franklin, K. S. (1991). Supposed employment and assistive technology-a powerful partnership. In L. Griffin & W. G. Revell (Eds.), *Rehabilitation counselor desktop guide supported employment*. Richmond, VA: Virginia Commonwealth University, Rehabilitation Research and Training Center on Supported Employment.

Frey, G. C., & Temple, V. A. (2008). Health promotions for Latin Americans with intellectual disabilities. *Salud Pública de México*, *2*, 167–177. doi:10.1590/S0036-36342008000800010 PMID:18470345

Friedman, D., Holmbeck, G. N., Jandasek, B., Zukerman, J., & Abad, M. (2004). Parent functioning in families of preadolescents with spina bifida: Longitudinal implications for child adjustment. *Journal of Family Psychology*, *18*(4), 609–619. doi:10.1037/0893-3200.18.4.609 PMID:15598166

Fudala, J. B., & Reynolds, W. M. (2000). *Arizona Articulation Proficiency Scale*. Los Angeles, CA: Western Psychological Services.

Fulcher, G. (1989). Disability: A social construction. In G. Lupton & J. Najman (Eds.), *Sociology of health and illness: Australian readings*. Melbourne: Macmillan.

Fulero, S. M., & Everington, C. (1995). Assessing competency to waive Miranda rights in defendants with mental retardation. *Law and Human Behavior*, *19*(5), 533–543. doi:10.1007/BF01499342

Fuller, T.E. (1997). Deinstitutionalization: A Psychiatric "Titanic". In *Out of the Shadows: Confronting America's Mental Illness Crisis*. John Wiley & Sons.

Gabel, S. (2004). South Asian Indian cultural orientations toward mental retardation. *Journal Information*, *42*(1), 12–25. PMID:14720098

Galil, A., Bachner, Y. G., Merrick, J., Flusser, H., Lubetzky, H., Heiman, N., & Carmel, S. (2006). Physician-parent communication as predictor of parent satisfaction with child development services. *Research in Developmental Disabilities*, *27*(3), 233–242. doi:10.1016/j.ridd.2005.03.004 PMID:15998579

Gallagher, S., & Hannigan, A. (2014). Depression and chronic health conditions in parents of children with and without developmental disabilities: The growing up in Ireland cohort study. *Research in Developmental Disabilities*, *35*(2), 448–454. doi:10.1016/j.ridd.2013.11.029 PMID:24361813

Gallagher, S., Phillips, A. C., Oliver, C., & Carroll, D. (2008). Predictors of psychological morbidity in parents of children with intellectual disabilities. *Journal of Pediatric Psychology*, *33*(10), 1129–1136. doi:10.1093/jpepsy/jsn040 PMID:18430761

Gallo, A. M., Breitmayer, B. J., Knafl, K. A., & Zoeller, L. H. (1993). Mothers' perceptions of sibling adjustment and family life in childhood chronic illness. *Journal of Pediatric Nursing*, *8*, 318–324. PMID:8271153

Gamble, W. C., & McHale, S. M. (1989). Coping with stress in sibling relationships: A. comparison of children with disabled and nondisabled siblings. *Journal of Applied Developmental Psychology*, *10*(3), 353–373. doi:10.1016/0193-3973(89)90035-X

Garber, H. (1988). *The Milwaukee project: Preventing mental retardation in children at risk*. Washington, DC: American Association on Mental Retardation.

Garber, H. L., & Hodge, J. D. (1989). Risk for deceleration in the rate of mental development. *Developmental Review*, *9*(3), 259–300. doi:10.1016/0273-2297(89)90031-2

Gath, A., & Gumley, D. (1987). Retarded children and their siblings. *Journal of Child Psychology and Psychiatry, and Allied Disciplines*, *28*(5), 715–730. doi:10.1111/j.1469-7610.1987.tb01554.x PMID:2959672

Gathercole, S. E., & Baddeley, A. D. (1993). *Working memory and language*. Hillsdale, NJ: Erlbaum Associates.

Gavidia-Payne, S., Richdale, A., Francis, A., & Cotton, S. (1997). *The Parenting Hassles Scale: Measuring stress in parents of children with disabilities*. Paper presented at the 121st Annual Meeting of the American Association on Mental Retardation, New York.

Gavidia-Payne, S., & Hudson, A. (2002). Behavioural supports for parents of children with an intellectual disability and problem behaviours: An overview of the literature. *Journal of Intellectual & Developmental Disability*, *27*(1), 31–55. doi:10.1080/13668250120119626

Gavidia-Payne, S., & Stoneman, Z. (2006). Marital adjustment in families of young children with disabilities: Associations with daily hassles and problem-focused coping. *American Journal of Mental Retardation*, *111*(1), 1–14. doi:10.1352/0895-8017(2006)111[1:MAIFOY]2.0.CO;2 PMID:16332152

Geffken, G. R., Morgan, S. B., & Rodrigue, J. R. (1992). Psychosocial adaptation of fathers of children with autism, down syndrome and normal development. *Journal of Autism and Developmental Disorders*, *22*(2), 249–263. doi:10.1007/BF01058154 PMID:1385591

Genesee, F., Paradis, J., & Crago, M. B. (2004). *Dual language development and disorders: A handbook on bilingualism and second language learners*. Baltimore, MD: Brookes Publishing Co.

Genesi, D. (2000). *Disability Discrimination against students in the classroom*. Retrieved from http://www.cedarville.edu/academics/education/classes/edsp202/examples/literature_review_genesi.htm

Geng-qing, C., & Qu, H. (2003). Integrating persons with disabilities into the workforce: A study on employment of people with disabilities in foodservice industry. *International Journal of Hospitality & Tourism Administration*, *4*, 59–83. doi:10.1300/J149v04n04_04

Gerstein, E. D., Crnic, K. A., Blacher, J., & Baker, B. L. (2009). Resilience and the course of daily parenting stress in families of young children with intellectual disabilities. *Journal of Intellectual Disability Research*, *53*(12), 981–997. doi:10.1111/j.1365-2788.2009.01220.x PMID:19874449

Ghai, A. (2002). Disabled Women: An excluded agenda of Indian feminism. *Hypatia*, *17*(3), 49–66. doi:10.1111/j.1527-2001.2002.tb00941.x

Giallo, R., & Gavidia-Payne, S. (2006). Child, parent and family factors as predictors of adjustment for siblings of children with a disability. *Journal of Intellectual Disability Research*, *50*(12), 937–948. doi:10.1111/j.1365-2788.2006.00928.x PMID:17100954

Giannouli, V. (2014). What do Greeks believe about elders and mental? *Agora International Journal of Juridical Sciences*, *8*(3), 1–5.

Giannouli, V., & Tsolaki, M. (2011). Competency and dementia: A challenge of today. [in Greek]. *Neurology*, *20*(6), 12–19.

Giannouli, V., & Tsolaki, M. (2015). A neglected drama for elders: Discrepancy between self-perception and objective performance regarding financial capacity in patients with cognitive deficits. *Psychological Thought*, *8*(2), 142–147. doi:10.5964/psyct.v8i2.130

Gillberg, C., & Geijer-Karlsson, M. (1983). Children born to mentally retarded women: A 1–21-year follow-up study of 41 cases. *Psychological Medicine*, *13*(04), 891. doi:10.1017/S003329170005162X PMID:6665104

Girimaji, S., Zahman, S., Wijetunja, P. M., Pejarasangharn, U., & Nagpal, J. (2001). *Mental Retardation: From Knowledge to Action*. Retrieved June 24, 2005 from http://whqlibdoc.who.int/searo/2001/SEA_Ment_119.pdf

Girolametto, L., Weitzman, E., & Clements-Baartman, J. (1998). Vocabulary intervention for children with Down syndrome: Parent training using focused stimulation. *Infant-Toddler Intervention: the Transdisciplinary Journal*, *8*(2), 109–125.

Glaser, W., & Deane, K. (1999). Normalisation in an abnormal world: A study of prisoners with an intellectual disability. *International Journal of Offender Therapy and Comparative Criminology*, *43*(3), 338–356. doi:10.1177/0306624X99433007

Glaun, D. E., & Brown, P. F. (1999). Motherhood, intellectual disability and child protection: Characteristics of a court sample. *Journal of Intellectual & Developmental Disability*, *24*(1), 95–105. doi:10.1080/13668259900033901

Gleeson, B. (1995). Disability: A state of mind? *The Australian Journal of Social Issues*, *30*(1), 10–23.

Glumbic, N., Kaljaca, S., & Brojcin, B. (2004). The attitude of future special educators towards inclusive education of children with mild intellectual disability. *Journal of Intellectual Disability Research*, *48*, 505–505.

Glumbic, N., & Zunic-Pavlovic, V. (2010). Bullying behavior in children with intellectual disability. *Procedia: Social and Behavioral Sciences*, *2*(2), 2784–2788. doi:10.1016/j.sbspro.2010.03.415

Goddard, H. H. (1912). *The Kallikak family: A study in the heredity of feeble-mindedness*. New York: Macmillan. doi:10.1037/10949-000

Gohel, Mukherjee, & Choudhary. (2011). *Psychosocial impact on the Parents of mentally retarded children in Anand District*. Indian Association of Preventive and Social Medicine.

Gohel, M., Mukherjee, S., & Choudhary, S. K. (2011). Psychosocial impact on the parents of mentally retarded children in Anand District. *Healthline*, *2*(2), 62–66.

Gold, M. W. (1975). Vocational training. In J. Wortis (Ed.), Mental retardation and developmental disabilities. An annual review (Vol. 7, pp. 254–264). Academic Press.

Gold, M. W. (1972). stimulus factors in skill training of retarded adolescents on a complex assembly task: Acquisition, transfer, and relation. *American Journal of Mental Deficiency*, *76*, 517–526.

Gold, M. W. (1972). Stimulus factors in skill training of the retarded on a complex assembly task: Acquisition, transfer and retention. *American Journal of Mental Deficiency*, *76*, 517–526. PMID:5012132

Gold, N. (1993). Depression and social adjustment in siblings of boys with autism. *Journal of Autism and Developmental Disorders*, *23*(1), 147–163. doi:10.1007/BF01066424 PMID:8463194

Goldsmith, T. R., & LeBlanc, L. A. (2004). Use of technology in interventions for children with autism. *Journal of Early and Intensive Behavior Intervention*, *1*(2), 166–178. doi:10.1037/h0100287

Goldstein, H., & Ferrell, D. (1987). Augmenting communicative interaction between handicapped and nonhandicapped preschool children. *The Journal of Speech and Hearing Disorders*, *52*(3), 200–211. doi:10.1044/jshd.5203.200 PMID:3455442

Goode, D. A. (1994). *A world without words: The social construction of children born deaf and blind*. Philadelphia, PA: Temple University Press.

Goode, D. A., & Hogg, J. (1994). Towards an understanding of holistic quality of life in people with profound intellectual and multiple disabilities. In D. Goode (Ed.), *Quality of life for persons with disabilities: International perspectives and issues* (pp. 197–207). Cambridge, MA: Brookline Books.

Gopalan, R. T., Sharma, R., & Unnikrishnan, M. P. (2014). Socio-Demographic and Clinical Features of Children with Intellectual Disability and Their Parents-an Indian Study. *International Neuropsychiatric Disease Journal*, *2*(6), 289–302. doi:10.9734/INDJ/2014/10610

Gordon, B. O., & Rosenblum, K. E. (2001). Bringing Disability into the Sociological Frame: A comparison of disability with race, sex, and sexual orientation statuses. *Disability & Society*, *16*(1), 23–44.

Gostason, R. (1985). Psychiatric illness among the mentally retarded. *Acta Psychiatrica Scandinavica*, *318*(suppl 71), 1–117. doi:10.1111/j.1600-0447.1985.tb10511.x PMID:3893045

Goudie, A., Narcisse, M. R., Hall, D. E., & Kuo, D. Z. (2014). Financial and psychological stressors associated with caring for children with disability. *Families, Systems & Health*, *32*(3), 280–290. doi:10.1037/fsh0000027 PMID:24707826

Govender, N., (2002). *Attitudes of Parents towards their Mentally Retarded Children: A Rural area Examination*. Academic Press.

Grace, N. C., Thompson, R., & Fisher, W. W. (1996). The treatment of covert self-injury through contingencies on response products. *Journal of Applied Behavior Analysis*, *29*(2), 239–242. doi:10.1901/jaba.1996.29-239 PMID:8682739

Graham, S., Bellmore, A. D., & Mize, J. (2006). Peer victimization, aggression, and their co-occurrence in middle school: Pathways to adjustment problems. *Journal of Abnormal Child Psychology*, *34*(3), 363–378. doi:10.1007/s10802-006-9030-2 PMID:16648999

Granic, I., & Patterson, G. R. (2006). Toward a comprehensive model of antisocial development: A dynamic systems approach. *Psychological Review*, *113*(1), 101–131. doi:10.1037/0033-295X.113.1.101 PMID:16478303

Grant, J., Karmiloff-Smidh, A., Gathercole, S. E., Paterson, S., Howlin, P., Davies, M., & Udwin, O. (1997). Phonological short-term memory and its relationship to language in Williams syndrome. *Cognitive Neuropsychiatry*, *2*(2), 81–99. doi:10.1080/135468097396342 PMID:25420198

Graves, T. B., Collins, B. C., Schuster, J. W., & Kleinert, H. (2005). Using video prompting to teach cooking skills to secondary students with moderate disabilities. *Education and Training in Developmental Disabilities*, *40*, 34–46.

Gray, K. M., Piccinin, A. M., Hofer, S. M., Mackinnon, A., Bontempo, D. E., Einfeld, S. L., & Tonge, B. J. et al. (2011). The longitudinal relationship between behavior and emotional disturbance in young people with intellectual disability and maternal mental health. *Research in Developmental Disabilities*, *32*(3), 1194–1204. doi:10.1016/j.ridd.2010.12.044 PMID:21295442

Grayson, J. (Ed.). (2000). *Parents with mental retardation* (Vol. 57). Virginia Child Protection Newsletter.

Grebler, A. M. (1952). Parental attitudes towards mentally retarded children. *American Journal of Mental Deficiency*, *56*, 475–483. PMID:14902885

Greef, A. P., & van der Walt, K. J. (2010). Resilience in families with an autistic child. *Education and Training in Autism and Developmental Disabilities*, *45*(3), 347–355.

Green, S., & Bake, B. (2011). Parents emotion expression as a predictor of child's social competence: Children with or without intellectual disability. *Journal of Intellectual Disability Research*, *55*(3), 324–338. doi:10.1111/j.1365-2788.2010.01363.x

Greenwald, C., & Leonard, L. (1979). Communicative and sensorimotor development of Down's syndrome children. *American Journal of Mental Deficiency*, *84*, 296–303. PMID:160755

Greve, B. (2009). *The labour market situation of disabled people in European countries and implementation of employment policies: A summary of evidence from country reports and research studies. Report prepared for the Academic Network of European Disability Experts (ANED)*. University of Leeds.

Griffin, C. C., Hammis, D., & Geary, T. (2007). *The job developer's handbook.Practical tactics for customized employment*. Baltimore, MD: Paul H. Brookes.

Griffith, G. M., & Hastings, R. P. (2014, September). Hastings RP. 'He's hard work, but he's worth it'. The experience of caregivers of individuals with intellectual disabilities and challenging behaviour: A meta-synthesis of qualitative research. *Journal of Applied Research in Intellectual Disabilities*, *27*(5), 401–419. doi:10.1111/jar.12073 PMID:24105755

Grigal, M., Hart, D., & Migliore, A. (2011). Comparing transition planning, postsecondary education, and employment outcomes of students with intellectual and other disabilities. *Career Development for Exceptional Individuals*.

Grissom, M. O., & Borkowski, J. G. (2002). Self-efficacy in adolescents who have siblings with or without disabilities. *American Journal of Mental Retardation*, *107*(2), 79–90. doi:10.1352/0895-8017(2002)107<0079:SEIAWH>2.0.CO;2 PMID:11853525

Groce, N., Gazizova, D., & Hassiotis, P. (2014). Forced Marriage among Persons with Intellectual Disability. *Journal of Intellectual Disabilities*.

Gudjonsson, G. H., & Henry, L. (2003). Child and adult witnesses with intellectual disability: The importance of suggestibility. *Legal and Criminological Psychology*, *8*(2), 241–252. doi:10.1348/135532503322363013

Gudjonsson, G. H., Murphy, G. H., & Clare, I. C. H. (2000). Assessing the capacity of people with intellectual disabilities to be witnesses in court. *Psychological Medicine*, *30*(2), 307–314. doi:10.1017/S003329179900149X PMID:10824651

Gupta, A., & Singhal, N. (2004). Positive Perceptions in Parents of Children with Disabilities. *Asia Pacific Disability Rehabilitation Journal*, *15*(1). Retrieved from http://english.aifo.it/disability/apdrj/apdrj104/positive-perceptions.pdf

Gupta, R.K., & Harpreet, K. (2010). Stress among parents of children with intellectual disability. *Asia Pacific Disability Rehabilitation Journal,* 21.

Gupta, V.B., Mehrotra, P. &Mehrotra, N (2012). *Parental Stress in Raising a Child with Disabilities in India*. Academic Press.

Guralnick, M. J. (1997). Effectiveness of early intervention for vulnerable children: A developmental perspective. *American Journal of Mental Retardation*, *102*(4), 319–345. doi:10.1352/0895-8017(1998)102<0319:EOEIFV>2.0.CO;2 PMID:9475942

Guralnick, M. J. (2004). Family investments in response to the developmental challenges of young children with disabilities. In A. Kalil & T. Deleire (Eds.), *Family investments in children's potential: Resources and parenting behaviors that promote success* (pp. 119–137). Mahwah, NJ: Lawrence Erlbaum.

Guralnick, M. J., Hammond, M. A., Connor, R. T., & Neville, B. (2006). Stability, change, and correlates of the peer relationships of young children with mild developmental delays. *Child Development*, *77*(2), 312–324. doi:10.1111/j.1467-8624.2006.00872.x PMID:16611174

Guralnick, N. J., & Paul-Brown, D. (1986). Communicative interactions of mildly delayed and normally developing preschool children: Effects of listener's developmental level. *Journal of Speech and Hearing Research*, *29*(1), 2–10. doi:10.1044/jshr.2901.02 PMID:3702375

Gustiatas, R., & Young, E. W. D. (1986). *A time to be born, a time to die: Conflicts and ethics in an intensive care nursery*. Reading, MA: Addison-Wesley.

Hackman, D. A., Farah, M. J., & Meaney, M. J. (2010). Socioeconomic status and the brain: Mechanistic insights from human and animal research. *Nature Reviews. Neuroscience*, *11*(9), 651–659. doi:10.1038/nrn2897 PMID:20725096

Hagopian, L. P., Wilson, D. M., & Wilder, D. A. (2001). Assessment and treatment of problem behavior maintained by escape from attention and access to tangible items. *Journal of Applied Behavior Analysis*, *34*(2), 229–232. doi:10.1901/jaba.2001.34-229 PMID:11421317

Hagopian, L., Fisher, W., Sullivan, M., Acquisto, J., & LeBlanc, L. (1998). Effectiveness of functional communication training with and without extinction and punishment: A summary of 21 inpatient cases. *Journal of Applied Behavior Analysis*, *30*, 229–237. PMID:9652101

Haley, W., & Perkins, E. (2004). Current status and future directions in family caregiving and aging people with intellectual disabilities. *Journal of Policy and Practice in Intellectual Disabilities*, *1*(1), 24–30. doi:10.1111/j.1741-1130.2004.04004.x

Hall, C.S., Lindzey, G., & Campbell, J.B. (2004). Sigmund Freud's Classical Psychoanalytic Theory. In *Theories of Personality*. John Wiley & Sons, Inc.

Hall, A. M., Neuharth-Pritchett, S., & Belfiore, P. J. (1997). Reduction of aggressive behaviors with changes in activity: Linking descriptive and experimental analysis. *Education and Training in Mental Retardation and Developmental Disabilities*, *32*, 331–339.

Halle, J. W. (1987). Teaching language in the natural environment: An analysis of spontaneity. *The Journal of the Association for Persons with Severe Handicaps*, *12*, 28–37.

Hall, S., Oliver, C., & Murphy, G. (2001). Early development of self-injurious behavior: An empirical study. *American Journal of Mental Retardation*, *106*(2), 189–199. doi:10.1352/0895-8017(2001)106<0189:EDOSIB>2.0.CO;2 PMID:11321609

Hallum, A. (1995). Disability and the transition to adulthood:Issues for the disabled child, the family, and the pediatrician. *Current Problems in Pediatrics*, *25*(1), 12–50. doi:10.1016/S0045-9380(06)80013-7 PMID:7720408

Halpern, A. S., Close, D. W., & Nelson, D. J. (1986). *On my own. The impact of semi-independent living programs for adults with mental retardation*. Baltimore, MD: Paul H. Brookes.

Hamana, R., Ronen, T., & Feigin, R. (2000). Self-control, anxiety, and loneliness in siblings of children with cancer. *Social Work in Health Care*, *31*(1), 63–83. doi:10.1300/J010v31n01_05 PMID:10989875

Hamdani, S., Atif, N., Tariq, M., Minhas, F., Iqbal, Z., & Rahman, A. (2014). Family networks to improve outcomes in children with intellectual and developmental disorders: a qualitative study. *International Journal of Mental Health Systems*. doi:10.1186/1752-4458-8-7

Handen, B. L., & Gilchrist, R. (2006). Practitioner review: Psychopharmacology in children and adolescents with mental retardation. *Journal of Child Psychology and Psychiatry, and Allied Disciplines*, *47*(9), 871–882. doi:10.1111/j.1469-7610.2006.01588.x PMID:16930381

Hanley, G. P. (2012). Functional assessment of problem behavior: Dispelling myths, overcoming implementation obstacles, and developing new lore. *Behavior Analysis in Practice*, *5*(1), 54. PMID:23326630

Hanley, G. P., Iwata, B. A., & McCord, B. E. (2003). Functional analysis of problem behavior: A review. *Journal of Applied Behavior Analysis*, *36*(2), 147–186. doi:10.1901/jaba.2003.36-147 PMID:12858983

Hanley, G. P., Piazza, C. C., & Fisher, W. W. (1997). Noncontingent presentation of attention and alternative stimuli in the treatment of attention-maintained destructive behavior. *Journal of Applied Behavior Analysis*, *30*(2), 229–237. doi:10.1901/jaba.1997.30-229 PMID:9210303

Hannam, C. (1975). *Parents and Mentally Handicapped Children*. London: Penguin.

Harbour, C. K., & Maulik, P. K. (2010) History of Intellectual Disability. *International Encyclopedia of Rehabilitation*. Retrieved from http://cirrie.buffalo.edu/encyclopedia/en/article/143/

Harmer Cox, A., Marshell, E., Mandlesco, B., & Olsen, S. (2003). Coping responses to daily life stressors of children who have a sibling with a disability. *Journal of Family Nursing*, *9*(4), 397–413. doi:10.1177/1074840703258328

Harris, J. C. (2006). *Intellectual disability: understanding its development, causes, classification, evaluation and treatment*. New York: Oxford University Press.

Harris, J. C. (2006). *Intellectual Disability: Understanding Its Development, Causes, Classification, Evaluation, and Treatment*. New York: Oxford University Press.

Harris, J. C. (2006). *Intellectual disability: Understanding its development, causes, classification, evaluation, and treatment*. Oxford University Press New York.

Harris, J. C. (2013). New Terminology for Mental Retardation in DSM-5 and ICD-11. *Current Opinion in Psychiatry*, *26*(3), 260–262. doi:10.1097/YCO.0b013e32835fd6fb PMID:23507999

Hassall, R., Rose, J., & McDonald, J. (2005). Parenting stress in mothers of children with an intellectual disability: The effects of parental cognitions in relation to child characteristics and family support. *Journal of Intellectual Disability Research*, *49*(6), 405–418. doi:10.1111/j.1365-2788.2005.00673.x PMID:15882391

Hastings, R. P. (2003). Brief report: Behavioral adjustment of siblings of children with autism. *Journal of Autism and Developmental Disorders*, *33*, 99-104. doi: 0162- 3257/03/0200-0099/0

Hastings, R. P. (2002). Parental stress and behaviour problems of children with developmental disability. *Journal of Intellectual & Developmental Disability*, *27*(3), 149–160. doi:10.1080/1366825021000008657

Hastings, R. P. (2003). Child behaviour problems and partner mental health as correlates of stress in mothers and fathers of children with autism. *Journal of Intellectual Disability Research*, *47*(4-5), 231–237. doi:10.1046/j.1365-2788.2003.00485.x PMID:12787155

Hastings, R. P., & Beck, A. (2004). Practitioner review: Stress intervention for parents of children with intellectual disabilities. *Journal of Child Psychology and Psychiatry, and Allied Disciplines*, *45*(8), 1338–1349. doi:10.1111/j.1469-7610.2004.00357.x PMID:15482495

Hastings, R. P., Huws, J. C., Reilly, D. E., & Vaughan, F. L. (2008). "When your child dies you don't belong in that world any more." Experiences of mothers whose child with an intellectual disability has died. *Journal of Applied Research in Intellectual Disabilities*, *21*(6), 546–560. doi:10.1111/j.1468-3148.2008.00427.x

Hastings, R. P., Thomas, H., & Delwiche, N. (2002). Grandparent support for families of children with Downs syndrome. *Journal of Applied Research in Intellectual Disabilities*, *15*, 97–104. doi:10.1046/j.1360-2322.2001.00097.x

Hastings, R., Horne, S., & Felce, D. (2004, January). Positive Perceptions Held by Support Staff in Community Mental Retardation Services. *American Journal of Mental Retardation*, *109*(1), 53–62. doi:10.1352/0895-8017(2004)109<53:PPHBSS>2.0.CO;2 PMID:14651449

Hatton, C. (2002). Psychosocial interventions for adults with intellectual disabilities and mental health problems: A review. *Journal of Mental Health (Abingdon, England)*, *11*(4), 357–374. doi:10.1080/09638230020023732

Hatton, C., & Emerson, E. (2003). Families with a person with intellectual disabilities: Stress and impact. *Current Opinion in Psychiatry*, *16*(5), 497–501. doi:10.1097/00001504-200309000-00002

Hauser-Cram, P., Warfield, M. E., & Shonkoff, J. P. et al.. (2001). Children with disabilities: A longitudinal study of child development and parent wellbeing. *Monographs of the Society for Research in Child Development*, *66*, 1–131. doi:10.1111/1540-5834.00151 PMID:11677873

Hauser-Cram, P., Warfield, M. E., Shonkoff, J. P., Krauss, M. W., Upshur, C. C., & Sayer, A. (1999). Family influences on adaptive development in young children with Down syndrome. *Child Development*, *70*(4), 979–989. doi:10.1111/1467-8624.00071 PMID:10446730

Havermans, T., & Eiser, C. (1994). Siblings of children with cancer. *Child: Care, Health and Development*, *20*(5), 309–322. doi:10.1111/j.1365-2214.1994.tb00393.x PMID:7988001

Hawker, D. S., & Boulton, M. J. (2000). Twenty years' research on peer victimization and psychosocial maladjustment: A meta-analytic review of crosssectional studies. *Journal of Child Psychology and Psychiatry, and Allied Disciplines*, *41*(4), 441–455. doi:10.1111/1469-7610.00629 PMID:10836674

Hawkley, L. C., & Cacioppo, J. T. (2010). Loneliness matters: A theoretical and empirical review of consequences and mechanisms. *Annals of Behavioral Medicine*, *40*(2), 218–227. doi:10.1007/s12160-010-9210-8 PMID:20652462

Hayden, M. E., & Heller, T. (1997, October). Support, Problem-Solving/Coping Ability, and Personal Burden of Younger and Older Caregivers of Adults With Mental Retardation. *Mental Retardation*, *35*(5), 364–372. doi:10.1352/0047-6765(1997)035<0364:SPAAPB>2.0.CO;2 PMID:9339065

Hayes, S. C., Strosahl, K. D., & Wilson, K. G. (2011). *Acceptance and Commitment Therapy and Mindfulness for Chronic Pain: Model, Process, and Progress*. Retrieved from the Web:https://www.apa.org/pubs/journals/releases/amp-a0035623.pdf

Hayes, S. (1996). Recent research on offenders with learning disabilities. *Tizard Learning Disability Review*, *1*(3), 7–15. doi:10.1108/13595474199600003

Hayman, R. L. (1990). Presumptions of justice: Law, politics, and the mentally retarded parent. *Harvard Law Review*, 103.

Headey, B., & Wearing, A. (1992). *Understanding happiness: A theory of subjective well-being*. Melbourne: Longman Cheshire.

Health Commission of New South Wales. (1981). *Circular 81/8*. Sydney: Health Commission of New South Wales.

Health Scotland, N. H. S. (2004). *Health Needs Assessment Report*. People with Learning Disabilities in Scotland. NHS Health Scotland.

Heather, S. (2013). Fighting the stigma caused by mental disorders: past perspectives, present activities, and future directions. World Psychiatric Association.

Heikura, U., Taanila, A., Hartikainen, A. L., Olsen, P., Linna, S. L., Von, W. L., & Järvelin, M. R. (2006). Intellectual disability: A prospective longitudinal population-based study. *Intellectual Disability Research*, *50*(4), 259–268. doi:10.1111/j.1365-2788.2005.00792.x PMID:16507030

Heilbronner, R. (2004). A status report on the practice of forensic neuropsychology. *The Clinical Neuropsychologist*, *18*(2), 312–326. doi:10.1080/13854040490501574 PMID:15587677

Heiman, T. (2002). Parents of Children with Disabilities: Resilience, Coping and Future Expectations. *Journal of Developmental and Physical Disabilities*, *14*(2), 159–171. doi:10.1023/A:1015219514621

Heller, T., Hsieh, K., & Rowitz, L. (2000). Grandparents as Supports to Mothers of Persons with Intellectual Disability. *Journal of Gerontological Social Work, 33*(4).

Heller, T., Miller, A., & Factor, A. (1997). Adults with mental retardation as supports to their parents: Effects on parental caregiving appraisal. *Mental Retardation*, *35*(5), 338–346. doi:10.1352/0047-6765(1997)035<0338:AWMRAS>2.0.CO;2 PMID:9339062

Hemphill, S. A., Tollit, M., Kotevski, A., & Florent, A. (2015). Bullying in schools: Rates, correlates and impact on mental health. In J. Lindert & I. Itzhak (Eds.), *Violence and mental health: Its manifold faces* (pp. 185–205). Springer. doi:10.1007/978-94-017-8999-8_9

Henninger, N. A., & Taylor, J. L. (2014, April). Family Perspectives on a Successful Transition to Adulthood for Individuals With Disabilities. *Intellectual and Developmental Disabilities*, *52*(2), 98–111. doi:10.1352/1934-9556-52.2.98 PMID:24725109

Henny, M. J., Schrojenstein, L. V., & Walsh, P. N. (2008). Managing Health Problems in People with Intellectual Disabilities. *British Medical Journal*, *337*, 1408–1412.

Henry, L. A., & Gudjonsson, G. G. (1999). Eyewitness memory and suggestibility in children with mental retardation. *American Journal of Mental Retardation*, *104*(6), 491–508. doi:10.1352/0895-8017(1999)104<0491:EMASIC>2.0.CO;2 PMID:10587731

Hernández, F. J., Zorrilla, A. M., & Zapirain, B. G. (2012). Management Platform to Support Intellectually Disabled People Daily Tasks Using Android Smartphones. In *Ambient Intelligence-Software and Applications* (pp. 119–128). Springer Berlin Heidelberg. doi:10.1007/978-3-642-28783-1_15

Hertz, M. F., Donato, I., & Wright, J. (2013). Bullying and suicide: A public health approach. *The Journal of Adolescent Health*, *53*(1), S1–S3. doi:10.1016/j.jadohealth.2013.05.002 PMID:23790194

Hewett, S. (1975). Telling the family; A review of some relevant research and opinion. In S. Berie & W. Cuy (Eds.), *Right from the start: A service for families with young handicapped*. London: National Society for Mentally Handicapped Children.

Hewitt, O. (2007). What is the effect on a child of having a parent with a learning disability? *Tizard Learning Disability Review*, *12*(2), 33–44. doi:10.1108/13595474200700015

Hewstone, M. (2003). Inter-group contact: Panacea for prejudice? *The Psychologist*, *12*(7), 352–355.

Hirisave, U., Oommen, A., & Kapur, M. (2002). Psychological assessment of children in the clinical setting - Introduction. In Psychological assessment of children in the clinical setting (pp 1-5) Bangalore: NIMHANS.

Hockley, O. J., & Langdon, P. E. (2015). Men with intellectual disabilities with a history of sexual offending: Empathy for victims of sexual and non-sexual crimes. *Journal of Intellectual Disability Research*, *59*(4), 332–341. doi:10.1111/jir.12137 PMID:24761788

Hodapp, R. M., Urbano, R. C., & Burke, M. M. (2010, February). Urbano RC, Burke MM, Adult female and male siblings of persons with disabilities: Findings from a national survey. *Intellectual and Developmental Disabilities*, *48*(1), 52–62. doi:10.1352/1934-9556-48.1.52 PMID:20503816

Hodgins, S. (1992). Mental disorder, intellectual deficiency, and crime: Evidence from a birth cohort. *Archives of General Psychiatry*, *49*(6), 476–483. doi:10.1001/archpsyc.1992.01820060056009 PMID:1599373

Hodgins, S., Mednick, S. A., Brennan, P. A., Schulsinger, F., & Engberg, M. (1996). Mental disorder and crime: Evidence from a Danish birth cohort. *Archives of General Psychiatry*, *53*(6), 489–496. doi:10.1001/archpsyc.1996.01830060031004 PMID:8639031

Hofer, S. M., Gray, K. M., Piccinin, A. M., Mackinnon, A., Bontempo, D. E., Einfeld, S. L., & Tonge, B. J. et al. (2009). Correlated and coupled within-person change in emotional and behavior disturbance in individuals with intellectual disability: Results from the Australian Child to Adult Development (ACAD) study. *American Journal on Intellectual and Developmental Disabilities*, *114*(5), 307–321. doi:10.1352/1944-7558-114.5.307 PMID:19928014

Hogg, J., Lucchino, R., Wang, K., Janicki, M. P., & Group, W. (2000). *Healthy Ageing: Adults with Intellectual Disabilities: Ageing & Social Policy*. Geneva: World Health Organization.

Hogg, J., & Sebba, J. (1987). Profound retardation and multiple impairment:*Development and learning* (vol. 1). Rockville, MD: Aspen Publishers.

Holburn, S., Nguyen, D., & Vietze, P. M. (2004). Computer-assisted learning for adults with profound multiple disabilities. *Behavioral Interventions*, *19*(1), 25–37. doi:10.1002/bin.147

Holland, T., Clare, I. C. H., & Mukhopadhyay, T. (2002). Prevalence of 'criminal offending' by men and women with intellectual disability and the characteristics of 'offenders': Implications for research and service development. *Journal of Intellectual Disability Research*, *46*(s1), 6–20. doi:10.1046/j.1365-2788.2002.00001.x PMID:12061335

Holroyd, J. (1974). The Questionnaire on Resources and Stress: An instrument to measure family response to a handicapped family member. *Journal of Community Psychology*, *2*(1), 92–94. doi:10.1002/1520-6629(197401)2:1<92::AID-JCOP2290020133>3.0.CO;2-A

Holroyd, J., & McArthur, D. (1976). Mental retardation and stress on the parents: A contrast between Down's syndrome and childhood autism. *American Journal of Mental Deficiency*, *80*, 431–436. PMID:129006

Holth, P. *(2003)*. Generalized imitation and generalized matching to sample. *The Behavior Analyst/MABA*, *26*(1), 155-158.

Hong, J. S., Davis, J. P., Sterzing, P. R., Yoon, J., Choi, S., & Smith, D. C. (2014). A conceptual framework for understanding the association between school bullying victimization and substance misuse. *The American Journal of Orthopsychiatry*, *84*(6), 696–710. doi:10.1037/ort0000036 PMID:25545436

Hong, J. S., Peguero, A. A., Choi, S., Lanesskog, D., Espelage, D. L., & Lee, N. Y. (2014). Social ecology of bullying and peer victimization of Latino and Asian youth in the United States: A review of the literature. *Journal of School Violence*, *13*(3), 315–338. doi:10.1080/15388220.2013.856013

Hopkins, H. L., & Smith, H. D. (1993). Willard and Spackman's Occupational Therapy (8th ed.). Philadelphia: J.B. Lippincott. Retrieved from http://www.sgh.org.sa/Portals/0/Articles/International%20Handbook%20of%20Occupational%20Therapy%20Interventions.pdf

Hoppes, K., & Harris, S. L. (1990). Perceptions of Child Attachment and Maternal Gratification in Mothers of Children with Autism and Down Syndrome. *Journal of Clinical Child Psychology*, *19*(4), 365–370. doi:10.1207/s15374424jccp1904_8

Hoppestad, B. S. (2007). Inadequacies in computer access using assistive technology devices in profoundly disabled individuals: An overview of the current literature. *Disability and Rehabilitation: Assistive Technology*, *2*(4), 189–199. doi:10.1080/17483100701249540 PMID:19263537

Hornby, G. (1992). A review of fathers' accounts of their experiences of parenting children with disabilities. *Disability, Handicap & Society*, *7*(4), 363–374. doi:10.1080/02674649266780431

Horner, R. H., Day, H. M., Sprague, J. R., O'Brien, M., & Heathfield, L. T. (1991). Interspersed requests: A nonaversive procedure for reducing aggression and self-injury during instruction. *Journal of Applied Behavior Analysis*, *24*(2), 265–278. doi:10.1901/jaba.1991.24-265 PMID:1890047

Horner, R. H., Dunlap, G., & Koegel, R. L. (1988). *Generalization and maintenance. Life-style changes in applied settings*. Baltimore, MD: Paul H. Brookes.

Horrell, S.C.V., MacLean, W.E., & Conley, V.M. (2006). Patient and parent/guardian perspectives on the health care of adults with mental retardation. *Mental Retardation, 44*(4), 239-248.

Hosseinkhanzadeh, A. A., & Yeganeh, T. (2013). A study of the siblings relationships in families with mentally disable children. *Procedia: Social and Behavioral Sciences*, *84*, 864–868. doi:10.1016/j.sbspro.2013.06.663

Howell, A., Hauser-Cram, P., & Kersh, J. E. (2007). Setting the stage: Early child and family characteristics as predictors of later loneliness in children with developmental disabilities. *American Journal of Mental Retardation*, *112*(1), 18–30. doi:10.1352/0895-8017(2007)112[18:STSECA]2.0.CO;2 PMID:17181387

Hsu, T.-H., Huang, Y.-T., Liu, Y.-H., Ososkie, J., Fried, J., & Bezyak, J. (2015, March). Taiwanese Attitudes and Affective Reactions Toward Individuals and Coworkers Who Have Intellectual Disabilities. *American Journal on Intellectual and Developmental Disabilities*, *120*(2), 110–124. doi:10.1352/1944-7558-120.2.110 PMID:25715181

Hughes, R. (1994). Psychiatric rehabilitation: An essential health service for people with serious and persistent mental illness. In An Introduction to Psychiatric Rehabilitation. Academic Press.

Hughes, K., Bellis, M. A., Jones, L., Wood, S., Bates, G., Eckley, L., & Officer, A. et al. (2005). Prevalence and risk of violence against adults with disabilities: A systematic review and meta-analysis of observational studies. *Lancet*, *379*(9826), 1621–1629. doi:10.1016/S0140-6736(11)61851-5 PMID:22377290

Hunt, P., & Goetz, L. (1988). Teaching spontaneous communication in natural setting through interrupted behaviour chains. *Topics in Language Disorders*, *9*(1), 58–71. doi:10.1097/00011363-198812000-00006

Hur, J. (1997). Review of research on parent training for parents with intellectual disability: Methodological issues. *International Journal of Disability Development and Education*, *44*(2), 147–162. doi:10.1080/0156655970440206

Hurley, A. D. (2006). Mood disorders in intellectual disability. *Current Opinion in Psychiatry*, *19*(5), 465–469. doi:10.1097/01.yco.0000238471.84206.0a PMID:16874117

Hymel, S., & Swearer, S. M. (2015). Four decades of research on school bullying. *The American Psychologist*, *70*(4), 293–299. doi:10.1037/a0038928 PMID:25961310

ICD 10. (1992). *Classification of mental and behavioural disorder: Diagnostic criteria for Research*. Author.

ILO Vocational Rehabilitation and Employment (Disabled Persons) Convention (No. 159) and Recommendation (No. 168). (2008). *United Nations Convention on the Rights of Persons with Disabilities / International Labour Office*. Geneva: ILO.

ILO. (2001). Influencing self-employment success for people with developmental disabilities. *Rehabilitation Review, 12*, 75–85.

Inge, K. (2006). Customized employment: A growing strategy for facilitating inclusive employment. *Journal of Vocational Rehabilitation*, *24*, 191–193.

Inge, K. (2008). Choice and customized employment: A critical component. *Journal of Vocational Rehabilitation*, *28*, 67–70.

International Labour Office. (2003). *Employment of People with Disabilities: The impact of Legislation.* India Country Profile. Retrieved March, 17, 2005 from http://www.ilo.org/publi/english/employment/skills/disability/download/cpindia.pdf

International Labour Organization (ILO). (1981). *Vocational rehabilitation and the employment of the disabled: A glossary*. Geneva: ILO.

Irazábal, M., Marsà, F., & García, M. et al.. (2011). Family burden related to clinical and functional variables of people with intellectual disability with and without a mental disorder. *Research in Developmental Disabilities*, *32*, 796–803. PMID:22245729

Ishizaki, Y., Ishizaki, T., Ozawa, K., Fukai, Y., Hattori, Y., Taniuchi, S., & Kobayashi, Y. (2005). Psychosocial problems among siblings of children with disabilities in Japan: Psychosocial association between mothers and siblings. *Journal of Developmental and Physical Disabilities*, *17*(2), 119–132. doi:10.1007/s10882-005-3684-5

Iverson, J. C., & Fox, R. A. (1989). Prevalence of psychopathology among mentally retarded adults. *Research in Developmental Disabilities*, *10*(1), 77–83. doi:10.1016/0891-4222(89)90030-9 PMID:2928581

Iwata, B. A., & DeLeon, I. (1996) The functional analysis screening tool. Gainesville, FL: The Florida Centre on Self-Injury, The University of Florida.

Iwata, B., Dorsey, M., Slifer, K., Bauman, K., & Richman, G. (1994). Toward a functional analysis of self-injury. *Journal of Applied Behavior Analysis, 27*, 197-209.

Iwata, B. A., & Dozier, C. L. (2008). Clinical application of functional analysis methodology. *Behavior Analysis in Practice*, *1*(1), 3–9. PMID:22477673

Iwata, B. A., Pace, G. M., Cowdery, G. E., & Miltenberger, R. G. (1994). What makes extinction work: An analysis of procedural form and function. *Journal of Applied Behavior Analysis*, *27*(1), 131–144. doi:10.1901/jaba.1994.27-131 PMID:8188555

Jaarsveld, A. V. (2007). Sensory Integration in mental retardation and pervasive developmental disorders. In R. Crouch & V. Alers (Eds.), *Occupational therapy in psychiatry and mental health* (pp. 369–391). Whurr Publishers.

Jackson, C., Richer, J., & Edge, J. A. (2008). Sibling psychological adjustment to type 1 diabetes mellitus. *Pediatric Diabetes*, *9*(4pt1), 308–311. doi:10.1111/j.1399-5448.2008.00385.x PMID:18466212

Jacobs, K. (1993). Work assessments and programming. Willard and Spackman's Occupational Therapy, 7, 272-299.

Jacobson, J. W., Mulick, J. A., & Rojahn, J. (2007). *Handbook of Intellectual and Developmental Disabilities*. doi:10.1007/0-387-32931-5

Jahoda, A., Pert, C., & Trower, P. (2006a). Socioemotional understanding and frequent aggression in people with mild to moderate intellectual disabilities: Recognition of facial affect and role-taking abilities. *American Journal of Mental Retardation*, *111*(2), 77–89. doi:10.1352/0895-8017(2006)111[77:SUAFAI]2.0.CO;2 PMID:16466287

Jahoda, A., Pert, C., & Trower, P. (2006b). Frequent aggression and attribution of hostile intent in people with mild to moderate intellectual disabilities: An empirical investigation. *American Journal of Mental Retardation*, *111*(2), 90–99. doi:10.1352/0895-8017(2006)111[90:FAAAOH]2.0.CO;2 PMID:16466288

Jakab, I. (1990). Neuropsychological evaluation and rehabilitation in mental retardation. *Neuropsychology Review*, *1*(2), 137–164. doi:10.1007/BF01108715 PMID:2152529

James, H. (2004). Promoting effective working with parents with learning disabilities. *Child Abuse Review*, *13*(1), 31–41. doi:10.1002/car.823

Jan, J.E., Owens, J.A., Weiss, M.D., Johnson, K.P., Wasdell, M.B., Freeman, R.D. (2008). Sleep hygiene for children with neurodevelopmental disabilities. *Ipsiroglu O.S Pediatrics, 122*(6), 1343-50.

Jan, S. (1999, September). Siblings of Adults with Mental Illness or Mental retardation: Current Involvement and Expectation of Future caregiving. *Psychiatric Services (Washington, D.C.)*, *50*(9).

Jansen, S. L., van der Putten, A. A., & Vlaskamp, C. (2013). What parents find important in the support of a child with profound intellectual and multiple disabilities. *Child: Care, Health and Development*, *39*(3), 432–441. doi:10.1111/j.1365-2214.2012.01381.x PMID:22515566

Jarrold, C., Baddeley, A. D., & Phillips, C. E. (2002). Verbal short-term memory in Down syndrome: A problem of memory, audition, or speech? *Journal of Speech, Language, and Hearing Research: JSLHR*, *45*(3), 531–544. doi:10.1044/1092-4388(2002/042) PMID:12069005

Jeevanandam, L. (2009). Perspectives of intellectual disability in Asia: Epidemiology, policy, and services for children and adults. *Current Opinion in Psychiatry*, *22*(5), 462–468. doi:10.1097/YCO.0b013e32832ec056 PMID:19625968

Jenkins, J., & Smith, M. A. (1990). Factors protecting children living in disharmonious homes: Maternal reports. *Journal of the American Academy of Child and Adolescent Psychiatry*, *29*(1), 60–69. doi:10.1097/00004583-199001000-00011 PMID:2295580

Jenkins, R., & Angrosino, M. V. (1998). *Questions of competence: Culture, classification and intellectual disability*. Cambridge, UK: Cambridge University Press.

Jessop, D. J., Riessman, C. K., & Stein, R. E. (1998). Chronic childhood illness and maternal mental health. *Journal of Developmental and Behavioral Pediatrics*, *9*, 147–156. PMID:3403730

Jeyachandran, P., & Vimala. (1983). *Madras Developmental Programming System* (3rd Ed.). Chennai, India: Vijay Human Services.

Jeyachandran, P., Gadkari, J. P., & Mishra, S. K. (2009). Mental Retardation, Status of Disability in India-2007. New Delhi: Rehabilitation Council of India. Retrieved from http://www.rehabcouncil.nic.in/writereaddata/mr.pdf

Jobling, A., Moni, K., & Nolan, A. (2000). Understanding friendship: Young adults with Down syndrome explore relationships. *Journal of Intellectual & Developmental Disability*, *25*, 235–245. doi:10.1080/13269780050144299

John, K. (2011). *People with disabilities and their siblings: Building Concepts of Support and Transition*. American Association on Intellectual and Development Disabilities Annual Conference.

Jones, G. (1997). Disabling Children: Autism, the Effect on Families and Professionals. *Educational and Child Psychology*, *14*(3), 71–76.

Jones, J. (2007). Persons with intellectual disabilities in the criminal justice system: Review of issues. *International Journal of Offender Therapy and Comparative Criminology*, *51*(6), 723–733. doi:10.1177/0306624X07299343 PMID:17636203

Jones, J. L., Oseland, L. M., Morris, K. L., & Larzelere, R. E. (2014, November). Parent report of conversations with their adolescents with intellectual disability. *Journal of Applied Research in Intellectual Disabilities*, *27*(6), 521–530. doi:10.1111/jar.12090 PMID:24677601

Jones, K. L., & Smith, D. W. (1997). *Smith's recognizable patterns of human malformation* (5th ed.). Philadelphia: Saunders.

Jones, K. M., Drew, H. A., & Weber, N. L. (2000). Noncontingent peer attention as treatment for disruptive classroom behavior. *Journal of Applied Behavior Analysis*, *33*(3), 343–346. doi:10.1901/jaba.2000.33-343 PMID:11051579

Jones, L., Bellis, M. A., Wood, S., Hughes, K., McCoy, E., Eckley, L., & Officer, A. et al. (2012). Prevalence and risk of violence against children with disabilities: A systematic review and meta-analysis of observational studies. *Lancet*, *380*(9845), 899–907. doi:10.1016/S0140-6736(12)60692-8 PMID:22795511

Jones, O. H. M. (1977). Mother-child communication with prelinguistic Down's syndrome and normal infants. In H. R. Schaffer (Ed.), *Studies in mother-infant interaction*. London: Academic Press.

Joseph, J. (2005). The 1942 'euthanasia' debate in the American Journal of Psychiatry. *History of Psychiatry*, *16*(2), 171–179. doi:10.1177/0957154X05047004 PMID:16013119

Kabra, M., & Gulati, S. (2003). Mental retardation. *Indian Journal of Pediatrics*, *70*(2), 153–158. doi:10.1007/BF02723745 PMID:12661811

Kagan, C., & Lewis, S. (1996). Families with parents who have multiple commitments. In M. Moore, J. Sixsmith, K. Knowles, C. Kagan, S. Lewis, S. Beazley, & U. Rout (Eds.), *Children's reflections of family life* (pp. 29–51). London: The Falmer Press.

Kagohara, D. M., van der Meer, L., Ramdoss, S., O'Reilly, M. F., Lancioni, G. E., Davis, T. N., & Sigafoos, J. et al. (2013). Using iPods® and iPads® in teaching programs for individuals with developmental disabilities: A systematic review. *Research in Developmental Disabilities*, *34*(1), 147–156. doi:10.1016/j.ridd.2012.07.027 PMID:22940168

Kahng, S., Iwata, B. A., Fischer, S. M., Page, T. J., Treadwell, K. R., Williams, D. E., & Smith, R. G. (1998). Temporal distributions of problem behavior based on scatter plot analysis. *Journal of Applied Behavior Analysis*, *31*(4), 593–604. doi:10.1901/jaba.1998.31-593 PMID:9891396

Kahng, S., Iwata, B. A., & Lewin, A. B. (2002). Behavioral treatment of self-injury, 1964 to 2000. *American Journal of Mental Retardation*, *107*(3), 212–221. doi:10.1352/0895-8017(2002)107<0212:BTOSIT>2.0.CO;2 PMID:11966334

Kahn, J. (1984). Cognitive training and initial use of referential speech. *Topics in Language Disorders*, *5*(1), 14–23. doi:10.1097/00011363-198412000-00006

Kail, R. (1992). General slowing of information-processing by persons with mental retardation. *American Journal of Mental Retardation*, *97*(30), 333–341. PMID:1449732

Kaiser, A. P., & Hancock, T. B. (2003). Teaching parents new skills to support their young children's development. *Infants and Young Children*, *16*(1), 9–21. doi:10.1097/00001163-200301000-00003

Kaiser, A. P., & Robert, M. Y. (2013). Parent-implemented enhanced milieu teaching with preschool children who have intellectual disabilities. *Journal of Speech, Language, and Hearing Research: JSLHR*, *56*(1), 295–309. doi:10.1044/1092-4388(2012/11-0231) PMID:22744141

Kaltiala-Heino, R., Rimpela, M., Marttunen, M., Rimpela, A., & Rantanen, P. (1999). Bullying, depression, and suicidal ideation in Finnish adolescents: School survey. *British Medical Journal*, *319*(7206), 438–451. doi:10.1136/bmj.319.7206.348 PMID:10435954

Kamhi, A. G., & Johnston, J. R. (1982). Towards an understanding of retarded children's linguistic deficiencies. *Journal of Speech and Hearing Research*, *25*(3), 435–445. doi:10.1044/jshr.2503.435 PMID:7176618

Kaminsky, L., & Dewey, D. (2002). Psychosocial adjustment in siblings of children with autism. *Journal of Child Psychology and Psychiatry, and Allied Disciplines*, *43*(2), 225–232. http://onlinelibrary.wiley.com/journal/ doi:10.1111/1469-7610.00015 PMID:11902601

Kandel, I., Morad, M., Vardi, G., & Merrick, J. (2005). Intellectual disability and parenthood. *TheScientificWorldJournal*, *5*, 50–57. doi:10.1100/tsw.2005.12 PMID:15674450

Karanth, P. (1986). *Language proficiency test*. Mysore: All India Speech and Hearing Institute.

Karlin, I. W., & Strazzulla, M. (1952). Speech and language problems of mentally deficient children. *The Journal of Speech and Hearing Disorders*, *17*(3), 286–294. doi:10.1044/jshd.1703.286 PMID:13053550

Karl, R., McGuigan, D., Withiam-Leitch, M. L., Akl, E. A., & Symons, A. B. (2013). Reflective impressions of a precepted clinical experience caring for people with disabilities. *Intellectual and Developmental Disabilities*, *51*(4), 237–245. doi:10.1352/1934-9556-51.4.237 PMID:23909585

Katz, M. M., & Warren, W. L. (1999). *Katz Adjustment Scales relative report form (KAS-R) manual*. Academic Press.

Katz, G., & Lazcano-Ponce, E. (2008). Intellectual disability: Definition, etiological factors, classification, diagnosis, treatment and prognosis. *Salud Pública de México*, *50*(2), 132–141. PMID:18470340

Katz, G., & Lazcano-Ponce, E. (2008). Sexuality in subjects with intellectual disability: An educational intervention proposal for parents and counsellors in developing countries. *Salud Pública de México*, *2*, 239–254. doi:10.1590/S0036-36342008000800018

Katz, S., Ford, A. B., Moskowitz, R. W., Jackson, B. A., & Jaffe, M. W. (1963). Studies of illness in the aged: the index of ADL: a standardized measure of biological and psychosocial function. *Journal of the American Medical Association*, *185*(12), 914–919. doi:10.1001/jama.1963.03060120024016 PMID:14044222

Kavale, K. A., & Forness, S. R. (1995). Social skill deficits and training: A meta-analysis of the research in learning disabilities. *Advances in Learning and Behavioral Disabilities*, *9*, 119–160.

Kavale, K. A., & Forness, S. R. (1996). Social skill deficits and learning disabilities: A meta-analysis. *Journal of Learning Disabilities*, *29*(3), 226–237. doi:10.1177/002221949602900301 PMID:8732884

Kay-Raining Bird, E., & Gaskell, A. (2000). Novel word acquisition in children with Down syndrome: Does modality make a difference? *Journal of Communication Disorders*, *33*(3), 241–266. doi:10.1016/S0021-9924(00)00022-8 PMID:10907718

Kazak, A. E., & Marvin, R. S. (1984). Differences, difficulties and adaptation: Stress and social networks in families with a handicapped child. *Family Relations*, *33*(1), 67–77. doi:10.2307/584591

Kazdin, A. E. (2012). *Behavior modification in applied settings*. Waveland Press.

Kebbell, M. R., & Hatton, C. (1999). People with mental retardation as witnesses in court: A review. *Mental Retardation*, *37*(3), 179–187. doi:10.1352/0047-6765(1999)037<0179:PWMRAW>2.0.CO;2 PMID:10473337

Keenan, B. (1992). *An evil cradling*. London: Vintage Press.

Keen, D., Brannigan, K. L., & Cuskelly, M. (2007). Toilet training for children with autism: The effects of video modeling. *Journal of Developmental and Physical Disabilities*, *19*(4), 291–303. doi:10.1007/s10882-007-9044-x

Keith, K. D., & Bonham, G. S. (2005). The use of quality of life data at the organization and systems level. *Journal of Intellectual Disability Research*, *49*(part 10), 799–805. doi:10.1111/j.1365-2788.2005.00755.x PMID:16162131

Kellems, R. O., & Edwards, S. (2015). Using Video Modeling and Video Prompting to Teach Core Academic Content to Students With Learning Disabilities. *Preventing School Failure: Alternative Education for Children and Youth*, 1-8.

Keller, F. S., & Schoenfeld, W. N. (1950). *Principles of psychology: A systematic text in the science of behavior*. New York: Appleton-Century-Crofts. doi:10.1037/11293-000

Kelly, C., Craig, S., & Kelly, F. (2010). *Annual Report of the National Intellectual Disability Database Committee 2009*. Dublin: HRB.

Kelly, D., & Rice, M. (1986). A strategy for language assessment of young children: A combination of two approaches. *Language, Speech, and Hearing Services in Schools*, *17*(2), 83–94. doi:10.1044/0161-1461.1702.83

Kelly, E. V., Newton, N. C., Stapinski, L. A., Slade, T., Barrett, E. L., Conrod, P. J., & Teesson, M. (2015). Suicidality, internalizing problems and externalizing problems among adolescent bullies, victims and bully-victims. *Preventive Medicine: An International Journal Devoted to Practice and Theory*, *73*, 100–105. doi:10.1016/j.ypmed.2015.01.020 PMID:25657168

Kelly, G., Crowley, H., & Hamilton, C. (2009). Rights, sexuality, and relationships in Ireland: "It'd be nice to be kind of trusted. *British Journal of Learning Disabilities*, *37*(4), 308–315. doi:10.1111/j.1468-3156.2009.00587.x

Kelly, G., & Parry, A. (2008). Managing Challenging Behaviour of People with Acquired Brain Injury in Community Settings: The first 7 years of specialist clinical service. *Brain Impairment*, *9*(3), 293–304. doi:10.1375/brim.9.3.293

Keltner, B., Finn, D., & Schearer, D. (1995). Effects of family intervention on maternal-child interaction for mothers with developmental disabilities. *Family & Community Health*, *17*(4), 35–49. doi:10.1097/00003727-199501000-00006

Keltner, B., Wise, L., & Taylor, G. (1999). Mothers with intellectual limitations and their 2-year-old children's developmental outcomes. *Journal of Intellectual & Developmental Disability*, *24*(1), 45–57. doi:10.1080/13668259900033871

Kemp, C., & Carter, M. (2002). The social skills and social status of mainstreamed students with intellectual disabilities. *Educational Psychology*, *22*(4), 391–411. doi:10.1080/0144341022000003097

Kempton, W., & Gochros, J. (1986). The developmentally disabled. In H. L. Gochros, J. S. Gochros, & J. Fisher (Eds.), *Helping the sexually oppressed* (pp. 224–237). Englewood Cliffs, NJ: Prentice-Hall.

Kennedy, C. H. (1994). Manipulating antecedent conditions to alter the stimulus control of problem behavior. *Journal of Applied Behavior Analysis*, *27*(1), 161–170. doi:10.1901/jaba.1994.27-161 PMID:8188556

Kerenhappachu, M.S., & Sridevi. (2014). Caregiver's Burden and Perceived Social Support in Mothers of Children with Mental Retardation. *International Journal of Scientific and Research Publications, 4*(4).

Kern, L., Choutka, C. M., & Sokol, N. G. (2002). Assessment-based interventions used in natural settings to reduce challenging behaviors: A review of the literature. *Education & Treatment of Children*, *25*, 113–134.

Kersh, J., Hedvat, T. T., Hauser-Cram, P., & Warfield, M. E. (2006). The contribution of marital quality to the well-being of parents of children with developmental disabilities. *Journal of Intellectual Disability Research*, *50*(12), 883–893. doi:10.1111/j.1365-2788.2006.00906.x PMID:17100949

Khadi, P. B., & Hidangmayum, N. (2012). Parenting stress of normal and mentally challanged children. *Karnataka Journal of Agricultural Sciences*, *25*(2), 256–259.

Khandelwal, S. K., & Workneh, F. (1986). Perception of mental illness by medical students Indian. *Journal of Psychological Medicine*, *9*, 26–32.

Khare,S. (2015). Impact of quality of life in parents of mentally retarded children: Research findings in a regional centre. *Innovation Journal of Nursing and Healthcare, 1*(3), 171 -178.

Kiernan, W. E., Gilmore, D., & Butterworth, J. (1997). Provider perspectives and challenges in integrated employment. In W. E. Kiernan & R. L. Schalock (Eds.), *Integrated employment. Current status andfuture directions* (pp. 97–105). Washington, DC: American Association on Mental Retardation.

Kiernan, W. E., Hoff, D., Freeze, S., & Mank, D. M. (2011). Employment first: A beginning not an end. *Journal of Intellectual & Developmental Disability*, *49*(4), 300–3004. doi:10.1352/1934-9556-49.4.300 PMID:21721982

Kijak, R. J. (2011). Desire for love: Considerations on sexuality and sex education of people with intellectual disability in Poland. *Sexuality and Disability*, *29*(1), 65–74. doi:10.1007/s11195-010-9184-2 PMID:21423325

Kimura, M., & Yamazaki, Y. (2013, October). Yamazaki Y., The lived experience of mothers of multiple children with intellectual disabilities. *Qualitative Health Research*, *23*(10), 1307–1319. doi:10.1177/1049732313504828 PMID:24022734

Kim, Y., & Lombardino, L. (1991). The efficacy of script contexts in language comprehension intervention with children who have mental retardation. *Journal of Speech and Hearing Research*, *34*(4), 845–857. doi:10.1044/jshr.3404.845 PMID:1956192

Kirkham, M. A. (1993). Two-year follow-up of skills training with mothers of children with disabilities. *American Journal of Mental Retardation*. PMID:7681675

Kirkham, M. A., & Schilling, R. F. II. (1990). Life skills training with mothers of handicapped children. *Journal of Social Service Research*, *13*(2), 67–87. doi:10.1300/J079v13n02_05

Kishore, M. T. (2011). Disability impact and coping in mothers of children with intellectual disabilities and multiple disabilities. *Journal of Intellectual Disabilities*, *15*(4), 241–251. doi:10.1177/1744629511431659 PMID:22158461

Kishore, M. T., Nizamie, A., Nizamie, S. H., & Jahan, M. (2004). Psychiatric diagnosis in persons with intellectual disability in India. *Journal of Intellectual Disability Research*, *48*(1), 19–24. doi:10.1111/j.1365-2788.2004.00579.x PMID:14675227

Kistner, J. A., & Gatlin, D. F. (1989). Sociometric differences between learning-disabled and nonhandicapped students: Effects of sex and race. *Journal of Educational Psychology*, *81*(1), 118–120. doi:10.1037/0022-0663.81.1.118

Klein, H. (1984). Procedure for maximizing phonological information from single-word responses. *Language, Speech, and Hearing Services in Schools*, *15*(4), 267–274. doi:10.1044/0161-1461.1504.267

Klein, H. B., & Moses, N. (1999). *Intervention planning for children with communication disorders: A guide for clinical practicum and professional practice* (2nd ed.). Boston: Allyn & Bacon.

Klimecki, M. R., Jenkinson, J., & Wilson, L. (1994). A study of recidivism among offenders with an intellectual disability. *Journal of Intellectual & Developmental Disability*, *19*(3), 209–219. doi:10.1080/07263869400035241

Knox, M., & Bigby, C. (2007). Moving towards midlife careas negotiated family business: Accounts of people with intellectual disabilities and their families "Just getting along with their lives together". *International Journal of Disability Development and Education*, *54*(3), 287–304. doi:10.1080/10349120701488749

Knox, M., & Parmenter, T. R. (1993). Social networks and support mechanisms for people with mild intellectual disability in competitive employment. *International Journal of Rehabilitation Research. Internationale Zeitschrift fur Rehabilitationsforschung. Revue Internationale de Recherches de Readaptation*, *16*(1), 1–12. doi:10.1097/00004356-199303000-00001 PMID:8486438

Koistinen, M. (2008). *Understanding experiences of vocational training and employment for persons with learning disabilities in Zambia: Lessons for the future*. Helsinki: FAIDD Finnish Association in Developmental Disabilities.

Kolevzon, A., Gross, R., & Reichenberg, A. (2007). Prenatal and Perinatal Risk Factors for Autism: A Review and Integration of Findings. *Archives of Pediatrics & Adolescent Medicine*, *161*(4), 326–333. doi:10.1001/archpedi.161.4.326 PMID:17404128

Konstantareas, M. M., & Lunsky, Y. J. (1997). Socio-sexual knowledge, experience, attitudes, and interests of individuals with autistic disorder and developmental delay. *Journal of Autism and Developmental Disorders*, *27*(4), 397–413. doi:10.1023/A:1025805405188 PMID:9261666

Kopecky, K. (2014). Cyberbullying and other risks of internet communication focused on university students. *Procedia: Social and Behavioral Sciences*, *112*, 260–269. doi:10.1016/j.sbspro.2014.01.1163

Kopelowicz, A., Liberman, R. P., & Zarate, R. (2006). Recent advances in social skills training for schizophrenia. *Schizophrenia Bulletin*, *32*(suppl 1), S12–S23. doi:10.1093/schbul/sbl023 PMID:16885207

Koskentausta, T., Iivanainen, M., & Almqvist, F. (2007). Risk factors for psychiatric disturbance in children with intellectual disability. *Journal of Intellectual Disability Research*, *51*(1), 43–53. doi:10.1111/j.1365-2788.2006.00871.x PMID:17181602

Koul, R., & Clapsaddle, K. C. (2006). Effects of repeated listening experiences on the perception of synthetic speech by individuals with mild-to-moderate intellectual disabilities. *AAC: Augmentative & Alternative Communication*, *22*, 112–122. PMID:17114169

Kozlowski, A. M., & Matson, J. L. (2012). Interview and observation methods in functional assessment. In J. L. Matson (Ed.), *Functional assessment for challenging behaviour* (pp. 105–124). New York, NY: Springer New York; doi:10.1007/978-1-4614-3037-7_7

Krauss, M. W. (1993). Child related and parenting stress: Similarities and differences between mothers and fathers of children with disabilities. *American Journal of Mental Retardation*, *97*(4), 393–404. PMID:8427694

Kregel, J., & Dean, D. H. (2002). Sheltered vs. supported employment: A direct comparison of long-term earnings outcomes for individuals with cognitive disabilities. In J. Kregel, D.H. Dean, & P. Wehman (Eds.), *Achievements and challenges in employment services for people with disabilities: The longitudinal impact of workplace supports monograph*. Available at: http://www.worksupport.com/ resources/viewContent.cfm/151

Kregel, J., Wehman, P., & Banks, P. D. (1989). The effects of consumer characteristics and type of employment model on individual outcomes in supported employment. *Journal of Applied Behavior Analysis*, *22*(4), 407–415. doi:10.1901/jaba.1989.22-407 PMID:2533194

Krupa, M., Perumal, R. C., & Kripa, S. (2009). *Semantic Intentions in normally developing children and children with Mental Retardation: A comparative study*. (Unpublished master's dissertation). Sri Ramachandra University, Chennai, India.

Krutchzer, S., Deluca, J., & Caplan, B. (2012). Encyclopedia of neuropsychology. Academic Press.

Kumar, A. (2013). Normalization: Guiding Principle of Equal Opportunities in Education for Children with Disabilities in India. *American Journal of Epidemiology*, *167*, 169–177.

Kumin, L. & Adams, J. (2000). Developmental apraxia of speech and intelligibility in children with Down syndrome. *Down Syndrome Quarterly, 5,* 1-6.

Kumin, L. (2006). Differential diagnosis and treatment of speech sound production problems in children with Down syndrome. *Down Syndrome Quarterly, 8,* 7-18.

Kumin, M. (2014). Speech intelligibility helping children and adults develop and maintain understandable speech. *Down Syndrome News, 37.*

Kumin, L., Councill, C., & Goodman, M. (1994). A longitudinal study of the emergence of phonemes in children with Down syndrome. *Journal of Communication Disorders*, *27*(4), 265–275. doi:10.1016/0021-9924(94)90019-1 PMID:7876409

Kumpulainen, K., Rasanen, E., & Puura, K. (2001). Psychiatric disorders and the use of mental health services among children involved in bullying. *Aggressive Behavior*, *27*(2), 102–110. doi:10.1002/ab.3

Kuo, S. H. (1993). Forensic psychiatry in Taiwan. *International Journal of Law and Psychiatry*, *6*(3-4), 457–472. doi:10.1016/0160-2527(83)90032-8 PMID:6679535

Kurth, J. A. (2014). Educational placement of students with autism: The impact of state of residence. *Focus on Autism and Other Developmental Disabilities*.

Kurtz, P. F., Boelter, E. W., Jarmolowicz, D. P., Chin, M. D., & Hagopian, L. P. (2011). An analysis of functional communication training as an empirically supported treatment for problem behavior displayed by individuals with intellectual disabilities. *Research in Developmental Disabilities*, *32*(6), 2935–2942. doi:10.1016/j.ridd.2011.05.009 PMID:21696917

Kwiatkowski, J., & Shriberg, L. D. (1992). Intelligibility assessment in developmental phonological disorders: Accuracy of caregiver gloss. *Journal of Speech and Hearing Research*, *35*(5), 1095–1104. doi:10.1044/jshr.3505.1095 PMID:1280309

Lagerheim, B. (1986). Preparing disabled children for coping with adolescent stress. *International Journal of Adolescent Medicine and Health*, *2*(4), 309–316.

Lakanna, S., Venkatesh, K., & Bhat, J. S. (2008). *Assessment of Language Development*. Bakersfield, CA: Omni Therapy Services.

Lakhan, R., & Sharma, M., (2010). A study of Knowledge, Attitudes and Practices (KAP) Survey of Families towards their Children with Intellectual Disability in Barwani, India. *Asia Pacific Disability Rehabilitation Journal,* 21.

Lalli, J. S., Browder, D. M., Mace, F. C., & Brown, D. K. (1993). Teacher use of descriptive analysis data to implement interventions to decrease students' problem behaviors. *Journal of Applied Behavior Analysis*, *26*(2), 227–238. doi:10.1901/jaba.1993.26-227 PMID:8331019

Lalli, J. S., Casey, S. D., & Kates, K. (1997). noncontingent reinforcement as treatment for severe problem behavior: Some procedural variations. *Journal of Applied Behavior Analysis*, *30*(1), 127–137. doi:10.1901/jaba.1997.30-127 PMID:9103988

Lamberts, R., & Weener, P. (1976). Children's competence in processing negation. *American Journal of Mental Deficiency*, *81*, 181–186. PMID:970417

Lamb, M. E., & Billings, L. A. L. (1997). Fathers of children with special needs. In M. E. Lamb (Ed.), *The role of the father in child development* (3rd ed., pp. 179–190). New York: John Wiley & Sons.

Lambrick, F., & Glaser, W. (2004). Sex offenders with an intellectual disability. *Sexual Abuse*, *16*(4), 381–392. PMID:15560418

Lamont, A., & Bromfield, L. (2009). Parental intellectual disability and child protection: Key issues. National Child Protection Clearing house. *Issues (National Council of State Boards of Nursing (U.S.))*, *31*. Retrieved from http://www.aifs. gov

Lampert, A., & Friedman, A. (1992). Sex differences in vulnerability and maladjustment as a function of parental investment: An evolutionary approach. *Social Biology*, *39*, 65–81. PMID:1514125

Lancioni, G. E., O'Reilly, M. F., & Basili, G. (2001). Use of microswitches and speech output systems with people with severe/profound intellectual or multiple disabilities: A literature review. *Research in Developmental Disabilities*, *22*(1), 21–40. doi:10.1016/S0891-4222(00)00064-0 PMID:11263629

Lancioni, G. E., O'Reilly, M. F., Singh, N. N., Sigafoos, J., Oliva, D., Antonucci, M., & Basili, G. et al. (2008). Microswitch-based programs for persons with multiple disabilities: An overview of some recent developments. *Perceptual and Motor Skills*, *106*(2), 355–370. doi:10.2466/pms.106.2.355-370 PMID:18556894

Lancioni, G. E., O'Reilly, M. F., Singh, N. N., Sigafoos, J., Oliva, D., Bracalente, S., & Montironi, G. (2007). Orientation systems to support indoor travel by persons with multiple disabilities: Technical aspects and applicability issues. *Technology and Disability*, *19*(1), 1–6.

Lancioni, G. E., Oliva, D., & Bracalente, S. (1995). An acoustic orientation system to promote independent indoor travel in blind persons with severe mental retardation. *Perceptual and Motor Skills*, *80*(3), 747–754. doi:10.2466/pms.1995.80.3.747 PMID:7567392

Lancioni, G. E., Sigafoos, J., O'reilly, M. F., & Singh, N. N. (2013). *Assistive technology: Interventions for individuals with severe/profound and multiple disabilities*. New York: Springer. doi:10.1007/978-1-4614-4229-5

Langdon, P. E., Clare, I. C., & Murphy, G. H. (2011). Moral reasoning theory and illegal behaviour by adults with intellectual disabilities. *Psychology, Crime & Law*, *17*(2), 101–115. doi:10.1080/10683160903392384

Lanovaz, M. J., Argumedes, M., Roy, D., Duquette, J. R., & Watkins, N. (2013). Using ABC narrative recording to identify the function of problem behavior: A pilot study. *Research in Developmental Disabilities*, *34*(9), 2734–2742. doi:10.1016/j.ridd.2013.05.038 PMID:23787117

Lapidot-Lefler, N., & Dolev-Cohen, M. (2015). Comparing cyberbullying and school bullying among school students: Prevalence, gender, and grade level differences. *Social Psychology of Education*, *18*(1), 1–16. doi:10.1007/s11218-014-9280-8

Larkin, P., Jahoda, A., MacMahon, K., & Pert, C. (2012). Interpersonal sources of conflict in young people with and without mild to moderate intellectual disabilities at transition from adolescent to adulthood. *Journal of Applied Research in Intellectual Disabilities*, *25*(1), 29–38. doi:10.1111/j.1468-3148.2011.00652.x PMID:22473946

Larrabee, G. J. (2005). *Forensic neuropsychology: A scientific approach*. New York: Oxford University Press.

LaVigna, G. W., & Willis, T. J. (2012). The efficacy of positive behavioural support with the most challenging behaviour: The evidence and its implications. *Journal of Intellectual & Developmental Disability*, *37*(3), 185–195. doi:10.3109/13668250.2012.696597 PMID:22774760

Laws, C. B., Kolomer, S. R., & Gallagher, M. J. (2014, December). Age of Persons Supported and Factors Predicting Intended Staff Turnover: A Comparative Study. *Inclusion*, *2*(4), 316–328. doi:10.1352/2326-6988-2.4.316

Lawton, M., & Brody, E. (1969). Assessment of older people: Self maintaining and instrumental activities of daily living. *The Gerontologist*, *9*(3 Part 1), 179–186. doi:10.1093/geront/9.3_Part_1.179 PMID:5349366

Leddy, M. (1999). The biological basis of speech in people with Down syndrome. In J. Miller, M. Leddy, & L. A. Leavitt (Eds.), *Improving the communication of people with Down syndrome* (pp. 61–80). Baltimore, MD: Paul H Brooks.

Lee. (2004). *Vocational Rehabilitation for People with Disabilities*. Department of Counseling, School and Educational Psychology, University at Buffalo.

Lee, J. (2013). Maternal stress, well-being, and impaired sleep in mothers of children with developmental disabilities: A literature review. *Research in Developmental Disabilities*, *34*(11), 4255–4273. doi:10.1016/j.ridd.2013.09.008 PMID:24080069

Lee, Y., & Vail, C. O. (2005). Computer-based reading instruction for young children with disabilities. *Journal of Special Education Technology*, *20*(1), 5–18.

Lemay, J. F., Herbert, A. R., Dewey, D. M., & Micheil, A. I. (2003). A rational approach to the child with mental retardation for the paediatrician. *Journal of Paediatrics and Child Health*, *8*(6), 345–356.

Leonard, H., Glasson, E., Nassar, N., Whitehouse, A., Bebbington, A., Bourke, J., & Bower, C. et al. (2011). Autism and intellectual disability are differentially related to sociodemographic background at birth. *PLoS ONE*, *6*(3), e17875. doi:10.1371/journal.pone.0017875 PMID:21479223

Leonard, H., Petterson, B., Bower, C., & Sanders, R. (2003). Prevalence of intellectual disability in Western Australia. *Paediatric and Perinatal Epidemiology*, *17*(1), 58–67. doi:10.1046/j.1365-3016.2003.00469.x PMID:12562473

Leonard, H., Petterson, B., De Klerk, N., Zubrick, S. R., Glasson, E., Sanders, R., & Bower, C. (2005). Association of sociodemographic characteristics of children with intellectual disability in Western Australia. *Social Science & Medicine*, *60*(7), 1499–1513. doi:10.1016/j.socscimed.2004.08.014 PMID:15652683

Leonard, H., & Wen, X. (2002). The epidemiology of mental retardation: Challenges and opportunities in the new millennium. *Mental Retardation and Developmental Disabilities Research Reviews*, *8*(3), 117–134. doi:10.1002/mrdd.10031 PMID:12216056

Lerman, D., & Iwata, B. (1996). Developing a technology for the use of operant extinction in clinical settings: An examination of basic and applied research. *Journal of Applied Behavior Analysis*, *29*(3), 345–382. doi:10.1901/jaba.1996.29-345 PMID:8926226

Lerner, J. (2003). *Learning disabilities: Theories, diagnosis, and teaching practices* (9th ed.). Boston, MA: Houghton Mifflin Company.

Lesar, S. (1998). Use of Assistive Technology with Young Children with Disabilities Current Status and Training Needs. *Journal of Early Intervention*, *21*(2), 146–159. doi:10.1177/105381519802100207

Lewandowski, L. J., & Barlow, J. R. (2000). Social cognition and verbal learning disabilities. *Journal of Psychotherapy in Independent Practice*, *4*(4), 35–47. doi:10.1300/J288v01n04_04

Lewis, T., Scott, T., & Sugai, G. (1994). The problem behaviour questionnaire: A teacher-based instrument to develop functional hypotheses of problem behaviour in general education classroom. *Diagnostique*, *19*, 103–115.

Liberman, R. P., Corrigan, P. W., & Schade, M. L. (1989). The interaction of drug and psychosocial treatment. *International Review of Psychiatry (Abingdon, England)*, *1*, 289–294. doi:10.3109/09540268909110419

Lifter, K., & Bloom, L. (1989). Object knowledge and emergence of language. *Infant Behavior and Development*, *12*(4), 395–423. doi:10.1016/0163-6383(89)90023-4

Lindfors, P. J., Kaltiala-Heino, R., & Rimpela, A. H. (2012). Cyberbullying among Finnish adolescents – a population-based study. *BMC Public Health*, 1. PMID:23176715

Lindsay, S., & McPherson, A. C. (2012). Strategies for improving disability awareness and social inclusion of children and young people with cerebral palsy. *Child: Care, Health and Development*, *38*(6), 809–816. doi:10.1111/j.1365-2214.2011.01308.x PMID:21880056

Lindsay, W. R. (2002). Integration of recent reviews on offenders with intellectual disabilities. *Journal of Applied Research in Intellectual Disabilities*, *15*(2), 111–119. doi:10.1046/j.1468-3148.2002.00112.x

Lindsay, W. R., Carson, D., Holland, A. J., Taylor, J. L., O'Brien, G., Wheeler, J. R., & Steptoe, L. (2013). Alcohol and its relationship to offence variables in a cohort of offenders with intellectual disability. *Journal of Intellectual & Developmental Disability*, *38*(4), 325–331. doi:10.3109/13668250.2013.837154 PMID:24279785

Lindsay, W. R., Law, J., Quinn, K., Smart, N., & Smith, A. H. (2001). A comparison of physical and sexual abuse: Histories of sexual and non-sexual offenders with intellectual disability. *Child Abuse & Neglect*, *25*(7), 989–995. doi:10.1016/S0145-2134(01)00251-4 PMID:11523873

Lindsay, W. R., Smith, A. H., Quinn, K., Anderson, A., Smith, A., Allan, R., & Law, J. (2004). Women with intellectual disability who have offended: Characteristics and outcome. *Journal of Intellectual Disability Research*, *48*(6), 580–590. doi:10.1111/j.1365-2788.2004.00627.x PMID:15312059

Lindsay, W. R., Taylor, J. L., & Sturmey, P. (Eds.). (2004). *Offenders with developmental disabilities*. Chichester, UK: John Wiley & Sons. doi:10.1002/9780470713440

Lindsay, W. R., Tinsley, S., & Emara, M. (2012). Alcohol use and offending in people with intellectual disability. *Alcohol-Related Violence. Prevention & Treatment*, 285–302.

Lindstrom, L., Doren, B., Metheny, J., Johnson, P., & Zane, C. (2007). Transition to Employment: Role of the Family in Career Development. *Council for Exceptional Children, 73*, 348–366.

Lin, L. Y., Orsmond, G. I., & Seltzer, M. M. (2007). Mothers of adolescents and adults with autism: Parenting multiple children with disabilities. *Intellectual and Developmental Disabilities*, *45*(4), 257–270. doi:10.1352/1934-9556(2007)45[257:MOAAAW]2.0.CO;2 PMID:17627373

Lin, L.-P., Hsu, S.-W., Kuo, M.-T., Wu, J.-L., Chu, C., & Lin, J.-D. (2014). Onset aging conditions of adults with an intellectual disability associated with primary caregiver depression. *Research in Developmental Disabilities*, *35*(3), 632–638. doi:10.1016/j.ridd.2013.12.013 PMID:24467811

Llewellyn, A. (2000). Perceptions of mainstreaming: A systems approach. *Developmental Medicine and Child Neurology*, *42*(2), 106–115. doi:10.1017/S0012162200000219 PMID:10698328

Llewellyn, G., McConnell, D., & Ferronato, L. (2003). Prevalence and outcomes for parents with disabilities and their children in an Australian court sample. *Child Abuse & Neglect*, *27*(3), 235–251. doi:10.1016/S0145-2134(03)00004-8 PMID:12654323

Lobato, D. J., & Kao, B. T. (2002). Integrated sibling-parent group intervention to improve sibling knowledge and adjustment to chronic illness and disability. *Journal of Pediatric Psychology*, *27*(8), 711–716. doi:10.1093/jpepsy/27.8.711 PMID:12403861

Lobato, D. J., & Kao, B. T. (2005). Brief report: Family-based group intervention for young siblings of children with chronic illness and developmental disability. *Journal of Pediatric Psychology*, *30*(8), 678–682. doi:10.1093/jpepsy/jsi054 PMID:16260437

Loewy, J., Hallan, C., Friedman, E., & Martinez, C. (2006). Sleep/sedation in children undergoing EEG testing: A comparison of chloral hydrate and music therapy. *American Journal of Electroneurodiagnostic Technology*, *46*, 343–355. PMID:17285817

Long, K. A., Kao, B., Plante, W., Seifer, R., & Lobato, D. (2015, March). Cultural and Child-Related Predictors of Distress Among Latina Caregivers of Children With Intellectual Disabilities. *American Journal on Intellectual and Developmental Disabilities*, *120*(2), 145–165. doi:10.1352/1944-7558-120.2.145 PMID:25715183

Longo, D. C., & Bond, B. (1984). Families of the handicapped child: Research and practice. *Family Relations*, *33*(1), 57–65. doi:10.2307/584590

Lopez, V., Clifford, T., & Minnes, P. et al.. (2008). Parental stress and coping in families of children with and without developmental delays. *Journal on Developmental Disabilities*, *14*, 99–103.

Lopez, V., Clifford, T., Minnes, P., & Kuntz, H. O. (2008). Parental stress and coping in families of children with and without developmental delays. *Journal on Developmental Disabilities*, *14*(2).

Lorenzo, L. A. (1991). Societal prejudice reflected in our courts: The unfavorable treatment of the mentally retarded. *Seton Hall Const. LJ*, *2*, 771.

Louhiala. (2004). *Preventing intellectual disability. Ethical and clinical issues.* Cambridge, UK: Cambridge University Press.

Lowe, K., Allen, D., Jones, E., Brophy, S., Moore, K., & James, W. (2007). Challenging behaviours: Prevalence and topographies. *Journal of Intellectual Disability Research*, *51*(8), 625–636. doi:10.1111/j.1365-2788.2006.00948.x PMID:17598876

Luckasson, R., Borthwick-Duffy, S., Buntinx, W. H. E., Coulter, D. L., Craig, E. M., Reeve, A., & Tasse´, M. J. et al. (2002). *Mental retardation: Definition, classification, and systems of supports* (10th ed.). Washington, DC: American Association on Mental Retardation.

Luckasson, R., & Reeve, A. (2001). Naming, defining, and classifying in mental retardation. *Mental Retardation*, *39*(1), 47–52. doi:10.1352/0047-6765(2001)039<0047:NDACIM>2.0.CO;2 PMID:11270213

Lukmanuel Hakeem & Subathra. (2013). A Study on the Attitude of Siblings Towards Their Mentally Retarded Brother/Sister. *Indian Journal of Applied Research*, *3*(1).

Lund, J. (1985). The prevalence of psychiatric morbidity in mentally retarded adults. *Acta Psychiatrica Scandinavica*, *72*(6), 563–570. doi:10.1111/j.1600-0447.1985.tb02655.x PMID:4083061

Lund, J. (1990). Mentally retarded criminal offenders in Denmark. *The British Journal of Psychiatry*, *156*(5), 726–731. doi:10.1192/bjp.156.5.726 PMID:2095951

Lunsky, Y., Bradley, E. A., Gracey, C. D., Durbin, J., & Koegl, C. (2009). Gender differences in psychiatric diagnoses among inpatients with and without intellectual disabilities. *Journal Information*, *114*(1). PMID:19143463

Lunsky, Y., Hastings, R. P., Hensel, J., Arenovich, T., & Dewa, C. S. (2014, August). Perceptions of Positive Contributions and Burnout in Community Developmental Disability Workers. *Intellectual and Developmental Disabilities*, *52*(4), 249–257. doi:10.1352/1934-9556-52.4.249 PMID:25061769

Luria, A. R. (1961). *The Role of Speech in the regulation of normal and abnormal behaviour.* New York: Pergamon Press.

Luria, A. R. (1963). *The Mentally retarded child.* Oxford, UK: Pergamon Press.

Luukkonen, A. H., Riala, K., Hakko, H., & Rasanen, P. (2010). Bullying behavior and substance abuse among underage psychiatric inpatient adolescents. *European Psychiatry*, *25*(7), 382–389. doi:10.1016/j.eurpsy.2009.12.002 PMID:20435448

Lyall, I., Holland, A. J., & Collins, S. (1995). Offending by adults with learning disabilities and the attitudes of staff to offending behaviour: Implications for service development. *Journal of Intellectual Disability Research*, *39*(6), 501–508. doi:10.1111/j.1365-2788.1995.tb00570.x PMID:8746737

Maccoby, E., & Martin, J. (1983). Socialization in the context of the family: parent-child interaction. In E. M. Hetherington (Ed.), Socialization, personality and social development. New York: Wiley.

MacDonald, E. E., Hastings, R. P., & Fitzsimons, E. (2010). Psychological Acceptance Mediates the Impact of the Behaviour Problems of Children with Intellectual Disability on Fathers' Psychological Adjustment. *Journal of Applied Research in Intellectual Disabilities*, *23*(1), 27–37. doi:10.1111/j.1468-3148.2009.00546.x

Macks, R. J., & Reeve, R. E. (2007). The adjustment of non-disabled siblings of children with autism. *Journal of Autism and Developmental Disorders*, *37*(6), 1060–1067. doi:10.1007/s10803-006-0249-0 PMID:17072750

MacLean, W. E. Jr, Tervo, R. C., Hoch, J., Tervo, M., & Symons, F. J. (2010). Self-Injury among a community cohort of young children at risk for intellectual and developmental disabilities. *The Journal of Pediatrics*, *157*(6), 979–983. doi:10.1016/j.jpeds.2010.05.052 PMID:20630541

Mactavish, J. B., & Schleien, S. J. (2004). Re-injecting spontaneity and balance in family life: Parents' perspectives on recreation in families that include children with developmental disability. *Journal of Intellectual Disability Research*, *48*(2), 123–141. doi:10.1111/j.1365-2788.2004.00502.x PMID:14723655

Madan-Swain, A., Sexson, S. B., Brown, R.T., & Ragab, A. (1993). Family adaptation and coping among siblings of cancer patients, their brothers & sisters and nonclinical controls. *American Journal of Family Therapy, 21*, 60–70.

Madhavan, T., Kalyan, M., Naidu, S., Pashwarla, R., & Narayan, J. (1999). *Mental retardation- a manual for psychologists*. Secunderabad, India: National Institute for the Mentally Handicapped.

Madhavan, T., Menon, D. K., & Kalyan, M. (1988). *Mental Retardation: A Manual for Village Rehabilitation Workers*. National Institute for the Mentally Handicapped.

Maes, B., Broekman, T. G., Došen, A., & Nauts, J. (2003). Caregiving burden of families looking after persons with intellectual disability and behavioural or psychiatric problems. *Journal of Intellectual Disability Research*, *47*(6), 447–455. doi:10.1046/j.1365-2788.2003.00513.x PMID:12919195

Mafifei-Almodovar, L., & Sturmey, P. (2012). Evidence-based practice and crisis intervention. In D. D. Reed, R. F. D. DiGennaro, & J. K. Luiselli (Eds.), *Handbook of crisis intervention for individuals with developmental disabilities*. New York: Springer.

Magaña, S., Li, H., Miranda, E., & Paradiso de Sayu, R. (2014). Improving health behaviours of Latina mothers of youths and adults with intellectual and developmental disabilities. *Journal of Intellectual Disability Research*, *59*(5), 397–410. doi:10.1111/jir.12139 PMID:24761812

Maggi, S., Irwin, L. J., Siddiqi, A., & Hertzman, C. (2010). The social determinants of early child development: An overview. *Journal of Paediatrics and Child Health*, *46*(11), 627–635. doi:10.1111/j.1440-1754.2010.01817.x PMID:20796183

Mahoney, G. J., & Snow, K. (1983). The Relationship of sensorimotor functioning to children's response to early language training. *Mental Retardation*, *21*, 248–254. PMID:6231449

Mak, W. S., & Ho, S. M. (2007). Caregiving perceptions of Chinese mothers of children with intellectual disability in Hong Kong. *Journal of Applied Research in Intellectual Disabilities*, *20*(2), 145–156. doi:10.1111/j.1468-3148.2006.00309.x

Malin, A. J. (1949). Manual of Malin's Intelligence Scale for Indian Children. Lucknow: Indian Psychological Corporation.

Mandleco, B., Olsen, S. F., Dyches, T., & Marshall, E. (2003). The relationship between family and sibling functioning in families raising a child with a disability. *Journal of Family Nursing*, *9*(4), 365–396. doi:10.1177/1074840703258329

Manion, M. L., & Bersani, H. A. (1987). Mental retardation as a Western sociological construct: A cross-cultural analysis. *Disability, Handicap & Society*, *2*(3), 231–245. doi:10.1080/02674648766780301

Mank, D. M., Rhodes, L. E., & Bellamy, G. T. (1986). Four supported employment alternatives. In W. E. Kiernan & J. A. Stark (Eds.), *Pathways to employment for adults with developmental disabilities*. Baltimore, MD: Paul H. Brookes.

Manolson, A. (1992). *It takes two to talk: A parent's guide to helping children communicate*. Toronto, Canada: The Hanen Centre.

March, R. E., Horner, R. H., Lewis-Palmer, T., Brown, D., Crone, D., & Todd, A. W. et al.. (2000). *Functional Assessment Checklist: Teachers and Staff (FACTS)*. Eugene, OR: Educational and Community Supports.

Marini, Z. A., Dane, A. V., Bosacki, S. L., & Cura, Y.-. (2006). Direct and indirect bully-victims: Differential psychosocial risk factors associated with adolescents involvement in bullying and victimization. *Aggressive Behavior*, *32*(6), 551–569. doi:10.1002/ab.20155

Marmot, M. G., Allen, J., Goldblatt, P., Boyce, T., McNeish, D., Grady, M., & Geddes, I. (2010). *Fair society, healthy lives: Strategic review of health inequalities in England post-2010*. Academic Press.

Marshall, K., & Ferris, J. (2012). Utilizingbehavioral family therapy (BFT) to help support the system around a person with intellectual disability and complex mental health needs: A case study. *Intellect Disabil.*, *16*(2), 109–118. doi:10.1177/1744629512443619 PMID:22496309

Martell, D. A. (1992). Forensic neuropsychology and the criminal law. *Law and Human Behavior*, *16*(3), 313–336. doi:10.1007/BF01044772

Martin, H., McConkey, R., & Martin, S. (1984). From acquisition theories to intervention strategies: An experiment with mentally handicapped children. *The British Journal of Disorders of Communication*, *19*(1), 3–14. doi:10.3109/13682828409019832 PMID:6733030

Martin, S. L., Ramey, C. T., & Ramey, S. (1990). The prevention of intellectual impairment in children of impoverished families: Findings of a randomized trial of educational day care. *American Journal of Public Health*, *80*(7), 844–847. doi:10.2105/AJPH.80.7.844 PMID:2356909

Martlew, M., & Hodson, J. (1991). Children with mild learning difficulties in an integrated and in a special school: Comparisons of behavior, teasing and teachers' attitudes. *The British Journal of Educational Psychology*, *61*(3), 355–372. doi:10.1111/j.2044-8279.1991.tb00992.x PMID:1786214

Marvin RS and Pianta RC. (1996) Mothers' reactions to their child's diagnosis: Relations with security of attachment. *Journal of Clinical Child Psychology, 25*(4), 436-445.

Maryland Coalition for Inclusive Education. (2011). *Quality indicators for inclusive building based practices*. Retrieved from: http://www.mcie.org/usermedia/application/8/quality-indicators---building-based-practices-(2011).pdf

Mary, N. L. (1990). Reactions of black, hispanic, and white mothers to having a child with handicaps. *Mental Retardation*, *28*(1), 1–5. PMID:2308509

Mascha, K., & Boucher, J. (2006). Preliminary investigation of a qualitative method of examining siblings' experiences of living with a child with ASD. *British Journal of Developmental Disabilities*, *52*(102), 19–28. doi:10.1179/096979506799103659

Mash, E. J., & Wolfe, D. A. (2002). *Abnormal Child Psychology* (3rd ed.). Belmont, CA: Wadsworth Group. American Psychiatric Association.

Mates, T. E. (1990). Siblings of autistic children: Their adjustment and performance at home and in school. *Journal of Autism and Developmental Disorders*, *20*(4), 545–553. doi:10.1007/BF02216059 PMID:2279972

Mather, N., & Goldstein, S. (2015). *Behaviour Modification in the classroom*. Retrieved from http://www.ldonline.org/article/6030/

Matheson, C., Olsen, R. J., & Weisner, T. (2007). A good friend is hard to find: Friendship among adolescents with disabilities. *American Journal of Mental Retardation*, *112*(5), 319–329. doi:10.1352/0895-8017(2007)112[0319:AGFIHT]2.0.CO;2 PMID:17676957

Matson, J. L. (2012). Functional assessment for challenging behaviors. New York, NY: Springer. doi:10.1007/978-1-4614-3037-7

Matson, J. L., & Coe, D. A. (1992). Applied Behaviour Analysis: Its impact on the treatment of mentally retarded emotionally disturbed people. *Research in Developmental Disabilities*, *13*(2), 171–189. doi:10.1016/0891-4222(92)90023-Y PMID:1574625

Matson, J. L., Horovitz, M., Kozlowski, A. M., Sipes, M., Worley, J. A., & Shoemaker, M. E. (2011). Person characteristics of individuals in functional assessment research. *Research in Developmental Disabilities*, *32*(2), 621–624. doi:10.1016/j.ridd.2010.12.012 PMID:21211941

Matson, J. L., & Vollmer, T. R. (1995). *User's guide: Questions About Behavioral Function (QABF)*. Baron Rouge, LA: Scientific Publishers, Inc.

Matthew, P. (2000). Characteristics of the Grandparents and the Children with Disabilities for Whom They Care. *Journal of Gerontological Social Work*, *33*(3), 35–55. doi:10.1300/J083v33n03_03

Maulik, P. K., & Harbour, C. K. (2010). Epidemiology of intellectual disability. *International Encyclopaedia of Rehabilitation.*

Maulik, P. K., Mascarenhas, M. N., Mathers, C. D., Dua, T., & Saxena, S. (2011). Prevalence of intellectual disability: A meta-analysis of population-based studies. *Research in Developmental Disabilities*, *32*(2), 419–436. doi:10.1016/j.ridd.2010.12.018 PMID:21236634

Mayer, G. R., Sulzer-Azaroff, B., & Wallace, M. (2014). *Behavior analysis for lasting change* (3rd ed.). Cornwall-on-Hudson, NY: Sloan Publishing.

Mayes, R., Llewellyn, G., & McConnell, D. (2006). Misconception: The Experience of Pregnancy for Women with Intellectual Disabilities. *Scandinavian Journal Of Disability Research*, *8*(2-3), 120–131. doi:10.1080/15017410600774178

Mazzucchelli, T. G., & Sanders, M. R. (2011). Preventing behavioural and emotional problems in children who have a developmental disability: A public health approach. *Research in Developmental Disabilities*, *32*(6), 2148–2156. doi:10.1016/j.ridd.2011.07.022 PMID:21831592

Mc Connel, D., & Llewllyn, G. (2002). Stereotypes, parents with intellectual disability and child protection. *Journal of Social Welfare and Family*, *24*(3), 297–317. doi:10.1080/09649060210161294

McAfee, J. K., Cockram, J., & Wolfe, P. S. (2001). Police reactions to crimes involving people with mental retardation: A cross-cultural experimental study. *Education and Training in Mental Retardation and Developmental Disabilities*, 160–171.

McCabe, M. P. (1999). Sexual knowledge, experience, and feelings among people with disability. *Sexuality and Disability*, *17*(2), 157–170. doi:10.1023/A:1021476418440

McCallion, P., Janicki, M., Grant-Griffin, L., & Kolomer, S. R. (2000). Grandparent carers II: Service needs and service provision issues. *Journal of Gerontological Social Work*, *33*(3), 57–84. doi:10.1300/J083v33n03_04

McCarthy, A., Cuskelly, M., van Kraayenoord, C. E., & Cohen, J. (2006). Predictors of stress in mothers and fathers of children with fragile X syndrome. *Research in Developmental Disabilities*, *27*(6), 688–704. doi:10.1016/j.ridd.2005.10.002 PMID:16361079

McCarthy, J., & Boyd, J. (2002). Mental health services and young people with intellectual disability: Is it time to do better? *Journal of Intellectual Disability Research*, *46*(3), 250–256. doi:10.1046/j.1365-2788.2002.00401.x PMID:11896810

McCauley, R., & Swisher, L. (1984b). Use and misuse of norm-referenced tests in clinical assessment: A hypothetical case. *The Journal of Speech and Hearing Disorders*, *49*, 338–348. doi:10.1044/jshd.4904.338 PMID:6389982

McConachie, D. A., McKenzie, K., Morris, P. G., & Walley, R. M. (2014, June). Acceptance and mindfulness-based stress management for support staff caring for individuals with intellectual disabilities. *Research in Developmental Disabilities*, *35*(6), 1216–1227. doi:10.1016/j.ridd.2014.03.005 PMID:24685937

McConachie, H. (1986). *Parents & Young mentally handicapped children: a review of research issues*. London: Croom Helm.

McConkey, R., & Mezza, F. (2001). Employment aspirations of people with learning disabilities attending day centres. *Journal of Learning Disabilities*, *5*, 309–310.

McConkey, R., Truesdale-Kennedy, M., Chang, M.-Y., Jarrah, S., & Shukri, R. (2008). The impact on mothers of bringing up a child with intellectual disabilities: A cross-cultural study. *International Journal of Nursing Studies*, *45*(1), 65–74. doi:10.1016/j.ijnurstu.2006.08.007 PMID:17022985

McConnell, D., Mayes, R., & Llewellyn, G. (2008). Women with intellectual disability at risk of adverse pregnancy and birth outcomes. *Journal of Intellectual Disability Research*, *52*, 529–535. doi:.01061.x10.1111/j.1365-2788.2008

McConnell, D. (2008). Parents labelled with intellectual disability: Position of the IASSID SIRG on Parents and Parenting with Intellectual Disabilities. *Journal of Applied Research in Intellectual Disabilities*, *21*(4), 296–307. doi:10.1111/j.1468-3148.2008.00435.x

McConnell, D., Feldman, M., Aunos, M., Prasad, N., & Westad, C. (2010). *Child welfare process and outcomes: Caregiver cognitive impairment*. Edmonton, Alberta: University of Alberta Press.

McConnell, D., & Llewellyn, G. (2000). Disability and Discrimination in Statutory Child Protection Proceedings. *Disability & Society*, *15*(6), 883–895. doi:10.1080/713662015

McConnell, D., Llewellyn, G., Mayes, R., Russo, D., & Honey, A. (2003). Developmental profiles of children born to mothers with intellectual disability. *Journal of Intellectual & Developmental Disability*, *28*(2), 122–134. doi:10.1080/1366825031000147067

McConnell, D., Savage, A., & Breitkreuz, R. (2014). Resilience in families raising children with disabilities and behavior problems. *Research in Developmental Disabilities*, *35*(4), 833–848. doi:10.1016/j.ridd.2014.01.015 PMID:24491480

McCormick, R., & McRae, J. (2005). *Job development in supported employment: A study of Dublin supermarkets*. National Disability Authority (NDA) Disability Research Conference, Dublin, Ireland.

McDonald, E. (2000). *Deep Test of Articulation*. Pittsburg: Stanwix House.

McDonald, K. E., Keys, C. B., & Balcazar, F. E. (2007). Disability, race/ethnicity and gender: Themes of cultural oppression, acts of individual resistance. *American Journal of Community Psychology*, *39*(1-2), 145–161. doi:10.1007/s10464-007-9094-3 PMID:17294120

McGaw, S. (2004) Parenting exceptional children. In Handbook of Parenting. Theory and Research for Practice. Sage Publications. doi:10.4135/9781848608160.n14

McGaw, S., Shaw, T., & Beckley, K. (2007). Prevalence of Psychopathology Across a Service Population of Parents With Intellectual Disabilities and Their Children. *Journal Of Policy And Practice In Intellectual Disabilities, 4*(1), 11-22. doi:. 00093.x10.1111/j.1741-1130.2006

McGillivray, J. A., Gaskin, C. J., Newton, D. C., & Richardson, B. A. (in press). Substance Use, Offending, and Participation in Alcohol and Drug Treatment Programmes: A Comparison of Prisoners with and without Intellectual Disabilities. *Journal of Applied Research in Intellectual Disabilities*. PMID:25754684

McGillivray, J. A., & Moore, M. R. (2001). Substance use by offenders with mild intellectual disability. *Journal of Intellectual & Developmental Disability*, *26*(4), 297–310. doi:10.1080/13668250120087317

McGrail, J. P., & Rieger, A. (2013). Coping humor and family functioning in parents of children with disabilities. *Rehabilitation Psychology*, *58*(1), 89–97. doi:10.1037/a0031556 PMID:23438005

McHale, S. M., & Gamble, W. C. (1987). Sibling relationships and adjustment of children with disabled brothers and sisters. In F. Fuchs Schachter & R. K. Stine (Eds.), Practical concerns about siblings: Bridging the research-practice gap (pp. 131-158). New York: Haworth Press.

McHale, S. M., & Gamble, W. C. (1989). Sibling relationships of children with disabled and nondisabled brothers and sisters. *Developmental Psychology*, *25*(3), 421–429. doi:10.1037/0012-1649.25.3.421

McHale, S. M., Updegraff, K. A., Jackson-Newsom, J., Tucker, C. J., & Crouter, A. C. (2000). When does parents' differential treatment have negative implications for siblings? *Social Development*, *9*(2), 149–172. doi:10.1111/1467-9507.00117

McIntyre, L. L. (2008). Adapting Webster-Stratton's incredible years parent training for children with developmental delay: Findings from a treatment group only study. *Journal of Intellectual Disability Research*, *52*(12), 1176–1192. doi:10.1111/j.1365-2788.2008.01108.x PMID:18671808

McIntyre, L. L., Blacher, J., & Baker, B. L. (2002). Behaviour/mental health problems in young adults with intellectual disability: The impact on families. *Journal of Intellectual Disability Research*, *46*(3), 239–249. doi:10.1046/j.1365-2788.2002.00371.x PMID:11896809

McIntyre, L. L., Blacher, J., & Baker, B. L. (2006). The transition to school: Adaptation in young children with and without developmental delays. *Journal of Intellectual Disability Research*, *50*(5), 349–361. doi:10.1111/j.1365-2788.2006.00783.x PMID:16629928

McKinlay & McGowan. (2003). Forensic issues in neuropsychology. In P. W. Halligan, U. Kischka, & J. C. Marshall (Eds.), *Handbook of clinical neuropsychology* (pp. 676–693). New York: Oxford University Press.

McLean, L. K., Brady, N. C., & McLean, J. E. (1996). Reported communication abilities of individuals with severe mental retardation. *American Journal of Mental Retardation*, *100*, 580–589. PMID:8735572

McLean, L. K., Brady, N. C., McLean, J. E., & Behrens, G. A. (1999). Communication forms and functions of children and adults with severe mental retardation in community and institutional settings. *Journal of Speech, Language, and Hearing Research: JSLHR*, *42*(1), 231–240. doi:10.1044/jslhr.4201.231 PMID:10025557

McLeavy, B. C., Tomey, J. F., & Dempsey, P. J. R. (1982). Nonretarded and mentally retarded children's control over syntactic structures. *American Journal of Mental Deficiency*, *86*, 485–494. PMID:7124802

McLeod, S. A. (2008). *Erik Erikson/Psychological Stages*. Retrieved from www.simplypsychology.org/Erik-Erikson.html

McNamara, J. K., Willoughby, T., & Chalmers, H. (2005). Psychosocial status of adolescents with learning disabilities with and without comorbid attention deficit hyperactivity disorder. *Learning Disabilities Research & Practice*, *20*(4), 234–244. doi:10.1111/j.1540-5826.2005.00139.x

McNaughton, D., & Light, J. (2013). The iPad and mobile technology revolution: Benefits and challenges for individuals who require augmentative and alternative communication. *Augmentative and Alternative Communication*, *29*(2), 107–116. doi:10.3109/07434618.2013.784930 PMID:23705813

McNulty, C., Kissi-Deborah, R., & Newsom-Davies, I. (1995). Police involvement with clients having intellectual disabilities: A pilot study in South London. *Mental Handicap Research*, *8*(2), 129–136. doi:10.1111/j.1468-3148.1995.tb00150.x

McVilly, K. R., Parmenter, T. R., Stancliffe, R. J., & Burton-Smith, R. M. (2004). Friendship experiences and aspirations of adults with intellectual disability (ID). *Journal of Intellectual Disability Research*, *48*, 428.

Mechling, L. C. (2011). Review of twenty-first century portable electronic devices for persons with moderate intellectual disabilities and autism spectrum disorders. *Education and Training in Autism and Developmental Disabilities*, 479-498.

Mechling, L. C., Gast, D. L., & Barthold, S. (2003). Multimedia computer-based instruction to teach students with moderate intellectual disabilities to use a debit card to make purchases. *Exceptionality*, *11*(4), 239–254. doi:10.1207/S15327035EX1104_4

Mechling, L. C., Gast, D. L., & Langone, J. (2002). Computer-based video instruction to teach persons with moderate intellectual disabilities to read grocery aisle signs and locate items. *The Journal of Special Education*, *35*(4), 224–240. doi:10.1177/002246690203500404

Meltzer, H., Gatward, R., Goodman, R., & Ford, T. (2000). *Mental health of children and adolescents in Great Britain*. London: The Stationery Office. doi:10.1037/e622732007-001

Mencap. (2007). *Death by indifference*. Mencap.

Mental Disability Rights International (MDRI). (2007). *Ruined Lives: Segregation from Society in Argentina's Psychiatric Asylums*. Washington, DC: Mental Disability Rights International.

Mercer, J. (1973). *Labelling the mentally retarded*. Berkeley, CA: University of California Press.

Merrill, E. C., & Mar, H. H. (1987). Differences between mentally retarded and non retarded persons' efficiency of auditory sentence processing. *American Journal of Mental Deficiency*, *86*, 485–494. PMID:3812610

Merrill, E. C., & Mar, H. H. (1987). Differences between mentally retarded and nonretarded persons' efficiency of auditory sentence processing. *American Journal of Mental Deficiency*, *91*, 406–414. PMID:3812610

Mesibov, G. B., Shea, V., & Schopler, E. (2004). *The TEACCH approach to autism spectrum disorders*. Springer Science & Business Media. doi:10.1007/978-0-306-48647-0

Metcalf, D. S., & De Marco, J. M. (2006). mLearning: Mobile learning and performance in the palm of your hand. Amherst, MA: HRD Press.

Meyer, D., Vadasky, P., & Fewell, R. (1982). Involving fathers of handicapped infants: Translating research into program goals. *Journal of the Division for Early Childhood, 5*.

Meyer, K. A., Ingersoll, B., & Hambrick, D. Z. (2011). Factors influencing adjustment in siblings of children with autism spectrum disorders. *Research in Autism Spectrum Disorders*, *5*(4), 1413–1420. doi:10.1016/j.rasd.2011.01.027

Michael, J. (1982). Distinguishing between discriminative and motivational functions of stimuli. *Journal of the Experimental Analysis of Behavior*, *37*(1), 149–155. doi:10.1901/jeab.1982.37-149 PMID:7057126

Michael, J. (2000). Implications and refinements of the establishing operation concept. *Journal of Applied Behavior Analysis*, *33*(4), 401–410. doi:10.1901/jaba.2000.33-401 PMID:11214018

Mickelson, P. (1947). The feeble-minded parent: A study of 90 family cases. *American Journal of Mental Deficiency*, *51*, 644–653. PMID:20267775

Miclea, D. L., Cuzmici, Z., & Pop, I. V. (2015). Genetic testing in patients with global developmental delay / intellectual disabilities. *A review Med.*, *88*(3), 288–292. PMID:26609258

Migliore, A., Grossie, T., & Rogan, P. (2008). Why do adults with intellectual disabilities work in sheltered workshops? *Journal of Vocational Rehabilitation*, *28*, 29–12.

Migliore, A., Mank, D., Grossi, T., & Rogan, P. (2007). Integrated employment or sheltered workshops: Preferences of adults with intellectual disabilities, their families, and staff. *Journal of Vocational Rehabilitation*, *26*, 5–19.

Miller, J. (1981). *Assessing language production in children*. Needham Heights, MA: Allyn and Bacon.

Miller, J. F., & Yoder, D. (1974). An ontogenetic language teaching strategy for retarded children. In R. Schiefelbusch & L. Lloyd (Eds.), *Language perspectives-Acquisition, retardation and intervention*. Baltimore University Park Press.

Miller, L. (1984). Problem solving and language disorders. In G. P. Wallach & K. G. Butler (Eds.), *Language learning disabilities in school-age children* (pp. 199–229). Baltimore, MD: Williams & Wilkins.

Mills, L. A. (2006). *Revitalizing integrated employment: A study of nationwide best practices for increasing integrated employment outcomes among people with developmental disabilities*. Madison, WI: Wisconsin Department of Health and Family Services/Pathways to Independence.

Mindell, J. A., Kuhn, B., Lewin, D. S., Meltzer, L. J., & Sadeh, A. (2006). Behavioral treatment of bedtime problems and night wakings in infants and young children. *American Academy of Sleep Medicine Sleep.*, *29*(10), 1263–1276. PMID:17068979

Miodrag, N., & Hodapp, R. M. (2010). Chronic stress and health among parents of children with intellectual and developmental disabilities. *Current Opinion in Psychiatry*, *23*(5), 407–411. doi:10.1097/YCO.0b013e32833a8796 PMID:20592593

Mishna, F. (2003). Learning disabilities and bullying: Double jeopardy. *Journal of Learning Disabilities*, *36*(4), 336–347. doi:10.1177/00222194030360040501 PMID:15490906

Mishna, F., Khoury-Kassabri, M., Gadalla, T., & Daciuk, J. (2012). Risk factors for involvement in cyber bullying: Victims, bullies, and bully-victims. *Children and Youth Services Review*, *32*(1), 63–70. doi:10.1016/j.childyouth.2011.08.032

Mitchell, C., McLanahan, S., Brooks-Gunn, J., Garfinkel, I., Hobcraft, J., & Notterman, D. (2013). Genetic differential sensitivity to social environments: Implications for research. *American Journal of Public Health*, *103*(S1), S102–S110. doi:10.2105/AJPH.2013.301382 PMID:23927507

Mitchell, D. B., & Hauser-Cram, P. (2008). The well-being of mothers of adolescents with developmental disabilities in relation to medical care utilization and satisfaction with health care. *Research in Developmental Disabilities*, *29*(2), 97–112. doi:10.1016/j.ridd.2006.12.002 PMID:17267176

Moeschler, J. B., & Shevell, M. (2006). Clinical genetic evaluation of the child with mental retardation or developmental delays. *Pediatrics*, *117*(6), 2304–2316. doi:10.1542/peds.2006-1006 PMID:16740881

Mohanty, G. (1989). Mental Retardation. In *Text Book of Abnormal Psychology*. New Delhi: Kalyani Publishers.

Mohanty, G. (1989). *The Ego and its DefenseMechanism. Text book of Abnormal Psychology*. New Delhi: Kalyani Publishers.

Mohapatra, S., & Mohanty, M. (2004). *Abuse and Activity Limitation: A Study on Domestic Violence Against Disabled Women in Orissa, India*. Retrieved: http://swabhiman.org/userfiles/file/Abuse%20and%20Activity%20Limitation%20 Study.pdf,10-11

Mohapatra, S., & Mohanty, M. (2004). *Abuse and activity limitation: a study on domestic violence against disabled women in Orissa, India*. Bhubaneswar, Orissa: Swabhiman.

Molteno, G., Molteno, C. D., Finchilescu, G., & Dawes, A. R. L. (2001). Behavioural and emotional problems in children with intellectual disability attending special schools in Cape Town, South Africa. *Journal of Intellectual Disability Research*, *45*(6), 515–520. doi:10.1046/j.1365-2788.2001.00368.x PMID:11737538

Mondal, A., Mete, J., (2011). *Education of Children with Disabilities in India: Concern and Policy Perspective*. Academic Press.

Mondal, A., & Mete, J. (2013). Education of children with disabilities in India.*Indian. The Journal of Educational Research*, *2*, 56–67.

Moore, K. A., & Keyes, C. L. M. (2003). Introduction. In M. H. Bornstein, L. Davidson, C. L. M. Keyes, & K. A. Moore (Eds.), *Wellbeing: Positive development across the life- course* (pp. 1–11). Mahwah, NJ: Lawrence Erlbaum.

Moran, G., Pederson, D. R., Pettit, P., & Krupka, A. (1992). Maternal sensitivity and infant-mother attachment in a developmentally delayed sample. *Journal of Infant Behavior and Development*, *15*(4), 427–442. doi:10.1016/0163-6383(92)80011-I

Mørch, W. T., Skår, J., & Andersgård, A. B. (1997). Mentally retarded persons as parents: Prevalence and the situation of their children. *Scandinavian Journal of Psychology*, *38*(4), 343–348. doi:10.1111/1467-9450.00044 PMID:9449195

Morin, D., Rivard, M., Boursier, C. P., Crocker, A. G., & Caron, J. (2015). Norms of the Attitudes Toward Intellectual Disability Questionnaire. *Journal of Intellectual Disability Research*, *59*(5), 462–467. doi:10.1111/jir.12146 PMID:25041088

Morin, D., Rivard, M., Crocker, A. G., Boursier, C. P., & Caron, J. (2013). Public attitudes towards intellectual disability: A multidimensional perspective. *Journal of Intellectual Disability Research*, *57*(3), 279–292. doi:10.1111/jir.12008 PMID:23279318

Morisse, F., Vandemaele, E., Claes, C., Claes, L., & Vandevelde, S. (2013). Quality of Life in Persons with Intellectual Disabilities and Mental Health Problems: An Explorative Study. *The Scientific World Journal*.

Morris, C. D., Niederbuhl, J. M., & Mahr, J. M. (1993). Determining the capability of individuals with mental retardation to give informed consent. *American Journal of Mental Retardation*, *98*(2), 263–272. PMID:8398085

Morris, J. (2005). *Citizenship and disabled People, Disability Rights Commission*. London: DRC.

Morrison, G. M., Furlong, M. J., & Smith, G. (1994). Factors associated with the experience of school violence among general education, leadership class, opportunity class, and special day class pupils. *Journal of Education and Treatment of Children*, *17*, 356–369.

Moss, S., Emerson, E., & Kiernan, C. et al.. (2000). Psychiatric symptoms in adults with learning disability and challenging behaviour. *The British Journal of Psychiatry*, *177*(5), 452–456. doi:10.1192/bjp.177.5.452 PMID:11060000

Moyson, T., & Roeyers, H. (2012, January). Roeyers H., 'The overall quality of my life as a sibling is all right, but of course, it could always be better'. Quality of life of siblings of children with intellectual disability: The siblings' perspectives. *Journal of Intellectual Disability Research*, *56*(1), 87–101. doi:10.1111/j.1365-2788.2011.01393.x PMID:21366753

Mulder, E., Tudor, M. E., & Walsh, C. E. (2013). Predictors of parent stress in a sample of children with ASD: Pain, problem behaviour, and parental coping. *Research in Autism Spectrum Disorders*, *7*(2), 256–264. doi:10.1016/j.rasd.2012.08.010

Mundt, J. C., Marks, I. M., Shear, M. K., & Greist, J. M. (2002). The Work and Social Adjustment Scale: A simple measure of impairment in functioning. *The British Journal of Psychiatry*, *180*(5), 461–464. doi:10.1192/bjp.180.5.461 PMID:11983645

Mung'omba, J. (2008). Comparative policy brief: Status of intellectual disabilities in the Republic of Zambia. *Journal of Policy and Practice in Intellectual Disabilities*, *5*(2), 142–144. doi:10.1111/j.1741-1130.2008.00163.x

Murphy, B. 2000 Australian WHOQoL instruments: User's manual and interpretation guide. Melbourne, Australia: Australian WHOQoL Field Study Centre.

Murphy, G., & Mason, J. (2014). Forensic and offending behaviours. In E. Tsakanikos & J. McCarthy (Eds.), Handbook of psychopathology in intellectual disability (pp. 281-303). New York: Springer. doi:10.1007/978-1-4614-8250-5_18

Murphy, S. T., & Rogan, P. M. (1995). *Closing the shop: Conversion from sheltered to integrated work*. Baltimore, MD: Paul H. Brookes.

Myers, J.S. (1962). Education and Rehabilitation. *The Journal of Education*, *145*(1), 3-34.

Myrbakk, E., & von Tetzchner, S. (2008). Psychiatric disorders and behaviour problems in people with intellectual disability. *Research in Developmental Disabilities*, *29*(4), 316–332. doi:10.1016/j.ridd.2007.06.002 PMID:17616450

Nabuzoka, D. (2003). Teacher ratings and peer nominations of bullying and other behavior of children with and without learning difficulties. *Educational Psychology*, *23*(3), 307–321. doi:10.1080/0144341032000060147

Nabuzoka, D., & Smith, P. K. (1993). Sociometric status and social behaviour of children with and without learning difficulties. *Journal of Child Psychology and Psychiatry, and Allied Disciplines*, *34*(8), 1435–1448. doi:10.1111/j.1469-7610.1993.tb02101.x PMID:8294529

Nachshen, J. S., Garcin, N., & Minnes, P. (2005). Problem behaviour in children with intellectual disabilities: Parenting stress, empowerment and school services. *Mental Health Aspects of Developmental Disabilities*, *8*, 105–114.

Nadeau, L., & Tessier, R. (2006). Social adjustment of children with cerebral palsy in mainstream classes: Peer perception. *Developmental Medicine and Child Neurology*, *48*(05), 331–336. doi:10.1017/S0012162206000739 PMID:16608539

Nalavany, B. A., Glidden, L. M., & Ryan, S. D. (2009). Parental satisfaction in the adoption of children with learning disorders: The role of behavior problems. *Family Relations*, *58*(5), 621–633. doi:10.1111/j.1741-3729.2009.00579.x

Nambi, S. (2005). Marriage, Mental health and the Indian legislation. *Indian Journal of Psychiatry*, *47*(1), 3–14. doi:10.4103/0019-5545.46067

Nankervis, K. (1997). *Keynote Address*. Paper presented at the Annual Conference, Australian Society for the Study of Intellectual Disability, Hobart, Australia.

Nansel, T. R., Overpeck, M., Pilla, R. S., Ruan, W. J., Simons-Morton, B., & Scheidt, P. (2001). Bullying behaviors among US youth: Prevalence and association with psychosocial adjustment. *Journal of the American Medical Association*, *285*(16), 2094–2100. doi:10.1001/jama.285.16.2094 PMID:11311098

Narayan, J. & Kurani, D.R. (1990). *Vocational training and employment of persons with mental retardation.* Academic Press.

National Legal Services Authority. (2010). *Legal services to the mentally ill persons and persons with mental disabilities: Scheme Sheet*. Author.

National Sample Survey Organization (NSSO) Ministry of Statistics and Programme Implementation Government of India. (2003). *Disabled Persons in India, NSS 58th round (July - December 2002) Report No. 485 (58/26/1)*. Available from: http://www.domain.b.com/economy/general/ 2005/pdf/Disability_in_India.pdf

National University of Educational Planning and Administration. (2012). *Status of Education in India National Report.* Department of Higher Education, Ministry of Human Resource Development, Government of India.

Navas, P., Verdugo, M. A., Gómez, L. E., & Schalock, R. L. (2012). The concept of quality of life and its role in enhancing human rights in the field of intellectual disability. *Journal of Intellectual Disability Research*, *56*(11), 1036–1045. doi:10.1111/j.1365-2788.2012.01585.x

Naylor, A., & Prescott, P. (2004). Invisible children? The need for support groups for siblings of disabled children. *British Journal of Special Education*, *31*(4), 199–206. doi:10.1111/j.0952-3383.2004.00355.x

Neece, C. L. (2014). Mindfulness-based stress reduction for parents of young children with developmental delays: Implications for parental mental health and child behaviour problems. *Journal of Applied Research in Intellectual Disabilities*, *27*(2), 174–186. doi:10.1111/jar.12064 PMID:23813562

Neece, C. L., Blacher, J., & Baker, B. L. (2010, July). Impact on Siblings of Children With Intellectual Disability: The Role of Child Behavior Problems. *American Journal on Intellectual and Developmental Disabilities*, *115*(4), 291–306. doi:10.1352/1944-7558-115.4.291 PMID:20597724

Neece, C., & Baker, B. L. (2008). Predicting maternal parenting stress in middle childhood: The roles of child intellectual status, behavior problems and social skills. *Journal of Intellectual Disability Research*, *52*(12), 1114–1128. doi:10.1111/j.1365-2788.2008.01071.x PMID:18513339

Neufeldt, A., & Albright, A. (1998). *Disability and self-directed employment. Business development models*. Concord, Canada: Captus Press.

Neufeldt, A., Sandys, J., Fuchs, P., & Logan, P. (2000). Economic integration and disability: A baseline benefits and costs study of supported and self-directed employment initiatives in Canada. *International Journal of Practical Approaches to Disability*, *23*, 24–36.

Neuwirth, G. S., Heisler, P. A., & Goldrich, K. S. (1974). Capacity, competence, consent: Voluntary sterilization of the mentally retarded. *Columbia Human Rights Law Review*, *6*, 447. PMID:11663600

New South Wales. Law Reform Commission. (1994). *People with an intellectual disability and the criminal justice system: Courts and sentencing issues* (Vol. 35). The Commission.

Ng, C. H. (1997). The stigma of mental illness in Asian cultures. *The Australian and New Zealand Journal of Psychiatry*, *31*(3), 382–390. doi:10.3109/00048679709073848 PMID:9226084

Nichols, M. L. (1989). *The self-esteem of normal children of mothers with mental retardation: An exploratory study*. (Unpublished doctoral dissertation). University of Oregon, Portland, OR.

Nihira, K., Mink, I. T., & Meyers, C. E. (1985). Home environment and development of slow-learning adolescents: Reciprocal relations. *Developmental Psychology*, *21*(5), 784–794. doi:10.1037/0012-1649.21.5.784

Nimbalkar, S., Raithatha, S., & Shah, R. (2014). *A qualitative study of psychosocial problems among parents of children with cerebral palsy attending two tertiary care hospitals in Western India*. ISRN Family Medicine.

Nirje, B. (1985). "The basis and logic of the normalization principle", in Australia & New Zealand. *Journal on Developmental Disabilities*, *11*, 65–68.

Nishina, A., Juvonen, J., & Witkow, M. (2005). Sticks and stones may break my bones, but names will make me sick: The consequences of peer harassment. *Journal of Clinical Child and Adolescent Psychology*, *34*, 37–48. doi:10.1207/s15374424jccp3401_4 PMID:15677279

No Child Left Behind Act of 2001, 20 U.S.C., Pub. L. No. 107-110 (2002).

Noorden, T. H. J., Haselager, G. J. T., Cillessen, A. H. N., & Bukowski, W. M. (2015). Empathy and involvement in bullying in children and adolescents: A systematic review. *Journal of Youth and Adolescence*, *44*(3), 637–657. doi:10.1007/s10964-014-0135-6 PMID:24894581

Norins-Bardon, Matsumoto, & Siperstein. (2005). *US students attitudes to students with intellectual disabilities at the Global Youth Summit, Nagano, Japan, February 2005.* Available at www.specialolympics.org

Norman, J. M., Collins, B. C., & Schuster, J. W. (2001). Using an instructional package including video technology to teach self-help skills to elementary students with mental deficiency. *Journal of Special Education Technology*, *16*, 5–18.

Norrgard, K. (2008). Human testing, the eugenics movement, and IRBs. *Nature Education*, *1*(1), 170.

Norwich, B., & Kelly, N. (2004). Pupils' views on inclusion: Moderate learning difficulties and bullying in mainstream and special schools. *British Educational Research Journal*, *30*(1), 43–65. doi:10.1080/01411920310001629965

Nota, L., Ferrari, L., Soresi, S., & Wehmeyer, M. (2007). Self-determination, social abilities and the quality of life of people with intellectual disability. *Journal of Intellectual Disability Research*, *51*(11), 850–865. doi:10.1111/j.1365-2788.2006.00939.x PMID:17910537

Novaco, R. W., & Taylor, J. L. (2004). Assessment of anger and aggression among male offenders with developmental disabilities. *Psychological Assessment*, *16*(1), 42–50. doi:10.1037/1040-3590.16.1.42 PMID:15023091

Nowicki, E. A. (2006). A cross-sectional multivariate analysis of children's attitudes towards disability. *Journal of Intellectual Disability Research*, *50*(5), 335–348. doi:10.1111/j.1365-2788.2005.00781.x PMID:16629927

NSW Ministry of Health. (2015). *NSW School-Link Strategy and Action Plan 2014-2017.* Sydney, Australia: NSW Ministry of Health.

Ntombela, T. (1991). *The family of a mentally retarded child* (Vol. I). Social Work Practise.

O'Brennan, L. M., Bradshaw, C. P., & Sawyer, A. L. (2009). Examining development differences in the social-emotional problems among frequent bullies, victims, and bully/victims. *Psychology in the Schools*, *46*(2), 100–115. doi:10.1002/pits.20357

O'Brien, I., Duffy, A., & Nicholl, H. (2009). Impact of childhood chronic illnesses on siblings: *A literature review. British Journal of Nursing (Mark Allen Publishing)*, *18*, 1360–1365. PMID:20081690

O'Callaghan, A. C., & Murphy, G. H. (2007). Sexual relationships in adults with intellectual disabilities: Understanding the law. *Journal of Intellectual Disability Research*, *51*(3), 197–206. doi:10.1111/j.1365-2788.2006.00857.x PMID:17300415

O'Keefe, P. (2009). *People with disabilities in India: from commitments to outcomes. Human Development Unit, South Asia Region.* The World Bank.

O'Neill, A. M. (1985). Normal and bright children of mentally retarded parents: The Huck Finn syndrome. *Child Psychiatry and Human Development*, *15*(4), 255–268. doi:10.1007/BF00706369 PMID:4042738

O'Neill, R. E., Horner, R. H., Albin, R. W., Sprague, J. R., Storey, K., & Newton, J. S. (1997). *Functional Assessment and Program Development for Problem Behavior* (2nd ed.). Pacific Grove, CA: Brooks/Cole.

O'Neill, R. E., Horner, R. H., Albin, R. W., Storey, K., & Sprague, J. R. (1990). *Functional Analysis of Problem Behavior: A Practical Assessment Guide.* Sycamore, IL: Sycamore Publishing.

O'Brien, G., Barnard, L., Pearson, J., & Rippon, L. (2002). Physical health and clinical phenotypes. *Physical Health of Adults with Intellectual Disabilities*, 35-62.

Office of Disability Employment Policy. (2001). Customized employment. In *Applying practical solutions for employment success* (Vol. 2). Washington, DC: United States Department of Labor.

Okahashi, P. (2001). Self-employment for people with disabilities. *Rehabilitation Record*, *12*, 1–2.

Oliver, M. (1996). *Understanding disability: From theory to practice*. London: Macmillan Press. doi:10.1007/978-1-349-24269-6

Olsson, M. B., & Hwang, C. P. (2001). Depression in mothers and fathers of children with intellectual disability. *Journal of Intellectual Disability Research*, *45*(6), 535–543. doi:10.1046/j.1365-2788.2001.00372.x PMID:11737541

Olsson, M. B., & Hwang, C. P. (2008). Relationships Among Risk, Sense of Coherence, and Well-Being in Parents of Children With and Without Intellectual Disabilities. *Journal of Policy and Practice in Intellectual Disabilities*, *5*(4), 227–236. doi:10.1111/j.1741-1130.2008.00184.x

Olthof, T., & Goossens, F. A. (2008). Bullying and the need to belong: Early adolescents' bullying-related behavior and the acceptance they desire and receive from particular classmates. *Social Development*, *17*(1), 24–46.

Olvera, D. R., Dever, R. B., & Earnest, M. A. (2000). Mental retardation and sentences for murder: Comparison of two recent court cases. *Mental Retardation*, *38*(3), 228–233. doi:10.1352/0047-6765(2000)038<0228:MRASFM>2.0.CO;2 PMID:10900930

Olweus, D. (1978). *Aggression in the schools: Bullies and whipping boys*. Washington, DC: Hemisphere Press.

Olweus, D. (1993). *Bullying at school: What we know and what we can do*. Blackwell Publshing.

Opperman, S., & Alant, E. (2003). The coping of the adolescent siblings of children with severe disabilities. *Disability and Rehabilitation*, *25*(9), 441–454. doi:10.1080/0963828031000069735 PMID:12745939

Orchard, A. (2013) *The burning issue: Why do people with intellectual disability commit arson?* (MSc dissertation). University of Portsmouth.

Orsmond, G. I., Seltzer, M. M., Krauss, M. W., & Hong, J. (2003). Behavior problems in adults with mental retardation and maternal well-being: Examination of the direction of effects. *American Journal of Mental Retardation*, *108*(4), 257–271. doi:10.1352/0895-8017(2003)108<257:BPIAWM>2.0.CO;2 PMID:12780337

Osborn, F. (1937). Development of a Eugenic Philosophy. *American Sociological Review*, *2*(3), 389–397. doi:10.2307/2084871

Ou, J.-J., Shi, L.-J., & Xun, G.-L. et al.. (2015). Employment and financial burden of families with preschool children diagnosed with autism spectrum disorders in urban China: Results from a descriptive study. *BMC Psychiatry*, *15*, 42–57. PMID:25608486

Ouyang, L., Grosse, S. D., Riley, C., Bolen, J., Bishop, E., Raspa, M., & Bailey, D. B. Jr. (2014). A comparison of family financial and employment impacts of fragile X syndrome, autism spectrum disorders, and intellectual disability. *Research in Developmental Disabilities*, *35*(7), 1518–1527. doi:10.1016/j.ridd.2014.04.009 PMID:24755230

Owens, R. E. (2004). *Language disorders: A functional approach to assessment and intervention* (4th ed.). Boston: Allyn & Bacon.

Owens, R. E. (2005). *Language development: An introduction* (6th ed.). Boston: Allyn & Bacon.

Owings, N. O., & McManus, M. D. (1980). An analysis of communication functions in the speech of deinstitutionalized adult mentally retarded client. *Mental Retardation*, *18*, 309–314. PMID:7253928

Ozdemir, M., & Stattin, H. (2011). Bullies, victims, and bully-victims: A longitudinal examination of the effects of bullying-victimization experiences on youth well-being. *Journal of Aggression, Conflict and Peace Research, 3*(2), 97–102. doi:10.1108/17596591111132918

Paransky, O., & Zurawin, R. (2003). Management of menstrual problems and contraception in adolescents with mental retardation: A medical, legal and ethical review with new suggested guidelines. *Journal of Pediatric and Adolescent Gynecology, 16*(4), 223–235. doi:10.1016/S1083-3188(03)00125-6

Parker, J., & Stimpson, J. (2002). *Sibling rivalry, sibling love*. London: Hodder & Stoughton.

Parmenter, T. R. (1980). *Vocational training for independent living*. New York: World Rehabilitation Fund Inc.

Parmenter, T. R. (2001). Intellectual disabilities. Quo vadis? In G. Albrecht, K. D. Seelman, & M. Bury (Eds.), *Handbook of Disability Studies* (pp. 267–296). New York: Sage. doi:10.4135/9781412976251.n11

Parmenter, T. R. (2008). The present, past and future of the study of intellectual disability: Challenges in developing countries. *Salud Pública de México, 50*, s124–s131. doi:10.1590/S0036-36342008000800004 PMID:18470339

Parmenter, T. R., Einfeld, S. L., Tonge, B. J., & Dempster, J. A. (1998). Behavioural and emotional problems in the classroom of children and adolescents with intellectual disability. *Journal of Intellectual & Developmental Disability, 23*(1), 71–77. doi:10.1080/13668259800033591

Parry, J., & Drogin, E. Y. (2007). *Mental disability law, evidence, and testimony: A comprehensive reference manual for lawyers, judges, and mental disability professionals*. American Bar Association.

Passey, J., & Feldman, M. (2004). Descriptive analysis of parent–child interactions in young children with or at risk for developmental delay. *Behavioral Interventions, 19*(4), 233–246. doi:10.1002/bin.164

Patterson, T. L., Goldman, S., McKibbin, C. L., Hughs, T., & Jeste, D. V. (2001). UCSD Performance-Based Skills Assessment: Development of a new measure of everyday functioning for severely mentally ill adults. *Schizophrenia Bulletin, 27*(2), 235–245. doi:10.1093/oxfordjournals.schbul.a006870 PMID:11354591

Paul, R., & Cohen, D. J. (1984). Responses to contingent queries in adults with mental retardation and pervasive developmental disorders. *Applied Psycholinguistics, 5*(04), 349–357. doi:10.1017/S0142716400005221

Paul, R., & Norbury, C. F. (2012). *Language Disorders: From infancy through adolescence*. Missouri: Mosby-Yera Book.

Pearl, R., & Bay, M. (1999). Psychosocial correlates of learning disabilities. In V. L. Schwean & D. H. Saklofske (Eds.), *Handbook of psychosocial characteristics of exceptional children* (pp. 443–470). New York, NY: Kluwer Academic / Plenum Publishers. doi:10.1007/978-1-4757-5375-2_17

Pena-Brooks, A., & Hegde, M. N. (2000). *Assessment & Treatment of Articulation and Phonological Disorders in Children*. Austin, TX: Pro-Ed.

Pena, E. D., Iglesias, A., & Lidz, C. S. (2001). Reducing test bias through dynami assessment of children's word learning ability. *American Journal of Speech-languag Pathology, 10*, 138–154. doi:10.1044/1058-0360(2001/014)

Pendergast, K., Dickey, S. E., Selman, J. W., & Soder, A. (1990). *Photo Articulation Test*. Danville, IL: Interstate Printers and Publishers.

Perkins, T., Holburn, S., Deaux, K., Flory, M., & Vietze, P. (2002). Children of Mothers with Intellectual Disability: Stigma, Mother-Child Relationship and Self-esteem. *Journal Of Applied Research In Intellectual Disabilities, 15*(4), 297-313. doi:.00140.x10.1046/j.1468-3148.2002

Perren, S., Dooley, J., Shaw, T., & Cross, T. (2010). Bullying in school and cyberspace: Associations with depressive symptoms in Swiss and Australian adolescents. *Child and Adolescent Psychiatry and Mental Health*, *23*(4), 28. doi:10.1186/1753-2000-4-28 PMID:21092266

Perry, J., & Felce, D. (2005). Factors associated with outcomes in community group homes. *American Journal of Mental Retardation*, *110*(2), 121–135. doi:10.1352/0895-8017(2005)110<121:FAWOIC>2.0.CO;2 PMID:15762822

Persha, A., Arya, S., & Nagar, R. K. et al.. (2007). Biological and Psychological Predictors of Developmental Delay in Persons with Intellectual Disability: Retrospective Case- File Study. *Asia Pacific Disability Rehabilitation Journal*, *18*(1), 93–100.

Perske, R. (1991). *Unequal justice?: What can happen when persons with retardation or other developmental disabilities encounter the criminal justice system*. Nashville, TN: Abingdon Press.

Perske, R. (2005). Search for persons with intellectual disabilities who confessed to serious crimes they did not commit. *Journal Information*, *43*(1), 58–65. PMID:15628935

Perske, R. (2008). False confessions from 53 persons with intellectual disabilities: The list keeps growing. *Intellectual and Developmental Disabilities*, *46*(6), 468–479. doi:10.1352/2008.46:468-479 PMID:19006433

Perske, R. (2011). Perske's list: False confessions from 75 persons with intellectual disability. *Intellectual and Developmental Disabilities*, *49*(5), 365–373. doi:10.1352/1934-9556-49.5.365 PMID:21905830

Peshawaria, R., Menon D.K., Ganguly, R., Roy, S., RajanPillay, P.R.S., & Gupta, A. (1998). A study offacilitators and inhibitors that affect coping in parents of children with mental retardation in India. *Asia Pacific Disability Rehabilitation Journal, 9*(1).

Peshawaria, R., Menon, D. K., Ganguly, R., Roy, S., Pillay, R.P.R.S., & Gupta, A. (1995). *Understanding the Indian Families Having Persons with Mental Retardation.* NIMH, Secundrabad. Retrieved from http://nimhindia.gov.in/Understanding%20Indian%20Families.pdf

Peshawaria, R., Menon, D.K., Ganguly, R., Roy, S., Rajan Pillay, P.R.S., Gupta, A., … Ayub, L. (1995). *Understanding Indian Families, having persons with mental retardation.* Academic Press.

Petalas, M. A., Hastings, R. P., Nash, S., Lloyd, T., &Dowey, A. (2009). Emotional and behavioural adjustment in siblings of children with intellectual disability with and without autism. *Autism, 13*, 417-483. doi: 10.1177/1362361309335721

Petalas, M. A., Hastings, R. P., Nash, S., Hall, L. M., Joannidi, H., & Dowey, A. (2012). Psychological adjustment and sibling relationships in siblings of children with Autism Spectrum Disorders: Environmental stressors and the Broad Autism Phenotype. *Research in Autism Spectrum Disorders*, *6*(1), 546–555. doi:10.1016/j.rasd.2011.07.015

Peterson, S., Robinson, E., & Littman, I. (1983). Parent-child interaction training for parents with a history of mental retardation. *Applied Research in Mental Retardation*, *4*(4), 329–342. doi:10.1016/0270-3092(83)90033-4 PMID:6670870

Pettigrew, T. F., & Tropp, L. R. (2000). Reducing prejudice and discrimination. *The Claremont Symposium on Applied Social Psychology.*

Petty, J. L., Bacarese-Hamilton, M., Davies, L. E., & Oliver, C. (2014). Correlates of self-injurious, aggressive and destructive behaviour in children under five who are at risk of developmental delay. *Research in Developmental Disabilities*, *35*(1), 36–45. doi:10.1016/j.ridd.2013.10.019 PMID:24216345

Piaget, J. (1997). The essential Piaget. In R. E. Gruber & J. J. Voneche (Eds.), *The language and thought of the child* (p. 85). New York: Basic Books, Inc. Publishers.

Pianta, R. C., Marvin, R. S., Britner, P. A., & Borowitz, K. C. (1996). Mothers' resolution of their children's diagnosis: Organized patterns of caregiving representations. *Infant Mental Health Journal, 17*(3), 239–256. doi:10.1002/(SICI)1097-0355(199623)17:3<239::AID-IMHJ4>3.0.CO;2-J

Piazza, C. C., Hanley, G. P., & Fisher, W. W. (1996). Functional analysis and treatment of cigarette pica. *Journal of Applied Behavior Analysis, 29*(4), 437–450. doi:10.1901/jaba.1996.29-437 PMID:8995829

Pic-ten Care, L. M., & Loors, G. M. P. (2000). Experiences of siblings of children with physical disabilities: An empirical investigation. *Disability and Rehabilitation, 22*, 399–408. doi:10.1080/096382800406013 PMID:10894203

Piecuch, R. E., Leonard, C. H., Cooper, B. A., & Sehring, S. A. (1997). Outcome of extremely low birth weight infants (500 to 999 grams) over a 12-year period. *Pediatrics, 100*(4), 633–639. doi:10.1542/peds.100.4.633 PMID:9310517

Pisula, E. (2011). Parenting stress in mothers and fathers of children with autism spectrum disorders. In A Comprehensive Book on Autism Spectrum Disorders. InTech. doi:10.5772/18507

Pixa-Kettner, U. (1998). Parents with Intellectual Disability in Germany: Results of a Nation-wide Study. *Journal of Applied Research in Intellectual Disabilities, 11*(4), 355-364. doi:.1998.tb00043.x10.1111/j.1468-3148

Pixa-Kettner, U. (1999). Follow-up study on parenting with intellectual disability in Germany. *Journal of Intellectual & Developmental Disability, 24*(1), 75–93. doi:10.1080/13668259900033891

Plant, A., McDermott, E., Chester, V., & Alexander, R. T. (2011). Substance misuse among offenders in a forensic intellectual disability service. *Journal of Learning Disabilities and Offending Behaviour, 2*(3), 127–135. doi:10.1108/20420921111186589

Plante, E. M., & Beason, P. M. (1999). *Communication and Communication Disorders: A clinical Introduction*. Needham, MA: Allyn & Bacon.

Plant, K. M., & Sanders, M. R. (2007). Predictors of care-giver stress in families of preschool-aged children with developmental disabilities. *Journal of Intellectual Disability Research, 51*(2), 109–124. doi:10.1111/j.1365-2788.2006.00829.x PMID:17217475

Plant, K. M., & Sanders, M. R. (2007). Reducing problem behavior during care-giving in families of preschool-aged children with developmental disabilities. *Research in Developmental Disabilities, 28*(4), 362–385. doi:10.1016/j.ridd.2006.02.009 PMID:16781115

Polder, J. J., Meerding, W. J., Bonneux, L., & Van Der Maas, P. J. (2002). Healthcare costs of intellectual disability in the Netherlands: A cost-of-illness perspective. *Journal of Intellectual Disability Research, 46*(2), 168–178. doi:10.1046/j.1365-2788.2002.00384.x PMID:11869388

Polloway, E. A., & Lubin, J. (2009). Feeblemindedness. Encyclopedia of American Disability History of children and adolescents with intellectual disabilities in Britain: A replication. *Journal of Intellectual Disability Research, 51*, 866–874.

Poppes, P., van der Putten, A. J. J., & Vlaskamp, C. (2010). Frequency and severity of challenging behaviour in people with profound intellectual and multiple disabilities. *Research in Developmental Disabilities, 31*(6), 1269–1275. doi:10.1016/j.ridd.2010.07.017 PMID:20728304

Poreddi, BIrudu, Thimmaiah, & Math. (2015). Mental health literacy among caregivers of persons with mental illness: A descriptive survey. *Journal of Neurosciences in Rural Practice, 6*(3), 355-360.

Powell, T. H., & Ogle, P. A. (1985). *Brothers & sisters: A special part of exceptional families*. Baltimore, MD: Paul H. Brookes Publishing.

Prasher, V. P., & Routhu, S. K. (2003). Epidemiology of learning(intellectual) disability and comorbid conditions. *Psychiatry*, *2*, 8.

Pring, T. G. (2004). *Evidence-based practice*. Buckingham, UK: Open University Press.

Psalti, A. (2012). Bullies, victims, and bully-victims in Greek schools: Research data and implications of practice. *Hellenic Journal of Psychology*, *9*(2), 132–157.

Quality of life of young people with an intellect disability in Ireland: Interim Report. (2003). Retrieved from: https://www.fedvol.ie

Rademakers, J., Mouthaan, I., & de Neef, M. (2005). Diversity in sexual health: Problems and dilemmas. *The European Journal of Contraception & Reproductive Health Care*, *10*(4), 207–211. doi:10.1080/13625180500279847 PMID:16448946

Radford, J. P. (1991). Sterilization versus segregation: Control of the 'feebleminded', 1900-1938. *Social Science & Medicine*, *33*(4), 449–458. doi:10.1016/0277-9536(91)90327-9 PMID:1948159

Radliff, K. M., Wheaton, J. E., Robinson, K., & Morris, J. (2012). Illuminating the relationship between bullying and substance use among middle and high school youths. *Addictive Behaviors*, *37*(4), 569–572. doi:10.1016/j.addbeh.2012.01.001 PMID:22277772

Raina, P., & Lunsky, Y. (2010). A comparison study of adults with intellectual disability and psychiatric disorder with and without forensic involvement. *Research in Developmental Disabilities*, *31*(1), 218–223. doi:10.1016/j.ridd.2009.09.008 PMID:19854026

Ramey, C. T., & Ramey, S. L. (2004). Early learning and school readiness: Can early intervention make a difference? *Merrill-Palmer Quarterly*, *50*(4), 471–491. doi:10.1353/mpq.2004.0034

Ramey, C., & Campbell, F. (1984). Preventive education for high-risk children: Cognitive consequences of the Carolina Abecedarian Project. *American Journal of Mental Deficiency*, *88*, 515–523. PMID:6731489

Ramey, C., & Campbell, F. (1987). The Carolina Abecedarian Project: An educational experiment concerning human malleability. In J. Gallagher & C. Ramey (Eds.), *The malleability of children* (pp. 127–139). Baltimore, MD: Brookes.

Randall, L. (2002). *Psychosocial aspects of functional capacity evaluations*. Paper presented at Vocational Rehabilitation Workshop, Pretoria, South Africa.

Randall, P. E., & Parker, J. (1999). *Supporting the families of children with autism*. Chichester, UK: Wiley & Sons.

Rao, L., Govinda, &Sivakumar, T.C. (2003). Vocational Training of the mentally retarded. *EDUTRACTS, 2*(10).

Ravindranodan, S., & Raju, V. (2007). Attitudes of parents of children with mental retardation. *Journal of the Indian Academy of Applied Psychology*, *1*, 137–141.

Rawlins, R. C. A. (1983). *Attitudes to Mental retardation: a cross cultural study.* (MA Counseling Psychology Thesis). University of Natal.

Ray, N. K., Rubenstein, H., & Russo, N. J. (1994). Understanding the parents who are mentally retarded: Guidelines for family preservation programmes. *Child Welfare League of America*, *73*, 725–743. PMID:7988279

Reardon, T. C., Gray, K. M., & Melvin, G. A. (2015). Anxiety disorders in children and adolescents with intellectual disability: Prevalence and assessment. *Research in Developmental Disabilities*, *36*, 175–190. doi:10.1016/j.ridd.2014.10.007 PMID:25462478

Reed, E. J. (1997). Criminal law and the capacity of mentally retarded persons to consent to sexual activity. *Virginia Law Review*, *83*(4), 799–827. doi:10.2307/1073749

Reed, V. A. (2005). *An introduction to children with language disorders* (3rd ed.). Boston: Pearson, Inc.

Rehfeldt, R. A., Dahman, D., Young, A., Cherry, H., & Davis, P. (2003). Teaching a simple meal preparation skill to adults with moderate and severe mental retardation using video modeling. *Behavioral Interventions*, *18*(3), 209–218. doi:10.1002/bin.139

Reid, M. J., Webster-Stratton, C., & Hammond, M. (2007). Enhancing a classroom social competence and problem-solving curriculum by offering parent training to families of moderate-to-high-risk elementary school children. *Journal of Clinical Child and Adolescent Psychology*, *36*(4), 605–620. doi:10.1080/15374410701662741 PMID:18088218

Reilly, P. R. (1987). Involuntary sterilization in the United States: A surgical solution. *The Quarterly Review of Biology*, *62*(2), 153–170. doi:10.1086/415404 PMID:3299450

Reiter, S., Bryen, D., & Shachar, I. (2007). Adolescents with intellectual disabilities as victims of abuse. *Journal of Intellectual Disabilities*, *11*(4), 371–387. doi:10.1177/1744629507084602 PMID:18029413

Reiter, S., & Lapidot-Leflet, N. (2007). Bullying among special education students with intellectual disabilities: Differences in social adjustment and social skills. *Journal of Intellectual & Developmental Disability*, *45*(3), 174–181. doi:10.1352/1934-9556(2007)45[174:BASESW]2.0.CO;2 PMID:17472426

Remington, B. (1998). Applied behaviour analysis and intellectual disability: A long-term relationship?1. *Journal of Intellectual & Developmental Disability*, *23*(2), 121–135. doi:10.1080/13668259800033631

Repp, A. C., & Karsh, D. (1994). A hypothesis-based interventions for tantrum behavior of person with developmental disabilities in school settings. *Journal of Applied Behavior Analysis*, *27*(1), 21–31. doi:10.1901/jaba.1994.27-21 PMID:8188561

Reschly, D. J. (1996). Identification and Assessment of Students with Disabilities. *The Future of Children Special Education for Students with Disabilities*, *6*(1). Retrieved from https://www.princeton.edu/futureofchildren/publications/docs/06_01_02.pdf

Rethink autism provides distance BCBA supervision to candidates seeking certification in behavior analysis . (2010). PR Newswire.

Revheim, N., & Medalia, A. (2004). The independent living scales as a measure of functional outcome for schizophrenia. *Psychiatric Services (Washington, D.C.)*, *55*(9), 1052–1054. doi:10.1176/appi.ps.55.9.1052 PMID:15345767

Reynolds, T., & Zupanick, D.M. (2013). *Intellectual Disability and Severity Codes*. Retrieved from https://www.mentalhelp.net/articles/intellectual-disability-and-severity-codes/

Reynolds, T., Zupanick, C. E., & Dombeck, M. (2013). *Historical and Contemporary Perspectives on Intellectual Disabilities*. Intellectual Disabilities.

Rhodes, P. (2003). Behavioural and family systems interventions in developmental disability: Towards a contemporary and integrative approach. *Journal of Intellectual & Developmental Disability*, *28*(1), 51–64. doi:10.1080/1366825031000086894

Rice, M. L., Warren, S. F., & Betz, S. K. (2005). Language symptoms of developmental language disorders: An overview of autism, Down syndrome, fragile X, specific language impairment, and Williams syndrome. *Applied Psycholinguistics*, *26*(1), 7–27. doi:10.1017/S0142716405050034

Richard, P. (2007). Hastings andTracey Lloyd, Expressed emotion in families of children and adults with intellectual disabilities, Mental Retardation and Developmental Disabilities Research Reviews. *Special Issue: Families of Children with Developmental Disabilities*, *13*(4), 339–345.

Richardson, S. A., & Koller, H. (1996). *Twenty-two years: Causes and consequences of mental retardation*. Harvard University Press.

Richardson, S. O. (1996). Coping with dyslexia in the regular classroom: Inclusion or exclusion. *Annals of Dyslexia*, *46*(1), 37–48. doi:10.1007/BF02648170 PMID:24234266

Richdale, A., & Wiggs, L. (2005). Behavioural approaches to the treatment of sleep problems in children with developmental disorders. What is state of the art? *International Journal of Behavioral and Consultation Therapy*, *1*(3), 165–187. doi:10.1037/h0100743

Riches, V. C., Parmenter, T. R., Llewellyn, G., Hindmarsh, G., & Chan, J. (2009a). I-CAN: A new instrument to classify support needs for people with disability: Part I. *Journal of Applied Research in Intellectual Disabilities*, *22*(4), 326–339. doi:10.1111/j.1468-3148.2008.00466.x

Riches, V. C., Parmenter, T. R., Llewellyn, G., Hindmarsh, G., & Chan, J. (2009b). The reliability, validity and practical utility of measuring supports using the I-CAN Instrument: Part II. *Journal of Applied Research in Intellectual Disabilities*, *22*(4), 340–353. doi:10.1111/j.1468-3148.2008.00467.x

Riddell, S. (2002). Work preparation and vocational rehabilitation: a literature review. Book Work Preparation and Vocational Rehabilitation: A literature. *RE:view*.

Ridley, A. M., Gabbert, F., & La Rooy, D. J. (2012). *Suggestibility in legal contexts: psychological research and forensic implications*. Chichester, UK: John Wiley & Sons.

Rigby, K., & Cox, I. K. (1996). The contributions of bullying and low self-esteem to acts of delinquency among Australian teenagers. *Personality and Individual Differences*, *21*(4), 609–612. doi:10.1016/0191-8869(96)00105-5

Rigby, K., & Slee, P. T. (1991). Bullying among Australian school children: Reported behaviour and attitudes to victims. *The Journal of Social Psychology*, *131*(5), 615–622. doi:10.1080/00224545.1991.9924646 PMID:1798296

Rigby, N. (Ed.). (1973). *The retarded: Pensions or progress?* Canberra: Australian Association on the Mentally Retarded.

Rimmerman, A. (1998). Factors relating to attitudes of Israeli corporate executives towards the employability of persons with intellectual disability. *Journal of Intellectual & Developmental Disability*, *23*(3), 245–254. doi:10.1080/13668259800033731

Risdal, D., & Singer, G. H. (2004). Marital adjustment in parents of children with disabilities: A historical review and meta-analysis. *Research and Practice for Persons with Severe Disabilities*, *29*(2), 95–103. doi:10.2511/rpsd.29.2.95

Ritzema, A.M., & Sladeczek, I.E. (2011). Stress in parents of children with developmental disabilities over time. *Journal of Developmental Disabilities, 17*, 21-34.

Rivers, J., & Stoneman, Z. (2003). Sibling relationships when a child has autism: Marital stress and support coping Disorders. *Journal of Autism and Developmental, 33*, 383-394. doi: 0162-3257/03/0800-0383/0

Robbins, F. R., Dunlap, G., & Plienis, A. J. (1991). Family Characteristics, FamilyTraining and the Progress of Young Children with Autism. *Journal of Early Intervention*, *15*(2), 173–184. doi:10.1177/105381519101500206

Roberts, C. M., & Smith, P. R. (1999). Attitudes and behavior of children towards peers with disabilities. *International Journal of Disability Development and Education*, *46*(1), 35–50. doi:10.1080/103491299100713

Roberts, C., Mazzucchelli, T., Studman, L. J., & Sanders, M. R. (2006). Behavioral family intervention for children with developmental disabilities and behavioral problems. *Journal of Clinical Child and Adolescent Psychology*, *35*(2), 180–193. doi:10.1207/s15374424jccp3502_2 PMID:16597214

Roberts, M. Y., & Kaiser, A. P. (2011). The effectiveness of parent-implemented language interventions: A meta-analysis. *American Journal of Speech-Language Pathology*, *20*(3), 180–199. doi:10.1044/1058-0360(2011/10-0055) PMID:21478280

Robertson, L., Emerson, E., Hatton, C., Elliot, J., McIntosh, B., & Swift, P. et al.. (2006). Longitudinal analysis of the impact and cost of person centered planning for people with intellectual disabilities in England. *American Journal of Mental Retardation*, *111*(6), 400–416. doi:10.1352/0895-8017(2006)111[400:LAOTIA]2.0.CO;2 PMID:17029498

Robinson, M., & Neece, C. L. (2015). Marital satisfaction, parental stress, and child behavior problems among parents of young children with developmental delays. *Journal of Mental Health Research in Intellectual Disabilities*, *8*(1), 23–46. doi:10.1080/19315864.2014.994247

Rodrigue, J. R., Geffken, G. R., & Morgan, S. B. (1993). Perceived competence and behavioural adjustment of siblings of children with autism. *Journal of Autism and Developmental Disorders, 23,* 665–674. doi: 0162-3257/93/0900-0665

Rodrigue, J. R., Morgan, S. B., & Gefken, G. (1990). Families of Autistic Children: Psychological Functioning of Mothers. *Journal of Clinical Psychology*, *19*, 371–379.

Roeleveld, N., & Zielhuis, G. A. (1997). The prevalence of mental retardation: A critical review of recent literature. *Developmental Medicine and Child Neurology*, *39*(2), 125–132. doi:10.1111/j.1469-8749.1997.tb07395.x PMID:9062428

Rogan, P., & Rinne, S. (2011). National call for organizational change from sheltered to integrated employment. Journal of Intellectual and Developmental Disabilities, 49, 248-260. doi:10.1352/1934-9556-49.4.248

Rogers, S. J., Hepburn, S. L., Stackhouse, T., & Wehner, E. (2003). Imitation performance in toddlers with autism and those with other developmental disorders. *Journal of Child Psychology and Psychiatry, and Allied Disciplines*, *44*(5), 763–781. doi:10.1111/1469-7610.00162 PMID:12831120

Rogner, J., & Wessels, E. T. (1994). Coping strategies of mothers and fathers with a first or second born mentally handicapped child. *Praxis der Kinderpsychologie und Kinderpsychiatrie*, *43*(4), 125–129. PMID:8016022

Rogner, J., & Wessels, E. T. (1994). Coping strategies of mothers and fathers with a first- or second-born mentally handicapped child. *Praxis der Kinderpsychologie und Kinderpsychiatrie*, *43*(4), 125–129. PMID:8016022

Romski, M. A., Sevcik, R., & Fonseca, A. (2003). Augmentative and alternative communication for persons with mental retardation. In L. Abbeduto (Ed.), *International review of research in mental retardation: Language and communication* (pp. 255–280). New York: Academic Press. doi:10.1016/S0074-7750(03)27008-7

Ronai, C. R. (1997). On loving and hating my mentally retarded mother. *Mental Retardation, 35*, 417–432. doi:<0417:OLAHMM>2.0.CO;210.1352/0047-6765(1997)035

Rondal, J. A., & Turnure, J. E. (1976). *Maternal speech to normal-hearing and down syndrome children matched for mean length of utterance.* Paper presented at the Annual meeting of the American Association on Mental Deficiency, Chicago, IL.

Roos, P. (1977). Parents of mentally retarded people. *International Journal of Mental Health*, *6*(1), 96–119. doi:10.1080/00207411.1977.11448758

Roseberry-McKibbin, C. (2007). *Language disorders in children: A multicultural and case perspective*. Boston: Pearson Education, Inc.

Rose, C. A., & Espelage, D. L. (2012). Risk and protective factors associated with the bullying involvement of students with emotional and behavioral disorders. *Behavioral Disorders*, *37*(3), 133–148.

Rose, C. A., Espelage, D. L., & Monda-Amaya, L. E. (2009). Bullying and victimization rates among students in general and special education: A comparative analysis. *Educational Psychology*, *29*(7), 761–776. doi:10.1080/01443410903254864

Rose, C. A., Forber-Pratt, A. J., Espelage, D. L., & Aragon, S. R. (2013). The influence of psychosocial factors on bullying involvement of students with disabilities. *Theory into Practice*, *52*(4), 272–279. doi:10.1080/00405841.2013.829730

Rose, C. A., Monda-Amaya, L. E., & Espelage, D. L. (2011). Bullying perpetration and victimization in special education: A review of the literature. *Remedial and Special Education*, *32*(2), 114–130. doi:10.1177/0741932510361247

Rosefeld-johnson, S. (1999). Oromotor exercise for speech clarity. Tucson, AZ: Innovative Therapists International.

Rose, J., West, C., & Clifford, D. (2000). Group interventions for anger in people with intellectual disabilities. *Research in Developmental Disabilities*, *21*(3), 171–181. doi:10.1016/S0891-4222(00)00032-9 PMID:10939316

Rosenbaum, P. L., King, S., Law, M., King, G., & Evans, J. (1998). Family-centred service: A conceptual framework and research review. *Physical & Occupational Therapy in Pediatrics*, *18*, 1–20. Retrieved from http://informahealthcare.com.ezproxy.lib.rmit.edu.au/loi/pop

Rosenberg, S. (1982). The language of the mentally retarded: Development, processes, and intervention. In S. Rosenberg (Ed.), Handbook of applied psycholinguistics: Major thrusts of research and theory (pp. 329-392). Hillsdale, NJ: Erlbaum.

Rosenberg, B. (1973). *The work sample approach to vocational evaluation.Vocational evaluation for rehabilitation services*. Springfield, IL: Charles C Thomas.

Rosin, M., Siwft, E., Bless, D., & Vetter, D. K. (1988). Communication profile of adolescence with Down syndrome. *Journal of Childhood Communication Disorders*, *12*(1), 49–64. doi:10.1177/152574018801200105

Rossiter, L., & Sharpe, D. (2001). The siblings of individuals with mental retardation: A quantitative integration of the literature. *Journal of Child and Family Studies*, *10*(1), 65–84. doi:10.1023/A:1016629500708

Ross, P., & Cuskelly, M. (2006). Adjustment, sibling problems and coping strategies of brothers and sisters of children with autistic spectrum disorder. *Journal of Intellectual & Developmental Disability*, *31*(2), 77–86. doi:10.1080/13668250600710864 PMID:16782592

Roux, G., Sofronoff, K., & Sanders, M. R. (2013). A Randomized Controlled Trial of Group Stepping Stones Triple P: A Mixed-Disability Trial. *Family Process*, *52*(3), 411–424. doi:10.1111/famp.12016 PMID:24033239

Rubin, S. E., & Roessler, R. T. (1995). *Foundations of the vocational rehabilitation process* (4th ed.). Austin, TX: Pro-Ed.

Rueda, R., & Chan, K. (1980). Referential communication skill levels of moderately mentally retarded adolescents. *American Journal of Mental Deficiency*, *85*, 45–52. PMID:7446568

Ruff, C. F., Templer, D. I., & Ayers, J. L. (1976). The intelligence of rapists. *Archives of Sexual Behavior*, *5*(4), 327–329. doi:10.1007/BF01542085 PMID:952615

Ruggeri-Stevens, G., & Goodwin, S. (2007). "Learning to work" in small businesses: Learning and training for young adults with learning disabilities. *Education + Training*, *49*(8/9), 745–755. doi:10.1108/00400910710834139

Rush, A. J., & Frances, A. T. (2000). The expert consensus guidelines: Treatment of psychiatric and behavioral problems in mental retardation. *American Journal of Mental Retardation*, *105*, 159–1228.

Rutledge, M. S., & Scott, M. H. (1997). Students' attitudes towards people with mental retardation. *Academic Medicine*, *72*(4).

Ryan, S. (2005). People don't do odd, do they? Mothers making sense of the reactions of others towards their learning disabled children in public places. *Children's Geographies*, *3*(3), 291–305. doi:10.1080/14733280500352920

Ryckman, D. B., & Henderson, R. S. (1965). The meaning of a retarded child for his parents—A focus for counsellors. *Journal of Mental Retardation.*, *3*(4).

Ryoo, J. H., Wang, C., & Swearer, S. M. (2015). Examination of the change in latent statuses in bullying behaviors across time. *School Psychology Quarterly*, *30*(1), 105–122. doi:10.1037/spq0000082 PMID:25111466

Sacks, O. (1995). *An anthropologist on Mars*. Sydney: Pan Macmillan Australia.

Sailor, W., Wolf, N., Choi, H., & Roger, B. (2009). Sustaining positive behavior support in a context of comprehensive school reform. In W. Sailor, G. Dunlop, G. Sugai, & R. Horner (Eds.), *Handbook of positive behavior support* (pp. 633–669). New York: Springer Publishing. doi:10.1007/978-0-387-09632-2_26

Salend, S. J., & Duhaney, L. M. G. (1999). The impact of inclusion on students with and without disabilities and their educators. *Remedial and Special Education*, *20*(2), 114–126. doi:10.1177/074193259902000209

Saloviita, T., Itälinna, M., & Leinonen, E. (2003). Explaining the parental stress of fathers and mothers caring for a child with intellectual disability: A double ABCX model. *Journal of Intellectual Disability Research*, *47*(4-5), 300–312. doi:10.1046/j.1365-2788.2003.00492.x PMID:12787162

Saloviita, T., & Pirttimaa, R. (2007). Surveying supported employment in Finland: A follow-up. *Journal of Policy and Practice in Intellectual Disabilities*, *4*(4), 229–234. doi:10.1111/j.1741-1130.2007.00126.x

Sameroff, A. E. (2009). *The transactional model of development: How children and contexts shape each other*. American Psychological Association. doi:10.1037/11877-000

Sameroff, A. J., & Seifer, R. (1983). Familial risk and child competence. *Child Development*, *54*(5), 1254–1268. doi:10.2307/1129680 PMID:6354632

Sandberg, N. M., & Ahlström, G. (2015). Prevalence of older people with intellectual disability in Sweden: A spatial epidemiological analysis. *Journal of Intellectual Disability Research*, *59*(12), 1155–1167. doi:10.1111/jir.12219 PMID:26306552

Sanders, M. R., Mazzecchelli, T. G., & Studman, L. J. (2003). *Practitioner's Manual for Standard Stepping Stones Triple P: For Families with a Child who has a Disability*. Brisbane, Australia: Triple P International.

Sanders, M. R., Mazzucchelli, T. G., & Studman, L. J. (2003). *Practitioner's manual for standard Stepping Stones Triple P*. Brisbane: Triple P International Pty. Ltd.

Sanders, M. R., Mazzucchelli, T. G., & Studman, L. J. (2004). Stepping Stones Triple P: The theoretical basis and development of an evidence-based positive parenting program for families with a child who has a disability. *Journal of Intellectual & Developmental Disability*, *29*(3), 265–283. doi:10.1080/13668250412331285127

Sansone, R. A., & Sansone, L. A. (2008). Bully victims: Psychological and somatic aftermaths. *Psychiatry*, *5*(6), 62–64. PMID:19727287

Satchidanand, N., Gunukula, S. K., Lam, W. Y., McGuigan, D., New, I., Symons, A. B., & Akl, E. A. et al. (2012). Attitudes of healthcare students and professionals toward patients with physical disability: A systematic review. *American Journal of Physical Medicine & Rehabilitation*, *91*(6), 533–545. doi:10.1097/PHM.0b013e3182555ea4 PMID:22596075

Sayce. (2011). *Getting in, staying in and getting on: Disability employment support fit for the future*. Presented to Parliament by the Secretary of State for Work and Pensions by Command of Her Majesty.

Scelles, R. (1997). The impact of a person's disability on his or her sibling. *International Journal of Rehabilitation Research. Internationale Zeitschrift fur Rehabilitationsforschung. Revue Internationale de Recherches de Readaptation*, *20*(2), 129–137. doi:10.1097/00004356-199706000-00002 PMID:9226496

Schalock, R. L. (1999, September). *The application of the concept of quality of life: IASSID Quality of Life Consensus Document: Discussion draft*. Paper presented at the 35th National Conference of the Australian Society for the Study of Intellectual Disabilities, Sydney, Australia.

Schalock, R. L. (2002, June). *The concept of quality of life: What we know and do not know*. Paper presented at the Inaugural IASSID [International Association for the Scientific Study of Intellectual Disabilities] Europe Quadrennial Conference, Dublin, Ireland.

Schalock, R. L. (2011, May 31). *Interview: Professor Robert Schalock*. Retrieved from http://enil.eu/2011/05/interview-professor-robert-schalock/

Schalock, R. L. (1997). The concept of quality of life in 21st century disability programmes. In R. I. Brown (Ed.), *Quality of life for people with disabilities: Models, research and practice* (2nd ed.; pp. 327–340). Cheltenham, UK: Stanley Thornes.

Schalock, R. L. (2004). Quality of life: What we know and what we don't know. *Journal of Intellectual Disability Research*, *48*(3), 203–216. doi:10.1111/j.1365-2788.2003.00558.x PMID:15025663

Schalock, R. L. (Ed.). (1990). *Quality of Life: Perspectives and issues*. Washington, DC: American Association on Mental Retardation.

Schalock, R. L., Bonham, G. S., & Verdugo, M. A. (2008). The conceptualization and measurement of quality of life: Implications for program planning and evaluation in the field of intellectual disabilities. *Evaluation and Program Planning*, *31*(2), 181–190. doi:10.1016/j.evalprogplan.2008.02.001 PMID:18394704

Schalock, R. L., Borthwick-Duffy, S. A., Bradley, V. J., Buntinx, W. H., Coulter, D. L., & Craig, E. M. (2010). *Intellectual Disability: Definition, Classification, and Systems of Supports*. Washington, DC: ERIC.

Schalock, R. L., Gardner, J. F., & Bradley, V. J. (2007). *Quality of life for persons with intellectual and other developmental disabilities: Applications across individuals, organizations, communities, and systems*. Washington, DC: American Association on Intellectual and Developmental Disabilities.

Schalock, R. L., Luckasson, R. A., & Shogren, K. A. (2007). The renaming of mental retardation: Understanding the change to the term intellectual disability. *Journal Information*, *45*(2). PMID:17428134

Schalock, R. L., & Ruth, A. (2007). The Renaming of Mental Retardation: Understanding the Change to the Term Intellectual Disability. *Intellectual and Developmental Disabilities*, *45*(2), 116–124. doi:10.1352/1934-9556(2007)45[116:TROMRU]2.0.CO;2 PMID:17428134

Schalock, R. L., & Verdugo, M. A. (2002). *Handbook on quality of life for human services practitioners*. Washington, DC: American Association on Mental Retardation.

Schalock, R. L., Verdugo, M. A., Bonham, G. S., Fantova, F., & Van Loon, J. S. (2008). Enhancing personal outcomes: Organizational strategies, guidelines, and examples. *Journal of Policy and Practice in Intellectual Disabilities*, *5*(4), 276–285. doi:10.1111/j.1741-1130.2007.00135.x

Schilling, R. F. II, & Schinke, S. P. (1984). Personal coping and social support for parents of handicapped children. *Children and Youth Services Review*, *6*(3), 195–206. doi:10.1016/0190-7409(84)90060-4

Schilling, R., Schinke, S., Blythe, B., & Barth, R. (1982). Child maltreatment and mentally retarded parents: Is there a relationship? *Mental Retardation*, *20*(5), 201–209. PMID:6757649

Schlossar, S. (2004). *Opening Doors*. Multicultural Disability Advocacy Association of NSW. Retrieved on June. 13.2015 from http://www.mdaa.org.au/publications/ethnicity/indian/IndianOpenDoors.pdf

Schoenberg, M. R., & Scott, J. G. (2011). *The little black book of neuropsychology: a syndrome-based approach*. New York: Springer Science & Business Media. doi:10.1007/978-0-387-76978-3

Schor, D. P. (1987). Sex and sexual abuse in developmentally disabled adolescents. *Seminars in Adolescent Medicine*, *3*, 1–7. PMID:2955493

Schuengel, C., Rentinck, I. C. M., Stolk, J., Voorman, J. M., Loots, G. M. P., Ketelaar, M., & Becher, J. G. et al. (2009). Parents' reactions to the diagnosis of cerebral palsy: Associations between resolution, age and severity of disability. *Child: Care, Health and Development*, *35*(5), 673–680. doi:10.1111/j.1365-2214.2009.00951.x PMID:19320906

Schuiringa, H., van Nieuwenhuijzen, M., & de Castro, B. O. et al.. (2015). Parenting and the parent–child relationship in families of children with mild to borderline intellectual disabilities and externalizing behavior. *Research in Developmental Disabilities*, *32*, 1–12. doi:10.1016/j.ridd.2014.08.018 PMID:25262097

Schulman, B. H., & Mosak, H. H. (1988). *Manual for Life Style Assessment*. Muncie, IN: Accelerated Development.

Schuntermann, P. (2007). The sibling experience: Growing up with a child who has pervasive developmental disorder or mental retardation. *Harvard Review of Psychiatry*, *15*(3), 93–108. doi:10.1080/10673220701432188 PMID:17510829

Schwartz, R. (2001). *Introduction to Internal Family Systems Model*. Trailheads Publications Oak Park.

Scior, K. (2011). Public awareness, attitudes and beliefs regarding intellectual disability: A systematic review. *Research in Developmental Disabilities*, *32*(6), 2164–2182. doi:10.1016/j.ridd.2011.07.005 PMID:21798712

Scior, K., Kan, K. Y., McLoughlin, A., & Sheridan, J. (2010). Public attitudes toward people with intellectual disabilities: A cross-cultural study. *Intellectual and Developmental Disabilities*, *48*(4), 278–289. doi:10.1352/1934-9556-48.4.278 PMID:20722478

Scott, H. (1998). Helping clients in their sexual expression. *British Journal of Nursing (Mark Allen Publishing)*, *7*(10), 568. doi:10.12968/bjon.1998.7.10.5678 PMID:9775763

Scott, M. H., & Rutledge, C. M. (1997). Students' attitudes toward people with mental retardation. *Academic Medicine*, *72*(4), 246–247. doi:10.1097/00001888-199704000-00005 PMID:9125936

Scruggs, T. E., & Mastropieri, M. A. (1996). Teacher perceptions of inclusion/ mainstreaming, 1958-1995: A research synthesis. *Exceptional Children*, *1996*, 59–74. Retrieved from http://ecx.sagepub.com/content/63/1/59

Seagull, E., & Scheurer, S. (1986). Neglected and abused children of mentally retarded parents. *Child Abuse & Neglect*, *10*(4), 493–500. doi:10.1016/0145-2134(86)90054-2 PMID:3791026

Seligman, M. (1975). *Helplessness. On Depression, Development and Death*. San Francisco: W.H. Freeman.

Seligman, M. (1983). Siblings of handicapped persons. In M. Seligman (Ed.), *The Family with a Handicapped Child: Understanding and Treatment* (pp. 147–174). Orlando, FL: Grune & Stratton, Inc.

Serrata, C. A. (2012). Psychosocial aspects of parenting a child with autism. *Journal of Applied Rehabilitation Counseling*, *43*(4), 29–35.

Sethi, S., Bhargava, S. C., & Dhiman, V. (2007). Study of level of stress and burden in the caregivers of children with mental retardation. *Eastern Journal of Medicine*, *12*, 21–24.

Sexuality and Disability in the Indian Context. (2010). TARSHI.

Sharma, A., & Chowhan, S. (2014). *The Neuropsychological Components of Visual Processing and Learning in High and Low Functioning Children Exhibiting Autism Spectrum Disorder: A Comparative Study*. Unpublished manuscript.

Sheard, C., Clegg, J., Standen, P., & Cromby, J. (2001). Bullying and people with severe intellectual disability. *Journal of Intellectual Disability Research*, *45*(5), 407–415. doi:10.1046/j.1365-2788.2001.00349.x PMID:11679046

Shearn, J., & Todd, S. (2000). Maternal employment and family responsibilities: The perspectives of mothers of children with intellectual disabilities. *Journal of Applied Research in Intellectual Disabilities*, *13*(3), 109–131. doi:10.1046/j.1468-3148.2000.00021.x

Sheeran, T., Marvin, R. S., & Pianta, R. C. (1997). Mothers' resolution of their child's diagnosis and self-reported measures of parenting stress, marital relations, and social support. *Journal of Pediatric Psychology*, *22*(2), 197–212. doi:10.1093/jpepsy/22.2.197 PMID:9114643

Sheridan, J., & Scior, K. (2013). Attitudes towards people with intellectual disabilities: A comparison of young people from British South Asian and White British backgrounds. *Research in Developmental Disabilities*, *34*(4), 1240–1247. doi:10.1016/j.ridd.2012.12.017

Sherman, B. R., & Cocozza, J. J. (1984). Stress in families of the developmentally disabled: A literature review of factors affecting the decision to seek out-of-home placements. *Family Relations*, *33*(1), 95–103. doi:10.2307/584594

Shipley-Benamou, R., Lutzker, J. R., & Taubman, M. (2002). Teaching daily living skills to children with autism through instructional video modeling. *Journal of Positive Behavior Interventions*, *4*(3), 165–175. doi:10.1177/109830070200 40030501

Shonkoff, J. P., & Phillips, D. A. (2000). *Committee on Integrating the Science of Early Childhood Development. From Neurons to Neighborhoods: The Science of Early Childhood Development*. Washington, DC: National Academies Press.

Shrivastava, S. P. (Ed.). (1970). Social Work and the Rehabilitation of the Physically Handicapped. *The Journal of Rehabilitation in Asia*, *11*(1).

Siddiqi, A., Irwin, L. G., & Hertzman, C. (2007). *The total environment assessment model of early child development. Evidence Report for the World Health Organization's Commission on the Social Determinants of Health*. OMS.

Siebelink, E. M., de Jong, M. D. T., Taal, E., & Roelvink, L. (2006). Sexuality and people with intellectual disabilities: Assessment of knowledge, attitudes, experiences, and needs. *Mental Retardation*, *44*(4), 283–294. doi:10.1352/0047-6765(2006)44[283:SAPWID]2.0.CO;2 PMID:16834465

Sieman, M. (1984). Siblings of the chronically ill or disabled child. *The Nursing Clinics of North America*, *19*, 295–307. PMID:6233538

Silver, H. (1957). *The Physically Handicapped*. Social Work Year Book.

Silverstein, A., Pearson, L., Colbert, B., Cordeiro, W., Marwin, J., & Nakaji, M. (1982). Cognitive development of severely and profoundly mentally retarded individuals. *American Journal of Mental Deficiency*, *87*, 347–349. PMID:7180897

Simpson, M. K., & Hogg, J. (2001). Patterns of offending among people with intellectual disability: A systematic review. Part I: Methodology and prevalence data. *Journal of Intellectual Disability Research*, *45*(5), 384–396. doi:10.1046/j.1365-2788.2001.00345.x PMID:11679044

Singal, N. (2009). *Education of children with disabilities in India.* Retrieved from http://unesdoc.unesco.org/images/0018/001866/186611e.pdf

Singer, G. H. S., Marquis, J., Powers, L. K., Blanchard, L., DiVenere, N., Santelli, B., & Sharp, M. et al. (1999). A multi-site evaluation of parent to parent programs for parents of children with disabilities. *Journal of Early Intervention, 22*(3), 217–229. doi:10.1177/105381519902200305

Singer, G. H., Ethridge, B. L., & Aldana, S. I. (2007). Primary and secondary effects of parenting and stress management interventions for parents of children with developmental disabilities: A meta-analysis. *Mental Retardation and Developmental Disabilities Research Reviews, 13*(4), 357–369. doi:10.1002/mrdd.20175 PMID:17979202

Singer, G., & Todis, B. (1991). Stress and stress management in families with adopted children who have severe disabilities. *The Journal of the Association for Persons with Severe Handicaps, 16*(1), 3–13.

Singh, A. (2004). *Hand book of Behavioral Sciences.* New Delhi: Galgotia Publishers.

Singhi, P., Malhi, P., & Dwarka, P. (2002). Psychological adjustment of siblings of children with disabilities. *Journal of Personality and Clinical Studies, 18*, 9–18.

Singh, N. N., Lancioni, G. E., Winton, A. S., Fisher, B. C., Wahler, R. G., Mcaleavey, K., & Sabaawi, M. et al. (2006). Mindful parenting decreases aggression, noncompliance, and self-injury in children with autism. *Journal of Emotional and Behavioral Disorders, 14*(3), 169–177. doi:10.1177/10634266060140030401

Singh, N. N., Lancioni, G. E., Winton, A. S., Karazsia, B. T., Myers, R. E., Latham, L. L., & Singh, J. (2014). Mindfulness-Based Positive Behavior Support (MBPBS) for mothers of adolescents with autism spectrum disorder: Effects on adolescents' behavior and parental stress. *Mindfulness, 5*(6), 646–657. doi:10.1007/s12671-014-0321-3

Singh, N. N., Lancioni, G. E., Winton, A. S., Singh, J., Curtis, W. J., Wahler, R. G., & McAleavey, K. M. (2007). Mindful parenting decreases aggression and increases social behavior in children with developmental disabilities. *Behavior Modification, 31*(6), 749–771. doi:10.1177/0145445507300924 PMID:17932234

Singh, N. N., Lancioni, G. E., Winton, A. S., Singh, J., Singh, A. N., Adkins, A. D., & Wahler, R. G. (2010). Training in mindful caregiving transfers to parent–child interactions. *Journal of Child and Family Studies, 19*(2), 167–174. doi:10.1007/s10826-009-9267-9

Sinson, J., & Wetherick, N. (1982). Mutual gaze in preschool Down's and normal children. *Journal of Mental Deficiency Research, 26*, 123–129. PMID:6213781

Siperstein, G. N., KeerthiSugumaran, D., Bardon, J.N., & Parker, R.C. (n.d.). *Attitudes of the Public in India towards People with Intellectual Disabilities.* Retrieved from: https://www.media.specialolympics.org

Siperstein, G. N., Sugumaran, K., Bardon, J. N., & Parker, R. S. (2001). *Attitudes of the Public in India towards People with Intellectual Disabilities.* Retrieved from www.specialolympics.org/uploadedfiles/.../india_full%20report.pdf

Siperstein, G. N. (2003). *Multinational study of attitudes towards individuals with intellectual disabilities: General findings and calls to action.* Special Olympics.

Siperstein, G. N., Hardman, M. L., Wappett, M. T., & Clary, L. (2001). *National Evaluation of the Special Olympics Unified Sports Program (Final Report for Special Olympics, Incorporated).* Boston: University of Massachusetts, Center for Social Development and Education.

Sirlopu, D., Gonzalez, R., Bohner, G., Siebler, F., Ordonnez, G., Millar, A., & De Tezanos-Pinto, P. et al. (2008). Promoting positive attitudes toward people with Down syndrome: The benefit of school inclusion programs. *Journal of Applied Social Psychology, 38*(11), 2710–2736. doi:10.1111/j.1559-1816.2008.00411.x

Sivakumar, T. C., & Kumar, R. (2009). *Selection and Training to develop adult independent living skills in the Indian context across socio cultural and economic levels*. Report of the National Seminar - Planning for Comprehensive Rehabilitation of Persons with mental retardation, Chennai, India.

Sjgafoos, J., Elkins, J., Kerr, M., & Attwood, T. (1994). A survey of aggressive behaviour among a population of persons with intellectual disability in Queensland. *Journal of Intellectual Disability Research*, *38*(4), 369–381. doi:10.1111/j.1365-2788.1994.tb00417.x PMID:7949789

Skapinakis, P., Bellos, S., Gkatsa, T., Magklara, K., Lewish, G., Araya, R., & Mavreas, V. et al. (2011). The association between bullying and early stages of suicidal ideation in late adolescents in Greece. *BMC Psychiatry*, *11*(1), 1–9. doi:10.1186/1471-244X-11-22 PMID:21303551

Skotko, B. G., & Levine, S. P. (2006). What the other children are thinking: Brothers and sisters of persons with Down syndrome. *American Journal of Medical Genetics*, *143*(C), 180–186. doi:10.1002/ajmg.c.30101 PMID:16823778

Smith, K., Landry, S., & Swank, P. (2000). Does the content of mothers' verbal stimulation explain differences in children's development of verbal and nonverbal cognitive skills? *Journal of School Psychology*, *38*(1), 27–49. doi:10.1016/S0022-4405(99)00035-7

Smith, T. B., Oliver, M. N. I., & Innocenti, M. S. (2001). Parenting stress in families of children with disabilities. *The American Journal of Orthopsychiatry*, *71*(2), 257–261. doi:10.1037/0002-9432.71.2.257 PMID:11347367

Smyer, M. A., McHale, S. M., Birkel, R., & Madle, R. A. (1988). Impairments, handicapping environments, and disability: A life-span perspective. In P. S. Van Hasselt, P. S. Dtrain, & M. Herson (Eds.), *Handbook of developmental and physical disabilities* (pp. 9–20). New York: Permagon.

Snyder, L. E., & Sherer, N. (2004). The development of symbolic play and language in toddlers in cleft palate. *American Journal of Speech-Language Pathology*, *13*(1), 66–80. doi:10.1044/1058-0360(2004/008) PMID:15101815

Sobsey, D. (1994). *Violence and abuse in the lives of people with disabilities: The end of silent acceptance?* Baltimore: Paul H. Brookes Publishing Co.

Sobsey, D., & Mansell, S. (1990). The prevention of sexual abuse and assault: Sexual exploitation of people with disabilities. *Sexuality and Disability*, *9*, 243–259. doi:10.1007/BF01102395

Söderholm, S., Meinander, M., & Alaranta, H. (2001). Augmentative and alternative communication methods in locked-in syndrome. Journal of Rehabilitation, 33, 235-239.

Sofair, A. N., & Kaldijian, L. C. (2000). Eugenic sterilization and a qualified Nazi analogy: The United States and Germany, 1930-1945. *Annals of Internal Medicine*, *132*(4), 312–319. doi:10.7326/0003-4819-132-4-200002150-00010 PMID:10681287

Sofronoff, K., Jahnel, D., & Sanders, M. R. (2011). Stepping Stones Triple P seminars for parents of a child with a disability: A randomized controlled trial. *Research in Developmental Disabilities*, *32*(6), 2253–2262. doi:10.1016/j.ridd.2011.07.046 PMID:21871779

Solomon, M., Ono, M., Timmer, S., & Goodlin-Jones, B. (2008). The effectiveness of parent–child interaction therapy for families of children on the autism spectrum. *Journal of Autism and Developmental Disorders*, *38*(9), 1767–1776. doi:10.1007/s10803-008-0567-5 PMID:18401693

Soltani, S., Khosravi, B., & Salehiniya, H. (2015). Prevalence of intellectual disability in Iran: Toward a new conceptual framework in data collection. *Journal of Research in Medical Sciences*, *20*(7), 714–715. doi:10.4103/1735-1995.166234 PMID:26622264

Søndenaa, E., Rasmussen, K., & Nøttestad, J. A. (2008). Forensic issues in intellectual disability. *Current Opinion in Psychiatry*, *21*(5), 449–453. doi:10.1097/YCO.0b013e328305e5e9 PMID:18650685

Søndenaa, E., Rasmussen, K., Palmstierna, T., & Nøttestad, J. A. (2008). The prevalence and nature of intellectual disability in Norwegian prisons. *Journal of Intellectual Disability Research*, *52*(12), 1129–1137. doi:10.1111/j.1365-2788.2008.01072.x PMID:18498332

Son, E., Parish, S. L., & Peterson, N. A. (2012). National prevalence of peer victimization among young children with disabilities in the United States. *Children and Youth Services Review*, *34*(8), 1540–1545. doi:10.1016/j.childyouth.2012.04.014

Sourander, A., Klomek, A. B., Ikonen, M., Lindroos, J., Luntamo, T., Koskelainen, M., & Helenius, H. et al. (2010). Psychosocial risk factors associated with cyberbullying among adolescents: A population-based study. *Archives of General Psychiatry*, *67*(7), 720–728. doi:10.1001/archgenpsychiatry.2010.79 PMID:20603453

Special Olympics. (2004). *A Study of Youth Attitudes about Intellectual Disabilities*. Retrieved from http://www.specialolympics.org

Special Olympics. (2005). *Multinational Study of Attitudes towards Individuals with Intellectual Disabilities*. Retrieved from www.specialolympics.org/...Studies.../Multinational_Attitudes_Study.asp

Sprafkin, J., & Gadow, K. (1987). An observational study of emotionally disturbed and learning-disabled children in school settings. *Journal of Abnormal Child Psychology*, *15*(3), 393–408. doi:10.1007/BF00916457 PMID:3668086

Srinath, S., & Girimaji, S. C. (1999). Epidemiology of child and adolescent mental health problems and mental retardation. *Nimhans Journal*, *17*, 355–366.

Stainton, T., Hole, R., Charles, G., Yodanis, C., Powell, S., & Crawford, C. (2006). Non-residential supports and intellectual disability: A review of the literature on best practices, alternatives and economic impacts. Vancouver: Community Living Research Project, University of British Columbia.

Stainton, T., Hole, R., Charles, G., Yodanis, C., Powell, S., Crawford, C., & Wilson, L. (2006, October). *Non-residential Supports and Intellectual Disability: A Review of the Literature on Best Practices, Alternatives and Economic Impacts*. Community Living Research Project School of Social Work and Family Studies, University of British Columbia

Stalker, K., & Connors, C. (2004). Children's perceptions of their disabled siblings: "She's different but it's normal for us. *Children & Society*, *18*(3), 218–230. doi:10.1002/chi.794

Standen, P. J., & Brown, D. J. (2005). Virtual reality in the rehabilitation of people with intellectual disabilities[review]. *Cyberpsychology & Behavior*, *8*(3), 272–282. doi:10.1089/cpb.2005.8.272 PMID:15971976

State of Nebraska Health and Human Services. (2006). *Nebraska developmental disabilities provider profiles*. Lincoln, NE: State of Nebraska Health and Human Services, Division of Developmental Disabilities.

Stawski, M., Auerbach, J. G., Barasch, M., Lerner, Y., & Zimin, R. (1997). Behavioral problems of children with chronic physical illness and their siblings. *European Child and Adolescent Psychiatry Journal*, *6*(1), 20–25. doi:10.1007/BF00573636 PMID:9112043

Stella, C. S. C., Forlin, C., & Lan, A. M. (2007). The influence of an inclusive education course on attitude change of pre-service secondary teachers in Hong Kong. *Asia-Pacific Journal of Teacher Education*, *35*(2), 161–179. doi:10.1080/13598660701268585

Steptoe, L., Lindsay, W. R., Forrest, D., & Power, M. (2006). Quality of life and relationships in sex offenders with intellectual disability. *Journal of Intellectual & Developmental Disability*, *31*(1), 13–19. doi:10.1080/13668250500488652 PMID:16766318

Sterzing, P. R., Shattuck, P. T., Narendrof, S. C., Wagner, M., & Cooper, B. P. (2012). Bullying involvement and autism spectrum disorders: Prevalence and correlates of bullying involvement among adolescents with an autism spectrum disorder. *Archives of Pediatrics & Adolescent Medicine*, *166*(11), 1058–1064. doi:10.1001/archpediatrics.2012.790 PMID:22945284

Stevens, H. (1967). Mental deficiency in an international perspective. In B.W. Richards (Ed.), *Proceedings of the First Congress of the International Association for the Scientific Study of Mental Deficiency*.

Stoel-Gammon, C. (2000). Down syndrome phonology: Developmental patterns and intervention strategies. *Down's Syndrome: Research and Practice*, *7*(3), 93–100. doi:10.3104/reviews.118 PMID:11721538

Stokes, S. (1990). Restaurant supervisors: Don't discount the disabled. *The Cornell Hotel and Restaurant Administration Quarterly*, *30*(4), 14–17. doi:10.1177/001088049003000405

Stoneman, Z. (2005). Siblings of children with disabilities: Research themes. *Mental Retardation*, *43*, 339–350. PMID:16131231

Storey, K., & Horner, R. H. (1991). Social interactions in three supported employment options: A comparative analysis. *Journal of Applied Behavior Analysis*, *24*(2), 349–360. doi:10.1901/jaba.1991.24-349 PMID:1890051

Straus, M. A., & Stewart, J. H. (1999). Corporal punishment by American parents: National data on prevalence, chronicity, severity, and duration, in relation to child and family characteristics. *Clinical Child and Family Psychology Review*, *2*(2), 55–70. doi:10.1023/A:1021891529770 PMID:11225932

Straus, M. S., & Donnelly, D. A. (2001). *Beating the devil out of them. Corporal punishment in American families and its effects on children*. New Brunswick, NJ: Transaction Publishers.

Strohm, K. (2002). *Siblings: Brothers and sisters of children with special needs. Kent Town*. Wakefield Press.

Stromme, P., & Diseth, T. H. (2000). Prevalence of psychiatric diagnoses in children with mental retardation: Data from a population-based study. *Developmental Medicine and Child Neurology*, *42*(04), 266–270. doi:10.1017/S0012162200000451 PMID:10795566

Strømme, P., & Hagberg, G. (2007). Aetiology in severe and mild mental retardation: A population-based study of Norwegian children. *Developmental Medicine and Child Neurology*, *42*(2), 76–86. doi:10.1111/j.1469-8749.2000.tb00050.x PMID:10698323

Stromme, P., & Magnus, P. (2000). Correlations between socioeconomic status, IQ and aetiology in mental retardation: A population-based study of Norwegian children. *Social Psychiatry and Psychiatric Epidemiology*, *1*(35). PMID:10741531

Sturmey, P. (2011). Functional analysis in clinical treatment. Amsterdam: Academic Press.

Sturmey, P. (1995). DSM-III-R and persons with dual diagnoses: Conceptual issues and strategies for future research. *Journal of Intellectual Disability Research*, *39*(5), 357–364. doi:10.1111/j.1365-2788.1995.tb00539.x PMID:8555711

SubbaRao, T.A. (1992). *Manual on developing communication skills in mentally retarded persons*. Secundrabad: National Institute for the mentally handicapped.

SubbaRao, T.A., & Srinivas, N.C. (1989). Speech and Language defects and mental retardation-A report on the analysis of 300 mentally retarded persons. *Indian Journal of Disability and Rehabilitation*, 31-43.

SubbaRao. (1986). *Language Assessment Tool*. Author.

Su, K. P., Yu, J. M., Yang, T. W., Tsai, S. Y., & Chen, C. C. (2000). Characteristics of mentally retarded criminal offenders in Northern Taiwan. *Journal of Forensic Sciences*, *45*(6), 1207–1209. doi:10.1520/JFS14869J PMID:11110172

Sullivan, P. M., & Knutson, J. F. (2000). Maltreatment and disabilities: A population-based epidemiological study. *Child Abuse & Neglect*, *24*(10), 1257–1273. doi:10.1016/S0145-2134(00)00190-3 PMID:11075694

Sultana, S. A. G., Lam-Po-Tang, T. R. L., Wright, F., Linderman, R., & Purvis-Smith, S. (1995). Fragile X mental retardation in an Indonesian family. *Medical Journal of Indonesia*, *4*, 17–17. doi:10.13181/mji.v4i1.885

Suresh, A. P., Benjamin, T. E., Crasta, J. E., Alwinesh, M. T., Kanniappan, G., Padankatti, S. M., & Russell, P. S. et al. (2014). Comparison of burden among primary care-givers of children with autism and intellectual disability against children with intellectual disability only in a hospital population in India. *Indian Journal of Pediatrics*, *81*(Suppl 2), S179–S182.

Suto, W. M. I., Clare, I. C. H., Holland, A. J., & Watson, P. C. (2005). Capacity to make financial decisions among people with mild intellectual disabilities. *Journal of Intellectual Disability Research*, *49*(3), 199–209. doi:10.1111/j.1365-2788.2005.00635.x PMID:15713195

Swart, L. (2007). Vocational Rehabilitation in psychiatry and mental health. In R. Crouch & V. Alers (Eds.), *Occupational therapy in psychiatry and mental health* (pp. 208–229). Whurr Publishers.

Swearer, S. M., Siebecker, A. B., Johnsen-Frerichs, L., & Wang, C. (2010). Assessment of bullying/victimization: The problem of comparability across studies and across methodologies. In S. R. Jimerson, S. M. Swearer, & D. L. Espelage (Eds.), *Handbook of bullying in schools: An international perspective* (pp. 305–327). New York, NY: Routledge.

Sweet, J. J., King, J. H., Malina, A. C., Bergman, M. A., & Simmons, A. (2002). Documenting the prominence of forensic neuropsychology at national meetings and in relevant professional journals from 1990 to 2000. *The Clinical Neuropsychologist*, *16*(4), 481–494. doi:10.1076/clin.16.4.481.13914 PMID:12822057

Swift, E., & Rosin, P. (1990). A remediation sequence to improve speech intelligibility for students with Down syndrome. *Language, Speech, and Hearing Services in Schools*, *21*(3), 140–146. doi:10.1044/0161-1461.2103.140

Taanila, A., Rantakallio, P., Koiranen, M., von Wendt, L., & Jarvelin, M. R. (2005). How do persons with intellectual disability manage in the open labour market? A follow-up of the Northern Finland 1966 Birth Cohort. *Journal of Intellectual Disability Research*, *49*(3), 218–227. doi:10.1111/j.1365-2788.2005.00648.x PMID:15713197

Tam, S. F., Man, D. W. K., Chan, Y. P., Sze, P. C., & Wong, C. M. (2005). Evaluation of a Computer-Assisted, 2-D Virtual Reality System for Training People With Intellectual Disabilities on How to Shop. *Rehabilitation Psychology*, *50*(3), 285–291. doi:10.1037/0090-5550.50.3.285

Tarbox, J., Wallace, M. D., Tarbox, R. S. F., Landaburu, H. J., & Williams, W. L. (2004). Functional analysis and treatment of low rate problem behavior in individuals with developmental disabilities. *Behavioral Interventions*, *19*(3), 187–204. doi:10.1002/bin.158

Tassé, M. J., Schalock, R. L., Balboni, G., Bersani, H., & Sharon, A. (2012). The Construct of Adaptive Behavior: Its Conceptualization, Measurement, and Use in the Field of Intellectual Disability. *American Journal on Intellectual and Developmental Disabilities*, *117*(4), 291–303. doi:10.1352/1944-7558-117.4.291 PMID:22809075

Taylor, C., Norman, D., Murphy, J., Jellinek, M., Quinn, D., Poitrast, F., & Goshko, M. (1991). Diagnosed intellectual and emotional impairment among parents who seriously mistreat their children: Prevalence, type, and outcome in a court sample. *Child Abuse & Neglect*, *15*(4), 389–401. doi:10.1016/0145-2134(91)90023-7 PMID:1959072

Taylor, J. L., Hatton, C., Dixon, L., & Douglas, C. (2004). Screening for psychiatric symptoms: PAS-ADD Checklist norms for adults with intellectual disabilities. *Journal of Intellectual Disability Research*, *48*(1), 37–41. doi:10.1111/j.1365-2788.2004.00585.x PMID:14675229

Tellegen, C. L., & Sanders, M. R. (2013). Stepping Stones Triple P-Positive Parenting Program for children with disability: A systematic review and meta-analysis. *Research in Developmental Disabilities*, *34*(5), 1556–1571. doi:10.1016/j.ridd.2013.01.022 PMID:23475006

Tervo, R. C., Azuma, S., Palmer, G., & Redinius, P. (2002). Medical students' attitudes toward persons with disability: A comparative study. *Archives of Physical Medicine and Rehabilitation*, *83*(11), 1537–1542. doi:10.1053/apmr.2002.34620 PMID:12422321

The Centre for Developmental Disability Health Victoria (CDDH). (2015). *Working with people with intellectual disabilities in healthcare settings: Fact Sheet*. Retrieved from: www.cddh.monash.org

The ICD-10 Classification of Mental and Behavioral Disorders Clinical descriptions and diagnostic guidelines. (2004). World Health Organization.

The UN Convention on the Rights of the Child. (n.d.). *Tenth Report of the session 2002-03*. House of Commons. London: The Stationery Office Limited.

Thompson, R. J., & O'Quinn, A. N. (1979). Developmental disabilities: Etiologies, manifestations, diagnoses, and treatments. New York: Oxford.

Thompson, A., Curtner, M., & O'Rear, M. (1994). The psychosocial adjustment of well siblings of chronically ill children. *Children's Health Care*, *23*(3), 211–226. doi:10.1207/s15326888chc2303_5

Thompson, J. R., Bryant, B., Campbell, E. M., Craig, E. M., Hughes, C., & Rotholz, D. A. et al.. (2004). *Support needs intensity scale (SIS)*. Washington, DC: American Association on Mental Retardation.

Thompson, R. H., & Iwata, B. A. (2007). A comparison of outcomes from descriptive and functional analyses of problem behavior. *Journal of Applied Behavior Analysis*, *40*(2), 333–338. doi:10.1901/jaba.2007.56-06 PMID:17624074

Timms, S., & Goreczny, A. J. (2002). Adolescent sex offenders with mental retardation: Literature review and assessment considerations. *Aggression and Violent Behavior*, *7*(1), 1–19. doi:10.1016/S1359-1789(00)00031-8

Tiong, S. J., Blampied, N. M., & Le Grice, B. (1992). Training community-living, intellectually handicapped people in fire safety using video prompting. *Behaviour Change*, *9*, 65–72.

Tizard, J., & Loos, F. M. (1954). The learning of spatial relations by adult imbeciles. *American Journal of Mental Deficiency*, *59*, 85–90.

Todd, S. (2007). Silenced grief: Living with the death of a child with intellectual disabilities. *Journal of Intellectual Disability Research*, *51*(8), 637–648. doi:10.1111/j.1365-2788.2007.00949.x PMID:17598877

Tolu, E.A., Temitayo, & Kofoworola, A. (2014). Exclusion of Children with Intellectual Disabilities from Regular Classroom: Nigeria Perspective. *African Journal for the Psychological Study of Social Issues*, *17*, 99-109. Retrieved from http://ajpssi.org/index.php/ajpssi/article/view/94/pdf_65

Tomasik, M. (2007).Effective inclusion activities for high school students with multiple disabilities. *Journal of Visual Impairment & Blindness*, *101*(10), 657–659.

Tommasone, L., & Tommasone, J. (1989). *Adjusting to Your Child's Diagnosis*. Bethesda, MD: Woodbine House.

Tonge, B., & Einfeld, S. (2000). The trajectory of psychiatric disorders in young people with intellectual disabilities. *The Australian and New Zealand Journal of Psychiatry*, *34*(1), 80–84. doi:10.1046/j.1440-1614.2000.00695.x PMID:11185949

Tonge, B., & Einfeld, S. L. (2003). Psychopathology and intellectual disability: The Australian child to adult longitudinal study. *International Review of Research in Mental Retardation*, *26*, 61–91. doi:10.1016/S0074-7750(03)01002-4

To, T., Guttmann, A., Dick, P. T., Rosenfield, J. D., Parkin, P. C., Tassoudji, M., & Harris, J. K. et al. (2004). Risk markers for poor developmental attainment in young children: Results from a longitudinal national survey. *Archives of Pediatrics & Adolescent Medicine*, *158*(7), 643–649. doi:10.1001/archpedi.158.7.643 PMID:15237063

Touchette, P. E., MacDonald, R. F., & Langer, S. N. (1985). A scatter plot for identifying stimulus control of problem behavior. *Journal of Applied Behavior Analysis*, *18*(4), 343–351. doi:10.1901/jaba.1985.18-343 PMID:4086416

Tower, C. (1989). *Understanding child abuse and neglect*. Boston: Allyn and Bacon.

Tracy, J., & McDonald, R. (2015). Health and Disability: Partnerships in Health care. *Journal of Applied Research in Intellectual Disabilities*, *28*(1), 22–32. doi:10.1111/jar.12135

Traustadóttir, R., & Sigurjónsdóttir, H. B. (2005). Adult children of mothers with intellectual disabilities: Three life histories. In A. Gustavsson, J. Sandrin, R. Traustadóttir, & J. Tøssebro (Eds.), *Resistance, reflections and change: Nordic disability research* (pp. 147–161). Lund, Sweden: Studentlitteratur.

Tremblay, K. N., Richer, L., Lachance, L., & Côté, A. (2010). Psychopathological manifestations of children with intellectual disabilities according to their cognitive and adaptive behavior profile. *Research in Developmental Disabilities*, *31*(1), 57–69. doi:10.1016/j.ridd.2009.07.016 PMID:19700260

Triple P is giving our parents help. (2015). *The Newcastle Herald (Newcastle, Australia).*

Trute, B. (1990). Child and parent predictors of family adjustment in households containing young developmentally disabled children. *Family Relations*, *39*(3), 292–297. doi:10.2307/584874

Tuckerman, P. (2008a). Job support: a demonstration of what is possible. *Interaction, 21*, 6-10.

Turnbull, A. P., Brown, I., & Turnbull, R. H. (Eds.). (2004). *Families and people with mental retardation and quality of life: International perspectives*. Washington, DC: American Association on Mental Retardation.

Turnbull, A., Turnbull, R., Erwin, E., & Soodak, L. (2006). *Families, professionals and exceptionality: Positive outcomes through partnerships and trust* (5th ed.). Upper Saddle River, NJ: Pearson/Merrill Prentice Hall.

Tyler, C. V. Jr, Snyder, C. W., & Zyzanski, S. J. (1999, October). Caring for Adults With Mental Retardation: Survey of Family Practice Residency Program Directors. *Mental Retardation*, *37*(5), 347–352. doi:10.1352/0047-6765(1999)037<0347:CFAWMR>2.0.CO;2 PMID:10581920

Tymchuk, A. (2001). Family life: Experiences of people with mild cognitive limitations. In A. J. Tymchuk, K. C. Lakin, & R. Luckasson (Eds.), *The forgotten generation: The status and challenges of adults with mild cognitive limitations* (pp. 249–274). Baltimore, MD: Brookes.

Tymchuk, A. J., & Andron, L. (1990). Mothers with mental retardation who do or do not abuse or neglect their children. *Child Abuse & Neglect*, *13*(3), 313–323. doi:10.1016/0145-2134(90)90003-C PMID:2207800

U.S. Census Bureau. (2007). *American with disabilities act: July 26*. Retrieved February 25, 2008 from the World Wide Web: vikaspedia.in/health/...disabilities/legal-rights-of-the-disabled-in-india

Underwood, M. K., Galen, B. R., & Paquette, J. A. (2001).Top ten challenges for understanding gender and aggression in children: Why can't we all just get along? *Social Development*, *10*, 248–266.

United Nations Educational, Scientific and Cultural Organization. (1994). *The Salamanca Statement and framework for action on special needs education*. Paris: Author.

United Nations Educational, Scientific and Cultural Organization. (2008a). *Inclusive education: The way of the future. 48th session of the International Conference on Education*. Genova: Author.

United Nations Educational, Scientific and Cultural Organization. (2008b). *Defining an Inclusive Education agenda: Reflection around the 48th session the International Conference on Education.* Retrieved from www.ibe.unesco.org/.../48th.../Defining_Inclusive_Education_Agenda_2

United Nations. (n.d.). Conventions on the Rights of the Persons with Disabilities. *Treaty Series.* Retrieved November 17, 2015, from UN Treaty Collection website: https://treaties.un.org/Pages/ViewDetails.aspx?src=TREATY&mtdsg_no=IV-15&chapter=4&lang=en

University Legal Services. (2012. *The Work Option for Individuals with Intellectual Disabilities: The Obstacles and the Possibilities.* Retrieved from www.ulsdc.org/Employment%20Report_FINAL.pdf

UNNATI. (2004). *Understanding Disability: Attitude and Behaviour Change for Social Inclusion.* Retrieved from http://www.unnati.org/pdfs/books/research-eng.pdf

Upadhyaya, G. R., & Havalappanavar, N. B. (2008). Coping in parents of the mentally challanged. *Journal of the Indian Academy of Applied Psychology*, *34*(2), 221–225.

US Government Accountability Office. (2001). *Centers offer employment and support services to workers with disabilities, but Labor should improve oversight.* Washington, DC: United States General Accounting Office.

Van Cleave, J., & Davis, M. M. (2006). Bullying and peer victimization among children with special health care needs. *Pediatrics*, *118*(4), 1212–1219. doi:10.1542/peds.2005-3034 PMID:17015509

Van Dyke, D. E., Mc Brien, D. M., & Sherbondy, A. (1995). Issues of sexuality in Down Syndrome. *Down's Syndrome: Research and Practice*, *3*(2), 65–69. doi:10.3104/reviews.53

Van Houten, R., Axelrod, S., Bailey, J. S., Favell, J. E., Foxx, R. M., Iwata, B. A., & Lovaas, O. I. (1988). The right to effective behavioral treatment. *Journal of Applied Behavior Analysis*, *21*(4), 381–384. doi:10.1901/jaba.1988.21-381 PMID:3225255

Van Riper, M. (2000). Family variables associated with wellbeing in siblings of children with Down Syndrome. *Journal of Family Nursing*, *6*(3), 267–286. doi:10.1177/107484070000600305

Vandevelde, S., Broekaert, E., Schuyten, G., & Van Hove, G. (2005). Intellectual abilities and motivation toward substance abuse treatment in drug-involved offenders: A pilot study in the Belgian criminal justice system. *International Journal of Offender Therapy and Comparative Criminology*, *49*(3), 277–297. doi:10.1177/0306624X04270779 PMID:15851508

Vaughan, P. J., Pullen, N., & Kelly, M. (2000). Services for mentally disordered offenders in community psychiatry teams. *Journal of Forensic Psychiatry*, *11*(3), 571–586. doi:10.1080/09585180010004829

Veerman, J. W., & Van Yperen, T. A. (2007). Degrees of freedom and degrees of uncertainty:A developmental model for the establishment of evidence-based youth care. *Evaluation and Program Planning*, *30*(2), 212–221. doi:10.1016/j.evalprogplan.2007.01.011 PMID:17689326

Venkatesh Kumar, G. (2008, July). Psychological Stress and Coping Strategies of the Parents of Mentally Challenged Children. *Journal of the Indian Academy of Applied Psychology*, *34*(2), 227–231.

Vera, H., Barnard, G. W., & Holzer, C. (1979). The intelligence of rapists: New data. *Archives of Sexual Behavior*, *8*(4), 375–377. doi:10.1007/BF01541880 PMID:475583

Verdonschot, M. M., De Witte, L. P., Reichrath, E., Buntinx, W. H. E., & Curfs, L. M. G. (2009). Impact of environmental factors on community participation of persons with an intellectual disability: A systematic review. *Journal of Intellectual Disability Research*, *53*(1), 54–64. doi:10.1111/j.1365-2788.2008.01128.x PMID:19093982

Verdonschot, M. M., deWitte, L. P., Reichrath, E., Buntinx, W. H., & Curfs, L. M. (2009). Community participation of people with an intellectual disability: A review of empirical findings. *Journal of Intellectual Disability Research*, *53*(4), 303–318. doi:10.1111/j.1365-2788.2008.01144.x PMID:19087215

Verdugo, M. A., Bermejo, B. G., & Fuertes, J. (1995). The maltreatment of intellectually handicapped children and adolescents. *Child Abuse & Neglect*, *19*(2), 205–215. doi:10.1016/0145-2134(94)00117-D PMID:7780782

Verdugo, M. A., Martín-Ingelmo, R., Jordán de Urríes, F. B., & Vicent, C. et al.. (2009). Impact on quality of life and self-determination of a national program for increasing supported employment in Europe. *Journal of Vocational Rehabilitation*, *31*, 55–64.

Verte, S., Roeyers, H., & Busse, A. (2003). Behavioral problems, social competence and Self-concept in siblings of children with autism. *Child: Care, Health and Development*, *29*(3), 193–205. doi:10.1046/j.1365-2214.2003.00331.x PMID:12752610

Vetere, A., & Dallos, R. (2003). *Working Systemically with Families*. London: Karnac.

Violence against Disabled Children: A summary report. (2005). UNICEF.

Visier, L. (1998). Sheltered employment for persons with disabilities. *International Labour Review*, *137*, 347–365.

Vollmer, T. R., Marcus, B. A., Ringdahl, J. E., & Roane, H. S. (1995). Progressing from brief assessments to extended experimental analyses in the evaluation of aberrant behavior. *Journal of Applied Behavior Analysis*, *28*(4), 561–576. doi:10.1901/jaba.1995.28-561 PMID:16795882

Vos, T., Barker, B., Stanley, L., & Lopez, A. (2007). *The burden of disease and injury in Aboriginal and Torres Strait Islander peoples 2003: Centre for Burden of Disease and Cost-Effectiveness*. School of Population Health, University of Queensland.

Vrijmoeth, C., Monbaliu, E., & Lagast, E. (2011). Behavioral problems in children with motor and intellectual disabilities: Prevalence and associations with maladaptive personality and marital relationship. *Research in Developmental Disabilities*, *32*, 1027–1038. PMID:22502827

Vyogotsky, L. (1962). *Thought and Language*. Cambridge, MA: MIT Press. doi:10.1037/11193-000

Waasdorp, T. E., & Bradshaw, C. P. (2015). The overlap between cyberbullying and traditional bullying. *The Journal of Adolescent Health*, *56*(5), 483–488. doi:10.1016/j.jadohealth.2014.12.002 PMID:25631040

Waldman, H. B., Swerdloff, M., & Perlman, S. P. (1999). A "dirty secret": The abuse of children with disabilities. *ASDC Journal of Dentistry for Children*, *66*(3), 197–202. PMID:10476359

Walker, A. (2011). CHECKMATE! A self-advocate's journey through the world of employment. *Intellectual and Developmental Disabilities*, *49*(4), 310–312. doi:10.1352/1934-9556-49.4.310

Walker-Hirsch, L. (2007). *The Facts of Life...and More Sexuality and Intimacy for People with Intellectual Disabilities*. Brookes Publishing Co.

Wallace, C. J., Liberman, R. P., Tauber, R., & Wallace, J. (2000). The Independent Living Skills Survey: A comprehensive measure of the community functioning of severely and persistently mentally ill individuals. *Schizophrenia Bulletin*, *26*(3), 631–658. doi:10.1093/oxfordjournals.schbul.a033483 PMID:10993403

Wallander,J.L., Dekker, M.C., Koot, H.M.,(1992) *Variations in prenatal sociodemographic factors associated with intellectual disability*. Academic Press.

Walsh, F. (2003). Family resilience: A framework for clinical practice. *Family Process*, *42*(1), 1–18. doi:10.1111/j.1545-5300.2003.00001.x PMID:12698595

Walter, J. (n.d.). From taboo to self-actualization–acceptance problems and learning processes in working with mentally handicapped patients. *Praxis der Kinderpsychologie und Kinderpsychiatrie*, *51*(8), 587–597. PMID:12425228

Wang, J., Iannotti, R. J., Luk, J. W., & Nansel, T. R. (2010). Co-occurrence of victimization from five subtypes of bullying: Physical, verbal, social exclusion, spreading rumors, and cyber. *Journal of Pediatric Psychology*, *35*(10), 1103–1112. doi:10.1093/jpepsy/jsq048 PMID:20488883

Wang, P. P., & Bellugi, U. (1994). Evidence from two genetic syndromes for a dissociation between verbal and visuo-spatial short-term memory. *Journal of Clinical and Experimental Neuropsychology*, *2*(2), 317–322. doi:10.1080/01688639408402641 PMID:8021317

Ward, J., Parmenter, T. R., Riches, V., & Hauritz, M. (1978). Adjustment to work: A follow-up of mildly handicapped adolescents who have undergone training in a Work Preparation Centre. National Rehabilitation Digest, 2(3-4).

Ward, L., & Tarleton, B. (2007). Sinking or swimming? Supporting parents with learning disabilities and their children. *Tizard Learning Disability Review*, *12*(2), 22–32. doi:10.1108/13595474200700014

Ward, R. L., Nichols, A. D., & Freedman, R. I. (2010, November). Uncovering Health care Inequalities among adults with intellectual and developmental disabilities. *Health & Social Work*, *35*(4), 280–290. doi:10.1093/hsw/35.4.280 PMID:21171535

Warner, G. (2010). *Good practices in economic empowerment programme for people with disabilities*. Paper presented to 3rd Malaysian Conference on Rehabilitation (MCR), Kuala Lumpur, Malaysia.

Warren, S. F. (1988). A behavioural approach to language generalization. *Language, Speech, and Hearing Services in Schools*, *19*(3), 292–303. doi:10.1044/0161-1461.1903.292

Warren, S. F., & Brady, N. C. (2007). The role of maternal responsivity in the development of children with intellectual disabilities. *Mental Retardation and Developmental Disabilities Research Reviews*, *13*(4), 330–338. doi:10.1002/mrdd.20177 PMID:17979201

Warren, S. F., Fey, M. E., Finestack, L. H., Brady, N. C., Bredin-Oja, S. L., & Fleming, K. K. (2008). A randomized trial of longitudinal effects of low-intensity responsivity education/ prelinguistic milieu teaching. *Journal of Speech, Language, and Hearing Research: JSLHR*, *51*(2), 451–470. doi:10.1044/1092-4388(2008/033) PMID:18367689

Warren, S. F., Fey, M. E., & Yoder, P. J. (2007). Differential treatment intensity research: A missing link to creating optimally effective communication interventions. *Mental Retardation and Developmental Disabilities Research Reviews*, *13*(1), 70–77. doi:10.1002/mrdd.20139 PMID:17326112

Watson, L. S. Jr. (1968). Application of behaviour-shaping devices to training severely and profoundly mentally retarded children in an institutional setting. *Mental Retardation*, *6*, 21–23. PMID:5705586

Webster-Stratton, C. (2000). The Incredible Years Training series. Office of Juvenile Justice and Delinquency Prevention Bulletin Review, 1–24.

Webster-Stratton, C. (2001). *The Incredible Years: Parents, teachers, and children training series, leader's guide*. Seattle, WA: Author.

Wehman, P., Inge, K. J., Revell, W. G., & Brooke, V. A. (Eds.). (2006). *Real work for real pay.Inclusive employment for people with disabilities*. Baltimore, MD: Paul H. Brookes.

Wehmeyer, M. L., Buntix, W. H. E., Lachapelle, Y., Luckasson, R. A., Verdugo, M. A., Borthwick-Duffy, S., & Yeager, M. H. et al. (2008). The intellectual disability construct and its relation to human functioning. *Intellectual and Developmental Disabilities*, *46*(4), 48–55. doi:10.1352/1934-9556(2008)46[311:TIDCAI]2.0.CO;2 PMID:18671445

Weikart, D. P., Deloria, D., Lawser, S., & Wegerink, R. (1970). *Longitudinal results of the Ypsilanti Perry Preschool Project*. Ypsilanti, MI: HighScope Educational Research Foundation.

Weikle, D. W. J. Jr. (2008). Achieving community membership through CRPs: A reaction to Metzel et al. *Journal of Intellectual & Developmental Disability*, *46*(1), 58–63. doi:10.1352/0047-6765(2008)46[58:ACMTCA]2.0.CO;2 PMID:18271613

Weissman-Fogel. (2015, March31). Pain experience of adults with intellectual disabilities - caregiver reports. *Journal of Intellectual Disability Research*.

Weissman, M. M., & Bothwell, S. (1976). Assessment of social adjustment by patient self-report. *Archives of General Psychiatry*, *33*(9), 1111. doi:10.1001/archpsyc.1976.01770090101010 PMID:962494

Weitzner-Lin, B. (2004). *Communication assessment and intervention with infants and toddlers*. St. Louis, MO: Butterworth Heinemann.

Weizman, Z. O., & Snow, C. E. (2001). Lexical Input as Related to Children's Vocabulary Acquisition: Effects of Sophisticated Exposure and Support for Meaning. *Developmental Psychology*, *37*(2), 265–279. doi:10.1037/0012-1649.37.2.265 PMID:11269394

Wells, T., Sandefur, D., & Hogan, D. P. (2003). What happens after the high school years among young persons with disabilities? *Social Forces*, *82*(2), 803–832. doi:10.1353/sof.2004.0029

Wenhua, L. (2005). Analysis of 294 cases of murder in forensic psychiatric expertise. *Journal of Clinical Psychosomatic Diseases, 4,* 25.

Werner, D. (2006). *Disabled Village Children: A Guide for Community Health Workers, Rehabilitation Workers, and Families*. Berkeley, CA: Hesperian Foundation.

Wert, B. Y., & Neisworth, J. T. (2003). Effects of video self-modeling on spontaneous requesting in children with autism. *Journal of Positive Behavior Interventions*, *5*(1), 30–34. doi:10.1177/10983007030050010501

Westling, D., & Fox, L. (2000). *Teaching students with severe disabilities*. Upper Saddle River, NJ: Merrill.

Wethervy, A., & Prizant, B. (1993). *Communication and Symbolic Behaviour Scales*. Chicago, IL: Riverside Publishers.

Whitehouse, A. J. O., Durkin, K., Jaquet, E., & Ziatas, K. (2009). Friendship, loneliness and depression in adolescents with Asperger's Syndrome. *Journal of Adolescence*, *32*(2), 309–322. doi:10.1016/j.adolescence.2008.03.004 PMID:18692233

Whitehouse, A. J. O., Watt, H. J., Line, E. A., & Bishop, D. V. M. (2009). Adult psychosocial outcomes of children with specific language impairment, pragmatic language impairment and autism. *International Journal of Language & Communication Disorders*, *44*(4), 511–528. doi:10.1080/13682820802708098 PMID:19340628

White, N., & Hastings, R. P. (2004). Social and professional support for parents of adolescents with severe intellectual disabilities. *Journal of Applied Research in Intellectual Disabilities*, *17*(3), 181–190. doi:10.1111/j.1468-3148.2004.00197.x

Whitman, B. Y., Graves, B., & Accardo, P. J. (1989). Training in parenting skills for adults with mental retardation. *Social Work*, *34*, 431–434.

Whitney, I., Nabuzoka, D., & Smith, P. K. (1992). Bullying in schools: Mainstream and special needs. *Support for Learning*, *7*(1), 3–7. doi:10.1111/j.1467-9604.1992.tb00445.x

Whitney, I., Smith, P. K., & Thompson, D. (1994). Bullying and children with special educational needs. In P. K. Smith & S. Sharp (Eds.), *School bullying: Insights and perspectives* (pp. 213–240). London: Routledge.

Whittingham, K., Sofronoff, K., Sheffield, J., & Sanders, M. R. (2009). Stepping Stones Triple P: An RCT of a parenting program with parents of a child diagnosed with an autism spectrum disorder. *Journal of Abnormal Child Psychology*, *37*(4), 469–480. doi:10.1007/s10802-008-9285-x PMID:19023654

WHO. (2011). *World Report on Disability*. Retrieved from: http://www.who.int/whosis/whostat/2011/en/

Wiig, E., Secord, W., & Semel, E. (1992). *Clinical Evaluation of Language Fundamentals (CELF)*. San Antonio, TX: Psychological Corporation.

Wikler, D. (1979). Paternalism and the mildly retarded. *Philosophy & Public Affairs*, 377–392.

Wikler, L. (1981). Chronic stresses of families of mentally retarded children. *Family Relations*, *30*(2), 281–288. doi:10.2307/584142

Williams, J. R., & Algozzine, B. (1979). Teachers' Attitudes toward Mainstreaming. *The Elementary School Journal*, *80*(2), 63–67. doi:10.1086/461173

Williams, P. D. (1997). Siblings and pediatric chronic illness: A review of the literature. *International Journal of Nursing Studies*, *34*(4), 312–323. doi:10.1016/S0020-7489(97)00019-9 PMID:9306166

Wilson, A. S. (2007). *Caregiver Attitude of Sexuality of the Intellectually Disabled Population*. Proquest Theses & Dissertation.

Wilson, M. C., & Scior, K. (2015). Implicit attitudes towards people with intellectual disabilities: Their relationship with explicit attitudes, social distance, emotions and contact. *PLoS ONE*, *10*(9), e0137902. PMID:26366575

Witwera, A. N., & Lecavaliera, L. (2008). Psychopathology in children with intellectual disability: Risk markers and correlates. *Journal of Mental Health Research in Intellectual Disabilities*, *1*(2), 75–96. doi:10.1080/19315860801988327

Wolberg, L. R. (2013). *The Techniques of Psychotherapy*. Chevy Chase, MD: International Psychotherapy Institute E-Books.

Wolfe, B., Song, J., Greenberg, J. S., & Mailick, M. R. (2014). Ripple effects of developmental disabilities and mental illness on nondisabled adult siblings. *Social Science & Medicine*, *108*, 1–9. doi:10.1016/j.socscimed.2014.01.021 PMID:24607704

Wolfe, P. S. (1992). Challenges for service providers. In P. J. McLaughlin & P. Wejman (Eds.), *Developmental disabilities: A handbook for best practice* (pp. 124–141). Boston: Andover Medical.

Wolfgang, C. H. (2001). *Solving discipline and classroom management programs: Methods and models for today's teachers*. New York: John Wiley.

Wolf, L., Fisman, S., Ellison, D., & Freeman, T. (1998). Effect of sibling perception of differential parental treatment in siblings dyads with one disabled child. *Journal of the American Academy of Child and Adolescent Psychiatry*, *37*(12), 1317–1325. doi:10.1097/00004583-199812000-00016 PMID:9847505

Wolf, M. M. (1978). Social validity: The case for subjective measurement or how applied behavior analysis is finding its heart. *Journal of Applied Behavior Analysis*, *11*(2), 203–214. doi:10.1901/jaba.1978.11-203 PMID:16795590

Wong, J. G., Clare, I. C. H., Holland, A. J., Watson, P. C., & Gunn, M. (2000). The capacity of people with a 'mental disability'to make a health care decision. *Psychological Medicine*, *30*(02), 295–306. doi:10.1017/S0033291700001768 PMID:10824650

Wood, L. W., Sherman, E., Hamiwka, L. D., Blackman, R. N., & Wirrell, E. (2008). Depression, anxiety, and quality of life in siblings of children with intractable epilepsy. *Epilepsy & Behavior*, *13*(1), 144–148. doi:10.1016/j.yebeh.2008.03.012 PMID:18456563

Woodman, A. C., Mawdsley, H. P., & Hauser-Cram, P. (2011). Parenting stress and child behavior problems within families of children with developmental disabilities: Transactional relations across 15 years. *Research in Developmental Disabilities*, *32*, 264–276. PMID:25462487

Woolfenden, S., Goldfeld, S., Raman, S., Eapen, V., Kemp, L., & Williams, K. (2013). Inequity in child health: The importance of early childhood development. *Journal of Paediatrics and Child Health*, *49*(9), E365–E369. PMID:23551940

Woolfenden, S., Williams, K., Eapen, V., Mensah, F., Hayen, A., Siddiqi, A., & Kemp, L. (2014). Developmental vulnerability–don't investigate without a model in mind. *Child: Care, Health and Development*. PMID:25088700

World Health Organisation. (2003). *Caring for children and adolescents with mental disorders*. WHO.

World Health Organisation. (2007). International Classification Diseases (10th ed). Geneva: WHO.

World Health Organisation. (2009a). *Mental health aspects of women's reproductive health. A global review of literature*. WHO.

World Health Organisation. (2009b). *Promoting Sexual and Reproductive Health for People with Disabilities*. WHO.

World Health Organization. (1992). International statistical classification of diseases and related health problems (10th ed.). Geneva: WHO.

World Health Organization. (1992). *The ICD-10 classification of mental and behavioral disorders: clinical descriptions and diagnostic guidelines*. Geneva, Switzerland: WHO.

World Health Organization. (1992). *The ICD-10 classification of mental and behavioural disorders: Clinical descriptions and diagnostic guidelines*. Geneva: World Health Organization.

World Health Organization. (1993). *The ICD-10 Classification of Mental and Behavioural Disorders* (10th ed.). Geneva: World Health Organization.

World Health Organization. (1996). *Psychosocial rehabilitation: A consensus statement*. Geneva: World Health Organization.

World Health Organization. (2000). Ageing and Intellectual Disabilities - Improving Longevity and Promoting Healthy Ageing: Summative Report. Geneva, Switzerland: WHO.

World Health Organization. (2001). *International classification of functioning, disability, and health (ICF)*. Geneva: Author.

World Health Organization. (2001). *International Classification of Functioning, Disability, and Health*. Geneva: Author.

World Health Organization. (2001). *The World Health Report 2001- Mental Health: New Understanding, New Hope*. Retrieved from http://www.who.int/whr/2001/en/

World Health Organization. (2007). *Atlas: global resources for persons with intellectual disabilities*. Geneva: World Health Organization. Retrieved from http://www.who.int/mental_health/evidence/atlas_id_2007.pdf

World Health Organization. (2007). *International classification of functioning, disability and health: Children & youth version*. Geneva: Author.

World Health Organization. (2011). *Rehabilitation. World report on disability*. WHO.

Wright, G. N. (1980). *Total rehabilitation*. Boston: Little Brown.

Wuang, Y. P., Wang, C. C., Huang, M. H., & Su, C. Y. (2008). Profiles and cognitive predictors of motor functions among early school-age children with mild intellectual disabilities. *Journal of Intellectual Disability Research*, *52*(12), 1048–1060. doi:10.1111/j.1365-2788.2008.01096.x PMID:18557969

Yamaki, K., & Fujiura, G. T. (2002). Employment and income status of adults with developmental disabilities living in the community. *Mental Retardation*, *40*(2), 132–141. doi:10.1352/0047-6765(2002)040<0132:EAISOA>2.0.CO;2 PMID:11925267

Yamaoka, Y., Tamiya, N., Moriyama, Y., Sandoval Garrido, F. A., Sumazaki, R., & Noguchi, H. (2015). Mental health of parents as caregivers of children with disabilities: Based on Japanese nationwide survey: E0145200. *PLoS ONE*, *10*(12), e0145200. doi:10.1371/journal.pone.0145200 PMID:26692344

Yang, X. (2015, March23). No matter how I think, it already hurts: Self-stigmatized feelings and face concern of Chinese caregivers of people with intellectual disabilities. *Journal of Intellectual Disabilities*, *19*(4), 367–380. doi:10.1177/1744629515577909 PMID:25801087

Yazbeck, M., McVilly, K., & Parmenter, T. R. (2004). Attitudes toward people with intellectual disabilities an Australian perspective. *Journal of Disability Policy Studies*, *15*(2), 97–111. doi:10.1177/10442073040150020401

Yeargin-Allsopp, M., Drews, C. D., Decouflé, P., & Murphy, C. C. (1995). Mild mental retardation in black and white children in metropolitan Atlanta: A case-control study. *American Journal of Public Health*, *85*(3), 324–328. doi:10.2105/AJPH.85.3.324 PMID:7892913

Yoder, P. J., & Warren, S. F. (1998). Maternal responsivity predicts the prelinguistic communication intervention that facilitates generalized intentional communication. *Journal of Speech, Language, and Hearing Research: JSLHR*, *41*(5), 1207–1219. doi:10.1044/jslhr.4105.1207 PMID:9771641

Yoder, P. J., & Warren, S. F. (2002). Effects of prelinguistic milieu teaching and parent responsivity education on dyads involving children with intellectual disabilities. *Journal of Speech, Language, and Hearing Research: JSLHR*, *45*(6), 1158–1174. doi:10.1044/1092-4388(2002/094) PMID:12546485

Yoder, P., & Stone, W. L. (2006). A randomized comparison of the effect of two prelinguistic communication interventions on the acquisition of spoken communication in preschoolers with ASD. *Journal of Speech, Language, and Hearing Research: JSLHR*, *49*(4), 698–711. doi:10.1044/1092-4388(2006/051) PMID:16908870

Yoder, P., & Warren, S. (2001). Relative treatment effects of two prelinguistic communication interventions on language development in toddlers with developmental delays vary by maternal characteristics. *Journal of Speech, Language, and Hearing Research: JSLHR*, *44*(1), 224–237. doi:10.1044/1092-4388(2001/019) PMID:11218105

York, J., Vandercook, T., MacDonald, C., Heise-Neff, C., & Caughey, E. (1992). Feedback about integrating middle school students with severe disabilities in general education classes. *Exceptional Children*, *58*(3), 244–257. PMID:1839896

Zablotsky, B., Bradshaw, C. P., Anderson, C., & Law, P. A. (2013). The association between bullying and the psychological functioning of children with autism spectrum disorders. *Journal of Developmental and Behavioral Pediatrics*, *34*(1), 1–8. doi:10.1097/DBP.0b013e31827a7c3a PMID:23275052

Zapf, W., Glatzer, W., Noll, H. H., Habich, R., Berger-Schmitt, R., & Breuer, S. et al.. (1987). German social report: Living conditions and subjective well-being, 1978–1984. *Social Indicators Research*, *19*, 1.

Zeanah, C. H., Boris, N. W., & Larrieu, J. A. (1997). Infant development and developmental risk: A review of the past 10 years. *Journal of the American Academy of Child and Adolescent Psychiatry*, *36*(2), 165–178. doi:10.1097/00004583-199702000-00007 PMID:9031569

Zeedyk, S. M., Rodrigeuz, G., Tipton, L. A., Baker, B. L., & Blacher, J. (2014). Bullying of youth with autism spectrum disorder, intellectual disability, or typical development: Victim and parent perspectives. *Research in Autism Spectrum Disorders*, *8*(9), 1173–1183. doi:10.1016/j.rasd.2014.06.001 PMID:25285154

Zeitlin, S., & Williamson, G. (1990). Coping characteristics of disabled and nondisabled young children. *The American Journal of Orthopsychiatry*, *60*(3), 404–411. doi:10.1037/h0079183 PMID:2143354

Zigler, E., & Hodapp, R. M. (1986). *Understanding mental retardation*. Cambridge, UK: Cambridge University Press.

Zimmerman, I., Steiner, V. G., & Pond, R. (2011). *Preschool Language Scale – 5*. San Antonio, Tx: Psychological Corporation.

Zisberg, A., Young, H., Schepp, K., & Zysberg, L. (2007). A concept analysis of routine: Relevance to nursing. *Journal of Advanced Nursing*, *57*(4), 442–453. doi:10.1111/j.1365-2648.2007.04103.x PMID:17291208

About the Contributors

Rejani Thudalikunnil Gopalan is currently working as a faculty in Clinical Psychology and she is specialized in child and adolescent mental health area. She has more than a decade experience in the area of intellectual disability. She did M.Phil and Ph.D in Clinical Psychology from National Institute of Mental Health and Neurosciences, India. She has academic and clinical work experience in both national and international levels and won many awards for contributions in the area of mental health. She is serving as an editorial board member and reviewer for many journals. Trauma and Sexual Abuse, Mental health issues among children, convicted offenders and juveniles are her predominant areas of research.

* * *

Prathibha Agustus is a clinical Psychologist and currently a PhD scholar.

Norharlina Bahar received her MD and MMed (Psych) from Universiti Kebangsaan Malaysia in 1997 and 2005 respectively. She worked and trained in Melbourne for her subspecialty in Child and Adolescent Psychiatry. Her special interests are in the area of Infant Mental Health; Early Childhood Emotional Development; Parent-Child Relationship; and Internet Addiction. She is an international Board Member of the International Society of Internet Addiction. She is now heading the Child & Adolescent Psychiatry Unit in Hospital Selayang. She is active in several non-governmental organizations and schools to advocate the needs of children, adolescents and people with mental health issues.

Priyanka Behrani did her masters in psychology from the Kanpur University, India in 1993 and doctorate in 2000 in the area of Personality Psychology. She completed her certificate course in Disability specializing in Mental Retardation. She was a visiting faculty for Diploma in Special Education till 2004. Then assistant professor in 2004 at the Department of Psychology, The Maharaja Sayaji Rao University of Baroda, . She is the coordinator of counseling cell and Diploma course on Human Resource development run at the Department of Psychology,. She has attended national and international conferences, seminars and workshops in the area of Educational and Industrial Psychology. She has published in different books and journals.

Swarnima Bhargava has attained her MPhil. in Clinical Psychology from the Institute of Human Behavior and Allied Sciences, Delhi. She has completed an M.A. in counselling from the Tata Institute of Social Sciences, Mumbai. She holds a B.A. (Hons) degree in Psychology from Lady Shri Ram College for Women, University of Delhi.

Prakash Boominathan is currently Professor in the Department of Speech Language and Hearing Sciences, Sri Ramachandra University (SRU), Chennai. He completed his Bachelors (1998) and Masters (2000) degrees in Speech and Hearing at the All India Institute of Speech and Hearing, Mysore. He received the prestigious Fulbright Research Fellowship for the year 2005-06. In 2008, he was awarded Ph.D degree from SRU. His publications are in the area of voice, speech and communication disorders. He has contributed book chapters in the area of voice and fluency disorders, and has published two self- instructional DVDs.

Sandamita Choudhury is currently pursuing M.Phil Clinical Psychology from Gujarat Forensic Sciences University. She received her M.Sc. in Clinical Psychology from Jain University, Bangalore in 2013. She worked with the special needs children and undertook training programs for creating awareness and understanding of disability among high school teachers in Assam under Rashtriya Madhyamik Shiskha Abhiyan (RMSA).

Sumita Chowhan received her PhD degree from Andhra University, Vishakhapatnam, India. She is a doctoral guide and assistant professor in Jain University, Bangalore, India. She is EAP (Employee Assistant Programme) Affiliate (Psychologist) working with Workplace Options. Astute, result oriented with proven success in counselling, research, training (SPSS) and teaching. She has international exposure both in education and job in US and UK. She received Cognitive behavioural therapy diploma from UK. She has five plus years of experience in versatile fields like Research (SPSS) /Teaching/Counselling/ Training and HR. She also attended and presented papers in national/international conferences. She had published research articles and chapter in journals and Book. She is peer reviewer and board of editorial member of different journals. Her areas of interest are Education, clinical, child psychology and developmental, positive psychology (character strength), Neuropsychology and Industrial.

Bijoy Kumar Dehuri graduated in Medicine and joined Indian Air Force. Later did MSc in Defence Studies from Defence Services Staff College, Wellington (India) followed by M Phil in Hospital & Health System Management, BITS, Pilani. In the past (more than 30 years) worked as Senior Medical Officer in practically all kinds of Air Force Bases in India which involved Medical administration and training including planning and projecting KRAs and accomplishing them. Worked as a Senior Instructor (Management Topics particularly applicable in Healthcare, Emotional Intelligence and Spiritual Intelligence etc.) at Officers Training College of Army Medical Corps Centre & College. Now retitred from active services. He has been counseling and practicing as a Life Coach for the past ten years.

Dorothy Bhandari Deka received her MA in Clinical Psychology from The Maharaja Sayajirao University of Baroda in 2013. She has also done a diploma course in Clinical and Applied Hypnosis from The Maharaja Sayajirao University of Baroda. Presently, she is pursuing her M.Phil training in Clinical Psychology from Gujarat Forensic Sciences University, Gandhinagar.

Valsamma Eapen (PhD, FRCPsych, FRANZCP) is the Chair of Infant, Child and Adolescent Psychiatry, University of New South Wales, Australia, and Head of the Academic Unit of Child Psychiatry, South Western Sydney Local Health District, Australia. She is also a practising Psychiatrist.

Jamila Firdaus holds an M.A. in clinical psychology degree and has completed her PhD in Education. She researched on Emotional Intelligence as a part of her PhD thesis work. She is a practicing psychologist for the last 19 years. She specializes in psychometric assessment, child and adolescent counseling, adult counseling and old-age counseling. She is actively involved in providing her services to NGOs with M.S. University and Airforce station in Vadodara.

Neerajana Ghosh has a Masters in Clinical Psychology from Calcutta University. Is currently MPhil trainee in Clinical Psychology from Central Institute of Psychiatry.

Vaitsa Giannouli received her PhD in Neuroscience from the School of Medicine, Aristotle University of Thessaloniki. She is a cognitive psychologist and neuropsychologist. She is currently a research fellow at Aristotle University of Thessaloniki (AUTh), Greece. She has received numerous accolades and scholarships for her work as an undergraduate and graduate student. She is working as a research assistant and is involved in several cross-cultural research projects focusing on issues of cognition and lifespan development.

Sanjeev Kumar Gupta received his MPhil in Medical and Social Psychology from the Central Institute of Psychiatry, Ranchi University, Ranchi. He is a trained Clinical Psychologist (Clinician & Researcher) and works at the Department of Clinical Psychology, All India Institute of Speech and Hearing, India. He is interested in the area of Clinical Psychology, Neuropsychology; Mindfulness based interventions, Cognitive Neuroscience, and Diagnostic assessment and intervention for children with developmental disabilities. He has published several articles in national and international journals.

Aili Hanim Hashim is Consultant Psychiatrist for Child, Adolescent and Adult Mental Health at the Department of Psychological Medicine, Faculty of Medicine, University Malaya, Kuala Lumpur. She received her initial training in medicine and psychiatry at the University Malaya, Kuala Lumpur, and did her advanced training in Child and Adolescent Psychiatry at the Mindful Center, Melbourne. Her work at the Psychiatry Adolescent and Child (PAC) Unit includes assessment of child and adolescent mental health issues and working with their families or carers. Through collaboration with relevant agencies in the community, early intervention is emphasized. Much of her work utilizes individual, parent work and family therapy.

Mythili Hazarika, Post-Doctoral Research Scholar (University of Florida, USA), PhD (Gauhati University), MPhil (NIMHANS, Bangalore), M.A. (Pune University), is a Senior Lecturer in Clinical Psychology Department of Psychiatry Gauhati Medical College & Hospital (GMCH).

Wan Salwina Wan Ismail is a consultant Psychiatrist for Child, Adolescent and Adult Mental Health She obtained her medical degree from the University of Adelaide, South Australia, in 1994. After completing her internship, she worked as a medical officer in a psychiatric institution in Ulu Kinta, Perak. She completed Masters in Psychiatry, from Universiti Kebangsaan Malaysia, in 2003. In 2006, she furthered her study in Advanced Masters in Child and Adolescent Psychiatry, Universiti Kebangsaan Malaysia, and had been working with children and adolescents since. She is currently a lecturer, Child and Adolescent Psychiatrist, and Head of Child and Adolescent Psychiatry Unit, Department of Psychiatry, Faculty of Medicine, Universiti Kebangsaan Malaysia.

Mansi Jadeja completed her graduation and Masters degree in Psychology from the Maharaja Sayajirao University in the year 2013. She is currently pursuing her M.Phil in Clinical Psychology from Gujarat Forensic Sciences University, Gandhinagar. Her research interests include positive psychology, clinical psychology and therapy. She has gained experience in working with children and adult patients during her internship periods.

Manveen Kaur, a Child and Adolescent Psychiatrist, works at the Department of Psychological Medicine, University Malaya. She is a Senior Lecturer, whose clinical duties at the PAC Unit (Child & Adolescent Psychiatry Unit), involve treating children and adolescents with mental health difficulties. In addition to this, she is active in research and teaching postgraduates in the field of both General and Child Psychiatry. An integral part of her work involves reaching out to the Community, where educating the public, and working with teachers and councilors, in order to better support children.

Aditi Lohan is pursuing a PhD in Clinical Psychology at the Parenting and Family Support Centre, The University of Queensland, Australia. She is an accredited provider of different Triple P variants.

Krupa M. pursued her bachelors (2003-2007) and masters (2007-2009) in Speech Language Pathology and Audiology at Sri Ramachandra University, Chennai, India. She also has graduated in the field of Psychology through distance education mode from the University of Madras. A speech language pathologist/therapist by profession, Krupa is currently a Senior Lecturer at the Dept of Speech Language and Hearing Sciences at Sri Ramachandra University, India. Her clinical, research and teaching work are predominantly in the area of children with communication disorders. She is also pursuing doctoral research in the area of caregiver-child communication in children with autism. Her work has been presented in national and international forums. She is a Hanen certified Speech Language Pathologist.

Preeti Mishra is a Ph.D (Clinical Psychology) From CIP, Clinical psychologist, Shai Mavant Indiresh hospital, Dehradun. Worked as research coordinator in "Project HIFAZAT" of CIP.

Bhavna Mukund graduated in Psychology from Lucknow University and did Masters from Delhi University. Has completed M Phil in Clinical Psychology from Institute of Behavioural Sciences, Gujarat Forensic Sciences University, Gandhinagar, Gujarat, India. Keen on working and contributing towards a significant breakthrough in the field of academics and Clinical Psychology in particular.

Jyoti Mishra Pandey completed Post Graduation (MSc in Clinical Psychology) from Punjabi university Patiala. Did M.Phil M & SP (Clinical Psychology) from Central Institute of Psychiatry, (CIP), Ranchi). First Rank holder in M.Phil (Clinical Psychology). Taught in CIP as Assistant Professor in the department of Clinical Psychology. Worked as Clinical Psychologist at Bharti Vidyapeeth Medical College and Hospital Deemed University in Dept of Psychiatry and Paediatrics in 2013. Presently perusing PhD from RINPAS, Ranchi. Has published papers in Various National Journals.

Plabita Patowary received her MSc in clinical psychology from Jain University, Bangalore in 2013. In 2014, she was selected as a trainee in M Phil in clinical psychology program in Gujarat Forensic Sciences University. She has published research papers and attended numerous conferences on mental health and related issues.

Shuvabrata Poddar has a M.Phil in Medical and Social Psychology from Central Institute of Psychiatry, M.Sc in Psychology from University of Calcutta Assistant, and is a Professor of Clinical Psychology, Central Institute of Psychiatry.

Babita Prusty is working as Asst. Professor in the dept of Psychology at Amity University, Uttar Pradesh. She has completed her M.Phil from Utkal University, Orissa. Presently Pursuing Ph.D from School of Social Sciences, IGNOU. Her interest areas are cognitive Psychology, Clinical Psychology, Developmental Psychopathology etc. She has many national & International publications to her credit. She is a regular writer in renowned news letters and news papers on different psychological issue in children and adolescents.

K. R. Santhosh, currently working as Assistant Professor in Jain University, completed his Ph.D. in Psychology from Bharathiar University, Coimbatore. He has 14 publications and 27 presentations. His research interests include Positive Psychology, especially resilience, prevention of child abuse etc. and Political Psychology focusing on the political behaviours and critical evaluation skills among the citizens in Democratic Nations.

Rajesh 'Jay' Sharma, M.A., BCBA, received his B.A. (Honours) Psychology in 1999, and M.A. Applied Psychology from Jamia Millia Islamia University 2001. He worked with mental health clinics and schools between the years 2001 to 2006 providing professional consultations on issues such as stress management, staff training, counselling, disabilities / special education service provisions, academic performance etc. In the year 2006, Jay moved to the U.S.A on a teaching assignment where his roles involved teaching adolescents with developmental disabilities and youths with challenging behaviours. To update his skills and knowledge in the area of Applied Behaviour Analysis (ABA) Jay completed his second master degree in Applied Psychology with a concentration in Applied Behaviour Analysis from McNeese State University, Louisiana in 2013. In 2014, Jay was hired by an Australian behavioural consulting company The Centre of Applied Behaviour Analysis as a Consultant Behaviour Specialist to provide professional behavioural services to individuals with developmental disabilities presenting challenging behaviours. Currently, Jay is employed with the Department of Community, Child Safety, and Disabilities as a Clinician to provide behavioural intervention services to individual presenting challenging behaviours. Jay also heads a behavioural consulting company Sunrise Behavioural Health Pty Ltd which provide ABA based interventions in Canberra, Sydney, and Brisbane through a network of dedicated behaviour therapists.

Vinod Kumar Sinha is a Professor of Psychiatry at Central Institute of Psychiatry, significant work on child population and various publications in national and international journals.

Daanesh M. Umrigar has completed his MPhil in Clinical Psychology from the Institute of Human Behavior and Allied Sciences (IHBAS), Delhi. He attained his Masters degree. in Psychology from the University of Pune. He has also completed a "One Year Post Graduate Certificate Course in Counseling" from The Maharashtra Institute of Mental Health (M.I.M.H.), Sassoon General Hospital, Pune. His major areas of interest include, Sexuality and Sexual Health, as well as Behavioural Medicine.

Krishna Shailesh Vora is a Counseling Psychologist who is currently working with children with learning difficulties. She is also involved in the development of a programme for gifted children. In future, she hopes to create differentiated curriculum for both children with learning difficulties as well as children with gifted needs.

Amelia Walter (DClinPsych/MSc, BA Hons) is an early career researcher in the Academic Unit of Child Psychiatry, South Western Sydney Local Health District, Australia. She is also a practising Clinical Psychologist, and holds a Conjoint Lecturer position with the School of Psychiatry, University of New South Wales, Australia.

Michelle F. Wright is a postdoctoral research fellow at Masaryk University. Her research interests include the contextual factors, such as familial and cultural, which influence children's and adolescents' aggression and victimization as well as their pursuit, maintenance, and achievement of peer status. She also has an interest in peer rejection and unpopularity, and how such statuses relate to insecurity with one's peer standing, aggression, and victimization.

Index

V

W

www.ingramcontent.com/pod-product-compliance
Lightning Source LLC
LaVergne TN
LVHW081249011026
849162LV00006BA/1247
* 9 7 8 1 5 2 2 5 0 0 8 9 6 *